Praise for Richard Wightman Fox's *Reinhold Niebuhr*:

REINHOLD NIEBUHR

A

BIOGRAPHY

RICHARD
WIGHTMAN
FOX

HARPER & ROW, PUBLISHERS, SAN FRANCISCO

Cambridge, Hagerstown, New York, Philadelphia, Washington
London, Mexico City, São Paulo, Singapore, Sydney

Grateful acknowledgment is made for permission to reproduce the following photographs:

Dr. Richard Niebuhr at Yale Divinity School, by Alfred Eisenstaedt, *Life* magazine. Copyright © 1955 by Time Inc. Reprinted by permission of Life Picture Service, a division of Time Inc.

March 8, 1948 *Time* cover of Reinhold Niebuhr. Copyright 1948 by Time Inc. All rights reserved. Reprinted by permission of *Time*.

Niebuhr with Senators Humphrey and Lehman at Roosevelt Day Dinner of ADA, January 1950, and Niebuhr in Retirement, early 1960s. Reprinted by permission of Wide World Photos.

1927 Lake Geneva Conference photo, Yale Divinity School Library, Archives of the YMCA, Student Division, Record Group 58. Reprinted by permission of Yale Divinity School Library.

For excerpts from *Leaves from the Noteboods of a Tamed Cynic* by Reinhold Niebuhr, grateful acknowledgment is made to Harper & Row, Publishers, Inc. Copyright 1929, © 1957 by Reinhold Niebuhr. Reprinted by permission of Harper & Row, Publishers, Inc.

Hardcover edition published in 1985 by Pantheon Books, a Division of Random House, Inc. First Harper & Row paperback edition published in 1987. Reprinted by arrangement with Pantheon Books, a Division of Random House, Inc.

Library of Congress Cataloging-in-Publication Data

Fox, Richard Wightman.
  Reinhold Niebuhr.

  Bibliography: p.
  Includes index.
  1. Niebuhr, Reinhold, 1892–1971. 2. Theologians —
United States — Biography. I. Title.
BX4827.N5F68 1987   230',092'4 [B]   86-45806
ISBN 0-06-250343-X (pbk.)

To My Parents
and to Diane's

M. Bernard Fox
Lucy Pope Hopman
Herman Niblack
Gena-Vera Niblack

The joys of parents are secret;
so are their griefs and fears.
—FRANCIS BACON

CONTENTS

Illustrations follow pages 84 and 212.

DAY
OF
THE LORD

I

James Chapel began filling up half an hour before the service. Townspeople emerging from an icy Hudson breeze on the Manhattan winter morning rubbed their hands and kept their coats buttoned. They squeezed gladly into pews beside the seminarians. It was Reinhold Niebuhr's turn to preach on February 3, 1952, and the Union Theological Seminary hall of worship that sat half empty on many Sundays was packed well before he appeared. Niebuhr swept in, draped in his flowing gown. The gothic sweep of the nave accentuated his height. He was tired, recovering from the flu, but when he rose for the sermon his eyes began to dance. He focused on one face and then another. The coughing in the congregation died down and many bent forward in concentration. "For he makes his sun rise on the evil and on the good, and sends rain on the just and on the unjust." He recited the text from Matthew's Gospel slowly and reflectively, caressing each word with care. Then he preached for thirty minutes on the impartiality of God's providence. Sometimes his voice receded into an intense whisper, sometimes it erupted in a gravelly bark. He used no notes and kept his hands free for vast circling motions, pointed jabs, for tugging at his gown, rubbing his bald crown: constant motion and an unremitting flow of words.

The problem with Christians, he observed, was their self-satisfaction. "When we say that we believe in God, we are inclined to mean that we have found a way to the ultimate source and end of life, and this gives us, against all the chances and changes of life, some special security and some special favor." Between such a religion and secularism he chose the latter;

•

with William James he scorned any "effort to lobby in the courts of the Almighty" for special treatment. He was challenging his listeners in the classic prophet's mode, but he also offered reassurance. God was ultimately "on our side." Not in the sense that he was "against somebody else," but in the sense that a trust in the ultimate meaningfulness of human existence permitted one to persevere despite "the impartial destinies of this great drama of life." Christianity was not a protection against misfortune, but a basic trust that put misfortune in perspective.

Niebuhr was always first a preacher, though he was always more than that: political organizer and commentator, religious thinker, social critic, seminary teacher. Students in his office on the seventh floor of Brown Tower at Broadway and 120th Street sat before an attentive listener but a frenetic one: he paced with long strides through clouds of cigarette smoke while pondering their projects and problems. He had to be up and about. Forty or more weekends a year, for more than a quarter-century, he bolted from one state to another, preaching at colleges, addressing student conferences, conferring at political meetings. His hastily packed suitcase sometimes sat poised beside the lectern at his Friday class. A delayed train, or later a weatherbound plane, drove him to distraction. He constantly checked his watch. There might not be enough time.

His admirers and opponents alike understood they were confronted by a man of uncommon gifts. Many sober-minded observers, not just among his friends, insisted on calling him a prophet—a label that always embarrassed him. But he knew it was on target. He grappled endlessly with the paradox of cultivating a prophetic identity while avoiding a pretentious pose. It was Amos he wished to follow. The Hebrew prophet had warned that the day of the Lord would be darkness and not light, that Yahweh had no use for solemn assemblies or burnt offerings. God would be impressed when justice rolled down like waters and righteousness like an everlasting stream. He scorned those who were at ease in Zion, who lay upon beds of ivory and ignored the urgency of the hour. Niebuhr shared Amos' sense of crisis. He also shared Amos' awareness of the risk of pride. Amos denied any special competence: "I am no prophet, nor a prophet's son, but a herdsman and a dresser of sycamore trees." Niebuhr yearned to speak with Amos' authority and to appropriate his humility.

He already had the prophet's intensity and single-mindedness. He spoke as one possessed, driven—not just in church, but with friends, in meetings, in the classroom. His charisma was no pulpit act; his gift was far less manageable than that. He was strikingly unselfconscious in public, unconcerned with social form. He was totally without ostentation, constitutionally unable to condescend. He was a pure democrat in personal relations, at home above all with the seminary students who flocked around him and called him Reinie. He answered all the letters he received, often writing thoughtful replies to penciled inquiries from unknown correspondents in the heartland. His many friends in the political and intellectual worlds marveled at his energetic presence and quick wit. Felix Frankfurter and Isaiah Berlin, both inspired conversationalists and masters of repartee, found themselves evenly matched. When the agnostic Frankfurter heard Niebuhr preach at a small church near his summer home in Heath, Massachusetts, he was

•

captivated. As they filed out the door he shook Niebuhr's hand and said, "May a believing unbeliever thank you for your sermon?" Niebuhr did not hesitate before replying, "May an unbelieving believer thank you for appreciating it?"[1]

II

I first encountered Niebuhr's thought as a Stanford undergraduate in the mid-1960s. Two devoted Niebuhrians—Robert McAfee Brown and Michael Novak—introduced hundreds of students to his work. Although I never saw or heard Niebuhr, I knew at once from the devotion of Brown and Novak that he had deeply marked their generation. Those who came to political awareness between the depression of the 1930s and the Cold War of the 1950s found in Niebuhr a "crisis" theologian for troubled times. He exhorted his readers and listeners to take "responsibility" for their world, while warning them against the temptation to try to perfect it. All Niebuhrians united on the bedrock conviction that there could be no ultimate fulfillment in the political realm and yet no salvation apart from the life of political commitment. Even in the 1960s, before Niebuhr's death, his followers were liable to dwell on different sides of his message. Brown (who actually studied and taught with Niebuhr) was more likely to emphasize the critique of complacency and the quest for justice; Novak (a former Catholic seminarian) was apt to stress the anti-utopianism of the political realist, the Burkean appreciation for tradition and community. Their differences were testimony to the complexity of Niebuhr's stance and a goad to my own thinking. As the split between Brown and Novak—between a left-liberal sympathetic to the theology of "liberation" and a right-liberal disposed toward "democratic capitalism"—deepened in the 1970s, I was drawn back to their teacher in order to clarify the rift between my own teachers. This is a quest for the historical Reinhold, to paraphrase Albert Schweitzer, an attempt to probe beneath the conflicting Niebuhrs of faith.

It is also an effort to write intellectual history. Too often historians treat ideas as free-floating essences evolving in proud disregard for mere social reality. Other historians try to compensate for that abstract view by examining the social function of thought: they typically restate the political and cultural debates intellectuals have had with each other and their fellow citizens. The real challenge is to put ideas in their full biographical and communal context. It is a thinker who produces thought, but not simply as an individual product; a set of communities, historic and contemporary, shapes the thought. So do events, public and private. In addition, the thought takes on a life of its own in society and in a group of intellectual traditions. Ideas emerge out of and develop in a complex series of overlapping fields. A biography must grasp its subject as a producer, but also as one produced by particular life circumstances and cultural resources. It must see him as one whose creativity, as T. S. Eliot suggested, is the fruit of tradition as much as it is the expression of individual talent. Autonomy is not canceled out by the determinisms that impinge on it; it is made possible by them. Freedom is creative because it is delimited, finite, contingent.

•

The student of Reinhold Niebuhr and his ideas confronts a special problem. His work transcends standard disciplinary categories. I do have some background in theology, but I am not a specialist. I was trained as a historian. Only a theologian could do full justice to Niebuhr's religious ideas. But even a study of his theology must begin with the central fact that it was intimately linked to his social and political views. He self-consciously eschewed the label "theologian"; he was, he insisted, a teacher of "social ethics." It will take a number of sustained inquiries from different perspectives to measure the full significance of his work. Taken together, however, they will still fall short. It is a sign of his stature that each generation will have to confront him anew.

Niebuhr himself was of two minds about biographies. On the one hand he thought they veered too often toward adulation. When Scribners asked him in the 1940s if they should publish a short study of his life by the English parson D. R. Davies, he said no, it was "quite uncritical and embarrassingly adulatory." When they asked him in the 1960s whether to publish another glowing introduction to his life and thought by his close friend June Bingham, he said yes, go ahead. The fact is that he disliked criticism as much as he was embarrassed by praise. He was always forthright in his criticisms of others, and strenuously insisted that disinterested observation was an integral component of true understanding. He knew that appreciation for other people's humanity meant holding their virtues and vices in tension. He knew he had flaws too, hard as it was for him, as for all of us, to admit them. The greatest danger in writing the biography of a religious leader—especially one of acknowledged eminence—is the danger of deification. Part of the quest for the historical Reinhold is to rescue his humanity from the inertia of glorification. The venerated master must take on flesh. I have been moved by the greatness of Niebuhr's person and the magnitude of his achievement. But exaltation diverts us from the task of grasping his character and contribution. He was a treasure, but like the rest of us a treasure in an earthen vessel. There is a sympathy that includes but transcends praise, and its starting point is impartial scrutiny.

A word about language. Niebuhr was untroubled by the use of the generic "man," as he made clear in the titles of several of his books. He was aware of the possible slight to women. On a radio panel in 1939 about the threat to "mankind" he prefaced his remarks with the warning that when he spoke of "men" he meant to include women. He saw no alternative to the male generic noun and pronoun. I share his view. *Moral Man and Immoral Society* and *The Nature and Destiny of Man* would have lost rhythm and power if he had titled them *Moral Selfhood and Immoral Society* or *The Nature and Destiny of Humankind*. I will trust to the context to make clear whether the generic or the masculine use is intended.[2]

ONE

NEVER FAR
FROM
THE TREE

(1892–1913)

I

For the prosperous Protestant farmers of Logan County in central Illinois, the summer of 1903 was a time for rejoicing. Bumper crops of corn and oats blanketed the flat, fertile fields all the way from Middletown in the west to Chestnut in the east. There had been several banner years in succession. The depression of the nineties—a bleak era of declining prices and receding personal horizons—was fading in memory. Fishing in the muddy Kickapoo was again an affair of leisure, not a task of putting catfish on the table.

The other good news that summer was the inauguration of the permanent Chautauqua grounds two miles outside Lincoln, the county seat. For years the annual Chautauqua had been the social and recreational high point of the midwestern Protestant calendar: communal camping, picnicking, ball games, study groups, lectures, music, theater, capped by the impassioned addresses of renowned orators. Fellowship, lofty ideals, the purifying waters of a lake or river: the Chautauqua was a dignified, secularized camp meeting. It was still Protestant, but not revivalist or sectarian. A sober, interdenominational celebration of the temperate way of life.

Before 1902, Logan County farmers and townspeople had to make a full day's journey to Petersburg, on the banks of the Sangamon River in Menard County to the west, in order to sip at the cleansing Chautauquan stream. But in 1902 a trial Chautauqua was held in Lincoln, a meeting so phenomenally successful that investors and subscribers rushed forward to make it permanent. On August 4, the final day of the two-week session, over 1,150 people bought season tickets for the 1903 meeting—their purse strings having been loosened by the unmatchable oratory of no less than

1

·

Illinois's own favorite son, William Jennings Bryan. In the morning it had rained heavily, and the organizers feared that Bryan's speech would have to be canceled—not because rivers of mud made the two-mile trek from downtown to Brainerd Park treacherous, but because a steady downpour on the main tent would drown out even the stentorian voice of the Great Commoner. But the rain let up about noon and a parade of wagons and pedestrians battled the mud and the derailed streetcars, put out of commission by excessive loads of pilgrims on rain-softened roadbeds. Three thousand listeners finally made it to the tent and put down their twenty-five cents for Bryan's two-hour, untitled address. When he was done, more than a third of the audience produced another dollar and a half for a 1903 season ticket.

The promoters went all out for 1903. They dug an artificial lake that connected with Salt Creek. They built stone and wooden cottages overlooking the water beneath the sprawling oak trees. And at a cost of $10,000 they erected a Gargantuan, circular steel auditorium, open on three sides, with only a single interior pole, that could seat five thousand visitors on straight, uncushioned benches. The Lincoln *Courier* was if anything understating the case when it remarked that the Chautauqua was now "the chief event of Lincoln's life." It was a transfiguring event. The whole town and much of the surrounding countryside were mobilized for the inauguration of the new grounds. On August 7, stores in Lincoln put up their shutters and ten thousand people—equal to the entire population of Lincoln—assembled to celebrate the opening of the session and their own heightened stature as a community. Lincoln township and Logan County had become a fixture on the Chautauquan circuit of enlightenment.[1]

Among the thousands of farmers and townsfolk who in the next two weeks saw and heard General Fitzhugh Lee, French's Military Band, the Gretna Green Company's Shakespearean drama, the latest moving pictures, and many other attractions was a young German-American family new to the town. The Reverend Gustav Niebuhr, a forty-year-old minister of the German Evangelical Synod of North America, was used to pulling up stakes. He had served several German-language churches since his ordination in 1885, including Saint John's in San Francisco, which he built up from almost nothing, and Saint John's in St. Charles, Missouri, a hundred miles to the southwest. With his wife and four children he had left St. Charles the previous fall for the bigger, more prestigious job in Lincoln, a post that combined the pastorate at Saint John's Evangelical Church with the directorship of the synod's new Deaconess Hospital. Gustav Niebuhr's star was rising within the synod; his superiors in St. Louis viewed him with great favor.

Saint John's had its own tent at the Chautauqua, a welcome haven from the searing prairie sun and the hovering hordes of gnats and mosquitoes. A roving photographer passed by the tent, and persuaded Gustav to buy photos of his family, which he sent back to his parents and siblings on the farm in Lippe Detmold, near the Dutch border. One of the pictures shows a lanky, puckish lad of eleven, Gustav's middle son, Reinhold, sitting in the tent beside the youngest child, Helmut, a dreamy-eyed boy just short of his ninth birthday. They both wear knickers, Reinhold sports a cloth

•

cap, and Helmut has a giant bow ribbon tied securely around his neck. A protective coterie of stern arch-backed churchwomen, all in long-sleeved blouses, sits around the two brothers in a semicircle; they are planted as straight and firm as the white sticks of a sturdy picket fence. There is a look of eager concentration and excitement on Reinhold's face. He relishes the moment. The camera has arrested the darting of his eyes only for an instant. Helmut by contrast looks distant, perplexed, uncomfortable in the thick, steamy August heat.

Another picture shows a group of picnickers spread across a patch of grass. Gustav, severe and unsmiling, stands beside them staring down the camera: the shepherd guarding his flock. His bald head is glistening in the sun. He has a thick, well-trimmed goatee and moustache, and holds a wide-brimmed hat in one hand. But the focal point of the picture is his piercing, deep-set eyes. They cut right through his wire-rimmed spectacles, and suggest a man of intense self-discipline and fierce rectitude. This is not a man who doubts himself.

II

Gustav Niebuhr had come to America in 1881 at the age of eighteen. He was the third child, and second son, of the *Grossbauer* (large farmer) Friedrich Niebuhr, who employed about twenty-five hands on a farm held by his family since the thirteenth century. Neither Gustav nor his next younger brother, Louis, who emigrated to Nebraska somewhat later, got along with their father. His autocratic ways, Gustav later informed his own children, were typical of the German *Vater*; to escape the tyranny he had departed for New York. Much later his children recalled that their father had also left Germany to escape military service, but that was not a point Gustav underlined in family discussion.

Like most late-nineteenth-century immigrants to the United States, Gustav had a specific destination in mind; he was not setting forth into the misty unknown. His cousin Karoline Lüttmann had gone to Illinois in 1876, the bride of another Lippe Detmold native, William Hummermeier, who had been farming near Freeport since 1874. Gustav arranged to stay with the Hummermeiers before sailing from Hamburg. They were delighted to have an extra hand on the farm, but before long Gustav, who had almost completed his *Gymnasium* education in Germany, tired of the routine and set out for Chicago. It is unclear how long he stayed in the fastest-growing metropolis in America, in which he worked for a time in a sewing-machine factory, but it was less than two years. Apparently his health gave way and he asked the Hummermeiers to take him back in. They readily agreed, but Karoline was shocked to discover that Gustav now sprinkled his speech with a liberal supply of profanities. In Karoline's eyes he was now a "wild" young man.

In later years she often told her children the story of a memorable ride to church in early 1883. It was early Sunday morning and they were all riding in a three-seat spring wagon to the Salem Evangelical Church in Freeport. Karoline withstood the usual dose of Gustav's vulgarities, and expected to have to put up with the same thing on the way home. But on the return trip, to her surprise, he made no sound at all. The sermon had completely silenced him. Not long after that he announced his intention to study for the ministry, a course that William Hummermeier had often urged on him because of his relatively advanced schooling.[2]

There is no indication that his own family had been particularly pious, although he and his six siblings were all baptized and confirmed in the Prussian Union Church—a body that combined many Lutheran and Reformed congregations by an 1817 edict of King Friedrich Wilhelm III and which eventually grew into the Evangelical Church of Germany. The sovereign believed church union would bolster Prussian strength, and saw no reason why the two groups should continue to split theological hairs. It was therefore natural that Gustav—once he had undergone his conversion experience on the road to Freeport—should seek admission to Eden Seminary near St. Louis, the training school for ministers of the Deutsche Evangelische Synode von Nord-Amerika. For the German Evangelical Synod, although of American origin, had followed the lead of the Prussian Union in refusing to call itself either Lutheran or Calvinist. Its founding confessional statement, issued in 1848, said simply that the synod "accepts the interpretation of the Holy Scriptures as given in the symbolic books of the Lutheran and Reformed Church . . . in so far as they agree; but where they disagree [it] adheres strictly to the passages of Holy Scriptures bearing on the subject and avails itself of the liberty of conscience prevailing in the Evangelical Church." The synod, like most frontier faiths, cared less about the fine points of dogmatic theology than about inner spirituality and practical results: conversions made, churches raised, welfare structures built.

In 1890, according to the US Census, the Evangelical Synod was a modest denomination with 187,000 members served by 680 ministers. It was thoroughly German. Even a quarter-century later, after a good deal of Americanization had occurred, only one-sixth of its congregations used any English at all in worship. The synod was heavily concentrated in Illinois, Ohio, and Missouri, which between them accounted for 40 to 50 percent of the faithful. In the next few decades, through the zeal of the synod's Home Mission Board, immigration, and natural population increase, the membership grew by 56 percent. By 1906 there were over 293,000 members served by 972 ministers. That was a ratio of 302 church members per pastor, by far the highest of any Protestant denomination. That ratio put an enormous burden on the synod's clergy, some of whom—like Gustav Niebuhr— would be called upon to serve a number of parishes in rapid succession. At times of peak stress certain energetic churchmen like Gustav would become de facto circuit riders.

The Evangelical Synod was typical of much nineteenth-century German and American Protestantism in its relative neglect of the intellectual content of the faith and its pietistic stress on the heart. The believer aspired above all to experience the immediate presence of Christ; doctrine was secondary. But in spite of its deep aversion to rationalism, it was a "liberal" church. Unlike most German immigrant bodies, such as the more numerous Lutheran churches, the Evangelical Synod encouraged a fundamentally open, accommodating, pragmatic attitude toward other denominations and even toward the American culture around them. The Evangelicals were by conviction ecumenical: even as they persisted in the use of German, they cooperated actively with Baptists, Congregationalists, Presbyterians, Methodists, and other American denominations. They had very little of the fortress mentality that marked, for example, the Missouri Synod Lutherans. They were not shielding a golden past from contamination by the present.[3]

With financial aid from William Hummermeier, Gustav breezed through Eden Seminary's three-year program in two years—his classmates did not have the advantage of a nearly completed *Gymnasium* education—and was ordained in 1885 at the age of twenty-two. After a brief tour of duty in a New Orleans church, he was sent to northern California to assist the synod's Pacific slope missionary, Edward Hosto, who had recently moved from San Francisco to found a settlement at Mount Shasta. Niebuhr took over the San Francisco church, Saint John's, but was a frequent visitor at Mount Shasta. He took a liking to Hosto's energetic fifteen-year-old daughter Lydia, and two years later they were married. Together they returned to Saint John's, a rented, crumbling structure on Telegraph Hill. Before the marriage Gustav had sometimes preached to congregations of two or three. With Lydia's full-time aid—and musical talent—his parish began to grow. Lydia, one of twelve children, knew all about church operations. She had already served her father as organist and Sunday School assistant. She lacked formal schooling, but ran her parish tasks with discipline and enthusiasm. Like her husband, she reveled in work. By the end of 1891, when the denominational Home Mission Board transferred him back to Missouri, he had built a small, stable congregation.

They left San Francisco with two children—two-year-old Hulda and one-year-old Walter (the third child, Herbert, died six weeks after birth in early 1891)—and Lydia was already a few months pregnant with another son when they set out by train for Wright City, Missouri. In that town on June 21, 1892, Karl Paul Reinhold was born. He was followed, in September, 1894, by their last child, Helmut Richard.

The young children did not see much of their father during their ten years in Missouri. His organizational prowess persuaded his superiors to rely on him for the creation of new parishes and welfare homes. Wright City was the base from which he traveled from one church to the next; he was continuously on the road, with only brief stops at home. Even after 1895, when he agreed to become pastor of Saint John's Church in St. Charles, Missouri, he kept up his traveling. And in 1899 he resigned from the parish altogether to become the *reisende Vertreter* (traveling representative) of the synod's Emmaus movement, which established homes for the epileptic and feebleminded. While the family remained in St. Charles, he was away for months at a time, including periods of service as pastor to Evangelical churches as far west as Utah.

His decision in 1902 to accept the call as pastor of Saint John's in Lincoln was therefore also a choice of the family over the open road. Perhaps at the age of thirty-nine he was ready to settle down to a more domestic existence; perhaps he was eager to know his children, one of whom was already a teenager. The congregation's promise of a sparkling new parsonage—a nine-room, two-story frame house on a shady lot beside the church (completed in 1903 for the sizable sum of $4,500)—made the idea all the more attractive. So did the fact that he would be not just pastor of the church, but director of the parochial school and superintendent of the Evangelical Deaconess Hospital. Gustav Niebuhr was ambitious and possessed of such unusual energy that all who met him remarked on it. The more responsibilities he acquired the better he felt.[4]

III

Lincoln, Illinois, in 1902 was a modest county seat and commercial center; it was also, in summer, a town walled with corn. By mid-July the stalks were over six feet high and their sweet odor could already be detected from the center of town. Most city streets dead-ended in cornfields. "Corn is king in Logan County," wrote a prominent resident in 1911, "and his dynasty is eternal." It was Lincoln's task to serve the needs of the thousands of county farmers who produced, by 1900, the colossal figure of nine million bushels of corn a year in a county with a total area of less than 400,000 acres—a production unmatched by any other Illinois county. Provisions, equipment, seed, insurance, medicine, schooling for the children eight months a year, religious fellowship for the family on Sunday—except during the hottest weeks of the summer, when the horses could not fairly be asked to make the round trip—these and other services Lincoln provided for a farm population that exceeded its own population by several thousand.

Lincoln itself had 9,000 residents in 1900, of whom a third were either born overseas or the children of immigrants. Roughly two-thirds of that group, or about 2,000 people, were Germans, nearly all of whom still spoke German as their first language. Logan County, which stretched over 610 square miles, had 29,000 people, about half of whom lived on the 2,400 small farms (an average of 158 acres per farm) that produced not only huge yields of corn, but substantial amounts of oats and dairy goods, and a little wheat. In the county as a whole, as in Lincoln, one-third of the people were of foreign stock, and two-thirds of the latter were German. In all, about 7,000 Logan County residents were first- or second-generation German-Americans.

With such a sizable German population, it did not take a dynamic German churchman like Gustav Niebuhr long to emerge as a prominent public figure. Two of the local daily papers, the morning *Courier* and the afternoon *News-Herald*, carried regular stories about his activities even before 1910, when his oldest son Walter became part-owner of the *Courier*. Gustav was a forceful pastor to a congregation of more than a hundred families (by 1910) and a powerful force within the synod, whose top officials frequently stayed in his home. He was also superintendent of the more modern of Lincoln's two hospitals and the leader of the socially and politically active Lincoln Ministerial Association, which in good "progressive" fashion stood for "a clean civic life." Only Gustav Niebuhr of the four German ministers in town—there were also two Lutherans and one Catholic—worked closely with the native-born clergy, in both religious and secular affairs.[5]

Paradoxically Gustav was both liberal and Evangelical in his faith. He was liberal in his conviction that the Gospel was social as well as individual, that the Christian had to work for social improvement, not simply religious conversion. He was also liberal in his unconcern for doctrinal precision. He told his parishioners and his children that it was better to define faith as trust, not belief. And he was liberal in his ecumenical interest, his determination to break down artificial walls between the denominations. But unlike those liberal ministers who tended to reduce theology to philosophy or ethics, and to strip Jesus of his divinity in favor of calling him a perfect human being, he insisted on the divinity of Christ, the supernatural inspiration of the Bible, and the centrality of prayer in the religious life. He was a pietist, not a fundamentalist—not every word or episode in the Bible was literally true. Yet while he dismissed the fundamentalists, he was also enraged by liberal modernists who discounted the New Testament miracles. In his review of Harnack's *Wesen des Christentums* in 1902 he praised the celebrated church historian's open-mindedness but ridiculed his contention, in Gustav's words, that "the stilling of the storm at sea is a violation of the laws of nature which no one should be expected to accept." Harnack was "a child of his times" who was prone to "subjectivism." "Like Schleiermacher in his time, [Harnack] feels impelled by the prevailing philosophy to declare as impossible a certain class of miracle, thereby limiting the omnipotence of God instead of defending the thoroughly Christian and true-to-the-Gospel proposition that God the law-giver stands above all law, including the laws of nature."

Gustav did not hesitate to speak out on controversial public issues, at a time when many liberal ministers preferred to stick to platitudes about social progress. He was especially outraged by the local saloons, which in his view undermined family life. Perhaps it was his six years in San Francisco, one of the "wettest" American cities, that filled him with animus on the subject of public drinking. His was not a popular stance in a German community that often viewed the temperance movement as an Anglo-Saxon plot against German culture. But it probably did endear him, by contrast, to the town's Protestant leaders, who were appalled not only by German drinking, but by the drinking of the several hundred Irish and Polish Catholic miners who worked the three local coal mines and periodically let loose in Lincoln.

For all the vigor of his public pronouncements, and his strenuous liberal effort to relate Christian faith to society and politics, Niebuhr was very far from being a radical. At a time when the democratic-socialist movement was profoundly influential within liberal Protestant ranks, it had no impact at all upon Gustav. He was a firm defender of the rights of property. The socialist contention that the gap between rich and poor, and the conflict between labor and capital, might best be overcome by a redistribution of wealth and power struck him as an anarchistic delusion. His liberalism was that of Teddy Roosevelt: efficiency, social order, and a bigger role for the federal government in bringing that order about. There was nothing wrong with wealth, or even with absentee ownership of land. Indeed, one of

Niebuhr's leading laymen, Gustav Briegel—a member of the board of the Deaconess Hospital—was an absentee landlord with substantial holdings in Logan County.

One other gauge of the moderation of Niebuhr's progressivism was his stand on the movement for women's rights: he viewed it with horror. He was a firm believer in woman's special sphere—the gentle realm of home, nurture, and charitable service—and was a major force behind the promotion of the Deaconess order within the Evangelical Synod. In 1906 he began to edit a quarterly journal about the Deaconesses, and in the November, 1908, issue he leveled a blast against female emancipation that minced no words. He granted that "the average girl is just as intelligent as the average boy," but argued that "long years of study on the part of women could only lead to the destruction of family life." He was sure that the "emancipated English or American woman is in no way superior to the much more modest German girl. True, she has learned to speak up boldly and to express her opinions freely, to be quite uninhibited in writing any- thing and everything that comes into her head, thus to impress those with weak minds. But in heart, spirit, and soul, she is only the more impov- erished." The beleaguered tone of his polemic suggests he may have feared for the future of the Deaconess order itself, which was premised upon the distinctive female gift for soothing, selfless service. Niebuhr was on the whole a force for more rapid Americanization within the Evangelical Synod. It was he, for example, who introduced a monthly English-language service on Sunday evening and English-language confirmation classes at Saint John's. But he stridently drew the line at the aspirations of "English and American women."

He may also have been implicitly resisting the aspirations of his own eldest child, Hulda, who graduated with high marks from Lincoln High School in 1906. For his three sons he envisioned college educations; for Hulda he most emphatically did not. Her proper model was to be her mother, Lydia—tireless parish assistant, first to her father at Mount Shasta, then to her husband in San Francisco and the midwest. Whatever Hulda's own wishes, she remained at home after graduation and took on a succession of parish tasks: teacher in the parochial school, instructor in the Sunday School, vice-president of the Young People's Society, organist and member of the mixed choir. She was a mirror image of her mother, who was also an organist, secretary of the Ladies' Society, superintendent of the Home Visitation Department, and member of the administrative board of the Deaconess Hospital. Only after her father's death would Hulda resume her education.[6]

Walter, Reinhold, and Helmut were twelve, ten, and eight when the family moved to Lincoln. In St. Charles they and Hulda had gone to the church's own elementary school, where the day began with German- language Bible study. They memorized German hymns and recited their German catechism. They did study English, but made little progress until they got to Lincoln. Soon after arrival the boys entered Central School, the three-story grammar school two blocks from their home. They each com- pleted the seventh grade at Central and then went on to Lincoln High School, which had two eighth-grade classrooms. But while Reinhold and

•

Helmut would both ɪeave ᴌɪɪʟʋɪɪ ɪ ɪɪɡɪɪ aɪʟer the ninth grade to enter the synod's boarding school for prospective ministers, Walter remained to graduate, as Hulda had done. He had no interest in following his father's path into the ministry.

Family oral tradition makes clear that Walter, a strong-willed, impetuous youth, did not see eye-to-eye with his father. Their conflict probably stemmed less from the rejection of the ministry by the firstborn son—a ranking with critical significance in the German family—than from Walter's active pursuit of secular American mores. Photographs of Walter in adolescence show a tall, well-dressed, strikingly handsome but somber young man. With his flowing, carefully brushed hair he cut a dashing figure. Lincoln newspaper stories began praising his athletic prowess as early as 1903, and by 1907, his senior year, they were raving about his exploits on the track and football teams. One wonders if Gustav sat in the high school bleachers and heard the 175 students cheer Walter on with the Lincoln High yell:

Slickety, slab, gobble and grab,
High, high, squeeze 'em dry,
Ricket, rock, water the stock,
We win tonight!

Walter's immediate ambition was to be a college fraternity man, and after that to be a success in business. From Gustav's point of view this was Americanization run amuck; Walter was breaking a bit too eagerly with his heritage. Yet in a sense Walter was merely following his father's own example. Gustav had turned against his father and carried his rebellion even to the point of self-exile. Before his conversion experience he had been secular in spirit, indeed profane. Walter resurrected that earlier identity, and Gustav doubtless did not like the reminder. He did not attempt to block his son's chosen course, but he did withhold his approval. Walter carried his father's silently scornful judgment through adulthood and eventually could not bear its weight.

But he did manage for a time to fulfill his dual dream. He entered Illinois Wesleyan in the fall of 1909, two years after graduating from Lincoln High, and promptly pledged as a member of the Phi Delta Phi fraternity. A year later he and a friend bought the Lincoln *Morning Courier*, an eight-page paper with a circulation of 1,000, and in 1912 they took over the afternoon *News-Herald* as well. Walter served as president of the *Courier-Herald* Company and managing editor of the papers. The departing publisher of the *News-Herald*, Morris Emmerson, called him "a man of wonderful energy and resources," and praised his intention, as a good progressive, to do away with partisanship in daily journalism. Walter may have sought to stay free of party labels, to work only for the "public interest," but that did not prevent him from trying to put the Democratic *Evening Star* out of business. John Edmonds, editor of the *Star*, even claimed in print that Walter used cut-rate advertising practices to do him in. When Walter read that, he stormed over to the *Star* office and in good frontier fashion struck Edmonds "several blows with his flat hand and also afterwards with his fist." Edmonds threatened to shoot him but instead took him to court, where only a few

•

minutes later Niebuhr was fined five dollars for assault and forced to sign a "peace bond" with Edmonds for "a period of four months." Although Walter never managed to put the *Star* out of business, the *Courier-Herald* Company did apparently thrive up to 1915, when he suffered other business reverses and was forced to sell out.[7]

IV

Reinhold, by complete contrast to Walter, was the polished apple of his father's eye: ebullient but disciplined, spontaneous yet cooperative. Like his father he was the third child and second son in his family. Unlike Gustav and Walter, he displayed no hint of rebellion. Both his own recollections and those of his contemporaries at Saint John's agree that Reinhold strove to imitate his father from the earliest age. Florence Denger, the daughter of Adam Denger, a leading church member and respected downtown merchant, saw a lot of Reinie, as everyone called him then and later. "I remember him as a bright eager boy with a zest for life," she wrote in a 1959 letter. "His face was usually wreathed in smiles, he was a battery of energy, he was very popular with young and old alike in the church, and he never left any doubt in anybody's mind that he would be a preacher. We all took it for granted."

As a young boy Reinhold was already a tireless worker. As a twelve- or thirteen-year-old he worked for a time in Adam Denger's grocery store on Lincoln's central square, where Florence, who was a few years older, worked as a cashier. He worked not only on Saturdays and after school, but before school too. "The man whose duty it was to open the store at 6:00 A.M. found Reinie already waiting at the door." But Reinhold made such a racket every day getting up at 5:00 A.M. that his family finally insisted that he quit. He had no trouble obtaining another job in a shoe store, which opened at 9:00 A.M., and where he impressed everyone as a salesman. He was also a born impersonator. "I remember when I was a guest in the Niebuhr home," Florence Denger recalled,

> Reinie was imitating peculiarities of some member of the church. I laughed heartily, although I was old enough to know better. His mother frowned on this kind of thing but I noticed his father smiling slyly behind the book he was reading. Another time a crowd of young people went out to the Chautauqua on the closing day for a picnic. The session had just closed and the last speaker had been very pompous and over-developed in the stomach. Reinie, skinny fellow of about 13, got up on the platform, with all the pompousness of the speaker, walked back and forth with his stomach sticking out, used all the same pompous phrases until the rest of us were in stitches. He was always the life of the party wherever he was, but we all still knew he was going to be a preacher.

His mother may have frowned on his satirical imitations, but she was the pivotal force in developing his imagination. She knew how to set up children's games that sparked creativity. She gave them ropes and mattresses for the buggy shed and they transformed it into one arena after another: a

•

circus, a World's Fair, a Chautauqua. They mounted their own theatrical skits: Walter and Reinhold conferred on the plot; Hulda, Helmut, and other neighborhood kids took their assigned roles. Reinhold, by common consent the best actor, was always given the lead. One of his favorite roles, Hulda later recalled, was "preacher." "He loved to officiate at 'weddings' and 'baptisms.' "

Young Reinhold was utterly fascinated by his father. He was thrilled by his sermons, awestruck by the steady stream of high synod officials who passed through the house. It was in his preteen years, he repeatedly stressed in later recollections, that he made up his mind to be a minister. His father's vocation was more interesting, as he explained to an inquiring stranger in 1957, than that of anyone else in Lincoln. His motivation was as straight-forward as that, he believed, and he had never had second thoughts about his choice. What is most remarkable about this explanation for his decision is not that he should have found his father the most interesting man in a prairie town of ten thousand residents. The striking thing is that he should have limited his arena of choice to small midwestern towns. Both Gustav and Walter went to Chicago to work before coming to firm career decisions. Something about his father so overwhelmed Reinhold that he could not follow their example: leave home, seek his fortune, gain some experience of the world before making a decisive life choice.

What may have been most irresistible about his father was that he treated his middle son differently from the other two. He "constantly flattered me in my adolescence by taking me into his confidence and asking for advice on decisions which he faced," Reinhold recalled in the 1950s. "I have a very vivid memory of the impression he made upon me . . . in consulting me about whether or not he should accept a call to a church in another town. . . . I have only pleasant memories of my father and the sense of partnership he established with an adolescent boy." Hulda remembered the same thing: "Father talked to Reinie quite early about all the problems of the ministry. I don't think he talked to the rest of us." By comparison to his siblings Reinhold was a favored child. Gustav had caught his own reflection—the reflection of his mature identity—in this exuberant son. Even before adoles-cence Reinhold must have picked up subtle signals about his special place in his father's affections.

Reinhold grew up thinking that Gustav was "far from being a typical authoritarian German father." He knew his father was stern on some sub-jects. No shirking of chores. No newspaper in the house on Sunday. (The children snuck over to a neighbor's to read the funnies.) No dancing. (Walter alone defied the ban.) But Reinhold was shocked when in the 1930s Helmut informed him that his own memory of father was decidedly different. For Reinhold Gustav was something of a senior colleague; for Helmut (as for the other boys at Saint John's) he seemed a wrathful tyrant. Reinhold later told a friend about their "almost diametrically opposed" memories. He remembered his father as "rigorous" but "just" and "fair." His brother, however, "excessively shy and given to tantrums in his shyness," recalled being somewhat afraid of him. The fear could be traced, Reinhold thought, to "early punishment for bed-wetting and [to] locking him in a closet to cure him of a tantrum." Helmut was not the only one locked in a closet.

Hulda recalled that Walter met the same fate, and once was forgotten in the closet when his father went out to deliver a sermon. Gustav, it turned out, was not so far from being the "typical authoritarian German father." He had simply, like many parents, had a favorite child. Reinhold was the chosen one.[8]

Despite Niebuhr's retrospective claim that he had only pleasant memories of his father, his "partnership" with Gustav did have its strains. His mother recalled in the 1950s, for instance, that Gustav had campaigned strenuously against Reinhold's left-handedness. One night at the dinner table, in the presence of guests (there were always guests at the Niebuhrs' table), Reinhold reached for a plate of cheese with his left hand. Before he got to it his father rapped him with a stinging blow to the knuckles. Reinhold was enraged and ran upstairs to his room. When his mother, not his father, came up after the meal to offer comfort, he vowed to her tearfully, "I'm going to get rich some day! I'm going to buy myself all the cheese I want! And I'm going to buy *you* all the cheese *you* want."

Gustav later apologized for not making clear that his objection was to left-handedness, not to the consumption of more cheese. But he was not apologetic about the war on the left hand. Reinhold, meanwhile, had given voice to the forbidden wish to provide for his mother in a way that his father could not. For an instant he dared to express the son's deep-seated desire to strike back against his omnipotent father by allying, uniting, with his mother. This suppressed wish to take his mother away was the underside of his conscious desire to be exactly like his father, to take his father's place in the world. Even as a seven-year-old he displayed the same burning intensity and assertiveness that were Gustav's trademarks. One of his father's acquaintances recalled Reinhold riding in a wagon in St. Charles "asking more questions than a dozen wise men could answer"—a striking reference to Luke's Gospel story of the young Jesus querying the teachers in the temple. From an early age Reinhold had begun to resolve his ambivalent feelings about his father by imitating him in order ultimately to transcend him.

Walter had his father's assertiveness—which, as in the incident with the editor of the *Star*, he had great difficulty controlling—but he showed no interest in his pursuits. Helmut, though eventually, and only after much soul searching, a minister and a theologian, took on his mother's outward pose of quiet, self-deprecating passivity—under which there raged an intense will and devotion to work. Reinhold alone inherited and cultivated his father's outlook and style. He was the one who fulfilled the German proverb *"der Apfel fällt nicht weit vom Stamm,"* which German-Americans rendered "the apple never falls far from the tree." When at the age of thirteen he was confirmed into the membership of Saint John's, his father selected a verse from Jeremiah 31:3 for Reinhold to memorize. The particular choice may not have been accidental, since it expressed the unique fondness Gustav felt for his middle son and the unwavering devotion Reinhold had shown his father. At the Palm Sunday service, April 8, 1906, at which a class of seventeen was confirmed, Reinhold looked at his Pastor and recited the words of Yahweh to Israel: "I have loved you with an everlasting love; therefore have I continued my faithfulness to you."[9]

•

V

After his confirmation Reinhold spent one more year in Lincoln, during which he completed the ninth grade at Lincoln High. His teachers were mightily impressed by his performance. The *Courier* reported on October 24 that along with three other freshmen (in a class of about seventy) he would be exempted from semester exams in four subjects—Latin, English, algebra, and zoology—because of superior conduct and classwork. At the end of the year he had top marks in every subject: 97 in Latin, 96 in geography, 94 in zoology, 93 in civics, 92 in algebra and English, and 90 in physiology. (The science and math courses he took that year at the age of fourteen were the last he would ever take.) His Latin teacher, Eva Paine Carnes, was particularly taken with Reinhold. She served as a judge for one of his school debates, and after the decision went against Reinhold, for whom she had voted, she spread the word that he had in truth been far superior. For that breach of decorum she was summoned to the office of the superintendent of schools and upbraided. In later years Niebuhr recalled that she was the single high school teacher who had made a substantial impact upon him.

Despite his successful debut at Lincoln High School—success restricted to the classroom and debate team, since he did not have Walter's athletic gifts—he was not reluctant to leave after the ninth grade. In a few years he would express keen regret that he had missed a solid high school education, but in the spring and summer of 1907 he was eagerly anticipating his departure for Elmhurst College, the "pro-seminary" designed to prepare boys for Eden Seminary. He loved the thought of being on his own, even though at Elmhurst his life would be closely supervised. Reinhold's eye had always been firmly fixed on the future. There would be no standing still, no adolescent turmoil, no visible storm and stress. On the surface at least he seemed to vault over adolescence altogether. When he left Lincoln by train on September 2, 1907, he was more mature by far than most fifteen-year-olds; in some respects he was already an adult.

Elmhurst College, fifteen miles west of Chicago, was in those years a college only in name. In fact it was a second-rate boarding school with eight teachers who offered a stale curriculum of classics and ancient history to 140 pupils in the four high school grades. Niebuhr entered the second-year class of twenty-five boys since he had already completed the ninth grade. He encountered nothing to stimulate his mind. Elmhurst passed over the sciences, English, and modern history. Even with the stress given to the classics, his Latin teacher was so poor that in his last year, at the age of seventeen, Reinhold led a movement to have both him and an English professor dismissed. His classmate Theophil Twente recalled that Reinhold astutely mobilized a hard core of students for the protest, then enlisted his father, who made inquiries at higher levels. The teachers were dismissed that spring, and Niebuhr, who all the students anticipated would be chosen valedictorian, was shunned by the six remaining faculty members. He graduated in 1910 having learned little and applied himself sparingly. His 87 grade-average was not enough to earn him a merit citation at commencement.

Reinhold may have learned as much in these years from his father—

•

who introduced him to Harnack, Macaulay, and others during his vacations—as he did from his Elmhurst teachers. Although Gustav did not have the time to become a scholar, he was a widely read man with deep respect for the traditions of German learning. He did write a few articles for the synod's theological journal, but he conveyed his ideas primarily in conversation with the synod visitors who were always in the house, and with his own children. Although he was a thoroughgoing pietist—and hence a determined foe of rationalism and relativism—he was nevertheless intellectually curious. He took pleasure, as Florence Denger remembered, in repeatedly informing his congregation, "I am by nature a Doubting Thomas." Hulda, Reinhold, and Helmut all picked up from him this urge to subject traditional ideas and practices to critical scrutiny.

The Lincoln Chautauqua, which Reinhold never missed in the Elmhurst years, was another key educational resource. It introduced him to the broad currents of American Protestant moral and intellectual life that transcended the traditions of his own denomination. It was his first exposure, in the somewhat parochial isolation of the Evangelical Synod, to the cosmopolitan life of a continental nation. It was also an incomparable lesson in the arts of oratory and rhetoric, disciplines in which he displayed evident talent. Even in the summer of 1909, when he remained in Chicago to peddle books for a local publisher, he quit work in time to be at the Chautauqua. The *Courier* went to the trouble of announcing his homecoming in a separate note entitled "Here for Chautauqua"—the children of Pastor Niebuhr being by this time newsworthy in themselves. Reinhold was without any question an early arrival at Brainerd Park that week. William Jennings Bryan, still probably the greatest living American orator, was appearing again in Lincoln. So was Billy Sunday, former major-league baseball player and now an accomplished revivalist, whose sermonic antics included "sliding home" to Jesus on the stage.[10]

VI

In September, 1910, Reinhold left for Wellston, Missouri, on the outskirts of St. Louis, to begin his three-year stay at Eden Theological Seminary, from which his father had graduated in 1885. He was in a class of twenty, and was one of the youngest at age eighteen. All but two of his classmates were nineteen or older; most were already in their twenties. His youth did not prevent him, however, from emerging without delay as a leader among his peers. It was his public-high-school experience, according to Theophil Twente, that led his classmates to look up to him. Not only was he better prepared academically; from their standpoint he was further along the path to Americanization, toward mastering a mysterious and tempting environment.

Once again he majored in extracurricular activities and scarcely had to crack a book to maintain good marks. He took courses from all five professors, but actually put in an effort for only one, Professor Samuel Press, a man who in a short time would become a second father to him. Press had come to Eden in 1908 to occupy the "English chair." He was the first native-born scholar appointed to the faculty, and the first to teach his courses in English. From the start he exerted a powerful magnetic attraction upon Reinhold, as he would two years later upon Helmut. Reinhold recollected, decades later, that Press struck all his classmates with his openness and seriousness. He took both his theology and his students seriously; he expected them to perform to their capacity and in return gave a full, considered hearing to their views. His colleagues still relied on recitation and rewarded memorization; he used discussion and rewarded originality. Niebuhr found the combination irresistible.

Two other things about Press drew Reinhold toward him. One was his ease with the English language. Reinhold may have looked Americanized to his classmates—several of whom were in fact German immigrants, not second-generation—but he was still much more comfortable writing and thinking in German. He was quite aware of how incompletely acculturated he was. Professor Press was a critically important model for a young man groping after a firm identity as an American. The other striking fact about Press was his insistence that his students educate themselves outside the classroom. He organized the Lincoln Lyceum, a campus literary society which published *Keryx* ("Messenger") and provided for many of the boys a first exposure to English and American literature. The Lyceum sponsored essay contests starting in Reinhold's senior year (when he was editor of *Keryx*). His entry on the assigned topic—"Religion: Revival and Education"—was a thoroughly pedestrian discussion of emotional revivalism and rational education as competing modes of Christian pedagogy. Each had its place, he argued safely. Revivals could attract nonbelievers to religion, but it took education to hold them and deepen their commitment to the church. The young author did not distinguish between the personal "growth" of the believer and the numerical "growth" of the church. He saw no tension between the faithful person and the institution, no danger that the church might impede spiritual growth in the very complacency of its devotion to missionary advance. The essay was a typical adolescent effort: a stilted statement of what the young writer imagined adult authorities were thinking.

He produced a much more original and energetic piece of writing in an unpublished short story that he probably also wrote for Press's literary club. In fact it was a retelling of a story that had won him a prize in Lincoln. The Lincoln version was a harrowing account of a boy being chased by a bull—based on his own run-in with a bull at a Hosto relative's farm in Alhambra, Illinois. The Eden version is about an adult—and it reveals a good deal more about his own preoccupations than his essay on revivals versus education. The four-page tale entitled "Before and After" opens with a disgustingly fat, self-satisfied man of wealth sitting languidly beside his wife in front of the fire. She needles him about his weight and orders him to take up golf. He dutifully agrees, outfits himself with the latest golf fashions, and reports regularly to the links. One day a bull gives chase to him on the course; he falls and rolls down a vast slope, and emerges magically, despite his wounds, with a lean frame and an admiring wife. She rejoices that he is "at last a man [about] whom the whole town does not talk."

The story is about personal transformation to manliness and respectability. The growth is threatened by the enraged bull, but paradoxically the bull is the effective agent of the final victory over complacent passivity. The animal exhibits both more power and more intensity of conviction than the man: "he seemed to have a determination in his face to land such a victim even if it should cost him his horns." Even a non-Freudian reader of the story would have to grant that deep-seated feelings were struggling for expression. Niebuhr was launched on his own quest for success and maturity and he sensed there were imposing obstacles in his path. The bull perhaps stood not simply for some powerful male figure who might resist his advance, but for mysterious internal impulses and passions that he might need but not know how to control. He looked to the future with outward exuberance, but the story suggests a current of foreboding. He would have to mobilize hidden potencies, direct them to his chosen goals. He would have to remain in command when he felt "the hot breath of the bull." The ultimate threat was that the bull would seize him, as it had tried to seize the golfer, and "sever the cord that united his sole [sic] with his body." Niebuhr resolved to avoid that fate by appropriating in imagination the determination of the bull itself—a determination so intense the animal was willing to surrender "his horns."

Professor Press superintended the fledgling literary life at Eden and was also responsible for starting a program of debates, which turned out to be Niebuhr's particular forte. Press contemplated a casual program limited to Eden. But the debaters were soon bold enough to challenge a team from Concordia Seminary, the much larger school of the archrival Missouri Synod Lutherans. Concordia accepted and suddenly the prestige of the entire German Evangelical Synod seemed to be on the line. The big debate was scheduled for February 12, 1912. The topic: resolved, that arbitration is a practical means to abolish war. In January Eden held a trial debate to select the two gladiators who would go off to battle. Niebuhr and two others took the negative—the position Niebuhr actually believed in—and soundly thrashed the three men on the affirmative side. Niebuhr and a member of the affirmative team, Paul Schroeder, won the right to represent Eden.

On the night of the debate the auditorium of St. Louis Central YMCA was jammed. Both faculties and student bodies were there, along with battalions of alumni, church members, admiring parents (including Lydia Niebuhr), and musicians whipping up spirit for each side. A well-known St. Louis judge, draped in black robes, took the chair to lend the proper air of gravity. Senator S. P. Spencer and a professor from each school made up the panel of judges. This time Niebuhr and Schroeder had the affirmative side, while Concordia's team of Friedrich and Lehenbauer had the negative. Schroeder began for the affirmative, and Friedrich followed for the negative, each taking three minutes. Then Niebuhr, who had been nonchalantly munching on a toothpick, rose to speak. He hammered mercilessly at the pessimists who dared not give arbitration a chance. Hissing from the Concordia faithful spurred him to mightier rhetorical flights. "Before he had spoken three minutes," Friedrich later recalled, "I knew we were going to be licked. He was too good for us. He was better informed, had excellent command of the language, and clinched every point in a way that convinced the audience he was right. His rebuttal was devastating." The judges voted

2–1 for the affirmative, Evangelical honor was preserved, and Niebuhr emerged a hero to his peers. The Evangelical boys sang all the way home on the streetcar, and insisted that their professors celebrate with them into the night.

A half-century later, when asked to offer their recollections of Reinhold at Eden, his classmates invariably mentioned the "great debate," when this nineteen-year-old David slew Goliath with a dazzling display of logic, facts, and rhetorical barbs. His fellow students had not always admired him before the debate. Some resented his dominance, his natural assumption of authority. His practice sermons struck some of his peers as condescendingly erudite and self-important. But after the debate all that changed. He was thereafter almost worshiped. The *Keryx* report on the victory declared with a new tone of pride that now Eden Seminary "need not remain in the background and be content to hide her light under a bushel. . . . Our first intercollegiate debate succeeded in directing the attention of the public to the fact that there does exist such a place as Eden Theological Seminary."

Niebuhr was active in at least one Eden organization with which Press apparently had nothing to do: the Bachelor's Club, dubbed ironically by its members as *Sans Souci*. Reinhold was a co-founder in his junior year, and president in his senior year. *Keryx* suspected editorially that "the rules of the club are not as strict as the name would indicate," but admitted to being uncertain, since "the members are sworn to secrecy. . . . The absoluteness of their vows of celibacy is a matter of mystery." Whatever the absoluteness of his vow, Niebuhr never had a date, it appears, through the age of twenty, and quite possibly for a considerable time after that. "So far as I know," Twente wrote decades later, "in all his school days he never really had a date with a girl. He was always neatly dressed, but not flashy. He kept his person clean. The only distinguishing mark about him was that his fingers were sometimes spilt with ink. Being an energetic writer, he would sometimes jam the paper too hard when making a period, so the ink splashed on his fingers."[11]

Florence Mittendorf, who grew up in Lincoln and eventually married Helmut, remembered that Reinhold "just wasn't the type" to go on a date. "He was too serious for it, always thinking about profound things." Walter was of course surrounded by girls. And Helmut himself, though shy and retiring, dated frequently while home on vacations from Elmhurst and Eden. He took girls roller skating (but not dancing) on the second floor of Klatt's Livery Barn, and then to Ferucci's Ice Cream Parlor (run by Lincoln's single Italian family). Occasionally he would invite a date to the movies at the Nickelodeon, or rent a buggy from Klatt's and take a female companion for a tour of the countryside. He had a strong aesthetic streak, nurtured by his mother, and he loved to relax in contemplation of nature. Reinhold was too busy for such frivolity. While Helmut was writing nature poetry, some of it published in *Keryx*, Reinhold spent his vacations from the seminary churning out editorials on world affairs for Walter's papers.

One major campus organization Niebuhr repeatedly declined to join: the Student Volunteer Movement, a nationwide group of those pledged to foreign mission work. In American seminaries of many denominations prior to World War I, the Student Volunteer Movement, led by the indefatigable

•

John R. Mott, was an exceedingly popular cause. Its motto was "the evangelization of the world in this generation." Anyone with even a shred of idealism thought seriously about joining it. Niebuhr had much more than a shred of idealism, but something made him hold back, even when several of his best friends—including Twente, Theodore "Sox" Seybold, and Armin Meyer—signed their pledge cards (all three went on to have long careers in India). It was not that he rejected the idea of mission work. He was not merely lukewarm on the subject; he supported it enthusiastically. Niebuhr was not a cultural relativist who saw compensatory strengths and weaknesses in all world religions. Outside the Judeo-Christian tradition there was, in effect, no salvation—not because he judged other religions deficient in particular ways, but rather because they were totally beyond his mental horizon. What made Niebuhr shy away from the mission field was the overriding sense that he had something else to do first. He had to prove himself as an American, to ground himself securely in American soil. He was a deeply bifurcated soul: profoundly German, yet somehow fundamentally American, in America but not of it. He needed time to sort out his loyalties, to comprehend his roots and his goals.

During his last year at Eden he and his father agreed that he ought to do further graduate work at a major east-coast institution, despite the synod's wish that he take immediate charge of one of the many Evangelical churches that lacked a pastor. His father was persuaded, Niebuhr recalled, "that an eastern university would be like a German university, and that one should get a university training." Reinhold was primed to test himself in a thoroughly "American" environment, one far removed from the Evangelical Synod, the German-American community, and his own family.

There were two problems: being accepted by a major east-coast institution without having a BA from an accredited college, and financing his studies once he was accepted. Fortunately Yale Divinity School was then drawing students, as Niebuhr put it later, from "second-rate denominational colleges . . . because [it] was in the process of enlarging numerically." By contrast, "the standards of Union [Theological] Seminary"—which required a BA for admission—"were too high for me." The money problem was even more serious. The Niebuhrs were living in "genteel poverty": his father's salary never topped $1,400 a year. (When Gustav came to Lincoln in 1902, the Saint John's church council raised the pastor's salary to $800 a year.) With the aid of a grant from Yale he scraped together the funds to pay his way.[12]

VII

In early 1913 the future looked bright for Reinhold Niebuhr, as it always had. No one doubted that he would be selected valedictorian for the June commencement; the honor that he had deserved but been denied at Elmhurst would now be his. After that he would become the first synod boy to go to Yale. The twenty-year-old champion debater, editor of *Keryx*, winner of the Lyceum essay contest, and president of the Bachelor's Club was certainly his peers' unspoken choice as "most likely to succeed." But just

•

as the spring flowers were joining the rest of the world in paying him tribute, one of the most devastating shocks of his life took place.

His father had taken sick during his sermon on Sunday, April 13. No one was seriously alarmed, since Gustav had had frequent bouts of ill health in adulthood and had always bounced back. In 1907, during a conference of the Northern Illinois Synod held at Saint John's, he had collapsed completely from nervous exhaustion, and had then sailed alone for Europe, for a six-month convalescence on the family farm in Germany. This attack in the spring of 1913 did not seem, in light of the earlier episode, to be a grave matter. Even when a doctor diagnosed it as diabetes, there was thought to be little cause for concern. He was ordered to rest and change his diet (insulin was not available until years later). He insisted on keeping up with his pastoral work during the week despite the doctor's command, and the following Saturday he grew worse. Reinhold and Helmut, who was now in his first year at Eden, were summoned home. Sunday morning, April 20, as Reinhold occupied his father's pulpit and led the congregation in prayer for the stricken pastor, Gustav entered a comatose state. On Monday morning, April 21, after regaining consciousness long enough to call for his wife and children, he succumbed. He had just passed his fiftieth birthday. The bell in Saint John's tower tolled solemnly fifty times, and could be heard far into the surrounding countryside.

The funeral on Wednesday, April 23, drew over a thousand mourners from Saint John's and other local churches. Synod ministers and officials came in from more than a score of cities. The service lasted all afternoon; fifteen ministers, beginning with Samuel Press, gave memorial addresses. Four Lincoln pastors, all members of Lincoln's Evangelical Union, to which Saint John's belonged, spoke in turn. W. N. Tobie of First Methodist stressed Gustav's patriotism and ecumenical spirit: "German though he was, he impressed his brethren with his Americanism in thought and sentiment. . . . He cooperated with his American brethren in all good work." Charles A. Galloway of Cumberland Presbyterian alluded to Gustav's public forcefulness: "No doubt many who at times in the past thought that our deceased brother was too plain[spoken], too aggressive, or perhaps too harsh in some instances, can ever now see the great blessings which have come to them on account of the courage of his convictions of right." Then he stressed one of the key themes of the afternoon. "As Joshua succeeded Moses and carried on the work of the Lord, God will raise up a leader who will carry on the work so well begun and carried thus far by our brother." N. J. Hilton of First Baptist looked toward the Niebuhr family in the first pew and made the point more explicit. "It gives me joy to know that the work our brother can no longer carry on will be continued by two of his sons."

Only one of his sons would be called upon to take his father's place immediately. Before leaving Lincoln the synod leaders excused Reinhold from the rest of his classes at Eden and urged the Saint John's church council to appoint him interim pastor. They did so unanimously and on Sunday, April 27, Reinhold occupied the Saint John's pulpit for the second time in two weeks, this time as pastor. He preached a memorial service for his father: "The Eternal Glory of Eternal Deeds." His father was to be praised, he said, not for those things that will be written on his tombstone, but for the small acts of charity that he constantly performed even for the least of his brethren. He had been an important man in his town and denomination, it was true, but more importantly he had cared for the sick and the feeble. Florence Denger later recalled that "this happy lively boy we had known [was now] standing before the weeping congregation, clear-eyed, almost stern, though there was an almost imperceptible quiver of his youthful chin. He had grown up overnight." Reinhold wrote a somber account of the mourning of his family and his parish in the synod's regional German-language newspaper. He urged everyone "in this time to learn to say again in faith: *Der Herr hat's gegeben, der Herr hat's genommen, der Name des Herrn sei gelobet* (The Lord has given, the Lord has taken away, Blessed be the name of the Lord)."

In early May he wrote his Eden classmates to inform them that he would be forced to miss his graduation and that they would need to pick another graduation speaker to replace him. But they voted unanimously that either Reinie would address them or nobody would. On June 11, therefore, he returned to St. Louis long enough to deliver his speech and receive his diploma. On June 29, a week after his twenty-first birthday, he was ordained into the ministry of the German Evangelical Synod by a battery of leading officials, all of whom had been close to his father, and by Samuel Press, to whom he now felt closer than he did to any other man. Rev. W. T. Jungk of St. Louis, editor of the *Messenger of Peace*, to which Gustav had contributed, performed the rite of ordination and concluded with the words: "We are about to lay the mantle of a father upon the son."[13]

As a child Reinhold had always fantasized about taking his father's place in the world. Now that role had been thrust upon him with terrifying suddenness. The Saint John's parishioners and synod leaders were depending on him to be what his father had been. Had his father lived on, another decade or more, perhaps Reinhold would have second-guessed his early decision to imitate him. With Gustav struck down prematurely, there was no room for future doubts. He came to see his own life as the completion of his father's. Again and again in later years Niebuhr remarked that he had never wanted to be anything but a preacher like his father, that he had never wavered from the firm career decision he made in childhood. He winced when others implied that he had ventured into the ministry without thinking. His reasons for the choice, he said in one of his last interviews in 1966, "my friends think are inadequate." His first published answer to their gibes came in 1927. It was, he wrote, the "beauty and romance in my father's life and character" that attracted him. He never met Gustav's equal among "the great and the near-great of our town" or even in later adolescent years among those "who were more pretentious than our village notables." But he ceded substantial ground to the "cynics" and "determinists" when he went on to note that "whether I drifted into the ministry or not I have . . . [had] numerous opportunities to leave it." The reflection that he might indeed have drifted into the ministry reveals his own awareness of the combined paternal constraints: his father's dominant will and sudden death. They had blocked critical reflection about his future. For all the "numerous opportunities" to leave his calling thereafter, his freedom of choice was severely curtailed after 1913 by the demands of his church and by the overriding fact that his mother was a young widow—forty-three years old at Gustav's death—with no continuing means of support.[14]

Reinhold was the son with whom Gustav was well pleased. As a child he no doubt relished this favored treatment. As an adult he was nourished by the warm memory of his father's trust. But there must have been times when he felt guilty about having been elevated over his two brothers and his sister. Beginning in his young adulthood, he would go to exceptional lengths to provide for his mother and siblings. Until his health gave way completely in 1952, he toiled at a furious pace, with utter disregard for his own physical well-being. One can see in this reckless abandon not merely the inheritance of Gustav's overflowing energies, and the desire to complete his father's work, but a determined effort to justify the privileged position he held in his father's house. To whomsoever much is given, of him shall much be required.

T W O

A MONGREL
AMONG
THOROUGHBREDS

(1913–1915)

I

For five months in 1913, between his father's death at the end of April and his departure for Yale in late September, Reinhold Niebuhr was a practicing minister. Even before his ordination on June 29 he was busy with pastoral duties. He preached weekly, and instructed the confirmation class of thirteen-year-olds. He was active in the Lincoln Evangelical Union, which Gustav had helped establish. This ecumenical body brought together Lincoln's five biggest Protestant churches—the First Christian, First Baptist, First Methodist, Cumberland Presbyterian, and Saint John's—which between them had over seven hundred member families. Membership in the union was one of the many ways that Saint John's Evangelical Church, unlike its neighbor on Kankakee Street, the German Evangelical Lutheran Zion Church, expressed its will to adapt to American society.

The group's main activity was its annual series of Union Services on Sunday evenings in the late summer. With some of the town's clergy on vacation, and with church attendance dwindling in the drenching heat, the union services were both a consolidation of the churches' forces in the slowest months of the year and an effort to spark new interest in the Christian faith. In 1913 Reinhold Niebuhr became a fixture at the services. He gave the benediction at the Baptist church on July 20, the invocation at Cumberland Presbyterian on August 3, and at the Methodist church on August 17—the final night of the series—he gave his first public address to an interdenominational audience. It was a sermon based on Matthew 10:39, a verse certainly chosen in part with his father's example in mind. "He that findeth his life shall lose it; and he that loseth his life for my sake shall

22

find it." In his son's view Gustav had put the well-being of the least of his brethren ahead of his own. He had found his life in giving it up for others.

Niebuhr's typescript of the sermon reveals a young man still struggling with English spelling and idioms—the passage from Matthew had "more truth in less space than any sentence or peace [sic] of philosophy that I know"—but it also reveals a preacher already at home with the dissection of paradoxes, a method that would later become his trademark as a speaker and a thinker. Matthew 10:39, he urged, "expresses the paradox of all life: that self-preservation means self-destruction and self-destruction means self-preservation. . . . As a mirage in the desert the happiness we seek will disappear when we seek it, we will lose our life when we attempt to find it. What sport life has with us, what fools it makes of us." The solution to the problem of life, Niebuhr proposed, was love and self-sacrifice. "Selfishness, that is our sin, to overcome it, that is the problem of our life. . . . The image of God that is still within us will never be satisfied until it is satisfied by the principle that made it—love."

By portraying God as a principle of love rather than a principle of judgment Niebuhr had taken the first standard liberal Protestant step—one common to Biblically oriented "evangelical" liberals like his father and to more rationalistic "modernist" liberals. But in the next part of the sermon he moved decisively toward the modernists, who debunked theological dogma and ridiculed the notion of the supernatural. The logic of the sermon text was unanswerable, he claimed. "It has been to me. There was a time when I did not believe in the divinity of Christ, the two natures of Christ, the trinity of God, and the communion of the spirit and I do not understand them now. Maybe you don't either. But the moral and social program of Christ can be understood." Traditional dogma was not necessarily false, but it was irrelevant to the Christian's primary job of overcoming selfishness and losing himself in love. Like other militant liberals Niebuhr was on the verge of reducing belief to morality, theology to ethics, the divine Son to a model human being. And like the Social Gospelers among the liberals, he was convinced that love was the answer to both "the personal problem" and "the social problem."

The raging battle between capital and labor was caused, he asserted, by human selfishness. Granted, capital earned too much and labor too little. But socialism was no better than capitalism since it merely put the selfishness of the "underclass" in place of that of the "upper classes." As long as most people were selfish there could be no solution. Capitalists would have to "voluntarily release some of their fat profits, . . . to lose themselves for their employees." On both sides love was the answer. The twenty-one-year-old Lincoln pastor believed love and self-sacrifice to be both the essence of the individual's faith and the basis of a social program—liberal sentiments that he would later deride as "utopian."

Gustav's liberalism had combined both a flexible attitude toward dogma and strong interest in social and political questions, with an orthodox commitment to the divinity of Christ and the supernatural character of saving grace. Reinhold, in the summer of 1913, had begun to secularize, naturalize his father's message. He was reaching out to the interdenominational audience at Lincoln's First Methodist Church, but also beyond it to the cosmopolitan, Protestant world he was about to enter. It was a world in which the "reasonableness" of Christianity, and the primacy of the natural over the supernatural, was taken for granted. As he prepared to depart geographically from his family and his synod he announced a theological departure as well. He would continue his father's work, but modify Gustav's faith by stressing the modernist, not the evangelical, side of Protestant liberalism.

Niebuhr's sermon spelled out his emerging liberal convictions, yet it also suggested a current of self-doubt. Several of his Eden classmates, including Theophil Twente and "Sox" Seybold, were preparing to leave shortly for missionary careers in India. He sensed that it was they who were on the road toward losing, and therefore finding, themselves. "The man who leaves his country to be a missionary," he preached, "is always reported to be happy. Why, because he has solved the problem of life. He wasn't afraid to lose his life and so he found it." By contrast his own chosen path, that of finding his life in the larger world beyond the Evangelical Synod, may have seemed fraught with spiritual risks. His sermon was addressed as much to himself as to his listeners. In seeking his life he would be in danger of losing it. Repeating the paradox to himself in a public forum may have helped ease his impending confrontation with the wider world. Perhaps it also assuaged whatever guilt he felt over "extricating" himself from his "implied promise" to the synod that he would accept a pastoral assignment right after finishing Eden.

On August 31 Niebuhr gave his last sermon (in German) at Saint John's on the Labor Day theme of "Christianity and the Workingman." Samuel Press came up from St. Louis to spend the day with his family and to preach at the English service in the evening. Press was already a father-substitute for Reinhold, the first in a life-long series of older men from whom he would seek counsel, favors, and encouragement. But his relationship with Press was unique: the first model for an English language vocation, an ever attentive adviser who helped smooth his passage to the national Protestant arena. He spent another three weeks at home, negotiating in vain with synod officials for a successor at Saint John's (all they would offer was a rotating group of seminarians for Sunday services), and helping Walter make inquiries with local builders for a new house for his mother. That project would in the course of the next year exhaust the benefits from Gustav's life insurance and leave Lydia and Hulda with a respectable roof over their heads at 535 Union Street—a stylish section of Lincoln—but no income whatsoever.[1]

II

He arrived in New Haven on September 23, two days before the start of classes at Yale's "School of Religion." New Haven he immediately found "disillusioning because it looked like a middlewestern industrial town. . . . It had nothing of the romance that my imagination [had] invested it with." It may have been ordinary, but at least it was familiar. Yale by contrast was a shock. He found himself in an elite bastion where men's middle

•

names were even more distinguished, if that were possible, than their last names. With classmates like Frederic Wyllys Eliot, Jr., Wallace Dwight Humiston, Mylon Dickinson Merchant, and Aiken Augustus Pope, who were on the average two years older than he was, plain Reinhold Niebuhr felt intimidated. "I remember being conscious," he would still reflect forty years later, "that the easterners would detect my middlewestern accent, which was at the time a little more marked than it is today."

Yale Divinity School, however imposing to a young German-American from the provinces, was in the decade before the First World War trying to re-establish its reputation. Founded in 1822 as a means of professionalizing the training of Connecticut ministers—who previously had apprenticed themselves after college to practicing pastors—Yale Divinity School in the early nineteenth century was the prestigious center of America's Congregational education. Its graduates supplied not only the vast majority of the Congregational pulpits in southern New England, but a large and growing number of those in the West. Its faculty included Nathaniel W. Taylor, the leading exponent of the liberalized Calvinism of the "New Haven Theology," and its alumni included Horace Bushnell of Hartford, the most important American theologian at midcentury.

By the end of the century, however, the faculty had lost its distinction and New England Congregationalism had lost its denominational vitality. Its raison d'être had always been the defense and development of Calvinism in New England and, through the home mission movement, the newly settled West. But the rapid secularization of American thought in the late nineteenth century, in response both to Darwin's theories and to the expansion of the capitalist marketplace, undermined the unique mission of the Congregationalists, even in the eyes of many of its own clergy. Some, like Henry Ward Beecher of Brooklyn's Plymouth Church (son of Lyman Beecher, prominent Yale College graduate and Connecticut pastor), made their Congregational pulpits interdenominational, and preached therapeutic gospels that stressed this-worldly health and fulfillment. Others, like Washington Gladden of the First Congregational Church in Columbus, Ohio, preached a "social gospel" and engaged in progressive politics. But whether they stressed individual betterment, "social salvation," or a combination of both, they tended to minimize the previously central issues of divine judgment, human frailty, and individual culpability. The old Calvinist refrain "there is no good in us" had been shelved in favor of the upbeat theme of positive thinking: both individual and society could be remade through reason, sympathy, and goodwill.

Yale Divinity School failed to keep up with the times. The future lay with interdenominational seminaries like Union Theological Seminary in Manhattan, which was less reticent about introducing psychological and sociological perspectives, about training ministers to be educators, social workers, and therapists, rather than merely interpreters of the Word of God. Attendance at Yale dropped sharply in the 1890s and by 1906 only thirteen men entered for the Bachelor of Divinity degree. The school, according to the *Yale Alumni Weekly*, was in a state of "stagnation not to say recession." Of the thirty Yale College graduates headed that year for the seminary, not one chose Yale Divinity School. President Arthur Twining

·

Hadley (the first lay president of the university) decided that the Divinity School was an embarrassment he could no longer tolerate and promised funds to upgrade its faculty, library, and physical plant. The faculty simultaneously determined to update its course offerings by abandoning the uniform core curriculum and the by-now onerous requirement of Hebrew language instruction. They introduced the elective system and new courses on contemporary issues began to appear, like William Bailey's Welfare, Work, and Practical Philanthropy in 1906. In 1907 the school declared itself nonsectarian, and in 1909 it hired Douglas Clyde Macintosh—a young Canadian Baptist and strongly modernist liberal—to teach systematic theology and the philosophy of religion.

By 1909 enrollment was on the rebound. Sixty students were now in the three-year BD program, compared to forty-six in 1906. By 1911, when Charles Reynolds Brown was appointed dean, Yale Divinity School had decisively embraced the new era. A Congregational minister from Oakland, California, Brown was a perfect symbol of Yale's liberal face-lift. He was a social activist, a labor mediator, and a proponent of popular psychic therapies. He had been so fascinated by Christian Science that he had trained under Mary Baker Eddy herself and been licensed as a practitioner. Later he decided that Christian Science was "a colossal humbug." But he remained sympathetic to mind-cure programs like the Emmanuel Movement and to mass-market counselors like Ralph Waldo Trine (*In Tune with the Infinite*) and Annie Payson Call (*Power Through Repose*). He cautioned the average minister against turning his church into a "clinic"—only "specialists" should handle serious health problems, mental or physical—but he was a prime mover in the widespread campaign to connect the realms of "faith and health," as he titled his major book in 1910.

His earlier *Social Message of the Modern Pulpit* (1906) had made clear that the up-to-date liberal Christian's concerns were social as well as psychological. He lamented the spread of tenements, tuberculosis, child labor, and unsafe coal mines, and then dressed his analysis in the rhetoric of uplift. The industrial system would become a genuine expression of God's will when all social groups acted together in the interests of all. The job of the Christian minister was to help bathe the entire social arena in love and goodwill. Brown brought a rush of new activity to the Divinity School. Having earlier lost its connection to the fiery faith of its Calvinist ancestors, the seminary was finally renouncing the role of transmitting revealed wisdom. It was becoming a combined training center for practical work and a school for the scientific study of religion and social problems.

Beginning in the fall of 1911 Dean Brown was constantly on the road drumming up new students for what was now officially designated (until 1920) the Yale School of Religion. He was often in the midwest, including St. Louis. Perhaps he even visited Eden during one of Reinhold Niebuhr's last two years there. By the fall of 1913, when Niebuhr arrived as a third-year BD student (Eden's diploma was not accepted as the equivalent of Yale's BD), Yale was recruiting and attracting students from all over the nation and several foreign countries. Their academic preparation—like Reinhold Niebuhr's—was often below par. Of the thirty-two members of Nie-

•

buhr's senior class, thirteen were from west of the Ohio River and eight were foreigners; the intimidating easterners were actually a minority. In the school as a whole there were thirty-two Methodists, twenty-seven Congregationalists, twenty-five Disciples of Christ, eight Presbyterians, six Baptists, and four from denominations that did not merit mention, including the Evangelical Synod. Yale had just over 100 divinity students, compared to more than 250 at Union Theological Seminary, the largest school in the north (Southern Baptist in Louisville had 375). Union required a BA of all its applicants; Niebuhr could not have qualified for the seminary he would later make famous throughout the world.[2]

III

Niebuhr moved into his single room in the Divinity School's five-story Taylor Hall, directly across from Battell Chapel and the undergraduate campus on Elm Street. Elm Street was in fact lined with billowing elm trees, as was the large New Haven Green one block away. Though the school was in the heart of the Yale campus, and hence of the city, it had only a slight touch of the urban atmosphere that surrounded Union Seminary in Manhattan. It was easy to spend several years at Yale without ever noticing the industrial and immigrant character of the nearby neighborhoods. New Haven made apparently no impression on Niebuhr, apart from his initial discovery that it had no more romance than a midwestern industrial town. His thoughts, to judge by both his later recollections and his contemporary letters to Professor Press, were restricted to his family, his future, and his course work, for which he felt miserably prepared.

Niebuhr elected the "sociology" concentration within the Department of Pastoral Service, which was distinct from the Departments of Missions, Religious Education, and Social Service. The "sociology" option was perhaps somewhat less demanding than either the "historical" field, which required Hebrew, or the "philosophical" field, which required a year-long course in the history of doctrine. In the sociology field he could coast through Professor Bailey's required Practical Philanthropy, and still choose as an elective Professor Macintosh's Philosophy of Religion, the class to which he devoted most of his energy. For all his interest in contemporary social issues, he eschewed the many recommended courses in sociology itself—systematic sociology, labor problems, immigration, and American social conditions and municipal problems. For his electives he chose, besides Macintosh's course, Benjamin Bacon's Johannine Writings and Hershey Sneath's History of Ethics. His other main course was Frank Porter's New Testament Theology, required of all seniors.

Academically Niebuhr did well, but not brilliantly, in his first year. On a scale of four (4 = A, 3 = B) he averaged 3.4. He got a 3.6 from Macintosh, 3.4 from Porter and Bacon, 3.3 from Sneath, and 3.0 from Bailey. Ironically his worst mark, in view of his later pulpit eminence, was his 2.9 in Henry Tweedy's Advanced Homiletics, a one-unit required course. Perhaps his marks would have been even higher had he not in the late fall come down with scarlet fever. The illness forced him to miss classes for a couple of weeks and cost him (in an era before student health insurance) $300 in savings and a good deal of the hair on his head—precipitating the baldness that, to judge by his father and two brothers, would have come in any case. But even with perfect health his grades would probably have remained at best in the high B or low A range. For he was struggling with both the content of the courses and the English language, as he reported dejectedly to Press.

"I have bluffed my way through pretty well by industrious reading," he wrote on March 2, 1914, his second letter in two days. "But I feel all the time like a mongrel among thoroughbreds and that's what I am." He was bitter about being "cheated out of a college education" at Elmhurst and Eden. In part he was embarrassed by the visible lack of a degree. As he reported the following year to the readers of *Keryx*, "even the Mennonites" came to Yale armed with BAs and were thus prepared to "take their place among the chosen." Synod boys, by contrast, were "forced to look on naked of those garments without which a man is considered a barbarian in the academical world." Niebuhr was one student who resonated to the proud calculation of the Divinity School's own information flyer. "Why choose Yale Divinity School?" it asked. Because, among other reasons, "it confers upon its graduates a Yale degree, good for its face value in any part of the world." But he also realized, as he told Press, that being deprived of the BA meant missing what lay behind it: "philosophy, ethics, science, and a real course in English." The Evangelical Synod was inexcusably lax. Other denominations valued scholarship; his own was "pennywise." The synod's "substitution of piety for critical inquiry" made him "boil."

Niebuhr's lengthy, soul-searching letter to Press—the first of several in 1914 and 1915—raised two other vital issues about his future. They were so personally touchy that he could discuss them freely only with his mentor. First there was the painful subject of his German-American identity, and his place in a German-American denomination. Press, the first native-born professor at Eden and the first to teach his courses in English, was living proof that one could attain a leading position in the synod without being outwardly "German." But Niebuhr needed reassurance. He was prepared to make a conscious break with his past but he could not do so unassisted. In a remarkable paragraph he began with the reflection that one reason for not spending a second year at Yale was his rapid loss of facility in German. He still read some German theology, but he had no chance to speak or write it. "I'm afraid," he lamented, "I won't have any German left by the end of next year." The following sentence, however, released a torrent of justification for abandoning German. "But at that I've about made up my mind that I will have to do most of my work in English. I'm tired of this half-way business." At Eden he had suffered from knowing neither English nor German adequately. His English was now improving, and since he could master only one language, he had made up his mind to "cast my lot with the English." He wondered what Press thought of his "desertion." He was pleading with Press to deliver him from his last residual doubts

•

about leaving his childhood world behind. Only Press had the authority to validate the renunciation of his inherited culture.

The second issue he broached was money: he wondered if he could afford the second year at Yale. He was $300 in debt, and although Walter could help him, he was reluctant to ask. His brother's income at the *Courier* was sizable for the moment, but he was also several thousand dollars in debt. Perhaps, Reinhold thought, a one-year pastorate would supply the funds he needed, but he was loathe to postpone his study. As he put it to Press in April, he was "extremely anxious to get out in life and make it worthwhile by doing something." And he wished to get out in life with a credential few young ministers could match: a Yale Master's degree. He did not have much hope that Yale would give him one. The dean of the Graduate School scoffed at the prospect of granting the MA in the absence of a BA. But Divinity School faculty members encouraged him in his quest for the graduate degree, and also assured him that Sunday preaching could fund a second year. By spring, as he settled down to work on his required BD thesis, he knew he would be back for graduate courses in the fall.[3]

IV

"I have read I believe about fifty books," Niebuhr told Press proudly in reporting on his thesis work. His topic as of April was "The Validity of Religious Experience and the Certainty of Religious Knowledge," but when he handed in the thirty-eight-page essay at the end of May it was entitled simply "The Validity and Certainty of Religious Knowledge." His adviser was Macintosh, the single faculty member to whom he seems to have taken a real liking. Perhaps Niebuhr sensed he had something in common with the young assistant professor, since Macintosh—a Baptist and a Canadian— was also in many respects an outsider at Yale. Macintosh, for his part, took a strong liking to the effervescent, hardworking midwesterner.

Had there been a dynamic professor of Christian ethics at Yale Niebuhr might never have gravitated toward Macintosh. But aging Professor Sneath was unoriginal and uninspiring: he produced abstract classifications of ethical systems. Macintosh was a very productive thirty-six-year-old and a magnet for intellectually vigorous students. He was a thoroughgoing liberal of the modernist persuasion. It was too late, he argued, for Christians to appeal to the authority of Biblical revelation to buttress their faith. Christian apologetics needed a surer basis: belief had to be grounded in a systematic analysis of universal human experience. More than any other modernist, Macintosh supposed that theology could become an "empirical science." But his reach exceeded his grasp, as Helmut Niebuhr (later another of his star students) was to point out. Macintosh unwittingly reintroduced culturally conditioned assumptions into his "universal" science. He innocently imagined that concepts like "rationality," "beauty," and "personal goodness" were objectively "divine" values. Reinhold too found his teacher's metaphysical program uncongenial—not, as in Helmut's case, because it was unpersuasive, but because it was irrelevant and boring. It took the vital

•

juices out of the philosophy of religion, turned it into an intellectual game. Reinhold was never drawn to theoretical enterprises: they smacked of passivity, lacked an aura of crisis. But in 1913 he was still drawn to Macintosh. He winced at his systematizing, but found his starting point very attractive: human experience, not inherited revelation.

Niebuhr's BD thesis was rambling and Teutonic, filled with unwieldy phrases and egregious misspellings ("ruffly" for "roughly" and many others). But it exhibited a certain raw capacity for philosophical argument. He was trying to establish rational grounds for religious belief, since "authority religion" (a term borrowed from Auguste Sabatier, the premier French Protestant theologian in the late nineteenth century) had been eaten away by the twin acids of Biblical criticism and evolutionary naturalism. The first had caused men to doubt some aspects of Biblical revelation, while the second had led them to doubt the possibility of revelation itself. In the face of modern skepticism Niebuhr set out to demonstrate that belief in a personal God, a belief he found indispensable, was rationally justified. The essay was an exercise in Christian apologetics. Its starting point was belief, not doubt. He was attempting to prove that he had a right to believe what he had been taught, and what he still wanted, to believe.

Religious certainty could no longer be based upon "superhuman revelation"; it had to be grounded in a philosophy of human needs and in the actual experience of belief. At bottom human beings needed two things: an assurance that divine "personality" had a place in an apparently "impersonal universe," and an assurance of personal contact with that eternal standard. The first need was for an "efficient God," the second for "an intimate God who appreciates our personal and moral values and helps us develop them." Neither "naturalism" nor "idealism," in Niebuhr's view the key rivals to Christian belief, could supply such a God—a God both transcendent and ever present, "a God who is sufficiently separated from the world and from man himself that he might have intercourse with him." Naturalists could not conceive of an intimate God because they "devalued" personality. Idealists were more likely to posit an intimate God, but in pantheistic fashion they tended to eliminate the distance between God and man. They sacrificed individuality to their quest for spirit.

Niebuhr's preoccupation with "personality" was typical of liberal Protestant thinkers in both America and Germany. It was the banner under which evangelical and modernist liberals all could unite. Confronted in the late nineteenth century by Darwin's theories and Biblical criticism, they turned to personality as a lifeline. The essential human being, they insisted, was not subject to the laws and vicissitudes of nature. Humanity occupied a privileged realm of spirit that scientific naturalism could not touch. For the modernists like Niebuhr, who followed Harnack in surrendering a supernaturalist worldview, personality provided an added benefit: it permitted them to salvage a special place for Christ. If Jesus was not quite the "true God and true man" of historic orthodoxy, he was at least the perfect embodiment of "personality." He revealed to human beings the spiritual heights to which they could themselves aspire. As the liberals used the term, personality had nothing to do with the personal winsomeness that secular success manuals were touting. For the hucksters of self-advancement, personality was the key to getting ahead. For the liberal Protestants, personality was the realm in which the Christian "died to self," sacrificed selfish desires to loftier goals. Personality was a disciplined, long-term self-giving, not a grooming of appearances for self-boosting.

What was remarkable about Niebuhr's discussion of personality was his total neglect of the social dimension that the liberal Social Gospelers had been stressing for a generation. He had stressed it himself in his first Lincoln sermon. But the thesis, reflecting Macintosh's interests, implied that the development of personality was an individual, not a collective, project. That focus is surprising, since the Social Gospel was at its peak in the wake of Walter Rauschenbusch's *Christianizing the Social Order* (1912) and the tremendous enthusiasm among left-liberal Protestants for the Socialist presidential candidacy of Eugene Debs, who received a million votes in the fall of 1912. Rauschenbusch was pushing the Social Gospel further and further toward socialism, toward outright support of the working class—"the most modern of all classes," which "embodies an immense fund of moral energy." He saw in "the tramping hosts of labor" a collective expression of "the miraculous power of the human personality." This enthusiasm for the working class went far beyond the more respectable liberalism of Dean Brown and others on the Yale faculty, like William Bailey and Henry Tweedy. But even they emphasized that Christian faith meant transforming social structures, not simply working on one's relationship to God. Later Niebuhr would mine Rauschenbusch in earnest, join the party of Debs, and mock the tepid politics of men like Brown. For the moment he was not inclined to go even as far as they did: he was immersed in matters of individual belief and unbelief. That was the tack his adviser encouraged, but it was also one that conformed to his own expressed need for personal legitimation as a preacher of the Gospel.

The God Niebuhr knew he needed—the one in whom he wished to justify his belief—was at once transcendent and immanent. Transcendent enough to leave human beings their individuality and to enter a "relationship" with them. Immanent enough to empower them to act freely and responsibly, the only kind of action that befit "persons." In Niebuhr's view God was himself like a person in having a range of capacities and limitations. He resembled man in not being completely free; he could not do anything he pleased, at any time or in any field. "He is limited by the determinism and necessity of fields which he enters." In human consciousness, where "determinism is at its minimum," God's freedom of action was the greatest. Personality was the realm of unpredictable encounters between man and God. In the natural world, subject to observed laws, God's freedom was most limited. Like other modernist Christians, Niebuhr ceded important ground to modern science: even God had to obey its laws. Had Gustav lived to hear his son speak of God's limits he would have been horrified. It was precisely the argument of Protestant modernism that upset him the most, as he made clear in his review of Harnack's *Das Wesen des Christentums*. Reinhold would never return to his father's supernaturalism on the question of natural miracles, though he would come to echo his father's polemical dismissal of those who put their ultimate faith in science and reason. Gustav's concluding put-down of Harnack—a man "who speaks as a priest of sci-

•

ence" and yet "is unable to find satisfaction in the finding of science"—
would be matched many years later in Reinhold's attacks on John Dewey,
Bertrand Russell, and others.

Having decided what type of God he needed, Niebuhr proceeded to
invoke William James's pragmatism to justify the act of belief itself. James's
"will to believe," even in the absence of strict verification, was rooted in
the conviction that the act of knowing was not an "outward look." Truth
was not something to be possessed once and for all, not a final apprehension
of reality, but something to be worked toward, approximated, in action.
Men did not have the right to believe whatever they wanted, but whatever
was not contrary to established facts and desired consequences.

> The revolt of men like William James against the determinism of the uni-
> verse . . . is the revolt of a growing moral consciousness in men, that is be-
> coming increasingly impatient with a universe in which its struggles are without
> effect and its powers not its own. Man wants to know that the battle of life is
> not a sham battle.

Niebuhr agreed with the "later Ritschlians" (disciples of the German liberal
theologian Albrecht Ritschl) that religious knowledge was "theoretical
knowledge" based not on "complete verification" but on "value judgments." Religious ideas, he concluded,

> are based upon what man believes to be necessary for the existence of personality
> in the universe. We need, or think we need, immortality, God, freedom, re-
> sponsibility, for our soul and therefore we believe them to be true, and in so
> far as we can verify our needs and values we have a certainty that they are true.
> We argue: I have a soul; it is a certain reality; there must be a universe in which
> such a reality with its attendant realities are possible. It is an induction based
> upon facts. Future knowledge may change our conception of the nature of the
> facts from which we start or may prove our induction to have been false but
> the proceedings have been entirely justified.

Niebuhr was aware of the obvious objection that could be made to his
anthropomorphic starting point. He granted that "one can go too far in . . .
making everything conform to human needs. There is something admirable
in the stoicism, James calls it 'toughmindedness,' that is willing to let truth
prevail even if it seems to rob the human being." Yet he still insisted "that
in the main we may hold on to our personal values and demand that the
universe appreciate them." We may believe, that is, whatever we consider
it important to believe, as long as our belief does not contradict verifiable
facts or entail undesirable consequences. Niebuhr grasped the intellectual
possibility of skepticism, of agnosticism, but was not tempted by it. He
was spared the grueling experience of relativity, of groundlessness, of noth-
ingness, that afflicted many of his intellectual contemporaries, including his
brother Helmut.

Later in life he did write to a friend that in early adulthood he had had
"a rather general experience [of doubt] pervading everything." He found
no "rest for this condition," shared by "all the young people of my gen-

eration," until he realized that "there cannot be 'rational' validations of religious experience. . . . Pascal, living in a rationalistic century dominated by Descartes, was incidentally my best guide." His BD thesis had agreed that there were no rational validations of religious experience; there was simply a rational justification for religious belief. But the thesis disclosed no fundamental experience of doubt; it revealed only a doubt about the best means of buttressing revealed religion in an age of pervasive intellectual uncertainty. There is no contemporary evidence to suggest that Niebuhr struggled without "rest" over the issues of belief and unbelief. Indeed, what is striking and perhaps distinctive about Niebuhr is that whereas many members of his generation grew up with the experience of doubt, while understanding the appeal of (and even yearning for) faith, he grew up with the traditional experience of faith while understanding the appeal of doubt. That permitted him to speak to the intellectuals of his generation with a compelling force that few if any other Christian preachers could match.[4]

In early June, 1914, Niebuhr left Yale for Lincoln. He had a summer job, according to the *News-Herald*, "assisting on the *Courier* staff," and he also preached several times at Saint John's and at the First Methodist Church. His sermon there on July 19, "Religion as the Fight for Personality," came right out of his BD thesis; his June 28 sermon at Saint John's on "Morality and Religion" was already one of his well-worn homiletic themes. But in August his focus shifted, for the international arena had exploded. His Niebuhr grandparents, aunts and uncles, and cousins were citizens of the nation that by August 4 was occupying Belgian territory and formally at war with Russia, France, and Britain. President Wilson pleaded with Americans on August 19 to be "impartial in thought as well as in action." There is no way to know how impartial Niebuhr was in his September 13 sermon at First Methodist on "The Dangers of National Peace," but as a German-American strongly committed to Americanizing himself, he may well have cautioned Lincoln's Germans against undue sympathy for the *Vaterland*.

Just before the outbreak of war, Niebuhr found himself confronting the offer of a job in the federal government in Washington. Walter, a strong Wilsonian progressive and a vigorous foe of the state Democratic machine of Roger Sullivan, had actively campaigned in the fall of 1913 and winter of 1914 for Carl Shurz Vrooman of Bloomington, wealthy "scientific" farmer and progressive reformer. Vrooman appeared to have a chance of defeating Sullivan in the primary, but when Secretary of State William Jennings Bryan failed to support him, Vrooman withdrew from the race. Wilson thereupon appointed Vrooman to the post of Assistant Secretary of Agriculture. Before leaving for Washington Vrooman came to Lincoln to thank his supporters, including Walter Niebuhr. He had certainly known Walter since 1912, when Walter ran unsuccessfully in the Democratic primary for Congress. During his visit in 1914 he met Reinhold for the first time. The young minister must have made an unusually strong impression since Vrooman, according to Niebuhr, immediately asked him to become his personal secretary. Niebuhr recollected years later that Vrooman "thought it was rather foolish for me to go into the ministry of this rather immigrant church," and sweetened the offer with the promise of a "tempting" salary.

In later life he periodically wondered if he should have chosen a more "political" career, but even in 1914 he knew it was too late to reconsider his vocational choice.[5]

V

Niebuhr returned to Yale in late September, a week before the start of classes. He moved into a larger room in Edwards Hall overlooking the New Haven Green—a room he shared with two new recruits from Eden, Henry Dinkmeyer and Cornelius Kruse. He also began searching for a Sunday preaching job, which he was counting on to fund his final year's study. The search proved fruitless for several months, and he sank further into debt. Despite the financial problems he was able to enjoy Yale more than he had in his first year. Enjoyment for Niebuhr did not mean recreation. Fellow-student Ferdinand Poffenberger later recalled that Niebuhr was always in the Day Mission library seated before a stack of books, and "Skip" Kruse remembered that "Reinie's old typewriter was going long after Dinkmeyer and I had gone to bed." Kruse found him more "serious-minded" than most of his peers. That did not prevent Niebuhr from engineering an occasional prank. Once he surreptitiously removed crackers from the dinner table and sprinkled them liberally in Kruse's and Dinkmeyer's beds. But he rarely wasted time on frivolous pursuits, and never went on a date or to a dance. He was busy trying to catch up with the better-prepared students in his philosophy classes at Yale College—one of whom was Archibald MacLeish. (When they became good friends in later years MacLeish had to admit he had never noticed him at Yale.) But he no longer felt quite the "mongrel" he had during the previous year. He was happy to report to *Keryx* that he had made contacts both in the Divinity School and in the more intimidating College. "Of course a great proportion of the 'undergraduates' are sons of New York plutocrats . . . but there is nevertheless a large number with whom even a poor divinity student can strike up friendships, or at least acquaintances that are helpful to him in many ways."

Niebuhr was now a graduate student at Yale Divinity School. He was not enrolled in a degree program at Yale Graduate School, which actually conferred the advanced degrees of MA and PhD. Decades later he recalled that in the fall of 1914 the dean of the Graduate School promised him admission for the following year (1915–1916)—if he maintained an A average during 1914–1915. He claimed that in the course of the year he lost interest in advanced study: he was hankering after the challenges of the "real" world, and had grown increasingly weary of Macintosh's enterprise. "The more I threw myself into these philosophical studies," he recollected with a sure comic touch, "the more I got bored with all the schools of epistemology that had to be charted—the realists, the idealists, the logical idealists, the psychological idealists, the psychological logical idealists, and the other different kinds of idealists and realists."

What he did not tell his interviewer was that his fall term grades—a combined 3.27 average—did not add up to the requisite A average. His hankering after the real world may have been intensified by the suspicion

•

that his full-year grades would not qualify him for graduate-school admission. In the spring he again got a B+ (3.37). But even if his grades had been higher, he probably would not have taken Macintosh's advice and pursued the PhD. His "hankering" was temperamental. The scholarly life seemed too passive. When he wrote to *Keryx* about life at Yale Divinity School he praised the daily prayers, the weekly devotional meeting, and the classroom devotions, on the grounds that they were "very helpful in what might otherwise be an atmosphere of cold scholarship." He lauded Dean Brown—"the biggest spiritual force in Yale"—for putting scholarship in the context of "real spirituality." "Critical studies" were important, but they were lacking in "inspiration." Scholarship seemed desiccating. He needed another sort of outlet, one that combined the use of the mind with the cultivation of spirit. Brown's career was an attractive model: respected and wide-ranging writer, renowned preacher, reassuring counselor.

His best marks of the year (above 3.5) were in Benjamin Bacon's Old Testament Theology, Macintosh's Religion and Contemporary Philosophy, and an undergraduate logic course. He did less well in the four courses he took in the philosophy department of the College—Platonic Idealism and Modern Idealism, both taught by Charles Montague Bakewell, and Pragmatism and Metaphysics, both taught by Arthur K. Rogers. Nor did he shine in the three church history courses he took from Williston Walker. His major commitment was to Macintosh, for whom he wrote not only his MA thesis in the spring, but also a paper called "Patriotism and Altruism" in the fall. During the winter he rewrote it, titled it "The Paradox of Patriotism," and submitted it to the student essay contest of the Carnegie Endowment for International Peace. In March he was declared the third-prize winner and received a $200 check (of which Yale deducted $25 for "overhead"). It was his first experience of earning cash through writing, and it may have suggested to him that his financial future was linked to his pen. At one stroke he had earned the equivalent of two or three months of a minister's salary.[6]

Just as Niebuhr's BD thesis leaned heavily on William James's "will to believe," his essay on patriotism took as its point of departure James's "moral equivalent of war." James's essay by that title, published a few weeks before his death in 1910, chided liberal pacifists for failing to understand that despite its undoubted brutality, war answered an ineradicable longing in the human heart—for service, sacrifice, and heroism. Unless a moral equivalent for war could be devised—James somewhat lamely suggested "a conscription of the whole youthful population to form . . . [an] army enlisted against Nature"—the peace movement would bear no fruit. "So far, war has been the only force that can discipline a whole community, and until an equivalent discipline is organized, I believe that war must have its way."

Niebuhr seconded James's diagnosis in a formulation strikingly suggestive of the structure of his own *Moral Man and Immoral Society*, still eighteen years in the future. "The moral charm that war still holds for many as an opportunity for the expression of some of man's noblest passions" guaranteed its hitherto secure place among human institutions. "As a collective undertaking war is primarily selfish and immoral without excuse. But for the individual it often means the highest expression of his altruism and the greatest opportunity for the development of his nobler passions." In war the individual soldier could aspire to moral achievements that the entire army and nation could not; in that extreme case individual morality and group morality were radically different. In *Moral Man* Niebuhr would extend his point to the life of man in society as a whole, precisely because by the early 1930s it appeared to him that all of society had been reduced to warfare in the form of class struggle.

But in 1914 he still believed it possible to abolish war, to build a "civilization of peace," a society in which the individual and the collectivity would both be committed to the same standard of love and self-sacrifice. The problem was that "many of the issues with which men busy themselves in times of peace are not genuine enough and not momentous enough to enlist the complete devotion of men. . . . Too many of their issues are trivial and too many of their battles are sham." Niebuhr, who also protested against the "sham battles" of modern life in his BD thesis, noted that the pacifists were on the right track in calling for active devotion to the international community as a substitute for the national community. He agreed that "humanity as a whole may become the object of man's sincere devotion." But he remained skeptical about transcending the nation-state altogether: "of course men will always have a particular sense of devotion to that part of humanity which is best known to them."

If people would always preserve a residual identification with and devotion to "their own particular race and nation," the only way to ground a "militant altruism" was by creating a voluntary, international body independent of races and nations.

> There is one agency, one special community that ought to be particularly effective in providing adequate moral substitutes for war. That agency is none other than the Christian Church. If its purposes and ideals are not great enough to interest men, they ought to be, and if its call to service has been too softspoken this is certainly not because of its true nature. . . . It is more universal than most agencies and its ideals are more unique and therefore more challenging than are those of any other special community.

In his BD thesis Niebuhr had argued that men needed to believe life was not a "sham battle" and that of the various alternative faiths—naturalism, idealism, and personal religion—the latter was the only acceptable foundation for genuine battle. Now he was again calling for a vision of life as a struggle for high moral stakes and arguing that of the few collective institutions capable of generating militant devotion—the state, an international community, or the church—only the latter could promote real self-sacrifice in the interest of humanity.

Between the lines Niebuhr was also saying that only a militant church was capable of enlisting his own complete devotion. Whether or not the Christian church could really mobilize humanity for the abolition of war, it might provide a haven for those who, like himself, could commit themselves to life only if the stakes were high, if the individual's beliefs and actions were eternally significant. His essay was another *apologia pro vita* sua—a justification for his choice of the ministry—and a personal call to arms. If the church was to become militant it would have to be made militant by men like himself. He took heart from the examples of "Amos and Elijah, Calvin and Luther, Loyola and Huss, all these heroes of religion, all these prophets of righteousness," who had in earlier epochs "compete[d] with the heroes of war for places of honor." It was time for "the heroes of moral struggles [to] take the places of the heroes of war in our [own] halls of fame."[7]

VI

After Christmas, 1914, with the school year half over, a debt-burdened Niebuhr finally managed to land a job as a Sunday preacher. The First Congregational Church of Derby, an industrial town ten miles west of New Haven on the banks of the Housatonic River, agreed to try him out temporarily after its pastor resigned. It did not take the church members long to decide that they liked what they heard. At the beginning of March the congregation of one hundred thirty-seven families voted to offer him the pastorate. But he replied that he was firmly bound to "the West": his mother could not be expected to move "to a country altogether strange." The church council decided to keep Niebuhr on as long as he was willing to stay. For the next three months Niebuhr was an acting pastor. But until the end of classes in May he traveled to Derby only on Sundays. He was buried in his MA thesis for Macintosh, though he had no assurance of receiving the MA degree for his trouble.

His forty-page essay on "The Contribution of Christianity to the Doctrine of Immortality" was much better written than his BD thesis had been. His English was now thoroughly idiomatic and his spelling only rarely faulty. Yet the essay was much less "existential," much more an academic exercise than the earlier thesis. He apparently did not care as much about the issue of immortality as he had about the question of religious certainty. Only at the end of the essay, when he shifted the argument from the Christian idea of immortality to the Christian idea of personality, did he appear to have something vital at stake.

The essay began in what was already typical Niebuhrian fashion: the outlining of two antithetical and predictably unacceptable alternatives to the Christian viewpoint. In his BD thesis these had been naturalism and idealism; in the essay on patriotism they had been the nation-state and international community. In the MA thesis they were the Greek and Hebrew doctrines of immortality, both of which contributed to Paul's distinctively Christian synthesis. The Hebrews, according to Niebuhr, failed to distinguish clearly between the future life of the individual and that of the nation. Moreover, when they did speak of individual immortality they linked it to the resurrection of the physical body, considered it not as a natural continuation of life on earth but as a special miracle of God. The Greeks improved on the Hebrews, in Niebuhr's view, by regarding the immortality of the individual as a natural extension of life on earth and by eschewing the "crass" notion of physical resurrection. (By "crass" he seems to have meant not

•

that physicality in general was crass, but that the hope of preserving the earthly body after death was crassly wishful thinking.) But they split the immortal soul so completely from the body that they could not ultimately maintain the individuality of that eternal human element. The individual soul tended to become submerged in the universal Nous.

It was the "religious genius" of Paul, Niebuhr wrote, to effect a synthesis based on the apparently outlandish notion of "unphysical corporeality." "Paul was not particularly concerned with the fine logical implications of his dogma. What he did was simply to assert on the one hand that the life after death could not be a crassly physical existence, and on the other that it must nevertheless really be the persistence of the individual personality in all the marks of its individuality." Niebuhr granted that Paul's unphysical corporeality appeared to be "an impossible concept," but contended that "it is no more impossible than the idea of a disembodied soul." Paul rose above logic to embrace an ultimate paradox that alone did justice to the idea of individual immortality.

At bottom, however, Niebuhr was not really interested in pushing Paul's speculations about the afterlife. His real concern was to defend personality not after death but in life. As in his BD thesis he was asserting in modernist liberal fashion that Christianity was "the religion of a person rather than the religion of a book." The "chief contribution" of Christianity was its "championing the cause of personality in its unequal struggle with the unappreciative forces of nature. . . . With Jesus, the individual receives a new place in the world. The soul of the individual is so valuable that no detail of its fate escapes the Father in heaven." With a wry personal reference to his bout with scarlet fever, Niebuhr added that "He knows even the hair that falls from a man's head." For Niebuhr only "a God that loves the soul" could guarantee "a universe that appreciates the individual." Only such a universe could provide an arena for battles that were real and not sham. What modern man needed—and what Niebuhr himself needed—was the assurance that his personal struggles mattered, that they were observed, recorded, appreciated in an ultimate scheme.[8]

VII

Professor Macintosh and other readers were plainly impressed with the thesis. Despite his B+ average and his lack of a BA, Yale Graduate School bestowed the Master's degree on him in June. It must have been an eleventh-hour decision: on the June 7 commencement program Niebuhr was not listed among the candidates presenting theses for the MA degree. After leaving the east coast on June 15 and arriving in Lincoln, Niebuhr sent the good news to Press on July 1. He admitted he had no idea how the MA had come through, since other students "with perfectly good AB degrees" had been turned down. "For some reason or other they were lenient enough to let me by."

The good news out of the way, Niebuhr unloaded two long paragraphs of current troubles, ecclesiastical and financial, on his mentor. First, the gap between his own modernistic liberal theology, which had been deepened

•

at Yale ("one would have to go to Princeton to escape it"), and the evangelical liberalism of the synod now seemed unbridgeable. "I am a good deal worried," he wrote, "that my liberalism will not at all be liked in our church and will jeopardize any influence which I might in time have won in our church." The problem was not just that others in the synod would suspect him of being unorthodox, but that he might be prevented from rising to a position of authority. Niebuhr was not simply seeking a niche within which to do his preaching, thinking, and writing. He was seeking "influence."

But his financial worries were weighing on him even more heavily. The synod was proposing to send him to Detroit as pastor to a fledgling congregation that could pay only $600 a year. That was out of the question, Niebuhr announced. Whatever he might owe his church—and he was not sure he owed it anything—he was not about to take a vow of poverty. His two years at Yale had cost him "a great deal of money." Besides his debts he would now have to assume some of the family burden. Walter had "nobly carried" them since Gustav's death, but "I owe it to him and to the family" to "earn to the limit of my earning capacity." Walter had in fact not just carried the financial burdens, but been crushed by them and by some of his own investments. Carl Vrooman came to see Walter's *Courier* colleagues on July 10 and recorded in his diary that he had "looked into financial condition of Courier-Herald Co. and of Niebuhr. Paper seems OK but N. apparently owes twice his assets. Had conferences with . . . R[einhold] Niebuhr and the Bus. Mgr.—laid out plan of action." That plan called for Walter's removal as editor upon his return from Europe—where he had been since late May reporting on the war for the *Courier*, the United Press, and the Chicago *Tribune*.

Reinhold's role in the affair is unknown, but he must certainly have regretted his brother's departure from the paper, which had been his own first journalistic outlet. For years he had contributed unsigned editorials and stories. Walter's financial demise was the demise not just of an older brother, but of a role model and even a comrade in arms. Though Reinhold had never imitated Walter's rebelliousness, he had admired his worldly exploits, his political know-how, his secular ease. Respected town editor, Congressional hopeful in 1912, member of the press at national conventions that year, campaign manager for progressive Democrats: Walter's career represented for Reinhold the path of practical accomplishment and access to power in mainstream America. There had even been talk in the spring of 1915 about Reinhold's joining Walter as a reporter in Europe for the summer. The *Courier* went so far as to claim in mid-May that "Reinhold Niebuhr . . . plans to sail later in the summer for Berlin to take care of the transmission of official dispatches to a western news agency." The plan must have collapsed along with Walter's own position at the *Courier*. Reinhold had to postpone his journalistic career, but Walter had given him his first intoxicating exposure to political reportage. When in the 1920s Reinhold began to establish himself as a preacher and a journalist, he was carrying on both the tragically interrupted vocation of his father and the suspended career of his older brother.

Once the extent of Walter's financial failure was revealed in July, 1915,

•

Reinhold knew that by default he was to be the family's chief breadwinner. The process by which he became the family's surrogate father was now complete. He was to be both spiritual leader and material provider—in reality, though not in birth rank, the eldest son. But how to provide on the minuscule salary of the Detroit church? He set about the task of persuading his superiors to raise it. By the time he wrote to Press on July 11 he had extracted a promise from the synod's Mission Board of a total annual salary of $900. But even that would not be enough to support himself and his mother, since the Detroit congregation had no parsonage and a two-bedroom apartment in housing-scarce Detroit would be out of reach. He was "very desperate to be so impotent" after two years of advanced study, and felt entitled "to something a little better than the ordinary." Outside the synod he could easily find a pulpit that would pay him adequately. "Now I am thrown into a curious complication of ethical considerations, duty to family, duty to church and friends. . . . I am burdening you again simply because I must unburden myself to someone."

After two years of relative freedom from obligation to either his family or his church, he was being claimed by both institutions. He felt "impotent" in the face of his duty to care for his mother, to accept the assignment President-General John Baltzer gave him, and perhaps also to help with the settlement of Walter's debts. His life seemed suddenly to be an oppressive network of restraints. He put off leaving for Detroit as long as he could. When the secretary of the church wrote to him in early July urging him to come right away, he replied that *"dringende Geschäfte"* (pressing business) made it impossible to come until August. Remaining in Lincoln until August would give him more time to plead with synod authorities for a higher salary, and also save him a month's room and board in the much more expensive metropolis. But the synod refused to budge, even attempted to reduce his salary below the promised $900, a turn of events that embittered Niebuhr for months. On August 8—without his mother, who remained in Lincoln until after Christmas—he dutifully reported to Detroit's Bethel Evangelical Church for his first sermon.[9]

THREE

IF I WERE
NOT OF
GERMAN BLOOD

(1915–1919)

I

Bethel Evangelical Church was the newest and smallest of the synod's congregations in Detroit. Founded in August, 1912, by a group of thirteen laymen, Bethel was designed to serve Detroit's northwestern residential frontier. The founders, like the other members who joined during the rest of the decade, were with few exceptions middle-class German-Americans. Like other middle-class Detroiters, they were anxious to find homes on the outskirts of what was rapidly becoming—thanks to the assembly-line ingenuity of Henry Ford and his competitors—a densely congested, working-class city. Once they had relocated, it was natural enough to resign from their congregations in the city proper and establish a church of their own. Bethel was ever after a resolutely respectable parish. Contrary to the later, widespread rumor that Niebuhr did very little to quash, it was never in any sense a working-class parish. Even in the 1920s, when under Niebuhr's tutelage the congregation took a growing interest in social and political questions—including the racial and industrial crises in Detroit—the membership self-consciously safeguarded its white middle-class character.

By 1915 Bethel's membership had risen to sixty-five and the congregation owned its own small chapel on the southwest corner of Linwood and Lothrop avenues, one block north of West Grand Boulevard, a tree-lined thoroughfare that cut through the northwestern section. But Bethel's minister, Paul Zwilling, decided in April that he could no longer make do with the $1,000 annual salary he had been receiving. He announced his intention to depart as soon as possible for a greener pastorate in Buffalo. The six-man church council immediately requested from the synod a re-

41

placement, but the shortage of ministers was so acute that no one could be found. As late as June 10 the president of the Michigan District of the synod informed the council that he had no idea when or even if a replacement would appear, although he was "using every effort to find an efficient and competent man." Still a "mission church," Bethel was at the bottom of the synod's pecking order; it would be lucky to obtain even a graduating seminarian. Young Reinhold Niebuhr, much to his dismay, found himself in a similar dilemma. He could expect nothing more than a low-paying mission church for his first assignment, despite his "extra preparation."

When Niebuhr reminisced forty years later about his arrival at Bethel for his first sermon, he recalled only the amusing fact that when he entered the church it was filled almost uniquely with children and old people. He spent the entire service wondering why the congregation was so demographically odd. Later he found out that the church council had invited all the residents of the nearby German Protestant orphanage and old people's home in order to provide a numerically impressive welcome. What he did not recall in his later reminiscences, or record in his published "diary" of the Detroit years—*Leaves from the Notebook of a Tamed Cynic* (1929)—was that in August, 1915, and the months that followed he was both bitterly disillusioned with the synod and deeply disappointed that his Bethel parishioners were so "German."

His true feelings he disclosed, as usual, to Professor Press. "I know you will think me an incorrigible calamity howler," he wrote in November, but he had to tell someone what he thought of his work. He had absolutely nothing in common with the other synod ministers in Detroit, who formed a "nest of reaction." There was little hope for a young "progressive" in their midst. "To be very candid with you I do not feel at all at home in our church. I do not know whether Yale is the cause of this. I hope that I would have had enough sense without Yale influence to resent the imbecile standpatism of some sections of our church."

His Bethel flock gave him some comfort, since it was growing slightly and contained a strong "progressive" contingent. But he was disappointed about their ethnic makeup: "contrary to what I had been led to expect, the congregation is three-fourths German so that after spending two extra years in English study I am forced to take a church more German than most of the Eden graduates get and have to throw all my ambitions of perfecting myself in English to the winds."

Niebuhr's campaign of self-improvement through Americanization—his resolution, as he had put it to Press, to "cast his lot with the English"—had struck a sizable snag. The major problem was not the Germanness of Bethel but the standpatism of the synod. His own parishioners were "progressive" enough to acquiesce in his Anglicizing measures. His very first suggestion to the church council had been that English services be held every week (along with German ones), not on alternate Sundays. The council had gone along, as it did a few months later when he urged the purchase of English-language hymnals. Yet even if he succeeded in modernizing Bethel, the synod itself would, he was convinced, look complacently the other way. He would have created nothing more than an island of cosmopolitanism in a dark sea of ignorance.

·

What Niebuhr was facing in the Evangelical Synod in the fall of 1915 was not simply a deeply rooted tradition, but a resurgent wave of German pride sparked by the war with England and its allies. Raw feelings of loyalty to the Fatherland were re-emerging after decades of submersion. For Niebuhr the problem of Americanization—for himself, his congregation, and his church—took on grave new meaning. It was no longer a matter of replacing one language with another, but of rooting out one preconscious emotion in favor of another. It was a question of politics and ideology as well as culture. It was a matter of casting his lot with the English, and ultimately the American, war effort. "The German propaganda is so hysterical among many of our ministers," he told Press, "that largely by reaction I am getting to be a violent American patriot. . . . There is no real interest in the welfare of this country and no genuine American patriotism." At Yale Niebuhr had grasped that creating an American identity meant leaving his cultural inheritance behind. Now it was time to declare his political independence by standing up to the first generation of German-Americans. He understood the feelings of those born in "the other country," and was sure that if his father was alive he would differ even with him on the war. But the church had nevertheless failed its second generation by expressing no sentiment acceptable to them. It was evident to Niebuhr that "it would be wrong for them to hold the same views that their fathers hold."

Niebuhr had thrown down the gauntlet: he would work to rid the synod of the benighted reactionaries who sought to preserve a link to Germany. His personal struggle with his Germanness entered the heated new phase of a public battle. Becoming a militant spokesman for the patriotic second generation allowed him to dramatize the character of his new self. For one burdened with "an inferiority complex" due to the small size of his denomination, as he put it in his diary in 1916, a public struggle to Americanize his church was a sure means of overcoming isolation.[1]

II

His flag-waving enthusiasm was in part the typical immigrant's response to war: leap to the defense of one's new nation to prove one's allegiance. Irish and German immigrants of the 1840s and 1850s had shown by their blood sacrifices in the Civil War that their hearts belonged to America. Niebuhr was demanding that his elders in the synod act like true immigrants, proclaim their faith in the new republic as the earlier generation of Carl Shurz and other '48ers had done. They had become disciples of Lincoln, advocates of national unity. In his belief that there could be no dual allegiance, no hyphenating of identity in an hour of crisis, Niebuhr was appealing to their example—and mirroring the views of many young German-Americans outside the synod. The poet Hermann Hagedorn, ten years his elder, was a national leader of the German-American patriots, and a typical example of their zeal: determined to make it in America, devoted to the strutting nationalism and moderate progressivism of Teddy Roosevelt. He and his colleagues were bitterly opposed to the pro-German propaganda of their

•

contemporary George Sylvester Viereck, editor of *The Fatherland*. The old-fashioned loyalty of young men like Viereck made them all the more irate, for it offered painful proof that the battle had not even been won in the ranks of their own generation. It also presented a symbolic rebuke to their aims of recognition and status in mainline Anglo-America. Niebuhr was too young and too provincial to circulate in Hagedorn's national coterie of patriots, but in the circumscribed sphere of the synod he was fighting the same war.

Niebuhr's public career could get off the ground only after his mother's arrival in Detroit in January, 1916. She immediately took over much of the day-to-day conduct of the parish, including the Sunday School and the choir, activities which had become second nature in her three decades of work for her father and her husband. They moved into an apartment at 1950 West Grant Boulevard, where he chained himself to his typewriter. Aside from writing his weekly sermon, and an occasional sick visit or council meeting, he could devote most of his week to devouring magazines and drafting letters and articles, which he began to produce in profusion. In part the barrage of prose was an effort to augment his minuscule income. More important than money was influence for his ideas and notice for his person. He could feel "at home in our church" only if one foot was firmly planted outside it.

By spring he had become a regular columnist for the synod's *Evangelical Teacher*, a new English-language monthly. Writing about good Sunday School methods was a start, and gave him a certain visibility in the synod, especially when he became an associate editor in 1917. But it was scarcely the outlet he was hoping for. The *Atlantic* was, and he shook with pride when editor Ellery Sedgwick accepted two manuscripts in 1916. He still recalled with delight, forty years later, that these pieces had brought in the colossal sum of $120, the equivalent of seven weeks' salary. This was a sizable pot of gold for him and his mother, who he later claimed were living at the time on $75 a month, of which $45 had to go for rent.

The cover of the July, 1916, number of the *Atlantic* listed its contents by title and author—with one exception. The author of "The Failure of German-Americanism" was identified only as "A German American." One had to turn to page 13 to discover the author's name. The editor was of course trying to highlight the irony that this indictment was composed by a member of the group indicted. To Niebuhr the absence of his name from the cover was a reminder of just how unknown he was. But it was this article that was to introduce a national audience to a memorably and stereotypically Teutonic name. Niebuhr made sure it was read. He wrote letters to prominent German-Americans humbly beseeching them to read it and convey their reactions by return mail.

"The Failure of German-Americanism" was a ringing repudiation of his own past, a firm assertion of his adult course, a promise of adherence to liberal ideals. German-Americans, he argued, had failed in two ways: they had neither embraced American principles nor expressed allegiance to the best traditions of their own homeland. By a shrewd twist he brought Germanness to bear against the German-Americans. Real Germans, he wrote, were liberal, forward-looking, progressive in both politics and religion.

They had created a society of unparalled efficiency, "a clinic for the world in the methods of humanizing industry." Their theologians had taken the lead "in reinterpreting the old truths of the Christian faith in the light of modern scientific discovery."

In utter contrast to the "brilliancy" and "ingenuity" of the "German mind," the German-American was marked by "stolidity," "sluggishness," "conservatism in all his mental processes." He doggedly pursued his own economic respectability, his own individual well-being, and firmly turned his back on the wider community. It was no wonder, Niebuhr concluded, that when German-Americans finally came to express themselves publicly as a group in defense of Germany in the World War, the rest of America looked on with "suspicions of disloyalty." Those suspicions, he clearly implied, were thoroughly justified. They could have been prevented only if German-America had been "less indifferent to the ideals and principles of this nation, and more true to its own."

Niebuhr did not bother to defend his judgment that mainstream America would have tolerated German-Americans' support for the Kaiser if they had only displayed progressive tendencies at an earlier date. Nor did he meet the obvious objection that in pursuing their individual economic interests, they were doing no more than assimilating the dominant American ethic. His lofty generalizations about the "German mind" rested, moreover, on the dubious assumption that the true German character was revealed in the nation's modernizing, professional elites. In the elegant tendentiousness of the article it was hard to miss a rather anxious justification of his own personal course. By departing from the German-American world in his own life he was fulfilling the destiny of the true German. He was not content to be more American than his provincial brethren in the Evangelical Synod— he would be more German too.

Niebuhr apparently did not realize how blatantly his article seconded the Theodore Roosevelts and Oswald Garrison Villards in accusing the German-American community of disloyalty for supporting the German cause against the British and the French. On August 14 he wrote to German-born Professor Hugo Münsterberg, noted Harvard psychologist and author of "The Impeachment of the German-Americans" in the New York *Times Magazine* the previous September. "I am writing to you," Niebuhr told him, "in the hope that some of the views I express may meet your approval." Niebuhr had good reason to expect an approving reaction from Münsterberg, whose own article had made much the same argument. It had called on German-Americans to offset suspicions of disloyalty by making clear that their goal was to contribute to the "inner life of the American nation" their own "racial ideals." They had to inject German ideals of order and rationality into an American democratic system threatened by a "spirit of carelessness and recklessness." Working for a more efficient democracy would enable German-Americans to show that they were in no sense partisans of German autocracy.

What Niebuhr got from Münsterberg was general agreement on the contrast between Germans and German-Americans but sharp criticism for having published the piece at all in mid-1916. It gave too much ammunition to the opponents of German-America and of the German cause. Niebuhr

•

was taken aback at the charge and replied on September 4 in a defensive letter that was at once apologetic and aggressive. "I wrote the article in all good faith as a friend of the German cause," he began disingenuously. "If I should have done anything in support of the campaign of calumny against German-Americanism I should be genuinely sorry." He was distressed that his piece had created the suspicion that he was "a Rooseveltian hiding behind a German-American pseudonym." He was far from being "anti-German." Proof of that was easy to provide: "most of my friends are German-Americans and I think I have done more to preserve German culture in this country than many of my critics who cannot even speak the German language which I use fluently." But Niebuhr protested too much. And even he had to admit that there was much more to his article than that.

> I will not deny that I wrote my paper not only as a friend of Germany. . . . As an American who was born in this land and has never seen another I have been pained as much by the unwarranted criticisms that some Germans have made of everything American as I have been hurt by the slanders against my father's country on the part of so many Americans. The Germans of this country are undoubtedly more sinned against than sinning but that they also have sinned there can be no question. . . . We must regard them as enemies of that national unity and cohesion for which every nation strives. I am frank to confess that I get very tired and sometimes impatient with their constant attempts to belittle every American virtue and magnify every American evil.

The vehemence of his "confession" suggests that he felt German-America had sinned not only against America in general, but against him in particular—by making his Americanness problematic in the first place.[2]

Niebuhr's second contribution to the *Atlantic*, "The Nation's Crime Against the Individual," appeared in November, 1916. That same month Woodrow Wilson, running on the platform "He kept us out of war," edged Supreme Court Justice Charles Evans Hughes to win a second term. But the article made no mention of the election campaign, of the debate over American intervention in the war, of the failure of German-Americans. Instead Niebuhr returned to the theme of his Peace Prize essay on "The Paradox of Patriotism." In wartime, he argued, nations had no trouble obtaining the full sacrifice of their soldiers because "loyalty and courage are made ultimate virtues for which men are honored. . . ." The battlefield provided one of the few arenas in modern life for unselfish, impassioned service to the community. But there had been another brutal year of blood-letting in Europe since "The Paradox of Patriotism," and Niebuhr detected a "tragedy" that the earlier essay ignored. In warfare conducted by modern centralized states, loyalty and courage were made ultimate virtues "without regard to the ends which these virtues may serve." He was giving historical flesh to his abstractions about nations and individuals. Modern states attracted the undivided allegiance of their subjects, he wrote, because they had earlier broken down traditional loyalties to church, region, or class. But once a man was in uniform, the state could offer nothing to "hallow his sacrifices" except "the selfish and material [value] of securing his nation's prosperity." Now Niebuhr believed that the sacrifices were objectively in vain, however

•

understandable they might be in view of the individual's yearning for personal achievement, community service, or lasting glory.

> The willingness of men to die in struggles that effect no permanent good and leave no contribution to civilization makes the tragedy of individual life all the more pathetic. The crime of the nation against the individual is not that it demands his sacrifices against his will, but that it claims a life of eternal significance for ends that have no eternal value.

After America entered the war in 1917—and President Wilson hallowed American sacrifices with the rhetoric of "making the world safe for democracy"—Niebuhr changed his tune. But in 1916, and again after the war, he was sure that the national community could not provide the basis for "a life of eternal significance." In "The Paradox of Patriotism" he had supposed that a militant international church could project ends of eternal value. In the *Atlantic* he no longer spoke of an ideal church because the actual churches of the world had succumbed so shamefully, in his opinion, to the war spirit. His unpublished 1916 essay, "The War and Religion," pointed out that in each of the belligerent nations a revival of religion had occurred. But in each case religion had been "nationalized." God had been reduced to "a ready ally"; theism had degenerated into "polytheism." Even Turkey, an Islamic nation, had undergone a "religious awakening." That proved to the Eurocentric and Christocentric Niebuhr that "the religious needs of the hour have been such that almost any religion was able to satisfy them." Faith had been distorted into a merely utilitarian creed at both national and individual levels: a tool for securing national victory, a salve for soothing personal pain. He was determined to resist utilitarianism on both levels. If a transnational church was an impossible dream, he would be a free-lance critic of the national churches. If other preachers were reducing Christianity to a limp, therapeutic painkiller, he would stress stoicism.

> It would be a distinct gain to Christian character if religion were not so persistently used to nullify the wholesome effects of our pains and sorrows by offering quick and easy consolation for them. . . . The weakest point in the Christian "Weltanschauung" is its tendency to produce a whining unwillingness to meet the fortunes of life without some assurances of recompense for the pains they inflict.[3]

III

He would also stress that God was a Judge, not just a succoring Spirit, as he made clear in his first article for a Detroit audience. H. M. Nimmo, editor of the city's elegant weekly *Saturday Night*, had liked "The Failure of German-Americanism" enough to reprint most of it. That entrée led to an original assignment: an analysis of the preacher Billy Sunday, who brought his revival to Detroit in September, 1916. Niebuhr was captivated by Sunday, the former major-league baseball player whom he had first heard as a youth at the Chautauqua in Lincoln. Most enlightened, liberal ministers scoffed at Sunday's stage antics: strutting, shrieking, shedding coat and shirt, "sliding home" to Jesus. Niebuhr did not. Nor did the 40,000 Detroiters who packed the old Detroit Athletic Club grounds for the opening day of his revival on September 10, or the hundreds of thousands of others who trooped in from Michigan, Canada, and Ohio before his act closed in October. Sunday was one of the nation's leading popular evangelists and perhaps the single most influential crusader against the saloon. His encampment in one of the "wettest" cities in America gave a powerful final boost to the Prohibition campaign in Michigan, where the sale of alcohol was outlawed beginning May 1, 1918. Niebuhr did not wish to join Sunday's uncritical "eulogizers," but he even more emphatically dissociated himself from his strident "detractors." He counted himself among those "neither passionately for him or very strongly opposed to him," because there was a "peculiar mixture of good and evil in Sunday and his work."

Yet the article underlined the good Niebuhr perceived much more than the evil. What most impressed him was Sunday's "personal magnetism"— "Sunday seems to have more of it than even the most successful men on platform and pulpit." Sunday understood the homiletic truth that "religious enthusiasm is produced as much by the personal power of the prophet as by the power of his message." His theatricality was integral to his evangelism. It was not an end in itself, but a potent pose designed to dramatize his message of "the hideousness of sin, particularly of personal sin." On that subject Sunday had "the true instincts of a prophet, for as the prophets of old, he is an accelerator of the community conscience. . . . Like the prophets he ridicules the forms and symbols of religion and has no use for religion that exists for its own sake. Without a doubt he is without a peer as a denunciator of intemperance and immorality." True, he was silent on the risky subject of social ethics—especially "the application of Christian principles to the conduct of business"—and many of his views, like that on evolution, were "medieval." But Niebuhr stressed that "there is much in his theology to commend it."

> He maintains that fundamental paradox of Christian faith that God is both righteous and merciful and he preaches both judgment and forgiveness with force. Perhaps he emphasizes judgment more strongly than the modern church is wont to, but this emphasis is a wholesome antidote against the "tender-mindedness" of modern Christianity.

Against the growing liberal Protestant tendency to reduce religious faith to therapeutic positive thinking, Sunday insisted on the doctrine of future retribution, on the wrath of divine judgment. His apocalyptic literalism had its dangers, Niebuhr granted, but on balance it was salutary; unlike liberal "universalism," which assumed that salvation was for everyone who sought it sincerely, Sunday's stance preserved the "zest" of the "moral struggle."

Niebuhr's discussion of Sunday provides a revealing glimpse of his early attitudes toward the ministry—much more revealing in fact than the seven diary entries marked "1915" and "1916" published in 1929 in *Leaves from the Notebook of a Tamed Cynic*, his account of a "typical" young parson in "the modern ministry." (Only fourteen of ninety-eight entries treat the five years before 1920.) In the early "leaves" he portrays himself as "a callow young fool" who knew "little about life's problems," lacked "great convictions," and "almost dread[ed] the approach of a new sabbath" for want of anything to preach about. Perhaps from the vantage point of the thirty-seven-year-old author of *Leaves* the young parson of twenty-three seemed an ignorant, faltering fool. But at the time he had a good number of settled convictions and the confidence to express them, not only with firmness but with wrath—as his letters about Bethel and the synod, never alluded to in *Leaves*, make clear. The article on Sunday shows that he already had serious doubts about liberalism in the ministry and about calm reasonableness in the pulpit. Sunday was right in his eyes to attack the liberal Social Gospel for minimizing the gravity of personal sin and divine retribution. And he was right that the minister's task was not so much to enlighten or persuade, to call forth either the rational processes or latent psychic energies of his hearers, as to call down God's Word in a dialectic of judgment and reassurance. He discerned in Sunday the link between the preacher's posturing and his prophecy. Perhaps he was not yet an accomplished preacher himself, but he knew what to do: put his own "personal magnetism" to work in the service of the Gospel message.

Sunday was a significant model for Niebuhr in another respect: he was a touring public figure held down neither by parish duties nor even by denominational ties. Niebuhr craved the same freedom and the same renown. His mother had already freed him from most of the tedious parish tasks, but as an arena for his preaching Bethel was inadequate. A column in the synod's Sunday School magazine, and an occasional piece for a secular periodical, did not make up the difference. "Doesn't this denominational business wear on one's nerves?" he asked his diary in 1916.

> If I were a doctor people would consult me according to the skill I had and the reputation I could acquire. But being a minister I can appeal only to people who are labeled as I am. . . . Perhaps if I belonged to a larger denomination this wouldn't irk me so much. I suffer from an inferiority complex because of the very numerical weakness of my denomination. If I belonged to a large one I might strut about and claim its glory for myself. If I give myself to religion as a profession I must find some interdenominational outlet for my activities. But what?[4]

The answer came in mid-1917. Shortly after Wilson's declaration of war against Germany in April, the synod established a War Welfare Commission to oversee pastoral services for the Evangelical boys in military training camps. Evangelical volunteers and draftees were pouring into camps— ultimately more than ten thousand would serve—and the synod's President-General John Baltzer wanted an agency with a full-time staff to help shepherd them. He appointed six men to join him on the commission. As a public critic of disloyalty, Niebuhr was an obvious choice. What better way to allay suspicions directed against the church—a body still officially known as the German Evangelical Synod of North America? Baltzer and the other members pleaded with Niebuhr to accept the full-time post of executive secretary based in St. Louis. He needed no selling to be tempted by a job that would require extensive travel and high-level conferences with officials

•

of the Federal Council of Churches in New York—which assisted the War Department in the assignment of chaplains. But his mother's welfare made him hesitate. She was subject to periodic bouts of anxiety, and heavily dependent on Bethel Church for her equilibrium. Niebuhr persuaded the commission members to let him have the post yet remain formally in Detroit. He would spend most Sundays at Bethel, Hulda would move to Detroit to help Lydia with parish tasks, and Helmut would assist with the preaching whenever his MA studies at Washington University permitted. In November, 1917, Niebuhr assumed charge of a major synod agency. He was twenty-five years old and had the base he had been looking for—a base from which to roam far beyond the confines of Bethel and the Evangelical Synod. Moreover, it was a position within the church from which he could exert strong pressure for greater Americanization.

Niebuhr took to the road without delay. In November and December he toured camps in Arkansas, Louisiana, Texas, Oklahoma, and Kansas, addressed Evangelical congregations to raise funds, put the soldiers in touch with nearby churches, and sent lengthy reports back to the commission and the denominational press. He found the soldiers eager to show off their new skills to clerical visitors. "One of the boys," he wrote back to the youth magazine, "entertained me for a while with instructions in the use of gas masks. . . . These gas masks are very hideous things, and make a soldier look like a huge frog." Moral conditions in the camps appalled him. "Again and again," he told the commission members, "good Christian boys complained to me of the vulgar tone of the general camp conversation, of which I can myself bear witness. This is the least of the soldier's temptations." The trip was exhausting for Niebuhr—in Texas he "had a warm time traversing the miles of camp roads in order to find the men for whom I was looking"—and in mid-December he came down with a severe case of pneumonia. He was not restored to full strength until the end of January, 1918.

As he lay in Detroit recuperating, he learned that a problem more serious than vulgar conversation had arisen. Two synod soldiers at Camp Lewis in Washington State had complained about receiving in the mail copies of the *Evangelical Herald*—on the cover of which was printed in small letters the phrase "published by the German Evangelical Synod of North America." The soldiers had expressed their anxiety about the word "German" to the Reverend Eugene Baltzer, nephew of the president-general, and he passed their worry on to the commission. "They would hate," Baltzer wrote, "to become marked men or be held in suspicion even in the slightest degree since they are anxious to advance." Perhaps it might be possible, "without evident disloyalty or ungratefulness to our beloved church," to drop the word "German" from synod periodicals. Without knowing it, the young Baltzer had launched the first missile in what was shortly to become a fratricidal exchange between old and new guards in the church. His uncle, the head of the synod, would soon emerge as the chief behind-the-scenes supporter of the "progressive" wing. His key lieutenant and "point man" in the campaign would be Reinhold Niebuhr, who had already impressed him with his "college-bred" eloquence. Niebuhr became the most significant single soldier in the war to prove the synod's loyalty to America by

•

discrediting its diehard adherents of the German name, the German language, and in a few cases the German cause.[5]

IV

Baltzer's and Niebuhr's assault on "German" elements in the synod can be understood only in relation to the broader repression of German culture sponsored by the federal government in 1917 and 1918. Ever since the sinking of the *Lusitania* in 1915, the American press had been warning of German bomb plots in the United States, and calls for "100 percent Americanism" had echoed from the White House and Congress to July Fourth harangues at village squares. But it was only after the creation in early 1917 of a technically efficient propaganda agency, George Creel's Committee on Public Information, that the anti-German hysteria approached the dimensions of a wave of terror. Its seventy-five thousand speech-makers, called "Four Minute Men," fanned out across the country to whip up a spirit of vigilance. Armed with propaganda films for local movie houses, they made sure that everyone grasped the full import of President Wilson's 1917 Flag Day address. "The military masters of Germany," he said, "have filled our unsuspecting communities with vicious spies and conspirators and have sought to corrupt the opinion of our people."

State and community officials took the hint. Laws banning or restricting German-language instruction in the schools rapidly appeared in half the states. Some restricted the right to speak German in public or on the telephone. Others forced German magazines and newspapers—of which there were more than five hundred in the United States—to publish translations of all articles relating to the war. There was a contagion of name changes: Germantown, Nebraska, became Garland; East Germantown, Indiana, became Pershing; Berlin, Iowa, became Lincoln. But even more important than the anti-German legislation was the campaign by German-Americans to purify themselves. Many changed their own names, stopped speaking German at home, resigned from German singing societies. Americanization amounted to the excision of German influence through the organized efforts of the state and the active cooperation of many German-Americans. Not that they had a great deal of choice. Even if the campaign of intimidation had not erupted in violence in several localities, German-Americans were well advised to make outward gestures of inward allegiance to the nation. Especially if, like the Camp Lewis trainees, they were "anxious to advance" in the world. Reinhold Niebuhr, along with older brother Walter, made a noteworthy contribution to the wave of cultural repression. Walter, after covering the first part of the war from Europe, returned to make anti-German films as an employee of the Creel Committee itself. While his brother assisted the government effort, Reinhold went to work at rooting out disloyalty in the church.[6]

In response to the Camp Lewis complaint, the War Welfare Commission in January, 1918, sent out a "Memorial to the Officers of the German Evangelical Synod of North America." It granted that a majority vote at a General Synod Conference in August, 1917, had opposed dropping the

"German" from the title of the church. But new conditions demanded "simplifying the official title of our denomination." The present name implied an official connection to the German church, and therefore invited "criticism and possibly suspicion." Change came immediately to the cover of the *Evangelical Herald*, where the "German" disappeared with the February 21 issue. Change also came to its contents, since Niebuhr put together a vigorously patriotic issue on April 18. He wrote several of the articles, of which "Love of Country" was a typical example. "Patriotism," Niebuhr began in an abrupt departure from his views of 1916, "is one of the oldest forms of love."

> In many primitive societies it antedated family affection. . . . This war has proven that though patriotism may be old it still retains the vigor of youth. Its power over the lives of men is immeasurable. In spite of the fact that nations have often misused the loyal services of their citizens and have thus put their patriotism to ignoble uses it yet remains true that the individual patriotism is something sublime and noble. A man must be dead of soul indeed if he has no love for the land of his birth or adoption.

One "unfailing test of patriotism," Niebuhr went on, "is TOLERANCE." But he did not have in mind tolerance of those who dissented from the reigning war spirit. He meant forbearance in the face of the nation's faults. "If you love it you will be as tolerant as possible in your criticism of its faults. There are many men going about eternally criticizing everything their country does, belittling its virtues, magnifying its faults, and then they wonder why their patriotism should be impugned." He did not mean to advocate total blindness to national shortcomings.

> But you will have to prove that your criticisms are criticisms of love. . . . It is generally not difficult to determine whether people who criticize individuals are doing it out of love or out of spite, and it will be no harder if a nation is the subject. Love has ineffable ways of making itself manifest to men.

It was not enough, Niebuhr cautioned, to love the country's "body" alone. As in "conjugal love," mere "admiration for physical beauty and charm . . . never lasts." What really mattered was love of the spouse's, or nation's, "soul."

> If you have no appreciation for the American ideals of democracy, if you cannot see that in spite of some faults there is a potent strain of idealism in American life, you do not really love America. America is more than fields of grain or rich mines of ore or prosperous industries; it is an ideal not yet fully realized but in the process of realization. If you do not appreciate that you do not know and you cannot love America.

Of course "Love of Country" was public propaganda, not private confession, and Niebuhr may have tailored his presentation in order to win the hearts and minds of the thousands of servicemen who received the *Herald*. But he was genuinely seized by the spirit of sacrifice and service. His private letters and diary are full of it. He had momentarily found a

·

cause that went beyond mere national self-interest and came close—if one can trust his most effusive rhetorical flights—to embodying ends of eternal value. Niebuhr was *plus royaliste que le roi* in his paeans to Wilson and his war aims. "I do not believe that any nation ever tried more diligently and honorably to avoid a conflict than our nation did," he informed *Evangelical Teacher* readers during the summer,

> and, being forced finally to enter, that any nation has ever placed the issues of a conflict upon a higher moral plane than ours. American entrance into the war has given the conflict a new meaning. What began as a crime is ending as a crusade and for the first time in the history of the world we have the inspiring spectacle of a nation making every sacrifice of blood and treasure for aims which do not include territorial ambitions or plans for imperial aggrandizement. Except to the hopelessly prejudiced the word of the President that "we wish nothing for ourselves except what we may share with all free peoples," is convincing.

Niebuhr needed Wilson badly. The world-saving rhetoric of the President, himself a minister's son, permitted Niebuhr to reconcile his critique of merely "nationalized" religion with the need to prove his own and his synod's loyalty to the nation.[7]

The regular editor of the *Evangelical Herald*, J. H. Horstmann, contributed only a brief editorial to Niebuhr's special issue: a mild criticism of government censorship that stopped short of challenging American war aims. Yet it caught the eye of an intelligence officer at Camp Funston in Kansas. He informed the synod that such remarks were, in Niebuhr's words, "a sop to disloyalty and proved how much disloyalty there was in our church." Niebuhr had to agree with the officer. An editorial on "the press and the truth served no good purpose in a German American paper." It was time for the *Herald* to start expressing "out-and-out loyalty." The War Welfare Commission acted immediately "to take stricter surveillance . . . to guarantee an unequivocal American attitude in our periodicals." President-General Baltzer took an especially strong stand, and Niebuhr lauded his "splendid leadership in this crisis." He praised his superior for grasping "that nothing else but heroic action, let the chips fall where they may, will save the church."

Horstmann, meanwhile, was furious. He and Niebuhr had been at loggerheads before. After "The Failure of German-Americanism" appeared in the summer of 1916 Horstmann had rebutted it point by point, concluding that "whether or not German Americans have failed depends altogether on what Americanism really is. If Americanism means sympathy with England and the aims of a British world-empire, then German Americans have failed. But then the Declaration of Independence . . . ha[s] also failed." They had also had a confrontation over Horstmann's rejection of an article Niebuhr submitted in 1916 in support of Prohibition. Niebuhr indirectly accused Horstmann of "cowardice, fear of the many members of our church who like their beer." Approval of Prohibition was for Niebuhr a litmus test of both Americanism and progressivism. Horstmann dismissed it as "legalistic and therefore unchristian." In the present crisis Horstmann accused the War Welfare Commission of condemning him with no prior hearing—and of

•

kowtowing to a nameless military bureaucrat. Baltzer began to have second thoughts: perhaps they had indeed wronged the *Herald*'s editor. But Niebuhr was unrepentant, and acted to steel the president-general's will for further battle. Horstmann's resistance made his hackles rise. For the rest of the spring and summer of 1918 he was more than patriotic. He was positively bellicose.[8]

In mid-May Baltzer sent Niebuhr on a speaking campaign that lasted until the end of July. He was to explain the meaning of loyalty to synod congregations in the east and midwest. Baltzer was uneasy about Niebuhr's aggressiveness, but knew he needed it. "There is a kind of innate modesty about our synod," he reflected. "We do not like to meddle in politics and all that sort of thing, but these extraordinary times call for extraordinary measures." He cautioned Niebuhr that he did not want "to do these things topsy-turvy." He would ask senior synod ministers like Samuel Press to reassure local pastors before Niebuhr unsettled their congregations. "Wherever you speak," he admonished him, "be not hasty but lenient, long-suffering, and careful."

Baltzer supplied Niebuhr with ammunition for his speeches: historical episodes that documented the services the synod had rendered the nation—including the story of a military company of Eden students who stood guard by the Missouri River during the Civil War—and a new "declaration of loyalty and patriotism." Niebuhr himself had revised it prior to its release by the president-general's office. "The Evangelical Synod of North America," it began, omitting the "German" that was still officially in its title, was "a purely American institution."

> [The synod] takes occasion to declare both to its constituency and to the public at large that it fully ascribes to the principles and aims which dictated American participation in the world war. It endorses the democratic ideals as announced by the President of the United States. . . . namely the defense of international treaties and rights, the self-determination of nations, a league of nations and the overthrow of militarism and imperialism. . . . It herewith disclaims responsibility for any disloyal utterances or actions on the part of its members and demands a complete and unequivocal loyalty from them.

Baltzer, with Niebuhr's firm encouragement, was staking the synod's future on a policy of cooperation with the federal authorities and deliberate provocation of conflict within the church.

Niebuhr set off on his grand tour, leaving Helmut, who was waiting to hear about his application for a chaplaincy, in charge of Bethel. He visited New York, Philadelphia, New Orleans, and Kansas City—and dozens of other cities, towns, and military camps in between. One diary entry provides a revealing glimpse of what may have been going through his mind during the trip. After visiting Camp Funston, Kansas, Niebuhr confessed that "I hardly know how to bring order out of confusion in my mind in regard to this war. I think that if Wilson's aims are realized the war will serve a good purpose. When I talk to the boys I make much of the Wilsonian program as against the kind of diplomacy which brought on the war. But it is easier to talk about the aims of the war than to justify its methods." He was especially unsettled by bayonet practice. "It was enough to make me feel like a brazen hypocrite for being in this thing, even in a rather indirect way." Assuming that this passage was in his original diary, and was not added after the war, it is a fascinating disclosure of second thoughts at a time when both his private correspondence and public statements bristled with militancy. Whatever his secret doubts, he returned immediately even in the diary to the elemental matter of loyalty. "Yet I cannot bring myself to associate with the pacifists. Perhaps if I were not of German blood I could. That may be cowardly, but I do think that a new nation has a right to be pretty sensitive about its unity." The loyalist buried the skeptic for the remainder of the war.

While he was in New York, Niebuhr met with officials of the General War-time Commission of the Churches to seek their help in getting synod ministers into the chaplaincy corps. The officials informed him repeatedly, he told Baltzer, that the appointments were more likely to come through if the synod dropped the "German" from its name. Niebuhr made sure that Baltzer understood the depth of his personal feeling on the matter. As a "loyal and uncompromising American" he was "beginning to feel irritated over the constant aspersions cast upon us . . . I really would like nothing better than to be able to serve my country without these constant questions." If the name change did not come soon, disaffected progressives might well "leave and enter other bodies." The implication was plain that Niebuhr might be among them.[9]

V

After two months in the field, Niebuhr came to the conclusion that he ought to follow Helmut into military service as a chaplain. The step would depend, he informed Baltzer, upon finding a way to take care of his mother. But his commitment to military service was firm. He could no longer tolerate the inequity of pursuing a safe vocation, however important to the war effort, while others were under fire. "As a young man of draft age I no longer feel it right that I should stay out of the struggle." Yet a nearly simultaneous diary entry reveals that Niebuhr was troubled not only by feelings of inequity, but by the strong feelings of inferiority that had risen to the surface several times before.

> What makes me angry is the way I kowtow to the chaplains as I visit the various camps. Here are ministers of the gospel just as I am. Just as I they are also, for the moment, priests of the great god Mars. As ministers of the Christian religion I have no particular respect for them. Yet I am overcome by a terrible inferiority complex when I deal with them. Such is the power of a uniform. Like myself, they have mixed the worship of the God of love and the God of battles. But unlike myself, they have adequate symbols of this double devotion. The little cross on the shoulder is the symbol of their Christian faith. The uniform itself is the symbol of their devotion to the God of battles. It is the uniform and not the cross which impresses me and others. I am impressed even when I know that I ought not be.

Baltzer and Vice-President-General Becker refused for two months to consider his departure from the War Welfare Commission. They believed

•

him indispensable to the loyalty effort on the home front. But Niebuhr was adamant. On September 9 he informed his superiors that he would offer his resignation on October 1, though he would be willing to remain in his post until a replacement was found. "When I am called upon to speak upon patriotism, as I am called upon so often nowadays, my words seem to have a hollow and insincere ring. . . . Nothing can change the fact that it is a safe job while half of the manhood of the world in my age is in physical peril." His own manhood would be questioned by others even if he did not doubt it himself. But it was not so much suspicions of effeminacy that he wished to erase. It was the subtler suspicion that he was unprepared to offer the ultimate sacrifice of laying down his life. He had offered it rhetorically for some time, as in his September letter to Horstmann that carried their feud to a new pitch of vituperation: "If you do not know I shall inform you that there is a large number of men in our church who are sincerely for America, for America so devotedly that they would gladly lay down their lives for her." Baltzer was adamant too. "Niebuhr can you conscientiously leave our W.W. work? . . . Has not the Lord called you and prepared you for that time when you could be of great service in this extraordinary branch of work?" The "greater sacrifice" was to stay put. At the end of September Niebuhr turned down Baltzer's final appeal. A month and a half later, however, before a replacement had been found for him at the commission, the war was over.[10]

The end of hostilities in Europe by no means put an end to hostilities within the synod. If anything the in-fighting grew more bitter, as the old guard mounted a last desperate effort to maintain a German identity. Led by a group of conservative Chicago pastors, they clamored for retention of the German name and the German language. But some went to the new extreme of proposing eventual merger talks with the conservative United Lutheran Church, which was already busily adding smaller Lutheran bodies to its ranks. The progressive wing of Baltzer and Niebuhr immediately recognized the gravity of this threat to Americanization. Of the two historic ecclesiastical and theological traditions which the Evangelical Synod had brought together—the Lutheran and the Reformed (Calvinist)—the Lutheran was in the United States the more conservative, high-church, and "European," the Reformed the more liberal, low-church, and Anglo-American. Merger with the Lutherans meant greater isolation from the main currents of "American" Protestant culture. Even Horstmann was troubled by that prospect. He put the *Evangelical Herald* firmly in the Americanization camp, which he had conscientiously refused to do as long as Americanization meant support for American war aims.

Niebuhr realized that the best defense against the old guard was an aggressive offense. Instead of letting merger with the Lutherans monopolize the synod's attention he counterproposed eventual merger with the Calvinists of the Reformed churches. He thus shrewdly put the conservatives into the position of having to oppose a progressive measure—a measure which Niebuhr knew stood no chance of realization in the near future. Baltzer was so impressed with Niebuhr's political sagacity that he took him even more completely into his confidence by giving him access to his personal correspondence. He also took the unprecedented step of asking Nie-

•

buhr, at age twenty-six, to serve on the synod's powerful Commission on Church Relations, made up for the most part of distinguished senior ministers like Professor Press of Eden and Professor Irion of Elmhurst. In Baltzer's view Niebuhr had a critical role to play in the future of the synod, one that would take him far beyond the confines of Bethel Church.

> Let me be candid with you, Niebuhr. . . . You are the college-bred man, who has access in this circle. . . . You are the youngest, that is no sin, we will honor you for your youth. . . . I know some of the reactionaries in Chicago will feel very uncomfortable when they read my appointments, but this cannot bother me any longer. I am going to give you a chance and some more men like you, to not only grow up in the history of our church, but to live in it and one day, the Lord grant it, be of great value to the good old Evangelical Church.

Niebuhr was honored by Baltzer's confidence but felt he would be out of place on a committee of senior ministers. "I am really too young for it," he replied, and "perhaps too radical with the radicalism of youth for such a place." For the ongoing fight against the advocates of a "little Germany" in America, he needed to keep his independence. To underline the urgency of striking quickly against reaction, he told Baltzer once again that he might otherwise leave the church. "I do not mind saying that if I am going to stay in our church I would like to have a free hand to fight that crowd. Because if they win out our church would offer a poor field of labor for a young American who had his whole life before him." Baltzer accepted his declination, and agreed with his plan for attacking "Little Germany." But he chided his protégé for hinting at a possible departure from the synod. "One single little 'if,' dear Brother, in your letter I did not like. You are going to stay with us and stick it out no matter how the storm howls."[11]

VI

In his letter rejecting the commission appointment Niebuhr also gave voice to a major turn in his political thinking. Until November, 1918, he had been preoccupied with victory, and with loyalty as a means of victory. He had in fact been a self-conscious agent in the process by which the "nation" broke down parochial loyalties in the interest of loyalty to the state—a process which he had earlier identified, and viewed with apprehension, in "The Nation's Crime Against the Individual." But November brought both victory for the Allies in Europe and victory for the Republicans in the Congressional elections. That conservative resurgence was matched by the British Conservatives' smashing victory in December. The threat to Wilsonian idealism—which Niebuhr still, like many Europeans and Americans on the liberal left, identified with the cause of democracy in the world— was no longer German autocracy but Anglo-American conservatism.

Niebuhr was asking Baltzer for a free hand to take on American and European reaction. It was time to move beyond Americanization, and beyond mere patriotism. He saw "dangers ahead for American patriotism." The main threat was "complacent satisfaction" in the "small measure" of

•

democracy Americans had attained. "We have political democracy but we seem to be getting further away from social democracy just at a time when all the rest of the world is adopting it. . . . We are rapidly becoming the most conservative nation in the world." Niebuhr wanted the dual freedom to attack conservatives inside and outside the synod, in religious and political spheres. The contours of his early-adult career were coming into view, and Baltzer—who by this time had replaced Press as Niebuhr's mentor and father confessor—played the key role of encouraging him at this critical juncture. He did not share Niebuhr's interest in secular politics, but he understood that having his protégé's continued aid in the religious arena meant liberating him for political activity too.

Niebuhr had come to adopt the same general position on loyalty that his nemesis Horstmann had long been urging. Strong criticism of national policy was compatible with patriotism. Defense of ideals required not just aggressiveness toward the sworn enemies of those ideals, but vigilance against the ruses of their apparent defenders. As Horstmann, twenty years his senior, wrote to him in December,

> I have always been an idealist and am ready to go almost any length for ideals I can accept, but the forces that [pushed] for our entry . . . did not seem to have much idealism about them. When the Spanish[-American] war was on 20 years ago I was as much an idealist about it as you and others are now, but the things that came to the surface within a year or two afterward sobered this enthusiasm considerably. Since then I am somewhat shy on war ideals.

Shy on "war ideals," but not on "true American ideals as they have been worked out in the glorious history, traditions, and development of my country," as he put it in October. "I also am an American of the second generation, and I yield to no one in my devotion."

As the Paris Peace Conference progressed in the winter and spring of 1919—as Wilson's idealistic war aims were modified to accommodate the other victors' demands for spoils—Niebuhr went through a gradual disillusionment that matched Horstmann's of twenty years before. He had never, even in his most militant moments in the summer of 1918, believed in total victory over Germany. He had imagined that Wilson could throw the weight of the American nation behind the Allies and then enforce a new world order based on reconciliation, democracy, and open markets. Like other liberals he failed to notice that such a world order was on one level a Pax Americana of direct political and economic advantage to the United States. Wilson's idealism was also a very shrewd realism. Nevertheless that idealism was indeed giving way in Wilson's face-to-face encounters with Clemenceau, Orlando, and Lloyd George. "Wilson is evidently losing his battle," he wrote in his diary in early 1919.

> What seems to be happening in Paris is that they will let Wilson label the transaction if the others can determine its true import. Thus realities are exchanged for words. There will be "no indemnities" but of course there will be reparations; and, since the damage was great, the reparations may be made larger than any so-called indemnity of the past. There will be "no annexations" but there will be mandates. Wilson is a typical son of the manse. He believes

•

too much in words. The sly Clemenceau sneaks new meanings into these nice words, in which task he is probably ably helped by Mr. Lloyd George, who is an admirable go-between, being as worldly wise as M. Clemenceau and as evangelical as Mr. Wilson.

Niebuhr still shared Wilson's faith that "words have certain meanings of which it is hard to rob them, and ideas may create reality in time. . . . Realities are always defeating ideals, but ideals have a way of taking vengeance upon the facts which momentarily imprison them." But by late spring even that residual hope was ebbing. There was no point in planning a peace celebration in the synod, he wrote Baltzer in mid-May. "To celebrate peace implies that we as Christians can glory in reconciliation but since this peace does not mean reconciliation but a forced concession it does seem to me, and you are undoubtedly surprised to hear me talk this way, that any great celebrations would be out of place."

In his somber, post-Versailles mood, Niebuhr was prepared to question liberalism itself. He was not ready to jettison liberal "ideals," but he detected a fatal flaw in liberal methods. In a letter to the *New Republic*—for whose main pages he had vainly tried to write during the war—he indicted liberalism's "gray spirit of compromise."

> [Liberalism] lacks the spirit of enthusiasm, not to say fanaticism, which is so necessary to move the world out of its beaten tracks. [It] is too intellectual and too little emotional to be an efficient force in history. It is the philosophy of the middle aged, lacking the fervency of youth and its willingness to take a chance and accept a challenge. It approaches the old order with friendly mien, tries to blindfold it and lead it upon a new track without hurting the old order's feelings or losing its friendship. But the old order is never the doting fool that it seems to be. Either it humors and fools liberalism . . . or, if liberalism proves itself too persistent, it gets angry and gives the reformers a slap in the face. In the peace treaty the old order seems to have defended itself quite successfully by both methods. We need something less circumspect than liberalism to save the world.

To imagine that the goal of politics was still "to save the world" showed how deeply Niebuhr still adhered to the proclaimed purpose of Wilsonian idealism. The *New Republic* editors must have smiled at this encomium to youth, risk, and efficiency; it was no doubt a touching reminder of what they now had to consider their own innocent enthusiasms of five years before. They shared Niebuhr's disgust with the Versailles Treaty, but their disillusionment went further: they could generate no glowing sentiments about the future. Croly, Weyl, and Lippmann, and perhaps most other liberal intellectuals, put less store by politics after the peace conference.

Niebuhr by contrast was politicized, and gradually radicalized, by the apparent failure of liberal ideals. His youth may in fact explain part of the difference. He was just young enough to have missed the euphoria of militant prewar liberal progressivism, of which the early *New Republic* (founded in 1914) was the crowning expression. Books like Herbert Croly's *The Promise of American Life* (1909) and Walter Lippmann's *Drift and Mastery* (1914) were clarion calls for a tougher, more uncompromising, and hence more "efficient" politics and culture. They too had condemned "liberalism" for being too intellectual and unemotional, for lacking the rhythm and energy of "real life." It was precisely their "toughened" liberalism that died at Versailles, leaving them no clear path ahead in progressive politics. What Niebuhr lost was only his naive faith that "ideas may create reality," that they might take "vengeance upon the facts." His was a liberating discovery, one that ironically gave him renewed faith in liberal ideals—as long as they were tied to militancy and risk taking in the realm of action. His new realization he expressed quite pointedly in the last sentence of his diary entry on the Versailles Treaty. The sentence may well have been written much later in 1919 than the passage about "vengeance" which precedes it. "On the other hand," he wrote, "it is always possible that diabolical facts will so discredit the idea which they ostensibly incarnate that they will necessitate the projection of a new idea before progress can be made."[12]

VII

For the last year of the war, and the first year of the peace, Niebuhr saw little of Bethel Church. As late as the fall of 1919 he was so immersed in plans for a memorial library at Elmhurst that he was still a very part-time pastor. He did preach most Sundays after the end of the war, but he felt guilty about focusing so rarely on the needs of his congregation. Writing to the editor of a synod magazine in October, 1919, he noted that he had done no work for his congregation in more than a year, and no serious reading for months. It was actually two years since he had done any work for his congregation. He and Baltzer had known all along that it was physically and mentally impossible to direct both Bethel and the War Welfare Commission. That is why Baltzer proposed in 1918 that Helmut take over permanently at the church. There is no way to know why he did not. In all likelihood neither Lydia nor the parishioners themselves were comfortable with the idea; Helmut was not the dynamic preacher or paterfamilias that Reinhold was. Moreover, Helmut himself—who lived out his life under the gigantic shadow cast by his older brother—may well have resisted stepping into a framework constructed completely by Reinhold.

Niebuhr did stay in close enough touch with Bethel to be sure that it was progressing with adequate speed toward Americanization. At the church council meeting of May 7, 1918, the issue of German services came up. The congregation was not prepared to abandon German forever, as Niebuhr was urging, but the council did go on record "in favor of discontinuing [the] German language during the present war." It also agreed to appropriate five dollars for an American flag to be displayed in the church. A special meeting of the entire congregation on May 22 voted to accept the council's recommendation to suspend German Sunday services for the duration of the war, but only at the price of a compromise: "it was also decided to hold a German mid-week service on each Wednesday evening as long as enough members would attend."

Two months after the Armistice the language question came to a final climax. Niebuhr now had enough supporters to call another special meeting on the issue of eliminating German altogether. The secretary's minutes make a point of recording the momentous character of the proceedings of January 14, 1919.

> The most important question or matter concerning the welfare and future of this church was then taken up. It was with much anxiety, deep thought and feeling, that this very vital subject was approached, it was to be a turning point for better or worse of this church and every member was deeply interested. The question: shall we discontinue German service, and have a one language church, the English language only? The matter was not touched lightly by any member present. Almost everyone having something to say regarding it. Discussed, debated, dissected from all possible points and angles in the most brotherly and Christianlike spirit, with malice towards no one, with only one point in view, that being, the success, welfare, and future of this church, the congregation finally decided to use the English language only. The only vote taken resulted—34 for English and 9 against, there being 43 members present. Rev. Niebuhr then arose. The die is cast he said solemnly.

Although Niebuhr was not to return to full-time shepherding of his flock for another year, the stage had been set for the phenomenal growth of Bethel Evangelical Church in the 1920s—a gain in membership that paralleled, and was made possible by, the extraordinary population growth of Detroit itself. Having broken its last visible link to its German past, Bethel could become a thriving, interdenominational, middle-class community.[13]

FOUR

A NEW KIND
OF
MONASTICISM

(1920–1925)

I

The growth of Detroit in the early 1920s was explosive. Already the nation's fourth largest city in 1920, with a million residents, it had a million and a quarter by 1925. That growth rate of 25 percent was by far the highest of any large American city—Cleveland at 17 percent and Chicago at 11 percent were next in line. An average of almost a thousand new residents were arriving every week, many of them rural southern migrants (black and white) destined for the booming auto works. Middle-class flight from the city core, made possible by the very vehicles the new working-class Detroiters produced, picked up its pace. Like the other suburbs, the northwestern neighborhood— the home of Bethel Evangelical Church—was inundated with new settlers.

Bethel's own population growth was colossal. From just over one hundred members at the end of the war, it rose to two hundred by early 1920, four hundred by the end of 1922, five hundred in 1924, six hundred in early 1926. Some growth would have been expected in an area of such rapid settlement. But Bethel's 300 percent expansion in the first six years of the decade went far beyond the expected. The key to the church's swelling rolls was Niebuhr's determined campaign to make Bethel much more than a parish of the Evangelical Synod. By the early 1920s Niebuhr had created an interdenominational congregation of liberal-leaning Christians from a variety of backgrounds. Bethel was now a mirror of Niebuhr himself, who years before had made up his mind to transcend the boundaries of the Evangelical Synod. Not only did a large proportion of his faithful come from other Protestant denominations; one-third of the adults in his flock, he claimed in 1924, had no prior Christian commitment at all.

•

Niebuhr was a committed church builder throughout his thirteen years at Bethel. He could be very disparaging about ministers who succumbed to a "success" mentality—who maximized their salaries, their church "plants," their membership rolls. His *Leaves* are full of his distaste for it. He decried the spread of statistical measures of achievement. He bemoaned the practice of luring pastors from one church to another with "cynical" offers of "ten thousand dollars" a year. He rhapsodized about "a wonderful parson in the little village" who lived "very modestly in a little parsonage" and was still "undeniably the real leader of the community." This "young fellow" had no desire for a "big pulpit"; he was content to bask in the village's "higher type of fellowship." The moral of this pastoral parable was that "privilege and power"—and "the kind of obvious success which the world knows how to measure"—"tend to corrupt the simple Christian heart." But Niebuhr's professed aversion to institution building and upward mobility was not a sign of his own intention to seek the simple life. It was not a proclamation of his own rectitude but an implicit expiation, an indirect confession of guilt. Although he had no desire to maximize his financial advantage in the clerical marketplace, he had nothing against requesting salary increases, and he certainly dreamed of a "big pulpit," which he knew was a path to power in the synod and the wider community. One could not be a "real leader of the community" at the metropolitan or national level without a substantial base. His strictures against false gods were warnings to himself that the quest for influence which he had consciously chosen was morally perilous. "May the good Lord deliver me," he wrote in his journal in 1922— as hordes of new parishioners were flocking into Bethel—"from ever being a popular preacher."[1]

The Bethel Church minutes show that membership growth preoccupied Niebuhr from the start. At the church council meeting in October, 1915, just after his arrival in Detroit, "Reverend Niebuhr explained that he had surveyed the field and believed that a result of twenty-five new men should be forthcoming . . . in November, and asked the Board's hearty cooperation." In midsummer 1916 he "pleaded with the congregation and urged good attendance during the hot days, as it would cause strangers . . . to take notice of the interest displayed, . . . make a decided good impression and further the growth of the church." By February, 1918, the church council was debating how best to enlarge the church, since "the present chapel [is] proving too small to successfully conduct the fast growing Sunday school," the pet project of Niebuhr's mother. In January, 1919, the annual meeting of the congregation adopted the goal of a completely new church by 1921.

Thanks to the largesse of a new and very wealthy parishioner, William J. Hartwig, the new church was not only built in 1921, but built on a choice lot fronting the northwest's most impressive boulevard. Hartwig, a boyhood friend of Henry Ford and a manufacturer of electrical components, had come into his several millions when Ford gave him a lucrative contract. Raised in the Evangelical Synod by his immigrant parents, Hartwig joined Bethel upon moving into the neighborhood in 1920. He was distressed, however, about worshiping in the old church at Lothrop and Linwood; it was "too small" for him, his wife, and three daughters. He therefore pre-

•

sented the congregation with a $40,000 parcel on West Grand Boulevard—on which he himself resided—and added another $30,000 for the building fund. With the sale of the old property for $80,000, Bethel was able to afford an imposing English Gothic structure and a modern parish house. When the final charges put the parish $25,000 in debt, Hartwig offered to settle the account immediately; Niebuhr refused, on the grounds that the congregation should pay *something*.

During the construction Niebuhr predicted to Baltzer that the church would shortly be "one of the nicest in Detroit." When he dedicated the 750-seat edifice on February 12, 1922, the local press echoed his sentiment. Reporters were awed by the plush oak woodwork, the hand-carved pulpit, the $12,000 organ. Although the earlier Bethel church had been perfectly respectable, the new one was positively elegant. It must have eased the task of attracting new members. On dedication day itself Niebuhr welcomed fifty new parishioners and announced that he expected fifty more by the end of the Lenten season six weeks later. A visiting synod minister forwarded the good news to Horstmann's *Evangelical Herald* and a wide denominational readership: after breathlessly admiring each of the building's opulent details, he stressed "the promise this church gives of being one of the largest in the city." For all Niebuhr's doubts about the moral value of "the kind of obvious success which the world knows how to measure," he had campaigned hard for Bethel's expansion and was reaping where he had sown—not only a booming parish, but a spreading reputation in the synod as a miracle worker.

However attractive the new church may have been to prospective members, Niebuhr's preaching was the chief magnet that drew people to Bethel. By the early 1920s he was an accomplished pulpit performer, the educated Protestant's Billy Sunday. One did not merely listen to Niebuhr: one watched him lunge, gyrate, jerk, bend, and quake. He whirled his arms, rubbed his ears and his balding scalp, stretched his hawkish nose forward. His whole lanky frame was in motion. One did not merely listen to Niebuhr: to catch the stream-of-consciousness flow of analysis and anecdote—sometimes shouted, sometimes whispered, but always at the velocity of an undammed flood—demanded a concentration that few could sustain during an entire sermon. Adelaide Buettner, who joined Bethel in 1924, remembers the dizzying experience of hearing Niebuhr for the first time. She understood only part of what he said, and ran home to look up in her dictionary some of the words he had used. Like the rest of the congregation she was firmly hooked by Niebuhr's charisma; in the pulpit he was fired, inspired with the Word, yet thoroughly rational, "intellectual." To her and her young adult friends he was "a hero," a "father figure," although he was only in his thirties himself.[2]

II

Niebuhr's preaching was by no means just an act. It was a well-crafted blend of drama and argument, a constant dialectic of comfort and challenge. His sermons consistently combined priestly and prophetic postures: a priestly

•

gospel of hope for coping with the everyday perplexities and tragedies of earthly life; a prophetic gospel of repentance for confronting personal sin and social evil. He laid out his philosophy of homiletics in an anonymous article in 1922.

> A true gospel will at the same time encourage men to hope and persuade them to repent. . . . We need prophets who know all about man and yet believe in him, whose faith in his destiny as a son of God has been won without ignorance of his real crimes and sins. Like Jesus they must hate sin while loving the sinner; and like Jesus they must be able to apprehend sin in the respectable conventions and traditions of society no less than in individual departure from them.

At Bethel Niebuhr set out consciously to be that sort of prophet: to challenge his flock to confront their personal and collective sins, but to assure them of God's mercy in the face of their fumbling efforts and creaturely limitations. Judgment graced by forgiveness. Above all he avoided accusation—it was not Niebuhr judging, but Niebuhr calling down God's judgment on himself and his congregation together.

His most recurrent sermon topic in the early 1920s—the pursuit of happiness—illustrates how he blended reassurance and reproof. His version of reassurance was the opposite of the positive thinking that he believed had taken over too many Protestant pulpits. True happiness, he repeated in one sermon after another, was akin to what the world called unhappiness. Real contentment was a costly achievement, one that eluded most of those who sought it. Most religious and secular counselors, he noted in November, 1921, advised people that happiness was to be found when they felt no pain. To that doctrine Niebuhr counterposed, in his rough sermon notes, the paradox of the Sermon on the Mount.

> Happy are they who hunger and thirst. Happy are the poor in spirit. . . . Happy are those not who have but who are seeking. . . . Happy are they that mourn. The more spiritual power increases the more pain increases. The capacity to love also produces the capacity to grieve. Peculiar paradox . . . If you have drugged your conscience you are not bothered but you are not happy. If your conscience is quick and active . . . it will cause you many an anxious moment. . . . The joy of loneliness in serving a great ideal. The world is not really Christian. We easily assume it is.

In a December, 1922, sermon he repudiated the notion of "a completer revelation in some other person [than Jesus], as for instance in Mary Baker Eddy"—the founder of Christian Science and the prime propagator of religious mind cure. Against Eddy and the secular theorists of self-fulfillment through personal growth Niebuhr proposed what he considered Jesus' final, unsurpassable "revelation of life": "Who seeks his life will lose it. Who loses it will find it." Again and again he returned to that paradox—the one he had chosen in 1913 for the sermon in Lincoln that followed his father's death. "A paradox is always foolish," he said in October, 1923, "until you begin to analyze it and then you see that it is fundamental and irresistible. Those who seek their life do lose happiness, and those who forget their happiness in some great cause do achieve life."

The following month he argued that for Americans, "more comfortable" than other peoples, spiritual growth was especially difficult; they reduced happiness to ease, rest, leisure. "The world in which labor has decreased and leisure increased is a better world and we will not disparage the victory. But woe unto man if leisure alone is the source of his happiness." His October sermon concluded: "Every great saint had his cross. . . . The cross is central. You can't be happy in an easy way." The cross stood for more than the abstract atonement; it stood for the way of life that combined Stoic acceptance of the tragic with active striving for the ideal. Real happiness demanded suffering and struggle. His Good Friday sermon in 1925 was the culmination of his many sermons on this theme. In his journal that evening he wrote, "I don't think I ever felt greater joy in preaching a sermon." The theme of the homily had been the cross as "symbol of ultimate reality." He summarized its central point in his diary.

> It seems pathetic to me that liberalism has too little appreciation of the tragedy of life to understand the cross and orthodoxy insists too much upon the absolute uniqueness of the sacrifice of Christ to make the preaching of the cross effective. How can anything be uniquely potent if it is absolutely unique? It is because the cross of Christ symbolizes something in the very heart of reality . . . that it has its central place in history. Life is tragic and the most perfect type of moral beauty inevitably has at least a touch of the tragic in it. . . . Love pays such a high price for its objectives and sets its objectives so high that they can never be attained. There is therefore always a foolish and a futile aspect to love's quest which give it the note of tragedy. What makes this tragedy redemptive is that the foolishness of love is revealed as wisdom in the end and its futility becomes the occasion for new moral striving.

Preaching "Christ crucified, to the Jews a stumbling block and to the Gentiles foolishness," made sense to Niebuhr because it meant challenging the moral complacency of a leisure culture. He was taking "orthodoxy's" stress on the brokenness of human life and grafting it onto "liberalism's" quest for a new society. The cross symbolized both cultural withdrawal and political engagement. "When I see how Protestantism is being engulfed in American luxury," he wrote to a friend in early 1926, "I am convinced that what we need is a kind of new 'monasticism' that restores a sense of tension between the soul and its environment, which was the characteristic of monasticism at its best." Restoring that tension meant resisting both the moral laxity and the political apathy of twenties America.[3]

Niebuhr's sermons had always, since his first efforts in Lincoln, had a strong social and political content. Occasionally he would devote his entire Sunday morning sermon to a political question, as in his "Are Nations Anarchists?" in November, 1921. But with the opening of the new church in February, 1922, he inaugurated a weekly Sunday evening service in which he preached—actually lectured—on the pressing issues of the day. The Bethel "Forum," which in 1925 became a lecture/discussion, was a key attraction for the young, educated, liberal Protestants who joined the church in large numbers throughout the twenties. The Forum sermons, grouped in thematic series of three or four talks, covered subjects like war, industrial conflict, prohibition, evolution, divorce, the family, race, lynching, capital

•

punishment, health, and leisure. They were often advertised in the Saturday press under the boldface heading "Popular Sunday Evening Service"—an odd practice in view of Niebuhr's written denunciation of "the spirit of commercialism [that] has invaded the church and vulgarized it." While the ads for his own talks were appearing, surely with his approval, he wrote of his yearning for English clerical reticence, which restricted church notices to announcing the hours of services and the name of the preacher. English parsons presumably cared less about growth than the pastor of Bethel, who in practice made his peace with the "consumptionism" that in theory he condemned. While his ads avoided the cheap ballyhoo of some other churches' promotions, they were still designed to lure as well as inform.

Whatever the drawing power of the advertisements, the Forum itself may have been the main cause of the "demographic transition" that set in at Bethel in the 1920s. Those who had joined the church in the 1910s had been for the most part German-American shopkeepers, salesmen, and small businessmen. Among the church's lay leaders, for example, William Kemnitz was a savings bank officer, George Ruttmann a jeweler, Paul Jans a manager of a furniture company, and Otto Pokorny a general contractor. They were part of an "old middle class" of independent retailers and small-time entrepreneurs and managers. But those who came after 1922 were largely "new middle class": teachers, social workers, and other salaried professionals whose frame of reference was as much national as local. These cosmopolitans transformed Bethel into a prime Detroit outpost of enlightened, liberal Christianity. The *Christian Century* displaced the *Evangelical Herald* on the church magazine rack. Bethel was a microcosmic case of the process of modernization that transformed the American middle class itself in the late nineteenth and early twentieth centuries.

There was naturally a good deal of tension between the two groups since the old-timers watched their congenial if parochial fellowship dissolve before their eyes. Few pastors would have been able to counteract the bad feeling as effectively as Niebuhr. He had enormous personal charm and strong powers of persuasion; his sermons, moreover, kept everyone entranced. But one issue that deepened the rift within the congregation was Niebuhr's own frequent absences from the city. Even after the completion of his war welfare work in 1920 he was often on the road. He was in constant demand as a speaker for student conferences inside and outside the synod; each charismatic performance lent greater prestige to his name and brought in more invitations. The "cosmopolitans" at Bethel took delight in his growing national renown. Ironically, the more he was absent from Bethel—the more famous he became—the more nationally oriented liberal Protestants in Detroit flocked to join his church. It was the "locals," the older German-Americans, who bewailed his trips. They wanted a pastor who not only showed up for his sermons but was available for counseling during the week. Niebuhr was constantly apologizing for his peregrinations. "My schedule for the rest of the year," he assured the men's club in February, 1924, "calls for two weeks at home in every month." "That ends my wanderings for the time being," he added in April, after a one-week trip east. "In May I shall be gone for one short conference at Princeton University." The president of the men's club could only advise acquies-

•

cence. "We hope the Bethel folk appreciate what a privilege is ours to have our minister for ourselves Sunday after Sunday, and also to share him with others during the week from time to time."[4]

III

The "others" included three important figures who in the first half of the decade did their best to draw Niebuhr away from Bethel and into their own operations. President-General Baltzer, *Christian Century* editor Charles Clayton Morrison, and YMCA evangelist Sherwood Eddy were all captivated by Niebuhr's abilities as organizer, speaker, and writer. Through the 1920s they conducted a triangular contest for his services. Niebuhr relied on all of them for advice and encouragement—and for opening doors to wider worlds. His "new monasticism" was the reverse of a withdrawal from the public sphere. It was a heated pursuit of public leadership, and a resourceful cultivation of men of influence. Niebuhr had enormous ambition along with extraordinary talent. But he also had the wisdom to detect the subtle spread of self-satisfaction. He was a deep believer in the sin of pride because he was so sensitive to his own. There was nothing he hated more than pretentiousness—unless it was passivity. He felt called to take up a trumpet and vanquish the complacent, yet he feared the complacency that the prophetic vocation itself might produce in him. What appealed to him about prophecy was the unending tension of it: constantly raising himself in righteous indignation, constantly abasing himself by invoking God's judgment upon everyone, including himself. The cynic might suggest that prophetic garb was a convenient disguise for self-aggrandizement. But it was not so very comfortable to be locked into a permanent program of self-criticism. The new monasticism meant "restoring a sense of tension" to American culture, and also admitting a churning tension into his own life.

Niebuhr compensated for the strong self-assertion in his public life not simply through prophetic self-accusation but through the rigid self-denial he practiced in one segment of his private life. He abstained altogether from close relationships with women. There was a profoundly celibate character to his new monasticism. At Bethel his parishioners always took him as a confirmed bachelor. Several young women at the church were known to be very interested in him, but it was also plain, as one former parishioner puts it, that "he was above all that." He never dated, though as an old man he recalled having had a "romantic attachment" to Emily Meister, a German-American who had joined the church with her parents in 1919. His diary reveals that he did have a longing for fatherhood, though he admitted there to no yearning for a wife. "The old Methodist preacher who told me . . . that I was so cantankerous in my spirit of criticism about modern society because I am not married may be right," he wrote in 1923. "If I had about four children to love I might not care so much about insisting that the spirit of love shall dominate all human affairs. And there might be more value in loving the four children than in paying lip service to the spirit of love as I do." His way of formulating the dilemma—family nurturing

•

set off against social responsibility—determined his resolution of it. If the choice was that stark he was bound to select the social sphere. His vision of peripatetic leadership in the cause of "personality" left no place for the time-consuming, home-centered duties of family. The irony is that his program of promoting personality came at the cost of suppressing his own merely "personal" life. The further irony is that his self-suppression may have made him all the more vigorous in preaching the benefits of personality—the ideal form of the personal existence he had relinquished but still craved.

His choice of public over private life was in one sense not a choice at all. It was not a decision he came to after lengthy deliberation about his adult course. It was a pattern that evolved gradually after 1915 as he adjusted to life with his widowed mother. Lydia did not want him to start a family of his own. As she adapted to widowhood she came to identify her very survival with her position at Bethel. That position meant taking care of a large organization—a Boy Scout troop, a Ladies' Aid Society, and countless ad hoc activities had been added to the original Sunday School and choir. But in her mind it also meant running Reinhold's household. She could not contemplate living outside it. Niebuhr acquiesced in the face of this emphatic desire. He granted his mother the central place in his household and buried his own desire for a family and for an independent adulthood. Yet there were decided advantages for him. With a live-in assistant, cook, and maid who expected no intimacy in return, he was free to travel, write, lecture, organize, and consult. She was the essential material foundation for his public career. All she asked was not to be displaced. Her implicit plea that he remain celibate did not confront him as an unacceptable demand. In its absence he might have developed a relationship with one of the Emily Meisters in his midst. But out of habit, loyalty to his mother, and a calculation of both his interest and his responsibility, he settled down to an ascetic young adulthood.[5]

When the War Welfare Commission dissolved in 1920 Baltzer took steps to keep Niebuhr close at hand. He kept him on as his chief emissary to the Federal Council of Churches in New York, a position that Niebuhr welcomed. Then he tried to persuade him to come to St. Louis full-time to oversee the synod's participation in the Interchurch World Movement (IWM), a grandiose ecumenical body funded primarily by John D. Rockefeller, Jr. Niebuhr was not excited about taking on more administrative work for the synod. "I am really not cut out for organization work," he advised his superior. He was cut out for the life of a "pseudo-scholar, writing and studying." Moreover, his congregation was in the midst of a boom and needed him. He expected a hundred new members during the year, and thirty at Easter alone. Changing pastors would be a serious setback: "I don't know how to get away from here without losing their goodwill."

The president-general was not impressed with these excuses, especially since Niebuhr had been pressuring him for months to affiliate with the IWM. "Is this movement, I ask myself, really in the heart and mind of those men who had been talking about it for some time but who are not willing to put their shoulder to the wheel?" If the Bethel congregation's resistance was the problem, he would come personally to Detroit to explain

·

why he needed their pastor more than they did. "We must find ways and means to relieve you from your young and sturdy congregation, and you will have to serve in a greater cause, for some time at least." Faced with Baltzer's stony insistence, Niebuhr agreed to leave Bethel in Helmut's temporary care and reported for duty after Easter.

The Interchurch World Movement was the liberal churches' means of putting some of their social and evangelical enterprises, and much of their fund-raising, under a single umbrella. Rockefeller, who donated the bulk of the funds, was a liberal Baptist who believed that religion could spark a reconciliation between labor and capital, and help put capitalism back on a moral foundation. Niebuhr found himself defending the IWM not only from synod conservatives who considered it another "Americanizing" plot by the aspiring "Yankees" in their midst, but from younger liberals who believed it was a capitalist plot to mollify labor. It was easy to counter the reactionaries' charge that the IWM was "the most pernicious attempt ever made to undermine the authority of individual denominations." The only formal obligation the synod had to the movement was a levy of 5 percent on its anticipated five million dollars in annual fund-raising receipts. "The Interchurch Movement has no authority over our policies and makes no attempt to influence our action in any way," he told the *Evangelical Herald*. But justifying Rockefeller's role took all of Niebuhr's well-honed debater's skills. Niebuhr admitted it was a "strategic blunder" to "feature Mr. Rockefeller so prominently in the campaign." But opposition to him was based on "ignorance" of his work and "general prejudices aroused by the name of Rockefeller."

> Do the critics know that the younger "oil king" has practically nothing to do with the oil business; that his entire time is given to civic and philanthropic enterprises; that in a recent labor conference called by the President he went further in urging a just attitude toward labor than any capitalist present . . . ; that the Colorado strike several years ago, which brought his name in disrepute, was really the means of his "conversion" to a social gospel? He may not now have a viewpoint as free from prejudice as that of thinkers who are in no way connected with wealth production, and not subject to the atmosphere of the "capitalist class," but he evidently has a sense of stewardship far surpassing that of many a rich man. . . . Those who have seen Mr. Rockefeller at close range cannot but be impressed by his evident sincerity. . . . It is easy to cast suspicion on motives, but to appreciate the best in motives and character is a Christian duty and one that we owe all fellow-Christians.

Niebuhr assured "the critics" that he too held "quite liberal and even radical political and economic opinions." But his readiness to defend Rockefeller on the grounds of "sincerity" revealed that his radicalism did not go very deep. He failed completely to address the objection that Rockefeller was quite sincerely inviting the churches to join him in creating a more stable, morally based social order—one that would better buttress the interests of the "capitalist class" and allow it to engage in "stewardship" from a socially and financially secure position.

Niebuhr was in no sense a defender of business interests. He was a Christian left-liberal: to the moderate liberal Christian conviction that love was the solution to the social problem he was now adding the slightly more radical view that "some kind of democratization of industry and some degree of socialization of property are the ultimate goals toward which our whole political and social life is tending." He believed that "democracy in industry must be guaranteed by something better than the capricious benevolences of individual employers." But he was still convinced that "unselfishness" was the key force in progressive politics. The role of the church was to place itself resolutely between labor and capital, preaching patience to the former, sacrifice to the latter, and justice to both. It must speak "without compromise" but also "without malice." That was the only way to liberate the "unselfish instincts of the holding classes," the "love that is willing to sacrifice not merely surpluses of wealth but the very economic power by which inequitable surpluses have been created." To spark a voluntary renunciation of wealth and power on the part of the capitalist class required steering clear of "the class hatred of the proletarian movement," with its "cynical contempt for the power of altruism in human nature."[6]

He had no sooner penned his defense of Rockefeller and the IWM than the organization folded for failure to meet its debts. Its member churches had not contributed their 5 percent and Rockefeller decided not to rescue the movement single-handedly. By July, 1920, Niebuhr was back at Bethel, though still on call for Baltzer. As the most eloquent Americanizer in the synod he traveled frequently to speak to congregations in the midwest and east, to confer with officials in St. Louis, to powwow with Federal Council dignitaries in New York. When Baltzer wanted to persuade the Federal Council to address a reconciliatory letter to the churches of Germany, for example, he entrusted the task to Niebuhr. At twenty-eight years old Niebuhr was already master of the diplomatic missive that pressured and cajoled, fumed and cooed. He informed Robert Speer, president of the council, that reasons both principled and expedient supported the sending of an olive branch. It was of course the Christian thing to do. More to the point, a gracious overture to the German churches would help silence anti-American elements in the synod. "It may surprise you to know that many of our older men are hoping to effect a secession from the Federal Council. . . . Many of us feel so strongly upon this matter that we would resign from a denomination that cut itself loose from organized Protestantism. . . . Our problems are made more difficult by the reluctance of the Council to take any action." Speer could forestall both secession and schism with a single letter. Niebuhr added sternly that he "was not alone in resenting" opposition to the letter within the council. But he softened his wrath with a pledge of personal faith in Speer. "As a young man who often sat at your feet while in college (I often heard you at Yale in 1913–1915) I have absolute confidence in your Christian spirit and sincerity of purpose." At its next meeting the council approved the letter.

With Baltzer's support Niebuhr obtained in January, 1921, an established forum from which to battle the old guard within the synod: a monthly column in the *Evangelical Herald* entitled "Christian America." Ostensibly a series of notes about what was happening in the other churches, the column criticized standpatters who would keep the synod from becoming a modern American denomination. The Presbyterians and Methodists, he noted in

January, 1922, had managed despite the "financial depression" to allot increased funds to foreign missions. "Will our people ever learn to give with real generosity to Kingdom purposes?" The United Lutheran Church, "conservative" in "thought and religious outlook," was far more progressive in action than the Evangelical Synod. Month after month he chastised the synod for not holding a candle to the United Lutherans: they launched a vast recruitment campaign during Lent, while the synod mounted no "organized effort"; Lutheran women were zealous in support of missions, while Evangelical women displayed a "woeful lack of missionary interest"; the Lutherans had built twenty-eight colleges and seminaries, while the synod had only Elmhurst and Eden and still lacked "a full college course." Niebuhr kept up the barrage of information and criticism until the summer of 1923. Although he wrote occasional pieces for the *Herald* after that, he was by then too busy writing editorials and articles for the *Christian Century* to produce the column.[7]

IV

Charles Clayton Morrison, editor of the *Century*, was always on the lookout for new talent. He had bought the *Century* at a sheriff's sale in 1909 and struggled for a decade to transform it from a house organ of the Disciples of Christ—the denomination he had served as a minister from 1892 to 1908—into the nondenominational voice of liberal Protestantism. He was a stickler for vigorous, opinionated, authoritative prose, and demanded that his writers address the full range of connections between religion, culture, and society. By the start of the twenties he had gathered a prominent group of contributors—Harry Emerson Fosdick, Charles W. Gilkey, Charles A. Ellwood, Harry F. Ward, Bishop Francis McConnell, and others—and established the *Century* as the central arena of Protestant debate in America. But since most of his articles were unpaid—"service to the cause is its own reward," he explained—he relied on a motley array of nonprofessional writers to fill the bulk of the magazine. He kept his eye open for literate clergymen with distinctive viewpoints and forceful styles for whom publication was reward enough.

When Niebuhr submitted a manuscript on "The Church Vs. the Gospel" in July, 1922, Morrison was delighted. He had read and admired Niebuhr's few published pieces; as a leading pacifist he was particularly impressed with a recent letter to the *New Republic* in which Niebuhr apparently embraced "a position of unequivocal opposition to all warfare." Although he turned down the manuscript, he detected in Niebuhr the turn of mind he coveted. "I have every respect for you as a writer and thinker, and I feel morally sure that if you submit something else which passes your own judgment it will receive a more favorable consideration." Niebuhr responded a month later with a fifteen-hundred-word article on "Romanticism and Realism in the Pulpit" which Morrison liked so much he proposed using it as an unsigned editorial—at an honorarium of ten dollars. Offered the choice of being an unpaid author or an anonymous editorialist, Niebuhr picked the latter.

•

For Niebuhr "service to the cause" was necessary, but it was far from sufficient; he was still having trouble making ends meet even though his Bethel salary had risen to $2,000 a year (plus a rent-free parsonage). Morrison, for his part, knew he was getting a bargain. He could easily afford ten-dollar editorials, which, unlike signed submissions, lent prestige directly to the magazine's staff. He asked Niebuhr for more of the same. "You have somehow impressed me with your singular ability to work with us in this fashion." After "Romanticism and Realism" was published under the title "Repentance and Hope," he positively pleaded for more. "Please let me repeat my request that you send us some editorial material," he wrote in November. "Just send them in," he clamored early in 1923, "as many as possible and as often as possible." During the winter Niebuhr began to sense that he was in a position to request more money. "If you would like to write with some degree of regularity," the editor replied, "we should be pleased to take up the matter of compensation on a somewhat more satisfactory basis."

For the next half-decade Niebuhr anonymously authored a steady flow of *Century* editorials—short ones of a few hundred words, longer ones up to twenty-five hundred words. But his desire for recognition was not wholly eclipsed by his need for payment: he also submitted signed articles, beginning with "The Church and the Middle Class" published in December, 1922. Each year he wrote five or six signed pieces, dozens of editorials, and several book reviews. The *Century* was the outlet he had been waiting for: near-total freedom to write what he wanted, a sizable supplement to his income, a national, interdenominational readership of some thirty thousand who soon came to expect regular illumination or provocation from his pen. His *Century* experience was the rehearsal for his own later ventures as editor at *The World Tomorrow*, *Radical Religion*, and ultimately *Christianity and Crisis*; indeed, it made those ventures possible by creating a loyal audience of friends and even foes, who followed his writing from one journal to another in the decades to come.

No contributor to the *Century* rivaled Niebuhr for topical range or aggressive prose. He moved with ease from domestic politics to foreign policy, to ecclesiastical affairs, to philosophy of religion, to social trends. His ability to roam all over the religious, political, and intellectual map allowed Morrison to center his own editorial writing on a few pet subjects—especially the modernist-fundamentalist theological conflict and the national campaign to "outlaw" war—while ensuring that the *Century* would continue to report and generate debates in all areas of Christian life. Niebuhr was "point man" for Morrison in much the same way he had been for Baltzer. He had served the president-general as both trusted aide-de-camp in denominational battles and emissary to the larger American Protestant world. Now his fields of action had expanded: he served Morrison as gifted controversialist in national, liberal Protestant debates and interpreter of the broader secular and European Protestant worlds.

Niebuhr might just as well have signed his anonymous editorials. In retrospect, and for attentive readers at the time, his distinctive stamp could not be mistaken. He was hard-headed, vehement, satirical. A dash of disillusion, a sprinkling of hope; mild cynicism moderated by firm faith in

•

future action or conversion. Where Morrison's editorials were long-windedly sincere, lofty in sentiment, and laced with Victorianisms—"lest," "evermore," the frequent exclamation point for proof of earnestness—Niebuhr's were self-consciously pointed, "realistic," "masculine." Where managing editor Paul Hutchinson's editorials were temperate, straightforward, and brimming with facts, Niebuhr's were rhetorically explosive and determinedly paradoxical. He was forever aghast at the "perils" facing modern civilization, discouraged over the "fathomless sentimentality" and "impotence" of the churches in the social arena, angered by the "hypocrisy" and "complacency" of the rich, of Christians, of America. But he was heartened by the "prophetic" potential of the student movement, rhapsodic about the "promise" of British labor and German Christian socialism, dazzled by the "sublime" witness of this or that lonely bishop or minister. He was always detecting saving "virtues" in acknowledged "vices": true, the fundamentalists were reactionary, but at least they did not worship scientific reason, like many shortsighted liberals; true, the Catholics were a threat to democracy all over the world, but they had a sense of the organic character of social life that put individualist Protestants to shame. And there were flaws in every vaunted piety: of course Prohibition ought to be enforced, but clerical supporters of the Eighteenth Amendment were strangely silent about enforcing the Fifteenth Amendment—on Negro suffrage; of course war ought to be outlawed, but Christians were irresponsible if they never turned their gaze from ultimate ideals to address concrete crises that lead to war, such as the French occupation of the Ruhr.

Morrison soon came to the conclusion, as Baltzer had just after the war, that he needed Niebuhr more than Bethel Church did. In early 1925 he offered to bring him to Chicago as associate editor. Niebuhr was at first delighted—at least that was the reaction he conveyed in April to Baltzer, who along with the Bethel congregation was anxious to keep him in Detroit. All his friends agreed, he wrote, that he should go to Chicago, and he intended to take their advice. He hoped that Baltzer, who had always been "a good friend and father," would not interpret the move as "disloyalty to the church." In Niebuhr's casuistic flip-flop it was just the reverse: the synod had very few men in interdenominational activities, and he would be free to serve it as a roving troubleshooter. Baltzer was not biting at that bait. And he was not prepared to lose Niebuhr to Morrison without a fight. "Do you wish to exchange your pulpit where the Lord certainly has blessed you and given you the opportunity to influence a great many people connected and not connected with your church for an editorship? Would you rather use your pen continually than speak the living Word to an audience? The Lord has given you a good gift in that direction also, not that I want to tickle your six-foot-long Self."

It may have been Baltzer's reaction that gave Niebuhr second thoughts. Or perhaps Baltzer intervened directly with the Bethel church council, which soon in Niebuhr's words "made almost every kind of offer"—including the funding of a full-time assistant—to get him to stay. But it is also possible that Sherwood Eddy, the YMCA evangelist who had been trying desperately to persuade Niebuhr to join his personal staff in New

•

York, found a way at least to make him defer his decision. At any rate, when Niebuhr wrote in May to Kirby Page, a close friend of his and a key aide to Eddy, he had changed his mind. A three-day visit to the *Century* office convinced him, he told Page, that he could not work with Morrison at close range. The *Century* staff was completely preoccupied with the outlawry-of-war issue; Morrison could think of nothing else and was increasingly subservient to Salmon Levinson, a Chicago lawyer and the originator of the outlawry campaign, a man whose view of the world arena was abstractly legalistic. Niebuhr could tolerate sharing the *Century*'s columns with Morrison, but not its corridors. He did not see how "poor little me could successfully buck up against" Levinson's influence. Page was vastly relieved. He and Eddy were still in the fight for Niebuhr's future.[8]

V

Sherwood Eddy, like Charles Clayton Morrison, was always in the market for another bright young man. An old-stock American of inherited wealth, he had served the YMCA as an unsalaried preacher since 1895. Before the war he had been the Y's chief evangelist in Asia. When the war broke out, he enlisted young Kirby Page, a recently ordained Disciples of Christ minister, as his personal secretary and set out to tour the war camps in Europe. By war's end, like Morrison and many other liberal Christians, they were both committed pacifists, determined to work not simply for the elimination of war but for the transformation of the industrial capitalist society that produced war. Their quest for the Kingdom was continuous with the earlier Social Gospel, but the war experience had given it a new sobriety and a deep, though still very vague, conviction that more thoroughgoing social and political changes were essential. At a time when secular liberals, disillusioned by Versailles or intimidated by officially sanctioned repression of dissent, tended to give up on politics in general and radicalism in particular, religious liberals edged further left in large numbers. Eddy and Page were in the front rank of the many churchpeople galvanized by the war and groping in the postwar era for some radical means of applying the Gospel to the social realm. At the YMCA in New York Sherwood Eddy brought together a cluster of young social evangelists who toured colleges across the nation and helped generate the powerful student Christian movement of the twenties—a decade stereotyped wrongly as a time of uniform youthful frivolity and hedonism.

In 1921 Eddy and Page decided to organize a national Fellowship for a Christian Social Order (FCSO), an educational organization of liberal Christians who would study industrial capitalism and develop a Christian approach to reforming it. The time was right: a widely circulated exposé of working conditions in the steel industry, authored by a committee of the defunct Interchurch World Movement, had brought church awareness of labor-capital conflict to a peak. Church progressives were beginning to side with labor, to abandon the standard view of the church as a neutral buffer, a moral leaven, in the social struggle. But the movement was gradual, and those who favored labor's cause did not consider themselves anti-business. For the moment liberal churchpeople had questions, not answers; the idea of an educational fellowship, a federation of local chapters with occasional national conferences, caught on quickly. By November Page had lined up 125 members, many of whom fanned out to secure new recruits. By 1923 about 1,200 had joined; by 1928, about 2,400. Among the earliest members were such renowned churchmen as Bishop Francis McConnell, chairman of the committee that wrote the steel report; Dean Charles Reynolds Brown of Yale Divinity School, whose *Social Rebuilders* (1921) called for the democratization of industry; Samuel McCrae Cavert of the Federal Council of Churches, author of the council's 1920 report *The Church and Industrial Reconstruction*, and one of the leading voices of social Christianity in the Episcopal Church; and Bishop Charles D. Williams of Detroit. It was Williams who in 1922 called Reinhold Niebuhr to the attention of Eddy and Page as a first-rate organizer; together Williams and Niebuhr established the Detroit branch of the FCSO, which at its first meeting in November, 1922, attracted thirty recruits.[9]

Had the FCSO done nothing else it would still be historically important for having brought Niebuhr and Williams, and then Niebuhr, Page, and Eddy, into close personal contact. Niebuhr's relationship with Williams, which lasted only six months—Williams died of a heart attack at age sixty-three in February, 1923—was nonetheless a turning point for him. In Williams he saw a vision of the Christian prophet he wished to become. Not since his studies with Samuel Press a decade before had he been so captivated by a Christian model. Press had pointed the way to an American identity; Williams marked out the path toward a prophetic ministry. Indeed, the bishop's death itself may have been a transformative event for Niebuhr. He may have sensed that it was his duty to pick up this fallen mantle just as he had his father's ten years before. "Bishop Williams is dead," he wrote in his diary. "I just sit and stare at the floor while I say that to myself and try to believe it."

> Nowhere have I seen a personality more luminous with the Christ spirit than in this bishop who was also a prophet. . . . His fearless protagonism of the cause of democracy in industry won him the respect and love of the workers of the city as no other churchman possessed it. . . . He did not change Detroit industry but he left many of us holding our heads more upright.

To the bishop's widow, whom he did not know, Niebuhr wrote a letter expressing his grief. Only two nights before his death, he wrote, "we were planning together for the Fellowship for a Christian Social Order. Now he is gone. . . . Prophets such as he are not born every year or every generation." In the magazine of the Michigan Episcopal diocese, he summed up the meaning of the bishop's "voice crying in the wilderness."

> Religion rises only periodically to the heights of prophetic ardor and vision, but the deathlessness of the prophet's influence compensates for the infrequency of his appearance. Your diocese has lost a great bishop, but the church universal has lost infinitely more; it has lost a prophet who had the courage to challenge the complacency of a very self-righteous civilization.

In late 1922 and early 1923, as Niebuhr's writing moved from the columns of the *Evangelical Herald* to those of the *Christian Century*, it took on an urgent tone very characteristic of Williams. "Industry is warfare," the bishop had written in 1921.

> Industry as at present operated violates the fundamental human teaching of Jesus Christ, that the individuality of man is sacred. Factory industry today makes an animated tool out of laborers. There is nothing which the present commercialized conscience of America with its regime of reaction and invisible government of the "business man" . . . more dreads than the real Christianity of the Gospel.

In his first signed *Century* article in December, 1922, Niebuhr moved beyond his earlier vision of the church as moral umpire between labor and capital, and toward Williams's combative, prolabor stance. "If industrial strife is to be abolished," he argued, "the whole motive power of our modern industry" must be changed. "Industrial warfare" would provoke more and more strikes, which most Christians considered "anti-social." But "the organization of modern industry, which the strike disturbs and challenges, is as anti-social as the strike itself." It was time to take the side of labor; capitalists could no longer be counted on to respond to moral appeals for the voluntary redistribution of their wealth. Labor strikes merited Christian support because they were attempting "to make the benefits of modern industrial civilization more equally available to all men." In an article that appeared the week of Williams's death, he restated the bishop's central theme: "There is no Christian basis to modern industry. It is based upon a purely naturalistic conception of life and cynically defies every spiritual appreciation of human beings. Christianity has had nothing to do with the organization of industrial civilization. It ought therefore to have no pride in it."[10]

Niebuhr's increasingly forceful and prolabor calls for Christianizing industry made Sherwood Eddy—himself a frequent contributor to the *Century* on the industrial question—take notice. He invited Niebuhr to join his "American Seminar," an annual group-study tour of Europe in which Williams had taken part in the summer of 1921. Bethel's church council reluctantly approved his ten-week vacation and Niebuhr sailed for England on June 23, 1923, in a party that included, in Page's words, "ten ministers, ten college presidents and professors, and ten miscellaneous (labor leaders, businessmen, writers, YMCA and YWCA secretaries)." The first stop was the Toynbee Hall settlement house in East London, where for three weeks the group had two lecture discussions a day with such dignitaries as Labour Party leaders Ramsay MacDonald and Arthur Henderson, writers like Gilbert Murray, Bernard Shaw, and H. G. Wells, Liberal Party philosopher Richard Haldane, and church figures from the archbishop of Canterbury to acclaimed preacher Maude Royden of City Temple. Lady Astor had the group over for dinner; Lloyd George had them for tea. The heady company was exhilarating. But for Niebuhr, Page, and Eddy the most awe-inspiring guest was MacDonald: a functioning political leader (soon to be Prime Minister) who managed to combine vigorous social idealism with hardheaded practical wisdom. They marveled at his cool, nearly aristocratic

•

blend of prophecy and statesmanship; they lamented the lack of such a figure in America. The British Labour Party itself became for them the symbol of the successful application of Christianity to politics: all the idealism of liberal Christianity without the sentimentality; all the realism of Marxism without the cynicism. For liberal Americans seeking a Christian way of moving to the left, the Labour Party was a perfect halfway house; they would appeal to its example for many years to come.

Much of the talk at Toynbee Hall focused on the French occupation of the Ruhr, Poincaré's six-month-old effort to extract unpaid German reparations by seizing control of the country's major industrial center. The British speakers and American visitors took turns condemning the invasion as a threat to peace and aggravation of the German people's suffering. Neither group saw any justice in the French claim that their economy was also a shambles thanks to an earlier German invasion. In the conflict between the two continental powers, Niebuhr's ancestral allegiance came to the surface. His dislike for the French was intense; the British attitude of leniency toward the Germans on the reparations issue was for him one more proof of their superior political wisdom.

In early July, after hearing that the French were about to close access routes into the Ruhr, Niebuhr, Page, and another member of the group, St. Louis Episcopal Dean William Scarlett, decided to skip a few days of lectures to observe the occupation firsthand. They sailed for Holland July 5 and arrived at Dortmund in the Ruhr Valley the next day. The French troops had indeed stopped Germans from going in or out of the Ruhr, but American passports got the travelers through the barbed wire. For three days they roamed through Dortmund, Essen (where they toured the Krupp Works), and Düsseldorf; Niebuhr's "mastery of the German language," according to Scarlett, amazed the people they met. The stories they told him, he noted in his diary, were "horrible tales of atrocities, deportations, sex crimes, etc."

> Imagination fired by fear and hatred undoubtedly tends to elaborate upon the sober facts. But the facts are bad enough. . . . The Ruhr cities are the closest thing to hell I have ever seen. I never knew that you could see hatred with the naked eye, but in the Ruhr one is under the illusion that this is possible. The atmosphere is charged with it.

Niebuhr was so shocked at the stories, at the near starvation of German children at Red Cross centers, at separated family members calling to one another across the barbed wire, that he entered a firm resolution in his diary. "This is as good a time as any to make up my mind that I am done with the war business." The vindictive Versailles settlement had already made him skeptical about wars fought for liberal ideals; the hatred and suffering that flooded the Ruhr valley in 1923 persuaded him to reject all war, to call himself a pacifist.

> One would like to send every sentimental spellbinder of war days into the Ruhr. This, then, is the glorious issue for which the war was fought! I didn't know Europe in 1914, but I can't imagine that the hatred between peoples

could have been worse than it is now. . . . The times of man's ignorance God
may wink at, but now he calls us all to repent. I am done with this business.
I hope I can make that resolution stick.

He was even determined to become a more trusting, loving person "in all
human relations." It was dawning on him that his prior willingness to
countenance war between nations was connected to an instinctive distrust
of others. "I am not going to let my decision in regard to war stand alone.
I am going to try to . . . experiment with the potency of trust and love
much more than I have in the past."

For one who prided himself on his realism about human nature and
society this was an uncharacteristic sentiment. It was also one that he kept
carefully buried in the privacy of his journal. His published account of "A
Trip Through the Ruhr," which appeared in both the English and German
magazines of the Evangelical Synod, made no mention of his resolution,
nor even of the hatred and brutality that had so unsettled him. In fact his
published report was so fundamentally at odds with his diary entry that he
had good reason for doubting, as he put it in the journal, that "I can make
that resolution stick." What dominated his public thinking was the realization that only strong American diplomatic intervention could save Germany from catastrophe. "The only hope of Germany is America," he wrote
in his next report to the synod readership. England and America, he argued,
"are the only nations who are not animated by motives of revenge. But
England is practically powerless because America has withdrawn from European affairs and has left the continent to the tender mercies of French
chauvinism." The only way Europe could "learn to overcome its hate and
learn the divine art of forgiveness" was through the American example.
"We have no virtue above Europe but we have good fortune, and if we
were to exploit it morally we could save Europe." Perhaps he spared synod
readers his feelings of nausea—and his pacifist resolution—because such
sentiments could only reinforce the general American revulsion from European affairs that made "the complete disintegration of Germany . . . imminent." Niebuhr never made a good pacifist, even when his emotions
were most predisposed, as they were in the Ruhr. He was too aware of the
possibility, as he had put it in the *Century* the month after the Ruhr invasion,
that "the principle of nonresistance is too ideal for a sinful human world."

Page, Scarlett, and Niebuhr returned to London from Cologne on
July 9—by airplane. It was the first time aloft for all three. Before departure
they solemnly shook hands and said their adieux; they took mild reassurance
from the pilot's claim that he had not had a "fatal" accident in five years
of flying. They were in the air for three hours at two thousand feet, inching
westward at ninety miles per hour, stunned by the landscape—an ideal
position from which, in Niebuhr's words, "to forget [our troubles] and
those of Europe." Along with the rest of the Eddy group they spent another
three weeks at Toynbee Hall, then proceeded to Paris for meetings with
French cabinet ministers, journalists, and scholars. The Americans were in
a belligerent mood after a month of discussing the Ruhr occupation with
the British. They forthrightly protested to each of the Frenchmen they met,
with apparently explosive results. According to Scarlett's account, when

they suggested that the policy was "injuring England, which had helped to save France in the war, the owner of the most important Paris newspaper at the time looked steadily at us saying, 'As far as England is concerned she can go to hell!' There was no apparent dissent from the others." Niebuhr shared Scarlett's weariness with the "repetitive exposition of a selfish nationalistic point of view." "The purposes of France," Niebuhr wrote after the group had departed for Berlin, "may be too mad" to be challenged by rational diplomacy.[11]

VI

After a week of conferences in Berlin, where the group heard the same message it had received in Britain—that "American participation in European affairs is the only hope"—the seminar members split up. Most left on a tour of Prague, Vienna, and Geneva. Scarlett, Page, and a few others went to Amsterdam. Niebuhr alone remained in Germany. He ran some errands for President-General Baltzer, sought out church leaders (including Otto Dibelius) to whom Baltzer had provided letters of introduction, surveyed the relief operations organized by American churches, "examined all the places connected with Luther" in Wittenberg and Eisenach. He then set out for his first (and only) visit to Lippe Detmold, his ancestral German home near the Dutch border in northern Germany. He made no contemporary reference to the trip, in either his diary or published articles; his only account of it was in a manuscript written in the 1950s and never published in his lifetime. The reminiscence is a remarkable revelation of Niebuhr's deepest feelings about Germany, about his family, about his own (and his father's) rejection of German "autocracy" in favor of American democracy. It is further evidence that he viewed his own adult career as a continuation of his father's.

At the very start of the account, which takes up three typewritten pages in a fourteen-page manuscript of meandering, stream-of-consciousness thoughts on Germany, Niebuhr expressed the primary conclusion to which the visit had led him: Gustav's revolt "against his rather tyrannical father" and his emigration to America were both "amply justified" by what he found at the family farm. Reinhold's grandfather Friedrich had only recently died, during the World War, and had therefore outlived his errant son Gustav. But the old man's autocratic legacy lived on. "The *Hof*," Niebuhr wrote, with a strong air of intrigue and conspiracy, "was in control of my cousin, ably assisted by his mother, the widow of the heir." The deceased heir Paul Niebuhr was Friedrich's youngest son, "though the law of primogeniture was the general rule. The oldest son [Simon] had been disinherited because he was addicted to drink and because he married the kitchen maid. I don't know which offence was worse in his father's eyes, or whether they were equally heinous." Paul's son now governed the 250-acre "manorial estate" with its twenty-five laborers. (Niebuhr noted that he later became a Nazi sympathizer.) Simon had been given 10 acres, but these were tilled for him by the "minions" of the *Hof*; "he lived a life of idleness but on a very much lower social scale."

•

The tyranny, the hierarchy, the idleness, all combined to justify his father's youthful revolt—which Niebuhr himself proceeded to re-enact by launching a small-scale rebellion of his own. His aunt had organized a party so that all the relatives and neighbors could meet the American cousin. The village parson appeared on the scene, and displayed traits strongly reminiscent of Friedrich: he was intolerant, uncharitable, and undemocratic. The parson "proved himself a bigoted and benighted man. . . . He attributed the ills of postwar Germany to the machinations of a 'Jew' in the cabinet. That Jew, Walter Rathenau, a particularly enlightened industrialist who might have saved Germany if there had been more like him, was one of my heroes. My temper flared up at this manifestation of pious anti-Semitism and I spoiled my aunt's party." But perhaps the hapless parson had provoked an outburst that welled up from deeper sources. Niebuhr's wrath may have been directed as much against the German autocracy embodied in his family's *Hof* as it was against the visiting cleric. It was a blast of rage that ritually reinforced his link to Gustav.[12]

Even before the American Seminar split up in Berlin in August, Eddy and Page decided that Niebuhr was too valuable to be allowed to return to a full-time pastorate in Detroit. His gift as a speaker, his energetic amiability, his knack for joining religious and political issues, his ready knowledge of European affairs both secular and ecclesiastical, made him a perfect choice as a traveling secretary of the Fellowship for a Christian Social Order. Niebuhr leapt at the chance to keep speaking, to go on tour on the liberal Protestant circuit, all without formally leaving Bethel. Eddy provided $2,500 for the year—enough to cover travel expenses and an assistant pastor, Theodore Braun of the Evangelical Synod, who assumed charge of Bethel six days a week. Baltzer was hardly ecstatic about the arrangement, but was powerless to resist. What bothered him the most was not Niebuhr's absences from Bethel, but the heavy itinerary that prevented him from traveling for the synod. When Baltzer asked him to go to Philadelphia for a meeting in November, Niebuhr sent his regrets: he already had six speeches on the agenda that week.

The engagements were not all outside Detroit. There were some speeches to Detroit groups, like the Vortex Club—a 245-member "commercial exchange organization" which Niebuhr served as chaplain. He appeared at the club's Wednesday luncheon on September 12 to report on his "seventy-eight conferences with the greatest men in the Old World" and to plead for American involvement in Europe. Not to intervene meant in fact intervening in favor of France; "real intervention will mean cooperation with England, . . . politically the most sagacious country in the world, . . . incarnating the political sanity of Europe." There were monthly meetings of the small Detroit Fellowship group. But the bulk of his time and energy were consumed by outside activities. Despite Kirby Page's claim that Niebuhr was a "real force" in Detroit, his driving concerns were overwhelmingly national and international.

In January, 1924, Eddy made his first pitch to Niebuhr about his leaving Bethel altogether to become part of a high-powered team of evangelists on the college circuit. At a weekend "retreat" in New York Niebuhr and Henry P. Van Dusen—who had just graduated from Union Theological Seminary and whom Eddy considered "the strongest student that he knows in America at the present time"—were invited to join Sam Shoemaker of Princeton, another Eddy favorite, as the nucleus of the team. But as the weekend wore on, Niebuhr and Shoemaker—an evangelist who argued for less "social gospel" and more "supernatural gospel," for real old-fashioned personal salvation as the key to college evangelizing—got increasingly on each other's nerves. Niebuhr departed in a huff. Page begged Eddy not to let Niebuhr, whom authorities like Morrison and Scarlett swore was "one of the most brilliant young men of this day," slip through their fingers.

The meeting provoked in Niebuhr a limpid declaration of his present and future path. Eddy wanted to know if he could devote himself to "personal work." Niebuhr replied that he had "personally won" four of the men on Bethel's board. But he was not, for all that, a good personal worker because he was "not very good in dealing with people at close range." He realized that it was important to save souls as well as to "save the world." Yet he thought there were already enough "specialists" on the personal side. His own task lay in the more neglected social field: "to study some of the implications of liberalism and see whether spiritual power cannot be developed squarely upon the basis of modernism." The future belonged to the church only if it could infuse its liberalism with moral potency. In fact, by all accounts, Niebuhr was quite good "in dealing with people at close range." The problem with "saving souls" was not any incapacity on his part, but his conviction that creating believers was not enough. His "new monasticism" was taking shape in his mind as a social movement for which he would provide intellectual and organizational leadership. He would turn away from individual counseling just as he had submerged his "private" self. Others like Shoemaker could settle for saving souls. He would die to self and "help save the world." [13]

Eddy was momentarily piqued by Niebuhr's treatment of Shoemaker. "You overestimate his intellectual ability. . . . Time and prayer will show about Reinie," he told Page. But when it came time to set up the European visit for 1924, Eddy wanted him back. Niebuhr demurred: he could not afford it since he was still paying off debts from the 1923 trip. Eddy quickly responded with a $500 check, and Morrison, himself a member of the party, promised generous terms for Niebuhr's written reflections on the tour. On June 28 all three men left for England in a group of one hundred which included John Nevin Sayre, editor of the pacifist monthly the *World To-morrow*, and radical Methodist Harry F. Ward of Union Theological Seminary. This summer Niebuhr detected, in his reports to Evangelical Synod readers, "a dawn in Europe" by comparison with "the imminent catastrophe" he had observed in 1923. Ramsay MacDonald was now Prime Minister in England—"the rise to power and prestige of this man is a romance more wonderful than anything found in fiction"—Poincaré had fallen in France, and German liberals had held off threats from both extreme nationalists and Communists. The reparations issue was no longer a hopeless quagmire; the Dawes Report, while still demanding "the impossible sum" of $33 billion from Germany, at least afforded a means of getting the French out of the Ruhr and restoring German economic unity. The most troubling aspects

•

of the European scene were social and economic, not political. The German working classes continued to suffer from near-starvation, but did not express their alienation in political revolt. "One marvels at the comparative patience of these people." Yet the moral life of Germany was deteriorating rapidly. "Sex purity was once the pride of the German people." But urban "eroticism" had corrupted the entire culture.

> Street girls by the hundreds ply their ancient profession brazenly in every principal thoroughfare, and lascivious literature bedecks every newsstand and book store. The little push carts from which books are sold on the street display the works of Schiller and Goethe on the same shelf with unmentionable titles which betray the diseased imagination.

Ironically, both Germany and the United States, in Niebuhr's view, were becoming morally dissolute societies—the first from economic adversity, the second from economic abundance. America was languishing in luxury, dissipating its inherited virtue. "The young people of America," he had written in 1923, "are sacrificing the [sex morality] standards of the fathers with a gay abandon that sickens the heart of every careful observer." What each country lacked was a "potent" Christian church informed by both moral austerity and social idealism, and a Christian political party that combined moral and social concerns with practical statesmanship. Only Britain, which he idealized as the perfect embodiment of a stable culture and a mature religion and politics, could face the future with confidence. There were some promising stirrings in Germany and America. He singled out Arnold Wolfers's group of religious socialists in Berlin as one hopeful sign, his own FCSO in America as another. But neither country was close to matching England's unique juxtaposition of social Christianity and a religiously inspired Labour Party. "Only in England do democratic tendencies give promise of approximating the Christian ideal." In both Germany and the United States "religious idealism is constantly betrayed into fatuity by its very naiveté" about the social and economic arena.

The problem of how to create in America and Germany the morally potent Christianity and the politically potent labor movement which he found in England dominated Niebuhr's thinking for the next decade. What force, what set of resources, could Americans and Germans draw upon to produce a powerful church and a powerful politics which "appreciates the human personality as the end of all political effort"? What alternative was there to the "cynical" Marxian view that "all men are selfish and always selfish and that the social order can be changed only by a struggle in which the selfish interests of those who would profit from a change would be enlisted against the selfish interests of those who benefit from the status quo"? Idealism alone was not enough. The idealism of the war liberals in 1919 and the peace liberals after 1920 shared a common flaw: too great a faith in the power of reason in human affairs. Reason was essential for analysis— whether of the Bible or of the world situation—but it was woefully insufficient as a motive force. To be moved to moral action, to summon up hidden reserves of will, people needed not just appeals to reason but pro-

•

phetic religion, "irrational" religion. "Religion is the permanently irrational factor in civilization," as he put it in early 1923.

> The progress of civilization depends upon . . . growing intelligence and improved opportunities for intercourse between larger social groups. . . . Yet the modern world has become a neighborhood without developing into a brotherhood. Widening social contacts will not alone develop the love which the world needs for its salvation. Such love is the fruit of religion. . . . Reason and experience will contribute to the attainment of the ideal of human brotherhood; but spiritual religion must make the major contribution. Every essential of that contribution is in the gospel of Jesus.

He expanded his appeal to "super-rational" religion a month later in an unsigned critique of Herbert Croly's religious views.

> The best answer to Mr. Croly's plea for a purely humanistic and naturalistic religion is that it is a questionable therapeutics which imperils the life of the patient with its cures. Religion must be relieved of its elements of superstition and magic if it is to serve modern civilization, but if that can be done only by destroying every vestige of supernaturalism and absolutism, against which Mr. Croly contends, it is doubtful if religion could survive. Religion is the champion of personality in a seemingly impersonal world. This advocacy is the source of both its strength and its weakness. . . . [It] has inevitably developed an attitude of defiance for immediate evidences of experience in the hope that ultimate evidences would validate its sublime affirmations of faith; and such an attitude easily betrays religion to cling to totally discredited creeds and absolutely disproven facts. Being bound to be super-rational, religion easily becomes unreasonable. But if it capitulates to reason completely its doom is sealed. The intellect is too closely wedded to the senses to be an entirely trustworthy witness of truth.

Niebuhr had already laid out the problem he would address in *Does Civilization Need Religion?*—not published until 1927 but written in short spurts beginning in 1923—and sketched a provisional answer. How could one both embrace liberal religion in its rejection of "superstition and magic," that is, in its appeal to reason as the standard of truth, and yet transcend its faith in reason? By following the example of Immanuel Kant and William James: grant the primacy of reason in its proper sphere, then proceed to demarcate another sphere—that of "morality" or "personality"—within which not scientific reason but "practical reason" or "religious experience" operates as a standard of truth. Niebuhr was a thoroughgoing Jamesian pragmatist, as he had revealed in his BD and MA theses at Yale. Truth in the moral realm was personal, vital, a product of will as much as mind, confirmed not in logic but in experience. Truth was what "worked"—as long as it contravened no known facts—in the furtherance of desired ends. Christians could spark human brotherhood only by liberating the hidden resource contained in liberal Protestantism itself: Jesus' prophetic, paradoxical Gospel, a message not of propositional truths, but of poetic, dramatic, "irrational" truths. Armed with that Gospel radical Christians could stand resolutely against the moral complacency of the secular culture and of the churches themselves. They could strive, moreover, to establish links to the

Lydia (age seventeen) and Gustav (age twenty-four) on their wedding day, May 8, 1887.

Reinhold at about age three.

The Lincoln parsonage.

Helmut, Walter, Reinhold, and Hulda on the parsonage porch.

Walter (out of focus) and Helmut on grass, Reinhold in chair, Lydia and Hulda standing behind him.

AT THE LINCOLN CHAUTAUQUA, 1903.

Reinhold in chair, Helmut with large bow tie, inside Saint John's tent.

Reinhold (third from left) and Gustav at 1906 confirmation ceremony.

Sibling portrait (clockwise):
Walter, Hulda, Helmut, Reinhold.

Yale Divinity School Yearbook, 1914.

Walter, the foreign correspondent,
at the German front, 1915.

Lydia and Hulda, both Bethel
parish assistants during the war.

Lydia with her Bethel Boy Scouts (Reinhold at left), mid-1920s.

*Niebuhr reading prayer at laying of cornerstone
for the new church, June 5, 1921.*

*Lake Geneva, Wisconsin, student assembly, 1927. Niebuhr
with striped sweater at left. At far right, Sherwood Eddy
(bow tie and glasses) and, on his left, Kirby Page.*

U. S. CONGRESS AGAINST WAR

FRIDAY, SEPT. 29·

8 P. M.

MASS RECEPTION OPENING SESSION

"We have been depending on statesmen and diplomats
to preserve the peace of the world. We can do so no
longer. The time has come when we must act ourselves."

GUEST SPEAKER: **HENRI BARBUSSE** Author of "UNDER FIRE". Secretary, World
Committee for Struggle Against War and Fascism

Devere Allen

William N. Jones

Harriet Stanton Blatch

A. J. Muste

Earl Browder

William Pickens

SAME SPEAKERS AT BOTH MEETINGS

MECCA TEMPLE, 135 West 55th Street   **REINHOLD NIEBUHR,** Chairman

ST. NICHOLAS ARENA, 69 West 66th Street   **J. B. MATTHEWS,** Chairman

OPENING OF MEETINGS BY DONALD HENDERSON
Secretary, Arrangements Committee, U. S. Congress Against War

CONGRESS SESSIONS — SEPT. 30-OCT. 1
IN ST. NICHOLAS ARENA

BUILD A MASS CONGRESS

DELEGATES REGISTER ALL DAY FRIDAY
IN ST. NICHOLAS ARENA

AGAINST WAR!

ELECT   DELEGATES!

ADMISSION:
25c — 35c
RESERVED SEATS
ONE DOLLAR

TICKET STATIONS:
U. S. CONGRESS AGAINST WAR, 104 FIFTH AVE., Room 1610
WORKERS BOOKSHOP, 50 East Thirteenth Street
LEAGUE FOR INDUSTRIAL DEMOCRACY, 112 E. 19th Street

Socialist broadside, 1933.

labor movement, setting the stage for a British-style Labor Party—the only real hope for long-term social and political advance.[14]

VII

After returning from Europe in September, 1924, Niebuhr again traveled "half-time" for the FCSO, leaving Theodore Braun in charge of Bethel during the week. Eddy and Page persisted in contriving a plan to bring Niebuhr to New York. The idea of attaching him to the Van Dusen–Shoemaker evangelistic team was abandoned; they offered instead to subsidize him as a free-lance writer and speaker working out of their YMCA office in Manhattan. Niebuhr would be part of Eddy's "inner circle," meeting weekly with "outstanding men of the country." Niebuhr mulled the proposition over as other job offers arose in competition: the associate editorship of the *Christian Century*, a professorship at a seminary that Niebuhr identified only as "conservative," and Bethel's counteroffer, its own subsidy for an assistant pastor. Niebuhr decided to "stick it [out for] another year" at Bethel and settled down to get to know Detroit. For a decade he had called it home, but it had been mainly the base from which he ventured out into the national and international arenas. By 1925 his solid reputation in wider worlds gave him the confidence to restrict himself temporarily to his own city, to dig deeply into the local terrain. There was no better laboratory than Detroit for observing the industrial conflicts of modern America; there was no better place for putting the church on record against the moral status quo and for laying the foundation of a Labor Party on the British model.

Momentarily defeated in his campaign to transplant Niebuhr, Page secretly joined in another plot affecting his friend's future. It was a direct assault on the defenses Niebuhr had erected against the consuming diversions and wasteful emotions of private life. In early 1925 he consented to help Anne Guthrie, a Chicago YWCA secretary and member of the 1924 American Seminar, lure him into making a marriage proposal. After watching Niebuhr perform at a church conference in Columbus, Ohio, in April, 1925, Guthrie "told me frankly," Page informed his wife, "that she was in love with Reinie and asked my advice as to what she should do."

> Anne says she is almost sure she could win him if she went after him in earnest. He is so all-fired self-centered and diffident that it may never occur to him to get married. I told Anne I did not know of a single rational reason why a woman should not woo a man as readily as a man should woo a woman. Reinie needs Anne desperately and she needs him. She has a deep yearning for a home and babies. At the very first opportunity I am going to have a long heart-to-heart talk with Reinie about marriage and home life. Reinie shines above every other intellect at our Conference. He is certainly going to be a really great leader. Anne can help him immensely. Pray earnestly that they may receive guidance.

When Niebuhr came to Chicago in mid-May for his three-day visit to the *Century* office, he and Anne spent part of an evening together. "We moved on a step—a little step," she told Page. But the following night she began to doubt her judgment. When they were alone, she realized, he had kept himself carefully protected behind a shield of intellectual conversation. It was a dazzling display of brainpower.

> Yet—he's empty and cold and unemotional—unstirred in the depths of his being—at least only a little stirred. *Surely* with the tremendous capacity of mind—there must be this other thing dormant somewhere. But what will stir it, what will arouse it! I don't know. Or has so much gone into intellect that the other side has paid the penalty and become warped and dwarfed—and we must expect only mind! I don't know. He can *never* satisfy me as he is today— *never*. Perhaps I could mean in part what he needs—but he too must mean what I need.

After another week had passed she was cautiously hopeful, as she explained to Page's wife, Alma. She had turned down an offer to go to China in order to give Niebuhr more time to come around. "I *really* do agree with you, Alma, that once he wakes up he'll be *wide* awake! He doesn't go at anything in a half-hearted fashion." Whatever the final outcome, "it's been great fun sharing the plot with you and Kirby."

By summertime, however, Guthrie's dream had evaporated. Page informed her that his "heart-to-heart talk" with Niebuhr had ended in defeat for their plan. Guthrie was not surprised. "Theoretically," she responded, "Reinie and I are quite an ideal combination. . . . But—life doesn't go that way."

> He's not hopeless, Kirby. Far from it. Tho' we have been only friends I've had a few glimpses along the way of what there is smoldering way down *very* deep that someday will flash forth. But he's the *youngest* man I've ever known; emotionally youthful. While he's about a hundred years old in mind—he's not seventeen yet in other ways. Of course that's why he's gone so far intellectually; his mind has been absolutely unhampered by his emotions. . . . Someday something will hit hard. Someone will come into his life and knock him flat—and he'll dash forth to conquest in the same startling fashion in which he goes after ideas now. . . . But I don't believe it will come for a few years until he has decided what he himself wants to do permanently. . . . The girl whom Reinie falls for someday will be one much younger—just as the man who will mean most to me someday perhaps is apt to be one much older than I. . . . I can help a bit to wake him up and make him realize what he's missing. Already I've been able to do that more than he wants to admit even to himself. He's a bit afraid of waking up. That's one reason why it's so hard for him to stand the jollying of his friends.

What Niebuhr thought of Anne Guthrie is unknown. The idea of marriage was plainly on his mind. His diary entry in 1923 had made clear that having a family—"about four children to love"—appealed to him in principle. But Anne Guthrie was right. Whether or not he was a seventeen-year-old emotionally, he was not prepared to settle down with a woman in 1925. He may have had more to give even then than he was willing to reveal to Guthrie herself. Yet his adult career was approaching its takeoff point; he had pushed himself in a frenzy of writing and speaking ever since the war, and the job offers pointing the way to still greater renown were proliferating. It was no time to think of the domestic life.

Niebuhr's emerging analysis of culture and society worked against his accepting that sort of life. America was losing its thrust as a productive nation; it was languishing in leisured contemplation of its bourgeois achievements. Marriage, like leisure culture, might be pleasant, but it threatened to sap one's moral vigor, to pacify rather than provoke one's soul. Niebuhr's commitment to a new monasticism—to a prophetic church which set itself consciously against culture—did not require celibacy in principle, but for the moment, in his case, it demanded it. "The family is not . . . invariably opposed to larger ventures in fellowship," he noted in his diary in 1927, "but it may easily become so."

> Jesus' ruthless words, "He who loveth father or mother more than me is not worthy of me, he who loveth son and daughter more than me is not worthy of me," have more meaning than most Christians have realized. Celibacy may be wrong because it escapes rather than solves this problem. But the invariable tendency of religious movements of great moral sensitiveness to experiment with celibacy is significant. Thus speaks a bachelor. Let the cynic make the most of the private prejudice which colors this judgment.[15]

FIVE

HENRY FORD
IS
AMERICA

(1925–1928)

I

In the spring of 1925, as the Guthrie-Page conspiracy was unfolding, Niebuhr erupted in a bitter tirade against the American culture of consumption. Was it possible, he wondered in a Methodist magazine, even to preach the Gospel in America, where "happiness is gauged in terms of automobiles and radios," where "the love of possession controls our home life," where in Emerson's words " 'things are in the saddle and ride mankind'?" In a culture of such deep complacency "idealistic motives perish. . . . It is not possible to attain the kingdom of God if you think you are already in the kingdom." The pious bourgeoisie of the Protestant churches made "short shrift of any teacher of religion who trie[d] to teach them the way of God." There could be no security for such a teacher. "It seems that now, as in ancient times, the only safety for a prophet lies in itineracy. . . . Undoubtedly the Christian religion will not seriously challenge the conscience of America until it is presented to the nation by men with such conviction and passion that a few martyrdoms will become inevitable." For the prophet there would be not merely "tension" with culture, but a fight to the death. "For us, as for the time of Amos, the day of the Lord must be darkness, and not light, and things must become worse before they can be better."

Advertising man Bruce Barton's new book, *The Man Nobody Knows* (1925), was one sign that things were getting worse. It portrayed Jesus as "a regular he-man," a "typical Rotarian go-getter," "a kind of sublimated Babbitt." In Barton's own words Jesus was "the founder of modern business. . . . He picked up twelve men from the bottom ranks of business and forged them into an organization that conquered the world." He was not the anemic and long-suffering, passive and feminized Lord of the Victorians; he was virile, youthful, successful, a back-slapping man of affairs. Niebuhr was all for picturing Jesus as potent and masculine, but he blasted Barton for touting him as a worldly success, a prototype of the hardworking American executive. "The gospel of Jesus is not a gospel of obvious success, but of ultimate success through obvious failure." That paradoxical message was nearly incomprehensible in a nation "where every condition of life tempts the righteous man to seek the Kingdom not for its own sake but for the sake of things that will be added unto him." The Protestant clergy made matters worse by applauding Barton's boosterism. They sanctified their parishioners' money-getting and invited them to seek health instead of salvation. "Thus a church which has lost the spiritual passion to command the respect of men, stands in the marketplace and pleads with the indifferent multitudes to come inside its tent for a moment on the promise that it has a panacea for whatever ill of body or mind may afflict them at that moment."

For all Barton's babbling about Jesus as businessman, and his reduction of the Kingdom to the things of this world, he at least interpreted the moral life as active struggle for achievement, not as passive enjoyment of it. More disturbing to Niebuhr than Barton's strenuous quest for self-satisfaction was the sense of languid ease that was seeping into American culture. When he traveled to Los Angeles for an appearance at the Pacific Palisades Chautauqua in July, 1925, he was overwhelmed by California's stagnant "paganism of pleasure," its "state of complete relaxation." Angelenos "vegetate on these pleasant shores," and "lose all moral vigor in the process." In his diary he recorded his choice of Detroit over Los Angeles. "Detroit is typical of the America which works feverishly to get what it wants, while Los Angeles is typical of the America which has secured what it wants. On the whole I prefer the former to the latter."

For Niebuhr the danger posed by the consumer culture—whether in Barton's active form or California's passive version—was its undermining of "idealism." "This excessive emphasis on the possession of things," he told the Methodists, "is bound to thwart the idealism of many a young soul." To the readers of the *Atlantic* he insisted that the "world can be saved only by a spiritual ethics which will inspire men to trust human nature as essentially good," despite "how essentially evil good men can be." The role of religion was to project ideal ends—service, self-sacrifice, benevolence— and generate the passion to realize them in society. The Protestant middle class had lost both the ideals and the passion. Niebuhr took the growing respectability of the birth-control movement as a telling sign of bourgeois prudence at war with passion. The lower class procreated with little thought of the future. The middle class was "so overcome by consideration for the future of their offspring that the race practically dies with them." He was appalled by "the cautious and selfish tendencies of mere rationality." Life at its best always had "an element of abandon and irrationality in it. To be perfectly rational means finally to destroy life." Mere instinct, of course, was not sufficient. By itself it led to "vice and misery." But rationality by itself was even worse. "When rationality assumes control over instinct it dries up the sources of energy." A potent religion had to show that the real struggle was not between reason and instinct, but between supra-rational ideals on the one hand, and mere reason and mere instinct on the other.[1]

This perceived battle between supra-rational love and the debilitating forces of calculating reason and unalloyed instinct was standard Social Gospel doctrine. What distinguished the Niebuhr of 1925 from the earlier generation of Washington Gladden and Walter Rauschenbusch was the stridency and breathlessness of his prose—as if verbal vigor alone could turn the tide against the culture of bourgeois contentment. But as Niebuhr settled down in the fall of 1925 to get to know the burgeoning industrial city in which he had lived for a decade, his mental horizon began to change. He soon confronted social problems of such apparent intractability that his inherited liberal standpoint started to crack. Racial conflict and the struggle between labor and capital led him to wonder whether idealism could still undergird an adequate social perspective. The "spiritual ideals" that he had preached since his first Lincoln sermon began to seem impotent, as complacent and vacuous as the consumer culture they were meant to challenge.

II

The black population of Detroit had increased with extraordinary speed during and after World War I. It shot up from only 5,700 in 1910 to 81,000 in 1925. Industrialists had turned to southern black migrants as a cheap labor supply when European Catholic and Jewish immigrants were first barred by the World War and later restricted by postwar legislation. The availability of unskilled blacks helped keep Detroit safely open-shop; labor organizers would make little headway in the face of the labor surplus and the cultural gaps that divided workers. But the manufacturers, who lured blacks north with wages that by southern standards were generous, made no provision for housing. Each year thousands of new migrants squeezed into the "East Side Colored District," where rents for substandard flats soon became exorbitant. By 1917 the crowding was already unbearable. Editor H. M. Nimmo of *Detroit Saturday Night* noted in April, as the United States entered the war, that the arrival of 10,000 blacks during 1916 had stretched the colored district to the breaking point. "The new colored population must needs seek quarters in sections heretofore considered outside the colored belt." But the Detroit Real Estate Board, the banks, and many white residents did not agree. Neither did the Ku Klux Klan, which by 1923 claimed more than 20,000 members in the city.

Until the mid-1920s, to judge by his Bethel sermons and his published and unpublished writing, Niebuhr failed to notice the black migration at all. But the rapid postwar rise of the Klan in Detroit did attract his attention by the fall of 1924. In November his local branch of the Fellowship for a Christian Social Order put on a conference to call attention to mounting racial prejudice. A total of 530 people turned out for the conference's three sessions. Niebuhr's indefatigable typewriter, however, which was churning out editorials for C. C. Morrison on the subjects uppermost in his mind, produced nothing about the conference or the issues it had raised.[2]

•

It was not until the fall of 1925 that he preached about race, even to his own congregation. What provoked his outcry against the "Nordic Protestant heritage of racial pride" was the Klan's highly publicized and liberally funded entry into the Detroit mayoral contest of 1925. Catholic incumbent John W. Smith was opposed by Protestant lawyer Charles Bowles, whose major source of support was the KKK. Klan Kleagle Ira W. Stout came to Detroit to assume charge of strategy. Each Klan member was assessed five dollars for the campaign chest, and 400,000 leaflets preaching white Protestant unity against black, Jewish, and Catholic intruders were passed out door to door. The contest was exceedingly tense because it took place in the immediate wake of a serious racial incident. Ossian Sweet, a black doctor, had managed to buy a house in a white neighborhood near the black district. On September 9 a white mob armed with bricks assembled outside the house and threatened to remove Sweet's family and friends, who watched from windows with rifles in hand. When it appeared that the crowd was making its move, Sweet, his brother Henry, and several others fired "warning shots," one of which killed a member of the crowd. The police, who had been standing by, finally intervened; eleven blacks, including Ossian and Henry Sweet, were charged with murder. In the next few weeks white Protestants throughout the city's middle-class strongholds, including the northwestern neighborhood around Bethel, flocked into local Bowles clubs. Smith, though no advocate of full black equality, courted the black vote by proclaiming the duty of the police to protect homeowners. Clarence Darrow and Arthur Garfield Hays, fresh from the Scopes trial in Tennessee, arrived to defend Henry Sweet—the first person brought to trial—and to continue their battle against Protestant reactionaries.

As the campaign drew to a close several liberal Protestant ministers decided to speak out. Though none of them was entirely comfortable endorsing a "wet" Catholic, and a "machine politician" to boot, they agreed that the threat from the Klan was more serious than the threat from the saloon or the smoke-filled room. In their sermons on the Sunday before the election, Niebuhr, Lynn Harold Hough of Central Methodist, Joseph Vance of First Presbyterian, and others "urged their hearers," according to the Detroit *Times*, "to administer a body blow to that hooded organization." Both the *Times* and the *Free Press*, supporters of Smith, featured Niebuhr's sermon at the top of their page-one stories. "We fair-minded Protestants cannot deny," the *Free Press* quoted him as saying,

> that it was Protestantism that gave birth to the Ku Klux Klan, one of the worst specific social phenomena which the religious pride and prejudice of peoples has ever developed. . . . I do not deny that all religions are periodically corrupted by bigotry. But I hit Protestant bigotry the hardest at this time because it happens to be our sin and there is no use repenting for other people's sins. Let us repent of our own. . . . We are admonished in Scripture to judge men by their fruits, not by their roots; and their fruits are their character, their deeds and accomplishments.

Niebuhr's stand was not forgotten by Smith. When the mayor squeaked back into office by a thirty-thousand-vote margin, he put the Bethel pastor on his list of those who might be useful in the future. Niebuhr was by this

•

time a visible force in the Protestant community—he had recently become head of both the Detroit Pastors' Union and the Industrial Committee of the Detroit Council of Churches. He was therefore a valuable contact for Smith in a constituency that regarded him with distaste at best, loathing at worst. The following March Smith tapped him to become the new chairman of his Interracial Committee, which had been meeting to little effect since the Sweet incident the previous September. Unlike philanthropist Tracy McGregor and Circuit Judge Ira Jayne, the first two chairmen of the committee, Niebuhr brought energy and commitment to the job. Charged by Smith to determine the causes of the "dangerous civic condition" and propose "such a cure as seems best," the committee used its $10,000 grant from the Detroit Community Fund to sponsor a four-month research project by sociologist Robert Lansdale of the University of Michigan and social worker Forrester Washington, former director of the Detroit Urban League and author of a 1920 report, *The Negro in Detroit*. For all his doubts about the ultimate validity of "scientific reason," Niebuhr was an eager sponsor of the plan to produce an empirical study of black community organization and living conditions. "We are going to employ experts to make a real survey of race conditions here," he told Sherwood Eddy. "Then we are going to try to liberalize the mind of the community on race relations."[3]

For the first time in his life Niebuhr was rubbing elbows with leaders of the secular world. He had spent a decade moving up the ladder of influence in the ecclesiastical sphere, and was intimate with men of power in that realm. Now he occupied a position of leadership outside the church. Although he had worked on the LaFollette Presidential campaign in 1924, the mayor's Interracial Committee was the real starting point of his career in secular politics. He was running a blue-ribbon body. Among the six whites on the committee were Frederick C. Gilbert, president of the Detroit Citizen's League, Jefferson B. Webb, former president of the Detroit Board of Commerce, and Fred G. Dewey, president of the Wayne County Bar Association. Among the six blacks were the vice-chairman, William T. Vernon, bishop of the African Methodist Episcopal Church; Dr. E. A. Carter, a physician; Walter Stowers and Hayes McKinney, both lawyers; and Donald Marshall, an Episcopal layman and ex-policeman who wielded enormous power in the black community as a labor agent for the Ford Motor Company. Niebuhr judged the group "a little too official," but told Page that "on the whole the spirit is good."

The spirit was good in Niebuhr's eyes because of the Jewish lawyer and philanthropist Fred M. Butzel, who worked so closely with him that in later years he always referred to him erroneously as the committee vice-chairman. It was Butzel's élan that made it possible for one with prophetic aspirations to tolerate the stuffy dignitaries. In the 1950s Niebuhr remembered that he "was in many ways the most remarkable man I have ever encountered, either before or since."

He was the moving spirit in every Jewish charity and the guiding genius of the community fund. But Butzel was no ordinary philanthropist. . . . [He] analyzed for me without emotion, the realities of power in the city and the foibles of the powerful. Sometimes his cynicism, which was absolutely without malice, shocked even his young parsonic friend who had learned so much from him. While we were working together on the race commission the parsons of the Negro "store front" churches all approached him for a contribution. He gave each applicant a hundred dollars. I remonstrated with him and told him that there were some very good Negro churches, who could make more creative use of his money than these corybantic sects. "I don't know what corybantic means," said Fred, "but if you are a specialist in religion I am a specialist in amusements and I know these churches offer the laundresses the rousements which are the only amusements in their dreary lives."

Niebuhr's retrospective account was a parable and an act of contrition—a story of a hard-nosed cynic who had more compassion than the religious "specialist." Butzel had no religious belief, only "an ethical creed in which charity and integrity were the prime components; the charity was at once so broad and so free of condescension that he broadened every religious and moral horizon of the young parson who became his friend." Butzel was the first Jew Niebuhr knew intimately; from that time on Niebuhr constantly celebrated "the very great resources that the Jewish community has in their passion for practical justice." He rarely came across a Protestant equivalent of Butzel: unsentimental, unpretentious, benevolently tough-minded, gifted with practical wisdom. He more than anyone else gave Niebuhr his lifelong conviction, as he expressed it in his journal in 1928, of "the superior sensitiveness of the Jewish conscience in social problems."

> The Jews are after all a messianic people, and they have never escaped the influence of their messianic, or if you will, their utopian dreams. The glory of their religion is that they are really not thinking so much of "salvation" as of a saved society.

As the committee wrapped up its survey in the fall of 1926 and the winter of 1927, Niebuhr spoke repeatedly to secular and religious groups in Detroit about the race problem. His four Bethel forums on race in January, 1927, were advertised in oversized print in the Saturday press. Now he preached not just about race prejudice in general, but about the much more ticklish question of "Where Shall the Negro Live?"—as he titled his January 9 talk. It took courage to broach that question even at liberal Bethel; many of his flock were as worried about preserving the whiteness of their neighborhood as the average white homeowner. The committee's report, *The Negro in Detroit,* came out in March, 1927, and in May Niebuhr summarized its findings for the national *Century* audience. His unsigned editorial "Race Prejudice in the North" was the only article he wrote in the twenties on the racial conflict, when the question was most urgent in Detroit and other northern cities. It was also, by his standard, tame, methodical, and detached; it lacked the passionate momentum of the typical Niebuhr editorial. In straightforward, almost clinical prose he itemized the problems black Detroiters faced: overcrowded housing, usurious rents, refusal of white neighborhoods or the banks to countenance moves beyond the Negro district, police "severity, not to say brutality," exclusion of black women from factory work and of all blacks from certain professions such as high school teaching, failure of white churches to assist black congregations even of their own denominations. Reading the report filled him "with a feeling akin to despair." Though he claimed that the report "makes some recommendations which may prove helpful"—like increasing the number of black policemen, teachers, and girls certified "in the household arts"—he saw no way out of the housing dilemma, "the crux of the race problem in every city."

Niebuhr believed that his feeling of despair stemmed from the complexity of the race problem itself. But there was more to it than that. There was also his own inability to incorporate a critique of American race relations into his overall critique of modern industrial civilization. His Christian prophecy was so completely rooted in his reading of the industrial conflict between skilled white workers and their employers—in his hope that the American worker could join with enlightened professional people to form a Labor Party on the British model—that it had no place for the black struggle for equality. As he revealed in a diary entry the following year, he believed that northern urban life had so devastated the spirit of black Americans that they could hardly be approached as allies in the rebuilding of American society. Their "misery and pain" were so acute because they were "unadjusted to our industrial civilization. Hampered both by their own inadequacies and the hostility of a white world, they have a desperate fight to keep body and soul together, to say nothing of developing those amenities which raise life above the brute level." As long as circumstances conspired, in Niebuhr's view, to keep American blacks cut off from industrial civilization itself—to keep them at "the brute level"—they could be objects of Christian charity, but not participants in the reform of that civilization. There was certainly a place for some other prophet to flail America for its racial sins. But Niebuhr put his own prophetic energies elsewhere—where he could have visible impact, where problems were not structurally resistant to practical reform.[4]

III

Even during his year-long tenure as chairman of the Interracial Committee, Niebuhr devoted himself much more assiduously to the industrial question than to the race issue. While Lansdale and Washington were writing the report on the Negro in Detroit in the fall of 1926, he was assaulting—thanks to data provided by them—the humanitarian pretensions of Henry Ford. His series of three articles (two of them signed) in the *Christian Century* established his reputation as an intrepid rebel slinging stones at an industrial giant. But by the fall of 1926 it was hardly daring to attack Ford's heroic posture. Had the pieces appeared in the early twenties, when Ford's image as the philanthropic five-dollar-a-day Christian manufacturer was still largely intact, their publication by a Detroit minister would have been an act of courage. But in those years Niebuhr, like the rest of the Detroit clergy, considered the Ford Motor Company a relatively enlightened firm. Between 1915 and 1921, one of their own peers, Dean Samuel Marquis of the Episcopal Cathedral, personal pastor and intimate friend of Henry Ford, was the head of Ford's welfare bureau. The "Sociological Department," as it was called, was in part a spy agency to regulate workers' private lives, but it did sometimes defend employees—especially older men for whom the ever faster assembly line was a hardship—against capricious dismissals. As long as Marquis was in charge of the Ford experiment in welfare capitalism no respectable Detroit pastor would publicly second-guess the company's humanitarianism. Niebuhr did express dismay in early 1923 over Ford's "huge profits," but still accepted the myth that Ford paid "big wages." That had been true in 1915, but wartime inflation and postwar recession had reduced the Ford worker's wage advantage to almost nothing. Only after Marquis resigned in a dispute with another Ford lieutenant and published a critical book about his former boss and parishioner did liberals inside and outside the church take Ford on. The *New Republic* and *Nation* led the way. The *Christian Century* followed with a series of five short editorials between August, 1925, and March, 1926—pieces written not by Niebuhr but by Hutchinson or Morrison. They were the immediate inspiration for Niebuhr's more substantial attacks.[5]

Niebuhr's articles tried to puncture the "pretensions of the world-famed Henry Ford." By his standards they were heavily researched, since he had privileged access to the unpublished findings of his race committee on wage rates in Ford plants. He relentlessly documented the falsity of Ford's claim that the reduction of the work week in 1925 from six days to five had resulted in wage increases. He angrily noted that during the previous year "the average Ford man has lost between $200 and $300." Ford sped up the assembly line, shortened the work week, and produced as many cars as he had before. Meanwhile his "highly paid publicity experts" cranked out the news that he had "made his workers a present of an extra holiday each week." Niebuhr was not sure "whether Mr. Ford is simply a shrewd exploiter of a gullible public in his humanitarian pretensions, or whether he suffers from self-deception." He was probably "at least as naive as he is shrewd." In his "combination of sentimentality and shrewdness" Ford struck Niebuhr as an apt symbol of America itself, a nation which "applies the social intelligence of a country village to the most complex industrial life the world has ever known." Henry Ford was not malevolent but a deluded innocent with flashes of exploitative genius. He truly believed that unemployment insurance, old-age pensions, and disability compensation were superfluous when men were taught thrift and paid a generous wage—which he convinced both himself and an adoring public he was still paying. "Henry Ford," Niebuhr concluded, "is America": well-intentioned, mechanically gifted, exuberantly backward-looking in matters of social responsibility. "What a civilization this is!" he told his diary in 1927.

> Naive gentlemen with a genius for mechanics suddenly become the arbiters over the lives and fortunes of hundreds of thousands. Their moral pretensions are credulously accepted at full value. No one bothers to ask whether an industry

•

which can maintain a cash reserve of a quarter of a billion ought not make some provision for its unemployed. . . . The cry of the hungry is drowned out in the song, "Henry has made a lady out of Lizzy."

The remarkable irony about Niebuhr's three articles on Ford—all written while he was chairing the mayor's Interracial Committee—is that none of them even mentioned Ford's pioneering policy on black labor. He had taken the lead not only in hiring blacks in the twenties—there were about ten thousand, all male, at Ford in 1926—but in employing them at all levels of the manufacturing process. These facts were surely not unknown to Niebuhr; Donald J. Marshall, Ford's key labor agent in the black community, was on his committee. A full discussion of Ford's "philanthropy" had to address the race issue, since Ford claimed to be fully egalitarian in his hiring practices—even to the point of making room for ex-convicts and the physically handicapped. Perhaps Ford was motivated in part by Christian idealism in his personnel policy. But he was also committed to an open-shop Detroit, and playing the paternalist with southern black migrants was a sure means of undercutting labor organization. Segmenting one's labor force into different racial and ethnic groups was a time-honored tactic for capitalist control; black workers in particular had frequently proven themselves to be anti-union, naturally enough, since most unions had proven themselves anti-black. Niebuhr's avoidance of the whole subject is inexplicable, unless he was simply determined not to let his pessimism on solving the racial issue interfere with his hope that industrial conflict could be settled in labor's favor. To dwell on the impediments to unionization when it was a primary condition for social advance might have seemed thoroughly self-defeating.

The Ford articles caused a stir at Dearborn and Highland Park; no less a Ford official than Ernest Liebold, the boss's "confidential secretary," wrote to William Hartwig—former Ford intimate and present Bethel benefactor—to get help in straightening out, or at least silencing, the upstart clergyman. Liebold got little solace from Hartwig, who quickly replied, according to Niebuhr's later recollection, "I am sorry to learn that my pastor has given offense to the Ford Motor Co. I have consulted with him and he authorizes me to assure you that if there are any inaccuracies in his articles he will be glad to correct them." Some other members of the Bethel congregation did feel that Niebuhr was getting too mixed up in politics, as they had when he publicly supported Robert LaFollette in 1924. But the church council backed his right to engage in political activity as long as he did so only in his own name, not in theirs.[6]

Bethel's Sunday night forum was by this time a well-established arena for social and political debate, and in October, 1926—as Niebuhr was finishing the first of his Ford pieces—it attracted the national spotlight. The AFL convention was meeting in Detroit. A month earlier five liberal Detroit ministers, Niebuhr among them, had agreed to invite "labor speakers" to occupy their pulpits during the convention, and the local YMCA had offered AFL President William Green its Sunday afternoon forum. But Detroit's vociferously open-shop Board of Commerce went quickly to work. Wealthy

•

manufacturers threatened to withdraw from the YMCA's building program (to which Ford alone had pledged $1.5 million), and businessmen paid courtesy calls on their own pastors. The YMCA abruptly canceled its invitation to Green; only Bethel and Augustus Reccord's First Unitarian kept their original promise to accept speakers. Niebuhr was lauded on the floor of the convention and in the editorial pages of Walter Lippmann's New York *World*. Rabbi Stephen Wise told the delegates that Niebuhr was one man "resolved that the church shall not be chiefly the Sunday club of the foes of organized labor." *World* editorialist James M. Cain praised him for standing firm. Other papers, including the New York *Times*, called him for comments.[7]

The most important lesson Niebuhr drew from the convention was not that the Board of Commerce was capable of intimidation, but that the AFL itself was hopelessly conservative. "The idea that these AF of L leaders are dangerous heretics is itself a rather illuminating clue to the mind of Detroit," he wrote in his journal. "I attended several sessions of the convention and the men impressed me as having about the same amount of daring and imagination as a group of village bankers." The delegates could think of nothing but wages, hours, anti-communism (they hooted derision at Sherwood Eddy's mildly favorable remarks about the Soviet Union), and the success of their own organization. In his Ford articles Niebuhr registered his disgust not just with deluded magnates, but with bloated labor unions. He granted that the AFL was starting to grasp the urgency of organizing on industry-wide lines, as opposed to craft lines, but argued it would go nowhere until it transcended merely material demands. It failed "to fire the imagination of workers so that they might claim their birthright as human personalities." It swallowed Henry Ford's own argument that workers ought to pursue self-realization in leisure, not work, and therefore clamored only for higher pay and shorter hours. But that course led directly to the destruction of "personality," the loss of self-directed, autonomous existence. "Even an industry which grants all that the workers might ask in wages and hours and gives them no share in determining the conditions of their work and no opportunity for the exercise of personal initiative is perilous to civilization."

Niebuhr pursued the point at greater depth in another article on Ford, written for an international student audience. Ford, he noted, was turning factory work into the province of the young—only they could keep up with the assembly line—and compensating them for their boring, frenetic regime with the promise of leisure fulfillment. Some workers did perceive that "leisure alone will not solve the problem."

> In my own city hundreds of workers may be found who have transferred from an automobile factory which pays comparatively high wages and speeds up its production to a point beyond human endurance to another concern which has the policy of paying slightly lower wages and maintaining a slightly slower tempo of work. Yet as far as America is concerned it must be said that the general reaction to machine industry is not sullen revolt but unimaginative compliance. The one virtue of the machine, cheap production, benefits the

worker as consumer, and he seems to be willing to accept the things which he may own as adequate substitutes for the personal satisfactions which the work might bring him.

The overriding task at hand was "to save the machine process for the use of personality," not to leave the development of "creative enterprise" to the leisure realm alone. "It may not be possible to make the machine process itself interesting, but if some of the efficiency of the industry is sacrificed for the sake of introducing democratic procedure in the factory, it may be possible to give the worker some sense of personal relationship to the entire manufacturing process, and some satisfaction in the total product manu-factured."[8]

IV

The "Battle of Detroit," as the *Century* labeled the AFL affair, explains much of the animus of Niebuhr's attack on Ford. He was no longer a clerical commentator gazing at labor-capital conflict from the sidelines and leading a few morale-boosting cheers for labor. The manufacturing elite of the Motor City had broadened the battle by taking on the liberal churches themselves. Niebuhr and his peers were under siege; they could either retire from the field or return the fire. The Ford pieces were Niebuhr's first acts as a combatant. They prepared the way for the next step: a tentative, oral commitment to socialism as the only adequate answer to Ford. At a major Christian student conference in Milwaukee just after Christmas, 1926, he appeared in a symposium with Henry Sloane Coffin, the new president of Union Theological Seminary, and G. A. Studdert-Kennedy, a famous lib-eral pastor from London whom Niebuhr had met during the American Seminar in England in 1923. The Milwaukee students were well aware of his critique of Ford; his first signed blast had come out in the *Century* three weeks before. After their scheduled talks were finished, Studdert-Ken-nedy—himself a charismatic extemporaneous speaker—engaged Niebuhr in an ad hoc debate on the industrial question. No account of the exchange appeared in reports on the conference, but Niebuhr later recollected that he went on record for abolishing private property in major productive indus-tries. He was no longer willing to accept Henry Ford and his colleagues as arbiters of the public weal. He believed, as he had written anonymously in the *Century* a few weeks earlier, that the problem which "imperils an ethical civilization is not the dishonest acquisition of wealth but the tremendous centralization of wealth and power in the hands of a few."

> A man who has the power to control the lives of thousands of workingmen in his factory may have come by his property honestly according to traditional standards; and the privileges which his industrial enterprise is throwing into his lap each year by way of income are honest too. But the important problem in regard to his power and his privilege is whether it is itself ethical.

He was no longer impressed by the "stewardship" of the pious rich; their benefactions, which he had praised five years before in his defense of Rock-

•

efeller, were "veils of decency hiding essential indecencies." Disproportionate power and privilege were themselves unethical, "destructive of real
brotherhood."

By tiptoeing gingerly beyond liberalism—beyond reformist appeals for
more welfare measures, beyond industrial cooperation, beyond stewardship, beyond moral support for labor in the abstract—Niebuhr was beginning to politicize his "new monasticism." "Almost all of us," he told the
twenty-five hundred delegates at Milwaukee in his main address,

> are a part of a system of mutual exploitation that works fairly well, and par-
> ticularly so in America, partly because there is so much wealth that everybody
> gets a little; and if we outrage personality by this mutual exploitation, we
> compensate people by bestowing upon them the dubious blessings of a radio
> or an automobile.

It was no longer enough for Christians to protest against American luxury
or complacency; it was time to disengage from "exploitation." "It is our
business to expatriate ourselves, . . . to learn again what those simple words
mean, 'Be ye not conformed to this world.' "[9]

In Niebuhr's liberal pacifist circle it was not yet common to call oneself
a Socialist; he did not join the Socialist Party until 1929. American socialism
still seemed too akin to communism, which Niebuhr firmly condemned in
his Milwaukee address as an irremediable "strategy of hate." How could
Christians countenance a political philosophy premised not on brotherly
goodwill but on confrontation and even the use of force? One side of him,
outraged by Henry Ford's pious pretensions and by the standpat complacency of the AFL, was moving steadily toward socialism. It was the only
political position that did justice to his recent insight into the unethical
character of power and privilege. The other side of him was applying the
brakes because of his liberal Christian belief that the law of love had to be
invoked across the board in all human relationships, individual and collective. Yet he knew it was pointless to oppose a Henry Ford with moral
idealism; Ford himself was a world-famous moral idealist. Since he could
not imagine advocating force, much less violence, he did the next best
thing: he began to attack those on the liberal Christian left who naively
expected love to work. Lacking a positive alternative to pacifism, he leapt
all the more energetically into the negative task of proving pacifism fatuous.

He had always expressed reservations about pacifist strategies, even as
he was signing resolutions on the outlawry of war. He was dismayed by
Morrison's obsession with the outlawry movement, and subtly mocked his
boss's mania in the Century's editorial columns as early as 1924. But his
article "A Critique of Pacifism" in the May, 1927, Atlantic was his most
forceful rejection of what Morrison held dear. Niebuhr stressed that he was
still a pacifist—a claim on which Morrison and others may have gagged.
He came down firmly on the naiveté of those who proposed reasonableness
and goodwill as strategies of political action. Just as he had earlier minimized
the role of reason in attaining religious truth, he now minimized its place
in practical affairs. He of course valued it as a tool of analysis, but he
repudiated it as a means of building a just world order. It made no more

·

sense to preach reason and trust to the nations of the world than it did to preach them to Henry Ford. Pacifism was egregiously ignorant of the structures of international power.

> There are Continental cynics and shrewd observers in other parts of the world who slyly suggest that pacifism is a virtue that only the two great Anglo-Saxon nations are able to enjoy. The implication is that England and America are the only two really solvent nations in the Western world, and that, since they have what they want and need, it is to their interest to preach peace. The hungry nations will meanwhile fail to react to this moral idealism. They will shrewdly and cynically observe that it is always the tendency of those who have to extol the virtue of peace and order and to place those who have not at a moral disadvantage.

The dispossessed, whether auto workers or hungry nations, could be excused if they refrained from celebrating the moral purity of their philanthropic employers or the preachers of peace. Europeans were right to distrust the outlawry movement, since its American instigators lived "in a paradise that is protected by the two walls of the tariff and immigration restriction." The movement was "an ethical sublimation of an essentially selfish national position."

But when it came to offering an alternative to reason and trust, Niebuhr was stuck. Since "force" was inadmissible, he took refuge in vague calls for "sacrifice," moral "robustness," and other masculine, muscular stances. Professions of moral idealism had to be validated in action, he urged, in abandonment of the privileged position from which American idealists always pontificated. Yet when he tried to imagine a manly, Christian substitute for pacifism all he could conjure up was the voluntary renunciation by a nation of its own power in the world. Once a nation had sacrificed its own self-interest, then other nations would be able to listen to calls for trust and brotherhood. What was so striking about this sentimental resolution was that he had long since rejected it in the industrial sphere; he did not need to be told that industrialists were uninterested in voluntary giveaways.[10]

V

In the summer of 1927 Niebuhr sat down to complete the long-delayed manuscript of his first book, which he had begun in 1923. Macmillan brought out *Does Civilization Need Religion?* in December. The book did nothing to extricate him from his impasse. For regular *Christian Century* readers the book offered nothing new; most of it had already been published as articles, unsigned editorials, and book reviews in the *Century* between 1923 and 1926. Indeed, the book displayed no signs whatsoever of the major developments in his thinking since the summer of 1926: the critique of the AFL, of Ford, and of unethical power and privilege; the "despair" over the racial issue; the stress on workers' autonomy; the hesitant movement leftward to the ideological outskirts of socialism. It was a polishing of his earlier thoughts. It made no effort to incorporate his most recent insights.

Yet it had undeniable power as a piece of writing. Bishop Francis McConnell, a "social justice" Methodist who was one of Niebuhr's idols and the *Century*'s friendly reviewer, rightly pointed out that Niebuhr had an unmatched "gift of generalization." The book was not a linear progression of theses and evidence building toward a conclusion, but a loosely connected series of conclusions. It read like a lengthy sermon, a densely packed digest of maxims, not a treatise. One could open it at any page and start reading; it moved along like a succession of ocean waves, smooth but rumbling. It was hard not to respond to the musical rhythm of sentences that combined simplicity and majesty: "Religions grow out of real experience in which tragedy mingles with beauty and man learns that the moral values which dignify his life are embattled in his own soul and imperiled in the world." Niebuhr had the rare capacity to produce analysis that inspired, critique that reassured. Liberal religion was deeply flawed, he intoned, but eminently redeemable. "Modern religion is, in short, not sufficiently modern. In it eighteenth-century sentimentality and nineteenth-century individualism are still claiming victory over the ethical and religious prejudices of the Middle Ages. Meanwhile life has moved on and the practical needs of modern society demand an ethic which is not individualistic and a religion which is not unqualifiedly optimistic."[11]

Most of what Niebuhr wrote for the *Century* in 1925 and early 1926 reappeared in the manuscript of *Does Civilization Need Religion?*, as did some of his earlier pieces like his 1923 critique of Herbert Croly. Civilization needed religion, he argued, because religion alone could posit ultimate ethical goals and supply the passion to reach them. Liberal religion had to be "rational and irrational": rational in rejecting "superstition and magic," irrational in pursuing love and self-sacrifice, values undemonstrable and unattainable by reason alone. Niebuhr's basic formulation had not changed since his BD thesis of 1913: the point of religion was to preserve and promote the ideal realm of personality in an impersonal universe and an impersonal society.

Niebuhr invoked the authority of Alfred North Whitehead and Albert Schweitzer to buttress his belief in a protected sphere of spirit. Whitehead was "a Daniel come to judgment" against skeptics like his co-author of *Principia Mathematica*, anticlerical activist Bertrand Russell. In *Science in the Modern World* and *Religion in the Making* Whitehead confirmed "the metaphysical validity of the concept of God," Niebuhr asserted, while admitting "the moral inadequacy of any purely metaphysical concept." For Whitehead "God is the ideal which is always becoming real, but is never completely real in the actual world. Thus God is transcendent. Yet God is immanent for he is the principle of concretion in every specific epoch and situation." Whitehead steered clear of the pantheistic pitfall that bedeviled liberal philosophers; they invariably reasoned that if God was both good and omnipresent, everything in existence must despite appearances be fundamentally good. If the universe seemed inhospitable to God and his creatures, liberals chose the easy expedient of asserting that at a deeper level the personal and the divine held undisputed sway. The natural was suffused with the spiritual, they claimed. Christian Science was the logical end point of liberal metaphysics. It was "religious optimism gone mad." For Whitehead, by contrast,

•

God stood—in his own words—"behind, and within, the passing flux of immediate things, . . . a remote possibility and yet the greatest of present facts, . . . the ultimate ideal and the hopeless quest." The spiritual intersected the natural, but the two spheres remained distinct. Niebuhr was ecstatic over the discovery of a real scientist and respected philosopher who shared his propensity for paradox.

Yet on the whole he preferred Albert Schweitzer's frank disavowal of any metaphysics at all. It was better to concede the irrelevance of metaphysics to religion—thus subtly undercutting Russell's anti-metaphysics—and passionately assert the relevance of religion to morality. "To make God responsible for the universe is to rob him of his goodness. The facts of life are simply too confused to warrant faith in a God who is at once good and omnipotent." Schweitzer represented a return to the refreshingly "naive dualism" of Hebrew prophecy—"a picture of the world . . . in which personality is in conflict with nature, divine and human personality sharing in the conflict. The resources of the divine are available to the soul but they will guarantee only its integrity and not its immediate victory." As Schweitzer acknowledged, his philosophy had "many loose ends" as a "world view"; he defended it not as a *Weltanschauung*, but as a *Lebensanschauung* (life view). Niebuhr did not doubt the inadequacy of dualism "from the standpoint of the intellectualists," but applauded its moral fruits. It made life a battle, a contest for high stakes with no guarantee of easy or immediate victory. Ultimate victory followed apparent defeat, as at Calvary. Schweitzer like Whitehead was a kindred spirit—even more kindred since Niebuhr had himself abandoned metaphysics at Yale, on the grounds that it was irrelevant to life. Schweitzer appreciated Niebuhr's support. "From afar I shake your hand," he wrote from Lambarene. "Since my youth I have agonized over these questions and have now found peace and joy in activity." That was the alternative to "dilettantish skepticism."[12]

The key obstacle to a potent Protestantism, Niebuhr made clear, was not the intellectual challenge of the Bertrand Russells, but the moral complacency of Christians themselves. Drawing on Tawney and Weber, and in fact introducing most readers to the untranslated Weber, he explored the historic conjunction between Protestant religion and capitalist enterprise. In America in particular the Calvinist sanctification of secular activity became, as he put it in 1925, "the dominant spiritual and moral force." There Protestantism "built a little paradise on earth in which people are decent but not kind, and honest but not sacrificial. And the very certainty of having their virtues crowned with obvious success beguiles them from seeking higher virtues which promise less tangible rewards." The path toward the ethical reconstruction of society lay therefore in withdrawal from bourgeois complacency. But in *Does Civilization Need Religion?* and in the articles of 1925 and 1926, this new monasticism (in the book he called it "new asceticism") had none of the political content he had given it at the Milwaukee student conference. It was a general moral stance, a proclamation of radical intent. The "Christian radical," he wrote in 1925, was a "human maverick . . . sure to be scorned." His distinctive mark was his refusal to succumb to cynicism, his determination to affirm the power of love in social relationships.

The only chance of proving the cynic's estimate of man false is to assume it untrue even in the face of immediate evidence in its favor. Love must create its own evidence. . . . No one who does not love [man] can prove him lovable. It is the genius of true religion that it not only searches for but actually creates fact in support of its high assumptions. The function of the Christian radical, of the true prophet, is thus to be ruthless in revealing the weaknesses of man but determined to trust him in spite of his sins.

If civilization needed religion, Christians needed passion, daring, and sacrifice. "We may be able to put God back in nature by a little serious thought," he noted in 1926, "but we cannot put God back in society without much cross-bearing."[13]

Beneath the surface of *Does Civilization Need Religion?* and the earlier articles there were nevertheless some signs of the dead end his cross-bearing idealism had reached by 1927. There was a tone of persistent doubt about whether modern man could in fact put God back in society. The problem was not just the historic link between Protestantism and capitalism. The problem was man himself, at least in his collective relationships. The cynics were not entirely wrong. "Man is cruel on slight provocation," he mused in 1925.

His economic activities are largely dominated by the instinct of greed; he has been unable to organize his family life in even the most civilized communities without the shadow of prostitution falling on his home . . . ; his womankind are less cruel but probably more petty; and his herd instincts are so untamed that he cannot live with any other race upon terms of decency.

Niebuhr was tempted by the "cynical estimates of man's capacities and potentialities." But he could see no way of incorporating those estimates into a Christian philosophy of social reconstruction. "All this may be true about man, and yet to lose confidence in him is to commit the basest sin against him. For though man is always worse than most people suspect, he is also generally better than most people dream." That rhetorical solution had a faint-hearted ring to it. It was still his only defense against "the prophecies of the cynics." If those prophecies were true, "we can hope for no better future for mankind than that class wars shall be substituted for race wars and that the distrust which men have for people in other nations and races shall be eliminated by enlightened distrust of every man by every man irrespective of color or creed." That outcome was inadmissible on the face of it. He had no choice therefore but to proclaim his "robust" faith in man even when all "immediate evidences" disputed it.

Does Civilization Need Religion? never got beyond that dilemma; it rested finally on the very sentimentality about man that the book ostensibly condemned. "Sentimentality is a poor weapon against cynicism," he urged in the penultimate chapter. But so was his own book. It failed to take any account of his realization late in 1926 that the battle for an ethical society required not only moral robustness, but the taking of sides in a concrete political and economic struggle. He could have offered a telling critique of *Does Civilization Need Religion?* by quoting from his own previously published work of late 1926 or early 1927.

It ought not require an undue amount of spiritual imagination to perceive that a kingdom of God cannot be built in a society in which a few exercise power, however benevolently, and in which a few gain unequal privileges, however generously they may return a portion of their wealth. The kingdom of God, if it means anything in terms of modern life, means brotherhood developed in all human relationships. The basis of brotherhood is equality of opportunity and uncoerced cooperation. Is the church ready to advocate an ethical idea as thoroughgoing as that?

Reinhold Niebuhr himself was not ready to do it in his first book. The manuscript was so rooted in an earlier stage of his thinking that his only choice was to scrap it altogether and start from scratch, or issue it as a statement of that earlier stage. Niebuhr was rarely one to linger over manuscripts; his tendency was to publish what he had and rework it if necessary in a later article or book. His precarious financial status was certainly one force exerting pressure in the direction of publication. And for a somewhat forbidding essay, *Does Civilization Need Religion?* did sell well. By the end of March, 1928, it had already gone over the five-thousand-copy mark, thanks to its adoption by the twenty-five-hundred-member Religious Book Club.[14]

VI

The publication of his book brought Niebuhr a host of new invitations. The Detroit *Times*, a Hearst daily that catered to a working-class clientele, signed him up in January, 1928, as a biweekly columnist, a position he would hold for four years. Local organizations scrambled to reserve his free speaking dates. The Women's Council for Education in International Relations hired him for its elegant luncheon forum. On five consecutive Tuesdays in January he gave four hundred Statler Hilton diners a rapid-fire commentary on the world's hot spots, along with general reflections on nationalism, economic empire, and world peace. The response was so ecstatic that he realized he had risen to new heights as a public figure in Detroit. He was not just one of a number of well-known liberal pastors; he was now sharing the spotlight with the long-time darling of Detroit's liberal Christian intelligentsia, Lynn Harold Hough of Central Methodist.

New offers streamed in from outside Detroit too. The *Intercollegian*, a monthly magazine of the Student Christian Movement, secured him as a monthly columnist beginning in December, 1927. Boston University, where Hulda was now an assistant professor of Christian education, "called" him to a permanent post; he made clear to his friends that a seminary job was appealing, but not at BU. He turned down more speeches than he delivered, though he was speaking all the time. He was the main attraction at the quadrennial convention of the Student Volunteer Movement held in Detroit at the Masonic Temple just after Christmas. To the forty-five hundred delegates, present and future missionaries of the Christian churches, he proclaimed that "Western civilization is not Christian. It has embraced Christianity and used it to sanctify its acts. Our nationalism is only tribalism

•

raised to the n*th* degree. . . . Some day the Christianity we have forgotten will come back to us from the peoples who got it from our missionaries."[15]

Niebuhr ignited the students in Detroit, just as he had those in Milwaukee in 1926. For half a decade he had been a main draw at the winter conferences and summer retreats of the student Christian movement. Undergraduates squeezed into the largest armories and municipal halls in the Midwest to hear him challenge bourgeois piety. They massed in the bucolic woods of Lake Geneva, Wisconsin, and Olivet, Michigan, to savor his earnest, explosive talks. The tumultuous response of the Detroit students was not lost on Union Theological Seminary President Henry Sloane Coffin, who had shared the platform with him in Milwaukee in 1926 and was again in the crowd at the Masonic Temple. Sherwood Eddy was also at the conference. Before Niebuhr's address, Eddy conveyed to Coffin his and Kirby Page's interest in bringing Niebuhr to New York. Their previous offer of a subsidy for free-lance work had been upgraded to include an associate editorship of the *World Tomorrow*, of which Page was editor and Eddy a $5,000-per-year backer, but Niebuhr had still not acceded. Eddy knew that if a job at the country's most prestigious seminary could be added to the package, it might tip the scales. Niebuhr had made known his interest in an academic position. No doubt Coffin too was interested—though with a man of Eddy's wealth he must have struck a calculatedly detached pose. There was no point appearing too eager for something that Eddy might consider a large favor.

Coffin's chief goal in his second year as Union's president was to restore the training of ministers to its traditional primacy. The previous president, leading church historian Arthur McGiffert, had made Union a bastion of graduate research; many of the current students had no intention of becoming ministers and did much of their course work at Columbia University. Coffin—himself a renowned preacher and pastor of Madison Avenue Presbyterian from 1905 to 1926, while also a professor of practical theology at Union—knew what Niebuhr could do for him. Like Baltzer, Eddy, and Morrison, Coffin saw the greatness in him and knew that to help Niebuhr was to help himself. Niebuhr could inspire just the kind of student Coffin hoped to attract: intelligent, liberal, committed to Christian fellowship. Of course Niebuhr was on the rhetorically wild side at times, but Coffin was untroubled by youthful stridency. Niebuhr's charisma would do for Union what it had done for the *Christian Century*—build its eminence as a center of liberal Protestant debate.

Coffin told Eddy that the seminary had no funds for a new position in ethics or practical theology. No problem, Eddy quickly replied. He would fund Niebuhr's entire salary: part-time at the *World Tomorrow*, part-time at Union. Coffin sought out Niebuhr at the convention and asked him if he might like to teach in New York. Niebuhr was awestruck: what, he queried, could he possibly be qualified to teach at Union? All he would have to teach, Coffin answered, was "just what you think." When the Union faculty got wind of the Eddy-Coffin idea they were not uniformly thrilled. Left-wing ethicist Harry F. Ward was enthusiastic, but others were troubled by the absence of scholarly credentials. After Niebuhr had paid a visit, for an interview and a sermon, several older professors raised eyebrows about the excited pulpit behavior and the decided midwestern twang. But President Coffin, Yale '97, whose social contacts and breeding were unsurpassed, countered the wave of elegant dissent by insisting that the matter be handled as a business proposition: the post would cost the seminary nothing. In the end the faculty apparently approved the offer by a single vote. Niebuhr was invited to join the seminary as associate professor of Christian ethics.[16]

Niebuhr's own decision did not come easily either. Several highly placed friends and advisers—among them F. Ernest Johnson and Samuel Cavert of the Federal Council, and Socialist Norman Thomas, former editor of the *World Tomorrow*—thought it would be a mistake to leave Detroit. He had recently had such "phenomenal support" in the Motor City, he told Page, that he might be able to do more for social reconstruction there than in New York. "I don't want to let myself be influenced too much by other people, but I can't help wondering whether these fellows have the right dope." There was, he acknowledged, one strong factor pushing him away from Detroit. "My personal problem still demands my leaving. But have I the right to let a purely personal problem determine the choice?" There is no telling what the personal problem was, though it is clear it had nothing to do with his desire for a seminary post. Was it a relationship to a woman that he could break off only by moving away? Was his mother exerting so much pressure on him to stay in Detroit that he felt it was time to take her away—in order to safeguard his personal independence and authority within the family? Was it a need to augment his income in order to bail out his brother Walter—who had gone to Europe after the war to work as a film-maker and journalist, but was now having trouble making ends meet? Niebuhr made sure that no other reader of his letter to Page would know what he was talking about.

The personal problem, combined with the prestige of Union and the literary outlet at the *World Tomorrow*, did determine the choice. When the announcement was made public in Detroit—in the Bethel Church bulletin of April 22—the accolades poured in. The Detroit *News* put the story on Monday's front page. On Tuesday the editorial writer noted that Niebuhr was leaving "after having built up one of the city's great churches. . . . While his fearless frankness won him many opponents, it also gained him thousands of admirers . . . who found in him a champion of progressive and enlightened ideals." Black leaders privately echoed the *News*'s senti-ment. H. S. Dunbar, executive secretary of the YMCA, wrote that "to us in particular it seems almost a calamity that you should feel called upon to remove yourself from Detroit. . . . You know too well how thoroughly you are respected and loved by members of my race." John C. Dancy, director of the Detroit Urban League, assured him that "I express the feeling of the great majority of Negroes in Detroit when I say that there is genuine regret in the minds of the colored group of this city at your leave-taking."

H. M. Nimmo's *Detroit Saturday Night*, by contrast, was glad to see him go. It was the elegant city weekly, its pages dominated by financial news, political comment, and the latest comings and goings of the Motor City's proud entrepreneurs and their wives. Its readers did not appreciate the views of one who believed, in Nimmo's editorial phrase, that Detroit was an "industrial hell." At the farewell banquet in his honor—a luncheon

•

for five hundred at the Statler—Niebuhr took the offensive against his elite detractors. He was reluctant to leave Detroit, he claimed, because "the rich industries" of the city still encountered minimal resistance. They "have never thought of unemployment insurance and old age pensions," and his own and others' prophetic efforts seemed not to have changed "by a hair's breadth anyone's fundamental attitude toward this town and its industries." Niebuhr wished he could stay because "I feel I've been a failure in the very thing in which I've had most interest." Toastmaster Warren Rogers, Episcopal bishop of Cleveland and former Detroiter, expressed the ambivalent feeling that many liberal Protestants must have had in seeing Niebuhr go: "He is a revolutionary. I can't go all the way with Niebuhr, but I believe in him."[17]

VII

Dedicated entrepreneur C. C. Morrison, who had lost the battle for Niebuhr's editorial services to Kirby Page and the *World Tomorrow*, saw in his departure from Detroit the makings of a book. He persuaded Niebuhr to contract with Willett, Clark, and Colby, the *Century*'s publishing company, for a volume of selections from his diary. The idea of publishing his journal had always been in the back of Niebuhr's mind; many of the entries were composed after he knew they would be made public. Yet as the manuscript of *Leaves from the Notebook of a Tamed Cynic* progressed he grew dubious about releasing it. In the "Preface and Apology" written before he left Detroit at the end of the summer he explained that "the book is published with an uneasy conscience, the author half hoping the publishers would make short shrift of his indiscretions by throttling the book." Niebuhr claimed embarrassment over how "inane" some of the entries were, and over their author's "tendency to be most critical of that in other men to which he is most tempted himself." The publishers' own explanatory note—which appeared in the first Chicago edition of 1929 but was removed from the New York edition of 1930 and later reprintings—began with the assertion that "the author's reluctance to have this book published is all the more reason for the publishers' desire to have it see the light of day. The author felt that the book would be regarded as presumptuous criticism. It is natural that he would feel that way, for he is one of those rare men who see more error in themselves than they see around them." The publishers explained the choice of title as an effort to express their view of Niebuhr's growth from youthful cynicism to mature sympathy. "Page by page the cynic—the same cynic that is in us all—is tamed—not broken, not forced into compromises, but tamed by the release of impulses of sympathy, of maturer observation, of sincere analysis."

Niebuhr's own preface, however, made clear that the journal disclosed no such evolution. He was no less cynical in 1928 than he had been in 1915; if anything he was more cynical since he had come to believe that the ministry was inevitably a wrenching series of compromises. The pastor could never live out the ideals of love and sacrifice that he preached. What may really have made Niebuhr so uneasy about the book was its very

•

portrayal of himself as a sensitive modern pastor grappling with the inevitable compromises of the local urban ministry. Even that role was an "ideal" he had rarely attained. Throughout the first decade of his Bethel pastorate he had fled the pastoral vocation whenever he could. Once he had become a national figure he did spend more time in Detroit, but that time did not go into making the rounds among his parishioners. He still left most pastoral duties to his mother, his assistant pastor, and his eighteen lay "leaders"— one man and one woman chosen from each of the church's nine residential districts. That decentralized system had been created in 1925 when membership passed the five hundred mark. The most fundamental compromise Niebuhr made during the thirteen years of his Bethel pastorate—between being a pastor and being a writer, lecturer, and man of influence in metropolitan and national affairs both religious and secular—was left out of the account altogether. *Leaves* did mention many of his travels and outside activities. But the book portrayed him as a super-shepherd who had plenty of time for his travels and his flock. In truth he was himself one of the "itinerant prophets" whom the preface chastised for criticizing, but not experiencing themselves, all the struggles of the local pastor. It was indeed somewhat presumptuous of him to judge those pastors whose vision extended no further than the needs of their congregation; the needs of his own were frequently left to others while he wrote editorials and articles, made diary entries in Pullman cars, bowed to the plaudits of admiring student crowds, conferred with men of power at home and abroad. As President-General Baltzer pointed out to him in 1926: "You are burning the candle at both ends. You need time at home . . . for real congregational work in order to become a real spiritual adviser of individuals. . . . To spend too many hours on RR trains in the company of passing friends surrounded by compliments and entertainments does not deepen the spirit."

What made *Leaves* such an engaging and profound volume was not any account of "the typical problems of a modern minister in an industrial and urban community"—Niebuhr's expressed intention. What made it stand out was its relentless record of a unique man's attempt to become a prophet without succumbing to the obvious threat of pride and self-satisfaction. His embarrassment as the date of publication approached was genuine: a prophet needed to broadcast his thoughts, but it was obviously self-serving and arrogant to parade about as one. The book is a perpetual battle between Niebuhr's sense of calling and his sense of humility; he takes himself at all times both seriously and as an imposter. The diary is the revelation of a modern consciousness—relativist, fragmented, unsure of its standpoint, doubting its motives—but also the assertion of a traditional faith—dogmatic, unified, confident. The power of the book lies in the apparent contradiction between the alternating postures of decision and indecision, commitment and skepticism, and the oscillating voices of contempt and thanksgiving, mordancy and serenity. It is a portrait of the young man as a paradox: doubting believer, self-critical prophet.

Leaves is also a gallery of the many men he measured himself against as he tried to devise his humbly prophetic ministry. There was Lynn Harold Hough, silver-tongued Methodist, former president of Northwestern, pastor to Detroit's Christian literati, whose book learning impressed and intimidated him. Hough could not be dismissed as an intellectual isolated from real life. He too "convict[ed] Detroit of her sins," and managed to maintain "a robust religious vitality which I seem to lack." Hough was living proof that one could be "sophisticated and naive, critical and religious, at one and the same time." Reflecting on Hough, Niebuhr knew he had to return to the seminary. Prophecy demanded both the theological sophistication and the "appreciation of the mystical values in religion" that Hough possessed and he did not.

Another model of how to be both prophet and philosopher, to be wise without succumbing to "the endless antinomies of intellectualism," was Methodist Bishop Francis J. McConnell, former president of DePauw, outspoken advocate of social reforms. McConnell not only combined prophetic vigor and intellectual rigor; he blended prophetic detachment and the organizational responsibilities of the "statesman." "Here is a Thomas Aquinas and an Innocent III and something of a [Saint] Francis all under one hat." McConnell knew that the prophet had to "take account of the limitations of human society" if he was to escape "irresponsibility"; but he also understood that mere "statesmanship easily degenerates into opportunism." Niebuhr too would strive for a realistic prophecy.[18]

Above all there were the three figures of such significance in his Detroit experience that they took on mythic stature. For the rest of his life, when his thoughts turned to Detroit they turned to Bishop Williams, Fred Butzel, and Henry Ford. Charles Williams, the high-church bishop who despite his ceremonial robes condescended to no one and excoriated the exploiters of human labor; lawyer Fred Butzel, the ostensibly cynical, secular Jew who was in fact a selfless seeker after justice; Henry Ford, the naive gentleman whose idealism was so pure it was akin to cynicism. Williams was the transcendent model, like his own father removed so suddenly by death but his constant inspiration thereafter. Butzel was the ever-present alternative: the secular saint for whom religious trappings were superfluous. In imagination he became Niebuhr's secular "pole"; the image of Butzel was a constant challenge to his prophetic pretensions. The Butzel in him kept the Williams in him from becoming self-satisfied, grandiloquent.

Henry Ford was their antithesis. They each had authority which came from their office, their profession, but both had a gift of spirit which let them laugh at their office while using it. Ford was the man of limitless authority whose spirit was as mechanical as his product. His identification of his own and God's purposes was so complete that he was a danger to civilization. The real significance of Ford for Niebuhr—the real explanation of his fixation on the Ford image—was that he caught in him not just a glimpse of America, but a glimpse of himself. Ford's self-delusion was only an extreme form of the pretentious sentimentality to which Niebuhr believed liberal Protestants fell prey. Ford brought home to him the full social meaning of modern idealism, his own and that of his pacifist friends. It was ideology, false consciousness: Ford's idealism was a cover for power; his own—his calls for industrial cooperation, for a peaceful world order—was a cover for impotence. He was perhaps not a cynic by the time he left Detroit, but he was a bitter antagonist of the seductive moral idealism whose logical end he perceived in Henry Ford. Ford was his constant reminder

•

that prophecy was to be rooted not merely in voicing ideals but in exposing the realities camouflaged by ideals.

Niebuhr's overriding fear as he left the itinerant ministry of the Detroit years to settle into the position of part-time professor was that he would become a "professional," a "specialist." He sensed that religion might become his line of "business" instead of his calling. "The new world is filled with men who are pathetically incapable of doing anything with life outside the rounds of their specialization," he informed his Detroit *Times* readers on May 5. He had long condemned what he called the professionalization of the parish ministry too: as he put it in 1925, "the tendency to apply professional standards of success to it and to prompt its members to achieve success by tantalizing [them] with purely commercial rewards."

> There was a great moral advantage in the proud boast of the prophet Amos that he was neither a prophet nor the son of a prophet, that he was not a professional religionist, but an amateur. The apostle Paul found occasion to press the same advantage and remind his congregations that he did not depend on them for his sustenance. The professional ministry is at best a necessary evil and our Quaker friends may not be wholly wrong in regarding it as an unnecessary evil.

Religion, he wrote in 1926, had always been sparked "by God-intoxicated amateurs and corrupted by professionals who made a living out of its resources." As he assumed the office of salaried professor he took heart from the example of William James, "who was in many respects an amateur philosopher rather than a professional." He vowed not to succumb to the institutional demands and worldly rewards of teaching at the nation's most celebrated seminary. He wanted the visibility, the prestige, the influence, but feared losing his sting. His attacks on professionalism were cautions against back-sliding into respectability. He wanted to avoid the fate of "most budding prophets," who, he lamented in 1924, "are tamed in time to become harmless parish priests."[19]

SIX

A STATE
OF
JOY AND PAIN

(1928–1932)

I

Union Seminary's Gothic Revival towers, built in 1910, stood calmly above the frenzied Manhattan din at Broadway and 120th. A flawless stone sanctuary rising incongruously out of scarred asphalt, an outpost of the sacred on the boisterous urban frontier. Screeching subway trains took surface tracks south out of Harlem, but passing 125th Street they slowed to a crawl, groped up the Morningside Heights slope, and as if in deference to the solemn sphere of the seminary, plunged silently at 122nd into the bowels of Manhattan. The rush and rhythm of the city streets did not unsettle Union's dim chiseled corridors.

But in September, 1928, the rush and rhythm of Reinhold Niebuhr, associate professor of Christian ethics and philosophy of religion, penetrated the hush. Already a celebrity on the Protestant circuit, he instantly drew circles of students around him. They dogged his steps as he careened through the hallways, they sat wide-eyed in the Common Room after lunch and dinner while he issued rapid-fire commentary on world events, they struggled to record even a small portion of his lectures as his words raced ahead to keep up with his mind. They flocked to chapel to hear him roar and watch him gesticulate: his words rolled down like waters, his ideas like a never-ending stream. Thoughts piled up on other thoughts with such speed that sentences were often abandoned halfway through, overwhelmed by the more potent images that followed. He worked usually from a one-page outline, having long before found it difficult to read aloud from a text— perhaps a touch of dyslexia, he thought. Certain vital items like Biblical passages or literary allusions he memorized. Otherwise it was the free flow of an inspired mind, summoning a favorite Old Testament verse in an affectionate whisper, playing excitedly with some key irony of human living or paradox of Christian belief, clamoring with fists clenched for an end to Christian complacency and the dawn of a militant church fighting eyeball to eyeball with the powers and principalities.

Niebuhr's charging style, brash, outspoken, vehement, did not sit well with most of the senior faculty, who favored the clipped, understated, Scotch reserve of seminary tradition. James Moffatt, professor of church history, Ernest Scott, professor of Biblical theology, and William Adams Brown, professor of systematic theology (and blue-blooded scion of New York's Brown Brothers), judged it improper for students to address a professor as "Reinie." They also shook their heads when Niebuhr turned up for a tuxedo affair in honor of a visiting German dignitary in his everyday rumpled suit and carelessly knotted tie. They swallowed hard when they saw him eating an artichoke and a dish of Hollandaise sauce: instead of dipping the leaves one by one in the sauce, he dumped the sauce all over the artichoke. An uncouth country bumpkin with decidedly dubious scholarly credentials, an indecorous pulpit style, a nasal midwestern twang, and a growing reputation for political radicalism. Niebuhr's future at the seminary might have seemed dim. But President Coffin, his ear always close to the ground of student opinion at Union and nationwide, kept the guardians of tradition in check. Niebuhr's manner was no act of rebellion or disrespect; it was the sign of a prophetic sensibility that was in the world but not of it. Even his sternest detractors came eventually to cherish his spirit.

In his first year Niebuhr was also in the seminary but not completely of it. He taught only part-time, as Eddy and Coffin had agreed: one full-year course called Religion and Ethics, along with duties as an assistant to Harry Ward in Ethics. He shared a small apartment at 99 Claremont Avenue with his mother and sister, who moved to New York from Boston. Hulda had been teaching religious education at Boston University, where she had taken both BA and MA degrees after the war, and decided to pursue further graduate work at Union and Columbia. Her presence helped Lydia cope with the uprooting from Bethel, which she never fully got over—and gave Reinhold the freedom to roam the metropolis without worrying about his mother's state of mind.

He set out frequently for working lunches at the *World Tomorrow* or meetings with Sherwood Eddy, Norman Thomas, John Haynes Holmes, Edmund Chaffee, or other members of New York's Protestant-Socialist-pacifist nexus. Much of his appeal to Union students came from his immersion in political life outside the seminary. After dinner in the refectory he would sit for an hour or two surrounded by seminarians; clouds of cigarette smoke rose along with passionate analysis from the center of the circle. Niebuhr brought the inside story from the outside world, poked holes in the stone wall that separated the seminary from "real life." For many of the students he was a peerless model: the professor who acted as well as thought, who challenged the apparent monklike passivity of many cloistered Christian scholars. He was not the only professor who preached worldly engagement, but he had a charisma all his own. At nine or ten in the evening, when he had taken leave of his disciples, he retreated to his typewriter and turned out an article or two—rarely writing more than a single draft—before retiring in the early morning. The following week's *World Tomorrow*, *Christian Century*, or *New Republic* would buttress his standing as man of the world, offer further proof of his secular prowess.

In the fall of 1928 his prime concern was the Presidential campaign and the deepening debate over Prohibition. A decade before, as a young German-American seeking respectability in national Protestant circles, he had abandoned the laissez-faire position of the Evangelical Synod on alcoholic consumption. Prohibition was good liberal progressive doctrine; it was far from being the special property of small-town fundamentalists. Liberals such as Niebuhr considered the temperate life to be an essential foundation for a politically conscious working class. He was scarcely a true-blue Prohibitionist. He hated the narrow anti-Catholic animus of many politically active Protestants, and had argued publicly in 1925 that "wet" Catholic Mayor John W. Smith of Detroit was far preferable to the "dry" Protestant candidate who had cozied up to the Ku Klux Klan. But while he bemoaned many churchpeople's fixation on Prohibition to the exclusion of other issues, he joined the chorus of support, as he put it in 1923, for "educating the common variety of democrat in the purity ideals of the churches." He regretted excessive reliance on the police, but affirmed the principle of compulsion. "Now that we have won Prohibition," he told a meeting of the Detroit Pastors' Union in 1925, "some people seem to think we should content ourselves with standing behind, egging on the police, and getting people into jail, instead of doing our work of moral education." As late as the end of 1927 he was unable to countenance the coming candidacy of "hopelessly wet" Governor Al Smith of New York. He applauded Smith's liberalism in every other sphere, but still bristled at the governor's "blindness" to the "great moral problem with which Prohibition deals." Those "democrats" who, like himself, had "an appreciation of puritan virtues and values" were for the moment politically homeless.

But the 1928 campaign provoked a major reorientation in his thinking on Prohibition—a shift that accompanied and added further steam to his ongoing quest to move beyond social idealism. In late August the *Christian Century* went on record for Hoover, despite misgivings about his stand on labor and Latin America. C. C. Morrison was determined to keep Prohibition at center stage; even a bellicose pro-business candidate was superior, he felt, to one who would weaken the Volstead Act and repeal the eighteenth amendment. Protestants had to stand up for their most precious ideals when subjected to such direct challenge. Sacrificing Prohibition meant giving up on the progressive moral transformation of society. Hoover was undesirable in certain respects, but Smith was the sort of political operator who cared nothing for the ideals of moral purity or social cooperation. Prohibition was an essential step in advancing toward both goals.

Niebuhr took the lead in answering Morrison's stark argument by accepting his premises and reversing his conclusion. If preserving Prohibition required swallowing "Coolidge prosperity dogmas" and "imperialism" on "Latin America and Nicaragua in particular," then Prohibition would have to go. It was not worth jettisoning the entire liberal program on account of a single issue—a shrewd debater's formulation on Niebuhr's part, since Morrison's whole stance rested on the unspoken assumption that Prohibition was not just one discrete issue among others, but the center-piece, along with pacifism, of a strategy for social renewal. Niebuhr con-fessed that his own vote would go to Socialist Norman Thomas, a personal acquaintance and former editor of the *World Tomorrow*, but between Smith and Hoover the choice was clear. It was time for liberal Protestants to put issues of economic justice ahead of issues of personal purity; the wet Catholic Smith was far superior to the dry Protestant Hoover, even though Smith had shown political ineptitude and "quite probably imperiled his chances for election" by needlessly brandishing the liquor issue in his appeal to urban workers. If church liberals could not rise to the occasion and back Smith, they "merely prove[d] that the church is still enmeshed in an anach-ronistic puritanism which sees the sins of individuals but never the sins of society."

Only a year earlier Niebuhr had rejected Smith because of his own allegiance to "puritan values and virtues"; now, in the face of Hoover's across-the-board assault on the liberal agenda, he decided that the Protestant quest for moral purity was "anachronistic." As in his "Critique of Pacifism" in the *Atlantic* the year before, he proclaimed that it was too easy for self-satisfied, middle-class Protestants to preach ideals to the less fortunate, whether hungry nations or working-class Americans. Indeed, preaching ideals was problematic in itself; Henry Ford and other higher-ups were themselves spouting ideals ad nauseam in order to deflect attention from unpleasant realities. The point was to deflate mere ideals, roll up one's sleeves, work for true economic and social justice. Niebuhr was vague—as in his critique of pacifism—about what concrete steps a real advocate of justice ought to take, but he was sure that declarations of moral purity were beside the point.[1]

On the eve of the election, editorializing in his own *World Tomorrow*, he made clear that as a Thomas supporter he held "no brief" for Smith. "Nevertheless," he added,

> it is obvious that he is as truly the spokesman of the newer democracy of the cities as Andrew Jackson was . . . of the democracy of the "backwoods." The pharisaic tendency of respectable religion is revealed by the opposition of the "best people" to such political symbols of democratic forces as Jackson and Smith. The best people seem always to be interested in minutiae of personal habits or cultural achievements and insensible to the weightier matters of the law, social justice, and economic righteousness.

Morrison could have been forgiven for finding this paean to the new de-mocracy more akin to Democratic Party campaign literature than to serious political analysis, and for taking offense at Niebuhr's simplistic reduction of the prohibitionists' stand to a plea for personal purity at the expense of social justice. Progressives had for decades realized that alcohol was at the heart of a broader institutionalized oppression of the lower orders; drinking was in many cases an embodiment at the individual level of social injustice. Niebuhr's most effective point was that a major political realignment was in progress and serious reformers would have to take account of it. "The arrogant Nordic majority" needed to recognize the growing strength of "our newer immigrant groups." As he explained to the *New Republic's* liberal readership just before the election, Protestants could no longer expect to create a morally uniform culture based on middle-class Protestant ideals of temperance and restraint. He considered those ideals demonstrably superior to both traditional "Latin" Catholic license and contemporary American hedonism, and still held out the remote hope that religiously "vital" Protestants might carry the culture their way. But that sentimental aside was overwhelmed in the article by his realistic assessment of cultural diversity—a fundamental fact of life in polyglot New York City.

Before they could reform "culture," before they could strive to perfect "personality," Christians would have to help create a "new economic order." The modern industrial system, in which "socially created" capital was "privately owned," was incapable of distributing its profits "with any degree of fairness." True, American workers were highly paid by contrast to Europeans, but "compensation for injury, unemployment insurance and old age pensions are practically unknown." He did not envision any "absolute equality of income"—"human nature may not be equal to such a venture"—and he did not advocate "violent change." But a radical redistribution of wealth was a prerequisite of democratic progress and even of continued stability.

> The question is whether society can gain sufficient social intelligence to modify the present system step by step as the need arises . . . or whether through the stubbornness and blindness of the holders of power and privilege and through the ignorance of the masses the system will be permitted to disintegrate until change can come only through revolution and social convulsion.

Niebuhr's dual concern was for justice and cohesion, each the ultimate guarantor of the other. Only a stable social order could institutionalize justice; only a just social order could avoid disintegration. What remained unclear in Niebuhr's account was how a "society" could "gain social intelligence"—an exceedingly abstract formulation for one who prided himself on being realistic and concrete. He was sure that sweet reasonableness and loving trust had no more place in the social struggle at home than they had in international affairs. He was also prepared to concede that nonviolent "force"—as in Gandhi's boycotts or industrial strikes—might occasionally be justified. The vague call for "social intelligence" left all the difficult questions unanswered.[2]

II

What he could not answer theoretically he did his best to answer in practice. After the election, in which Hoover swamped Smith and they both pulverized Thomas—whose 267,000 votes was low even for a Socialist—Niebuhr committed himself increasingly to the Socialist cause. At first he remained aloof from the Socialist Party itself. Instead he joined George

•

Counts's left-leaning New York Teachers' Union, the pacifist Fellowship of Reconciliation, Norman Thomas's Socialist educational organization (the League for Industrial Democracy), and University of Chicago economist Paul Douglas's League for Independent Political Action. Like many other liberal professors and ministers, Niebuhr believed that only a third party could restore "social control." Neither Republicans nor Democrats could mobilize the expertise and political support to enact social insurance, public ownership of the major means of production, or the taxation of unearned wealth. Only a third party—perhaps a farmer-labor alliance like Robert LaFollette's Progressives of 1924, perhaps the Socialist Party itself—would be willing to approach social problems experimentally. The appeal of the Socialist movement for Niebuhr and other left-leaning liberals was not its Marxian heritage of social analysis or political action—they viewed Marxism as a "violent" creed and a form of "European" dogmatism—but the Socialist potential for gradualist reform.

It was the non-Marxist Norman Thomas's rapid rise in the Socialist ranks in the 1920s that made it possible for men like Niebuhr, Douglas, John Dewey, and John Haynes Holmes to gravitate toward the Socialist cause and in some cases enter the Socialist Party. Although the New York City branch of the Party was still, under Morris Hillquit's leadership, a bastion of the Social Democratic Marxism of the Second International, Norman Thomas's youthful, native-born forces were the emerging power in the national Party. Niebuhr had been hoping for a British-style Labor Party since the end of the war. It could bring together workers and intellectuals in a two-front campaign of "economic action" at the workplace and "political action" at the ballot box. Thomas, a Presbyterian minister who had resigned from his Manhattan church in 1917 to push pacifist and Socialist principles, was also impressed by the Labour Party after its electoral gains in 1923. In the eyes of Niebuhr and other young Socialists, Thomas stood a good chance of becoming the American Ramsay MacDonald. He was earnest, eloquent, intellectual, a fair-haired Princetonian with a wide-grinning common touch. When the British Labourites swept the elections in May, 1929, the Thomas Socialists saw a new day dawning.

Norman Thomas's personal charisma may have been the primary magnet that drew Niebuhr toward the Socialist Party, but the Party itself was a perfectly tailored outlet for his political energies in 1929. It was widely regarded as radical and militant on the one hand, but as responsible and nonviolent on the other. It symbolized exactly that mix of patience and impatience that Niebuhr wished to express: controlled vehemence, dissent grounded in affirmation, a mature middle road between the tinkering reformism of the liberals and the romantic revolutionism of the Communists. The Socialists were also a declining political party in great need of new blood in leadership positions. Hard workers, good speakers, and persuasive writers could be put to immediate use; a man of Niebuhr's talents could rise rapidly to a position of prominence in party affairs. Most of all, it was a party which put great value on "ideas" but at Thomas's insistence no longer demanded the maintenance of correct "doctrine." Niebuhr had energy and ideas in abundance, but a constitutional distaste for dogmatism— a distaste first acquired in the theologically ecumenical German Evangelical

Synod. By the end of the summer of 1929 he had signed his membership card.[3]

The abhorrence of dogmatism that governed Niebuhr's political thinking also marked his theological reflections in 1929. He was disturbed both by Marxism—which he considered dogmatic by definition—and by the growing influence of the Swiss theologian Karl Barth, who had just been translated into English for the first time. Niebuhr was no theologian, but he did not hesitate to disparage Barthianism as a "new kind of fundamentalism." A few years later Niebuhr would ironically acquire a reputation as an American adherent of European (and Barthian) "neo-orthodoxy." He did not deserve it in 1929, or later. He did approve of Barth's rejection of "immanent" theologies that minimized God's transcendence, but he was appalled by Barth's "absolute Christ-idea." It was no better than "magic." Niebuhr was not interested, then or later, in making a careful study of Barth's work. He had little patience with a theology based squarely on Biblical revelation, or with a theologian who wrote in dry, erudite prose. But he did grasp the essential character of Barth's challenge to liberal Christianity. And despite his own misgivings about liberalism, he jumped to defend its bedrock assumptions against Barth.

Barthianism, he wrote, was "a new and more terrifying subjectivism" because at bottom it was "dogmatically asserted," subject to no historical, rational, or experiential validation. It was totally innocent of Harnack's and Troeltsch's insights into the historical and cultural determinants of human consciousness. He was aghast at "the whole pathos of this kind of abstruse theological thought." It sapped the vitality from the moral life, robbed religion of its adventure and risk by providing phony assurances. Niebuhr mustered much more enthusiasm for the thoroughly secular visions of Walter Lippmann's *A Preface to Morals* and Joseph Wood Krutch's *A Modern Temper* than he did for Barth's *The Word of God and the Word of Man*. Better a complete and noble skepticism that rejected both traditional faith and the modern world's trivial illusions than a theology which challenged the latter but uncritically reaffirmed the former. In his theology as in his non-Marxian Socialist politics, Niebuhr was convinced, as he put it in denouncing Barth, that "we can escape relativity and uncertainty only by piling experience upon experience, checking hypothesis against hypothesis, correcting errors by considering new perspectives, not by the mere assertion of an absolute idea that is beyond experience." [4]

Niebuhr's membership in the Socialist Party did not endear him to Union's board of directors or to conservative faculty, but neither did it shock them. William Adams Brown had seen his own star pupil Norman Thomas—who graduated first in his class at Union in 1911—embrace the Socialist cause over a decade before. In their view Niebuhr was one more in a long line of mistaken Christian idealists. His apostasy from common sense was deplorable but not particularly threatening. Far from fretting over Niebuhr's politics, Henry Sloane Coffin was worried about losing his young prophet to Yale Divinity School. Yale's Dean Luther Weigle was in hot pursuit. After Niebuhr's scintillating sermon at Yale's Battell Chapel in November, 1929, Weigle offered him not only a full professorship, but an endowed chair, in Christian ethics. Niebuhr had been teaching for just a

•

year, and part-time at that, but Coffin judged him indispensable. He countered by persuading Gaylord White to vacate his Dodge Professorship in Applied Christianity, in exchange for the dean of students post, then gave Niebuhr the chair.

Niebuhr chose to stay in New York, but Yale was not reconciled to the loss. In the fall of 1930 the Yale College chaplaincy was dangled before him, complete with what Yale President James Rowland Angell termed "generous financial arrangements, including a house and entertainment fund." Niebuhr told him he wanted to remain a professor, but Angell persisted. Yale, he pointed out, had "one of the most extraordinary groups of young men that you could possibly hope to meet. The influence which these men are bound to exert on the life of their times, it would be difficult to exaggerate." Niebuhr needed no instruction on the elite makeup of the Yale student body; it was only fifteen years since he had sat self-consciously in their midst trying to hide his midwestern accent. Angell's arm-twisting was in vain; like Weigle he went away empty-handed.

Whatever Niebuhr's interest in either Yale job—it appears to have been minimal—he was very interested in promotion to a permanent post and higher salary. As usual he was striving to make ends meet, relying on his writing to stay in the black. Walter continued to struggle financially in Paris; Reinhold sent him $3,000 in 1929, and gave him another $3,000 when he returned from Europe in 1930 to look for work in filmmaking. Reinhold also had to support his mother and Hulda, since neither of them had any income until 1930, when Hulda was hired as associate director of Christian education at President Coffin's former church, Madison Avenue Presbyterian. Lydia, still an energetic woman as she passed her sixtieth birthday in December, 1929, was despondent, languishing in idleness. She was depressed by her lack of productivity, by the drain she exerted on her son's pocketbook, but most of all by the end of her partnership with him in the work of the Lord. She could not help feeling abandoned.[5]

III

While Coffin and Weigle were working overtime to outfox one another in December, 1929, Niebuhr himself was preoccupied with developments at Bethel Evangelical Church in Detroit. The church that he still considered his own had split acrimoniously over the issue of admitting Negroes to membership. He was drawn into the fray because each faction wanted his support. He also had his own reputation to protect. He was deeply troubled that papers around the country were running stories about "Niebuhr's church" excluding blacks. In September two Negroes had applied for membership with the strong backing of Reverend Adelbert Helm, the twenty-nine-year-old liberal activist who had replaced Niebuhr as pastor the previous year. When Helm got wind of opposition to the blacks in the church council, he took the offensive and made admission of the blacks a test of the church's adherence to the Gospel. His manner was so judgmental that even some of the members who favored admitting the Negroes lost faith in him. Niebuhr

•

went to Detroit in late October, and argued at the Sunday evening forum—for Helm's edification—that "racial prejudice never can be wiped out by preaching against it." Helm declined to back off. He claimed to be fulfilling Niebuhr's own ministry and vilified those willing to compromise with prejudice. Following a fiery Helm sermon in December, the church council, with Niebuhr's implicit support, forced him out. Niebuhr issued a blistering postmortem on Helm and his ilk in the *Century*; the anonymous editorial mentioned no names, but castigated those self-deluded "martyrs" who resigned from church posts with lofty declarations of their superior Christian insight.

Helm's departure ended the conflict between minister and congregation, but it did not resolve the issue of admitting the blacks to membership. Niebuhr feared the congregation would actually decide to exclude them, and suggested to his friend and church council member William Kenmitz that the vote be taken out of the congregation and restricted to the council, where there would be "fairly unanimous action" to admit. But his worst fears were realized in January, 1930, when the annual meeting of the congregation voted to bar the blacks. Niebuhr was profoundly shaken. "I never envisaged a fully developed interracial church at Bethel," he wrote the church council.

> I do not think we are ready for that. But I do not see how any church can be so completely disloyal to the Gospel of love as to put up bars against members of another racial group. . . . The number who would apply would probably never be large. We would never have been forced to meet the ultimate test, which I am willing to admit no congregation at the present time would be able to face. But to refuse to take the next step seems to me to be clearly an act of apostasy.

What pained Niebuhr most was the revelation that some of his closest friends in the church—men he had relied upon for years and had indeed brought to Christianity in the first place—were among the apostates. He now understood that Helm's "unpedagogical methods" were not the primary cause of the church's ignominy.

> These methods may be criticized but it remains a fact that prominent members of the church did everything in their power to fan latent race prejudices into a hot flame. . . . I am hurt and pained to my innermost being by your action. Whether I shall ever preach in your pulpit again is a real question in my mind. Whether you will ever invite me may be a question in yours after this letter. . . . Meanwhile I will hope and pray that the Lord will soften your hearts and help you to see how much harm has been done by your action to the cause of Christ everywhere.[6]

Niebuhr still found fault with Helm's uncompromising histrionics, but confessed to the young minister that he might have "thrown too much blame" on him in trying to "excuse" a church with which he was "sentimentally pretty much bound up." In his Detroit *Times* column in February he let his parishioners know that the primary flaw was theirs, not Helm's. "Any institution of the ideal, such as the church," he wrote, without men-

•

tioning Bethel by name, "must deal with the problem of interracial conflict if it is to justify the pretensions of moral leadership which it continually makes. It cannot deal with the problem if it will not offer the possibility of interracial contact within its own fellowship. Social attitudes yield very little to preachment and do yield to social experience." Through the spring he supported a conciliatory move on the part of some council members to rehire Helm. In July the council decided to reinstate him, but two weeks later the full congregation overruled the council. Just over half of the parishioners did vote for Helm, but a two-thirds-majority requirement—enacted the year before at Niebuhr's urging—defeated him. The church therefore reaffirmed its ethnic purity as a white and largely German-American body. By upholding the firing of Helm and the barring of blacks it repudiated the liberal, cosmopolitan identity that Niebuhr had fashioned, but never in his own ministry put to the racial test. A hard core of older German-Americans, among them some of Niebuhr's closest associates, had never been comfortable with that progressive identity; now they could take Bethel back from its forward position on the liberal vanguard.

To some observers Niebuhr himself did not appear blameless in the affair. Yale Divinity School professor Jerome Davis, a close acquaintance, even questioned the social idealism of Niebuhr's own Detroit pastorate. He drew a curt response. "I am not particularly anxious to challenge anyone on his interpretation of the Detroit situation even if it is critical of my ministry because I know very well that it was not perfect." Niebuhr did not tell Davis in what sense it had been imperfect. But *Leaves*, published the previous July, repeated over and over again that at Bethel he had been too tepid. "I have myself too frequently avoided the specific application of general principles to controversial situations," he admonished himself in a 1928 entry. "There must be something bogus about me. Here I have been preaching the Gospel for thirteen years and crying, 'woe unto you if all men speak well of you,' and yet I leave without a serious controversy in the whole thirteen years." In the wake of the debacle of 1929–1930, he must have wondered if he had set Bethel up for the fall by neglecting the issue of interracial membership in his own ministry. "There are probably not more than two score congregations in the nation," he wrote in the *Century* at the height of the Helm dispute, "which could receive Negroes into their membership without suffering either serious defections from their ranks or actual disintegration of their organization." But perhaps he, with his charisma and superior pedagogy, could have succeeded where Helm had not.

A quarter-century later he recalled to a friend that a few black professional people had in fact applied for membership near the end of his ministry. They were regular visitors to the evening forum, and the Bethel council, he claimed, was quite willing to have them join. But their own ministers objected on the grounds that they were needed for leadership in their black churches. From the vantage point of the 1950s it was evident to Niebuhr that Bethel itself had offered no obstacle to their admission. In retrospect he may have underestimated the racial fears of his congregation, or overestimated his own powers of persuasion. Yet it does seem likely that he could have secured the blacks' acceptance. Had he known in 1928 that

Bethel's survival depended on it, he might have put his persuasive powers to work on the black ministers.

In 1930 there was one thing of which he was sure: he was no longer in a mood to temporize with standpatters. There was "a certain softness" in the modern minister, he noted in the *Century* in June, 1930, and he had his own softness plainly in mind. Ministers were ill served by "a spirit of generosity which loves not wisely but too well and cannot preach [the] Gospel without tempering its wind to the shorn sheep. . . . Sometimes we cannot be honest with people because we love them too much. More frequently we cannot be honest with them because we are not honest with ourselves." With that act of contrition Niebuhr once again convicted himself of preaching mere ideals. He was determined to pass over to action, to controversial commitments of the sort he had avoided at Bethel. Just as the Wall Street crash in the fall of 1929 had revealed "the unethical character of our entire civilization," the Bethel collapse in the winter had disclosed the ethical failings of the church and its ministers. The local and national crises combined to prompt him to a new militancy.[7]

Not only did the times demand action; his own spirit demanded it. Niebuhr's personal needs, as he well understood, coincided with the social needs of the hour. Lingering unduly in the realm of thought led to "morbid introspection." He must have wondered if psychic distress was a family curse: his mother and all three siblings suffered periodic bouts of depression. Losing himself in a flurry of activity allowed him to ward off morbidity while keeping up the flow of financial and emotional sustenance to his family. Helmut, like Reinhold, was quite conscious of these family psychodynamics. When Hulda was mired in depression in 1930, he wrote Reinhold to report the advice he had given her. He had told her that "we were all inclined to introversion, and that it wasn't a good plan to introspect too much when we got into some psychical difficulty, because we found too many symptoms, and thought ourselves to be suffering from lots of things which were after all nothing but normal manifestations. I still think that's true and that Sis is finding a lot of complexes which are normal." Helmut then generalized from her case to that of the family.

> We've just got to get along with some of our complexes. There are some that can't be solved save by moral victory. . . . I'd better leave my fingers out of psychotherapy. All I know from observation on myself and on a number of students is that the old-fashioned advice to get busy on something external, preferably something manual, has very real therapeutic value.[8]

IV

In the summer of 1930 Niebuhr went beyond talking about controversial action and started taking some: he accepted the Socialist Party's request that he stand for office in the fall. Since the start of the year he had become more active in Party circles, speaking at gatherings of the faithful and offering political analysis to the readers of the Party's *New Leader*. Some Party members wanted him to run for governor of New York, but Niebuhr did not want to travel outside Manhattan during Union Seminary's fall term. He was placed instead on the State Senate ticket from the city's Nineteenth District, which included his home turf of Union and Columbia University. The state legislature was no minor item on the Socialist agenda. It held major symbolic significance for them, since five Socialists had been elected to it in 1920 and then been barred from taking office by antiradical legislators. The Party was determined to right that wrong. The *New Leader* identified Niebuhr as one of the Party's four strongest candidates, and reassured those readers who feared his campaign might be halfhearted since he had joined the Party less than a year before: "Prof. Niebuhr's acceptance of the Senatorial nomination is part of a decision he has taken to enter the local political arena in an active and continuous manner." [9]

When his candidacy was announced Niebuhr was in Germany scouting the political and religious terrain, reporting on each of those spheres for the *New Leader* and *Christian Century* respectively. He had found it much harder to free himself for the trip in 1930 than he had in 1924, when he last crossed the Atlantic, with Sherwood Eddy. Just short of his thirty-eighth birthday, he was so much in demand that he left Hulda behind in his apartment to answer the "three dozen invitations of various kinds" that had to be declined. His mother joined him for the voyage, and they met Helmut and his wife Florence in Germany. It was Reinhold's check for $250 that had permitted his brother to spend the spring and summer there studying theology; thus Niebuhr funded Walter's return from Europe and Helmut's departure for Europe in the same year. Helmut was uncharacteristically emotional when the check arrived.

> That check is 250 bucks and what a world more. It's Germany, it's a chance to get out of my provincialism, it's education, it's brotherhood, it's the memory of childhood and youth indebted to you, it's confidence and trust. Well, I don't want to get sentimental, but you must know how I feel about it. Still, I don't suppose you can, since no one has ever done for you what you are constantly doing for others. . . . I wish I had the grace to return it to you and to say, I love you for it old man but I don't need it as much as you do. But I haven't got that kind of guts or whatever it is.

His gratitude momentarily blotted out the darker currents of envy and jealousy that he had often felt but seldom expressed. He had always been forced to follow in the wake of Reinhold's exploits: first at Elmhurst and Eden, then at Yale Divinity School as a student and ultimately as professor of Christian ethics—the same post (without the chair) that Reinhold had turned down. He had to fight the feeling of being second-best that his father had unmercifully instilled in him and that others unintentionally reawakened. *Evangelical Herald* editor J. H. Horstmann—for whom Reinhold had filed dispatches during his trips in the early 1920s—did not grasp the hurt contained in his request to Helmut in July, 1930: please send us articles just like those Reinhold does for the *Century*.

Niebuhr's reports from Tübingen, where he spent ten days with Helmut reading and writing at the university library, stressed the social basis of

•

political and religious developments in Germany. Mounting unemployment underlay the political crisis: the Socialists were determined to expand benefits to those out of work, but the center parties formerly in coalition with the Socialists were determined to balance the budget. The breakup of the Weimar coalition guaranteed the National Socialists more parliamentary seats in the September election, but he considered them no "permanent threat to Republican Germany." Hitler and "his crowd of fascists" were "as impossible an aggregation of political freebooters as can be imagined." They were a dying force, "the unhealthy and decaying residue of old Germany." On the religious front he perceived a lackluster church from which the masses of German Protestants, despairing over their national fate, were thoroughly alienated. A small band of "religious socialists," including Frankfurt's "young philosopher of religion Paul Tillich," offered some hope, but theological conservatives were carrying the day. "There seems to be a general feeling that liberalism runs into the sand of relativism, and from this fate escape is sought by a new emphasis upon the church or the creed or the person of Jesus or, as in the case of the Barthians, upon a new dogmatism."

He tried debating a group of Barthians but gave up. "A positivism which stands above reason is not debatable so what's the use?" he wrote to his friend John Bennett. "It is really hopeless to argue with Barthians." They abstracted from the political realm and imagined a salvation "effected above the area of history"—a natural response to the social and historical defeats of an "old nation." His few days of dialogue with them revealed to him how liberal he still was. They altogether dispensed with the Enlightenment in their hasty retreat to the Reformation. He wanted to save what was good in the Enlightenment—its conviction that faith and redemption were intimately connected to actual social and moral experience in the secular world. To deny the legitimate role of human reason in spiritual life—to separate completely the realms of nature and grace—produced an ethical quietism typical of the Lutheran tradition. Barthianism was "sanctified futilitarianism." [10]

In mid-August Reinhold and Helmut both joined Sherwood Eddy's European Seminar for a two-week trip from Berlin to the Soviet Union. All self-respecting American radicals and left-liberals visited Russia at some point in the late twenties or early thirties to see Socialist reconstruction firsthand. Eddy made it possible for many of them to go: this was the fifth group he had led to Leningrad and Moscow since 1923. Reinhold's five dispatches to the *Century* and Helmut's two reports to the *Evangelical Herald* brought in the cash to pay part of their expenses; but to have Reinhold along was payment enough for Eddy. Since 1925 Niebuhr had declined Eddy's yearly entreaty that he accompany the group. Finally he had made time to go, and braved the omnipresent bedbugs and toilet paper cut from *Pravda* to catch a glimpse of revolution in the making.

The Niebuhr brothers made exactly the same points in their articles about Russia, though Reinhold was predictably lively, forceful, and quick to generalize, Helmut dry, roundabout, and tentative. "Reinie has been in Europe a few weeks," Helmut complained to his wife, "and he thinks he knows all about it." Helmut valued circumspection over the authoritative

•

pose. Each of the brothers was appalled by the drabness of the cities and the monotony of the life, yet each was captivated by the "energy" and "vitality" of the revolutionary effort. They granted that the vitality was (in Reinhold's words) "shot through with brutality" toward "every representative and symbol of the old order," but they were deeply impressed by the commitment average Russians seemed to make to the collective task. Their participation was uncoerced; it was "not the product of communism at all, but simply the vigor of an emancipated people who are standing upright for the first time in the dignity of a new freedom." As Reinhold wrote to the *New Leader* after returning to Berlin, "I doubt whether any generation in the history of the world has ever sacrificed itself (or is being sacrificed) so completely for the welfare of future generations as these Russians." It was the apparent vigor and determination of virtually all Russians to build a new society that held Niebuhr spellbound. He wondered if that kind of social energy could be mobilized in America.[11]

Building a nondogmatic Socialist Party informed by the Christian prophetic tradition was the institutional place to start. As classes began in his third year at Union (his first as a tenured professor), he went on the local stump in his race for the State Senate. The board of directors of the seminary was not amused; preaching idealistic social principles was one thing, standing for office as a Socialist was another. Niebuhr may have received some sort of dressing-down, judging by Helmut's letter of sympathy about "the difficulties in which you were plunged [at the seminary] after the summer's absence." But the Wall Street lawyers and other wealthy Presbyterians on the board had little to worry about aside from two months of unfortunate publicity. On November 4 Niebuhr got a minuscule 1,480 votes. The Democrat Duncan O'Brien got 20,271, and the Republican Wilbur Murphy 10,947. Niebuhr might claim to John Bennett that "none of our people were elected though the vote in each case was doubled or trebled," but in his case it was not true. He received 190 fewer votes than the Socialist candidate in the district had polled in 1928. The reassuring thing about the low vote, however, was that he could not help but do better in 1932.[12]

V

The academic year 1930–1931 was a pivotal one in the history of the seminary and a turning point in his own relationship to it. Not only was Niebuhr now a permanent member of the faculty who would keep Union squarely at the center of Protestant developments over the next generation. Three foreign scholars arrived at the seminary, each of whom was to have a significant impact on Niebuhr's life: John Baillie, William Adams Brown's successor as Roosevelt Professor of Systematic Theology; Dietrich Bonhoeffer, "German fellow" for the year; and Ursula Keppel-Compton, "English fellow" for the year. The Scottish Baillie, six years Niebuhr's senior, was already a well-known theologian and immediately put Union at the cutting edge of theological scholarship: the encounter with Barth. Moreover, unlike the older triumvirate of Brown, Scott, and Moffatt, Baillie took a rapid liking to Niebuhr. Their friendship not only made life at Union somewhat more comfortable for Niebuhr; it also increased his appreciation for theology as such. Baillie vindicated theology in Niebuhr's eyes because he preserved the standard liberal starting point of man's own natural potential for knowledge of God. Here theology was not a flight to other-worldly dogmatism, but a discriminating study of concrete man in relation to the transcendent. Baillie's thoughtful critique of Barthianism showed Niebuhr the way to the more sophisticated level of theological reflection that he reached during the late 1930s—after Baillie himself had departed for a professorship of divinity at the University of Edinburgh.

Dietrich Bonhoeffer was a brash, twenty-four-year-old post–doctoral student who quickly judged the intellectual capacities of the students and their favorite professors—Niebuhr and Ward—laughably undeveloped. "The theological education of this group is virtually nil," he reflected, "and the self-assurance which lightly makes mock of any specifically theological question is unwarranted and naive." He found the informality of social relations at Union not only jarring, but positively antithetical to serious thought. Community at the seminary was "founded less on truth than on the spirit of 'fairness.' One says nothing against another member of the dormitory as long as he is a 'good fellow.' " The result was a "leveling in intellectual demands and accomplishments." Seminars, lectures, and discussions were equally "innocuous"; they "crippled" critical thinking. When Baillie invited him to present a paper on Barth in his seminar, Bonhoeffer prefaced it by warning the students to forget, "at least for this one hour, everything you have learned before." All in all he felt that the theological atmosphere at Union was directly "accelerating the process of the secularization of Christianity in America."

Niebuhr was part of the problem. His lectures on religion and ethics were in Bonhoeffer's eyes refreshingly lively but deplorably shallow. He began to take notes—"Religion is the experience of the holy, transcendent experience of Goodness, Beauty, Truth and Holiness"—but then his pen fell still. He liked Niebuhr's and Ward's course on Ethical Viewpoints in Modern Literature better, but less for Niebuhr's contribution than for the reading list, especially the inclusion of black writers like James Weldon Johnson. Niebuhr was critical of Bonhoeffer too. Commenting on one of his papers, he summoned James's pragmatism to counter the ethical implications of Barthian theology.

> . . . in making grace as transcendent as you do, I don't see how you can ascribe any ethical significance to it. Obedience to God's will may be a religious experience, but it is not an ethical one until it issues in actions which can be socially valued. Any other interpretation of "ethical" than one which measures an action in terms of consequences and judges actions purely in terms of notions empties the ethical of content and makes it purely formal.

Bonhoeffer resisted Niebuhr's argument for the time being, but once back in Germany found himself more and more drawn to questions of politics

•

and ethics—perhaps in part because of Niebuhr's example. For Niebuhr, Bonhoeffer was one more force that pressured him to take theology more seriously, if only to defend himself more convincingly against his detractors.[13]

The third foreigner new to Union in 1930–1931 was Ursula Keppel-Compton, a physician's daughter and an Oxford theological graduate with a keen mind and a lilting, loquacious tongue. Uncertain about what career to pursue, she thought a year at Union would help her decide. She first heard about Niebuhr on the ship coming over, and it did not take her long, after arrival, to dispute Bonhoeffer's judgement: unlike the German, she found Niebuhr inspiring. Most of all she was drawn to his spirited, critical temper. Herself a devout Anglican, she was also irreverent about churchly pretensions—including the exclusion of women from the priesthood. She shared Niebuhr's impatience with ecclesiastical cant and admired his enthusiasm for applying the Gospel to the social sphere.

It was hardly a matter of indifference to the hundreds of male seminarians and dozen male faculty members that Miss Keppel-Compton was not merely intelligent and religious, but shapely and blonde—an awesome array of virtues for Christian bachelors to contemplate. Older students locked horns in pursuit, but she evinced little interest in their game, which included a betting pool on who would win her affections. As the year progressed she settled her own gaze on the most confirmed bachelor at Union, one who appeared never to give women a thought. Niebuhr had apparently not dated since coming to New York, although several women there, as in Detroit, had revealed their eagerness to know him better. Ursula managed to penetrate his defenses. Niebuhr was guarded about the whole matter, but did manage to divulge to Myles Horton, another one of his students, that he liked "the way her mind works." He apparently had nothing more to say about what turned into a spring courtship. Years later he did frequently invoke the adage "in courtship it is the man who pursues— until the woman catches him," implying it was relevant to his case. There is no question that Ursula took much of the initiative. She was determined to have him for a husband. Reinhold took his time but eventually responded in kind. Not only was she extraordinarily attractive and witty, smart and well versed in theology, she was English—the nationality he had long associated with maturity and wisdom in affairs both secular and sacred. To marry Ursula was to choose a transatlantic future.

As the end of the school year and Keppel-Compton's departure for England approached, they decided to act. Niebuhr was predictably reticent, even in private. To John Bennett he scrawled a secret note at the bottom of a dictated letter—so his secretary would not read it. Congratulating Bennett on his own engagement, he confessed that he "might get in a similar state of joy and pain on slight provocation. But don't say anything to anyone for the time being." At a weekend graduation party at Bennett's cottage on Heron Island, they announced their engagement. Niebuhr was overcome with delight, nearly mystified, as he now dictated openly to Bennett, by "the new happiness into which I have literally been catapulted." Helmut too was "almost delirious with joy over your good fortune. . . . I didn't know this thing could stir me as profoundly as it does." The Niebuhr brothers were both erupting with emotion, celebrating the hidden pleasures of the human heart; it may have been the only event in their lives that produced such an immediately shared rapture. "Life acquires new depths, new meanings, new dimensions for you and her and so for all who love you. . . . Please tell Miss Keppel-Compton (can we say Ursula?) how we rejoice with you, how happy we are over her conquest which is your victory. What a grand and glorious feeling it is to know that Reinie has found his great joy. Could I sing I would sing. Could I write poetry I would do that."

But Helmut understood what Reinhold meant when he told Bennett in May that he was entering a state of joy and pain. For his mother was not able to share the ecstasy. She let Reinhold know that she could not bear to leave his home; it would kill her, she warned. "I know," wrote Helmut, "that the joy has its tragic connotations for you because of all that is involved. But that mustn't and won't stop you. I do wish that mother would come to live with us"—in New Haven, to which Helmut and his wife Florence were moving to take up the post at Yale. Perhaps she might "consent to come with us" if the matter were presented to her not as a change in home, but as a question of who needed her most. "Our need of her, which took second place these many years while your need of her was greater, and which is now increased by our new adjustment, now has a chance to make itself felt." Whatever his mother's destination, "I'm with you to see this thing through to its beautiful consummation with joy for all." The problem for Reinhold, however, was his own desire not to have his mother leave. She had grown deeply dependent on him, but he had also grown used to living with her. He suggested to Ursula that perhaps Lydia could remain with them. But Ursula was having none of it. Never one to soft-pedal her feelings, she recalls telling her betrothed that while he might not be able to do without his mother, she—Ursula—was quite capable of doing without him. She also remarked acidly that while it was possible to marry the church, it was not possible to marry one's mother. "That's incest," she reminded him. Yet it was a painful time for Ursula too. She had done all she could to make him marry her right away, she wrote during the summer to fellow Union student James Dombrowski. But the "old gentleman," as they fondly dubbed him, wanted to wait until Christmas. She could not bear the thought of spending the fall without him, though she supposed there was some advantage to waiting until she was appreciated. For his part, Niebuhr needed the extra time to prepare for the break with his mother. He had to coax her into accepting the change, but more difficult still, perhaps, was coping with the guilt he must have felt at finally putting his personal desires ahead of his mother's. Their fifteen-year symbiotic relationship had been built upon his rigid suppression of any merely personal existence. With her devoted support he had developed a thoroughly, uncompromisingly public identity. Ursula awakened long submerged instincts in him. She prompted a new euphoria that was as unsettling as it was pleasurable. It was from his own experience that he preached on "The Common Root of Joy and Pain" to one congregation after another in 1931:

•

Profound sorrow and great happiness have the same root. . . . It is because pain and joy have this same root that it is quite impossible to make happiness the sole end of life. The very capacities which make for happiness also subject the soul to greater grief and more poignant pain.[14]

VI

After Ursula's ship sailed at the end of May, Reinhold raced through a torrid schedule of appearances: a series of talks at Negro academies in the south under the auspices of the American Missionary Society (he did his best to radicalize the quiescent black pupils, he wrote to Ursula); a week at the YMCA student camp at Lake Geneva, Wisconsin; a brief stint at the University of Missouri Summer School (to raise some cash); more talks in New England. By the Fourth of July he was ready for a rest and joined his mother, sister, and Kirby Page's family at the YMCA retreat at Blue Ridge, North Carolina. "Rest" for Niebuhr meant constant activity in one geographical spot. Page did persuade him to play some tennis, and Hulda got him to go berrying with her, a sortie he regretted. He "got into a dispute," she wrote to Union professor Pit Van Dusen, "over a particularly fruity spot with a lot of bumble bees and came away with five stings and not many more berries." Most of the time he wrote articles and worked on a new book, which Page told Eddy he was calling "The Ethics of Social Change," an early title for *Moral Man and Immoral Society*. He also wrote frequent letters to Ursula which dwelt on the travails their radical seminarian friends were experiencing in trying to organize black farmers and white workers in the south. James Dombrowski was harassed in Pennsylvania, and Allen Keedy and Arnold Johnson were both jailed on criminal syndicalism charges in the coal region of Harlan County, Kentucky. Niebuhr was distressed by their plight but only partially supportive of their stance. Their commitment to justice was laudable, but over the past year they had gotten so wrapped up in the class struggle that they were close to embracing communism. They were leaving Niebuhr's gradualist socialism for Harry Ward's newfound revolutionary Marxism.

Losing some of his close friends to the extreme left had made Niebuhr redouble his efforts to stake out a position to the left of liberalism but short of communism. In the bitterly depressed winter of 1930–1931, he and some close friends from the old Fellowship for a Christian Social Order pooled ideas for a more radical Fellowship of Socialist Christians (FSC). Eddy, Page, and Niebuhr were again at the center, joined by fellow Socialists John Bennett, Roswell Barnes, Buell Gallagher, Francis Henson, and Frank Wilson, all of whom became members of the executive committee. The FSC decided to demand sacrifices from its members: they voluntarily taxed their own salaries to provide relief for the unemployed, a practice that was made obligatory for all members two years later. As Niebuhr had argued in print the previous fall, anyone on a fixed salary was "really better off in times of depression than in times of prosperity. . . . He is profiting from the misery of others if he does not get rid of at least his 17 percent additional value." Besides their personal sacrifice, FSC members pledged to support the Socialist Party and to "recognize the essential conflict between Christianity and the ethics of capitalistic individualism." As with the FCSO, local chapters were encouraged, but few were established. There were never more than several hundred members, held together above all by the charisma of Reinhold Niebuhr. Its organizational life depended on his presence.[15]

The FSC was premised on the belief that time was short. Property had to be brought under social control without delay; otherwise, Niebuhr predicted in early 1931, "the disinherited, in whom bitter need is bound to generate more passion than circumspection, will make short shrift of the whole of our civilization." Although American workers were acquiescent for the time being, he thought they might soon follow the lead of the more radical German proletariat. Writing to Ursula in August, he predicted that upon her return the following winter there would be revolts akin to those of the nineteenth-century British Chartist movement. He did not relish that prospect. While he believed workers' radicalism essential to the Socialist cause, he also feared that it might easily get out of hand. Socialism could be brought about only by workers' pressure; but socialism was also the means of saving society from the disorder of the disinherited. It would transform society, but in transforming it preserve it. "We cannot save our civilization at all except we change its whole basis," he remarked in *The Unemployed*, a magazine put out by the New York Chapter of the League for Industrial Democracy (LID), of which he was now president. "Nothing less than that will save us."

The rhetoric was fiery, but his personal manner was mild. When the temperature plummeted in early 1931, the LID encouraged its unemployed street-corner salesmen of *The Unemployed* to descend into the subways. The New York police chased them out and John Herling, circulation manager of the magazine, suggested to Niebuhr that he send a strongly worded message to Edward Mulroney, commissioner of police. Niebuhr promised to take care of it and the next day showed Herling a copy of what seemed to the latter a "namby-pamby" plea for special consideration. Herling shook his head over Niebuhr's lack of militancy, but two days later Mulroney acceded. The salesmen went on to sell half a million copies of five monthly issues to which famous writers and cartoonists donated their work.

Niebuhr was also the voice of reason on the NBC Blue Network in the spring of 1931. On alternate Saturday afternoons at the Woodstock Hotel he presided over high-powered discussions of politics and economics featuring such well-known authorities as his friend Paul Douglas, an economist, and his Socialist superior Norman Thomas. Niebuhr was one radical who believed that "the cultivation of social intelligence" was "an urgent necessity," as he told an audience of social workers at Columbia University. But he added that social intelligence had to make use of a power that lay beyond reason. As he put it in the *Atlantic*, in a classically Niebuhrian formulation, a procession of thundering Latinisms, "some kind of religion is the basis of every potent social programme. Those who fear too much the fanaticism which is the inevitable by-product of religiously created energy are consigned to social impotence by the multitude of their scruples." With his Soviet visit of the previous summer firmly in mind, he asserted

•

that religious energy was dangerous—it was closely akin to fanaticism—but essential. It alone could transform a society and therefore preserve it. Yet for all his vehemence, his commitment to "social intelligence" preserved his own respectability in liberal circles. *Time* magazine considered him no threat. It identified him approvingly in May, 1931, as "38-year-old, athletic Dr. Reinhold Niebuhr, one of socialism's ablest, most trustworthy advocates."[16]

In August, 1931, he left his "folks"—Lydia and Hulda—at Blue Ridge and sailed for England to visit Ursula. He was determined to use his trip to political and intellectual advantage. He wrote ahead to his fiancée to request four days in London. Gandhi himself was to be there starting September 6 and Niebuhr wanted an interview. He wished to ask Gandhi his views on the difference between violent and nonviolent resistance to evil, and the difference between nonresistance and any form of resistance: the key questions he was mulling over for his book on social change. He got his four days in London—Ursula had already learned that he could not be taken out of circulation for a genuine vacation—but not the interview. He was stuck with the other reporters outside Kingsley House while John Haynes Holmes—Niebuhr's ultimate symbol of the sentimental liberal pacifist, but a faithful publicist for Gandhi in the United States—went inside for a personal appointment. Niebuhr nevertheless reported to the *Century* that Gandhi was a rare example of the combined prophet-statesman who understood the need for "force" in the quest for justice.

When he got back to Union for the fall term—Ursula remained in England to prepare for the December wedding—he found himself caught between conflicting forces. The radical students were leaning all the more toward Ward, who was on leave for the year, and were beginning to be unfriendly. Meanwhile President Coffin was angry about student radicalism and strongly implied that Niebuhr was duty-bound to end it. With Ward gone Niebuhr felt lonely and isolated, as he wrote to Ursula. If Coffin continued to carry on, his own days at the seminary might be numbered. But Niebuhr was not one to dwell on such feelings—at least not with those outside his family. He threw himself into his course work, his writing, and his political tasks in the Socialist Party, the Fellowship of Socialist Christians, and the Fellowship of Reconciliation, whose executive council he had joined in 1929 and chaired beginning in 1931. He wanted to be more vigorous than ever in "action," less marooned in "thought." When he came upon a group of seminarians discussing the differences between him and Ward, he answered them in a public confession: the simple difference was that he did not have Ward's guts for the real social battle. He mused to Ursula that teaching ethics from the safety of the seminary took the adventure and vigor out of life. He doubted whether he could ever be a scholar anyway, so why put up with all the pretensions and hypocrisies that went along with being a professor? Ursula was a sounding board for self-doubts that he often brought to consciousness but rarely expressed.[17]

The political situation in the fall of 1931 also gave Niebuhr cause for dismay. Norman Thomas had received only 48,000 votes in the race for borough president of Manhattan—where his strength was supposed to lie—and the Socialists were shell-shocked. Why, Niebuhr wondered, were

•

Americans so politically naive? He could only suggest to Ursula that they were still novices in political development. Perhaps it was futile to work through the Socialist Party after all. Maybe the League for Independent Political Action (LIPA) ought to launch a new party for 1932, a "farmer-labor" party like LaFollette's 1924 Progressives. But after meeting on November 24 with John Dewey, Oswald Garrison Villard (editor of the *Nation*), and other fellow members of the LIPA's executive committee, he realized that a new party was out of the question. They had not understood how strictly academic a group they were; they had ideas but no strength. The depressing array of political forces made Niebuhr feel so impotent, he claimed to Ursula, that he had difficulty giving speeches; it seemed impossible to awaken Americans to their fate, so why try? Perhaps Niebuhr was exaggerating his plight to solicit comfort from his distant fiancée. But some of his moroseness was genuine. He was afflicted by the thought that teachers and political activists could perhaps do little about the brutalities and injustices of group life. He might be better suited, he speculated occasionally to Kirby Page and others, to a pastorate in a workers' church; there he could share the life of the proletariat and witness to the tragic tangle of human hopes and historic realities. "Nothing that is worth doing seems ever possible of accomplishment," he had intoned the year before to his audience of social workers. "Certainly nothing that is worth doing can ever be completed in the life of one generation." He meant it not as a counsel of despair, but as a goad to realistic action that could not be overwhelmed by inevitable disappointments.

In December Niebuhr sailed alone to England for the wedding; Lydia, Hulda, Helmut and his wife Florence, and Walter all remained behind for financial reasons, but their absence fittingly symbolized the severe break the marriage signified. He was not just leaving his childhood home; for Lydia at least it was abandonment, if not desertion, divorce, and remarriage. On December 22 Reinhold and Ursula were married according to the rites of the Church of England in a ceremony at Winchester Cathedral. Niebuhr was wearing, as he complained to a group of students before sailing for England, "a damned pink vest." A week after the wedding they were on their way back to New York, where they debarked on January 4. Lydia was still not reconciled to moving into a separate apartment, even though he had found her and Hulda another one at 527 Riverside Drive. As it turned out they all had to move since 99 Claremont was being rebuilt: the "folks" to Riverside, the newlyweds to 114 Morningside Drive.

The married state had no impact on Niebuhr's itinerant life-style. Weekend commitments took him all over the east and midwest, and Ursula accompanied him only occasionally on the shorter trips. In Chicago for his annual appearance at Clifford Barnes's Sunday Evening Club at the end of January, he told Kirby Page that he could not afford to bring Ursula on the four-day trip because he was speaking mostly for almost nothing. She again had to stay home two weeks later when he departed for Iowa College to pick up an honorary Doctor of Divinity degree—his first apart from the in-house degree Eden Seminary presented to him in 1930. Not only was Niebuhr frequently away on weekends; during the week he scarcely slumbered by the hearth. Besides the daily demands of classroom teaching and

•

office hours—he was now lecturing in a religion course at the New School for Social Research too—he was forever going to evening meetings. For Ursula, and no doubt for Reinhold too, it was a difficult time. His frenetic schedule, combined with the lingering hurt to Lydia, which flared up whenever she and Ursula were in the same room, produced a monumental family tension. Looking back years later, Reinhold and Ursula agreed that in marriage "the first two years are hell." [18]

VII

It was a remarkable coincidence that the only published disagreement Reinhold and Helmut ever engaged in took place at the height of this familial conflict. In March, 1932, Reinhold accepted C. C. Morrison's invitation to answer Helmut's article "The Grace of Doing Nothing," a discussion of Christian responsibility in the face of the Japanese invasion of Manchuria.

Ever since the invasion in September, 1931, Christian pacifists had painfully pondered the proper response. The Japanese had flown in the face of solemn nonaggression pacts and many pacifists felt that it was time for coercive measures by the League of Nations and the United States. Niebuhr and Page joined Sherwood Eddy, who had been in Manchuria when the attack occurred, in supporting an economic embargo despite Secretary of State Stimson's claim that it might lead to war. After Japan bombed civilians in Shanghai in January, many war resisters took a further step: they called for a consumer boycott against Japanese products. That might seem innocent enough, but it posed a severe moral dilemma for Christian pacifists. It was an indiscriminate weapon that hurt an entire population. "The question was difficult," Niebuhr confessed to a Methodist readership, "because a boycott is a kind of war. Shall we use a modified form of warfare to stop a war of violence?" Niebuhr answered in the affirmative. It would be unfortunate "if we permitted every venture of imperialism in the world merely because we were afraid to use any but purely ethical means to stop it." Japan's defiance of the League of Nations gave the lie to "pure pacifism."

> It has shown that a mere pacifist promise to abstain from war is not an adequate social policy, whatever may be said for it from the standpoint of personal Christian ethics. . . . Perhaps this is the proof of the theory that inter-group relations require a different ethic from that which applies to individuals within a group.

The point was not to eschew coercion, but to find the mode of coercion that was least destructive and most "redemptive," most likely to preserve some "sense of community between nations." [19]

Helmut's "The Grace of Doing Nothing" was one pacifist's response to the coercive posture already adopted by the editors of the World Tomorrow, including Reinhold. The brothers had squared off in their own living rooms on the question many times: Reinhold would pace back and forth, gesticulating and dominating the floor; Helmut would sit awaiting his turn, eyes downcast, then gently present his alternative view—to the accompaniment of Reinhold's impatient huffing and puffing. For Helmut "the history of the world is the judgment of the world and also its redemption." God had His own plans for human history; "our wishes for a different result do not in the least affect the outcome." Christians should not expect to bend history to their will. They should instead prepare for the future—for the day when "this God of things as they are" establishes a reign of peace. They should gather into cells of those committed to "a higher loyalty which transcends national and class lines of division." This was the path of repentance, renunciation of self-interest, confession of our own sins instead of judgment of the sins of others. At the center of his vision was Jesus' command that he who was without sin should cast the first stone. Helmut's pacifism was not one of pious hope for the spread of goodwill but one of hope against hope that God truly meant to save man from his own frailties and futilities. It was a pacifism purposely forged to escape Reinhold's strictures against sentimental sermons on the power of human love.

Reinhold's response was ostensibly full of respect, appreciation, and evenhandedness—a spirit he did not ordinarily cultivate in public debate—but Helmut must have caught its tone of big-brotherly tolerance for the errant naïf. To take Jesus' Gospel command as literally as Helmut did meant that "we will never be able to act" as a nation. No conceivable long-run guidance by God could bring about "a society of pure love as long as man remains man."

> The relation of nations and of economic groups can never be brought into terms of pure love. Justice is probably the highest ideal toward which human groups can aspire. And justice, with its goal of adjustment of right to right, inevitably involves the assertion of right against right and interest against interest until some kind of harmony is achieved. . . . The ethical and spiritual note of love and repentance can do no more than qualify the social struggle in history. It will never abolish it.

Since justice "qualified" by love was the highest social goal for man in history, Reinhold suggested that rather than leaving God to manage the brutalities of nature and society as He saw fit, men ought to intervene.

> I should think it would be better to come to ethical terms with the forces of nature in history, and try to use ethically directed coercion in order that violence may be avoided. The hope that a kingdom of pure love will emerge out of the catastrophes of history is even less plausible than the communist faith that an equalitarian society will inevitably emerge from them.

Granted, Helmut's faith was closer to the Gospel than his own; it matched Jesus' own ethical perfectionism. Reinhold would not abandon Jesus' "pure love ideal," but he would have to relegate it to the status of an unattainable standard. Political and ethical responsibility meant making "judicious use of the forces of nature in the service of the ideal."

Morrison invited Helmut to make a last rebuttal, then consigned it to the rear letter columns, where it had little impact. Helmut disclaimed any interest in "demolishing my opponent's position—which our thirty years' war has shown me to be impossible," and lucidly restated their differences.

•

For Reinhold, God was outside history and history itself was "no more than tragedy." For Helmut, God "is always in history. . . . He is the rock against which we beat in vain, that which bruises and overwhelms us when we seek to impose our wishes, contrary to His, upon Him." The job of Christians was not to "qualify" the brutalities of life with "a homeopathic dose of Christian 'love,' " but to repent of their sins, forgive the sins of others, and have faith that in the end God would bring fulfillment out of tragedy. In his undemonstrative, soft-spoken way—buried in the small print at the back of the issue—Helmut pointed out what Reinhold's other critics had not yet seen. Despite his fulminations against sentimental liberalism, against complacent faith in the redemptive character of human goodwill, Reinhold remained a thoroughgoing liberal. His God did not act in history. His faith was built not upon abandoning himself to God's will but upon the old liberal dream of transforming human society. Helmut's position was carefully constructed as an alternative to his brother's. It was one means by which he could construct an adult identity beyond the reach of his brother's ever lengthening shadow.[20]

The exchange with Helmut, along with the broader debate over pacifism generated by the Manchurian crisis and Gandhi's nonviolent campaign, prepared Reinhold for his primary summer projects: revision of his social-work lectures delivered at Columbia in 1930–1931, and completion of his manuscript on the ethics of social change, now with the title, after a phrase from Ernst Troeltsch, *Moral Man and Immoral Society*. Howard Chandler Robbins, a leading Episcopal divine, made available a cottage on his own property at Heath, Massachusetts, in the foothills of the Berkshires. With a quiet place to write beginning in late June, Niebuhr quickly disposed of *The Contribution of Religion to Social Work*, for which Columbia University Press had been waiting for over a year. His editor was holding out for a bibliography, since other books in the series listed sixty or seventy sources. Niebuhr pleaded inability to complete the task—not because he had left his list of sources at home, but because he had none. His lectures, like all his speeches, had been based on his own thinking, not on research. He offered to look up some sources when he got back to New York in September, but the editor preferred to produce the list himself. His revised manuscript of 1932—which became a ninety-four-page book in the fall—was a full-dress rehearsal for *Moral Man*. It still represented the Niebuhr of 1930 in its praise of "social intelligence" and its tone of calm reasonableness. But his stance of 1930 already anticipated *Moral Man*: "vital religion" could contribute to social justice in a way that dispassionate analysis could not. He urged social workers to learn from the most vital religion of the day: communism. The Communists understood that justice followed struggle; it demanded beliefs so intense that they could not be generated or confirmed by "experimental reason." [21]

By early July he was immersed in *Moral Man*—his book held him in slavery, he wrote to Page—and he begrudged every interruption. He resisted Ursula's pleas for walks through the woods; his only voluntary interaction with nature came when he periodically emptied the skunk traps. One intrusion he could not resist. The New York State branch of the Socialist Party was meeting in Utica over the July Fourth weekend to select candidates for the fall election. He had been active in the so-called Militant wing, pledged to Norman Thomas and devoted to discrediting the Old Guard New York City leadership. Despite his poor showing in 1930, other Militants were pushing him for a major office. One powerful member of the Old Guard, Louis Waldman, remembered a decade later that Niebuhr was the "favorite" of the Militants' "inner circle." They launched a Niebuhr-for-Governor boom, according to Waldman's recollection, but it fell short and Waldman was nominated. Niebuhr himself spoke to Page of a Niebuhr-for-US-Senate boom, which may have occurred after his loss to Waldman. He told Page he did not want a statewide office—too many upstate speeches—and therefore accepted the nomination for Congress from his home Nineteenth District.

After the convention he closeted himself at Heath to write *Moral Man*. He finished the fifth of ten chapters by the end of July, then produced five more in August, an extraordinarily fast pace for a manuscript of almost seventy thousand words. The book was literally in his head waiting to be released; he needed other books only to supply illustrations or quotations. He had hoped to be completely done before leaving on a three-week trip to England in September, but it was not until the end of the month that Scribners was able to begin setting type for a pre-Christmas publication date.[22]

As classes began Niebuhr dove into the Socialists' campaign. He seemed to be everywhere at once: in the pages of the *New Leader*, *World Tomorrow*, and *Christian Century* chastising those who still hoped for a "disinterested" third party; churning out short articles at Party request for newspapers around the country; serving as treasurer and chief publicist for Norman Thomas's "Committee of Five Thousand," made up of his non-Socialist supporters; mobilizing college students to canvass for Thomas; addressing large rallies and taking his regular turn on the soapbox on windy Manhattan street corners. At the "Greens and Beans" luncheon for Thomas he wielded the gavel that limited thirty-two consecutive speakers to one minute each; Thomas rose to speak exactly thirty-two minutes later. At a banquet in his own honor on October 2, John Dewey, Heywood Broun, and Morris Hillquit all spoke. The irony of Dewey's appearance was known only to Niebuhr, since only he knew that the manuscript of *Moral Man* singled Dewey out as an impotent liberal unacquainted with power and struggle. Socialist hopes ran especially high as the election neared, since only the Socialists had a clear plan for using government intervention to end the depression. At Madison Square Garden on Thursday, November 3, twenty-five thousand people heard twelve Socialist speakers predict a massive show of support. Five thousand others listened to loudspeakers outside. Surely a Congressman or two would actually be elected, and Thomas's vote would dwarf all previous Socialist counts.

Niebuhr knew he stood no chance of victory, though he hoped for a respectable percentage. President Coffin wanted firm assurances that he would not win, since the seminary board of directors had expressed grave concern. Niebuhr reassured Coffin, and Coffin reassured the board. Their fears proved baseless. Niebuhr was soundly trounced, as was Thomas. Thomas got only 881,951 of the nearly 40 million votes cast: 2.2 percent, compared to Debs's 6 percent in 1912 and 3.5 percent in 1920. Niebuhr got 3,550 (4.4 percent) of the Congressional vote, but that was a slight percentage decline over 1930, when the Socialist Julius Gerber received 4.8 percent in losing to the same Democratic incumbent, Sol Bloom. Bloom took 70 percent of the 1932 total compared to 67 percent in 1930; the hapless 1932 Republicans managed once again to poll six times more votes than the Socialists. The Socialist Party was devastated by the loss. It had been thrashed before, but this time political and economic conditions had been ideal for a record result. All over New York Socialists gathered for morose postmortems. The Fellowship of Socialist Christians met at Union Seminary to make "a serious examination of the poor showing." "The Socialist vote was very disappointing," Niebuhr pronounced in his newly inaugurated, anonymous *World Tomorrow* column "Ex Cathedra." "The American people seem to be very inert in the face of the sufferings to which they are being subjected." [23]

VIII

If the Socialists and their thousands of left-liberal supporters were shocked by the election, many of them were equally shocked by the appearance in early December of *Moral Man and Immoral Society*. "Doctrine of Christ and Marx Linked," announced the New York *Times* news story that heralded its publication. Doctrine of Christ totally buried, thought many religious Socialists; doctrine of Marx excessively glorified, thought many secular Socialists. The book caused an immediate furor because Niebuhr was apparently condoning not only coercion, which many pacifists had come to accept since Manchuria, but actual violence. In addition, he did not just discuss the drawbacks of liberalism, he sneered at liberal heroes like John Dewey. His rhetoric was icy, his argument aggressive; many of his friends and colleagues took it as a personal assault. Certainly Niebuhr did not mean it personally. But *Moral Man* was a conscious declaration of independence from the pacifist circle—liberal and Socialist—in which he had worked for the previous decade. He was rejecting ideas, not people, but he could not help implying that the people who held the ideas were fools.

The tone of *Moral Man* was an integral part of its message. Niebuhr wanted to take a decisive step toward revolution without landing in Communist ranks; rhetorical vehemence was indispensable for generating a sense of crisis, sparking militant commitment, signaling a radical break with the past. The book rumbles and thunders along, cerebral and pugnacious. Only three pages into it he has dismissed America's greatest living social philosopher, John Dewey, as a tepid apostle of rational experimentation and political gradualism. Dewey was "platitudinous" and left Niebuhr upset over "the confusion of an analyst who has no clear counsels about the way to overcome social inertia." It was too late to put much stock in "reason," since "reason is always, to some degree, the servant of interest in a social situation"—an assertion with which Dewey, Niebuhr ought to have known, would have heartily agreed. But like most debaters Niebuhr was not making a close study of his opponent's thought; he was constructing an ideal-type opponent who was easy to take down. The overriding problem of the day, and of the book, was how to overcome "social inertia"—the inertia revealed in the terrible Socialist showing—and to build a just society. Radicals needed a "motive force" which could not be found in a commitment to scientific reason.

> Contending factions in a social struggle require morale; and morale is created by the right dogmas, symbols and emotionally potent oversimplifications. . . . [Industrial workers] will have to believe rather more firmly in the justice and probable triumph of their cause than any impartial science would give them the right to believe, if they are to have enough energy to contest the power of the strong.

Niebuhr had already, since the winter of 1930–1931, made this point many times: intellectuals had to go beyond using reason, Christians had to go beyond using love, in the social struggle. Since Manchuria, he had incorporated "coercion" into his ethical repertoire. What was new about *Moral Man* was his contention that it might be necessary to use violence. One can see in retrospect that Niebuhr was likely to arrive at this point sooner or later. In the aftermath of the Wilsonian debacle in 1918 he had committed himself, along with his pacifist mentor Sherwood Eddy, to preaching radical ideals. He sensed all along that preaching ideals was risky business—it promoted complacency, it diverted attention from the realities of power—but he felt that ideals had power themselves. They were catching; if believed in strongly enough they would spread like a contagion across national and class lines, creating the very world they dreamed of. But the experience of Henry Ford had led to the turning point of "A Critique of Pacifism" in 1927. Ideals were not enough. They deceived, both by hiding realities and by giving the believer the illusion that he was acting, not just dreaming. Niebuhr moved toward condoning the use of "force" in 1928, on the grounds that groups, unlike individuals, were inherently selfish. By 1931 "force" had become "coercion," a code word for a slightly more militant and worldly-wise stance. *Moral Man* completed the progression by asserting that the responsible Christian had to accept the use of force— otherwise he would have to withdraw from politics altogether—and that the use of force logically implied the use of violence in certain situations.

Niebuhr's argument about violence was actually a good deal more supple than his liberal critics allowed. After taking pains to prove that violence was not intrinsically immoral, that there was no absolute distinction between violent and nonviolent coercion, he asserted that the choice of violent or nonviolent force was dictated by circumstances. In the concrete situation of 1932, violence had to be ruled out as counterproductive; the proletariat in western countries was in no position to seize power through revolution. If it were in such a position—where it could use violence with "the tempo of a surgeon's skill" so that "healing" could "follow quickly upon its wounds"—revolution would be ethical. For the time being it was out of place, even though the Communists who called for it should be "welcomed" for challenging the "sweet reasonableness" of gradualists, ra-

·

tionalists, and parliamentarians who were prone to "opportunism and futility." Far from preaching violence, *Moral Man* was actually less sanguine about the use of violence than some of Niebuhr's shorter pieces written in 1932. His conclusion in *Harper's* in June that "it will be practically impossible to secure social change in America without the use of very considerable violence" went beyond anything in *Moral Man*; the book was a forceful challenge to such hard-line prophecies.[24]

Moral Man was unquestionably a book of uncommon brilliance. It was a bold polemic with its distinctive air of portentous omniscience, an intricate argument of breathless urgency and analytical skill. He shrewdly appropriated alternative viewpoints for his own cause. Communism, for example, he defined as a religion, then discounted as a religion: it had religious vitality but not the transcendent perspective from which it could itself be criticized and held accountable. He never bothered to show that communism was best understood as a religion. By centering the analysis on the question of communism's adequacy as a religion he deftly brought the reader into his camp: civilization needed some religion, but communism did not fit the bill. Likewise he appropriated Gandhi for his argument by showing that the Indian leader not only practiced coercion but even accepted violence in some situations—as in his support for the British cause in World War I. Gandhi had chosen nonviolence as a pragmatist, not as an absolutist; therefore, whether Niebuhr supported violence in a concrete case or not, he was a true Gandhian. Even his straw-men opponents, the rationalist educators, were brought slyly into his fold. Education itself utilizes subtle modes of coercion, he argued; no social activity is purely peaceful or disinterested. Thus the very reformers from whom he took pains to dissociate himself were in fact much closer to him—since they also used coercion—than they believed. Stylistically too the book was engaging. Some found it turgid, but there was rhetorical power in its dense construction: wave after wave of firepower directed at the liberal, pacifist ramparts. And it was frequently memorable in its rhythmic play with paradox: "Hypocrisy [is] an inevitable by-product of all virtuous endeavor"; "the will-to-power uses reason, as kings use courtiers and chaplains, to add grace to their enterprise"; "society remains man's great fulfillment and his great frustration"; "self-deception . . . is the tribute which morality pays to immorality."

The most questionable part of the book was not its condoning of violence, on which Niebuhr's critics tended to focus, but its condoning of a particular role for intellectuals: that of mythmakers to provide the illusions and "emotionally potent oversimplifications" that workers needed to pursue justice. Given "the stupidity of the average man," he followed not logic but myth.

> The naive faith of the proletarian is the faith of the man of action. Rationality belongs to the cool observers. There is of course an element of illusion in the faith of the proletarian, as there is in all faith. But it is a necessary illusion, without which some truth is obscured. . . . These illusions are dangerous because they justify fanaticism; but their abandonment is perilous because it inclines to inertia.

It was time for Christians and other progressives to "redeem" the "total human enterprise" of its "excesses and corruptions." In the final words of the book:

> In the task of that redemption the most effective agents will be men who have substituted some new illusions for the abandoned ones. The most important of these illusions is that the collective life of mankind can achieve perfect justice. It is a very valuable illusion for the moment; for justice cannot be approximated if the hope of its perfect realization does not generate a sublime madness in the soul. Nothing but such madness will do battle with malignant power and "spiritual wickedness in high places." The illusion is dangerous because it encourages terrible fanaticisms. It must therefore be brought under the control of reason. One can only hope that reason will not destroy it before its work is done.

Niebuhr was so concerned about sparking action and avoiding mere thought that he did very little to show how "reason" might "control fanaticism." *Moral Man* gave strong support to the reigning assumption on the American left in the 1930s that the social struggle would be decided by the most persuasive propaganda, not the most compelling argument. It left unanswered the question of how, if intellectuals engaged in producing propaganda, they would ultimately be able to distinguish truth telling from mythmaking at all. If intellectuals did not act to preserve the culture's critical rationality, who would? Dewey certainly had some reason to insist that the radical movement commit itself to a belief in "intelligence" if it was to build a just social order. It might be an "illusion" to imagine intelligence in control of society, Dewey granted in his response to Niebuhr. But "illusion for illusion, this particular one may be better than those upon which humanity has usually depended." [25]

Like many radical intellectuals in the 1930s, Niebuhr managed at one and the same time to believe in "the stupidity of the average man" and "the redemptive mission" of the working class. "Mass society" assumptions intermingled with "class struggle" assumptions: the ordinary American was rootless, disoriented, "mechanical" on the one hand, but capable of acting in his real interest as a member of an "organic" collectivity on the other hand. The two sets of assumptions struggled for supremacy in *Moral Man*, with the class-struggle premise emerging victorious. Unlike nations or privileged classes, the workers in Niebuhr's view possessed a relatively "universal" viewpoint. The proletarian (somewhat like Niebuhr's transcendent God) stood outside of bourgeois society. The laborer's vantage point, as Rauschenbusch had argued twenty years before, was less corrupted by self-interest, more in tune with collective needs. But Niebuhr's proletarian was totally abstract, a cartoon character analogous to the muscle-bound heroes of Socialist Realism. He never examined the concrete cultures of American working people: their ethnic diversity, their dreams of "making it," the individualist hopes that many of them shared with middle-class Americans. He did not see the cultural cement, the ideology, which held most Americans of all classes together as a nation. His economic determinism was if anything more all-encompassing than Marx's: "the full maturity of American capitalism will inevitably be followed by the emergence of the American Marxian proletarian." Like other radicals Niebuhr had to believe in the future proletarians; otherwise there was no social role for him in their midst, or in their genesis. However forthright Niebuhr was about the need of social movements for illusions, he was not very perceptive about the need of radical intellectuals for social movements, real or imaginary. He was convinced that since Germany had a class-conscious proletariat, America would have one too. Modern industrial society had its unalterable laws; Germany was simply further down the historical track.

The real historic significance of *Moral Man* lay not in its call for proletarian fortitude or even its justification of violence as an ethical resource. Many other radical Christians were making use of the same arguments, although none were doing so with the same rhetorical and analytical power. Its chief importance lay in Niebuhr's biting repudiation, in the name of Protestantism itself, of the historic liberal Protestant quest for the Kingdom of God. He dismissed with utter derision the deepest hope that animated thousands of radical and liberal Christians, including Sherwood Eddy, Kirby Page, Charles Clayton Morrison, Harry Ward, John Haynes Holmes, Norman Thomas, and scores of his other friends and acquaintances: the hope that human history would eventually see the inauguration of a community of love. Many of them did not realize until Niebuhr's blast how profoundly devoted to the ideal they were. They leapt to the defense of their belief, and of the central heritage of American social thought, both Protestant and secular. Most American thinkers between 1880 and 1930 had Protestant roots even if they disclaimed Protestant orthodoxy. They yearned for a future cooperative commonwealth that would transcend the brutal confines of industrial society. Only a few seconded William Graham Sumner's celebration of the virile entrepreneur forged by marketplace battles. Fewer still were willing to resign themselves like Henry Adams or Mark Twain to cultural despair. Most clung to the dream that an organic community would one day displace the impersonal mechanisms of modern capitalism—through the spread of scientific expertise, aesthetic sensibility, and Christian love.

Niebuhr was alien to the Anglo-Saxon Protestant tradition that gave rise to this transformative dream. His own formative tradition, more Lutheran than Calvinist, was less sanguine about conforming the world to God's law. *Moral Man* revealed that philosophically he was much closer to the cosmopolitan Jew Walter Lippmann—despite his abhorrence for Lippmann's conservative politics during the depression—than he was to his erstwhile comrades. Like Lippmann he saw society as a realm of power blocs to be adjusted, not a garden in need of regeneration. America was culturally pluralistic, devoid—as he had argued in the Prohibition debate— of moral consensus. "We are merely a vast horde of people let loose on a continent with little to unify us by way of common cultural, moral, and religious traditions. . . . We are held together mechanically by our means of production and communication." In the first chapter of *Moral Man* he drew his battleline. "The dream of perpetual peace and brotherhood for human society is one which will never be fully realized." Society is "in a perpetual state of war."

Niebuhr no longer spoke of building the Kingdom of God. He no

·

longer spoke of realizing "personality." In the midst of class conflict, political
disarray, and economic breakdown, the term that had been constantly on
his lips in the 1920s fell from favor. As an ideal it seemed to him slightly
archaic, irrelevant to the pressing crisis at hand. It was a time for reforming
the hard massive structures of the public realm, not for cultivating the spirit.
With millions out of work it seemed beside the point to wonder whether
modern work was personally fulfilling. He did not abandon the ideal of
personality altogether; he confined it to a narrow sphere beyond society.
The rare individual might submit his will to Jesus' perfectionist rule of self-
sacrifice and nonresistance to evil. That course was heroic, he granted, but
open only to those who acknowledged their impotence in the social struggle.
Jesus' perfectionist turning of the cheek—unlike Gandhi's nonviolent resistance—had no place in the worldly conflict of interest against interest.
Justice, not love, was the chief goal of Christian action in society—and
revolution, not love, was the Christian's final social appeal. No wonder so
many of his friends and colleagues turned on him with a vengeance. He
had ridiculed their most precious presuppositions. Some never forgave him
for what they considered a vicious personal blow.[26]

SEVEN

LIKE
A LONELY
SOUL

(1933–1935)

I

Pacifist liberals and socialists mounted their barricades for the counterattack. *Century* reviewer Theodore Hume, a Chicago pastor whom Niebuhr counted a "good friend," lamented the "cynicism" and "unrelieved pessimism" of *Moral Man*. "To call the book fully Christian in tone is to travesty the heart of Jesus's message to the world." *World Tomorrow* reviewer Norman Thomas tried valiantly to mince his words but found the book "a disappointing contribution" because of its "defeatism." John Haynes Holmes, having read Thomas's piece, agreed: "Religious Defeatism," he titled his angry *Herald Tribune Books* review. Francis Pickens Miller, another friend and a leading official of the World Student Christian Federation, drafted two lengthy critiques and circulated them among the "Younger Theologians"—a semiannual discussion group formed by Henry Van Dusen, Niebuhr's Union colleague, in 1931. Both Niebuhrs were members, along with Miller, John Bennett, Robert Calhoun of Yale, John Mackay of Princeton, and a dozen others. Miller, who for years had relied on Niebuhr's services at world student assemblies, challenged him to "face the full implication of the fact" that he had "abandon[ed] the idea that Christianity has a unique function to fulfill in the process of social transformation. You have apparently no theory of the Church or of its function and task in the midst of modern civilization." Nor a real God, added Calhoun in his *Intercollegian* review. How could Niebuhr pretend to discuss the "religious resources for social living" and not even mention "the presence and influence of God"? Van Dusen was with them. "It will interest you to know, confidentially," he

•

wrote to Miller, "that I have not heard one single enthusiastically favorable criticism of Reinie's book. Our faculty group here seems to be very luke-warm for the most part."

Niebuhr did not lie back and suffer their slings. He tried to plug all the holes in the dike with letters to editors and accusers alike. "I have dis-covered," he complained to the *Century*, "that the liberalism of American Protestantism has turned into a rather hard orthodoxy which turns vehe-mently upon every heretic who questions its assumptions." Having staked out his position as the aggrieved party, he swung swiftly to the offensive. Those who found him "unduly cynical and pessimistic" were "immersed in the sentimentalities of a dying culture." Addressing all of his critics at once from the columns of his own *World Tomorrow*, he for the first time labeled himself a "Marxian" as well as a "Christian"—the better to distin-guish himself from the likes of John Haynes Holmes, now his chief nemesis on the religious left. Holmes's idolizing of Gandhi had long bothered him; now he committed to print his view that Holmes was on the verge of "conscious self-deception" since he granted that Gandhi used "force" but denied he used "power."

Niebuhr was so defensively polemical that he was plainly disingenuous more than once. Responding to George A. Coe's criticism that he had discounted the power of rational and moral force, he denied any such thing. "I believe that once rational and religious idealists stop fooling themselves and recognize the basic fact of a social struggle in society they will be the more able to direct it morally and rationally"—a sentimental hope quite at odds with the dominant tone of *Moral Man*. In answer to the layman Francis Miller he was professorially condescending. Miller suffered from one "con-fusion" after another. Yet after rebuffing each of Miller's charges he turned around and implicitly granted the main contention that *Moral Man* had no doctrine of the church. His book was for liberals in general, he wrote, not for the Christian Church. He would discuss the church in his Taylor lectures at Yale the following month, and would try to meet Miller's objections in that forum. At this point Niebuhr could not give much positive content to his ecclesiology. He told Miller he did want "a church which will assert the demand for justice of the proletarian class without equivocation. It must do this even at the expense of a schism in the church though this need not be inevitable." Yet the church must also be committed to more than justice: "I will not have it believe that the social passions and political strategies of [the proletarian] movement are the last word about life, its hopes and possibilities." Political goals could not be achieved by "purely ethical action," but there were other goals in life besides political ones. Niebuhr was scrambling to prove that he really did value intelligence and love, but his irate colleagues rightly noted that *Moral Man* minimized their social impact.[1]

Niebuhr's exchange with his critics was a fine demonstration of *Moral Man*'s thesis that reason is always the servant of interest in a social situation. Men of high education and goodwill went for one another's jugular. Yet there was one critic who knew how to deliver a probing assessment of Niebuhr's work without excommunicating him from the Christian fellow-

•

ship. Helmut Richard Niebuhr, who was going by his "American" middle name since becoming a Yale professor in 1931, was himself disturbed by *Moral Man*. But he kept his critique private and stroked his brother's ego all along the way. For years they had criticized each other's work outside the public eye; Reinhold had been a chief critic of the manuscript of Richard's first book, *The Social Sources of Denominationalism*, in 1928. Richard was not about to add to the chorus of outrage that greeted *Moral Man*. Despite his strong misgivings about the book, he did not want to be identified with one group of Reinhold's vocal detractors—"the good democrats, liberals, orthodox believers in the efficacy of goodwill and intelligence who are horrified not only because their dogma is attacked but also . . . because their dogma is a defense against all disturbances of law and order, by which they profit more or less." Richard had predicted the liberal and pacifist outcry as soon as he had seen the manuscript, and had hastened to distinguish his own views from those of the "idealists." "I have no defense of idealism to offer. I hate it with all my heart as an expression of our original sin." But Reinhold had to understand that there was another body of critics with which he did associate himself. These readers were "as cynical or almost as cynical and skeptical as you are." But they were dissatisfied with *Moral Man* because "they have hope—not much but a little, and faith, not a great deal but some."

> They criticize you not for what you said but for what you could not say. They await a Messianic word of release which has not been given to our time. You are so much of a Christian that you can understand and appreciate them. . . . These men though they criticize you are your best friends and they would not hurt you were they not wounded themselves. I continue to regard your book with Lippmann's *Preface* [*to Morals*] as the two most important religious books since the war. But neither of them are finality. They are the death of the old man and insofar the harbingers of a new birth. They are defeatist, but let John Haynes Holmes realize that he was defeated long ago and that he and all his kin have been consoling themselves with romantic poetry about forlorn hopes.

Richard had another good reason for keeping his response private. In his eyes the character of their own fraternal relationship cast grave doubt on the book's central thesis. Reinhold was "still too romantic about human nature in the individual" and "in face-to-face relationships."

> I am convinced that there is quite as much hypocrisy in this idealization of our personal relationships as there is in our collective behavior. Take such a thing as brotherly love. I hate to look at my brotherly love for you to see how it is compounded with personal pride—I taking some kind of credit for the things you do and basking in reflected glory—and with selfish ambition—trying to stand on my own feet, trying to live up to you, being jealous of you, to use a harsh and brutal term. Enough to make one vomit. If I *being evil*—in no metaphysical sense—can nevertheless love you, it isn't because any ideal or will to love prevails over my putrid instinct and desire, but because something else which is not my will was at work long before I had a will or an ideal. . . . The moral gift man has is not a gift of goodness, but a gift of judging right and wrong. "Moral man" if he is moral knows he's bad. Therefore I must dissent

•

from the whole argument that "individuals (as individuals) have a moral code . . . which makes the actions of collective man an outrage to their conscience." They have a code which makes their own actions an outrage to their own conscience. . . . I'll go a step further with you and say that what keeps men halfway decent in face-to-face relations is coercion, particularly the coercion of public approval and disapproval. There is of course another factor— enlightened self-interest—and a third—identification of self with another, which as you are never tired of saying becomes predatory on those outside the area of identification. But in no case is there love of the other as oneself on this basis. It seems to me then that the apparently more decent behavior of men in face-to-face relationships is not due at all to any element of reason or of moral idealism, any inclination of the will, but to the fact that there is more coercion, more enlightened self-interest (because the relations are more easily seen) and more possibility of identifying ourselves with the other man and loving ourselves in him or her. I do not deny the presence of ideals. I deny their efficacy in influencing action.

Not only was Reinhold too romantic, too "liberal," about human nature, he was also too liberal about religion itself.

You think of religion as a power—dangerous sometimes, helpful sometimes. That's liberal. For religion itself religion is no power, but that to which religion is directed, God. . . . I think the liberal religion is thoroughly bad. It is a first-aid to hypocrisy. It is the exaltation of goodwill, moral idealism. It worships the God whose qualities are "the human qualities raised to the nth degree," and I don't expect as much help from this religion as you do. It is sentimental and romantic. Has it ever struck you that you read religion through the mystics and ascetics? You scarcely think of Paul, Augustine, Luther, Calvin. You're speaking of humanistic religion so far as I can see. You come close to breaking with it at times but you don't quite do it.

In Richard's view therefore Reinhold was still, for all his rhetorical militancy, a thoroughgoing liberal. He had rigidly preserved the liberal conception of the self—the rational agency of goodwill—and the liberal idea of religion as a power for social transformation. To Richard neither view was defensible if one was "realistic." Reinhold was still "a moralist where the individual is concerned, and also where the social groups of the future are concerned. You expect the proletarian ideal to be effective even when the industrial workers seize power, because somehow it must. I don't believe it. You are skeptical, but hope against hope."

In the "Grace of Doing Nothing" exchange, Richard had disclaimed any interest in converting Reinhold to his point of view. In his critique of *Moral Man* he pulled out all the evangelical stops: he wanted Reinhold as a comrade in the fight for a realistically radical Christianity. Perhaps they did not "see eye to eye," perhaps they were not "soldiers in the same division," but they were already "allies." And Richard was bold enough to predict that his brother would move his way.

I agree wholly with you on the amorality of violence and nonviolence. A pacifism based on the immorality of violence hasn't a leg to stand on. But I do think that an activism which stresses immediate results is the cancer of our

•

modern life. It is betraying us constantly into interfering with events, pushing, pulling, trying to wriggle out of an impassable situation, and so drawing the noose tighter around our necks. We want to be saviors of civilization and simply bring down new destruction. . . . You are about ready to break with that activism. I think I discern that.

Richard was wrong about Reinhold giving up on "teleological" politics. Reinhold would never stop "interfering with events," never renounce the liberal view of religion as power, as energy for the social struggle. In that respect he was always a liberal modernist Christian, true heir to the German liberal theologians Harnack and Troeltsch. He was right when he singled out Troeltsch to John Bennett in 1929 as one of the major formative influences on his intellectual outlook. Like Troeltsch his starting point was always human needs, human powers, human responsibilities. Christianity was a resource for man in the world, not a call for man to transcend the world. The progression of his thought went from humanity to God, not—as with Barth and to some extent Richard Niebuhr—from God to humanity.

But Richard's prediction about his brother's "break" was nevertheless very astute in light of Reinhold's subsequent course. There is no direct way to assess Richard's own impact on that course, since later in life he burned all of his correspondence—including his letters from his brother. But a basic shift in Reinhold's focus did become clear in 1933, just after the exchange with Richard. His personal involvement in Socialist Party politics diminished. No more running for office; no more jostling in the corridors at Party conventions; no more writing articles at Party request. He did remain wedded for several more years to the teleological Weltanschauung of socialism, but he was no longer the direct participant in Party battles. For the rest of the decade he concentrated his day-to-day labors on the FSC, the FOR, and other explicitly religious groups. He began to devote himself much more assiduously to theology, much less to social or economic theory. He continued to publish political commentary by the ream, but it was commentary that blasted all political parties, including his own Socialists. He was taking up a prophetic position on the hilltop— a place from which all politics could be subjected to judgment. In effect he was answering Richard's call, outlined in a 1932 letter to Kirby Page, for "religious action" as opposed to the "political action of socialism." Richard wanted to create a "close compact organization" of radical Christians "with a literary branch. That is almost a Christian Communist party pattern. But the Communists borrowed it from early Christianity." Religious action meant developing "theory and profound theory," resisting "temptations to premature revolt by the disciples of an activism which wants to act without having a clear-cut notion of what its action is all about." Richard's proposal became FSC policy in 1934 and 1935 with the establishment of a strict internal discipline and the founding of a new journal, Radical Religion. But even in 1933 Reinhold moved in his direction by plunging into theology, a course that would culminate six years later in his Gifford lectures on "The Nature and Destiny of Man." Embracing theology was Reinhold's way of countering the charge of defeatism leveled by all of his critics, including Richard: he had to show that there was a place for faith, a reason to hope, a role for the church. He had to show that life did go "beyond tragedy"—as Richard had argued in "The Grace of Doing Nothing"—and toward fulfillment.[2]

II

There is no doubt that Richard was a vital catalyst for Reinhold's shift toward theology and religious action after *Moral Man* and the Socialist electoral debacle of 1932. He seems to have helped unlock a part of his brother's identity, undam a current that had been backing up during the previous two decades. He spoke with the authority of one who had kept alive in his own work the evangelical theology of Gustav Niebuhr. He was the agent who brought Reinhold to an adult rendezvous with his father's Biblically centered faith. The creative outburst in Niebuhr's intellectual work over the next decade can perhaps be explained in part by that rendezvous: he was able to draw on submerged paternal elements in his self to challenge and transcend the standpoint of his young adulthood. In 1913 Reinhold had left his German heritage behind in his zeal to master the national, liberal Protestant world. For all his attacks on that liberalism in the 1920s, his vision had remained firmly liberal: human experience over divine revelation, social reform over individual salvation, ethics over theology. *Moral Man* was the crowning expression of liberal ethics because it took that perspective to its limit. Reform required propaganda, coercion, perhaps even violence. Liberal ends demanded antiliberal means. *Moral Man* was a combustible mixture, a powder keg that had either to explode or to be defused. Niebuhr would either have to follow Harry Ward to the fringes of communism or reexamine and reassert his liberal Christian commitment. Under Richard's prodding he took the second path. As he passed his fortieth year he came back, the prodigal son, to reappropriate his father's Biblical heritage. That act of repossession produced the intellectual fire that led ultimately to a new synthesis in liberal theology, his classic *The Nature and Destiny of Man*.

In his Taylor lectures at Yale in April, 1933, Reinhold took immediate steps to correct the romantic view of human nature that Richard had detected in *Moral Man*, and to insist that the Christian church was indeed an indispensable force in the social struggle. He titled his five lectures "Christianity in a Decadent Civilization," and predicted that Christianity would survive the inevitable collapse of bourgeois society—as it had earlier survived the deaths of the Roman empire and medieval feudalism. It would survive "by offering the new civilization spiritual insight and moral discipline"—insight most especially into the intensity of "human egoism." Niebuhr was silent on the question of why the empowered workers of Socialist civilization would care to listen to sermons about human selfishness. He merely asserted that the church would be able to "prove" to "the disinherited class" that "a religiously inspired analysis of human nature is psychologically the truest one." No social order could eliminate the individual's quest to aggrandize himself. The church would survive by speaking the truth about human selfhood. And ministers like Reinhold Niebuhr, the lectures strongly im-

•

plied, would survive by remaining prophets, by "teaching" their compatriots about the limits of human nature and the relativities of human history. Beneath the surface of his scathing denunciation of bourgeois civilization and his ruminations on the future Socialist order, a decisive shift in his stance on the present role of the Christian intellectual was evident: his task was less to mobilize the proletariat than to hold both workers and capitalists under judgment. The prophet was taking to the mountain for a broader view and covering his tracks with the usual denunciation of liberal hypocrisy and middle-class ineptitude. He continued to defend *Moral Man* down to the last comma even as he was leaving it behind. Only Richard seems to have known what was happening. Reinhold was indeed "ready to break" with his recent past.[3]

Charles Clayton Morrison was certainly in the dark. Niebuhr published a version of one of the Taylor lectures in the *Century* in June. It moved far beyond the standpoint of *Moral Man*, yet when Morrison found fault with it in his editorial column he took it as a restatement of the book. The article was blunt about the evil in human nature, even in people's most intimate relations. Following Richard's lead, he argued that "we may love wife, child, father, or mother as much as we love ourselves. But such love is always to some degree an extension of the self." The evil in people, on the other hand, was partly offset by their capacity to seek the good even in a world of sin. For the first time he introduced the concept of "natural law" into his writing. The traditional doctrine of natural law, derived from the Stoics and developed by Catholic and Protestant theology, was a "theory of compromise." It knew that social relations could not be governed by the "law of love." Niebuhr had never been enthusiastic about Catholicism, despite his praise for Catholic "social" sense: the Church was too dogmatic, hierarchical, undemocratic. Now the Catholic tradition—with its dual focus on natural, attainable standards of conduct and on a divine order which fulfills the natural—rose slightly in his estimation. "Christian orthodoxy" began to displace "Communist religion" as his chief rhetorical weapon for chastising liberal Christians. Liberal Christianity was flawed not just because it was timid in the social struggle, but because it ignored the insights of traditional theology. At the end of the *Century* piece he went so far as to speak of "the assurance of grace" that Christianity supplied—a notion totally foreign to the spirit of *Moral Man*.[4]

There was an obvious historical reason for Niebuhr's preoccupation in the Taylor lectures with the "survival" of Christianity. While he was discoursing in New Haven, Hitler was consolidating his power in Germany. He was rapidly domesticating the German Protestant church, and many observers feared for the future of independent Christianity. And for the future of progressive politics. Hitler was ruthlessly suppressing his opponents by dispensing with constitutional procedures. The Socialists upheld their long-standing commitment to democratic methods and parliamentary procedure, and thereby, in Niebuhr's view, helped Hitler dig their grave. The logic of his analysis led him to a political crossroads. Democratic socialism had revealed its impotence in the face of Fascist brutality. "If one is certain," he wrote, "that the enemies of labor will disavow democratic principles in the final combat, one is forced to the conclusion that labor

•

ought to beat them to it." The Communists were the only ones who understood that against Fascist cynicism legality was no defense. Yet he could not go with the Communists: they reduced life to politics, individual spirit to its social determinants, and put no limits on their own sense of righteousness. With the death of democratic socialism in Germany he could imagine only one remaining alternative to communism: prophetic Christianity. Not that socialism in America was dead. Rather, it had never left its infancy. The only way it could conceivably get out of its toddler's pants was through Christian "realism": use force and even violence if necessary in the battle for justice, but keep the workers' movement under constant judgment.

After a six-week stay in England in May and early June—where he got started on his new book, *Reflections on the End of an Era*—he spent a week in Germany and found his views confirmed. "The Socialist party is in a state of living death," he reported to the *New Republic.* "The Nazis have not proscribed it; they allow it to exist as a butt for their contempt."

> The party was sleepily constitutional in a day when its enemies, both Right and Left, were unconstitutional. . . . What good does it do to trust in elections when political issues are being determined by the power of private political armies? The impoverished middle classes who make up the backbone of fascism, were in fact more heroically revolutionary than the trade unions. At least they were more desperate, and against their desperation Socialist complacency had no power.

But reporting to the *Christian Century*, he revealed how politically unsettled he was. Socialists and liberals may have stuck too rigidly to democratic methods, but the rise of Hitler also demonstrated that "the liberal spirit" was a precious acquisition. The Nazi state was "totalitarian"—a newly devised word that Niebuhr placed in quotation marks. It imposed its authority across the entire range of cultural and political activity. "The insistence of liberalism that there are human rights which transcend any particular rights that are derived from adhesion to race, class, or nation, is not an illusion of the nineteenth century but belongs to ageless culture." The Germans needed a bit more "reason" and a bit less "political passion." Thus Niebuhr simultaneously berated the democratic forces for not dispensing with democracy and praised liberalism for its commitment to rights. He tried to evade the contradiction by praising liberalism as a "spirit" while denouncing it as a "creed." But that gesture begged the question of how the liberal spirit could ever underlie a realistic politics—a politics capable of girding itself for the final battle which Niebuhr continued to insist was coming in every western nation. In America Roosevelt's "amiable opportunism" was "arresting the decay of capitalism as effectively as that can be done." But the President could not remedy its "constitutional defects." Niebuhr took "the inevitability of fascism as a practical certainty" in America as well as Europe. How Americans could both cultivate the liberal temper and learn to dispense with it in the coming confrontation with fascism remained unexplained.[5]

Unable to escape the theoretical impasse, Niebuhr pointed to Britain's

•

example as a practical way out. Britain was a living paradox: traditional yet innovative, hierarchical but democratic. He was captivated by the unmatched political prowess of the English. As early as 1925 he had remarked that "in England a penchant for compromise serves to soften the asperities of class and race conflicts." In the late 1920s he and other American leftists saw Ramsay MacDonald as the embodiment of political virtues: intelligence, probity, loyalty to tradition, and commitment to justice. In 1931 MacDonald fell out of favor on the left—in both America and Britain—when he joined the Tories in the so-called National Government. But Niebuhr found another statesmanlike radical to take his place: Sir Stafford Cripps, whose left-wing Socialist League was trying by 1933 "to work out a philosophy which will do justice to both the democratic tradition and the general skepticism about democracy which recent events in Europe have prompted." Cripps's group was committed to taking power "by strictly democratic methods," but equally committed to holding power by force. Once in control it would use the police power to prevent "the instruments of democracy" from being used to defeat the socialization of finance and industry.

Cripps, who soon became a personal friend, was for Niebuhr typical of the British mind in politics: not interested in theoretical consistency, devoted to ideals but aiming for results. "The British are sane rather than intellectual," Niebuhr concluded. "They apply their intelligence directly to the situations in which they stand and they are thus able to gauge and apprehend the imponderables of politics in a way which no consistent political theory is able to do." But Niebuhr wavered on the exportability of the British model. British political sagacity had historical roots. Capitalism had not swept feudal and aristocratic traditions completely aside; British culture was still "organic," not "mechanical" like the American, where capitalism had razed the entire social field. Americans could not simply appropriate the English example. Rather, Britain could serve as a transcendent ideal for criticizing American and German practices. American Socialists ought to strive for the British ideal while realizing that for historical reasons they would never quite attain it. The goal was to be democratic whenever possible but nondemocratic whenever necessary. Legality was not an absolute, "since every legal system" was "a rationalization of a given equilibrium of political and economic power." Socialists would have to be "pragmatic rather than dogmatic in [their] parliamentarianism." [6]

III

After his month and a half in Europe Niebuhr hustled back to New York in late June to teach summer school again—and earn back some of the cash he had spent on his trip. Ursula was now pregnant, and Reinhold relished the thought of being a father in his forty-second year. But she suffered a miscarriage. "Our fond hopes are blasted," Niebuhr wrote to Page. They left for Heath so that she could recuperate—she felt ill for the rest of the summer—and he could finish his *Reflections* in time for a winter release. Their own familial misfortune may have contributed to the overwhelmingly

•

somber tone of the book. He took the high ground of Spenglerian judgment: civilizations rose up and then decayed, history was cyclical, western bourgeois society was crumbling from within. None of the ethical tension of *Moral Man*, where he had debated the boundaries of Chrisitian responsibility: was violence permissible, was mythmaking allowable, should one support the proletariat? There was no question of responsibility with history rumbling along on its chosen path. Niebuhr's voice was Olympian and detached, the cosmic commentator. Nature like history was brutal, antithetical to spirit. Human history and human life were littered with blasted hopes. No one would be able to accuse him of preaching violence this time—it was history, not man, that was violent.

The proletariat did not appear until the eleventh chapter: "The Executors of Judgment." The workers were "the ultimate arbiters of destiny," their future reign "inevitable." Yet from his vantage point on the mountain Niebuhr saw that the proletarian perspective was no more universal than that of any other class. He still pronounced that "the future belongs to the worker" but his support was formal, restrained. He was protecting his independence, preparing to bring down his judgment on the rising working-class forces. "History may also prove the proletarian to be mistaken in his belief that he is the herald and the author of the final form of civilization." The workers would rise and fall like every dominant class before them; Niebuhr would not let them bask in self-righteousness. They had a special mission to fulfill, but in the long view they had no special virtue: they were just another group trying vainly to tame the turbulent waters.

Niebuhr dedicated *Reflections on the End of an Era* to his brother. In the preface he noted that it was Richard's "stimulating analyses of the contemporary religious and social problem [that] prompted many of these reflections"—though he did not let on that the analyses had been delivered in private. *Reflections* was a disjointed, cumbersome, awkward volume because it was his first effort to bring together his own commitment to radical politics and Richard's commitment to Reformation orthodoxy. "Adequate spiritual guidance," he proclaimed in the preface, "can come only through a more radical political orientation and more conservative religious convictions than are comprehended in the culture of our era." On one level *Reflections* was his most radical, most "catastrophist" book—a lyric obituary to mark the final demise of the western bourgeoisie—but on another, more fundamental level it was a declaration of the end of an era in his own development. It was his announcement that he was turning to theology, to prophetic "religious" action, in order to create a truly viable alternative to liberal Protestantism. For over a decade he had concentrated on the study of society and the building of a political alternative to capitalism. He did not wish to believe that he was abandoning a sinking Socialist ship. He persuaded himself, despite the electoral debacle of 1932, that the decay of capitalism was irreversible and that the workers were safely on the road to victory. With history taken care of, he could afford to switch his sights to study the full mystery of human selfhood. He wished to stress (paraphrasing Richard) that "the blind forces of nature that frustrate the spirit are in the self as well as outside it." Only a "religious individualism" based firmly on Christian orthodoxy "recognizes the roots of society's evils in the self."

•

Moreover, only a religion that provided "the assurance of grace"—as he titled his concluding chapter—could make sense of the whole range of human experience, personal and political. Niebuhr was not turning into a Barthian. Grace was not a supernatural gift, but a mythological category that expressed in symbolic terms an experienced fact of human life.

> All men who live with any degree of serenity live by some assurance of grace. In every life there must at least be times and seasons when the good is felt as a present possession and not as a far-off goal. The sinner must feel himself "justified," that is, he must feel that his imperfections are understood and sympathetically appreciated as well as challenged. Whenever he finds himself in a circle of love where he is "completely known and all forgiven" something of the mercy of God is revealed to him and he catches a glimpse of the very perfection which has eluded him.

Beyond politics, beyond society, the individual confronted the stark brutality of existence. Perhaps with the recent miscarriage in mind, he observed that "people's hopes will be shattered by untoward fortune; family circles will be invaded by death." An assurance of grace supplied men and women with needed consolation in the face of absurdity and suffering. It was not a "magical" resource, but a "moral" interpretation of life which allowed people to cope, which left them, in Paul's phrase, "perplexed, but not unto despair."[7]

The reviews of *Reflections*, published and unpublished, were predictably diverse: some stressed Niebuhr's prophecies of doom, others his assurance of grace. In the *Century*, Morrison applauded his discovery of grace. Henry Van Dusen was pleased to advise his colleague that it was "definitely a stronger book than *Moral Man*" and that by the year 2034 it would be remembered as "a classic." He protested against Niebuhr's "insistence on the necessity of violence"—a curious comment in view of Niebuhr's careful avoidance of the term, his conscious retreat from *Moral Man* on that score. All he justified in *Reflections* was the workers' use of "political force" when faced with Fascist attacks on their rule. But Van Dusen too was delighted with Niebuhr's fledgling theological efforts, even if he found him equivocal on the question of whether "there is such a thing as an Objective God or [whether] the 'Christian myth' corresponds in any appreciable measure with the Reality which it tries to mythologize." The commonsensical Van Dusen did not comprehend that for a thoroughgoing Kantian like Niebuhr, "correspondence" with "objective reality" was a nonsensical way to formulate the problem.

John Haynes Holmes lost all patience with his former friend. In the *Herald Tribune Books* he blasted Niebuhr for his "growing dogmatism of temper, his flat repudiation of idealism, his cynical contempt for the morally minded, his pessimistic abandonment of the world to its own unregenerate devices, and his desperate flight to the unrealities of theological illusion." And he was not done yet. He then struck well below the belt.

> It is clear enough that Jesus' serene trust in human nature, his stern acclaim of the moral law, his utter reliance upon spiritual forces, his sunny optimism, his radiant passion, would all have seemed a little ridiculous to Niebuhr. The latter

·

would not have opposed the Man of Galilee, but he certainly would have despised him. And with what relief he would have turned to the "cynical and realistic" Pilate as the man of the hour!

Niebuhr had never been subjected to such a bitter attack. He shot back a letter decrying Holmes's "monstrous" unfairness and closed with an allusion to the end of their friendship. Holmes wrote back in all innocence to say there was no reason they could not continue to be great friends—it was just a difference of opinion—and then proceeded to judge Niebuhr's "recent writings . . . as a tragic instance of intellectual and spiritual bankruptcy," of "disintegration, confusion, and breakdown." Niebuhr again protested the string of insults, and Holmes again disingenuously affirmed his continued friendship. But Niebuhr was having none of it. He later told friends that Holmes was one man he truly despised.

For Van Dusen, Niebuhr was not yet theological enough, not yet in tune with the Christian doctrine of God. For Holmes, Niebuhr had already fallen into medieval superstition. Holmes's friend Harry Elmer Barnes, a "humanist" radical and a well-known figure on the New York left, agreed: Niebuhr had "revert[ed] still further toward intellectual fog and theological conservatism." Barnes had been singling out Niebuhr for criticism ever since 1929, praising his politics but dismissing his religion. Niebuhr had belittled Barnes's intelligence in turn, and continued to flail him for years to come as the epitome of liberal myopia. Barnes was another man whom Niebuhr had to admit he hated—sinful as he knew that feeling to be. The polemical savagery of his exchanges with both Holmes and Barnes was a revelation of the evil that men could not avoid doing, of "the law in their members" that warred against "the law in their minds"—a phrase of Saint Paul's that may be the most often quoted Biblical passage in all of Niebuhr's writings. The attacks of Holmes and Barnes hurt him deeply because they broached the forbidden territory of his private relationship to Jesus Christ; from Niebuhr's standpoint they were diabolical onslaughts against his deepest loyalty, his most sublime feelngs. There was an aura of sacrilege about the attacks. He could never forgive them.[8]

Richard Niebuhr was put in a difficult position as a critic of *Reflections*, since it was dedicated to him. "How does one properly thank an author for the gift of a book—not only of a copy, but of the thing itself?" he asked his brother. He did not know how to criticize it properly either. "It's a fine job, nobly done, better written I think than anything which has come before. I detect something of Ursula in that." He was plainly pleased about the book's effort to theologize, but had to admit he could not agree with it. "One reason we do not understand each other, as this book makes clearer than ever to me, is that our words mean different things to us."

Nature for you means mostly human nature, to me it means the sun, rain, grass, stars, climate, race, glands. You think in terms of psychology where I think in terms of biology and sociology. You think in terms of the absolute and the relative, where I think in terms of determinism and indeterminism. God for me is not so much the absolute, as he is the determining dynamic. You do not convince me because I do not recognize religion to be what you define—well, yes, I recognize it but there is a hitch. To me the trans-historical, absolute point of reference, the x beyond all x's, has no particular significance. This religion of the absolute remains to my mind an aspiration, not a faith, a trust, a hope, a surrender. On the other hand I remain an absolutist with the naive judgment that wrong is wrong and that thirst for power and balance of power are of the devil. That involves me in the acute dilemma of my life. But I hope to find my way out of that dilemma. Where I find myself in most conflict with you—if conflict it may be called—is in the conception of religion and God. But we've been over all this before.

Reinhold no doubt responded that his transcendent God was not a metaphysical essence beyond history, but a Judge who made man's own historic responsibility possible—by giving him the freedom to act for justice while condemning his pretensions and complacencies. Reinhold's image of God conformed to his view of man as historic actor in an apparently meaningless universe and visibly brutal society; Richard's to his view of man as historically acted upon though ultimately, through no action of his own, redeemed.

Reinhold was in a fighting mood, a state of siege, as the reviews piled up in early 1934. Richard's critique touched a tender nerve, and the brothers bickered back and forth through the spring. Without surrendering his viewpoint Richard nevertheless withdrew from the conflict in his letter of birthday wishes in June. With a forceful Hebraic reference he buoyed his brother up by abasing himself. "When I think of our brotherly relations," he wrote,

> I always recall that incident in our childhood—I hope you've forgotten it, though I can't—I was Cain to your Abel and chased you with a big poker. Probably chased is the wrong word. I doubt not that you overcame me in a pacific spirit. But I've been Cain ever since and gave after you with pokers because your sacrifices have been more acceptable in the sight of God than mine. But you're a forgiving Abel, whose blood doesn't cry for vengeance. . . . Your Abel-ity and my Cain-ishness have appeared again this past year, when I have been confounded by your book and it has appeared that my doubts of your position were ill-founded, and that my antagonism was premature. The next year will work you more than ever as a leader of American Christendom. . . . Of that I have no doubt. And if I can make a non-Cainish request, conserve your power for the big things which are coming to you and through you.

One does not have to embrace Freudianism to suspect that Richard's asking forgiveness for chasing his big brother with a poker represented an important psychological event, a deep affirmation of his subordination to an older brother who had become for him as for Hulda and Walter a surrogate father. There were limits to Richard's ability to engage Reinhold in debate: he might challenge his theology for a time, but not his authority.[9]

IV

Niebuhr had done his best in *Reflections* to stay away from the thorny ethical dilemmas that *Moral Man* had confronted. The term *violence*—the emotional code word that bedeviled the Protestant left—never appeared in the text. In part he was trying to mollify his pacifist accusers, but he was also at-

•

tempting to raise the debate above the emotional quagmire of social ethics to the lofty ground of theology and social philosophy. But after the manuscript was delivered to Scribners in the fall of 1933, Niebuhr found himself dragged right back into the ethical thicket. The Fellowship of Reconciliation (FOR), whose executive council he was chairing, had become a fellowship of recrimination by October. The thirty members of the council were split on the question of whether to retain Executive Secretary Joseph B. Matthews, a fire-eating radical who had gotten progressively bolder in his proclamations of the need for violence in resisting capitalism. He was also antagonizing other members of the board by his militant secularism; he claimed no religious basis for his standpoint. Christian pacifists in the leadership—John Nevin Sayre, Kirby Page, Edmund Chaffee, and others—decided he had to go. When the October meeting of the fellowship ended in a stalemate, the religious pacifists shrewdly moved to put the question to the whole membership by mail. In November a lengthy ballot went out to six thousand members asking their opinions about how much coercion of what kind was acceptable in which situation. Only one thousand replied, but they were overwhelmingly against Matthews's position: 90 percent absolutely ruled out "violence" in the social struggle; 53 percent even opposed "nonviolent coercion." At a six-hour meeting of the council on December 16, Matthews was ousted by a vote of 18 to 13, Niebuhr voting with the minority.

It was not that Niebuhr had any affection for Matthews. He thought him politically foolish for joining one Communist-front organization after another and religiously narrow-minded for wearing his secularism like a badge. Yet when pushed to decide the hypothetical question, Niebuhr still had to agree that the working class might some day have to use violence. "My political convictions are on the side of [Matthews]," he mused to Page, "but my personal friendships are on the other side, so I feel like a lonely soul." He had no choice but to resign from the council, as did ten others. He did keep his membership in the FOR itself, out of allegiance to his friends and his continuing belief that it could help keep the United States out of a European war. He regarded "international armed conflict as so suicidal" that he was "certain" he would not participate in it. There would be "such widespread destruction that any original reasons or motives for participation would be completely lost in the confusion. There would be neither victors nor vanquished." But if he was still a pragmatic pacifist on the international front, he was no longer able to associate himself publicly with absolute pacifists. "Pure pacifism" was fine as an "eschatological" sign—as a statement of the Christian ideal that could never be realized in history—but it was politically irresponsible. The only people who could ethically forswear coercion were "those who are willing to renounce the world (including the comforts and securities which come out of a coercive economic and political system)." [10]

Richard Niebuhr, himself not a member of the FOR, agreed completely with his brother's framing of the question. He had no sympathy, he told the World Tomorrow's readers, for social idealists who expected pacifism to "work" in history. "It seems much more consistent with the fundamental idealistic principle of the Fellowship to accept the non-pacifist position of

•

those who have left. . . . If we are going to be utilitarians let us be rational utilitarians and accept the principle that what matters is the ideal end and that whatever is necessary for its attainment is right." Richard proposed instead a "Christian non-resistance" that rejected "aggressive fighting for our ideals, whether by tongue and boycott or by sword. It rejects the whole humanistic faith upon which this idealism is built. It is as deterministic as communism is. But it knows that there is a divine teleology, and that the aggressiveness of the righteous runs counter to it as often as does the aggressiveness of the unrighteous." Richard and Reinhold could not have been further apart in their attitude toward worldly reform, but they were united in their opposition to what they called "idealism," the faith of the progressive pacifists. "The righteous idealists of the FOR do not stir me," Richard told his brother. "You are more realistic than they." In his antipathy toward social idealism Richard confessed he was increasingly tempted by Catholicism.

> You know I think we would both find ourselves at home in a Catholic church. You would make a good Pope, I would be at home in a friar's gown. Don't you really admire Hildebrand more than Lenin? I'm beginning to get worried about myself—to wonder whether I will end up in Catholicism. Neither the system of hierarchy and dogmatic authority nor the transcendental theology are my choices but I am weary to death of religious societies and clubs of reformers. And by and large I am convinced that there is no salvation outside the church. I am in an inner turmoil half the time.[11]

The FOR controversy brought Richard to the brink of conversion to a more rigorous, more demanding church within which he could more clearly submit his will to God's: freedom through self-abnegation, not self-assertion. The image of the humble friar suited his yearning for salvation through perfect dependency, obedience to his superiors. A few months short of his fortieth birthday, he was groping for a faith that could take the painful dependencies of his childhood and young adulthood—his relationships to his father and to Reinhold—and convert them into a pure trust, a serene surrender. *Thy Will, not mine, be done.* His personal salvation, he sensed, lay not in trying to match Reinhold's authority—that of the "good Pope"—but in abandoning the exercise of authority to him. Fulfillment lay not in pursuing ideals, trying to realize them in history, but in confessing his sins, his incapacity to realize ideals.

Reinhold was also fed up with the pacifists who thought that Christianity meant living out a set of ideals: invariably they sinned by believing that they were in fact living up to the ideals they professed. Niebuhr was going to deflate mere idealism. Together with a band of disciples who sided with him in the FOR affair, he transformed the Fellowship of Socialist Christians into a body which did not just profess ideals but translated them into practice. Fellowship members, beginning in the spring of 1934, were taxed. They each calculated their net taxable income—after deducting exemptions for dependents, educational costs, and medicine—and then assessed the tax: 10 percent of the first $1,000 of income, 20 percent of the next $1,000, 30 percent of the next $2,000, 40 percent of the next $4,000, and 100 percent of anything above $8,000. Each individual could contribute up to 90 percent of his tax to a social cause approved by the FSC; at least 10 percent went to the FSC itself for projects collectively chosen. Before the new discipline was enacted the FSC had over five hundred members; afterward it had one hundred.

In effect Niebuhr and his allies were purging the FSC, just as they had been purged from the FOR. They were building an organization premised on the reality of the social struggle, not on the reality of ideals. It was an organization conceived with the Communists clearly in mind, as Richard had urged in his letter to Kirby Page in 1932. At the start there were even "cells" of twelve members each, though they did not last long as the basic organizational unit. Semiannual retreats for the entire membership rapidly took their place. From 1934 until the end of the decade the FSC was Niebuhr's chief outlet for "action" in the world. While Christian action was not for him a means of progressively embodying ideals in history, it was certainly a matter of transforming the world in the light of ideals, and using those ideals as critical levers for generating commitment to action. But thanks to Richard's influence he no longer dissociated action from "thought": a key action of the FSC, Niebuhr wrote in laying out the new discipline, would be the effort to "relat[e] Christian and Socialist thought to each other."

Some FSC projects were designed to provoke social change, to radicalize the proletariat. These efforts were concentrated in the south, where the working class—whether black or white, sharecropper, miner, or factory hand—tended to be Protestant, not Catholic or Jewish. The FSC sent funds to the left-wing minister Claude Williams in Arkansas. It was the chief support for Howard Kester, former FOR secretary for the south, who was organizing cotton pickers and sharecroppers, and was a key figure in the formation of the Southern Tenant Farmers' Union. Niebuhr himself did most of the fund-raising for Kester; he started the Conference on Economic and Racial Justice in February, 1934, for the sole purpose of attracting non-Socialist contributions for Kester, and managed to draw in about $1,000 a year. But even more of the FSC's and of Niebuhr's energy went into the planning for a new journal, *Radical Religion*, which first appeared in the fall of 1935. It was the Fellowship's primary commitment for the rest of the decade: a visible bridge between the traditions of Christian and Socialist thought.[12]

The same debate over violence that split the FOR and produced the new FSC rocked the biennial Socialist Party convention in Detroit in June, 1934. Niebuhr followed it with interest and applauded when the "realists" this time came out on top. But he took no part in the Detroit deliberations and his comments from the sidelines bear the same tone of detached omniscience that marked his *Reflections*. He was zealous in criticizing the two tendencies in the Party that he disliked: the New York City Old Guard that forswore illegality in general, and violence in particular; and the "revolutionary party" —including J. B. Matthews, the FSC's own Howard Kester, and Niebuhr's former students Franz Daniel and James Dombrowski— which spoke of a revolutionary seizure of power. Niebuhr backed the middle-of-the-road Militants gathered around Norman Thomas: they felt some violence might be necessary to defend an elected workers' regime. But it

•

was his *World Tomorrow* colleague Devere Allen who played the key role for the Militants—writing their statement of principles, helping push it through the convention, saluting their victory for *World Tomorrow* readers. Niebuhr took a backseat in the Militant bandwagon. He also put a damper on the celebrating with a cautionary thrust in his own column. "The Socialist Party as now constituted," he wrote, "may not become the significant tool of Socialist principles in American politics. But Socialist principles are certain to play a role in our American life. This is just as certain as it is true that collective ownership of the means of production is a necessity of economic and social health in a technical civilization." He was not gravitating toward the New Deal or to any other third party; he had simply lost hope that the Socialists would ever manage to unite workers, farmers, and the middle class in a single political movement. Hence his greater commitment to the religious action of the FSC. It might bear immediate fruit by radicalizing the churches while he waited for a new political force to emerge.[13]

The rift over violence that split both the religious and secular left in 1934 put an end to the *World Tomorrow* in July—thereby clearing the decks for *Radical Religion*. Ostensibly the *World Tomorrow* fell victim to its financial plight. But financial woes had always threatened it since the depression began. The difference was that Page and Niebuhr were no longer making common cause. Their own disagreement on the social struggle mirrored and symbolized the break in the ranks of the readers. When Page sent out an emergency appeal in May it got no response: small donors and large benefactors alike turned their backs. Even Sherwood Eddy, who had always bestowed his favor equally on Page and Niebuhr, withdrew his support from Page's editorship. He had become a Niebuhrian in ethics and did not hesitate to lecture Page. Many of Page's "radical friends," Eddy informed him, regretted that he was " 'hipped,' or [had] a blind spot and emotional complex" when it came to Marx and class struggle. "Personally I think it is affecting the usefulness of your magazine." Eddy instructed him to wake up and see that "economic factors rather than ideas are dominant in shaping an age." Page went down swinging. He quoted Eddy's letter (without attribution) in one of his last pieces and insisted that violent revolution was by definition contrary to the Gospel.

But the real dispute between Page and Niebuhr went deeper than the hypothetical question of working-class resistance to capitalism. It went all the way to the innermost center of emotion and faith, to the precious core that Holmes had pierced in his tirade against Niebuhr: loyalty to Jesus, devotion to God. Each side had a different conception of Christian discipleship and could not sacrifice its vision without feeling sacrilegious. Yet there was no bitterness between Page and Niebuhr. They had worked closely for a decade, Page had been a sympathetic ear for Niebuhr in his personal travails, and Niebuhr felt nothing but gratitude in the end despite the parting of their paths. The day after their final *World Tomorrow* meeting Niebuhr wrote a letter that released a rare flow of emotion.

In the hurry of yesterday I never said any of the things that were really on my heart, partly because I was in a hurry and partly because I never say the right things face to face. . . . I have always felt very guilty doing so little for a venture

to which you gave so much. Yet I did enjoy this work with you greatly. I
would feel very badly if I thought that our cooperation would now cease. But
we are tied together in work in so many other ways that this need not happen.

Niebuhr did not want to lose Page's friendship. Hence his sentiments about
cooperation and continued ties. But the ties had already been severed, displaced into the realm of memory. With Page's move to California as an
organizer for the FOR they soon drifted apart.[14]

V

By 1934 Niebuhr was trying to back off from the revolutionary note he
had sounded in *Moral Man*, but Henry Sloane Coffin was among the many
observers who did not notice. In the spring semester he found himself
confronted with a rebellious band of students who claimed inspiration from
both Niebuhr and Ward. It was bad enough when they joined the picket
lines at the Waldorf Hotel service workers' strike. It was equally unfortunate
when they camped in protest before the door of a New York minister who
had issued a pro-lynching statement. It was still worse when the students
started to organize the underpaid blue-collar staff of Union's own refectory.
But what could not even be conceived of much less tolerated was the raising
of a red flag on the seminary flagpole on May Day. The students claimed it
was a prank but Coffin was beside himself. Weeks later he joked to an
alumni gathering he would not let the students "make this seminary the
guinea pig for some future soviet," but the humor scarcely concealed his
bitterness. He was fiercely angry at Niebuhr for even indirectly sparking
any of the incidents. He felt about Niebuhr as Niebuhr had about Helm in
the Bethel episode. His star professor of Christian ethics had no sense of
pedagogy, of ethical timing; he was bringing down the whole institution
with his ravings about force and violence in the quest for justice. Coffin
felt about the seminary—with which he had been associated for thirty years—
as Niebuhr had about Bethel: it was home, it was mother, it was a protected
sphere, it was the living symbol of the transcendent and holy. He did not
wish to cut its links to the world, indeed he wanted to nourish the seminary
by opening it to social concerns. Yet he drew the line at importing radical
politics into the internal life of the seminary.

Coffin had been silently stewing over Niebuhr ever since *Moral Man*.
When Sherwood Eddy had asked him in the summer of 1933 if he would
release Niebuhr for a series of talks in China the following winter, Coffin
said Niebuhr would be inappropriate: "No one knows where he stands,
having swung to the left in his justification of violence." Niebuhr was not
to be trusted in China, where American Protestants had close links with
the anti-Communist, heavily Christian Kuomintang. But until the spring
of 1934 Coffin did not upbraid Niebuhr in person. Niebuhr himself felt
pressured from both sides. He deplored the flagpole incident, and accepted
part of the blame for the train of events that led to it. Yet he considered
Coffin paranoid. He refused to climb aboard Coffin's antiradical juggernaut,
but also let the students know they had gone too far.

Coffin of course realized in his calm moments that for all Niebuhr's faults he was indispensable. He was both a presence that attracted many students and an internationally known writer with a growing reputation for theological as well as ethical reflection. He had just delivered the prestigious Rauschenbusch lectures at Colgate-Rochester Divinity School, and had peppered his predictable views on politics and religion, Marxism and liberalism, with Biblical analyses and scholarly thrusts into the philosophy of religion. He was showing signs of making his mark as a religious thinker. Moreover, he had been instrumental the previous fall in attracting the German refugee Paul Tillich to Union. Coffin was heavily indebted to Niebuhr in so many ways that he had no choice but to tolerate his errant ways. Niebuhr, for his part, tried to keep his students' minds focused on affairs outside the seminary. He was diplomatic enough to know that his position, however secure, could be rapidly undermined if he appeared to be part of an anti-Coffin vendetta. He had an extended family to care for—including a child if Ursula, once again pregnant, continued to do well. Job and family concerns exerted a subtle pressure on Niebuhr's rhetoric and ethical timing if not on his beliefs. They supported, even though they did not cause, his withdrawal from Socialist politics and his growing preoccupation with theology.[15]

Paul Tillich was another significant force that impelled Niebuhr toward deeper immersion in theology. Tillich had been professor of philosophy at Frankfurt, and a "religious Socialist," before he was suspended by the Nazis in the spring of 1933. He was little known in the United States, but the Niebuhr brothers had heard all about him while they were in Germany in 1930. Richard heard him lecture and was so impressed that he set about translating Tillich's *The Religious Situation* (1925). When the English edition appeared in 1932 Reinhold lauded it in the *World Tomorrow*. Tillich was a kindred spirit: he saw God as the absolute vantage point from which all human strivings were relativized; he castigated the bourgeois myth of progress; he viewed the proletarian movement as promising but threatened by its own sense of absolute righteousness. Tillich's book blazoned the path, said Niebuhr, in which "our thought must go if we are to have more than a merely political or superficially rationalistic interpretation of the realities of our decaying civilization and culture."

Naturally he was overjoyed when Union's faculty members voted to make a place for Tillich—by each contributing five percent of their salary for him. It was Niebuhr who, during his trip to Germany in June, 1933, telephoned the invitation to Tillich. Tillich, for his part, latched on to Niebuhr for support after arriving in New York in November, 1933. His English was primitive, Niebuhr could get along in German, and Tillich was cheered by their long walks down Riverside Drive. He would forget his anxieties, lose himself in rapturous contemplation of the sparkling Hudson, while Niebuhr shot off queries about Barthian theology or judgments on German politics. Tillich was always a borderline nature mystic and was amused by Niebuhr's "American" disregard for the aesthetic and pastoral. Niebuhr charged through life hacking away at the forest in good pioneer fashion. But he was also deeply attached to Tillich in those prewar years. He rightly saw himself as Tillich's advocate and protector. Later Tillich regretted that their friendship had been based so much upon Niebuhr's "helpfulness," so little upon Niebuhr's "sharing" himself with the more romantic, emotional German. In the thirties, however, he gladly accepted Niebuhr's aid: arranging lectures, essays, and book reviews, speeches at FSC meetings, and countless smaller favors around the seminary. Niebuhr was the key agent of Tillich's initial assimilation into the American and English-speaking world.

What Tillich had to offer Niebuhr in return was a compelling model of a non-Barthian *and* postliberal theology. John Baillie had already awakened Niebuhr to the need for more theological rigor in his war on Barth; it was not enough to moan about the ethical quietism which Barthianism supposedly produced. But Tillich gave him a particular language for coping with Barth—a language derived from Tillich's own early encounter with German liberalism. Like Niebuhr, Tillich had in the 1920s grown weary of liberal theology because it "lacked insight into the 'demonic' character of human existence," as he put it years later in an autobiographical letter to Thomas Mann. Like Niebuhr again, he remained loyal to Harnack and Troeltsch in his espousal of the "historical critical method": the traditional idea of revelation had to go. But where Niebuhr had followed the liberals into ethics—the realm which since Kant and Ritschl seemed to be well shielded from scientific and naturalistic doubt, a safe haven for religious and moral conviction—Tillich insisted on making the religious case in philosophy, in metaphysics itself. Marx, Nietzsche, and Freud had persuaded him that the ethical realm was no secure fortress for religion. Tillich thus devised a "theology of attack": vindicate religion as a real form of knowlege, not just a sphere of value. The Barthians proceeded to dismiss Tillich as a "humanist," while liberal American Protestants viewed him with suspicion as a closet supernaturalist. Niebuhr was immediately attracted to anyone who managed to draw attacks from both groups. When in the summer of 1934 he and Ursula took to the hills of Sharon, Connecticut, to prepare for their baby and to revise his Rauschenbusch lectures for publication as *An Interpretation of Christian Ethics*, he had Tillich's work—all of it untranslated except *The Religious Situation*—in front of him.[16]

VI

The tone of his *Interpretation* was extraordinary in light of his previous work. His blaring trumpet had become a melodious flute. Where his *Reflections* was Olympian and somber, the new book was measured and irenic. It had none of the uncompromising militancy that marked *Moral Man* and infused even the detached commentary on cultural decline in *Reflections*. It waived the urgency even of the Rauschenbusch lectures themselves, which had proclaimed the need for Christian action, including the creation of a specifically working-class church as a leaven within Protestantism. Tillich's example had shown him the way to a theological discourse, as Richard had long recommended—though Tillich's mythic view of God did not in Richard's opinion adequately express God's real presence in history. Tillich's vocabulary shone from virtually every page. "The life of every person is

•

religious," Niebuhr claimed, since "it is impossible to live at all without presupposing a meaningful existence." Only a rare skeptic could avoid any "concern for ultimate meaning and coherence." Religion provided "a transcendent source of meaning"—not just a transcendent ethical ideal, as Niebuhr had long argued. The "mythical symbols of transcendence in profound religion"—God as both Creator and Redeemer—pointed to "the ultimate ground of existence and its ultimate fulfillment." Niebuhr now detected a critical role for philosophy, which he had belittled as beside the point ever since he had grown bored with Professor Macintosh's epistemology twenty years before. It could mediate between science and religion, "bring the religious myth into . . . rational coherence with all the detailed phenomena of existence which science discloses." Reason was not to be disparaged or discounted; *Moral Man* had gone overboard on that count, though he admitted the point only implicitly. Reason and faith were mutually nourishing resources of Christian life.

Niebuhr was making use of Tillich to broaden his familiar assault on liberal Christian ethics, in which "the transcendent impossibilities of the Christian ethic of love became . . . the immanent and imminent possibilities of an historical process." Much of the book was by now second nature to his readers. But he broke new ground in his prolonged effort to justify the truth value of myth, a topic raised but not pursued in *Reflections*. What had been in *Moral Man* a vital social force, the driving power of proletarian revolt, now became a kind of knowledge alongside science: collective illusion had been transmuted into religious myth. It was "the genius of true myth to suggest the dimension of depth in reality and to point to a realm of essence which transcends the surface of history, on which the cause-effect sequences, discovered and analyzed by science, occur." Myth was to science, he asserted, as the portrait was to the photograph. Only the portrait could reveal "the transcendent unity and spirit of the personality," and only a myth could grasp "the world as a realm of coherence and meaning without denying the facts of incoherence."

Niebuhr's superficial view of photography as a merely objective record weakened his analogy, but the general point was clear enough: myths expressed ultimate truths about human existence that science was powerless to perceive. Myths were either stories which dramatized or propositions which asserted the essential realities of life—realities that scientific reason could not fathom. Yet it was reasonable to believe in such stories, or assent to such propositions, since they provided meaning—without which life could not be lived. Niebuhr made no effort to seek out other versions of his position, which was very close to John Henry Newman's discussion of the "illative sense" in *The Grammar of Assent*, a nineteenth-century Catholic work. He also did little to distinguish his viewpoint from the very different notion of early-nineteenth-century "demythologizers" like David Strauss, whose *Life of Jesus* tried to reduce the story of Jesus to a concocted "myth." He did not want to probe too deeply into the epistemological foundations of myth for fear of being caught in the quagmire. He rested his case with the claim that human beings lived not by scientific truth, but by "personal knowledge," in Karl Polanyi's later phrase. Even scientists in their concrete lives relied on some implicit faith that went beyond the canons of critical reason.

Niebuhr granted that "the vagueness of the boundary line between the art of portraiture and that of caricature" presented problems. All myths involved some exaggeration, some deception. It was difficult to distinguish "deception in the interest of a higher truth" from "deception which falsifies the ultimate truth." That was why "prophetic Christianity" was superior to both Marxism and liberalism, two "naturalistic" faiths equally dangerous because equally devoid of an ultimate perspective that could check their pretensions. Prophetic Christianity was built upon two central myths that kept it self-critical: the creation myth, which "sees the Transcendent involved in, but not identified with, the process of history," and the myth of the Fall, which assumed that evil entered the world through human responsibility and that human consciousness was flawed, sinful, prone to do evil as well as good. The idea of God as Creator was not a scientific conception since no evidence could be brought forward to demonstrate it. The notion of a prime mover or a first cause was more "rational." Yet it was reasonable to believe that God was a Creator because of the fruits of that belief. Niebuhr's apologetics came straight out of William James's pragmatism, as it had ever since his BD thesis. The Creator cared deeply about his people but also held himself aloof; he stroked them with affection but held them under judgment. Hebrew monotheism was an indispensable standpoint because its God was always present but could never be possessed, tamed, turned into a parochial cult figure. He was tender with his people but punished them severely if they grew proud of their relationship to him. The Creator-God systematically undercut human pretensions even as he called on his people to strive for justice.

The myth of the Fall was equally important because it avoided equating the origin of sin with the genesis of life. The Hebrews took the correct middle ground between "the optimism which conceived the world as possessing unqualified sanctity and goodness" and "the pessimism which relegated historic existence to a realm of meaningless cycles." Thanks to the myth of the Fall, the Judeo-Christian tradition compelled people to strive to do good and warned them to beware of the evil they would inevitably do in the course of doing good. Prophetic Christianity gave man responsibility in history but held him constantly under criticism. It braced him for unending struggle but prepared him for perennial disappointment. The major question raised by Niebuhr's analysis that he failed to confront was why this prophetic standpoint was specifically Christian and not also Jewish. His New Testament seemed a mere footnote to his Old Testament. But that was a central part of his crusade against Protestant liberals. Where they had often preached a religion of Jesus, the model human being with the perfectly sweet, sacrificial disposition, Niebuhr was resurrecting a religion of the prophets, spokesmen for the God of both Succor and Wrath.

In *An Interpretation of Christian Ethics* Niebuhr came down from the mountaintop detachment of his *Reflections*, from which he beheld the crumbling of civilizations but saw no individual human actors. He returned to the central ethical framework of *Moral Man*: what is the moral responsibility

·

of the Christian in the face of injustice? It was certainly no longer to help generate a potent proletariat. He was even more disparaging of the vanity of the working class than he had been in *Reflections*, which for all its misgivings still perceived a potential redemptive mission for the proletariat. Now he highlighted the "demonic element" (another Tillichian phrase) that all "rebels against injustice," not just Communists, displayed. Coffin must have nodded vigorously over this unspoken jab at the seminary flag raisers. Niebuhr was disgusted with their "intransigence" and "dogmatism," their ignorance of "wise statesmanship."

But he was also fed up with the confusions of the liberals, and made a point of returning to the debate over violence that he had prudently sidestepped in *Reflections*. He insisted once more that "a responsible relationship to the political order . . . makes an unqualified disavowal of violence impossible." The moral man was the one who fought for justice, used as little violence and coercion as possible, and conscientiously humbled himself all along the way. Niebuhr's overriding interest was in the moral disposition of the individual Christian, not in the social structures of classes and nations that historically framed the individual life—and to which he had paid much more attention in *Moral Man*. That gave his discussion of justice a more abstract quality than *Moral Man*, since there was much less sense of precisely what the moral man was fighting for. But it also based his ethics all the more firmly in a notion of moral responsibility, on which *Moral Man* had finally equivocated in its elevation of ends over means. The Christian was now above all the discriminating actor, carefully weighing his decisions, refusing to be swept along by temporary currents, yet willing to act in history. He was in politics but not of it. The pursuit of "responsibility" replaced the pursuit of "personality" for which Niebuhr had proselytized in the 1920s. It was a goal better suited to the relativities and injustices of the current epoch. It forced Christians constantly to re-examine their standpoints while maintaining their commitment to justice.[17]

VII

Niebuhr's growing self-conception as a theologian was evident in the new seriousness with which he approached his longtime adversaries, John Dewey and Karl Barth. He now tried to take them on as philosopher and theologian respectively, not as exponents of political or ethical views alone. He strode off to battle with a new suit of armor, thanks to Tillich's instruction, and a new sense of confidence as a thinker: less reliance on rhetorical put-downs, more effort at rational argumentation. Niebuhr tried to seize the middle ground between the supernaturalist Barth and the naturalist Dewey, author of the recent *A Common Faith*. He took Barth's claim to have produced a "dialectical" theology and argued that it was not dialectical enough. The prophets were truly dialectical: they saw that God was both in history and out of it, their people's active benefactor and angry judge. History for the Hebrews was a constant revelation of God's mercy and wrath. Barth's God was so completely "other," so qualitatively separate from man, that there was no dialectical interpenetration between natural and divine spheres. In

Barth the relation of God to man was not a dialectic, but an absolute paradox. As Niebuhr quoted Tillich in his support, "Between God and man [for Barth] there is a hollow space which man is unable to penetrate. If it were possible for him to do this he would have power over his relation with God and thus would have power over God himself." Niebuhr's criticism of Barth was also indebted to his brother's earlier criticism of his own view. Richard had cautioned him about making God totally "other," uninvolved in human history. Reinhold adopted his brother's position to gain leverage against Barth, but in doing so he mythologized that position. For Richard, God truly acted in the processes of history; for Reinhold the idea that God acted in history was "true" as a belief, because it allowed men to make sense of life and strive to create just societies.

The humanistic theism of Dewey's *A Common Faith* was inadequate, Niebuhr argued, because it equated the Christian viewpoint—which it rejected—with supernaturalism, with Barth. Had Dewey known about "profound prophetic religion" he would have understood that "its God is not a separate existence but the ground of existence," as Tillich held. He would also have grasped that its faith was not in a pre-existing set of ideals, already realized in a divine sphere; its commitment was to an historical quest for the realization of justice. In Niebuhr's view Dewey's credo actually came far closer to prophetic religion than Dewey himself could ever admit, since "he does believe in a world in which the possibility of realizing ideals exists."

> He believes in appreciating the world of nature as a realm of meaning even where it does not obviously support man's moral enterprise but is in conflict with it. This is the kind of faith which prophetic religion has tried to express mythically and symbolically by belief in a God who is both the creator and the judge of the world, that is, both the ground of existence and its *telos*.

All that stood in the way of Dewey's seeing the light was his assumption that myths were superstitions rendered anachronistic by modern science. True myth, purged of superstitious accretions like Adam's apple or the six-day creation, was a different matter, since it captured the paradoxical and dialectical realities at the heart of human existence.

What Niebuhr's analysis actually revealed, despite his intention, was how close his own prophetic faith was to Dewey, how far away it was from Barth. His starting point, like Dewey's, was man's drive for meaning and his quest to realize ideals in history. His religion and Dewey's were, as Richard had earlier shown, religions of human power. Niebuhr might put more stress on the pitfalls that men encountered—social structures, human pride—but Dewey was scarcely unmindful of them. Niebuhr could not have stomached the thought: his faith was shot through with the very liberalism that he flailed at and caricatured. Like Dewey he was a pragmatist, a relativist, and a pluralist at heart. He hated absolutism of any kind. Life was an adventure in which people could create their own world if they had the courage and intelligence to do so. Had Niebuhr unhardened his heart on the subject of liberalism he would have discovered that he was firmly cemented in the liberal tradition of John Stuart Mill: resistance to dogmatism, tolerance for diversity, openness to correction.

·

What he disliked about liberalism was that its intellectual openness, its commitment to free inquiry, often hardened into skepticism about ultimate meaning, or cynicism about ultimate values. Or else it took flight into utopian dreams about a new world to be established by scientific knowledge, technical efficiency, or (in its Marxist offshoot) proletarian virtue. But concentrating his fire on liberal skepticism or utopianism, "cynicism" or "sentimentalism," made Niebuhr miss the central point: a whole tradition of liberals from the Enlightenment onward had struggled to be as realistically hopeful as he. Mill and Dewey were his intellectual comrades-in-arms in the campaign to root human values securely in a scientific era. They were his colleagues in toppling all absolutisms, whether imposed by defenders of the past or created by worshipers of the future.

Niebuhr's almost willful failure to do justice to the liberal tradition was partly the product of his long-standing distaste for the hundreds of pious, syrupy religious liberals he had run into since his Yale Divinity School days. He was disgusted to think that at Yale he had become so much like them in their easy assertions about the power of love to harmonize human relations. Proclaiming his antipathy to "liberalism" let him blot out the memory of his own sentimentality. Still, he might have made a distinction between the smiling goodwill of many Protestant liberals and the more hard-headed realism of the secular liberal tradition. His lack of sympathy for that tradition may well have had deep roots in his personality. Liberal pluralism and pragmatism in the realm of thought implied liberal experimentation in the realm of politics. But it also implied tentativeness, which to Niebuhr seemed like hesitancy, inaction. He was afraid of keeping still, pondering endlessly; he thought he would dry up, lose the vitality that he had never ceased to acclaim as the crucial human attribute. He feared, as he put it in his weighty formulation of 1931, being "consigned to impotence by the multitude of his scruples." Beating the straw man of liberalism was a way of battling the threat of inactivity in his own being.

In 1935 he was by no means prepared to make peace with liberalism, but a decidedly tranquil tone became apparent in his writing. He was less caustic, less combative, more temperate, "liberal" in spirit. Perhaps the rhetorical serenity was in part the fruit of the birth, in September, 1934, of his first child. "It's great to be a father," he announced tersely to Page, "even though belated." He was relieved at age forty-two to have been given a son, whom they named Christopher. Niebuhr did not linger over the news. He never had time or inclination to be gushy about such things. Nor did Christopher's arrival alter his itinerant habits. Just as Gustav Niebuhr had been on the road during Reinhold's infancy, Niebuhr too kept to his punishing pace of appearances. But when he was at home he liked to give him his bath, feed him, show him off in the carriage. In his journal in 1923 he had wondered whether "I was so cantankerous in my spirit of criticism about modern society because I am not married." If he "had about four children to love" he might not be so insistent about transforming society. With one child bestowed upon him he was still insistent, but calming considerably.[18]

EIGHT

THIS SIDE
OF
CATASTROPHE

(1935–1940)

I

"We conceive our primary loyalty to be to Christianity," Niebuhr proclaimed in the inaugural issue of *Radical Religion* in the fall of 1935. The Fellowship was composed, he stressed, of "Socialist Christians," not "Christian Socialists." Too many young ministers had been seduced into "a complete capitulation to Marxian dogma." It was time for "a truly prophetic religion . . . to turn against the spiritual pretensions of a proletarian culture as well as against preceding cultures." Niebuhr did trot out some of the old rhetoric: the FSC agreed with the Marxians, he urged, that "capitalistic society is destroying itself" and "must be destroyed, lest it reduce, in the delirium of its disintegration, our whole civilization to barbarism." But that lofty pronouncement with its grating mixed metaphor rested incongruously among his second thoughts. The chief need of the day, in Niebuhr's view, was to distinguish Christianity from Marxism, to reaffirm the religious character of radical religion. He was distancing himself, and the FSC, from their earlier overwhelming sense of crisis.

Niebuhr *was* the FSC: head organizer, editorial director, guiding spirit, perennial leader by silent acclamation. Meetings revolved around his central presence. Many of the hundred members were the same former seminarians who had flocked around him in the refectory or lounged in his apartment at his Thursday evening "at homes." Union graduates like Albert Mollegen drove carloads of their own students from seminaries hundreds of miles away to attend semiannual FSC retreats in the Northeast. There was never any question who was in charge, or who was the magnet that drew the rank and file from the provinces. Nor was there any doubt who ran *Radical*

167

•

Religion. His colleagues were giving him something to which he had become accustomed: a regular outlet for his frenetic pen. Since the folding of the *World Tomorrow* in 1934 he had written frequently for the *Nation*, its close journalistic ally, and for other magazines. But *Radical Religion* gave him the editorship of four fifty-page issues a year. Each contained about ten pages of his own editorials, in addition to his occasional signed articles. The magazine was very much his own personal megaphone.

His editorial control did not do much for the literary quality of his own contributions. He would never bother with matters of style, whether in writing or in living. Words were vehicles for conveying ideas and sparking action, they were not aesthetic objects. Likewise clothes were for keeping warm and food was fuel to be rapidly taken in at the pit stop. In the world but not of it: he did not disparage elegance and polish, he just did not want to be burdened with them. "Cultured" behavior, like leisure, could only waylay a prophet intent upon spreading the word. There was no place for savoring a bottle of wine, admiring the cut of a coat, or reworking an essay. His writing in *Radical Religion* had none of the literary grace of his articles published simultaneously in *Harper's* or the *New Republic*. He was capable of poetic expression: his book manuscripts, which Ursula toiled over with red pencil in hand, contained some inspired passages. But calculated attention to form struck him as self-indulgent, diversionary. The point was to convince and mobilize, not beautify.

Despite the pedestrian writing, *Radical Religion* had the power that derived from the renown of its one dominant voice. By the mid-thirties Niebuhr was by far the most formidable man of the Christian left in America. His personal charisma was unmatched; his key ideas set the terms for debate. The journal could not help but lead the way in redefining the agenda for liberal and radical Christians after 1935. At its peak it had only a thousand subscribers—the operating deficit was covered by the wealthy and socially active Robert Paddock, a retired Episcopal bishop, and the ever loyal Sherwood Eddy—but its influence extended throughout the church. On the one hand it brought many radical Christians back to the study of theology; on the other hand it contributed to a major reformulation of the political task for the second half of the decade. The journal kept up the FSC's familiar barrage against "irresponsible" pacifists of the FOR stripe who imagined love to be a viable ethical strategy in the social and international arena. But it gradually transformed Christian "realism"—the willingness to use force and even violence when necessary—from an instrument of class struggle to a tool for resisting fascism and shoring up beleaguered bourgeois democracies. Niebuhr was one of the first radical Christians in America to insist that the main issue was no longer to transform capitalism by taking the workers' side in the social struggle, but to defend the relative justice of bourgeois society against "barbarians" in the international arena. *Radical Religion* was a leaven in the churches for the cause of a united democratic front.

The second issue of *Radical Religion* in the winter of 1935–1936 offered a clear signal of the shift. It abruptly dropped the "capitalism must be destroyed" atavism of the inaugural editorial and stoically announced that "the historic situation in western nations does not offer the possibility of breaking through to a new society. It offers only the immediate possibility

·

of defending democratic institutions, however corrupted, against the peril of fascism." The entire left—Christian and secular—could unite in that defense. Even the Communists, despite their illusions, could be valuable allies since they too stood for "universalist" principles. In effect they were wayward children of the Hebrew prophets, not tribalistic idolaters like the Nazis. "Communism may be a corruption of prophetic religion but it is not its antithesis. . . . It does not, at least, identify the principle of evil with a certain race but only with *the bearers of a particular form of social organization.*" The equivocal "at least" and the lengthy italics suggest a certain uneasiness about his own contrast. But as one who had very recently called himself a "Marxian" and admired the potency of Communist "religion," he wanted to underline what it had in common with Christianity: the belief that in principle all human beings are equal. That way he could both justify his own (and the FSC's) former self-description and provide theoretical legitimacy for the united front.[1]

Marxists themselves were hardly cheered by Niebuhr's analysis. Naturally they resisted the equation of their politics with "religion." Sidney Hook and V. F. Calverton, independent New York City Marxists, both issued cogent objections to Niebuhr's Tillichian assumption that all beliefs which give meaning to life are by definition "religious." "Marxism is not religious," Calverton wrote in his eclectic Marxist magazine *Modern Monthly*. "It is simply that a great number of Marxians tend to accept it in a religious manner and thus endow it with a religious aspect." He subscribed to fellow radical Corliss Lamont's view that "it is illegitimate to call any human activity religion unless there is . . . appeal to, reliance on, or faith in supernatural elements, powers, or states of being." Hook brought his legendary quick tongue into debate with Niebuhr at Christ Church in December, 1934, and insisted that Marxism was a critical theory of society, a faith in scientific method. It was empirical, experimental, self-critical—not religious. Both Calverton and Hook rightly sensed that Niebuhr was resorting to the debater's ancient ploy of presenting the opposition in simplistic terms, then rejecting their stance as simplistic. First he labeled Marxism a religion, then declared that as a religion it was shallow. They might have noted that he likewise reduced liberalism to a religion—to a faith in the perfectibility of man and society—then dismissed it as childishly sentimental. In each instance the initial act of definition was prejudiced. Niebuhr the Christian apologist had always begun by erecting unacceptable alternatives to the Christian faith—"naturalism" and "idealism" in his BD thesis, Greek and Hebrew notions of immortality in his MA thesis, Marxist cynics and liberal utopians in his writings of the 1920s and early 1930s. He always put more care into illuminating the Christian perspective than the rejected views.

By late 1935 the chief antipode to Marxist religion in Niebuhr's mind was not liberalism but fascism. He still had little good to say about liberalism. It was hopelessly enamored of scientific intelligence despite John Dewey's recent acknowledgment—in Niebuhr's words—that "conflicting interests in society prevent the method of experimental intelligence from being as effective in social problems as in the physical sciences." But "liberalism," to Niebuhr nothing more than the complacent, mechanical faith of the triumphant bourgeoisie, began to fade as an object of his antipathy. The new

•

pernicious pairing was communism and fascism: each utopian, religious, and unacceptable to Christians. Communism might have "the advantage over fascism that it affirms the future and not the past," he wrote in *Scribner's*, but he was worried about that future: "If we allow the western world to become engulfed in a social struggle between a consistent fascism and a consistent communism we will be involved in inconclusive civil wars for decades, and possibly for centuries, to come. The consequence will be neither the preservation of an old order nor the building of a new one but a progressive disintegration of our social life. . . . There is therefore a necessity of reconciling forces in the social struggle of our day." The west needed a political perspective that could "come to terms with the inevitable relativities of our western society." Communism and fascism both "endow[ed] partial and relative values of history with the prestige of the absolute"; only Biblical religion avoided that "demonic and dangerous" course by locating "the source and pinnacle of life's values above the partial values of history." At this point Niebuhr could not name an appropriate political alternative to communism and fascism; all he knew was that it had to be infused with Christian realism. But the way was left open for a return to liberalism—a "realistic" liberalism—as the only middle course between two demonic faiths.

Fascism was obviously the more demonic of the two for Niebuhr in 1935, but his love of paradox led him to find in fascism a hidden truth, if not a saving grace. The Fascists had a feeling for "the organic character of society," for the common sentiments and inherited traditions that bind people together. Liberals and Communists slighted those attachments. The Fascists perverted organicism, to be sure, by creating a "ridiculous romanticism" and "particularly atrocious forms of injustice and tyranny." But they saw a truth that both capitalists and Communists had expunged in their common aversion to feudalism. "Fascism is this outraged truth avenging itself," Niebuhr wrote in *Harper's*. "Like a Freudian nightmare, expressed in reality rather than dreams, it presents an extravagant expression of impulses and forces in society which have been unduly suppressed." No other politcal movement recognized the truth upon which the Fascists built their nightmarish terror. The Socialists were no better than the Communists or liberals; they all wallowed in their "rationalistic and mechanistic errors."

There was no political force that was realistic about power, committed to justice, sensitive to traditional loyalties, and humbly aware of its own temptation to self-righteousness. A tall order one might presume. It was not surprising that Niebuhr put more energy into his theological work and "religious action" in the late 1930s than he did into day-to-day politics. Had there been a vibrant national Farmer-Labor Party in 1935 he might have immersed himself in it. He and many other Socialists believed that building such a party was the only progressive alternative to the haphazard reformism of the New Deal and the demagogic pseudo-radicalism of Huey Long and Father Coughlin. A Farmer-Labor Party would take Americans where they were—individualists, aspiring property owners, factory hands looking for a raise or a steady job—and its Socialist members would educate them about collective ownership of major industry. The Socialist Party was finished, Niebuhr thought, as a prospective holder of power, but it could still teach farmers and laborers about modern society. On the other hand,

•

he sensed that farmers and laborers had just as much to teach Socialists. The farmers in particular had something to offer: an inbred appreciation for the organic. Mechanistic radicals had to learn that social fellowship depended on preserving inherited attachments, not acquiescing in their destruction. No national farmer-labor body developed, however, and Niebuhr and other Socialists were left wondering what might have been if they had resolutely backed the idea in 1932.[2]

II

In his newfound political isolation Niebuhr had a friend: the well-known radical writer Waldo Frank. Frank had been a wunderkind in literary New York during World War I, a Yale man with all the right connections, an associate of Van Wyck Brooks and Randolph Bourne at the *Seven Arts*. After the war he turned leftward, became involved in the pro-Communist *New Masses* in the late 1920s, yet also wrote glowing, rhapsodic studies of organic, Catholic, peasant cultures in *Virgin Spain* (1926) and *America Hispana* (1931). Those premodern cultures were collectivist by tradition, Frank believed; they had a lot to teach Marxist radicals, who imagined solidarity to spring magically from the industrial workplace. Solidarity was at bottom familial, national, religious—a thing of land and blood. Frank applied that view to the Soviet Union in *Dawn in Russia* (1932), a lyric hymn not to Soviet efficiency but to inherited Russian peasant culture. Niebuhr found the book offensive "in its sentimentalities" when he reviewed it just before the release of *Moral Man*. But by late 1934, when he was himself burning his bridges to "mechanistic" radicalism, he embraced both Frank and his work. Frank approached him for an endorsement of his recent novel *The Death and Rebirth of David Markand* and Niebuhr was delighted to oblige. He congratulated Frank for grasping the dilemmas of life at a depth that "the Malcolm Cowleys et al." failed to perceive. Frank, like Lewis Mumford, understood that "revolutionaries" needed "a sense of the organic character of life." Unfortunately the right-wing Fascists had so discredited the language of the "organic" that Frank's voice might not be heard. To judge by the reviews of his book it would not.

Radical reviewers did pan the novel—the story of a young intellectual's awakening to both mysticism and radicalism, to his oneness with "the people" and with "the whole" of ultimate reality—as contrived, gushy, and pedantic. But Niebuhr, in mailing a publisher's copy to a large number of friends, pleaded Frank's cause and signaled his shared sense of estrangement from the dominant radicalism of the time. Most radical reviewers, he asserted, had chastised Frank for seeking "an impossible combination of radicalism and mysticism. This really means that they are quite incapable of understanding the profundity of the problem with which Frank deals." He had a unique gift for depicting the spiritual tensions of the day, which could not be addressed by "any purely political approach." The only thing he disliked about the book, he told Frank, was that it "gives a pedestrian and prosaic academic a terrible inferiority complex. It proves that people without imagination really have no right to write about ultimate things." Their

•

common devotion to the paradoxical ideal of an organic radicalism became the bond of a long friendship, although Niebuhr never found time for the leisurely conversation or letter writing that Frank craved. Niebuhr always put his friends to a severe test since they could rarely secure his undivided attention. The friends who remained close throughout his life ceased to expect it.

The irony of his relationship to Frank is that Frank—a nonpracticing Jew—was in a real sense the more "religious" of the two. For him politics was a matter of both reforming society and transforming the self. Niebuhr had learned to be skeptical about enthusiastic professions of self-renewal; they smacked of cost-free, complacent piety. For him religion was not doing good, feeling holy, or experiencing the transcendent; it was grasping the evil in one's efforts to do good, recognizing one's finitude, realizing that the transcendent was unattainable. For Frank religion was an intensity of feeling, a pantheistic merging of the human with a divine spirit that suffused the world and nature. Niebuhr saw the utility of intense feeling for social movements—as long as it was controlled by self-criticism—but he distrusted it in the religious realm. His religion, for all its Biblical allusions and ethical drive—was more like a philosophy of life than a mystical encounter. It was much closer to the secular and relativist faith of William James than to Waldo Frank's rapturous quest for a merger with the Absolute.

Consequently the "organic" meant something quite different to Niebuhr than it did to Frank. For Niebuhr it was an historical reality that capitalism had all but expunged in America. The organic was that set of prerational loyalties and attachments which remained relatively untouched by the marketplace; they were not chosen by the calculating, self-interested operations of mind, but absorbed through community tradition, sucked in with mother's milk. The organic was not something reformers could inject into a culture. But it was a valuable resource that radicals should appreciate and preserve whenever they encountered vestigial fragments of it. Frank seconded Niebuhr's historical perspective but went beyond it. For him the organic was an actual spirit, a living reality, that human beings and human cultures could come to embody. Mechanical cultures could be inspirited, become organic—in America's case by cultivating the "great tradition" of Emerson, Thoreau, and Whitman. The organic functioned for Frank as a secularized Holy Spirit.

Niebuhr was hard pressed to give his "organic" a positive content. It was to be found in the realm of family, neighborhood, religion, and ethnic group, but he preferred to employ it as an abstract concept: a symbol of the wholeness, the gemeinschaft, that mechanistic bourgeois society could not attain. It was a reminder that human fulfillment lay beyond politics, indeed beyond social life. It was a humbling concept, a measure of how far modern men, especially Americans, were from living together in brotherly relations. "Our society is held together by mechancial forces of production and distribution," Niebuhr wrote in 1936. "The organic forces of common cultural traditions and sentiments are weak in it." The absence of such cultural cement was tragic, but clamoring for its restoration was pointless. History was not an arena for realizing ultimate goals. The organic, like the symbol of God himself, stood for the final reconciliation of man with man that lay beyond history. Niebuhr could not go along with Frank in wedding the organic to history itself—as Frank did in effusively embracing the Communist vision. When Frank took a leading role in organizing the pro-Communist American Writers' Congress in New York in 1935, he tried to interest Niebuhr in participating. Niebuhr did not refuse outright, but he demurred and in the end did not go. He doubted whether he had "anything to say that a group of predominantly communistic authors would be willing to listen to. If they should read my article in this month's *Harper's* ["The Revival of Feudalism"] they probably would have nothing to do with me." Frank, for his part, was chosen by the Congress to head the new League of American Writers, whose national council included Van Wyck Brooks, Lewis Mumford, James T. Farrell, Lincoln Steffens, Richard Wright, and Agnes Smedley. He was determined to teach the Communists about the "intuitive connection with soil and self and human past" that made possible "the organic growth of man." He and Niebuhr saw little of each other until he left the league's leadership in 1937.[3]

For Niebuhr, Britain was of course a more organic society than the United States; "feudal" attitudes, he felt, had softened the asperities of capitalist class relations in England. But he wavered on the question of whether the organic in England was merely a veil draped over cruel industrial realities or an actual living spirit of interclass harmony. He was sure only that Britain had something vital that America lacked; Britain was the transcendent model by which America could be judged. English rituals and assumptions were not transferable; the organic could not be imported. The nearly finished Episcopal cathedral in New York, for example, provided the imposing spectacle of Gothic arches, but it symbolized only "what is archaic in the church's message. . . . Let the emptiness of the unfinished cathedral symbolize that the message of the church is vacuous when it is not archaic." His "American" and "Protestant" sensibility was affronted by the "English" and "Catholic" tendency to "symbolize the eternal in church, edifice, altar, priest, and liturgy."

Niebuhr revealingly placed his discussion of the cathedral in the context of a mock "debate" between himself and Ursula, his English and Anglican spouse. "To compensate her for the number of times she has to hear me preach," he began, "I go with her on my two free Sundays of the year to the cathedral." He did not point out that most of his preaching took place on the road, far away from his wife and son. But that unacknowledged distance between them was implicitly mirrored in the gap that separated them as they strolled side by side into the cathedral. "We were off on an old argument," Niebuhr wrote. Ursula was the organic, "Catholic" party from whom he established his independence in the course of the debate. He was the "quasi-secular Protestant" and American for whom the prophetic Word sufficed. He did not want to be pinned down by her organicism, or by that of the church. Women, like the church, Niebuhr implied, were liable to domesticate the spirit, smooth its cutting edge. They were also liable to domesticate their men. But the image of Ursula was a good deal more dialectical than that. She was not just a mother figure like Lydia— one from whose smothering skirts he must escape—but an intellectual equal whom he must engage in debate.

In his portrayal she has a quick, ironic wit that disarms him even as he tries to mobilize his argument. He rejoices in her spirit even as he rejects her standpoint. He has met his match; she becomes the transcendent "organic" from whose perspective he is critically beheld. The superficial divisiveness of the debate, like the division between their two religious communions, is overcome finally by their respective openness to the truth that each of them embodies. Their "marital felicity" is "restored," he jokes in the last sentence. But it is a felicity that encompasses division, separation, and tension—theological, ecclesiastical, and personal. His relationship to Ursula reflects for him the ultimate paradox of man's relationship to God: a dialogue that in Niebuhr's view always implies disjunction before it means reconciliation. Ursula is a tangible symbol of the organic spirit that lies beyond human experience. The "family," which for Waldo Frank was a direct embodiment of the organic, was in Niebuhr's eyes much more complex: it both did and did not express the organic. The family was a sign of ultimate unity, but not its realization.

Ursula may well have symbolized something else to Niebuhr: a settled, stable, national identity rooted in centuries of geographical continuity. Just before writing his "Sunday Morning Debate" he unwittingly disclosed in a private letter how fundamentally insecure he still was about his own sense of nationality. One Elizabeth Kemlo had written President Coffin to complain about a sermon in which Niebuhr had taken the side of the workers in a New York elevator strike. "I do not know Prof. Neiburg [sic]," she wrote, "and know nothing of him or his nationality." She would have been willing to "overlook the speaker's poor American diction" if he had not given "but one side"—in the "falsifying" manner "peculiar to the German mind, and more in the spirit of Jewish cleverness than of broad-minded Christian tolerance." Niebuhr drafted a temperate reply, noting that he had preached six times a year for the past eight years in the Union Seminary chapel. She could check the posted sermon schedule in order to avoid him in the future. But in his one angry paragraph he referred to his own ancestry.

> You seem to think that because you do not agree with me that I must myself be unamerican. I am an American of the third generation. Would you suggest that only a fourth, fifth, or sixth generation American shall have the right to preach in an American pulpit?

It is revealing enough that he felt the need to take up his genealogy with her. It is still more revealing that he claimed he was a third-generation American when in fact his father was an immigrant and he had in young adulthood always said he was second generation. His relationship to Ursula, and through her to "organic" Britain, may have been one way he tried to make up for his deep sense of displacement.[4]

III

In the spring of 1936 England was for Niebuhr not only a symbol but a refuge. He had been tired in other years as classes drew to a close, but this time he was near exhaustion. For two months he had subsisted on a few hours of sleep per night, he confided to Page on June 3. He had canceled his June speaking schedule and booked passage to Britain on June 5. His sleeplessness had begun at the start of April—the very moment that Ursula had left for an extended stay in Britain. A doctor provided sleeping pills and commanded him to rest, but the spiral of tension and fatigue intensified. Niebuhr abandoned plans for the summer issue of *Radical Religion*—it never appeared—and packed his bags. "Either age is beginning to tell or I was busier than usual," Niebuhr suggested to Page. He did not suspect, or did not admit, that the sleeplessness and anxiety were provoked in part by Ursula's absence.

Once he had rejoined her in Surrey, he rested in the only way he knew how: poring over magazines on British politics and religion, accepting invitations to address student groups, calling on clerical and secular figures he had met since his first trip to Britain with Eddy, Page, and Scarlett in 1923. Seen at close range England displayed few marks of the ideally organic culture that he had so often lauded. The transcendent model he had invoked to humble American pretensions took on a fleshy imperfection. "Britain Bewildered," he titled his report back to the *Christian Century*. The usual political sagacity of the English had disappeared in the wake of the failure of League of Nations sanctions against Italy. Moralistic pacifism was mounting and the principle of collective security was losing favor. The British were coming to resemble the Americans: individualistic, perfectionist, hypocritical in imagining themselves driven by lofty ideals, not concrete interests.

Only Stafford Cripps's Socialist League was managing to remain realistic about power in world affairs and committed to thoroughgoing reform at home. Cripps was the very incarnation of organic radicalism for Niebuhr. Only three years Niebuhr's senior, he was the son of Lord Parmoor, a famous lawyer and Liberal leader, and a nephew of Beatrice Webb, a leader with her husband of the Fabian Society. He had served Ramsay MacDonald as solicitor-general (1929–1931) and been elected to Parliament from Bristol in 1931. After MacDonald joined hands with the Tories in 1931, Cripps sparked the left opposition, but also retained his ties to the centers of power. When he visited the United States in April, 1935, he saw not only Niebuhr and Socialist Party figures, but Roosevelt, Wallace, and other New Deal leaders. Cripps was rooted in the old England but adapted to the new; pragmatic statesman and farsighted prophet; skilled lawyer-economist and devout Christian. As principled as his bespectacled look-alike, Woodrow Wilson, as realistic as FDR, as passionately critical of capitalism as Norman Thomas, for Niebuhr he was an idealized image of worldly responsibility. He was deeply content to count him a friend. But he doubted whether Cripps's Socialist League could attract "the generally conservative workers." On the whole the "British political genius" was sadly absent as he surveyed the scene in 1936. His general tone of disillusion was a revealing sign of the crossroads he had reached in the mid-1930s. The British radicals were his last vestigial link to the notion of a responsible radicalism. In his eyes the summer experience of 1936 called even their future into question. He would always be personally attached to Cripps, and quick to defend the British Socialists against their American detractors, but the door was now firmly closed on his left-wing dreams of the early 1930s.[5]

Niebuhr's summer trip to England confirmed him in his recent choice of religious over political action. In the fall he naturally followed every twist of the presidential campaign and wrote constantly on the gathering international crisis. But he committed his extracurricular time not to Norman Thomas's never-say-die campaign, but to forming a United Christian Council for Democracy and to helping Sherwood Eddy set up the Delta Cooperative Farm in Hillhouse, Mississippi—each a key project of the Fellowship of Socialist Christians. The Delta Farm, Niebuhr urged, was "the most significant experiment in social Christianity now being conducted in America." Thirty families of evicted sharecroppers had settled on two thousand acres of land. They were black and white but uniformly Protestant: unlike the heavily Catholic and Jewish northern working class, the sharecroppers were a Protestant "proletariat." Niebuhr could not contain his pleasure at hearing a Southern Tenant Farmers' Union meeting opened with a prayer. He was awestruck at the STFU's "Ceremony of the Land," in which "the choicest Biblical passages are recited to give religious sanction to the cry 'Land to the Landless.' " He was gladdened by the "undissipated religious inheritance" of dispossessed southerners. Over the next several years he devoted a sizable portion of his energy to the Farm's problems.

The United Christian Council for Democracy (UCCD) was part of the same drive that produced the Delta Farm. The FSC decided in a joint meeting with the Fellowship of Southern Churchmen (many of them Niebuhr's students or disciples) to organize a new Protestant federation of social-activist bodies. The Delta Farm experience had brought home once again how conservative the mainline denominations were, north and south. Interracial mingling among sharecroppers and ministers alike had raised hackles even in ostensibly liberal circles. The UCCD was to be a socially progressive minority within the church. At the founding meeting in Columbus, Ohio, in November, eighty-five clerics and a handful of laymen answered the call. Niebuhr assumed the chairmanship by automatic consent, and William F. Cochran—a layman and benefactor for multiple Niebuhr causes—was chosen president. The group vowed to work toward a common weekly journal, UCCD pamphlets, and the establishment of new denominational social-action bodies, but it was too late in the game. By late 1936 the radical energies of the early 1930s had slackened and the UCCD made little impact during the rest of the decade. Religious activism like political activism sparked less and less enthusiasm in the churches. Even the FSC abandoned its self-taxation system in early 1937, a clear sign that social idealism had fallen victim both to the international crisis and to the prevalent perception that Roosevelt had out-reformed the reformers. Former activists slipped one by one into the New Deal coalition.

Niebuhr held out a good deal longer than most. In the fall election he went on public record for Norman Thomas and signed a Thomas-Nelson campaign letter sent to clerics, professors, and other intellectuals. Roosevelt was a cagey charlatan in Niebuhr's view, and a Socialist campaign, however quixotic, would at least help educate people about the proper course for the future: social ownership of the major means of production. Roosevelt's opportunistic shuffling from one compromise to the next was no substitute for carefully drafted policies. One of Niebuhr's friends who received the letter responded with a Niebuhrian critique. "You have pointed out very clearly what are the relativities of politics," wrote Dwight Bradley, an ethicist at Andover-Newton Seminary in Boston. "Is it sound judgment, then, to support a movement which seems to ignore these relativities?" Bradley was all for education, but the election was in fact a contest between Roosevelt and Landon, and Landon must be stopped. A Landon victory would do nothing to assist a long-range Socialist educational campaign.

Another defector from the Socialist column wrote with a deeper critique of Niebuhr's position. "I resigned my membership in the Socialist party today," announced his brother Richard on September 16. "I may vote for Roosevelt this fall, and go along with the LaFollette-LaGuardia-Norris progressives hereafter." It was time to stop the pretense that one had to be "on the right side in the class struggle." There was no right side. "I am a bourgeois, I make my life by capitalism, I live like a bourgeois, I think like one, and I am in [the] wrong. That doesn't make the proletarian right by a long shot. And my business is not to try to change sides but to admit that I am wrong, to live in daily repentance, to know that something is happening all the time whether or not I 'do anything about it.' " Radical religion meant resigning oneself to sin and imperfection, questing for repentance, not social redemption. The latter was the goal of the "religious radicals," those who put their radicalism first and their religion second.

Richard spoke to his brother with the authority that he alone possessed. He claimed to know the real Reinhold better than Reinhold himself.

> Really Reinie, you aren't a religious radical at all. You are primarily religious, and radically so. And as religious, better, as a Christian, you know that we are all in the wrong before God, and that there is no hope for us in the temporal, but only in the eternal. And that while we need to qualify all our temporal interests, even the relatively noble ones, by reference to the eternal setting, it is even more important . . . that "we so pass through things temporal as finally to lose not things eternal." You know my own doubts well enough to know that I am not speaking simply of an extension of life beyond death. In fact it was in the way you dealt with these doubts as well as in your conduct in family affairs, that the profundity of your Christianity came home to me.

Once again Richard the prophet was calling on his prodigal sibling to renounce the ways of the worldly reformers and return to the orthodox faith. Once again he was predicting that Reinhold would move toward his own position: reconciliation with the gradualist compromises of the New Dealers and other moderate progressives. If there was "no hope for us in the temporal," it made no sense to preach a gospel of social transformation.

There is no way to gauge the impact of Richard's or Dwight Bradley's critiques, but by election eve Niebuhr had reversed himself. In a talk to Yale students on October 31 he came out for the President. "Though himself a Socialist," the *Yale Daily News* reported the day before the election, "Mr. Niebuhr plans to vote for Roosevelt. He thinks the President the lesser of two evils." No doubt he remained ambivalent to the end. After contributing

•

to Roosevelt's smashing victory he was scarcely buoyed up. The President's second administration was "completely in the lap of the gods." The nation was stuck with "a messiah rather than a political leader committed to a specific political program." Despite his vote Niebuhr was still a man without a political home. He had not reconciled himself, as Richard had, to pragmatic compromise as the essence of politics in a fallen world. But he had taken a major step in that direction.[6]

IV

As in 1932, the national election convinced Niebuhr that the American populace was politically immature. With no organized outlet for his political energies, he immersed himself even more deeply in theological and ecclesiastical matters. During the winter he accepted an invitation—engineered by his old friend John Baillie, now a powerful figure in the Scottish church—to deliver the prestigious Gifford lectures at the University of Edinburgh in 1939. Only four other Americans—William James, Josiah Royce, John Dewey, and William Ernest Hocking—had been selected since Lord Gifford endowed the lectures with a grant of 80,000 pounds sterling in 1888. Niebuhr had reason to be anxious in that august company; he had never engaged in a long-term scholarly project in his life. The offer of 1,000 pounds for two sets of ten lectures each made the coming intellectual struggle somewhat more attractive—likewise the prospect of following hard on the heels of his nemesis Karl Barth, scheduled to finish his series of lectures in 1938. Yet Niebuhr was genuinely humbled and his self-doubt surfaced repeatedly. "The lectureship is somewhat of a doubtful blessing to one so poorly prepared as I," he confessed to Will Scarlett. "I will have to put myself into slavery to these lectures for years to come."

By the spring of 1937 he was beginning his background reading—Hegel, Schopenhauer, Nietzsche, Kant, and Freud—but his idea for the lectures was, he told Waldo Frank, "still pretty unformed." His classes were over in mid-April and he hoped to produce a rough outline over the summer. Yet other obligations continually pushed the Giffords off the front burner. As soon as Union shut down on April 18 he had to sail for England to deliver the Burge lecture at the University of London. Meanwhile Scribners was eager to get the manuscript of *Beyond Tragedy*, a collection of "sermonic essays." And in June he would be embarking for Britain again to attend the Oxford Conference on Church, Community, and State. It was one thing to resign himself to the "slavery" of the Giffords; it was another to find the time to slip on his chains.[7]

The Oxford Conference was a major event in the history of the Protestant church and demanded extensive preparation on Niebuhr's part. Over four hundred delegates from forty countries and a hundred Protestant bodies were to gather for two weeks to ponder the historical crisis and chart a course for Christian unity. Henry Van Dusen and John Bennett were put in charge of preparatory research in the United States, and they naturally secured Niebuhr's consent to produce a position paper. His essay on "The Christian Faith and the Common Life" was circulated in several languages

•

before the conference and had a considerable impact on the deliberations, as did his address to the delegates at the start of the meeting in Oxford's Sheldonian Theatre in July. His fifty-page typescript and his passionate speech centered neither on the world crisis nor on the injustices of bourgeois capitalism. They centered on the fact of sin in the individual life, a striking departure from Niebuhr's customary focus. Sin was an inevitable product of man's freedom, Niebuhr announced. One of the key errors of modern culture was its zeal to glorify that freedom, to ignore its potential for evil, to mistake "the image of God in man for God himself." Freedom, to be sure, was the ground of morality and the source of human achievement, but it was also the occasion for sin. Here Niebuhr went forcefully beyond the liberal Social Gospel of Gladden and Rauschenbusch: sin was not the result of the "natural" as opposed to the "spiritual" side of man. It was traceable not to man's finiteness, but to his pretentious effort to deny his limitations.

> It is not egocentricity which is sin. . . . Egocentricity is a natural limitation of nature. Sin is expressed not in making the self the center of the self, as in animal existence, but in the more spiritual enterprise of making the self the center of the world. Sin is not a quality of nature but of the spirit.

Niebuhr drew on the parable of the prodigal son to simplify his point for delegates confused by his philosophical exposition. The aggrandizing self of modern culture, like the prodigal son, was determined to extricate itself from the limits imposed by "fatherly" tradition. The modern self had come to glorify its self-sufficiency, but it was now encountering the "mighty famine," the social crisis of the 1930s. The role of the church was to call modern man back to humility, to sonship under the transcendent God. But the church had to avoid taking on the self-satisfied, superior air of the parable's elder brother. It needed "a contrite recognition of the shortcomings of historic Christianity."

Niebuhr's remarks displayed the evident influence of his brother's intrafamily preaching: the sinful self as the ultimate source of social disharmony. They also revealed the impact of his recent reading of Nicolas Berdyaev, whose *Freedom and the Spirit* he had reviewed in the *Herald Tribune* the previous summer. Berdyaev had stressed the spiritual root of sinfulness and its essential relation to human freedom: "The cause of evil," he wrote, "lies in a false and illusory self-affirmation and in spiritual pride which places the source of life not in God but in self." But Niebuhr was not calling on the delegates to embrace his brother's quietism or Berdyaev's mysticism. He was arguing that Christianity alone could get to the bottom of the world crisis because it alone could get to the bottom of man's paradoxical nature. The doctrine of original sin, at which liberal Protestants had learned to scoff, expressed the fundamental reality of human life: men had the capacity to do good, but they also had an inveterate drive to aggrandize themselves and do evil. Even Christians remained "under the law of sin." It was always possible that a contrite person might "make the Kingdom of God the norm of his behavior," but "the acceptance of the norm does not guarantee its realization." Religiosity was no sign of virtue. "Even in religion in which

•

man consciously seeks to submit himself to God, there is an element of sinful pretense, an effort to establish an exclusive claim upon God." The ultimate dilemma for the Christian was that he must act in the world despite the certainty that in acting he must sin.[8]

The delegates were no doubt ready by 1937 for a message that traced world disorder not to class oppression or national parochialism alone but to man's nature itself. Disillusionment with merely "social" explanations for human strife was pervasive by the late 1930s. Niebuhr's effort to go deeper was continuous with Sigmund Freud's pivotal *Civilization and Its Discontents*, published in English in 1930. In both cases the root was man himself, not economic organization or national rivalries. In both cases the argument was directed against the Communists, who imagined that new property relations would usher in a new era of freedom; and against the rationalist liberals, for whom the self was solid, unified, subject to conscious will. Of course Freud regarded religion as an "illusion," and put more stress than Niebuhr on the biological and cultural constraints that circumscribed human freedom. But both shared a profound sense of the self divided, unaware of its own deepest drives, destined to disappointment in its quest for happiness. The self was neither at peace with itself nor at home in the larger culture.

By all accounts Niebuhr's presence at Oxford was decisive in setting the conference's dominant tone of chastened expectations. The previous world assembly of Protestants, at Stockholm in 1925, had concluded with a clarion call for building the Kingdom with love and goodwill. Many of the delegates at Oxford had already been tutored by Niebuhr's writings, along with those of Emil Brunner and Karl Barth, to reject that Pollyannaish perspective: the conference planners chose Niebuhr as a speaker in order to help bury any lingering Kingdom talk. When C. C. Morrison complained in his reflections on the conference that the American delegation had been too heavily weighted toward Union Seminary, and away from the midwestern liberals, Van Dusen pointed out that Niebuhr was an international choice: "He was desired as the American thinker whose writings on the relation of the Christian church to the contemporary world have aroused the greatest interest among Christians in Europe and the Orient."

British participants recall Niebuhr as a galvanizing force at the conference. Economist John Maud (later Lord Redcliffe-Maud) presided over the economics commission—which included Tillich, Bennett, Baillie, R. H. Tawney, and T. S. Eliot, among seventy others—and remembers Niebuhr as "dominant, but angelically dominant." Eric Fenn, a secretary at the conference, was amazed at the energy Niebuhr generated in the largely staid gathering: "a volcano in constant eruption." It was not only the delegates at Oxford who resonated to the theme of man's sinfulness. Niebuhr's performance set off a wave of enthusiasm for his writings in British Protestantism as a whole. Older Christian liberals found themselves forced to confront the concept of sin for the first time in decades; for a generation it had been buried by liberal confidence in moral uplift. Even renowned Anglican Archbishop Temple of York, who was more aware of sin than most liberals, was unsettled. When he met Niebuhr for the first time he embraced him with the only half-jesting words, "At last I have met the disturber of my peace." Temple remained skeptical of Niebuhr's line, but the younger ranks of socially active ministers and students were swept completely along. By the time Temple appeared alongside Niebuhr at a student conference at Swanwick in 1939 he was feeling abandoned. He confessed to Fenn that he could not relate to a generation that had grave doubts about everything. "I never had any doubts," he said sadly.

Niebuhr by contrast told the British students what he had been telling their American counterparts for well over a decade: doubt was the necessary starting point for a revitalized Christianity, especially doubt about the liberalism of their fathers. Between the Oxford Conference and the outbreak of the war in 1939, there was a virtual cult of Niebuhr among younger British Christians, a cult that produced its own oral tradition of whimsical verse. Many young Niebuhrians had studied the Bible with C. H. Dodd at Oxford, which led one of them, Alan Richardson, to command: "Thou shalt love the Lord thy Dodd and thy Niebuhr as thyself." Another young minister, Oliver Tomkins, created a quatrain: "The true believer/ In Reinhold Niebuhr/ Is apt to mention/ The fact of tension." But Richardson's inspired limerick of 1936 became everyone's favorite. "At Swanwick, when Niebuhr had quit it/ A young man exclaimed 'I have hit it!/ Since I cannot do right/ I must find out, tonight/ The right sin to commit—and commit it.' "[9]

V

Many of the Oxford delegates proceeded to Edinburgh in August for the world assembly of the "Faith and Order" movement—an ecumenical body devoted to ecclesiastical questions. It was far too "churchy" for Niebuhr's taste, too institutional and inward-looking. He and Ursula returned to their summer cottage in Heath, Massachusetts, to put the finishing touches on *Beyond Tragedy*. The fifteen "sermonic essays" on "the Christian interpretation of history" spelled out his Oxford theme of man's sinfulness and followed the "prodigal son" precedent of his Oxford address: retelling well-known stories and parables from the Bible, exposing the perennial truth in time-worn Biblical phrases. The tower of Babel, for instance, stood for the partiality and the pretentiousness of even the highest human culture. "Human pride is greatest when it is based upon solid achievements. . . . Thus sin corrupts the highest as well as the lowest achievements of human life." And Jesus' command to become as little children meant that one must transcend "the adolescent sophistication of modernity" in a quest for a second childhood, "not the childlikeness of primitive ignorance but the childlikeness of a wisdom which has learned the limits of human knowledge . . . [and] approaches life with awe, hope, and fear."

Preaching was always Niebuhr's forte, not exhaustive analysis; the essays retain much of the flavor of his sermons. Stark, stabbing juxtapositions: "Man is mortal. That is his fate. Man pretends not to be mortal. That is his sin." A constant dialectic of unsettling and assurance: "The church is not the Kingdom of God. . . . The church is that place in human society where men are disturbed by the word of the eternal God. . . . But it is also the place where the word of mercy, reconciliation and consolation is heard." The essays are not linear arguments but circling forays in and out of the paradoxes of human life, in which man "sees the possibility of a truth which is more than his truth and of a goodness which is more than his goodness." More than any of his other books, *Beyond Tragedy* captures the play of his mind: unsystematic, restless, eruptive. It also reveals the character of his faith: acquainted with suffering and absurdity, yet built on an ultimate trust in the meaningfulness of life and the goodness of God.

Beyond Tragedy was a collection of essay-sermons, but it did claim to offer an overall thesis: Christianity went beyond a merely tragic vision of human life. "Christianity's view of history is tragic," he announced in the preface, "insofar as it recognizes evil as an inevitable concomitant of even the highest spiritual enterprises. It is beyond tragedy inasfar as it does not regard evil as inherent in existence itself but as finally under the dominion of a good God." Christians did not bewail their fate, but took responsibility for their own sins, repented of the evil they had themselves done. That distinguished them, according to Niebuhr, from the Greeks, whose tragic heroes were "always crying 'Weep for me.' " Jesus by contrast told the Daughters of Jerusalem to "weep for yourselves, and for your children." Repentance took the believer beyond tragedy since it accused not life or God but the self. "If the defect lies in us and not in the character of life, life is not hopeless." The defect was not "part of essential man," but the contingent result of his willful rebellion against God. Life was not a fore-ordained, everlasting battle between principles of good and evil. There was salvation through "hope and faith," which allowed one to "separate the character of life in its essential reality from life as it is revealed in sinful history."

But the critical reader may have wondered whether Niebuhr had marched as far "beyond tragedy" as he imagined, or whether he had fairly represented Greek tragedy in the first place. To equate tragedy with hopelessness made his Christian alternative seem more hopeful than his own account of it suggested. But if the "tragic" meant, as it did for Nietzsche, the quest for human excellence and meaning in the aesthetic, supra-rational realm, it was not so far removed from Niebuhr's own faith. For Niebuhr's Christianity, framed in the Tillichian terms he acquired in 1934, was "a faith in the meaningfulness of existence." It was not a faith in transforming the world, or a belief in supernatural revelation, or a conviction that God acted in human history. To argue that Christianity was beyond tragedy because it regarded evil as "finally" under the dominion of God conceded vital ground to the tragic view, since the "finally" was beyond human history altogether. The world of Niebuhr's Christian was scarcely more "redeemed" than that of Nietzsche's Aeschylus.[10]

Niebuhr was not pleased when academic and religious reviewers— among them his friends John Bennett, Cyril Richardson, and Joseph Har-outunian, all presently or formerly at Union—mixed praise of his "ethical" insight and "prophetic" urgency with strong dissent from his theological stance. Bennett and Richardson questioned his reduction of the Incarnation to the status of "myth." It was one thing to claim that the Fall was not an historical event, quite another to challenge the historicity of the Incarnation and Resurrection. If they were not historical events, if God had not decisively intervened in human history at precisely those points, then Christianity became, in Richardson's phrase, an "intellectualist" philosophy of life. Haroutunian concurred, calling Niebuhr a Platonist. Few labels could have upset Niebuhr more, since he conceived of himself as a Hebraist, not a Hellenist. He shot off an angry letter accusing his friend and former student of "polishing [him] off with simple *obiter dicta* hurled from some kind of Olympus." In reply Haroutunian was unrepentant and echoed Richard Niebuhr's earlier critiques.

> I called you a Platonist because your God is primarily the ethical ideal which passes judgment upon us by its sheer unattainable excellence. The "tension" between the ideal and the real seems to me to be the essence of your religion. Your God does not perform miracles; never has and never will; hence to you the Incarnation and the Resurrection of the dead are myths, not fantasies indeed (I never said so, nor made an "effort" to say so), and yet "trans-historical"—shall we say, unhistorical? . . . Reiny, for truth's sake, tell me, just what do you do with Paul, Augustine, and Luther, for whom sin and death, *together*, were what Christ saved us from? . . . Yours is a truncated Christianity, one that pushes aside the cry of the human heart for life with God in eternity.

The reviewers' critiques enraged Niebuhr in part because he was so committed emotionally to his self-image as a crusader against liberalism in theology. They rightly noted that his liberalism ran deep, deeper than he ever understood. He believed he was turning liberalism on its head by proclaiming man's sinfulness. But by conceiving of Christianity as the most reasonable philosophy of life available to twentieth-century, skeptically minded people, by seeing himself (like Schleiermacher) as an apostle to the "educated despisers" of religion, he had embraced the historic liberal mission of reconciling Christianity with the scientific world view. Haroutunian was right to distinguish Niebuhr's position from the orthodoxy of Paul, Augustine, and Luther. "The Incarnation is a fact and a miracle," he told Niebuhr. "That it cannot be undersood completely does not make it trans-historical." A mystery was not a myth. Niebuhr was abandoning Saint Paul for the post-Kantian German theology of Tillich and his ilk.

Niebuhr did not confine his rage to his friends. To Morrison at the *Christian Century*, whose reviewer dismissed *Beyond Tragedy* as unworthy of its author, Niebuhr addressed more than one scathing note. He assured Morrison that "I can stand criticism, such for instance as [Walter] Horton hands out in his *Christendom* review." But Horton's review was gentle in critique and bounteous in praise. It was no wonder that Niebuhr could take it. His inability to take more than that may have been a sign of insecurity as a scholar—particularly in view of his upcoming Giffords. If even his friends in the theological community were persuaded that he was not just wrong but, as Haroutunian suggested, "unintelligible," what response could he expect at Edinburgh? As he stewed in his state of anger and anxiety, his brother's early response may have given some solace. Richard admitted to having "read with a little dissent but very little."

> These sermons have your authentic ring in them. Of course I get them better than your critics because I remain more a preacher than anything else, despite

the fact that I preach little. There is more positive assurance, more faith, hope and love in this book than in anything I've seen in a long time. Your Gifford lectures will be more recondite but can't be deeper. . . . My present way of analyzing the difference between us is to say that you are now more transcendentalist, more orthodox, while I am more pietist. You said about the same thing for that matter about your reaction to my book [*The Kingdom of God in America*]. You are a bit more the idealist who regards finiteness as tragic; I remain a temporalist and a bit pantheistic or better Spinozistic.

No more campaigning to convert the transcendentalist, but a gentle call to live and let live.

Richard perhaps could be satisfied with *Beyond Tragedy*, for all its transcendentalist idealism, because he knew how far he had helped move Reinhold away from radical politics and "religious radicalism" since *Moral Man*. *Beyond Tragedy* was a book of sermons, not a statement of political views, but even the sermons made clear how completely he had changed his earlier position. His reading of Jeremiah 17—"Cursed be the man that trusteth in man"—was not just the usual rejection of liberal sentimentality, but a repudiation of the radical view that one should "trust the poor man," the belief that "since he has no interests to defend he can be trusted to see the truth." *Moral Man* had argued that the dispossessed were relatively less deluded about the meaning of justice in advanced industrial society because they had no need to legitimate a privileged position with deceptive slogans. But the preacher of *Beyond Tragedy* stressed the uniform sinfulness of all men. "The weak will not only sin when they become mighty, but they sin in prospect and imagination while they are weak." Distinctions between bourgeoisie and proletariat vanished in the pervasive darkness of human sin. As Richard had written to him in the 1936 election campaign, bourgeois wrongs did not make the disadvantaged right, "by a long shot."[11]

VI

Events in Europe and Asia, like Richard's fraternal pressure, contributed to the tone of dissipated hope that marked both the Oxford address and *Beyond Tragedy*. "Europe is even worse than I thought," Niebuhr wrote to Waldo Frank from Oxford. War was not imminent but a temporary peace permitted "the expansion of Germany all over central and southern Europe" and guaranteed "a more inevitable catastrophe. Terrible." British capitalism was seeking to save itself by sacrificing continental democracy to fascism; in classically tragic fashion its efforts to avoid disaster made the ultimate reckoning all the more horrible. Churchill looked better and better to Niebuhr. In his *Reflections* written in 1933 he had pilloried him for his "cynicism" and "unyielding imperial ambition." Now he perceived that Churchill was putting national survival ahead of short-term class interests, unlike most of his peers in the British ruling circles. He was a statesman, not an ideologue; he was a British analogue of Stalin, whose nationalistic "relativism and compromise" Niebuhr vastly preferred to Trotsky's "unstatesmanlike absolutism." But Churchill's practical wisdom was unavailing against

•

the pervasive complacency of the British. "The world seems to me to continue to wag to its doom," he lamented to Frank after returning to New York. "England has sold out to the enemy and is not honest enough to admit it."

Britain's head-in-the-sand response to Hitler was paralleled in Niebuhr's view by America's acquiescence in Japan's invasion of China—which took place five days before the start of the Oxford Conference. The mandatory neutrality legislation passed in 1935 and renewed in 1937 was perfectly suited to strengthening the Japanese at China's expense: they could still import raw materials which their factories could convert into weapons of war, while the relatively unindustrialized Chinese were forbidden to import manufactured war materiel. Once again sincere efforts to steer clear of conflict made an ultimate confrontation all the more certain. Niebuhr applauded Roosevelt's Jesuitical reading of the neutrality law, which barred shipments to belligerents whenever he "found" a state of war to exist. FDR refused to find a war in Asia, since none had been declared, and managed to send some munitions to the Chinese. Niebuhr disliked Roosevelt's own military buildup—the administration was "positively sinister in its navalism," he was still writing in 1938—but FDR's shrewdness was starting to strike him as statesmanlike. The conniving charlatan of the 1936 campaign was rising rapidly in Niebuhr's Presidential rankings—not yet near Lincoln's transcendent heights, but far above the moralizing Wilson, whose idealism had captivated Niebuhr at the start of the previous war.

He took his enthusiasm for "collective security" to the Thanksgiving weekend convention of the pro-Communist American League Against War and Fascism, whose chairman was Harry Ward. Niebuhr stirred the fifteen hundred delegates with his ridicule of the isolationists and neutralists who predominated on the American left. He distrusted the league itself—in his eyes "a very unnatural alliance between religious radicals and Communists, with no real support in the entire labor world" or in the churches—but he could not resist the opportunity to lecture full-fledged neutralists like A. J. Muste of the Workers' Party and many of his former Socialist comrades on the virtues of political realism. He did not call for American involvement in the event of war, only for vigorous American aid to the democracies. Granted, such aid might lead to participation in war. Granted, the democracies were not guiltless; they had helped produce fascism through their own imperialistic designs. Yet the destruction of European democracy would be an unthinkable catastrophe. Americans could retire to no pure, faultless vantage point where they could wait out the storm. If Robert Morss Lovett, a well-known left-wing activist, was typical of the rest of the audience, Niebuhr's pronouncements turned some minds: "I was converted by [his] eloquent address against isolation and in favor of collective security."[12]

If Niebuhr had been able to follow his natural inclinations he would have joined the international debate full-time. But the prospect of his Gifford lectures held him tightly in check. Thinking about them at all was "intellectually and spiritually painful," he confessed to Frank. "I have to force myself to keep at it because every time I try to work out the pattern I become afraid of the magnitude of the job and fear that I can never complete it." He withdrew completely from the New York state and city election

·

campaigns—"for the first time in ten years I refused to make political speeches this fall"—but even that infusion of extra time did not help. By the first week of 1938 his anxiety was beginning to look like panic—even though the lectures were still more than a year away. "Unfortunately I am still in the reading stage and have not begun to organize," he told Frank, whose relative ease with the pen made Niebuhr feel even worse. The more he read the more he felt he ought to read. He was looking for points of contact between Greek tragedy and the Hebrew prophets and found it "a devil of a job." He had already tossed out a dozen outlines. "Hitherto I have simply pitched into the subject and allowed the outline to grow as I write. This book is too big to build without a scaffold and I do not know how to build a scaffold."

Family burdens and disappointments doubtless reinforced his intellectual frustration. His brother Walter, who in the mid-1930s had found work in filmmaking, was once again a financial charge. Sherwood Eddy helped bail him out, but Niebuhr, assisted by an occasional $25 check from Richard, had to make regular payments on Walter's "account" with Eddy. Worse than the financial drain was the constant supervision he felt Walter needed. Reinhold and Richard had been trying to persuade him to see a psychiatrist, but they worried, in Richard's words, about "how to get him to go without breaking his hold." Meanwhile, Ursula suffered another miscarriage. "I don't know," he announced sadly to Frank, "whether we will ever have another youngster, much as we would like to." He added forlornly: "I enclose a snap of the only one." In the late winter his own health collapsed. By April he had been down twice with the flu and contracted an eye infection that kept him from reading for several weeks. "I'm just in a hell of a shape physically," he told Frank, all due to "foolish overwork." His personal problems combined with the world situation in a spiral of hopelessness. "The world is continuing to go to hell. I have never seen anything so cynical as Chamberlain's policy. It has written the doom of European civilization. . . . Britain has practically advertised the fact that Germany can have her way with Prague. . . . There seems no hope on this side of catastrophe for anything."

During the summer things improved on the personal front. Ursula was pregnant again and committed to remaining in bed, if need be, for the entire nine months. Her doctor ordered her to remain in New York City despite the heat. The price for her was heavy. "At present she has nausea about 24 hours a day," Niebuhr reported to Frank. "Nature is a little too unkind to her in increasing 'God's primeval curse upon Eve' as the old Calvinists put it." But the heightened prospect of another child, along with the enforced summer in the city, were just the right prescription for Niebuhr. He began to feel fecund himself. He burrowed in the Union library and the first ten Giffords, on "human nature," finally took shape in his mind. By July he had drafted rough versions of the first four lectures, which covered the historic alternatives in the west to the Christian view of man. There remained six lectures on the Christian view itself, but those he could write in the fall term, since he would be teaching a new course on the topic. What he had not counted on were physical troubles of his own. As Ursula emerged in August from the first four months of her pregnancy with improving health, he entered the hospital for a minor operation. He got over that quickly, but not over the spinal anesthetic. Six weeks later he was still bothered by headaches and nausea, could not work at night, and had fallen behind in his course prepartion. By the time he felt better in October he had to spend every weekend away from home on the college preaching circuit. "I haven't done a darn thing on my lectures for weeks," he complained to Scarlett in December. "The grind is too continuous." Finishing the first series would consume valuable days of his spring sabbatical—time he should spend writing the second series of lectures, on "human destiny," scheduled for October. Those would now have to be thrown together during the following summer in England, when he would have no regular access to a library.[13]

The last months of Ursula's pregnancy were uneventful and she gave birth in January to their daughter Elisabeth. "Baby and mother in excellent health," Niebuhr scrawled to Frank on a postcard. "I have to leave tomorrow for Cincinnati." No time-outs for the newborn. There were dozens of obligations to fulfill before leaving in March for seven months in Britain. There was also an unscheduled emergency that took a week out of his already clogged agenda. Sherwood Eddy's Delta Farm Cooperative in Mississippi, which Niebuhr served as chairman of the board of trustees, was under public attack—not just by the usual southern racists, but by one of its own trustees, Dr. William Amberson of the University of Maryland. Amberson, a professor of physiology and an active southern Socialist, believed that Eddy was siphoning funds out of the farm for his personal use. Niebuhr knew Eddy was no embezzler, but also knew that he was notoriously disorganized as a bookkeeper. He traveled to Mississippi to investigate, and to gather support for a repudiation of Amberson. "I can only explain your conduct in psychiatric terms," he informed Amberson, and repeated that clinical finding to other members of the board. The vigor of his counterattack was not simply a sign of loyalty to his perennial benefactor. He was himself indirectly implicated in any charges of wrongdoing. In February Amberson resigned from the board, but not before sowing doubts in the minds of some Niebuhr disciples, like radical organizer Howard Kester, about Eddy's behavior. When Kester wrote Niebuhr in partial defense of Amberson, Niebuhr erupted. If Amberson persisted in his public remarks, Niebuhr would, he assured Kester in the bluntest of terms, "enter a court for the first time in my life and sue him for libel. We are not a bunch of crooks and I am not going to allow Amberson to suggest that we are." Kester and Niebuhr were still sparring about Amberson over a year later, but Niebuhr never had to carry out his threat.[14]

VII

The Niebuhr family arrived in England in mid-March to find "war preparation the dominant note here everywhere," as he reported to Frank. Germany had just swallowed up Czechoslovakia, and the British were outraged. Niebuhr suspected that "we will be back before our time is up." A visit from his former exchange student Dietrich Bonhoeffer on April 3 confirmed his impression that war might intervene before his second series in October. According to Bonhoeffer, now a leader in the anti-Nazi Confessing Synod, German army sources were whispering about an invasion of Poland in September. Bonhoeffer himself expected to be drafted and asked Niebuhr to secure a position for him in the United States. With Niebuhr's contacts that was easy, and Bonhoeffer arrived in New York in June to find several offers awaiting him. But the safety of teaching in America plagued him, and he renounced it one month later; he went back to the German underground, in which he later helped organize the plot on Hitler's life and met martyrdom only days before the Allies liberated his prison camp. Bonhoeffer's precarious position even in April, 1939, made Niebuhr's own circumstances seem outrageously serene and risk-free. After arriving in Edinburgh in mid-April he confessed to Frank that "amidst this whole impending tragedy my little lectures seem futile and foolish. Even more foolish is my preoccupation with the task of trying to keep warm in Edinburgh with houses about ten degrees colder than the outside and fireplaces which warm a three-feet radius from the fire. Never knew a nation which made life so uncomfortable for itself by seemingly perverse design."[15]

The first series of ten lectures on "Human Nature" began on April 24 and continued, three per week, until May 15. Several hundred listeners turned out at 5:00 P.M. in Rainy Hall to marvel at the uncommon exploit of extemporaneous delivery. Gifford audiences were used to dull prose drily read, and also used to dropping out after the first few talks. With Niebuhr there was no need to switch the lectures to a smaller room. He had not been well known in Scotland before the lectures. The Edinburgh *Evening News* had had to reassure the Scots: "The fact that he is a German-American must not be understood to indicate that he has any sympathy whatever with the present political regime in his ancestral fatherland. On the contrary he is one of the doughtiest opponents of Nazism and all its works. Were he in Germany it is safe to say that he would be in a concentration camp." During the lectures he quickly established himself as a presence in Edinburgh; his Sunday sermons at the North Morningside Church also drew raves. Not that all his listeners knew what he was talking about. John Baillie, who introduced him and attended the lectures, claimed that "many hearers were hard put to . . . cling to even the extreme fringes of the lecturer's garment." After one of the lectures a woman told Baillie what she wanted to transmit to Niebuhr: "I dinna understand a word ye say when ye preach, but somehow I ken that you're makin' God great."

Niebuhr himself did not seem thrilled with the overall response. During the last week he wrote to Paul Lehmann, an old family friend from the Evangelical Synod, that he had "done as well as could be expected I suppose. Had a good audience all through but don't know much about how my stuff has been received." By the end he was "completely exhausted" and faced the depressing prospect of finishing the second series while meeting a score of other obligations he had incurred both in Britain and on the Continent. One side of him wanted to be rid of the intellectual pressure of the Giffords, to get back into the flow of day-to-day events. "During the past year I was driven by a demon because of my anxiety about these lectures," he confided to Frank. "I have allowed them to dominate my life completely." The other

•

side of him sensed that the scholarly challenge came first: he must establish himself as a thinker as well as a prophet. The conflict was to continue for several years. The strenuous labor of putting the lectures into publishable form warred with the natural desire to plunge into his regular diet of speeches, articles, and trips—a desire made all the more intense by the rush of wartime events.[16]

He set out first for two weeks in Oxford, where he delivered the four Dunkin lectures at Manchester College on "The Relation of Christianity to Marxism, Fascism, and Liberalism"—a topic on which he could by now expatiate in his sleep. He also gave a widely heralded sermon at the redoubtable Saint Mary's the Virgin, a "thrilling experience," he told Scarlett, "though I am [a] little [too] much of a Protestant to preach in Newman's pulpit." Then on to Sussex for a month to make notes for the second series of lectures. He had no doubt, as he put it to Frank, that they "will be very inferior and will have to be rewritten next summer." In mid-July he was off to the major Student Christian Movement conference at Swanwick, where his opening-day sermon on Saint Paul's text "Perplexed, but not unto despair" enlivened the assembled youth. Many of the men sensed they would soon be at war; decades later Niebuhr's inspiration was remembered as a key event in the effort of many of those present to steel themselves for the moral and physical battle to come.[17]

From Swanwick Niebuhr sailed at the end of July for Amsterdam to address the 2,200 delegates at the World Conference of Christian Youth. His invitation had almost been withdrawn at the last minute because Dutch authorities feared that Niebuhr, still widely considered a leftist, might say something offensive to the Nazis across the border. W. A. Visser 't Hooft, general secretary of the Provisional World Council of Churches and a Dutchman with close ties to the royal family, tried to reassure the government. The Giffords made clear, he said, that Niebuhr had no affection for the radical left. The minister of foreign affairs agreed to admit him if Union Seminary's William Adams Brown, a well-known ecumenist and member of New York's social elite, would certify in writing that Niebuhr was not a Communist. It was also agreed that Dutch security men would pore over an advance copy of the speech. The secret police shadowed him from the moment he got off the boat at Hoek van Holland, and turned up in the front row of the hall—advance texts in hand—for the address. They quickly discovered, as Visser 't Hooft knew all along, that Niebuhr did not read texts but hurled extemporaneous remarks from every spot on the stage. His rapid-fire midwestern English left them befuddled; they had no idea what he was saying. Unfortunately, most of the student delegates from the Continent did not either. As it turned out, both the prepared text and the spoken remarks were safely beyond politics.[18]

Niebuhr scurried back to Sussex in early August to pick up the lectures again. He hoped by the end of the month to have completed notes on all ten, since he was scheduled to lecture in Sweden for two weeks in September before returning to Edinburgh. He need not have worried about the time lost in Sweden. Stalin and Hitler signed their nonaggression pact on August 23, Germany invaded Poland on September 1, and Britain and France declared war on September 3. The Swedish trip was canceled and the US

•

embassy arranged passage home for Ursula, Christopher, and Elisabeth. Niebuhr was glad that the Giffords were not put off. He told Scarlett that as one who was persuaded "this thing had to be faced," he was "happy to be among a people who are facing it with grim determination and with a good deal of humility. None of the pride and vainglory of 1914 is evident." He was philosophical about the prospect of air bombardment. "The air defenses are pretty good now but the carnage may be bad nevertheless." In fact he had been shocked much more by the Nazi-Soviet pact than he was by the outbreak of war itself. "The announcement . . . has stunned everyone," he wrote to the *Century* on August 23.

For years he had been criticizing American leftists for failing to grasp that Stalin, like all great leaders, was a realist and nationalist. Even during the Moscow Trials, when many on the left expressed dismay at Stalin's brutalities, Niebuhr stressed that his machinations were to be expected and hardly besmirched his lasting achievements. Russia's revolutionary movement was composed of bickering power seekers just like any other ruling group; Stalin's deceptions might be excessive, but they were far less appalling than Trotsky's fanaticism. Niebuhr's political realism could not, however, accommodate the nonaggression agreement. He did grant a week later that "what Russia has done as a great power is understandable enough." But in this instance he was not willing to judge Russia like any other country. "What it has done as the fatherland of socialism, to which millions of united-fronters in every nation have given their devotion, is despicable." Niebuhr felt cheated. He had put in several good years on the united front and felt he deserved better. "The degradation of communism," he wrote a month later, was greater than that of fascism.

> For ideally . . . it does not glorify the nation but hopes to establish a universal culture with all particularism eliminated. Many of us were perfectly right in preferring it in principle. But we were also right in suggesting to our too enthusiastic friends that Russian nationalism was the lion who had insinuated himself into the sheep's clothing of communistic innocency. This is a bitter blow.

Here was a Trotskyist critique of Stalinism insinuated into Niebuhr's world-weary realism. The mix was unstable, a sign of defensiveness about his earlier view that communism was morally superior to fascism. Those who had been sympathetic to the new Russia "were perfectly right," though they might look foolish now. Niebuhr could tolerate Stalin's "statesman-like" compromises when they were confined to Russia's internal affairs. But striking a deal with Hitler was going too far. It rubbed Niebuhr's and thousands of other ex-radicals' faces in their former illusions.

Shortly after Britain's declaration of war, Niebuhr sat in Stafford Cripps's law office in London. Cripps, "one of the greatest lawyers of England," was abandoning his law practice; clerks were boxing up all of his books. Niebuhr asked if he was giving up the law for the duration of the war. "No," said Cripps, "forever."

> I'll help win the war, if I can, and then I will devote the rest of my life to trying . . . to bring about a decent solution of the international and social

•

problem. My law practice has become completely irrelevant. This war will destroy many good and some evil things in Europe. The destruction will be terrible. We have to defeat Hitler, but the question is can we really build a tolerable world after that defeat.

Niebuhr was enthralled with Cripps's vision. His report of Cripps's words to the readers of the *Century* was a means of underscoring his own silent vow to follow in his path. "He is one of the rarest spirits I know anywhere. . . . I came away heartened . . . , though he gave me a terribly dark picture of the international situation." Niebuhr suspected that his Giffords, like Cripps's legal work, were now irrelevant. But Cripps's example of Stoic resolution helped him cope with the short-term ordeal of the lectures by shoring up his long-term faith that "out of the chaos of power politics . . . decent men [may] rescue what little decency and justice there is in the world." After Edinburgh Niebuhr would box up his own books and embark upon the defense of Britain in the arena of American opinion.

Ursula and the children departed for New York on September 12 and Niebuhr assembled his "skeleton notes," as Baillie termed them, for the second series of Giffords. They started October 11 and ended November 1, and despite the war the audience remained faithful—even after Edinburgh itself was bombed in the middle of his third lecture. German planes were hitting a naval base a few miles away, and his listeners began to grow restive at the sound of anti-aircraft guns. Niebuhr was so wrapped up in his message that he heard nothing; he thought they were squirming about something he had said. Baillie was surprised they came back for the rest of the lectures. But they probably stuck it out precisely because these were not standard Gifford lectures; they were inspirational if sometimes dense sermons on the Christian view of human destiny. If bombs were going to fall it made sense to make time three afternoons a week for some stirring reflections that went beyond tragedy.[19]

Niebuhr had already missed nearly two months of the fall term when he got back to Union in November. He tried to make up for his absence by taking on extra class hours, and he immediately resumed his weekend preaching and lecturing trips. In addition he scheduled meetings to plan a new weekly journal of opinion, *Christianity and Crisis*. Not to mention gathering some of his published political essays for *Christianity and Power Politics*, and struggling to revise the first series of Giffords as volume one of *The Nature and Destiny of Man*. He was so overburdened that he grew testy even with those closest to him. He blew up at Richard, then wrote to apologize in a letter that released an unaccustomed flow of affection. Richard "treasured" the breakdown of his brother's reserve. "I have been frequently saddened in recent years," Richard wrote,

over the eternal preoccupation with affairs which left neither of us time for common and quiet meditation on the real issues in which we were interested. Perhaps the whole character of our relations since childhood determines that there will be nothing quiet about our meetings but that agreement should be only the background and interlude of our argument. But that makes argument with you so much more fruitful for me than agreement with others. . . . With

•

those whose fundamental interests we share we can afford to fight. Because I enjoy an Augustinian peace with you I can afford to quarrel.

The exchange with Richard relieved some of the intense pressure that had built up on Reinhold in the winter of 1940. By contrast, Waldo Frank's complaint that Niebuhr was forgetting his friends did not. "I wish you wouldn't always talk as if I didn't appreciate you," a perturbed Niebuhr replied.

> I feel myself more understood and understanding with you than anyone else. . . . But I'm not demonstrative and secondly I live in a schedule which requires all my wits to fulfill. I have 150 students here, see almost 35 per week personally, spend the weekends in the colleges, etc. Of course, you're right, it's too much. . . . But I can't change my mode of life completely.

By the late winter, however, his body intervened where his will would not. At the beginning of March he was felled by what his doctor termed "nervous exhaustion" and was forced to take a two-week leave from the seminary. When he got back he had enough energy only to teach his classes and then climb onto the couch. His doctor predicted that a summer of rest would restore him completely, but in July he was "so nervous," he told Frank, "that some of my old trouble has returned"—a chronic, undiagnosable pain in the lower digestive area which made it hard to sit down. He could put in only an hour a day on the Gifford revision. The rest of the day he spent, at Lewis Mumford's suggestion, gardening and gathering and sawing wood. "The ever present nightmare of the international situation may be a contributing cause," he wrote Mumford. The Allies were crumbling as the Nazis bludgeoned the French and pushed the British off the Continent at Dunkirk. The French were "sick" to have surrendered so quickly. The British were gravely imperiled, as much by American complacency as by German planes. Niebuhr was so agitated he could not sleep; his exhaustion deepened. As he passed his forty-eighth birthday he confronted an adversary that stalked him continuously thereafter: his own physical constitution and the nervousness and depression that intensified whenever his body was unable to keep up the fearsome pace.[20]

NINE

WISER
IN THEIR
GENERATION

(1941–1945)

I

The battle for Britain brought Niebuhr back to the secular political organizing that he had given up in the mid-1930s. It also brought him firmly into Roosevelt's camp, as it did many former radicals. For several years they had been cooling on socialism. The Socialist Party had failed to become the coalition of workers and intellectuals they had hoped for, and its European models had been destroyed, as in Germany, or discredited, as in Russia. The basic logic of socialism still seemed unassailable to Niebuhr and his peers: social order as well as social justice depended on social ownership of major enterprises. But history had mocked logic and sneered at social progress. Fascists shattered democracy in Germany, Italy, and Spain; Communists purged other Communists in trumped-up trials and then made peace with Fascists. Maybe someday one could dream again of a new society. To dream in 1940 was in Niebuhr's view to court catastrophe. It was time for retrenchment, for what Niebuhr and many others called "realism," "maturity," "responsibility." It was time to tailor one's hopes to the tragic limits of the historic moment: embrace the goal of salvaging the liberal heritage of the west by backing Britain against Hitler.

In the spring of 1940 Niebuhr was beating the drums furiously for the formula "all aid to the Allies short of war," a position sharply at odds with that of the Socialist Party. At its April convention the Party reaffirmed its neutral stance in the conflict between rival European imperialisms—and its determination to rid itself of interventionist backsliders. "May I call your attention," Party Executive Secretary Irving Barshop asked Niebuhr on May 22, "to the fact that you are serving as a sponsor on the Committee

•

to Defend America by Aiding the Allies"—William Allen White's well-known interventionist organization. "I am interested in getting your reaction on this matter. As you know, Party discipline demands conformance to Party policies." Niebuhr wasted no time drafting his reply. On May 24, he sent Barshop a curt resignation note. He had "no intention," he wrote, "of conforming to the discipline of the Party on the question of American responsibility in Europe."

In the *Nation*, which under Freda Kirchwey's editorship had become a key gathering place for radical and liberal interventionists, Niebuhr reported drily that "my mail this morning" contained the Party request to "give account of my nonconformity." His answer: "a quick resignation from the Party." The brusque, matter-of-fact rhetoric perfectly expressed his conviction that it was time for an "end to illusions," as he titled the piece: no sentimental salutes to past camaraderie, no regrets or apologies, an expeditious turning of the historical page. Neither the Party nor his own past association with it was worth dwelling on. Just a few staccato sentences to voice his weariness at the pacifism of former colleagues like Norman Thomas. "The Socialists have a dogma that this war is a clash of rival imperialisms. Of course they are right. So is a clash between myself and a gangster. . . ." Socialist "utopians" insisted on "measuring all significant historical distinctions against purely ideal perspectives and blinding the eye to differences which may be matters of life and death in a specific instance." Niebuhr was not being quite fair to Thomas and other pacifists who agreed that the specific instance was precisely the issue at stake, not the failure of the Allies to embody some faultless ideal. Thomas knew there were significant historical distinctions between Allies and Fascists, but argued that modern warfare would itself tend to erase those distinctions. He may have been wrong, but he was not simply "indulging," as Niebuhr alleged, "in the luxury of utopianism."

Niebuhr's oversimplification certainly had its political uses. It was vintage pamphleteering, as was the collection *Christianity and Power Politics*, which Scribners brought out in the fall of 1940. It contained several of his recent *Nation* pieces, including "An End to Illusions," and a number of other occasional papers published as early as 1934. Together they formed a polemical barrage against the "vapid" character of liberal Christian culture—a culture whose "will-to-live has been so seriously enervated by a confused pacifism, in which Christian perfectionism and bourgeois love of ease have been curiously compounded, that our democratic world does not really deserve to survive." In unacknowledged debt to Nietzsche, Niebuhr blasted the Christian tendency to reduce "love" to the mere avoidance of conflict, to equate self-assertion with evil, and self-sacrifice with good. "Civilized life" was sickly, impotent before the steely hordes of "barbarism." Christians had to be tough, to adapt to "the rough stuff of politics," to redefine love not as the "negative perfection of peace in a warring world," but as "responsibility for the weal and woe of others."

In the main Niebuhr stayed safely on the rhetorical high ground of the battle between "democracy" and "barbarism." One paragraph alone gave flesh to the disaster that he believed threatened America every bit as much as it did Britain. True, Americans did not have to worry about Hitler

•

"landing an army in New York." They had to worry instead about world markets. Hitler was an economic competitor "who will, for the first time in history, combine slavery with technical efficiency." A Europe under Nazi control was "bound to destroy all the living standards and . . . democratic rights which isolationists promise to maintain so confidently if only we stay out of the war." It was ironic that Niebuhr, after excoriating complacent Westerners for their "bourgeois love of ease," should be troubled about a threat to "living standards." Why would not an imposed Spartanism produce a hardier, tougher breed? Nor did he make clear how a Nazi Europe would threaten democratic rights in America. In the end his plea for American aid to the Allies was based less on a clear conception of the threat to the United States than on a passionate desire to rescue Britain. His pacifist antagonists insinuated as much: for family reasons, some suggested, he was putting British interests on a par with, or even ahead of, American ones, a claim that Niebuhr vehemently denied. Obviously he was not swayed by merely personal interests, but it was still disingenuous to write that "I am an American of pure German stock," without also mentioning that his wife was a British citizen.[1]

Niebuhr had hoped that *Christianity and Power Politics* would join Waldo Frank's *Chart for Rough Water*, Lewis Mumford's *Men Must Act*, and Archibald MacLeish's "The Irresponsibles" as key weapons in the interventionist arsenal. But the secular press generally ignored it, perhaps because almost all of it had been previously published in the United States, perhaps because they pegged it as a "religious" book. He complained to Frank at Thanksgiving that no one had noticed his book. He could expect a response only from the organs for which he himself wrote, the *Herald Tribune* and the *Nation*. Doubtless John Haynes Holmes would review it in the *Tribune*. "It's like asking a Mohammedan to give an objective review of Aquinas." If Holmes were given the book, Niebuhr announced, he would swear off writing for the *Tribune*. But Holmes's dismissive account appeared in December and Niebuhr failed to deliver on his threat; he was unwilling to surrender one of his few regular outlets to a secular readership. The *Nation*, in which five of the chapters had been published, gave it a belated, short, and unexpectedly negative review. W. H. Auden took him to task not for the attack on pacifism, which he found persuasive if unexceptional, but for his spiritual gloating, his air of easy superiority over his opponents. In fine Niebuhrian style Auden offered him a parable to chew on. "A brother once came to one of the desert fathers saying, 'My mind is intent on God.' The old man replied: 'It is no great matter that thy mind should be with God; but if thou didst see thyself less than any of His creatures, that were something.' I am sure Dr. Niebuhr knows this: I am not sure, though, that he is sufficiently ashamed." This was one critique that Niebuhr, according to his wife's later recollection, did not mind. They sought Auden out and it was the start of a long family friendship.

While the secular press yawned at the book, the Protestant press was up in arms. The controversy solidified his place as the primary Christian advocate of intervention: rallying point for some, symbol of Antichrist for others. Christian pacifists bordered on verbal violence in their denunciations of him—a fact he did not hesitate to use in accusing them of abandoning

•

their principles. With C. C. Morrison, one of his earliest boosters, his relations became irreconcilably bitter. Morrison read the volume "with a sense of the outrage you were committing against the pacifist," but offered the olive branch of continued friendship. Niebuhr was not soothed.

> Friendship does not exist by fiat but lives in life and deeds. You can get no moral advantage of me by generously claiming to be my friend when I say a friendship is ended. This whole business of covering up ugly realities with words is of no avail. The conflict between you and myself or between your side and mine is, in miniature, as tragic as the world conflict. But you cannot admit being in it; for if you did where would your nice warless world be, which you are trying to preserve.

He reconciled himself to a state of war with his former friends, a state not of hate but of the love of enemies: "something more transcendent than friendship, . . . namely the spirit of forgiveness in the 'body of Christ' which exists at least for fleeting moments when self-righteous combatants cease to be self-righteous and stand under a common divine judgment and know themselves in need of a common divine mercy." Loving one's enemies did not mean one had to like them, only that one recognized their ultimate sanctity as children of God.[2]

II

Morrison had been much on Niebuhr's mind in late 1939 and 1940 as he mulled over the idea of a new journal of Christian opinion with Pit Van Dusen and Francis Miller. All three were devoted friends of Britain (Van Dusen's wife was a Scot), and Van Dusen and Miller were longtime leaders in the world student and ecumenical movements. They agreed on a journal that would unite Christian interventionists of all political stripes, and quickly assembled an impressive board of thirty sponsors: Niebuhr intimates John Bennett, Sherwood Eddy, and William Scarlett, along with such ecclesiastical stars as Henry Sloane Coffin, William Adams Brown, John R. Mott, Francis J. McConnell, Robert E. Speer, his old Detroit model Lynn Harold Hough, and his summertime neighbor Howard Chandler Robbins. When the first number of *Christianity and Crisis* came out in February, 1941—with the lead editorial by Miller and lead article by Niebuhr—it was plain to all that Morrison's *Christian Century* was both target and model. From the alliterative double *C* of the title to the familiar layout—opening editorials, substantive articles, closing news of the Christian world—*Christianity and Crisis* was the *Century*'s conscious clone, except that it appeared biweekly, not weekly, and could not afford as many pages. The likeness of a blood relative, but the animus of a rebellious child: Niebuhr set out to discredit Morrison's Christian isolationism. *Christianity and Crisis*, which attracted seven thousand subscribers in the first six weeks, quickly deprived the *Century* of its longtime monopoly at the apex of the liberal, interdenominational press. But it delivered no mortal blow; Morrison's ideas were too deeply rooted in the northern and especially midwestern church.

•

If any magazine suffered from his new venture it was his own quarterly *Radical Religion*, which had been renamed in nondescript fashion *Christianity and Society* in the spring of 1940. It persisted through the war and into the postwar period, but with Niebuhr's energy focused elsewhere, it gradually shrank to a shadow of its former self. It breathed the borrowed air of early thirties social radicalism. As long as Niebuhr and his disciples remained persuaded that the socialization of major productive enterprises was an ultimate necessity—and they were convinced of it until the midforties—*Christianity and Society* had sufficient raison d'être to survive. It stood for the future beyond the defeat of Hitler, but that future appeared increasingly remote, abstract. The same passion could not be mobilized for both causes. Niebuhr put body, mind, and soul into the political, military, and ideological defense of bourgeois democracy; the Socialist critique of it was not explicitly denied but circumscribed, exiled to the little-read pages of *Christianity and Society*. His literary efforts were concentrated in *Christianity and Crisis* and the *Nation*, just as his day-to-day organizational work shifted from the Fellowship of Socialist Christians to the new group he helped found in 1941, the Union for Democratic Action.[3]

The UDA sprang up out of the disgust many New York leftists felt at the isolationism of the Socialist Party. After the Socialist convention in April, 1940, Niebuhr joined Murray Gross and Lewis Corey of the International Ladies' Garment Workers' Union, George Counts of the American Federation of Teachers, John Childs of Columbia's Teachers College, and Freda Kirchwey and Robert Bendiner of the *Nation* in a major recruiting effort. The goal was to gather those interventionists who were actively pro-labor—unlike the Henry Luces and James Conants of William Allen White's Committee to Defend the Allies and the Henry Coffins and Pit Van Dusens of *Christianity and Crisis*. Conservatives were excluded by definition; Communists were kept out by practical calculation. The UDA was zealous in barring party members, and as a result drew the scorn of the *Daily Worker* and many non-Communist progressives.

Niebuhr and Counts were especially adamant. It was not so much Marxist ideology that upset them, or the fear of being branded pink by association. Niebuhr for his part had shown he had no fear of such association when in 1938 he joined in a public defense of a young Communist, Simon Gerson, whom the New York press had tried to hound out of his job in the office of Stanley Isaacs, the Manhattan borough president. What bothered Niebuhr and Counts was the Communists' past behavior in the New York City Teachers' Union in the late 1930s. They had watched, and resisted, the Communist members' repeated efforts to take over the group through such stratagems as delaying votes until late at night, when ranks had thinned. What upset them even more—since delaying tactics were common in democratic bodies, including the US congress—was the Communists' devotion to the zigzagging of Moscow's line. After the Nazi-Soviet pact in August, 1939, the Soviet leadership ordered the American Party to cease its anti-Fascist activity; Niebuhr and Counts shook their heads as party members in the Teachers' Union turned 180 degrees overnight. A union resolution condemning the pact passed by only a single vote. "I have myself worked in dozens of organizations with Communists," Niebuhr wrote in

•

May, 1940, "but their present orientation is so completely under the control of Russian policy that I will not again knowingly have anything to do with any organization in which they function."[4]

In the UDA Niebuhr found a temporarily secure political home. Although it was not a political party, it offered some of the aura of the Labor Party that he had been dreaming of for two decades: intellectuals and labor leaders standing shoulder to shoulder for progressive change. He had shied away from the American Labor Party (ALP)—founded in 1936 by labor leaders David Dubinsky and Sidney Hillman to mobilize labor support for Roosevelt—because it lacked intellectuals, because it was too narrowly based in New York, and because he still had too many doubts about Roosevelt. As long as he believed that "a genuine farmer-labor party of national scope belongs to the inevitabilities of American politics," as he put it in mid-1940, he could not devote himself to the attenuated vision of the ALP. When it came time to vote in the fall, however, he quietly registered as a member of the ALP at the New York election board and gratefully cast his ballot for Roosevelt's third term. "He has anticipated the perils in which we now stand more clearly than anyone else," Niebuhr wrote on the eve of the election. After the victory, he concluded that "for eight years now the democratic will of the administration has shown more strength than the democratic forces in the country as a whole—a most paradoxical situation, a blow in the face of the easy theory that the government is a committee of the ruling class for keeping down the ruled." Thank God for the "common man," who was wiser than the "learned" in backing FDR.[5]

The final organizational meetings for the UDA took place in Niebuhr's Claremont Avenue apartment just after the election. He was given charge of collecting sponsors, the same task he was wrapping up for *Christianity and Crisis*. The initial "call" of the UDA—entitled "A Program for Americans"—was drafted by Lewis Corey and revised by Robert Bendiner, who had been Niebuhr's copy editor at the *World Tomorrow* in the early 1930s and was now managing editor of the *Nation*. By spring they were ready to go public: at New York's Town Hall on May 10 they unveiled a leadership comprised of Chairman Reinhold Niebuhr; Vice-Chairmen Robert Bendiner, John Childs, and Franz Daniel, an official of the Amalgamated Clothing Workers; Secretary Murray Gross; and Treasurer Freda Kirchwey. At the top, the UDA looked less like a coalition of intellectuals and workers than a merging of the New York clothing unions with the *Nation* magazine—of which Niebuhr himself became a contributing editor in September. But the more than one hundred other founding members and sponsors broadened it considerably: among them George Counts, Frank Graham, president of the University of North Carolina, A. Philip Randolph of the Sleeping Car Porters, Kenneth Crawford of *PM*'s Washington bureau (and until 1943 the *New Republic*'s anonymous TRB), Benjamin Davidson and James Loeb of the American Federation of Teachers, and such longtime Niebuhr stalwarts as Waldo Frank, King Gordon, and William F. Cochran, who helped pay the bills for this as for many other Niebuhr ventures.

In the spring of 1941 the UDA was not asking for a declaration of war against Germany, only for naval convoys to protect Lend-Lease shipments against German submarines. Niebuhr and his friends had been Roosevelt supporters on Lend-Lease itself; in January Niebuhr had backed it before the Senate Foreign Relations Committee. Proadministration senators had sought a church figure to neutralize the earlier isolationist testimony of Norman Thomas. In his Capitol Hill appearance Niebuhr admitted to skeptical senators like Hiram Johnson that Lend-Lease might lead to involvement in the war. But he argued that the defeat of Britain and Nazi hegemony over Europe and the Atlantic, followed by Fascist inroads in South America, was an intolerable prospect.

By May, 1941, his interventionist argument was much broader in range. Two days after the founding of the UDA he appeared on NBC Radio's "Town Meeting of the Air" to debate isolationist John T. Flynn. He began with his usual point about world markets, then dropped it for a moral argument. He agreed that the United States could in fact survive a Nazi victory in Europe if it were willing to "bear the stifling, staggering burden of many decades of military and naval expenditures and, in addition, subject its economy to the strain of meeting competition from a system which, for the first time in history, has combined slavery with efficiency." A calculation of pure national interest, a resolute reading of power politics, might well lead to an isolationist stance. But there was, he insisted, "no possibility of considering national interest without becoming involved in the more general moral questions of what we owe, as a people, to our common civilization." True realism was based on moral commitment, not just a determination of advantage. Americans bore a historic responsibility not only to defend their own shores, but to liberate Europe from oppression. Flynn, an economist and an official of America First, laid into Niebuhr's views on world markets. Of course we could compete with Hitler, he contended, of course we could bar him from South America. In the question period Niebuhr ceded the economic ground to Flynn and stuck to his theme of moral responsibility. One simple story probabably won him more supporters than all his earlier remarks.

> I remember a publisher friend of mine telling me some time ago, before the war began, that he was going to publish a German book, until he got the contract. He discovered that in this contract it was demanded that no Jew should have anything to do with the manufacture of the book. This is the kind of clause which would be written into all sorts of contracts. That is just a small matter, but that is the kind of world we would have to live in.[6]

The day-to-day office work of the UDA, which rented modest quarters on West 40th Street in New York, soon fell to James Loeb, who became executive secretary in the summer of 1941. A former New York City high school teacher with a PhD in Romance languages, Loeb toiled for $50 a week when he was paid at all. He rivaled Niebuhr for indefatigability: while Niebuhr did the fund-raising, recruiting, and major speechmaking, Loeb issued a steady barrage of press releases which the New York *Times* and *PM* often picked up. The UDA was in the news, but there is no way to assess what impact it may have had on policymakers or public opinion. Its historical role, in any case, should not be reduced to the question of influence. It was always a small organization—a few thousand members at most, a

•

budget ranging from $2,000 to $3,000 a month. Its real significance lies in its role as a haven for former radicals in transit toward the liberalism of the Democratic Party. The UDA provided a halfway house for anti-Fascists eager to defend Britain and groping for a non-Socialist yet still progressive vantage point on domestic issues. It supplied an early model of the liberal, anti-Communist organization—anti-Communist above all in the sense that Communists were not to be allowed to join, not in the sense that Communist ideas were purely evil or that Communist nations were invariably aggressive and not to be trusted. After the German invasion of Russia in June, 1941, it became very difficult to maintain the policy of barring Communists since the "united front" was once again Communist policy and many progressives, including some members of the UDA, argued for letting them in. Niebuhr and Loeb did repeatedly praise the Russian resistance, but they refused to bend on admitting Communists.

If the UDA's influence in the wider political world cannot be precisely measured, Niebuhr's own influence within the UDA can: he held it together by charismatic force. Also by the example of tireless devotion. He rarely missed presiding over weekly evening policy meetings at the office, and rarely refused to address fund-raisers in other cities. He worked closely with Loeb in drafting the UDA rating of Congressional voting records—ratings published in the *New Republic*—and took charge of defending the UDA against Congressman Martin Dies's charge that it was Communist inspired. Dies was troubled by the organization's tolerance for former Communists (Lewis Corey, for example, had under his real name Louis Fraina been a founder of the American Communist Party) and also by its campaign against conservative Congressmen like himself. It was politically advantageous to label the UDA "red." Niebuhr had to expend valuable energy in a defensive counterattack.

He also labored to goad the Roosevelt administration in 1943 to allow more European Jews to emigrate to the United States. While his friend Rabbi Stephen Wise struggled to make Americans comprehend the reality of mass murder, Niebuhr gathered the signatures of "fifty prominent persons" on an "Open Letter" from the UDA to the President and secretary of state. The letter did not mention the death camps themselves or call for American military action to save the Jews in Germany or Poland. It stuck to the more modest—and politically obtainable—goal of increasing European immigration totals. "In view of Hitler's campaign of extermination against the Jews," it read,

> we believe that the United States ought to follow a more liberal immigration policy within the limits of the present law. There are many Jews and other anti-Nazis in Spain, North Africa, Portugal, whose country of origin is some Axis or occupied nation and who are eligible under the respective quotas. Some Axis partners, such as Roumania and Hungary, contain many racial and other anti-Nazis who could come to us via Turkey. Since practically empty ships are coming back from North Africa, Spain and the Near East, transportation offers no difficulties for a more generous immigration policy.

The Roosevelt administration did make a gesture in the direction of a more generous policy a few months later when it created the War Refugee Board.

But the President did little to empower it. Niebuhr continued to toil on this issue—he and columnist Dorothy Thompson were two major exceptions to the rule of studied apathy among American intellectuals about the plight of the Jews. And he slogged on for the UDA on one issue after another. Bruce Bliven, editor of the *New Republic* and active in the UDA during the war, remembered his work a quarter-century later. "I recall at meeting after meeting seeing Reinhold looking as tired as I felt, but struggling on, like a man walking in thick sand."[7]

As if his labors for the UDA and *Christianity and Crisis* were not enough to overwhelm him, he also took charge of the American Friends of German Freedom. It had begun informally in the late 1930s when Niebuhr undertook fund-raising for exiled German Socialist Karl Frank (alias Paul Hagen), founder of the Neue Beginnen left-wing Socialists after Hitler's destruction of the Social Democrats. Hagen was in and out of Germany until the outbreak of the war, smuggling literature, helping comrades across the border, keeping up contacts with the underground labor movement and with other exiled Socialists in Lisbon and Stockholm. Niebuhr backed him on the advice of Norman Thomas and Stafford Cripps, who raised cash for him in Britain. When Hagen relocated to New York in 1940, the American Friends was organized formally with Niebuhr as chairman, Hagen as research director, and an executive committee made up of Lewis Mumford, Loeb, Bendiner, and others from the UDA, and former Socialist colleagues like Mary Fox, John Herling, and Joseph Lash. Like the UDA, the American Friends made do with $2,000 a month provided by Cochran and other benefactors who needed only to know that Niebuhr's name headed the list. Hagen organized short-wave radio broadcasts to Germany, oversaw two periodicals about German affairs, helped refugees arriving in New York, and kept up his ties in Europe. He regarded the American Friends as his personal instrument. Herling, for one, got tired of the one-man show, called Hagen "irresponsible" for acting without consulting the executive committee, and resigned. But Niebuhr supported Hagen, whose dynamism got things done. Where others saw a domineering prima donna, Niebuhr saw a forceful leader with enviable contacts in the German underground and the American State Department. Hagen was a Niebuhrian model for the 1940s: heroic action tied to the realistic, responsible goal of defeating Hitler.[8]

III

Niebuhr's stature as a spokesman for the American Friends of German Freedom, the UDA, and *Christianity and Crisis*—and as a much sought after sponsor for countless other groups—was enormously increased by the release in March, 1941, of the first volume of the Giffords, *The Nature and Destiny of Man: Human Nature.* If the secular press ignored *Christianity and Power Politics*, they hailed *The Nature and Destiny of Man* as an epochal work. "Sin Rediscovered," announced *Time*'s upbeat review of what it took to be a downbeat thesis. "The religious book-of-the-year was published last week," *Time* reported breezily, "and it puts sin right back in the spotlight." Niebuhr, "the high priest of Protestantism's young intellectuals," was lead-

•

ing "his legions back to an almost medieval emphasis on the basic sinfulness of man." *Time*'s reviewer Whittaker Chambers, until recently a Communist and still a fierce opponent of liberalism, lauded Niebuhr as a "belligerent" antagonist of the liberal doctrine of the goodness of man. He completely missed the tension in the book between man as sinner and man as image of God, a common mistake of friendly and unfriendly readers alike. Niebuhr's popular reputation was taking on a life of its own: the preacher of man's impotence to guide his fate. "Niebuhrian" was coming to mean "pessimistic," even "resigned." Meanwhile Niebuhr was working beyond endurance in one cause after another to help mold the fate that was supposedly beyond molding.

Niebuhr was partly to blame for the confusion; he had long been tossing off casual remarks about the stupidity of liberal hopefulness and the all-pervasiveness of sin. But Henry Luce, Whittaker Chambers, and other conservatives did their best to turn his thought to their advantage. If man was fundamentally flawed, liberal reformers ought to quit tampering with the free-enterprise system and make way, as Luce had put it in *Life* a few weeks earlier, for an "American Century" of economic and moral leadership. From Niebuhr's standpoint, the imperialist vanity of Luce was a classic instance of the sinfulness of human nature: proud, naive, relentlessly blind to its own limitations. "Mr. Luce is to be distrusted: he revels in . . . the new white man's burden. He does not show the slightest indication that our salvation can be worked out only in fear and trembling." Niebuhr conceded that Americans must take responsibility for future world order, and that the price of responsibility was the assuming of some "imperial" tasks. But America was menaced as much by its own pretensions to virtue as it was by world disorder. Luce's ignorant cheerleading for capitalism was poor preparation for mature statesmanship.[9]

The first volume of *The Nature and Destiny of Man* accepted the monumental challenge of surveying the history of classical and modern thought about man and expounding a "Biblical" perspective that did more justice to the observed facts of human existence. The fundamental structure of the work was already laid out in Niebuhr's BD thesis written at Yale almost three decades before. A succession of "naturalisms" and "idealisms" in western thought had tried to make sense of human nature, and they had always failed.

> The naturalist sees human freedom as little more than the freedom of *homo faber* and fails to appreciate to what degree the human spirit breaks and remakes the harmonies and unities of nature. The idealist, identifying freedom with reason and failing to appreciate that freedom rises above reason, imagines that the freedom of man is secure, in the mind's impetus toward coherence and synthesis. Neither naturalism nor idealism can understand that man is free enough to violate both the necessities of nature and the logical systems of reason.

Neither naturalism nor idealism comprehended man "in a dimension sufficiently high or deep to do full justice to either his stature or his capacity for both good and evil." As a Christian apologist Niebuhr was arguing that the Biblical view was contingently necessary since it was better than any alternative. It could encompass man in all his manifestations. "Man does not know himself truly except as he knows himself confronted by God. Only in that confrontation does he become aware of his full stature and freedom and of the evil in him."

The basic apologetic structure of the book was consistent with Niebuhr's earliest work, but the elaboration was the distinctive product of his maturity. In the decade since *Moral Man* he had come to understand that the self was not a simple entity set off against an impersonal universe, or against a complex and oppressive "society," but a paradoxical entity at odds with itself. Kierkegaard's notion of anxiety—the existential dread of the human being face to face with his own finitude and moral inadequacy—was the key addition to Niebuhr's conceptual armor. In his eyes Kierkegaard was a better psychologist than Karen Horney or Sigmund Freud, both of whom attributed anxiety to prior causes, either social or sexual. For Kierkegaard anxiety was primordial, the deep source from which flowed both human sin and human creativity. Niebuhr granted that self and society interpenetrated, as did self and nature. But he resisted the common behaviorist claim—a claim he wrongly assumed was shared by Freud—that man was fully determined by social, psychic, or natural forces. After all of those admittedly powerful forces were accounted for, man still stood face to face with his destiny, still possessed the power to act for good or for evil. More: he constantly undermined his efforts to do good by doing evil.

The final paradox of human nature was that man remained ultimately free as a moral agent despite the inevitability of his own sin. Indeed, "man is most free in the discovery that he is not free." Only those aware of the depth of their own sinfulness could be truly free, only they could act responsibly, in full appreciation of their limits. Only they could eschew the fanaticisms of the thirties and take one careful step at a time in the social and political arena. The dilemma of human life was the perpetual war of the self against itself, deluding itself, losing itself alternately to pride or despair, yet always capable of—indeed, "called" to—responsible action in the world. Human achievements, even human progress, were possible, but they always contained the seeds of their own destruction. The higher the good attained, the greater the potential for evil.

Robert Calhoun, historical theologian at Yale and fellow member of the Younger Theologians (now, in deference to the onset of middle age, renamed the Theological Discussion Group), made the most trenchant critiques of *The Nature and Destiny of Man*. He rightly observed that it was a prophetic, not a scholarly, work. "No cautious weigher of evidence here," he wrote, "but a preacher expounding the Word in line with his private revelation. . . . Other authors, Christian and nonChristian . . . are swiftly divided into sheep and goats. The former are treated with enthusiasm and insight, the latter dismissed as not worth much bother. Swiftness is the word always." Calhoun saw to the heart of Niebuhr's enterprise. The selective mining of the Christian tradition to illuminate and dramatize his personal vision: the prophets (especially Amos and Isaiah) preferred to the Wisdom literature; Paul to the Synoptic Gospels; the "Hebraic" to the "Hellenistic," a bias Niebuhr inherited from Harnack; a "Protestant" to a "Catholic" Augustine; Kierkegaard as the modern seer. At a more funda-

•

mental level: the passionate intensity, the urgency to speak, the carelessness with detail, the impatience with logical consistency. Speak now, discriminate later. Always on the run, suitcase packed, in dread of passivity. Obsessed with delivering his message; there might not be enough time. A spiritual vocation with evident if obscure psychological roots. The psychic battle does not explain away or invalidate the spiritual quest; it helps us grasp its cost. *The Nature and Destiny of Man* was no detached work of contemplation. It was as much the work of the insistent preacher as *Beyond Tragedy*. It was even in part a polemical tract for the times like *Christianity and Power Politics*. His mission in all three books was to justify Biblical religion as the only adequate foundation for self-understanding and political action in an age of lowered expectations and inexpressibly horrible disasters.

Niebuhr did not appreciate Calhoun's published judgment that "on its historical side this book cannot be taken seriously." He supposed that Calhoun was skewering him because of their disagreements on other issues (Calhoun was a pacifist). Calhoun replied that his critique was a purely professional judgment: "Your account of Christian and secular thought shows clearly that at various points you have lacked either time, equipment, or inclination to study the relevant data." Niebuhr might have responded that Calhoun had taken so much time to study the relevant data that he had never been able to publish a major work. Any writer had to call a halt to research before all conceivably relevant data had been assimilated. But Calhoun's conclusion, even if prompted partly by a desire to display his own mastery of historical theology, was surely on target. Niebuhr's historical survey was rudimentary in the extreme: a stringing together of uncautious judgments and random quotations, a sequence of straw ideas easily knocked down in his fuller but still highly selective treatment of the Biblical perspective. Yet even Calhoun went out of his way to praise the book for its insight into the human condition. "The real ground of the author's doctrine is not what he has read but what has happened to him as a struggling self"; his reflections on the mysteries of selfhood "must become a permanent part of any reader's thinking." Niebuhr had managed the uncommon feat of dissecting the intricacies of the self while communicating his own sense of wonder at its secrets. Analysis framed by amazement. He marveled at the capacity of the self to step back and examine itself; he shook his head at the thought of "a spirit who can set time, nature, the world and being *per se* into juxtaposition to himself and inquire after the meaning of these things." The book displayed the wisdom of one who knew what it meant to pass beyond knowledge and see again with the eyes of a child. He found the prophetic voice he had been seeking: authoritative and humble. Understanding human nature meant probing its paradoxes—the creaturely creator, determined yet free, sinful but responsible—and reveling in its mysteries.

The Nature and Destiny of Man was the mature flowering of the seed that Richard had planted ten years before in his critique of *Moral Man*. The self was fragmented, elusive, held together only by a mysterious force greater than itself. As Paul and Augustine put it, man did not so much know himself as feel himself known by another. Richard wished his brother a

•

happy forty-ninth birthday in June, 1941, applauded his achievement, and voiced his own sense of interconnected selfhood.

> This past year is one which even you, if you can look at it objectively and without false modesty, must regard as a year of creativity, as good, if not for you certainly for the world you serve. Your book opens a new chapter in American theology and by the grace of God may be the beginning of a new sanity in our religion. . . . You have been the man of the year in religious and moral matters, but your great year may yet be future and greater than this. All this sounds remote. Speaking personally, you're a damn fine brother and man and my affection for you surpasses my esteem, which is saying a lot. And affection has nothing to do with [my estimate of] your attainments though the latter give affection a special glow. May the Lord be with you, and you with me and us all the days of our life. You are my bow anchor, more than you can realize.

Reinhold was the model of resolve and decisiveness that armed Richard for the battle of everyday life. Paradoxically, Reinhold was both a major cause of the oppressiveness of his existence and a key to overcoming it. The Niebuhr brothers could probe the depths of human nature because they had their own interrelated selves to wonder at.[10]

IV

Niebuhr's readers were eager to see volume two, on human destiny—at last he would provide a doctrine of grace to accompany his doctrine of sin, a vision of salvation to complement his sense of human limits—but he was not eager to write it. When volume one appeared he was totally exhausted, as he was now every spring, and feared another nervous collapse. He was so tense he could not sleep, and his doctor urged the cancellation of all outside engagements. Niebuhr canceled only half of them, but agreed to quit working at seven o'clock in the evening. Although he was in no position to produce it, he did have the thesis of volume two clearly in mind: "an exposition," he told Mumford, "of the proposition that neither Aquinas nor Luther, neither Catholicism nor Reformation, are right." Catholicism viewed grace as the fulfillment of nature, the Reformation saw it as the negation of nature. In fact "the highest possibility" had to be conceived as both fulfillment and negation of the natural. Human reason, as Aquinas stressed, was capable of transcending mere egotism, but as Luther knew, it was always "tainted with self-interest." As usual Niebuhr was seeking the middle ground between extremes: "There can be an advance in truth and yet we never have universal truth but truth from a perspective."

But in 1941 his heart was not in it. The "literary work" of *Christianity and Crisis*, which was adding one hundred new subscribers a week, seemed far more pressing. Waldo Frank, Howard Robbins, and Henry Coffin all tried to goad him, and Scribners periodically pleaded. He could not get the war out of his mind even for a couple of hours a day; his voice might make a difference in keeping Britain afloat. The German invasion of Russia in June

•

gave the British a temporary respite, but still he could not relax. A serious family problem also added to his burdens and distracted him from his theological labors. Walter's health had deteriorated in the late thirties. In 1941 he broke down from alcoholism and depression, conditions traceable in part to his long-standing feelings of inadequacy. Over the summer Reinhold was, he told Frank, "very preoccupied with my psychopathic brother, whose state became very alarming and for whom I finally had to find institutional care." He placed him in the Rockefeller Hospital in Manhattan, where he stayed four months. That added considerably to the "heavy financial burden which requires a schedule from me, difficult to maintain." He was not only paying Walter's hospital bill, but subsidizing Walter's wife, Beulah, and his daughter, Carol, who was enrolled at a private school in Massachusetts.

There was fortunately now a second salary in the family to help balance the books. Ursula had been hired by Barnard College in 1940 to teach Bible and theology. With her Oxford training she was plainly qualified for the post and had not needed her husband's good offices. Nevertheless, he had intervened on her behalf. When he heard that Professor Horace Friess was opposing her appointment, he wrote him two blunt letters—against his wife's wishes. He underlined his own strong interest in seeing her have a chance to use her theological education. He was quite aware that Ursula had sacrificed her own career to his, and his guilt about having put limits on her life may have contributed to his animus toward Friess. The benefits of the Barnard position came, of course, at the cost of extra fatigue for Ursula herself, who still had the household and children to look after. The pace caught up with her in the fall of 1942, when she began teaching two new courses. "They proved a little too much for her," Niebuhr told Mumford, and in December she went away for a three-week "rest cure."

Ursula Niebuhr is quick to recollect that her husband was a big help around the apartment and with the children. He was not above scrubbing the floor, attacking a sinkful of dishes, or changing a diaper. But he well knew that he was leaving most of the chores to his wife: he marveled at how well she managed both household and career. He was away from home so much that most duties fell to her by default. Likewise his capacity for fathering was limited by his public preoccupations. He adored his children, and frequently referred to their youthful insights and exploits in his classroom lectures. But close family friends such as William Wolf emphasize that he lacked sensitivity as a father. He relied on Wolf to take Christopher swimming during the summer at Heath; Wolf believes that Niebuhr encouraged him to become a "substitute father" for the boy, a role he gladly played. Niebuhr later expressed remorse for having been such a "dreadful father"; he especially regretted the impatience he had displayed when Christopher was learning to tie his shoes. He had not yet understood that his son was dyslexic. But he exaggerated his own shortcomings. He was not dreadful, and certainly never a tyrannical or abusive parent, as Gustav had been for two of his sons. He was busy, frequently inattentive, and often absent. His bleak dedication of *The Nature and Destiny of Man* to Ursula, "who helped," and to Christopher and Elisabeth, "who frequently interrupted me in the writing of these pages," was meant to be humorous but

could not conceal his sense that being a parent, for all its undeniable pleasures, sometimes pulled him away from weightier matters.[11]

In the fall of 1941 the future looked dimmer than ever to Niebuhr. He
feared the Russians would "fold up" before winter's end, he told Scarlett,
leaving the anti-Nazi struggle "squarely up to us. I still don't know if we'll
have the resolution to carry it through." Niebuhr was subordinating his
Giffords and his health to the cause of mobilizing Americans behind the
President. Meanwhile the FBI was working overtime to protect the nation
from Reinhold Niebuhr. Right-wing zealots had been singling him out for
attack since 1934, when Elizabeth Dilling published her "Who's Who of
Radicalism," *The Red Network*, a book that lumped all Socialists and left-
liberals with the Communists as enemies of the Republic. Former radical
(and Niebuhr associate in the FOR) J. B. Matthews also pointed a finger
at him in his 1938 testimony before Congressman Dies's Un-American
Activities Committee. J. Edgar Hoover's agents had pored over the Dies
Committee findings, and were especially interested to note that in 1937
Niebuhr had chaired meetings of the American Friends of Spanish Freedom—an anti-Franco group. This "discovery" was ironic since Niebuhr
had never been deeply engaged in the Loyalist cause and had chaired the
meetings—and served on the group's executive committee—as a favor to
his benefactor Bishop Robert Paddock, chairman of the American Friends.

When Niebuhr's name turned up in 1940 as a sponsor for an émigré
scholar's visa application, the FBI told the State Department to reject it.
Friendly sources at State tipped Niebuhr off, and he protested to Supreme
Court Justice Felix Frankfurter, whom he knew through New York lawyer
C. C. Burlingham. He had been battling the Communists for years, he
wrote, and had never had any "contact" with them outside of the united-
front organizations. Even in those groups, he stressed, he was always "on
guard" against the Communists. If the State Department was seriously
interested in what former united fronters thought, it should "at least employ
snoopers who read our magazines to see what [we] are saying." Frankfurter
solicited strong character references on Niebuhr from Burlingham and Howard
Chandler Robbins—both active backers of *Christianity and Crisis*—and sent
them along with one of his own to Sumner Welles, FDR intimate and acting
secretary of state. Welles assured Frankfurter that it was all a big mistake
and that new measures would be enacted to "prevent completely unjusti-
fiable charges of this kind from carrying any weight." Frankfurter was
pleased: "I have every reason for believing," he told Burlingham, "that the
Niebuhr nonsense has been rectified."[12]

But government "snoopers" were not done with Niebuhr yet. A few
weeks before Pearl Harbor, Archibald MacLeish, Librarian of Congress and
head of the Office of Facts and Figures (OFF), invited Niebuhr to help draft
a "propaganda release"—Niebuhr's term—on Roosevelt's Four Freedoms.
Niebuhr gladly agreed to come to Washington for two weekends in January
to produce a document on freedom of religion. MacLeish, meanwhile,
without informing his new recruit, requested the usual security check required of all OFF personnel. The FBI dragged its feet and had not even
begun when Niebuhr turned up in Washington, interviewed Vice-President
Wallace and several Supreme Court justices, completed his report, and went

•

home. It was only at the end of January, when he filed a $45 travel-reimbursement claim, that the FBI went to work. They launched a "special inquiry investigation" out of the New York office: agents in St. Louis, Chicago, New Haven, Detroit, and New York scoured his past for evidence of disloyalty. They called at Elmhurst and Eden seminaries, at Yale Divinity School and the New Haven Police Department, at a Detroit credit bureau and the Detroit police (where they uncovered a 1926 speeding ticket), and trudged up apartment stairs all over Manhattan looking for former neighbors and acquaintances. They even went to 527 Riverside Drive, where Lydia and Hulda lived, to inquire about them; a neighbor called them "staunch Americans." On Niebuhr himself the Bureau's hearsay data was mixed: most informants believed him a loyal citizen, but others wondered how anyone could have belonged to so many "Communist fronts" without being disloyal or indeed a member of the Party.

The investigation was still in full swing when Niebuhr got wind of it in early March. He was amused, he told MacLeish and Frankfurter, but also deeply disturbed. MacLeish commiserated, but did not let on that he had ordered the security check in the first place. He did ask Attorney General Francis Biddle to put a stop to the inquiry—on the grounds that Niebuhr had long since finished his job—and promised to help arrange an interview with the FBI so that Niebuhr could answer the charges against him. But J. Edgar Hoover was now personally embroiled in the affair, and he instructed the New York office simply to record any statement Niebuhr wished to make, not to disclose any of the file's contents. An agent telephoned him at Union Seminary in late April, and when told the file would remain secret, Niebuhr deferentially backed down. Everything was "all right now," the agent quoted him as saying. He agreed with the agent that security inquiries were legitimate, claiming only that in his case they could have been waived: after all, his public views were well known. The agent did not bother to reply that it was his private views, if any, they were seeking. Niebuhr concluded that the whole episode was MacLeish's fault—for having him fill out the travel forms—and the agent wrote to Hoover with evident relief that Niebuhr bore the Bureau no ill will: "following his remarks, he did not seem greatly upset and said as far as he is concerned, the matter is a closed incident."

Niebuhr never did learn that MacLeish had been less than forthright about the imbroglio. He was decidedly uninterested in pursuing the case either in private or in public. Given his insistent manner on other vital issues his silence is surprising. In June the *Nation* reported that "some two hundred liberals have been dismissed from government jobs for such crimes as supporting the Loyalist government in the Spanish Civil War, advocating collective security, or criticizing the Dies Committee." It would have been fitting to put his substantial prestige on the line for them and against the government snoopers. Perhaps he figured that Freda Kirchwey was already taking care of Dies and the FBI in her frequent editorials. No doubt too he hesitated to jeopardize his ties to Frankfurter, MacLeish, and other powerful friends who would look askance at public crusades when their private influence was always available.

But some of his reticence has to be attributed to the deep-seated emotion

he had expressed twenty-four years earlier after America entered the Great
War: as a German-American he felt that "a new nation has a right to be
pretty sensitive about its unity." With America once again squared off
against his ancestral homeland, he would not be the one to challenge official
efforts, however perverse or inept, to root out the disloyal. Indeed, his first
contribution to the *Nation* after Pearl Harbor stressed the "greater measure
of coercion" required during a national emergency. Liberty was only one
principle of democracy; the other was unity. Liberals ought not to be troubled by temporary infringements on "the freedom of organizations to spread
subversive propaganda," or by community drives "to eliminate recalcitrant
and even traitorous elements." Roger Baldwin, director of the American
Civil Liberties Union, rightly complained that Niebuhr was much more
solicitous of unity than liberty. He might have balanced his concern for
community preservation with a strong warning against the danger of war
frenzy—as Francis Biddle himself did after the declaration of war. Neither
Niebuhr nor Baldwin were privy to the supreme irony that the FBI launched
its nationwide investigation of Niebuhr during the same week that his article
defending greater coercion hit the newsstands.[13]

V

Pearl Harbor put an abrupt and shocking end to the interventionist–isolationist debate. Nearly three thousand sailors were dead and the nation was
nearly unanimous in joining the Allies. It was not until six months later
that the Nazis began to suffer the reverses that gave the Allies assurance of
ultimate victory in Europe. But from the very start of American involvement Niebuhr was preoccupied with imagining the peace that would follow
victory. His first foray into postwar planning addressed the fate of the Jews,
whose plight had been for him one of the key arguments for intervention.
"Jews After the War" offered *Nation* readers—many of them anti-Zionist
Jews like contributing editor I. F. Stone—an eloquent statement of the
Zionist case: the Jews had rights not just as individuals, but as a people,
and they deserved not just a homeland, but a homeland in Palestine. Niebuhr
had come a long way in two decades. As a thirty-year-old Detroit pastor
in 1923 he was still in favor of converting Jews to Christianity, and blamed
the tiny number of converts on both "the unchristlike attitude of Christians"
and "Jewish bigotry." By 1926 he was ready to jettison missionizing altogether: liberal Jews like Rabbi Stephen Wise were speaking appreciatively
of Jesus, and Christians themselves needed the leaven of pure Hebraism to
counteract the Hellenism to which they were prone. After his move to New
York in 1928 he was drawn to Zionist currents of thought, though Jewish
leader Judah Magnes's commitment to a binational Palestine gave him pause.
Niebuhr's "personal pacifistic bias in favor of an end which can be carried
out without the use of coercion" inclined him toward Magnes. "Yet the
ideal of a political homeland for the Jews is so intriguing that I am almost
willing to sacrifice my convictions for the sake of it." By the early thirties
he had made the ethical leap to coercion, and grasped that Hitler was bent

•

on the cultural annihilation of the Jews. From that time on he was a firm, though sometimes qualified, backer of the Zionist cause.[14]

The American Palestine Committee, a Zionist support group, reprinted tens of thousands of copies of "Jews After the War," and by April Niebuhr had over two hundred invitations to speak to Jewish groups around the country. Felix Frankfurter and Isaiah Berlin, both European-born Jews, were delighted when they read advance copies. "Too many liberals, as you indicate," Frankfurter wrote, "are still enslaved by their romantic illusions, and cannot face your clean, surgeon-like exposition of reality. I find your essays as refreshing as cooling spring water to a parched throat." Berlin also found the articles scintillating and a timely corrective to the studied indifference of well-known commentators like Walter Lippmann. Niebuhr had in fact put his finger on a weak spot in the dominant liberal faith; liberals instinctively assumed that rights were possessed only by individuals, not collectivities. He had tried to make the same point in "The Limits to Liberty" by arguing that the community had a right to unity that counterbalanced the individual's right to liberty. But there he badly confused matters by ignoring the relationship between individual and community and by equating the latter with "order." Real unity depended on the interaction of free individuals; any infringement on liberty of expression, even if required by an emergency, was itself an attack on community, not simply a defense of it. It might be necessary to circumscribe both liberty and community during wartime, but restrictive measures imposed by the state were scarcely manifestations of community rights.

In "Jews After the War" he was on firmer ground. Liberals characteristically assumed, he asserted, that the Jewish problem was solved when Jews were guaranteed their rights as individual citizens. But there were collective rights too, such as the right of a people to exist and cultivate its unique identity. Perhaps it was his own origin in a minority cultural group that prepared him to reject a consistent cosmopolitan individualism—even though he had long before disavowed German-American ethnic consciousness and had in fact combated it tooth and nail alongside most other young German-Americans of his generation. Whatever his preparation, it was only after he had broken with Marxian socialism—an internationalist faith with no place for ethnic or national particularism—that he could come to see the Jewish problem as a national problem. It was a sign of his intellectual honesty that in "Jews After the War" he made plain that justice for the Jewish nation meant injustice for the Arab peoples. The west might try to sweeten the deal for the Arabs, but "it is absurd to expect any people to regard the restriction of their sovereignty over a traditional possession as 'just' no matter how many other benefits accrue from that abridgement."[15]

Creating a Jewish homeland would require the forthright exercise of American and British power: "The Anglo-Saxon hegemony that is bound to exist in the event of an Axis defeat will be in a position to see to it that Palestine is set aside for the Jews." Justice for the Jews depended on what Niebuhr soon began calling "imperialistic realism," the determination of the major Allied powers to assume responsibility for the reorganization of the world. Superior power bestowed greater responsibility; the victors alone could enact the peace. American and British "idealists" erred in supposing

•

that the moral course was to surrender excess power, to seek equal participation by all nations in a world government. Yet "balance-of-power realists" were also wrong in mocking the whole notion of international
organization and preaching a perpetual standoff between power blocks. As
he did in theology, Niebuhr fought a two-front war against those he termed
sentimentalists and cynics: his projected middle ground drew from both
the cynics' grasp of power relations and the sentimentalists' dream of equality and fellowship. The Soviets, Americans, and British would share world
leadership. The Soviets' role was pivotal. Their job was to prevent the
Anglo-Saxon powers from gloating in their supposed virtue and imposing
a purely Lucean imperialism, a free-enterprise capitalism, on the rest of the
world. The task of the Americans and English was to keep Soviets from
trying to dominate the European continent. But a "super-imperialism" of
the three great powers was not enough. Rooseveltian realism needed a
strong dose of Wilsonian idealism: the "voice and power" of the small
countries had to be brought into the councils of the Allied nations. Niebuhr's
middle ground was unstable, a roving vantage point from which he could
alternately chastise realists and idealists, his abstract antagonists.[16]

Once the United States had entered the war and begun the long mobilization of men and materiel, Niebuhr could take time out from his journalism and finish volume two of The Nature and Destiny of Man. He refused
all speaking engagements from May to September, 1942. He was so immersed in the book by mid-June, he informed Freda Kirchwey, that he had
"sidetracked everything else." Everything, that is, except the question of
whether to accept James Conant's recent offer of a university professorship
at Harvard. This was no ordinary offer, of which Niebuhr had received
many over the years—most recently a personal invitation from Robert G.
Sproul of the University of California to come to Berkeley. Conant, president of Harvard and a fellow member of William Allen White's Committee
to Defend America in 1940, wanted to appoint Niebuhr to a chair outside
of any department—and outside the scrutiny of any departmental hiring
committee. Conant liked Niebuhr's brand of religion: heavy on the preaching, topical, politically informed, intellectually vigorous, if not professionally polished. A regular appointment in either the Unitarian-leaning Divinity
School or the philosophy department, dominated by symbolic logicians
now that William Ernest Hocking and Ralph Barton Perry were approaching retirement, was out of the question. Niebuhr thought it would be a
challenge to see what he could do on such a "great campus," as he put it
to Scarlett. But his close friend Arnold Wolfers, Swiss émigré political
scientist at Yale, thought the faculty's resentment at his irregular position
and astronomical salary would undermine him. "I may be too old to take
the risk," he added to Scarlett. "At least Ursula thinks that's what is the
matter with me for she is more inclined to the job than I am." The salary
hike itself did not interest him. Although he was still putting Walter's
daughter through private school, he did not feel pressed financially. "He
[Walter] will probably be on my hands again," he predicted, "but never to
the amount of the past. I am able now to give most of my fees away. My
salary is quite sufficient for my family and my mother." Maximizing his
marketplace reward held no appeal.

•

His brother Richard urged him to go to Harvard for intellectual reasons. "You've fought the Deweyites etc. a long time," he wrote. "You'll probably get more new ideas, develop your thought more and on new subjects if you go to Harvard. . . . Besides, the challenge of a new situation is good for us at our age. I have about made up my mind that if I have a chance to change—what I have in view is not likely to materialize for a few years— I will do so. Because the groove gets too smooth after one has been in it for a dozen years." Henry Sloane Coffin naturally offered a contrary view: "It would be fatal for the seminary to lose you now." Coffin was an accomplished arm-twister. After assuring Niebuhr of still greater eminence in the religious world if he stayed put, he added the news that "the seminary is at present in a favorable financial position. If more assistance is needed in the field of Christian ethics, it ought to be provided." Coffin did come through with at least one major improvement in Christian ethics and systematic theology: the hiring for the fall of 1943 (as Harry Ward's successor) of Niebuhr's longtime friend and associate John Bennett, brought in from Berkeley's Pacific School of Religion. Bennett's appointment came independently, but it may have helped Niebuhr make up his mind.

When he finally decided in February, 1943—nine months after the offer— to turn Conant down, it was not because of potential animosity in the Harvard faculty. It was a choice of the familiar over the unpredictable. Ursula's explanation was right: he did feel too old, too set in his ways as a preacher, teacher, and thinker. He was not as adventurous intellectually as Richard; he wanted the security, as he put it to Scarlett, of the seminary's "specifically Christian foundation." At Harvard "one has to a certain extent the position of being a slightly queer exponent of the Christian faith among (to use Schleiermacher's phrase) 'its cultured despisers.' " Niebuhr had always been willing to address the cultured despisers, but he was not comfortable about living with them. He had never felt he had as much to learn from them as they did from him. And at age fifty, in the midst of war, he was not inclined to chart new paths.[17]

VI

It had taken even longer to make the Harvard decision than it had to finish volume two of *The Nature and Destiny of Man*, which Scribners released in January, 1943. *Human Destiny* recapitulated the central claims of *Human Nature*: the self was divided against itself, the cardinal human flaw was not finitude but sin, not ignorance but pretension. Yet it went well beyond volume one by elaborating on the historical framework of selfhood. God's self-disclosure in Christ, Niebuhr argued, gave new meaning to history. The essence of that self-disclosure was the Atonement, Christ's suffering love that led inexorably to the Cross. Perfect love must be suffering love, not triumphant love, when it enters history. God's revelation gives history new meaning, but does not bring it to fulfillment. Christ does not so much transform human existence as inject a new tension into it: love now transcends law but remains bound by the limits of human nature. God's grace is empowering, infusing culture and personality with new potential. Yet it

Ursula, Reinhold, and Christopher, c. Christmas, 1934.

With Christopher at Heath, c. 1940.

With Christopher and Elisabeth in Manhattan, c. 1944.

The Union Theological Seminary professor, 1930s.

*At Oxford Conference, 1937: J. H. Oldham,
William Temple, W. A. Visser t'Hooft, Niebuhr.*

March 8, 1948.

With John Foster Dulles and other members of the American delegation to the world Christian conference in Cambridge, England, 1946.

With Senators Hubert Humphrey and Herbert Lehman at ADA Roosevelt Day dinner, 1950.

As circus master in a summer skit at Heath, late 1940s.

Lecturing at Union Seminary, late 1940s.

H. Richard in Yale Divinity School chapel, 1955.

H. Richard in his Yale office, c. 1960.

Reinhold with Will Scarlett.

In retirement, early 1960s.

is also negative, condemning the swelling satisfaction that men take in their own achievements. And it is ultimately forgiving, showing men mercy for their transgressions. Human history is so significant, in the Christian view, that God himself takes flesh in it. But the Incarnation is paradoxical: God is present but absent. He remains hidden despite his intervention. Human history sits poised in the interim between First and Second Comings, between the revelation of meaning and the realization of it. In that charged atmosphere Christians attempt to embody Christ's love while also combatting their own temptation to self-righteousness.

Human Destiny was an elegantly written and beautifully structured volume. Henry Sloane Coffin, Howard Chandler Robbins, and Ursula Niebuhr had labored over its language. Its overall theme of historical selfhood was signaled in the organization of the book itself. It began with an initial distinction between those cultures where no Christ—no disclosure of transcendent meaning—is expected, and those where a Christ is expected. Then it moved chronologically through treatments of Jesus, Paul, Augustine, the Catholic "synthesis," the Renaissance, and the Reformation. Niebuhr was much fairer toward the Renaissance than he had been in volume one: its love of reason, its enthrallment with the world, was no longer to be derided as a superficial alternative to the wisdom of the Reformation. "Reformation insights," he noted, "must be related to the whole range of human experience more 'dialectically' than the Reformation succeeded in doing"—or than *Human Nature* succeeded in doing. Both "the 'yes' and 'no' of its dialectical affirmations" had to be held in tension. *Human Destiny* was a skillful balancing act, a nuanced assertion

> that the Christian is "justus et peccator," "both sinner and righteous"; that history fulfills and negates the Kingdom of God; that grace is continuous with, and in contradiction to, nature; that Christ is what we ought to be and also what we cannot be; that the power of God is in us and that the power of God is against us in judgement and mercy. . . . There is no area of life where "grace" does not impinge. . . . There are on the other hand no areas or experiences where historical insecurity and anxiety are completely transcended, except in principle.

Indeed, *Human Destiny* strived so hard for balance that it usually lacked the drama of Niebuhrian advocacy. No strident posturing, no dismissive oversimplification, but also no rumbling movement, no heated passion. It was respectable and decorous, a rhetorical design that sapped some of the vigor from his prose. The book exuded a calm deliberation typical of academic writing, but the equanimity tended to work against Niebuhr's message that the self was anxious, condemned to disappointment in its quest for historical security. The detached tone may have been an effort to accommodate the academic reviewers who had disparaged the aggressiveness of *Human Nature*. Perhaps too it was the product of repetition: Niebuhr had been restating these ideas for many years and may have had trouble mustering the dynamism of first discovery.

Yet there is no question that *Human Destiny* went further than *Human Nature* in probing the interpretation of "nature" and "grace" in individual and social existence. The penultimate chapter on "The Kingdom of God

•

and the Struggle for Justice" was typical of the rest of the book in the depth of its "dialectical affirmations." Now love was not just a transcendent ideal that stood as a critical lever by which to measure the relative attainments of human justice. Nor was love a possibility for individuals in their personal relations and an impossibility for them in their group relations. Justice and love interpenetrated, as did individuals and community. "Community is an individual as well as a social necessity; for the individual can realize himself only in intimate and organic relation with his fellowmen. Love is therefore the primary law of his nature, and brotherhood the fundamental requirement of his social existence." Love as "the pinnacle of the moral ideal stands both inside and beyond history: inside insofar as love may elicit a reciprocal response and change the character of human relations; and beyond history insofar as love cannot require a mutual response without losing its character of disinterestedness." The transcendent Word was made flesh.

In a radical departure from the perspective of *Moral Man*, he argued that human communities in some respects elevated disinterested love to higher levels than individuals could. The slow growth of custom and law made possible a growth of human brotherhood "without the interposition of superior coercive force." Of course the sense of social obligation and cooperation never completely displaced the spirit of egoistic interest, which always threatened to undo the achievements of love-informed justice. But collectivities could generate communal fellowship. The mobilization of the Anglo-Saxon democracies against Hitler prepared Niebuhr to perceive a heightened ethical potential for human groups. *Human Destiny* revalued not only liberal Protestant theology, but also liberal political theory, in which democracy promoted community even as it protected the individual against the false collectivism of fanatical political faiths. Liberal theory was for Niebuhr no longer an individualist ideology for camouflaging the interests of the bourgeoisie, but a realistic perspective that appreciated the potential for and limits upon human justice.

Most of Niebuhr's theological critics—Haroutunian, Bennett, Calhoun, and others—were impressed and reassured. The historical sections, said Calhoun, were much more discriminating than those in volume one. He was pleased to see the Renaissance rescued from the merciless pounding it suffered in the previous book. Bennett like Calhoun was gratified to witness an explicit return to liberalism, a firm rejection of the "errors of Luther and Calvin, Barth and Brunner." Niebuhr was glad to hear it, but surprised that anyone should ever have lumped him with "the continental neo-orthodox theologians."

> I have never thought of myself in their category. I think when it comes to the crux I belong to the liberal tradition more than to theirs. Whenever I read them or argue with them, Brunner for instance, I always feel that they are trying to fit life into a dogmatic mold and that they have hard and fast Biblical presuppositions which I do not share. Furthermore their indifference to and lack of understanding of political and social problems has always made them foreigners to me.

Haroutunian, no liberal, was also supportive. Volume two was "a landmark in the history of Christian thought" because it managed a "more subtle and complex" analysis of the relationship between justification and sanctification than did "traditional theologies, orthodox or liberal." Niebuhr managed, that is, to consider man simultaneously as a sinner in need of God's saving grace and as one already infused with that grace despite his sin. He captured the tension of human existence as it was judged and yet redeemed.

In the theological world volume two boosted Niebuhr's stature. Sophisticated readers found it an intellectual tour de force. The less sophisticated reveled in the new stress on Jesus himself, the incarnate Word. Volume one had forty-four Old Testament citations, thirty-three from Paul's letters, but only eight from the Synoptic Gospels. Volume two had thirty-four from the Old Testament, forty-nine from Paul, and thirty-five from Matthew, Mark, and Luke. But *The Nature and Destiny of Man* was scarcely a "popular" work and was no hit in the churches themselves—partly because it was too difficult, partly because there was, as Bennett complained, no doctrine of the church in it. In addition, for all its attention to Christ crucified and risen, the book offered only a very abstract Incarnation and scant assurance of the eternal life most believers yearned for. Niebuhr did not want to give "comfort to literalists," as he wrote to Norman Kemp-Smith, a Scot who had heard the Giffords. "I have not the slightest interest in the empty tomb or physical resurrection."

He could not reassure the ordinary believer about eternal salvation because, as he put it to Waldo Frank in 1938, "I do not believe in individual immortality." But he still considered the Christian doctrine of the Resurrection a vast improvement on the mystical doctrines that appealed to Frank— doctrines that in Niebuhr's view conceived of salvation as an escape from history or a merging into the one great Spirit. The wisdom of the Resurrection, as he explained to Kemp-Smith, was "the idea that the fulfillment of life does not mean the negation and destruction of historical reality (which is a unity of body-soul, freedom-necessity, time-eternity) but the completion of this unity." Perhaps there was some kind of life after death, Niebuhr thought, but since that life was totally beyond our experience, he would not count on it. He would, however, take pains to combat views of the afterlife that compromised worldly responsibility. "The body, the individuality, the particular," he told Frank, "is always the symbol of the meaningfulness of history as against the mystic idea of its meaninglessness." Frank, who like Ursula and Henry Coffin had worked over the manuscript to improve the style, continued to lament Niebuhr's blanket rejection of mysticism.[18]

The secular response to *The Nature and Destiny of Man* was a good deal more mixed than the religious one. Naturally friends like Mumford and John Herman Randall, Jr., professor of philosophy at Columbia, were delighted, even if critical in some particulars. Mumford, then at work on his *Condition of Man*, hailed Niebuhr and compared the two volumes to Aquinas's *Summa Theologica*. Randall lauded Niebuhr's dual vision of man's greatness and sinfulness, quarreling only with his rejection of "naturalism"; Niebuhr, he shrewdly noted, was a relativist and naturalist despite the God-

•

talk. John Dewey and his friends Sidney Hook and James T. Farrell did not read the volumes with the same pleasure. Niebuhr in their eyes was a prime culprit in "the new failure of nerve," as Hook put it. He was running to religion for reassurance when the world crisis demanded a thoughtful application of human reason, the time-tested tool of science. "A disgusting spectacle," remarked the uninhibited Farrell of volume one. "His fiddling around with Christianity is abhorrent and repellent." Dewey did not mention him by name in his 1943 attack on the "anti-naturalists," but had him plainly in mind. As he put it in a letter four years later, both Niebuhr and Kierkegaard had "completely lost faith in traditional statements of Christianity, haven't got any modern substitute and so are making up, off the bat, something which supplies to them the gist of Christianity." Niebuhr's foes like his friends considered *The Nature and Destiny of Man* a pivotal work that signaled a new direction in American intellectual life.

Dewey and Hook badly misconstrued the character of Niebuhr's thought, partly because they attributed to him the antirationalist, antinaturalist views of his close friends Frank and Mumford. In fact Niebuhr's stance was quite distinct from his friends', despite their common disdain for Dewey and all his works. When Frank and Mumford rejected naturalism and any reliance on Enlightenment reason, they did so in the name of a romantic faith in man's capacity to transform himself. They disliked "mechanical" reason and "naturalistic" determinism because these undermined the "organic" spirit that permitted human beings to transcend their limits. As Mumford concluded his *Condition of Man*, "The first step is a personal one: a change in direction of interest towards the person. Without that change, no great betterment will take place in the social order. Once that change begins, everything is possible." Mumford's personalism harked back to the old liberal Protestant veneration for personality—a devotion that Niebuhr had surrendered when faced with the social crisis of the early 1930s and his brother's intellectual assault on the notion of a sincere, solid self. Mumford and Frank actually shared with Dewey and Hook a certain confidence in human capacities that Niebuhr lacked. All four of them were disposed to view the future as a realm of limitless opportunity, and to conceive the self as a potent force in the renewal of society. Mumford and Frank might disparage the scientific reason that Dewey and Hook lauded, but that disagreement masked a deeper accord on the natural capacity of human beings to remake themselves and their world.[19]

Niebuhr by contrast was overwhelmed by the uncertainties of history, the unpredictability of the future, the fragility of the self. Like Freud he was attuned to the severe conflicts that raged within as well as outside the individual. His pivotal contribution to the intellectual life of the forties was the somber assertion of built-in limits to human existence. The "responsible" self struggled for justice but did not expect fulfillment; his commitments were qualified by skepticism about the delusions to which all individuals and groups were prone; human history was not an arena for perfecting communal fellowship. Responsibility connoted for Niebuhr a simultaneous engagement and retrenchment, a giving of commitment and a holding back, a willingness to act but only within the tragic boundaries of human life. Within those limits he was as devoted to instrumental reason, to the ap-

•

plication of intelligence to social affairs, as Hook or Dewey—and as sensitive to the nonrational passions, vitalities, and traditions that infused human culture as Frank and Mumford. But in his strenuous insistence on man's tangled destiny—on the unbridgeable gap between man's dreams and his deeds—he shared much more with thinkers such as Lionel Trilling, Richard Wright, and Dwight Macdonald than he did with either Frank, Mumford, Dewey, or Hook.

His Sisyphean perspective had points of contact with all of them, yet finally it was a unique and paradoxical mix: he was a religious modernist devoted to Biblical symbols; a political democrat infatuated with Burkean traditionalism; a skeptical relativist committed like William James to the life of passionate belief and moral struggle. He was a thoroughgoing naturalist despite his contempt for what he called "naturalism": the denial of human "spirit," the reduction of human nature to its psychic or physiological impulses. He had equal contempt for religious supernaturalism, which he thought voided man's native capacities and expunged man's own responsibility for his fate. His stance was naturalistic in the sense that his ultimate appeal in both politics and theology was always to the observed facts of human experience. His starting point was the community of concrete human beings confronted by the paradoxically free yet finite character of their nature.

VII

With the Giffords at last published and behind him, Niebuhr jumped at the chance to get closer to the war. John Baillie and William Temple, now archbishop of Canterbury, invited him to speak in Scotland and England, and the Office of War Information, when informed of his trip, added a request that he address the British public and the Allied troops on war aims. The Rockefeller Foundation provided financing, the government provided official status as a consultant (a fact duly noted in his FBI file), and he flew off in a bomber in the spring of 1943, for a stay of about ten weeks. The British people, as usual, he found resilient, organically connected to their past, and undeluded by abstract political theories: a nation of step-by-step pragmatists. He had a strong stake in locating wisdom and moderation among the British, for peace in the postwar era depended in his view on a mature and stable broker between two adolescent and unpredictable giants, the Americans and Russians.

For Niebuhr, Archbishop Temple himself was both an individual embodiment of wisdom and a revelation of the collective British genius. Only the British could have had the foresight to select a pro-labor, socially sensitive cleric as leader of their state church. Temple had the personal charisma that allowed him—like Niebuhr's first Anglican model, Bishop Williams of Detroit—to use his stately office while transcending it. Niebuhr may have doubted Temple's perceptiveness during the class struggles of the thirties, but he lauded his knack for symbolizing the unity of the nation in wartime. The British were so enlightened that even their soldiers in camp engaged in critical, open discussion of international affairs. After cursory

•

observation Niebuhr was confident in his global judgment that American soldiers by contrast consumed only Hollywood pabulum. They suffered from spiritual hollowness, he told Samuel Cavert of the Federal Council of Churches. The American War Department, and one wealthy supporter of *Christianity and Crisis*, were not pleased with his findings; General Osborn invited him to Washington to discuss them, but Niebuhr stood by his story.[20]

He flew home on a Pan American clipper in July and told a New York *Times* reporter at LaGuardia Airport about "the frictionless harmony" that united "people of all classes" in Britain, even in a period of strict rationing. He found no such unity in America: he was back in the real world of imperfection after many weeks of organic community. But the disjunction prompted him to redouble his political efforts, not to moan from the sidelines. He picked up his editorial chores and his duties as head of the UDA and the American Friends of German Freedom, and on top of all that became active in the state campaign of the American Labor Party. Earlier he had kept his distance from the Party because of its zeal for FDR and its heavily trade-union makeup. Now those objections faded, since he himself was touting FDR for a fourth term and since close friends from the UDA—George Counts, John Childs, and others—controlled the state branch of the Party organization.

In August he was appointed campaign manager for UDA member Pearl Willen, a former social worker and ALP candidate for city council. Willen managed to get the endorsement of the New York *Times,* but fell short of victory because the city branch of the ALP—controlled by Sidney Hillman, the head of the Amalgamated Clothing Workers—ran its own candidate. The city-state split in the Party grew steadily worse after the election, and in March, 1944, the "right-wing" state group seceded after being trounced in the Party primary. Counts, the state chairman, Alex Rose, the state secretary, Childs, A. Philip Randolph, Pearl Willen, and others accused Hillman's group of kowtowing to the Communists and founded a party of their own, the Liberals. Niebuhr hesitated before entering the new Liberal Party. He still approved of Hillman's National Political Action Committee—a broadly based progressive, pro-labor group—and wanted to maintain membership in it. When he was sure at midsummer that he could belong to both bodies simultaneously, he joined the Liberal Party and was quickly elected vice-chairman.[21]

While intensifying his political activities in 1943 and 1944, he also emerged as a regular on the radio talk-show circuit. George Denny's "Town Meeting of the Air" and William Benton's "University of Chicago Round Table" both found him indispensable because he offered a riveting blend of lofty pronouncement and caustic one-liner. During a 1942 appearance on "Town Meeting," an isolationist questioner in the Chautauqua, New York, amphitheater confronted him with the fact that 40 percent of America's ministers were still "not sure that we ought to participate in this war." Without missing a beat Niebuhr shot back with "Thank God for the laymen" and the audience erupted in laughter and applause. After his return from England in 1943 he debated Senator Taft and Sidney Hook on postwar policy. The stolid senator found himself left out as Niebuhr and Hook clawed each other amiably. Niebuhr pushed his notion of big-power responsibility balanced by small-power rights, which led Hook to borrow Niebuhr's favorite charge against the Deweyites and accuse him of utopianism. Niebuhr's big-power management would rapidly deteriorate into a new tyranny of nonprogressive states and provoke the death of democracy in Europe. "Does Sidney Hook," retorted Niebuhr, "want to leave the world in chaos until he can get the kind of order that he and I both desire?" and Hook was forced to parry with "That's not the only alternative" as he was drowned out by laughter.[22]

If Niebuhr was not quite a household word by 1944, he was at the very least an obvious presence in New York politics, a growing force in intellectual debate, and a surging sensation on college campuses across the country. Prestigious lectureships proliferated—Harvard's Dudleian lecture, Stanford's West lectures, Chicago's White lectures, Yale's Beecher lectures—though he had no time to prepare them. They were all quick spin-offs from *The Nature and Destiny of Man*, including the West lectures—delivered in January, 1944, reworked over the summer, and published at Christmas under the title *The Children of Light and the Children of Darkness*. The book flowed out of volume two, chapter nine, "The Kingdom of God and the Struggle for Justice." The Christian understanding of man as both sinner and image of God led in Niebuhr's view to the inescapable conclusion that "democracy" was a "perennially valuable" form of polity. As he put it in his most famous formulation: "Man's capacity for justice makes democracy possible; but man's inclination to injustice makes democracy necessary." Bourgeois culture had created democratic polity, but that culture itself had been built by "foolish children of light" who "underestimated the power of self-interest, both individual and collective, in modern society." To survive, democracy required a new "religious culture" that was realistic about power yet also humbly aware of the "fragmentary and broken character of all historic achievements." The "children of darkness"—the morally cynical Fascists and Stalinists—had been "wiser in their generation" (Luke 16:8) about the brutal realities of human existence than the "children of light"; it was time for the innocent to appropriate the wisdom of the shrewd without succumbing to their "malice."

The redeeming virtue of democracy, as Niebuhr had been urging since 1941, was its "openness." A democracy was an "open society," he argued in one of his first *Christianity and Crisis* pieces, because it "permits and even encourages criticism of itself in the light of universal standards." "Many of us," he wrote in the *New Leader* in the summer of 1941, "have become more devoted to democracy as a system of government than we once were," because "democratic checks and counterchecks are the best method of neutralizing special interests and of arriving at the truth by allowing various corruptions of the truth to destroy each other." Democracy provided the best chance to "eliminate ideology from culture" and to overthrow "tyranny, whether rooted in priestly, military, economic, or political power." He granted that inequalities of power were inevitable, but found them untroubling. "There is such a constant shift in the oligarchy, both in the political and economic sphere, through pressure from below," he observed in 1943, "that the oligarchy is kept fluid. . . . Furthermore, such justice as

•

a democracy has is achieved not only by pressure from below but by tension between various oligarchies." *The Children of Light* linked his by then usual defense of democracy to his doctrine of human nature and destiny. Democratic checks and counterchecks impeded the growth of disproportionate power that every group sought for itself; the free marketplace of ideas discouraged the self-righteous pretension to which every person was prone. Democracy built on men's virtues while protecting against their vices.

It was a reassuring vision for a time of liberal rebuilding. The despair of 1940 had given way to the resurgent if still chastened hope of 1944. The UDA, the Liberal Party, the National Citizens' Political Action Committee of the CIO, and the Henry Wallace Democrats were organizing for a renewal of the New Deal. *The Children of Light* was designed as a rationale for that resurgence: it was "about the UDA" in a general sense, Niebuhr told an interviewer years later. The book elevated gradualist experimentation and piecemeal reform to the level of a basic axiom. "The property issue" was no longer a "class" issue to be solved by confronting the bourgeoisie with demands for socializing large-scale industry; it was a dilemma that could be handled only by "continuous debate . . . between opposing factions." The "logic of history" might still support socialization, but that program always presented "some peril of compounding economic and political power." Therefore "a wise community will walk warily and test the effect of each new adventure before further adventures." The main thing was to preserve "a balance of forces" and prevent an "undue centralization of power." *The Children of Light* thus retraced much of the ground covered by *Moral Man* and offered a profoundly different conclusion. The struggle for justice was necessary but always a threat to social equilibrium. To reverse his portentous proclamation of 1931: those who feared too little the potency of religiously created energy were consigned to catastrophe by the multitude of their illusions. The sober Christian view of man that Richard had thrust on him after *Moral Man* implied a go-slow politics of "continuous adjustment"— precisely the pragmatic solution proposed by Richard in his pro-FDR letter of 1936. The New Deal notion of countervailing powers—business, labor, government, consumer—permitted a constant renegotiation of the social balance without upsetting the overall consensus. "Democracy," Reinhold concluded, "is a method of finding proximate solutions for insoluble problems."[23]

Niebuhr's about-face between the early thirties and early forties is understandable when one considers that scores of leading intellectuals made the same move in response to the rise of fascism, the Spanish Civil War, the Nazi-Soviet pact, and Pearl Harbor. But what is still surprising about *The Children of Light* is that the author of *Moral Man*, even if older and wiser, could have become so complacent about democratic processes in advanced industrial society. Had the younger Niebuhr reviewed *The Children of Light* he would have scoffed at its confidence in justice through adjustment, its belief that the debates of the "open society" operated equally in the interests of all. He would have chastised the author for his unspoken assumption that knowledge and information circulated "freely" when a private press relied on advertising revenue and packaged the news for a mass audience. No doubt the younger Niebuhr's objections could be met

•

by a skilled New Deal apologist, but the older Niebuhr made no effort to meet them. Like most former radicals he no longer thought such objections were to be taken seriously—if indeed he thought about them at all. In that way even a democratic society of apparently total openness operated ideologically: its respected intellectuals as well as its ordinary citizens ignored or dismissed potential challenges to its preferred self-images. As the younger Niebuhr had insisted, reason was always the servant of interest in a social situation. Reason was shaped by interest in selecting some topics for attention, others for the dustbin.

The younger Niebuhr might also have raised a skeptical eyebrow at the creation in early 1944 of a Commission on the Freedom of the Press. Henry Luce, publisher of *Time, Life,* and *Fortune,* had given University of Chicago president Robert Hutchins $200,000 to study the state of the free press, and Hutchins gathered fifteen intellectual dignitaries to help him reflect. Niebuhr joined Jacques Maritain, Archibald MacLeish, Arthur Schlesinger, Sr., Robert Redfield, Charles Merriam, William Ernest Hocking, and others for a four-to-six-hour meeting every six weeks; each of the fifteen "commissioners" collected $300 per meeting. The commission dragged its work out for more than two years, and Luce was far from pleased with the result. Niebuhr was one who pushed for the final document's emphasis on the dangers of press concentration, a point that Luce found unappealing. But Niebuhr also pushed successfully, with Luce's concurrence, for the view that concentration was inevitable; only quasi-Jeffersonians like MacLeish imagined the clock could be turned back. Press oligarchies might gain undue power, but a forced decentralization would require an even more baleful rise of state power.

The only solution, as Niebuhr put it to Hutchins after lunching with Luce, was to put "a tremendous burden upon the conscience of those who control the press." The younger Niebuhr would have found scant solace in moral appeals to men of power. He might also have wondered about participating in the Luce-funded study in the first place. Even though Luce did not control the proceedings, he did control the final disposition of the report. After withholding it until certain changes were made, he published it as a supplement to *Fortune,* accompanied by a lengthy editorial. The editorial praised his own financial largesse and breadth of mind in granting the commissioners total "freedom," chided them for their ivory-tower ignorance of the ways of the world, and assured his readers that the press was cultivating the moral responsibility for which the commission called. Luce had invested $200,000 in a brilliant display of the concrete operation of the free market in ideas—a market that *The Children of Light* had praised but draped in pious abstraction.[24]

Niebuhr mailed the manuscript of *The Children of Light* to Scribners at the end of August, 1944, and then took a fall semester leave from the seminary to campaign for the Liberal Party and to raise funds for the UDA. The UDA newsletter hailed his exploits as he spoke to audiences of up to one thousand people in more than twenty cities. He also went on the public attack against Norman Thomas, again the Socialist candidate for President. Thomas had addressed an open letter to him in late summer "because you stand for—yes, and lead—many men and women [who] are now supporting

•

the Democratic ticket, although by conviction they are democratic social-ists." Niebuhr's response on behalf of the UDA was predictable: that Roo-sevelt for all his faults was no Thomas Dewey and one had to go for the lesser evil.

After the election he was based at the University of Chicago, where he delivered his Alexander White lectures, "Changing and Unchanging Elements in the Human Situation," on six successive Wednesday afternoons to a crowd of four hundred listeners. It was fitting that in the historic bastion of liberal Protestantism, and the present home of religious naturalist Henry Nelson Wieman, he affirmed his own reconciliation with the liberal tradition. He of course rejected any naturalistic philosophy that banished the notions of spirit, sin, or faith. He made a naturalistic critique of natu-ralism: it was insufficiently empirical, too bound by absolutist views about man as a rational being, too zealous in limiting the realm of truth to the scientifically verifiable. It ignored the drama of the moral life: freedom perverted by pride. "He is, in truth," wrote the *Christian Century*'s appre-ciative reporter, "a radical empiricist if there ever was one."[25]

Between lectures he crisscrossed the midwest in a typical Niebuhr stampede. He slept little and was in frequent pain from his mysterious "neuralgia of the colon." Deep X-ray treatments offered only temporary relief. He pushed on despite his body's repeated pleas for rest. His brother Richard's hospitalization for severe depression in October may have spurred him on all the more. Richard's breakdown took place as he turned fifty in September—the age at which Gustav had died in 1913. As his own birthday approached he was overwhelmed with feelings of unworthiness: Why should he be permitted to outlive his father? The contrast to his brother could not have been starker. Reinhold's fiftieth birthday in 1942 had been an occasion for celebration. It coincided with an honorary doctorate from Yale, the offer from Harvard, the acclaim over *The Nature and Destiny of Man*. Richard felt doubly unworthy, undeserving of life itself. He voluntarily entered a mental facility and remained for two months.

Richard's despairing passivity, like his brother's restless activism, had intellectual as well as psychological roots. For Reinhold the war was a battle to believe in, nazism a diabolical force to eradicate; human beings were makers of their own history within the inescapable limits of their nature and destiny. For Richard the war revealed the inscrutability of God's pur-pose, the futility of human striving to transform the world. God Himself acted in history; man's puny efforts to affect its course evoked divine com-passion. Richard rebuked those who, like Reinhold, tried to join Christian repentance and worldly assertiveness. They were "di-theists" who honored God in private and forgot about Him in public. Richard preached by contrast a "radical monotheism" based on Jesus' faith that God acted "in objective, natural, and historical events." Faith in that God required a life of humility, not a shaky balancing act between internal confession and external arro-gance. "For me," Richard wrote, "the inner world is suspect and God must be objective before he can be subjective." For most men the war was an occasion for choosing sides and justifying their own; for the Christian it was a crucifixion in which "the death of the guiltless" becomes "a call to repentance—not to sorrow but to spiritual revolution." In itself Richard's

•

vision was not despairing. But it implied a disengagement from the world that reinforced the psychic impasse he had reached in 1944. His own suffering deepened as he contemplated the suffering of the innocent in Europe and the Pacific.

Reinhold did not share his brother's preoccupation with the theological meaning of the war. He preferred to dwell on geopolitics. But he too ruminated on the apparent injustice that, as Jesus observed, the sun is made to shine on the evil and the good and the rain to descend on the just and unjust. Unlike Richard, however, he believed that the suffering of the innocent was not merely spiritually but also historically fruitful, if only in the long run. When Lewis Mumford's son Geddes was killed in the European theater in late 1944, Niebuhr offered condolences of deeply felt poetic force. He regretted that his participation in Mumford's grief would be "only momentary compared to the hours and years in which one's friend bears the sorrow of a young life snuffed out, so full of promise and goodness." He rejoiced with Mumford that Geddes "had gone through the trying years of adolescence and found so fine a source of inner serenity." His life "was complete, though remaining horribly incomplete." Niebuhr closed by reaffirming his paradoxical faith, a faith strongly informed by Richard's quietism but driven by an ultimate confidence in man's capacity to make his own history. The work of their own and future generations would help atone for the suffering and death of millions of innocents.

> You say that we will have to be very good to be worthy of the goodness of such young men. To me the deepest tragedy of life is the certainty that we will not be. Not that their sacrifice will prove finally [unavailing]. But the world will obviously pass through some pretty terrible decades and perhaps a century before these sacrifices will bear fruit.[26]

TEN

THE HEAVENS
SHALL
LAUGH

(1946–1952)

I

"The surprise bombings of Hiroshima and Nagasaki," wrote the twenty-two theologians of the Federal Council of Churches' special commission on the war, "are morally indefensible. . . . As the power that first used the atomic bomb under these circumstances, we have sinned grievously against the law of God and against the people of Japan." Niebuhr was a member of the commission, chaired by Robert Calhoun, and a signer of the document. But his own published responses to the bombings were far more equivocal. "Historic forces more powerful than any human decision" may have been at play: since the Germans were at work on the bomb during the war, we had to develop it too; once built it was bound to be used if it would shorten the war. No solemn confession about transgressing the laws of God, no ink wasted on the sufferings of the victims or the infamy of the perpetrators. An insistence only upon the "moral advantage" the United States would have gained in first demonstrating the power of the bomb "without the wholesale loss of life." Dropping the bomb without warning made repentance difficult "for a vanquished foe who feels that he was defeated by the use of an illegitimate form of destructiveness."

When James B. Conant, a leading national defense policymaker during the war, challenged him to reconcile his signature of the Federal Council document with the pragmatism of his own *Children of Light,* Niebuhr was penitent. The report did not "make sufficiently clear what was the conviction of most of us—that the eventual use of the bomb for the shortening of the war would have been justified. I myself consistently took the position that failing in achieving a Japanese surrender, the bomb would have had to

•

be used to save the lives of thousands of American soldiers who would otherwise have perished on the beaches of Japan." Niebuhr, like Conant and other policymakers, took for granted that only unconditional surrender was acceptable. That perceived necessity made the bomb the weapon of choice. It was the quintessential revelation of "how much evil we must do in order to do good," of how much guilt accrues even to those who have "defeated tyranny."

The bomb was also a prime sign of the political and cultural irony of the mid-twentieth century. The science in which liberal rationalists put their faith had disclosed its Faustian explosiveness. The quest for the mastery of nature had climaxed in fear and trembling. It was one more proof that the human enterprise was laced with paradox: man's progress toward greatness was a simultaneous march toward weakness. Americans were now swelling with righteousness at the victory, fingering the Germans and Japanese for their treachery. But guilt and responsibility were shared. So was the capacity to forgive. "Be ye angry," Niebuhr preached following Saint Paul, "but let not the sun go down upon your wrath." After the war one of his favorite sermon texts came from the Psalmist: "He that sitteth in the heavens shall laugh, the Lord shall hold them in derision." God condemned man's hubris with a laughter that combined mocking derision and a forgiving smile. Human beings were haughty, but not irredeemable; despite their foolishness and pride they were worthy of divine love. Many of Niebuhr's liberal friends liked the somber tones and tempered hopes, but wondered with Harvard historian Arthur Schlesinger, Jr., if the part about God and sin was really necessary. To Niebuhr the theology and politics stood or fell together: it took a transcendent Judge, in whose eyes human beings were pretentious but precious, to prompt men to genuine contrition. Without prophetic judgment democratic politics like Communist politics veered toward self-satisfaction and hypocrisy.[1]

Niebuhr had political as well as religious grounds for feeling moderately hopeful despite the horror of Hiroshima. A month before the bomb was dropped the British Labour Party scored a stunning victory in parliamentary elections. It was "the most heartening single event since the beginning of the war." Not only would the English now achieve new levels of social justice at home and in the Empire; their example would bolster American liberalism, momentarily in disarray after Roosevelt's death. The English knew that respect for living traditions was compatible with "a more so-cialized society." They offered hope that "our conservative classes," with their "most curious nostalgia for the past of 'free enterprise,'" could be checked. In addition, a Labour Britain would help spark a real accord be-tween Russia and the west. Niebuhr no longer imagined that Britain pos-sessed the actual power to play the role of broker among the Big Three. But the Labour Party could articulate the middle-ground program of prag-matic socialization—the "Third Force"—between capitalism and commu-nism. It could teach the two ideological blunderers to trust each other—the minimum condition for postwar peace. Niebuhr flew to Britain at every opportunity during the late forties. It was his political home: he needed periodic infusions of British wisdom. His misty-eyed celebration of England did not make him a consistently reliable observer of the British scene. But it had the salutary effect of inoculating him against the uncritical celebration of American virtue that became increasingly common in the late forties and fifties.

On rare occasions Niebuhr did fault the British. The Labour government's performance on Palestine aped that of the Tories: bowing down to Arab "chieftains." A quarter of a million Jews were marooned in European camps for displaced persons and meanwhile the Jewish Agency's request for the admission of 100,000 to Palestine was languishing on Prime Minister Attlee's desk. Instead of granting permission he appointed a commission. The Anglo-American Committee of Inquiry heard testimony in Washington, Egypt, Palestine, and Europe as the government tried to buy time. When the committee came to Washington in mid-January, 1946, Niebuhr arrived uninvited to read a statement on behalf of the Christian Council on Palestine (and at the private urging of Rabbi Stephen Wise). He waited all day and was finally allowed to speak when an invited anti-Zionist witness— his boss Henry Sloane Coffin—failed to show up. His statement in vigorous support of "a Palestinian state with a Jewish majority" and against a "binational state" was a brilliant exposition of Zionist theory, in the view of one committee member, Labour Member of Parliament R. H. S. Crossman. A Zionist lawyer called the statement "the finest presentation of the Zionist case I have ever heard," and told Wise that Niebuhr's "closing of the case made all the difference in the world and may fundamentally affect the decision." In April the committee recommended that 100,000 refugees be admitted to Palestine immediately, but it rejected Niebuhr's notion of a Palestinian-Jewish state. Like the British government it was unwilling to choose between Jews and Arabs and therefore made no choice at all.

When he published his views on the Palestine impasse for British readers during his summer visit to England, he was critical but reverent. "Britain has a greater fund of both wisdom and experience in international relations" than America, he assured them. It had to be hard to be "yoked together with two giant but adolescent nations" like Russia and the United States. But the refusal to admit refugees in the wake of underground terrorism in Palestine was shortsighted. A Labour government above all should realize that long-range peace between Arabs and Jews depended on liberating "Jewish energy and skill" to help turn the Middle East into a "technical and dynamic civilization." Justice for the Arab masses, he was arguing, would actually be promoted by the founding of a Jewish state. Only the benighted "chieftains" would object to river development, soil conservation, and "a large-scale economic development of the whole region." As Niebuhr bluntly put it in his new syndicated column distributed by Religious News Service, the Arabs had a "pathetic pastoral economy." They might not immediately perceive the justice of the quid pro quo—a secure Jewish homeland (including forced relocation of some Arab Palestinians) in exchange for greater prosperity—but they would in the long run. Niebuhr's assumption that the Arab masses were yearning to breathe the free air of modernization was remarkable for its unalloyed economic determinism. But he may have been right that economic development was the only kind of "justice" left for Arabs deprived of their homes and livelihoods.[2]

In London at the end of July he addressed the International Council of

•

Christians and Jews on the Palestine question, then went to Cambridge with John Foster Dulles, chairman of the Federal Council's Commission for a Just and Durable Peace, for a planning meeting of the fledgling World Council of Churches. He and Dulles fought for a resolution urging a policy of forgiveness toward the defeated nations and were surprised to find themselves outnumbered by unforgiving British delegates—a depressing revelation for Niebuhr of the depth of collective resentment in human life. He stayed in England until late August, preaching about Britain's role as a Third Force and savoring his long dinners with energetic young MPs like R. H. S. Crossman, editor of the *New Statesman* and longtime admirer of *Moral Man*. They persuaded him that American hysteria about Russian intransigence on issues like controlling atomic energy was the key obstacle to international accord. The European delegates to the Cambridge conference had agreed: "Russian truculence" stemmed from "Russian fears." The Soviets deserved the benefit of the doubt. They were not Nazis after all, as Niebuhr had periodically stressed for over a decade. "Whatever the evils of communist totalitarianism," he once again assured his American readers, "Russian ideology is not morally nihilistic and does not worship force, race, and nation as final ends." It was therefore a fair assumption that "patience and lack of provocation may through the years allay Russian fears and mitigate Russian truculence." In the last year of the war and first year of the peace, Niebuhr had emphasized the equivalence of American and Russian foibles. Both were adolescent, insecure, liable to erupt unpredictably while spouting self-righteous rhetoric; each needed encouragement to trust the other. Now he concluded that America had the greater responsibility to be patient since it possessed the disproportionate power—the bomb.

He allowed himself only a brief return trip to the United States—a couple of days at home with Ursula and seven-year-old Elisabeth and a quick visit to eleven-year-old Christopher at summer camp. He was then off to Germany for five weeks as one of fifteen members of a mission jointly sponsored by the State and War departments to evaluate the educational system in the American-occupied zone. Niebuhr and T. V. Smith of the University of Chicago slept on the floor of the plane for the entire flight. No sooner had they landed, translator Beatrice Braude recalls, than Niebuhr was deep in discussion with a battery of German Socialists, conversing in his "execrable" midwestern German. The same evening he sent off his first dispatch to the *Nation*. He and Smith soon left for Wiesbaden, Stuttgart, Munich, and Berlin to visit universities. They were appalled by the cultural ignorance of the American army officers. But they were also put off by the cultural elitism of the German academics and the hierarchical structure of the educational system, which Germans of all classes seemed to support. Niebuhr again re-enacted his father's earlier revolt by lecturing the Germans about autocracy. "We tried unsuccessfully," Niebuhr recalled later, "to democratize the German universities and to persuade the German educational authorities to make less rigorous distinctions as early as the twelfth year of a child's life between those who would prepare for the university in a *Gymnasium* and those who were fated to be the hewers of wood and the drawers of water. The labor groups were as insistent on this distinction as the middle classes."

•

While he was in Stuttgart he received a telegram informing him that Walter, who had shuffled from job to job after his wartime hospitalization, had died suddenly of a heart attack. He withdrew from the mission's activities for a day to mourn and collect his thoughts. At lunch Donald Rohr, a civilian administrative liaison, found him in a reminiscent mood. He spoke not about Walter, but about his father, the democratic German who had fled Teutonic hierarchy. He remembered the remark of a German educator, earlier in the tour, that the turning point in a man's life was the moment when he rebelled against his father's authority. That might be true for Germans, Niebuhr said, but it did not apply in his own case. His father had always treated him as an equal and he had never needed to defy him. The implicit contrast was to Walter's rebellion turned sour, and the implicit criticism was of Gustav's unequal treatment of his sons. Reinhold was implicated, as Gustav's favorite, in Walter's tragedy. Guilt and responsibility were shared. To his widow, Beulah, he wrote of the mixed pain and relief they each felt.

> He was a person of great generosity of spirit which one sometimes forgot when he tried one's patience. . . . On the whole all of us erred on the side of leniency rather than severity and while none of us did all we could you did most. . . . Walter was not likely to improve greatly in mental or physical health and might have become an almost impossible burden to those who loved him. It was well that he could go while you can still have pleasant memories of his loyalty. We can leave him safely to the Father of mercies who will know how to complete our own sorry and incomplete lives.[3]

II

Niebuhr's reflection that with Walter he had "erred on the side of leniency rather than severity" mirrored precisely his thoughts about the Soviets after several weeks in Germany. His liberal and Socialist contacts in Germany had contradicted the message he had received in Britain. The Soviets, they insisted, were engaged in a systematic effort to impose a Communist regime in Germany. Socialists and Christian Democrats told him they needed American military and economic support if they were to avoid a repetition of their defeat in the early 1930s by another totalitarian party. Niebuhr left Germany at the end of September with a new view of Russia—and a partially completed draft of an article for *Life* magazine on "The Fight for Germany." There was "certainly no hope" in the conciliatory policy popular on the British left and among disciples of former Vice-President Henry Wallace— "a policy which assumes that Russian truculence is merely the consequence of fears aroused by our defensive measures." Like a debater summoned suddenly to argue an opposite viewpoint, Niebuhr declared that once upon a time there were "more creative elements in Communism than in Nazism. . . . But the actual tyranny which has emerged and the fanatical fury [generated] are, unfortunately, not distinguishable from the practices derived from the purer paganism and cynicism." The "absence of a race theory" in communism had always been its prime virtue for Niebuhr; now

·

he managed to assert that lack of such a doctrine "gives this new tyranny an advantage over the old one in bringing nations under its subjection." Communism was more dangerous than nazism because it was less heinous. He did still believe that the Russians had legitimate security grounds for controlling Eastern Europe. But "the Russians are not, and will not be, satisfied with any system of eastern European defenses but are seeking to extend their power over the whole of Europe." He was convinced, he wrote to Beardsley Ruml, that the way to avoid war was not to fear it too much. The Soviets were following Hitler's lead: trying to frighten us into a series of concessions.

Henry Luce liked what he read. Excerpts appeared in *Time* the same day that the full article came out in *Life*. Others were impressed too. The *Reader's Digest* ran it for its millions of readers around the world. James Loeb arranged for UDA distribution of five hundred reprints among political leaders in Britain, and David Dubinsky of the UDA and Liberal Party bought one thousand copies for CIO union members. Niebuhr, no doubt with an assist from the *Life* editorial staff's potent phrase-makers, had struck a militant note that rang true to an imposing array of liberals as well as conservatives. But in a *Christianity and Crisis* report one week earlier he had used much softer tones. "It may be," he concluded of his visit to Germany, "that the fear of Communism dominates both the Christian and Socialist life of Germany too much. But I would want to be sure that Western stupidity does not deliver Germany into the hands of Communism before I would allow myself such a criticism." And a week after the *Life* piece he tempered his message again. Henry Wallace was wrong to criticize "our increasing firmness" toward the Soviets. But firmness was not sufficient. We needed "firmness and patience," and massive economic aid should take the place of "hysteria and all undue and exaggerated strategic measures." He may already have realized that the hyperbolic rhetoric and bold-face subtitle of the *Life* article—"A distinguished theologian declares America must prevent the conquest of Germany and Western Europe by the unscrupulous Soviet tyranny"—contributed its share to the hysteria. In the months that followed he continued his retreat from *Life*'s unnuanced fist-shaking.[4]

Niebuhr's campaign to distance himself and the UDA from Henry Wallace's conciliatory tone was strong evidence of a deepening rift in liberal ranks, an impending breakdown in the liberal consensus of wartime. The split was already clear in April, 1946, when Niebuhr and Loeb blasted a Popular Front "Win the Peace" rally for opposing an American loan to the British. The UDA executive board, troubled by the strength of the Popular Fronters and by the dwindling balance in its own bank account, decided the time was ripe to launch a broader organization. Like the UDA it would bar Communists from membership; unlike the UDA it would attract major figures from New Deal Democratic ranks, people with access to money that the UDA—always a New York City–based group of intellectuals and labor unionists—had never been able to attract. Niebuhr and Loeb set about organizing, though Niebuhr's role was limited after he left for England in July. Loeb secured the services of Joseph Rauh, a young lawyer and assistant to Wilson Wyatt at the federal housing bureau. Rauh joined the recruiting

•

effort and brought his boss with him after Wyatt resigned from the Truman administration at the end of the year. James Wechsler, a well-known journalist who had resigned from *PM* in June because of the paper's alleged sympathy for the Communists, came aboard and proceeded to attract Averell Harriman, former ambassador to Moscow. Another young activist, Harvard professor Arthur Schlesinger, Jr., whose scathing denunciation of American communism had appeared in *Life* in July, made a major contribution to the groundwork. Even before the fall election, when the Republicans shocked the Democrats by taking control of Congress for the first time since 1930, the nucleus of a new organization had been assembled.

After the election crestfallen liberals tried to regain the political momentum. Popular Fronters flooded into the new Progressive Citizens of America, founded in New York at the end of December. Meanwhile Niebuhr and Loeb made final preparations for the founding conference of their own group. Loeb signed up Eleanor Roosevelt and Niebuhr solicited labor interest by addressing the November 19 CIO convention in Atlantic City on "Labor's Stake in the Fight for Europe." His arm-waving performance— despite his low blood pressure that almost forced cancellation of the speech— brought down the house, and brought leading union officials like Walter Reuther and James Carey, along with David Dubinsky of the UDA, enthusiastically into the fold. When Niebuhr, as chairman of the UDA, mailed out fifty invitations to the founding meeting scheduled for January, 1947, he was certain of a favorable response.

By January 4 the 50 liberals had grown to 130. They wasted no time in agreeing to establish the Americans for Democratic Action (ADA). They approved a statement of principles—which expanded the UDA's policy by excluding not only Communists but "sympathizers with Communism"— and appointed a twenty-five-person organizing committee, including Niebuhr and Loeb. The following day that body picked Wilson Wyatt and Leon Henderson, former head of the Office of Price Administration, as cochairmen. It may have been a bittersweet moment for Niebuhr. He had been instrumental in creating an organization that swallowed up the group of which he was chairman. He was to have presided over the January 4 meeting, but as it turned out he and Elmer Davis, former head of the Office of War Information and a leading news commentator, shared center stage— a fitting symbol of the transition from a New York–based group of former Socialists and middle-level union officials to a Washington-based group of former New Dealers, prominent CIO officials, popular journalists like Marquis Childs and the Alsop brothers, and rising Democratic politicians like Minneapolis mayor Hubert Humphrey. Loeb was not left behind: he was chosen executive secretary. But Niebuhr was to play an increasingly limited role in the ADA, despite his election (in absentia) to the executive board in March. He did help with fund-raising by allowing the use of his name, wrote occasional position papers on foreign policy, and delivered memorable speeches at some annual conventions. Thirty years later former ADA members still chuckled about his addresses, begun with salutations like "Ladies, Gentlemen, honored bigwigs and high brass," and peppered with adroit put-downs of adversaries like the Popular Fronters: "I never believed in my country right or wrong, especially when it wasn't my country."

•

But the ADA rapidly became absorbed in Democratic national politics, and Niebuhr preferred to devote his strictly electoral energies to New York State's Liberal Party, of which he was re-elected vice-chairman in 1947. When Loeb urged him to attend an important board meeting in June, 1947, Niebuhr—who had missed the first national conference in March because of his spring semester sabbatical in Europe—could not find the time. He needed to keep his agenda clear, he wrote, in order to finish a book. It would be his last chance for many years, he said, to do any scholarship. As excuses went, that one was not very persuasive. Loeb must have gotten the message that Niebuhr's involvement was to be intermittent. Later Niebuhr told him that he would have been more committed if the ADA had been more "educational," less consumed by day-to-day politics. Loeb replied that one could not organize a movement on the basis of ideas alone.[5]

III

Niebuhr might have finished a book in the summer of 1947 if he had used his spring sabbatical to revise his 1945 Beecher lectures—Scribners was waiting to publish them as *Faith and History*—and not to travel and lecture in Europe. He left for Scotland in late January, and after lectures there, flew to Holland and Sweden for more talks. He roamed as far as Basel, where he paid a call on his old nemesis Karl Barth. Niebuhr himself made no mention of the visit. Barth later remarked that he had nervously awaited his guest, unsure whether "we would sniff at each other cautiously like two bull mastiffs, or rush barking at each other, or lie stretched out peacefully in the sun side by side." Whatever they talked about—Barth simply called it a "good conversation"—he apparently persuaded Niebuhr to stop calling him a fundamentalist. In his published reflections on the European trip Niebuhr went out of his way to dissociate Barth from the "Biblicist literalism or fundamentalism . . . [that] seems to grip his followers."

Niebuhr was in Amsterdam on March 12, recuperating from a whistle-stop tour through four Dutch cities, at the time President Truman appeared before the Congress to appeal for $400 million in emergency military and economic aid for Greece and Turkey. Both "democracies," he claimed, were threatened by Soviet communism; it was the job of the United States to assist "free peoples who are resisting attempted subjugation by armed minorities or by outside pressures." Many liberals, including some in the ADA, were suspicious of Truman's move, since it completely bypassed the United Nations and bolstered hopelessly reactionary regimes. But Niebuhr, once again in daily contact with continental Socialists and democrats who feared Soviet machinations in Europe, was a strong supporter. He was "just as certain as most Europeans that the strategic measures which we are taking, in Greece and Turkey, for instance, are absolutely necessary; though it is rather silly to . . . talk of preserving 'democratic' governments in these two countries. . . . What is at stake is not the internal structure of these nations, but the peace of Europe, which cannot be preserved if the communist tide inundates it."

After returning home and scenting the depth of liberal skepticism, however, he modulated his view: "We may or may not agree with the specific policy taken in Greece and Turkey; but Europe was, on the whole, right in appreciating primarily the symbolic significance of that action. It was a symbol of our determination to remain in Europe, though there might well have been a more adequate token of this determination than what was actually done in Greece and Turkey." Niebuhr's litmus test for American policy was the reaction of the Western and Central European center-left. If it helped buoy them up in their battle with local, Soviet-assisted Communist movements, he was for it. Whether Greece or Turkey was actually threatened by the Soviets was a secondary question he did not bother to ask.

Despite his persistent use of the flood metaphor—"the one right decision we have made," he wrote in June, "is our evident intention to stay in Europe and prevent the Russian power from inundating the European continent"—he repeatedly stressed that the Russian threat was not military. The Russian waters would flow only if the European economy remained dried up and drove despairing citizens to turn to the Communists. Ever since the end of the war Niebuhr had been arguing for a "positive defense"; now he suggested "generous, interest-free loans [that] would not merely save the economy of western Europe but also insure our own economic health." Secretary of State George Marshall had the same idea. His Harvard commencement address, delivered just after Niebuhr's piece went to press, proposed an enormous aid package to reconstruct Europe, East and West. Once again some liberals were wary, since the plan bypassed the United Nations and in fact accepted the division of Europe as a fait accompli. But most, including Niebuhr, were delighted. In the wake of Marshall's speech even the Communist putsch in Hungary was untroubling: "That overthrow," he wrote in July, "has not altered the power realities of Europe. What is really important is to prevent France and Germany from becoming Communist."

On the eve of his departure for a Scandinavian lecture tour at the end of the month, he called the address a "turning point in postwar history. . . . The enthusiasm of the response of Western Europe" proved the wisdom of the nonmilitary approach. The remaining danger was that Americans—for whom libertarian democracy was too often a "religion"—might force free-enterprise doctrines on unwilling European nations. Americans had to learn that laissez-faire was not the only kind of freedom. Humility about their own ideological tradition was a vital part of the "positive defense." Niebuhr was shrewdly requisitioning prophetic self-criticism as a key weapon in the Cold War. Humility was strength, self-examination was preparedness. This was no ordinary anti-Communist doctrine. It stemmed from his conviction that Communists had to be kept out of power in Germany and France—just as he and Loeb had fought to keep them out of the UDA. Niebuhr was content to leave Eastern Europe to the Soviets, even after the coup in Czechoslovakia in early 1948. He insisted on the futility of military responses, the inanity of American ideology, the primacy of economic aid. He repudiated any simple dichotomy between an evil Soviet empire and a virtuous American democracy—even when, in moments of crisis, he escalated his rhetoric against the Soviet "tyrants." Niebuhr's was a Third Force anti–communism, one that implicitly accepted the division of the world into spheres of influence. The balance-of-power theorists against whom he had inveighed at the end of the war had been wiser than the children of light like himself, who had yearned for a new federative world order based on the United Nations.[6]

An anti-communism that preserved a critical attitude toward American pretensions had great appeal for American liberals in 1948. The ADA made Niebuhr the keynote speaker at its Roosevelt's birthday banquet in February. Introduced by Mrs. Roosevelt, he entertained a dinner crowd of eleven hundred with his torrent of gibes and thoughts on American adolescence and European maturity. One entranced delegate wrote to Loeb two weeks later that a movement should be started "to get Reinhold Niebuhr the Democratic Party's nomination for President this year. Many people have thought what a great President he would make—and this is the year that it might be done." Loeb certainly agreed that the Democrats were hard up for a candidate. Like most ADA members he felt sure Truman would lead a Democratic debacle in November and imagined that even the politically uncommitted Eisenhower would be a better bet. But a boom for Niebuhr made him smile. "I happen to think he is one of the greatest living Americans," he responded, "but I don't think enough other people think so." Not to be denied, his correspondent wondered if a Niebuhr candidacy would "be any more weird than, say, Willkie's was. . . . The liberal horizon simply does not have any other man of comparable stature."

Niebuhr's appearance on the cover of *Time* magazine's twenty-fifth anniversary number on March 8 may not have boosted his Presidential chances, but it did seal his reputation as the nation's leading theologian. Ernest Baker's cover portrait from a 1941 photograph showed his half-bald head resting uneasily against his tense left hand, and his prominent blue eyes peering with weary intensity at some weighty event outside the frame. Behind him, ominously swirling, dark-green clouds, barely distinguishable from a craggy, dark-green hillside; at the top of the hill, a small white cross in diagonal symmetry with the whites of his eyes. Niebuhr's vision occupied the plane between the viewer and the raging chaos in the rear. "Man's story is not a success story," the caption pronounced, but rock-strong, pensive "theologian Reinhold Niebuhr" would be able to salvage meaning, and perhaps some hope, from the wreckage of human history. Senior editor Whittaker Chambers provided a serviceable summary of his theology and a mostly accurate outline of his life, erring only in repeating the myth that Bethel Church had been a working-class parish "in a dingy district of Detroit." It was a much more nuanced discussion than Chambers's earlier review of *The Nature and Destiny of Man;* here he made clear that "Niebuhr's gloomy view of man and history does not inhibit his belief that man should act for what he holds to be the highest good (always bearing in mind that sin will dog his action)." The single photograph of Niebuhr to accompany the story showed him in uncharacteristic repose: squatting down with wife and children to admire the family dog. The caption was appropriately tongue-in-cheek: "Sometimes he relaxes." Overall, Niebuhr was pleased with the article's insights. He commended Chambers by repeating to him what his brother Richard had said in high praise: "Only a man who has deeply

•

suffered could have written it." Editor William Savage at Scribners was also pleased; weekly sales of *The Nature and Destiny of Man* doubled from forty a week to eighty a week after the cover story came out. Niebuhr was firmly ensconced as "the official Establishment theologian," in Richard Rovere's phrase, a position for which Time-Life bore much responsibility. Since the war *Time* had featured him two or three times a year in its religion section, and *Life* touted him in 1946 and again in 1948 as the resolute Christian defender of German freedom.

But he would never have caught on if there had not been a fundamental accord between his own sensibility and the crisis atmosphere of the times. His good friend and neighbor Lionel Trilling grasped this spirit of the age in his novel based on Whittaker Chambers's evolution from Communist operative to religious anti-Communist. In *The Middle of the Journey* he named the Chambers character Gifford Maxim (maxims of the Gifford lectures?) and contrasted Maxim's present Christian views to his earlier Marxist faith, which "had offered the possibility of heroism or martyrdom, made available the gift of commitment and virtue to those who chose to grasp it." In the forties, however, "the intellectual power had gone from that system of idealism, and much of its power of drama had also gone. The time was getting ripe for a competing system," one that dwelt on guilt and responsibility, spoke of sin and the forgiveness of sin. The times may have been "out of joint," as Niebuhr told the ADA banquet in February, 1948, but he was solidly in tune with them. The culture craved a spokesman for the tragic sense of life; Niebuhr had the intellectual skill, religious credentials, and personal charisma to step forward and seize the day.[7]

IV

Man of the hour in the secular political realm, he was equally dominant in the religious councils of America and Europe. He played a key role in the World Council of Churches' Commission on the Church and the Disorder of Society, which issued a major report at the council's First General Assembly in Amsterdam in the summer of 1948. Niebuhr wrote two of the preparatory papers and delivered two conference addresses. As usual he defined two prime antagonists to his own Christian realism: the laissez-faire pretensions of American ideology, and the implicit neutralism of the European Barthians, who narrowly limited the church's mission to the preaching of the Gospel. The Amsterdam assembly was a stage for a battle of the titans, Niebuhr and Barth, despite the *entente cordiale* they had reached in 1947 when Niebuhr called on him at Basel. Barth chastised the liberals, among whom he included Niebuhr, for reducing the Gospel to a sort of "Christian Marshall Plan," a worldly campaign to enact a good society. Echoing Richard Niebuhr's priorities, he declared that the church's business was not social reconstruction but repentance. Christians had to "free ourselves from all quantitative thinking, all statistics, all calculation of observable consequences, all efforts to achieve a Christian world order, and then shape our witness into a witness to the sovereignty of God's mercy, by which alone we can live." Niebuhr struck back in his main conference

•

address. "It is true that . . . repentance is always required even as evil always flourishes. But it is wrong to preach this Gospel *sub specie aeternitatis* as if there were no history with its time and seasons." Barth's "theology of crisis" bore fruit in times of dire emergency—as when Hitler launched a direct attack on the church—but it was impotent in times of subtler struggles for justice. The Barthians were "obliquely pro-Communist," Niebuhr wrote to the *Nation,* even if "not actively so." They had reverted to their prewar quietism, he argued in a published response to Barth's address. "Yesterday they discovered that the church may be an ark in which to survive a flood. Today they seem so enamored of this special function of the church that they have decided to turn the ark into a home on Mount Ararat and live in it perpetually."[8]

Niebuhr was so preoccupied at Amsterdam with Barth's apparent neutralism that he did not do much to spell out his attack on American laissez-faire ideology. His preparatory paper on "The Situation in the U.S.A." ran to a measly two-and-a-half pages, compared to his sixteen pages of general reflections on "God's Design and the Present Disorder of Civilization." He did at least note that American economic life was not nearly so laissez-faire as right-wing ideologues wished. Had he pursued that insight he might have found more merit in the views of one of the members of his own commission, French law professor Jacques Ellul. For Niebuhr was on the verge of arguing that the real danger in America was not a backward-looking libertarianism, but a new social order based on intricate systems of political and technological control. He granted in the abstract that it was hard "to maintain freedom under the intense and complex forms of social cohesion in modern technical society." He had long asserted that technology was man's peril as well as his promise. But he was so wrapped up in the rearguard defense of New Deal pragmatism against right-wing Republican dreams of free enterprise that he did not dwell on the threat posed by centralizing forces in modern life. For Ellul freedom was threatened in 1948 not by Soviet communism, but by the "machine," the technological society of which America was the vanguard. While Niebuhr was still vindicating political intervention in economic life, Ellul was warning about the ominous growth of political and technological control over social existence. In his eyes the machine was not a neutral entity, good or bad depending on the use made of it, as some members of the commission were claiming. Modern society exhibited totalitarian tendencies "even if no explicitly totalitarian doctrine is invoked." A "mass man" was emerging even in ostensibly democratic nations.

Niebuhr's perspective had important points of contact with Ellul's. For Niebuhr technology was never neutral, always simultaneously good and bad. But with the Soviets blockading Berlin in the summer of 1948 he was not interested in arguments that put the challenge to freedom anywhere but in the Kremlin. During the assembly he wrote another political tract for *Life,* which began predictably with the authoritative wisdom of a British member of Parliament. Did Americans realize, the MP wondered, that "to avoid war we must run the risk of war"? In Amsterdam Niebuhr queried "delegates from every European country, including many behind the Iron Curtain," and all but one insisted that the United States should stay in

Berlin "at all costs." The Russians were in fact weak, he suggested, and were attempting to force an American retreat by intimidation, the same tactic Hitler had used against the European democracies with such success. The article had none of the volatile rhetoric of "The Fight for Germany." If America stood firm the Soviets would waver and retreat: "Their policy of truculence is a sign of weakness rather than strength." Talks with assembly delegates convinced him that communism was waning in Europe even as it was rising in Africa and Asia. When his commission's final report made equally harsh criticisms of capitalism and communism, he concurred but feared that Third World delegates would go home ignorant of what Europeans had learned from bitter experience: communism's apparently dynamic quest for justice culminated in the sacrifice of liberty to equality, an equality of powerlessness beneath the ruling oligarchy. The Marxist sympathies of Asian and African Christians "prove[d] that the greatest triumphs of communism will be achieved in the non-European world."

In September, 1946, Niebuhr had returned home from Europe and sent off an attack on liberal hero Henry Wallace for publication by Henry Luce. In September, 1948, he went home and sent off a blast against Presidential candidate Henry Wallace for distribution by the ADA. The ADA had toyed with the idea of endorsing Eisenhower or William Douglas, but finally went reluctantly to bat for Truman, who seemed a guaranteed loser in November. It then stoically assumed the task of discrediting Wallace's Progressive Party candidacy, which was bound to draw some liberal voters away from Truman. James Loeb asked Niebuhr to write "An Appeal to American Liberals and Progressives" to be signed by "top-flight liberal and labor leaders." Niebuhr was glad to oblige, since he believed, as he put it to Scarlett, that "poor Henry is really a prisoner of the Commies." In the appeal he asserted only that the Communists were behind the Wallace candidacy, and that power in the Progressive Party was held by notorious adherents of the Communist line. Perhaps his appeal made some difference. Thomas Dewey snatched defeat out of the jaws of victory against the confident predictions of every informed observer, including Niebuhr. In October he had agreed to join Loeb after the election to assess the imminent disaster. His election-eve editorial announced the result: "Mr. Dewey will be elected. The outcome is obvious." Still he trudged to the polls to vote for Truman "without any enthusiasm." His first postelection column cleared the egg from his face with disparaging comments about public-opinion pollsters.[9]

Loeb had tried his best to get Niebuhr out on the stump for liberal candidates during the campaign—"innumerable requests" for his services had come in—but Niebuhr begged off for reasons of health. He would have to limit his political work, he told Loeb, to what he could do for the Liberal Party in New York. He was no doubt also eager to finish *Faith and History* at long last. With a guaranteed Democratic defeat in November he could afford to cut back on his speeches and complete the manuscript. It was done by Christmas. Like the lectures on which it was based, the book was a gloss on the Giffords. Once again he was writing Christian apologetics: the Biblical view of human history did a better job of grasping "man in his strength and in his weakness" than alternative "modern" views, whether optimistic (like Marxism and liberalism) or pessimistic (like recent French existentialism). Unfortunately, he reverted to the simplistic and formulaic treatment of the alternative views—the key flaw that had marred volume one of the Giffords. Remarkably, he was even more unfair to liberalism than he was to Marxism. He reduced it to a fatuous faith in the ability of "scientific method" to order society as successfully as it had comprehended nature. He cavalierly dismissed the disciplines of psychology and social science as myopic and rationalistic, unworthy of serious attention by those who wished to understand man in his fullness.

When *Faith and History* appeared in the summer of 1949 it was greeted with widespread apathy or disappointment. It was poorly organized, highly repetitive, and—as even friendly reviewer Perry Miller had to point out— completely unoriginal for anyone who had read *The Nature and Destiny of Man*. The book was a telling sign of the author's physical fatigue and intellectual stagnation. Irving Kristol rightly complained that "he is not saying anything he has not said before, and he seems to be less concerned with thinking problems through than with convincing others of truths with which he is well satisfied." Richard Niebuhr's warning in 1942 that he needed the mental stimulation of a new cosmopolitan environment had been amply borne out. Reinhold's superficial put-down of the social sciences must have especially perturbed his brother. No apologist for the social sciences himself, Richard approached them with intellectual humility and greatly enriched his own thought in the process. Reinhold's peremptory stance in *Faith and History* was one manifestation of the trait that Richard most disliked in his brother: his rush to judgment. He rarely gave voice to what irked him about Reinhold, but when a student once asked him why his brother published so much more than he did, Richard's anger erupted: "I think before I write," he snapped.

Faith and History provides a particularly clear case of one recurrent tendency in Niebuhr's intellectual vocation: the solitary, embattled apologist taking Christian truths into the lion's den of religion's "cultured despisers." He collected ideas from many sources, molded them into an original, passionately argued perspective, but mentioned other thinkers primarily as embodiments of untenable alternative views, not as contributors to his perspective. What Robert Calhoun noted of *The Nature and Destiny of Man: Human Nature*, Northrop Frye observed of *Faith and History*: "The people he disagrees with make up quite a large company, and after reading that the Catholics are wrong because they absolutize the Church, the Lutherans wrong because they believe in a rule of saints, the modern liberals wrong because they are infected with progressivism, one begins to reflect rather irritatedly that everybody seems to be out of step but our Reinhold." He tended not to see himself as part of a community of inquiry seeking a gradual elaboration of the truth, but as a prophetic judge of the complacencies of the scholarly Mandarins. Swiss theologian Emil Brunner was one who took umbrage at Niebuhr's frequent failure to acknowledge his intellectual debts. Niebuhr had used some of the ideas in Brunner's *Man in Revolt* (1938) in preparing his Giffords, thanked him personally, and forgotten to tell anyone else. "With us European scholars," Brunner finally protested in the fifties, "it is customary to give our readers some information as to the sources of our thought." Niebuhr quickly repented: "It was a grievous error not to acknowledge my debt to him."[10]

V

It is ironic that the publication of *Faith and History,* a weak book that did not augment his reputation in the theological and broader intellectual community, coincided with the peak of his stature as "Establishment theologian." By 1949 he was not only the mass media's pick as most influential American Protestant theologian; he was also the choice of the U.S. State Department. Since his government-sponsored tour of Germany in 1946— the same year that Allen Dulles nominated him for membership in the elite Council on Foreign Relations—he had met regularly with the State Department's Advisory Commission on Cultural Policy in Occupied Territories. In 1949 he became an even more frequent visitor to Foggy Bottom. George Kennan's Policy Planning Staff invited him to join its deliberations for two days in June. He did not know what they expected of him, he told Loeb, but the request was enticing enough to justify missing another ADA board meeting. Dorothy Fosdick, daughter of Harry Emerson Fosdick and an intimate friend of the Niebuhr family, was a member of Kennan's staff; Niebuhr's visit, she wrote to Coffin, was just like the old days at Union, when he would hold forth on world dilemmas. The conversations were general and global: "long-range ideas for Europe and Asia," Niebuhr explained to Schlesinger.

Whatever Niebuhr may have contributed to the discussion, it is unlikely that he influenced government policy. George Kennan recalls that Niebuhr had no discernible impact on the proceedings. Kennan may once have described Niebuhr as "the father of us all," as has been widely reported, but in 1980 he did not recall doing so. And the phrase does not accurately convey his feelings about him. It was Niebuhr's philosophical perspective that he found personally attractive; Niebuhr's political judgments and foreign-policy views he thought unexceptional. Niebuhr, for his part, found Kennan's "realism" a refreshing alternative to the legalistic moralism that had bedeviled American foreign policy since Woodrow Wilson. Yet he also feared that an unblinking calculation of national interest might err in the other direction. "Egotism," Niebuhr rejoined, "is not the cure for an abstract and pretentious idealism. Preoccupation with national interest can quickly degenerate into moral cynicism even if it is originally prompted by moral modesty. We must be concerned with the interests . . . of those whose lives are intertwined with ours and who are locked with us in a common destiny." Niebuhr's residual idealism was a sign of his persistent desire to place himself midway between the cynics and the sentimentalists. But for all his qualifying of Kennan's viewpoint, he was in practice much closer to the "egotists" than he was to the "moralists."

The State Department invitations kept coming, and he continued to give voice to his modestly idealistic realism. In September he was selected as a member of the American delegation to the Fourth Conference of

UNESCO in Paris, where he delivered a speech urging the organization to stick to the realm of culture, rather than imagine it could contribute directly to conflict resolution. "The intellectual and moral solidarity of mankind," which the UNESCO constitution proclaimed as the true path to peace, was in the immediate "an unattainable goal." Yet the organization could justify itself if it was satisfied with sparking communication between cultures "in order that a common social and cultural tissue may slowly develop." UNESCO "cannot guarantee the peace," he told NBC listeners in a panel discussion from Paris, "but it can provide some of the prerequisites for a peaceful world." A month after his return he reported to Washington again for a conference called by Secretary of State Acheson to consider, in the department's words, "various plans of the department for strengthening the non-Communist world without impairing the UN." Acheson himself was neutral about Niebuhr, but one of his assistants, Marshall Shulman, was in Acheson's words "much addicted to him." Again Niebuhr probably exerted no measurable influence on the policymakers. No doubt both he and the assembled foreign-service officers and department specialists learned something of value from one another. No doubt too he and the State Department officials lent one another a certain amount of prestige: he basked in the aura of high affairs of state, they lingered briefly in the presence of a celebrity intellectual. They helped augment his standing as a significant Establishment figure, he helped elevate their own image as intellectually vigorous officials, not narrow-minded technicians. If Niebuhr did not influence government policy, he did participate in a system of influence in which some individuals and agencies established themselves as authoritative voices.[11]

Two weeks after the Acheson conference Niebuhr discovered that he was being considered for a post at the very summit of the Establishment: president of Yale University. His State Department duties must have helped legitimate him as a serious candidate: they demonstrated that he was familiar with the corridors of power, attuned to lofty responsibilities. His intellectual credentials and proven fund-raising ability were added bonuses. One Fellow of the Yale Corporation, liberal New York lawyer Jonathan Bingham, pushed him from within while other liberal stalwarts with Ivy League pedigrees, like Chester Bowles (Yale) and Arthur Schlesinger, Jr. (Harvard), submitted letters of support. Bingham believed Niebuhr had a good chance. But an aging Henry Sloane Coffin still controlled the "liberal" faction of the Corporation—the very group whose support Niebuhr would need. Coffin was not about to start putting Yale's welfare ahead of the seminary's. He made clear he would vote against the man he had brought to New York twenty-one years before and kept there in the face of earlier Yale overtures. Still Niebuhr thought the offer might arrive. He found himself wishing it would not, he told Schlesinger, because "if a miracle should happen and it did come through . . . I might make the wrong [decision]. I think age, politics, and religion, plus personal prejudices all put together have killed, or will kill, every possibility." He was right that family breeding and low-church roots were scarcely in his favor. He was not surprised when Yale graduate and Harvard historian A. Whitney Griswold was selected for the job.

As the decade closed Niebuhr had reason to be satisfied. His personal

•

stature was at its apex, and even more pleasing was the weakness of communism in Europe. True, the Russians now possessed the atomic bomb,
but that was no reason for hysteria. Military might was ineffectual in the
absence of moral and political strength—both of which the Russians lacked
in Europe, including much of Eastern Europe. The military alliance of
NATO, established in the spring of 1949, had true power not because of
weaponry but because it was built on a bedrock of moral consensus. NATO
itself was relatively unimportant; it was worth having "primarily because
the European nations want it." It could do no harm as long as the western
allies did not "expect too much of it or sacrifice more important strategies
to it." There was little chance of that, the neophyte State Department
consultant stressed, because "our own State Department is much more in
charge of foreign affairs, and less under the pressure of the defense departments, than at any time since the close of the war." Niebuhr praised Acheson's leadership in resisting calls to save Chiang Kai-shek in his losing battle
with the Communists. "A Communist China is not as immediate a strategic
threat as imagined by some. The Communism of Asia is primarily an
expression of nationalism of subject peoples and impoverished nations. We
still have a chance to espouse their cause and help them to achieve independence and health." To have intervened militarily in Asia would have
been suicidal; on that continent America lacked the moral and political
resources that alone could buttress a military strategy. The balance sheet in
late 1949 was favorable: the United States had intervened successfully in
Europe with the Marshall Plan and NATO Pact, and had avoided a foolish
intervention in Asia. "We have a right to congratulate ourselves for a moment (though it must not be for more than a moment)."[12]

It was not for more than a moment. The new year began with Truman's
announcement of the hydrogen bomb and ended with disaster in Korea;
Niebuhr no longer spoke of "streaks of dawn in the night." The H-bomb
was perilous not because it was a thousand times more lethal than the
Hiroshima bomb, but because it might tempt military strategists to dream
of a quick fix. "We cannot afford, morally or strategically to confront the
world with such a weapon as the primary source of our defense." The new
bomb might also tempt the morally minded to fall back into a sentimental
idealism. After debating nuclear policy with a pacifist before Columbia
University students, Niebuhr told Schlesinger he was "dismayed to find
the student body not pacifist but yet so morally disturbed that they were
almost ready to turn to pacifism." He did not doubt the hydrogen bomb
had to be made, since the Russians would certainly make one. The moral
goal was to make it "only to prevent its use and of course to prevent our
subjugation." Niebuhr was instrumental in bringing a special Federal Council of Churches Commission on Weapons and Mass Destruction around to
his viewpoint. Joined by John Bennett, physicist Arthur Compton (a major
figure in the Manhattan Project), and others, he argued, as he reported to
Scarlett, that "no absolute line can be drawn on any weapon." Nor could
the United States promise never to use nuclear weapons in response to a
conventional attack—for example by Russian tanks in central Europe. A
preemptive first strike against the Soviets was plainly immoral, but first
use in response to aggression could not be ruled out as an option. The

•

commission report rested firmly on Niebuhr's paradoxical stance that atomic weapons were "our ultimate insecurity and our immediate security."

Niebuhr could be unalarmed about atomic weapons in the short run because the Korean war, which broke out in June, 1950, proved that conventional wars could still get along quite well without them. Korea posed a perilous threat to the United States, he thought, but it was not the threat of nuclear warfare. The danger was that America might be dragged into a land war in Asia, leaving Europe in a vulnerable position. When General MacArthur, commander of the UN forces, provoked the Chinese Communist intervention in October by approaching the Yalu River, it seemed to Niebuhr that all might be lost. MacArthur wanted to carry the battle to China itself; Niebuhr sensed that would mean the loss of America's European allies and a major political boost for the Communists in Europe. He proposed to bargain with the Chinese: they could have Taiwan in exchange for a cease-fire. To the readers of the New York *Times* he insisted that "becoming bogged down in a vast Asiatic war" meant "inviting aggression from Communism in Europe." Niebuhr was prepared to part with more than Taiwan. The "free world can live if we lose Asia, but we cannot live in security if Russia should come into possession of the economic and technical resources of Europe." Asia could go its own way: Europe must be defended at all costs.

For the first time Niebuhr actually feared a Soviet military invasion of Europe—or else he said he did to marshal support for a cease-fire in Asia. "The Soviets can overrun Europe at any time; and they could easily be tempted to a 'now or never' adventure." That speculation flew in the face of everything he had written about the Soviets for years. He backpedaled a few sentences later: "There is another possibility that Russia will not attempt a direct challenge in Europe but will seek for other 'soft spots' in the hope of increasing her gains without a war." That was the threat he emphasized to Scarlett several months earlier. The Russians did not want "a general war which they would lose." They were content to "harass us with political and military ventures all over the world, some of which they will win, particularly in Asia." The United States was right to defend Korea. It must "dismiss" its fears of atomic war in order to summon the fortitude to protect other "soft spots" for decades to come.[13]

The FBI was very interested to learn, in a report from the navy's intelligence office, that Niebuhr favored withdrawing the US fleet from the strait of Formosa and abandoning Chiang Kai-shek. It was one of many bits of information the Bureau collected in its "full-field loyalty investigation" of Niebuhr conducted in 1951. The State Department had asked him to become an official consultant in November, 1950, and the loyalty check was standard procedure under Truman's beefed-up security program. The New York office of the Bureau recycled all of the Dies Committee charges against him and came up with new items of its own: among them his evident tolerance for Asian communism; his open letter to Truman of May 15, 1951, which "was very critical of the Loyalty Program and of the Director [of the FBI, J. Edgar Hoover]"; his chairmanship of the Resettlement Campaign for Exiled Professionals, which dispensed hundreds of thousands of dollars in 1951 to bring displaced European intellectuals to the

United States. Several of the Bureau's new informants still contended that his activities in the thirties suggested actual Communist Party membership. One of them claimed that Niebuhr "belonged to at least forty CP front organizations and in all his experience [he] had never found anyone who was in as many as forty CP front organizations without being a CP member."

The New York office took all of 1951 to plumb Niebuhr's past and still was not done. J. Edgar Hoover fumed over the delay. Niebuhr's case was "among the most delinquent being handled by the Bureau," he wrote on December 13. "Remaining investigation must be expedited," he cabled a week later. "Unnecessary delay will not be tolerated." Hoover was in a poor position to complain. It was not the New York office's fault that Niebuhr had belonged to, spoken for, or signed the petitions of countless left-leaning groups that the attorney general's staff had seen fit to declare subversive. If left-wing politics was subversive, the New York office was only being diligent. In the end its labor, completed in February, 1952, was for naught; the Loyalty Review Board never made a judgment because Niebuhr had already left government service.

In the hysterical atmosphere that followed the news of the Russian atomic bomb and the "loss" of China in 1949, private groups like the American Council of Christian Laymen (ACCL) had joined the FBI in wishing to ferret out guilty parties. Their 1949 brochure, How Red Is the Federal Council of Churches?, pointed the finger at Niebuhr, John Bennett, Kirby Page, Will Scarlett, Henry Van Dusen, A. J. Muste, Harry Ward, and Harry Emerson Fosdick among many others, and claimed that Niebuhr had been affiliated with twenty-four "God-hating, unAmerican organizations." When Verne Kaub, president of the ACCL, wrote him during the FBI investigation with further insinuations of disloyalty, Niebuhr replied with an itemized denial. It is a striking indication of the anxieties of mid-1951—a year after the Hiss verdict and Joseph McCarthy's Wheeling speech had raised fears of communism in the State Department—that Niebuhr felt the need to deny Kaub's charges line by line. Unfortunately Niebuhr's memory for dates and events was deficient. He claimed he had left the Fellowship of Reconciliation in 1930 (he resigned from the executive board in 1934 but remained in the organization) and had dropped out of the Socialist Party in 1936 (he resigned in 1940). He also asserted he had "never had anything to do with the American Friends of Spanish Democracy," although (as a favor to his friend Bishop Paddock) he served in the late 1930s as a member of its executive committee. Kaub, who specialized in dates and events while ignoring the differences between casual contact and deep commitment, and between socialism and communism, no doubt deduced that all his charges were substantiated by Niebuhr's errors of recollection.

As the private and governmental investigations continued, Niebuhr made one anti-Communist commitment after another—enough of them, he might have thought, to clear his name. His first State Department duty as official consultant was to participate in a January, 1951, conference of "a dozen leaders of American thought" called, according to the title of a Sunday New York Times page-one story, "to help fight Red ideology." In April he resigned as contributing editor of the Nation, as did his friend Robert

Bendiner, because of pro-Soviet foreign editor Alvarez del Vayo's "incorrigibly tendentious . . . animadversions." As chairman of the Resettlement Campaign for Exiled Professionals he made sure the promotional literature was up-to-date. While his appeal letters in 1950 spoke of ending the needless suffering of thirty thousand refugees in displaced-persons camps—refugees from both fascism and communism—his May, 1951, letter argued only for saving writers and professionals from "behind the Iron Curtain" and inducting them into "our ideological counter-offensive against tyranny." In spite of his actions and the occasional vehemence of his rhetoric, Niebuhr's anti-communism was still discriminating and therefore suspect in the eyes of the patriotic zealots. He was not battling communism as much as he was fighting the Soviets and their American supporters. Anyone who publicly proclaimed that he could tolerate the loss of the whole of Asia to communism was bound to be found wanting in virtue—bound indeed to be taken as one example of further subversion in the State Department.[14]

VI

Niebuhr took a respite from the political frenzy in July, 1951, by escaping briefly to Europe, his first overseas jaunt since the UNESCO conference two years earlier. He was quickly reminded how complacently materialistic and arrogant America appeared to non-westerners and even some Europeans. Americans liked to think the Marshall Plan was an act of generosity. Europeans gave voice, he thought, to a deep well of legitimate resentment against American goodwill, along with some illegitimate envy. Americans would do well to expect the envy and expunge their own self-praise. It was "foolish for powerful nations to pretend to [generosity]. The pretension will merely elicit cynical reactions." At a ten-day World Council of Churches gathering in Geneva, Karl Barth made clear he could not stand the smiling American presence. "Yes, we sat there and talked for ten whole days," Barth recollected of the conference. "Americans (Niebuhr at their head!) with bright, healthy teeth, great determination and few problems." To Barth, Robert Calhoun remembered, the Americans were country bumpkins with too much self-assurance and too little capacity for serious thought. He erupted with anger when Niebuhr's remarks on the conference theme ignored the Christian's "final hope" of victory over evil in favor of a more worldly focus on incremental advances in social justice. Barth lamented that "we have to tear our hair so much over Christian hope, of all things, instead of rejoicing at it."

For Niebuhr Barth was being his usual irresponsible, ahistorical self. The Christian message was not the same in all contexts. Americans had to be cautioned against the pretensions of the powerful, Europeans against the despair of the powerless. These were not "different gospels. But different facets of the gospel are variously relevant." Barth's view was itself historically conditioned, "a natural expression of the Christian faith in those parts of the world where a Christian culture has broken down, where, as in France, the prevailing cultural mood is one of despair." American Christians, by contrast, "had no right to express their faith in such purely eschatological terms, that is, in terms which minimize the conquest of evil in particular instances and which place the whole emphasis upon God's final triumph over evil." It was up to them to uphold the historic liberal Protestant quest for a "responsible" society. Niebuhr was urging a pluralistic, shifting Christian prophecy that tailored its judgment to circumstances. God was beyond history, but the Christian witness was profoundly shaped by it. At the conference itself Barth's forces carried the day, perhaps because of his threat to bolt the meeting altogether. In the end, Niebuhr glumly recalled the following year, "we did nothing more than to capitulate more than was wise to Karl Barth."[15]

But even a lost round in his lifelong sparring match with Barth bore precious fruit. He returned to Heath for the month of August and sat down to begin the second half of a manuscript he was calling *This Nation Under God,* a short study of the curious amalgam of virtue and vice in the American experience. Eight of the ten chapters were based on lectures delivered in 1949 and early 1951, but the two most original chapters, "The Ironic Element in the American Situation" and "The Significance of Irony," were written after his return from Europe, and the entire text was then revised. His European sojourn provided the distance that allowed him to look at America as a whole; the argument with Barth made him freshly aware of the complexity of the American reality. The problem was methodological as well as substantive: one had to avoid pretension, as an American author, in order to understand the mix of pretension and achievement in the American past. By hitting upon the concept of irony, he was able to incorporate a principle of self-criticism into his own argument. "The ironic tendency of virtues to turn into vices when too complacently relied upon" became the major theme of the book, and supplied an internal corrective whenever he took occasion to praise the American performance. Once he had realized, in September, how central the concept of irony had become to his argument—and was told that Harpers already had a book under contract entitled *This Nation Under God*—he changed the title to *Ironic Elements in American History.* While the book was in production, editor William Savage proposed *The Irony of American History,* which Niebuhr feared—ironically—was too "pretentious." But he went along with his editor's judgment.

The Irony of American History had the passion and gathering force that *Faith and History* lacked; he was writing about his chief interest, America's place in the world. The book was a sharp attack on communism, which was to be expected in 1951. Less expected in this most frigid of Cold War years was the book's ringing indictment of American complacency. To be sure, *Irony* was a vindication of pragmatic democracy, as was *The Children of Light;* the wisdom of democratic politics lay in its capacity to restrain disproportionate power while stimulating gradual social reform. But Niebuhr was not issuing one more celebration of American uniqueness. Where a writer like Daniel Boorstin saw "the genius of American politics" in its lack of ideology, its distance from European abstractions, Niebuhr dwelt on the interrelatedness of American and European, liberal and Marxist, dogmas. One of the prime ironies of American life was that the very Communist creed against which Americans were contending was itself a distil-

•

lation of their own liberal utopianism: it was the liberal dream of justice run amuck.

We are more like our enemies than we think, Niebuhr asserted. Americans and Russians both portrayed themselves as innocent, misunderstood, unfairly libeled; Soviet bureaucrats and American social scientific planners both imagined they could create an efficient technical order without consulting their citizens; both nations conceived of their history as a new order of the ages. Where Boorstin saw an American consensus that set the New World off from the Old, Niebuhr saw an ironic consensus between two apparently antithetical giants. America was not a unique beacon of virtue in the world, but a telling refutation of its own original dreams of historical innocence. The American experience was not a revelation of progress, but a sign of the indeterminacy of history, of its potential for both good and evil. The same atomic bomb that symbolized technical proficiency and military power stood also for the crushing anxiety of modern life. In mastery there lay new forms of misery.

In most of the text Niebuhr used the term *irony* loosely, equating it with "paradox," any incongruous or apparently contradictory pairing of ideas. But in the opening and closing chapters he gave it a special meaning. The American experience was "ironic" at its core, he argued, not "pathetic" or "tragic." It was irony, not pathos, because Americans were not simply victims of their history. They had helped bring it about, bore responsibility for it; it had not just happened to them like some sequence of natural events. It was irony, not tragedy, because the unexpected disappointments and dilemmas of American life were the result not of fully conscious choice, but of partly unconscious stumbling. The American experience was best understood, that is, in terms of the paradox Niebuhr had elaborated in *The Nature and Destiny of Man:* human beings bore responsibility for their actions despite the inevitability of the sins they would commit. Americans were responsible for their history even though their historical choices as a nation had not been deliberative. Grasping their own past as "ironic," not "pathetic" or "tragic," could prompt them to a renewed sense of responsibility for their future. A pathetic experience provoked pity in an observer; a tragic experience, tears and admiration for the nobility of the doomed hero; an ironic experience, laughter and insight leading to deeper understanding. Irony was therefore an analytical device that pointed to an actual lived experience in the American past—an experience of paradox—and allowed a later generation to build on that past and bring forth a better future. Unlike pathos or tragedy, irony had the capacity to spark contrition; ironic awareness produced a knowing smile and a humbling nod of the head.

The ironic sensibility went "beyond tragedy" and brought a person to the verge of religious faith. Irony, he pointed out, was intrinsic to the Judeo-Christian conception of God. The Old Testament spoke of a God of wrath, but the Psalmist sang of a God who sat in the heavens to laugh. His laughter was derisive, judgmental, but also forgiving, merciful. The paradoxically angry yet smiling God was a model for the moral life: place a judgment upon evil-doers, but forgive them their sins. *Irony* enacted that moral stance by casting a stone at the Communists but immediately calling for humility and a recognition of how many of their illusions Americans shared. And how much of their humorlessness Americans shared. "No laughter from heaven could possibly penetrate through the liturgy of moral self-appreciation in which the religion of Communism abounds." But "a frantic anti-Communism can become so similar in its temper of hatefulness to Communism itself, the difference in the respective creeds being unable to prevent the similarity of spirit." Niebuhr had come a very long way from the progressive thirties in which his God of power and might called for cataclysm to topple the bourgeois lords; his God of humor and might corresponded perfectly to an era of tempered expectations. The ironic God still taught men to hate injustice, but also prodded them to laugh at their own pretensions. It was fitting that Niebuhr took leading roles in such postwar seminary satires as "Murder in the Seminary," a takeoff on T. S. Eliot's *Murder in the Cathedral*. He also starred in humorous summertime skits at Heath (once he was appropriately cast as a circus master), and was a much-admired player of charades at faculty parties. Humor was not mere diversion. It was a means of putting oneself and others in perspective.[16]

Reactions to *Irony* were vociferously pro or con. George Kennan and Arthur Schlesinger, Jr., were enthusiastic, as was historian Peter Viereck, who reviewed it on page one of the New York *Times Book Review*. Kennan and Schlesinger typified the growing band of secular liberals for whom "paradox" and "irony" had become substitutes for the older humanistic "faith in man"; Viereck stood contentedly for all the conservatives who could not believe their luck that even the liberals were talking about human limits. But the liberal community was still split. The writer Anthony West vilified Niebuhr in the *New Yorker* for deprecating "man's trust in reason"; the venom of the review may have been in retaliation for Niebuhr's disparaging of West's father, H. G. Wells, in *Faith and History*. Philosopher Morton White and historian William Leuchtenburg agreed that Niebuhr's doctrine was obscurantist and defeatist. Both lectured him for positing "a mocking God who laughs at our 'exertions,' " as Leuchtenburg put it, and for uttering the "monstrous falsehood" (White) that "nothing that is worth doing can be achieved in our lifetime." They were tone-deaf to Niebuhr's theology and preaching style. His God did not merely mock, and his counsel of patience was not a cry of despair. The two reviews were themselves cries of alarm over Niebuhr's mounting preeminence among liberals. They were last-ditch efforts to stop the swelling tide of those White labeled "Atheists for Niebuhr," those who "underrate[d]," in Leuchtenburg's phrase, "the power for good of a vision of human progress."

Niebuhrian ideas were attracting intellectuals in many fields, but *Irony* had a special impact on historians of the United States. Richard Hofstadter's *American Political Tradition* (1948) and other works had already played havoc with the "progressive" model dominant in the previous generation of Charles Beard and V. L. Parrington. For them the American experience had been shaped above all by a perennial battle between the popular forces of enlightenment and the privileged protectors of tradition; historical writing was an implicit call to arms. Hofstadter's book exploded those categories by demonstrating how conservative many liberal heroes had been, and how deeply rooted the capitalist consensus had been among all social groups.

•

Niebuhr's *Irony* put Hofstadter's post-progressive perspective on a firmer philosophical foundation and showed that the ironic stance could itself supply a kind of faith for the future. A somber faith, to be sure, as Lionel Trilling had already indicated in *The Middle of the Journey* (1947). Intellectual work was no longer to be a celebration of the people's unbounded potential, but a search for paradoxes, a statement of the tragic limits on human life. Within those limits human beings occasionally achieved beauty, excellence, responsibility, but always under the pressure of evil, treachery, despair. History was not a progressive march interrupted by temporary setbacks, but a drama of human weakness and strength. Many historians who came of age during the depression or Second World War—Perry Miller, C. Vann Woodward, Henry May, and David Brion Davis among others—were inspired by Niebuhr's vision.

It was a sign of the times that none of *Irony*'s liberal reviewers challenged his blanket denunciation of communism, one of the weakest points in the book. Niebuhr had carefully noted the similarity between Communist and liberal illusions, then boldly argued that western nations—America in particular—managed in practice to improve on their illusory theories. He might also have indicated, as he sometimes did in his occasional writings, that communism varied from time to time and place to place. Perhaps it was always and everywhere more oppressive than any democratic society, but it was not the monolith that *Irony* assumed. He knew very well that Tito was not Stalin and that neither was Mao. *Irony* reduced communism to a demonic religion while allowing democracy its historical diversity.[17]

VII

Irony was on the whole a remarkably acute performance for a man who was in an even more advanced state of physical exhaustion than usual. A photograph taken in June, 1951, when he testified to a Senate Ethics Committee shows a haggard fifty-nine-year-old Niebuhr with deeply circled eyes drying his brow with a handkerchief. His fervid mind dragged his careworn body from one commitment to another. While finishing the manuscript he was shuttling up and down the east coast for sermons and meetings, including the founding conference in Washington in September of a new organization of reform-minded Christians. Two hundred Protestant leaders heard his speech at the launching of Christian Action, a replacement for the Frontier Fellowship (the renamed Fellowship of Socialist Christians). Christian Action was to the FSC as the ADA was to the UDA: a broader-based reform group with no ties, even residual ones, to Socialist doctrines. No mention in its Statement of Purpose of socializing large-scale property; instead the liberal call for "a responsible society . . . which will give each person or group a fair and equal opportunity to develop his full potentialities." Niebuhr became co-chairman with Liston Pope of Yale Divinity School and remained as editor of *Christianity and Society,* which Christian Action took over from the FSC after the Fall, 1951, issue. But the new organization never took off. "We tried for several years to put life into Christian Action," John Bennett later recalled, "but

•

we failed." As Liston Pope put it, "It's difficult to have a parade for a mixed economy."[18]

Just after Christmas he came down with the flu, and returning to the seminary for the end of the semester in January he felt a bit weak. The new semester began at the end of the month, but he was buried under a pile of one hundred term papers from the fall. When he preached in James Chapel on February 3 he was obviously tired. He meditated on Jesus' conviction that the rain descends on the just and unjust alike. There was no "special Providence," Niebuhr claimed, no special intercession by God on behalf of the virtuous, no guarantee of reward for the moral life. "The prayers that many a mother with a boy in Korea must pray" were futile if they asked for special protection. He took the following Sunday off and went with Ursula to hear their friend James Pike preach at the Episcopal Cathedral of Saint John the Divine. He needed the weekend off to gather his strength for the following one: an all-day Christian Action meeting on February 16 and a Yale sermon on February 17.

But as he sat in his Brown Tower office at the seminary on Friday afternoon, February 15, he suffered a spasm in the limbs on his left side. He thought it might be a heart attack, and rushed to nearby Saint Luke's Hospital. Initial tests, President Van Dusen reported to the press the following Tuesday, showed "no basic ailment of the heart, brain, or circulatory system." Niebuhr was just overworked, and "with adequate rest, he should be restored to full health." His courses were canceled for the rest of the year, and all public engagements for six weeks. But the weakness persisted on his left side, and Dr. Herbert Parsons was called in to do exploratory brain surgery on March 5. No tumor was found, and in mid-March he felt and looked fine. It was the clearing before the storm. In the spring a series of spasms left him increasingly paralyzed on the left side and his speech impaired. Gradually the doctors deduced that a sclerotic artery was delivering insufficient blood to one part of the brain. They spoke reassuringly of future recovery, but Niebuhr knew the future was bleak.

The prospect of physical infirmity was crushing, and so was the realization that he was unprepared to deal with it. "I am ashamed that my convalescence proves to be spiritually so hard," he wrote to Scarlett, "because it reveals a certain lack in me, a reliance upon jobs and pressures rather than on inner calm."

> I think therefore with all the inner pain connected with it, it can be a means of grace. . . . Ursula says my difficulty is that I have insufficient faith in leaving the future, which I can't control, to the Lord. I am afraid that that is a case of preaching to others and myself becoming a castaway. For I am certain intellectually that modern man makes the mistake of trying to control the future and not living by faith and trust, but I break down in my own personal attitudes. So you see how I wrestle with problems which should have been solved.

Twenty-five years earlier, as he prepared to leave Detroit, he had written in his diary that "if I were physically anemic I would never be able to escape pessimism." In the two decades that were left to him he fought a protracted battle, with only partial success, to learn how to escape it.[19]

ELEVEN

QUITE
A DIFFERENT
PERSON

(1952–1960)

I

In the summer of 1952 Niebuhr worsened. The spasms continued at two-
or three-week intervals, and each time the paralysis and the speech im-
pairment were aggravated. His mother, Lydia, came for a visit in August,
and the tension of her arrival produced the worst attack of the summer.
When he went to meet his mother at an inn near Heath, he seemed to his
neighbor Louise Robbins "in great form, enthusiastic, quite sure he could
take up his work this autumn." But the following morning he had a terrible
spasm and could not speak. His speech soon returned and he was able to
"move about a little." Ursula told Scarlett that he was up for part of the
day, but quite weak and discouraged. His hope of going back to teaching
on a part-time basis was dashed. Niebuhr offered to resign if an early pension
could be provided. "I would be prepared to accept anything that would
keep me going," he wrote to Van Dusen. But the president was not about
to let him go if there was even a slight chance of recovery, and the doctors
thought the chance was better than that.

Niebuhr resigned himself to sitting briefly each day at the new electric
typewriter that John Bennett and others at Union had bought for him; he
could hunt and peck righthanded and produce a couple of letters a day.
Much of the day he spent watching ball games or election campaign news
on the new television set that Arthur Schlesinger and other ADA friends
had sent him. Television might be a peril to culture, as he had frequently
argued, but it was a godsend for a man of the world who was stuck at
home. He could watch an event like Vice-Presidential candidate Nixon's
Checkers speech and keep the literary and political juices flowing by typing

•

a short blast for the *Times* letter column. Eisenhower, who "was supposed carefully to weigh the evidence" about Nixon's expense account, had "yielded his prerogatives to a jury of the television audience." Nixon's "tear-jerking account of his personal history, involving his devoted wife, charming children, and even the family dog," was a "great show" inspired by talented "stage managers," but "what becomes of every rule of logic and reason in the proceedings?"

He did what little he could for Stevenson from the sidelines—Stevenson himself asked him to "say a prayer for me now and then"—but watching the action on television was a poor substitute for speechmaking. The doctors barred him from attending meetings even in New York City, so he urged political friends like Schlesinger, Wechsler, and Rauh to come by his apartment whenever possible. He grew more and more dependent on Schlesinger in particular for news of the political arena; the historian was willing to take the time to write, call, and visit. Niebuhr respected his judgment and saw in him a reflection of his own preferred self-image: the activist-scholar with a wide net of contacts among men of power and men of ideas. He confessed to a little jealousy when Schlesinger became active in the Stevenson campaign, "the enviable position of being both an observer of history in the making and a maker of history." But Schlesinger's history-making and Niebuhr's prayers were unavailing in the face of Eisenhower's charisma and his promise to "go to Korea" to settle the stalemated affair once and for all. Ike stormed into office with 55 percent of the vote and Niebuhr, Schlesinger, and their ADA colleagues found themselves in the unaccustomed position of a party in opposition.[1]

Niebuhr also found himself in the unaccustomed position of a home-body. No more weekend trips on the preaching circuit, no more meetings, only a reduced teaching load at the seminary beginning in February, 1953. Fourteen-year-old Elisabeth took pleasure in his presence and informed him that he was now a much better father. She had only rarely spent time with him alone before his stroke. Once he had taken her to Radio City Music Hall to see *Singin' in the Rain* (he enjoyed it, even while scribbling notes to himself during the show). Another time they had gone to a Giant game (they left early to beat the traffic). Elisabeth had inherited the puckish intelligence of the young Reinhold, and her mother's quick wit. When she was seven Niebuhr had written to his mother and sister that he especially liked her "dramatic appreciation of life, which Ursula says is a copy of me." Now Niebuhr watched with pride as his teenaged daughter developed an independent intellect—and began to find fault with him. He chuckled when she chided him for his ignorance of art: "Daddy, you're just an old aesthetic philistine!" He thought she was right and took delight in the gusto of her jab.

Ursula too was quietly pleased to have her husband home continuously for the first time in twenty years. John Smith, who lived in the Niebuhrs' seminary suite in calendar 1947 while teaching with Ursula in Barnard's department of religion, remembers her as having been "nearly bereft" during that time. Smith and his wife occupied the butler's quarters of the colossal apartment to which the Niebuhrs moved during the war: four bedrooms, two baths, and an enormous wood-paneled living room in which

•

Niebuhr held court during the Thursday evening "at-homes" for students. Niebuhr was constantly away lecturing, preaching, and doing seminary business; Presidents Coffin and Van Dusen each sent him on frequent trips that according to Smith and Ursula contributed to his ill health and ultimately to his stroke. When her husband returned home, Smith recalls, Ursula would make a point of inquiring about his doings, but Niebuhr did not often reciprocate. If he was home for the evening he would typically work on an article or attack the two piles his secretary Nola Meade assembled for him: books in one, papers and reports in the other. Frequently there were evening meetings. One friend recollects running into Niebuhr as he bolted with flushed face and furrowed brow from the apartment elevator on his way to a political affair; Ursula had just given him a tongue-lashing for stealing away once again. Even at Heath he would put up a fight before going with her on an occasional walk; five minutes into the hike he would suggest getting on home. "He was afraid he might miss the announcement of a new British tariff or something," she remembers, shaking her head. She also remembers that there was much laughter and gaiety when her husband was at home, and frequent visits from notable figures in politics, theology, and the arts. She thrived on the contacts and the conversation. She was one of the few who could match her husband's verbal skill.

He was already dependent on Ursula before his stroke, since it was she who kept the household going. But now he was dependent on her for physical care and mental encouragement. His condition stabilized in early 1953: a lame left arm, little energy, slightly slurred speech, recurrent depression. Ursula became an accomplished nurse, forceful yet lighthearted. The dominant personality she had had to subordinate to her husband's was now given freer play; she made more and more of the decisions about his activities. She willingly embraced her new role, but it put enormous pressure on her energies. Preparing her Barnard religion classes, managing the household, and attending to what she jokingly called "the care and feeding of Reinhold" drove her sometimes to the verge of exhaustion.

Christopher was already in his final year at Groton when Niebuhr found himself suddenly restricted to quarters. As a young child he had reminded Lydia and Hulda of the young Reinhold because of his loquaciousness. But they thought his disposition was sweeter, less stubborn and aggressive, than Reinhold's had been. His father had enjoyed reporting the boy's juvenile thoughts to his correspondents. "Christopher is busy speculating about time," he wrote when his son was five, "and worrying about the fact that there was a time when he was not, a nice example of hubris." As a teenager Christopher developed a consuming passion for politics, and eventually worked hard for the Democratic Party. Niebuhr's public career thus supplied his son with the model for one of his life pursuits; but that same career often took Niebuhr away from his son during the formative years. Christopher had experienced learning and speech problems because of his dyslexia. His IQ was high but he was handicapped in subjects requiring abstract ideas. After the stroke, when Niebuhr felt his own future threatened, he worried himself "sick" over Christopher's. Will Scarlett intervened with timely advice: he instructed his friend to stop trying to live his son's life for him. When Harvard accepted Christopher a month later, Niebuhr was

•

able to relax. He promised Scarlett he would concentrate on loving his son, not trying to control his fate. Christopher returned the affection by unselfishly nursing his father during the difficult summer of 1952. "He has grown into quite a young man," Niebuhr wrote to his friend in the fall, "and it gives us a good deal of joy."[2]

II

Limited on doctor's orders to the seminary in winter and the Heath cottage in summer, Niebuhr still found himself dragged into current controversies. In 1952 and 1953 the intellectual community was embroiled in debate over what was already called McCarthyism. Which was the greater danger, they wondered, communism or McCarthy himself? Niebuhr followed Schlesinger and others in the ADA in taking a middle ground: McCarthyism was a grave threat not so much because McCarthy lacked respect for civil liberties—as the left-progressives claimed—but because he was ineffective in fighting communism. His blunderbuss accusations brought ridicule on the serious business of rooting out Communists or Communist sympathizers from positions of influence. Before his stroke Niebuhr had never worried much about the activities of Communist agents in the United States; now he became more militant. Mercy for the Rosenbergs? Out of the question: "Traitors are never ordinary criminals and the Rosenbergs are quite obviously fiercely loyal Communists. . . . Stealing atomic secrets is an unprecedented crime." Europeans like Sartre—"only recently turned fellow traveler"—were deluded in imagining that this was another Dreyfus affair. The Rosenbergs ought to be executed.

Anti-Communist activist Irving Kristol, executive director of the American Committee for Cultural Freedom (ACCF), approached Niebuhr in January, 1953, for assistance in persuading theology professor Paul Lehmann, an old Niebuhr family friend, to resign from his leadership position in a key left-progressive organization, the Emergency Civil Liberties Committee. The ECLC had been founded in 1952 to protect the rights of Communists and non-Communists alike in a time of hysterical finger-pointing. There was no question, Kristol informed Niebuhr, that the ECLC was a Communist front. Already Paul Tillich had resigned. "Is Lehmann beyond the reach of persuasion?" he queried. "I know how impossible it is to demonstrate to someone who holds a high position in a Communist front organization that he really is in such an organization. . . . Lehmann and some of his friends are simply hopping mad at what they consider a slanderous assault. Is it within your power to open their eyes?"

Niebuhr had never been active in the American Committee for Cultural Freedom, an organization later revealed to have been subsidized by the CIA. But he did serve for a year before his stroke as one of several vice-chairmen of the American Committee, and was still one of the intellectual celebrities listed as an honorary chairman of the international parent body, the Congress for Cultural Freedom. His name had helped legitimize the group's activities even when he did not directly take part. In the case of the ACCF campaign against the ECLC he was, despite his illness, willing to help. He had known Lehmann and his father, an Evangelical Synod pastor and head of Elmhurst College, since the 1920s, but the battle against communism took precedence over family friendship: he told Kristol he would add his weight to the effort to persuade Lehmann of "the error of his ways in getting mixed up with these communist front personalities." Lehmann, organizer of the committee's highly publicized Carnegie Hall forum in January, 1953, insisted that the ECLC was not a front; the ACCF's charge, in his view, mirrored McCarthy's own scattershot attacks. He was appalled that Niebuhr, who had been for him a kind of "godfather," could believe that he was being manipulated by Communists.[3]

Until 1953 Niebuhr had rarely if ever expressed personal contempt for those he labeled fellow travelers, though he had disputed their judgment for almost two decades. But when the House Un-American Activities Committee called Methodist preacher (and former Union Seminary student) Jack McMichael to testify, Niebuhr released a stream of abuse in a letter to Schlesinger that was reminiscent of his polemical patriotic outbursts of the First World War.

> The Velde Committee [HUAC] is too stupid for words. They had one of the most notorious fellow travellers in the church before them, a thoroughly dishonest fellow whom the communists used because he was a facile and handsome Methodist preacher from Georgia who could be a good front. . . . The committee summons him and confronts him with previous testimony that he was a member of the party. He vehemently denies this with truth. None of these fellows were asked to become party members. Meanwhile they never confront him with the stream of abuse of America and adoration of Russia which he and Ward handed out in the past years. . . . Our precious Ward has written a letter to the Times saying that he was never a member (also a fact) and then declaring that as a Christian minister he considered himself above party loyalty. Could dishonesty go any farther?

It was one thing to drip vitriol in a private letter. It was another thing to toss off casual accusations of disloyalty in mass magazines like *Look*. In the summer of 1953 Ursula and Schlesinger had combated Niebuhr's boredom and depression by suggesting that he write a profile of professional anti-Communist J. B. Matthews, the former radical whom Niebuhr had known well in the Fellowship of Reconciliation in the thirties. Niebuhr liked the idea and collected reminiscences from Norman Thomas, Roger Baldwin, and Francis Sayre with an eye toward publication in the *Atlantic*. But he got stalled when he realized he did not know how to do a compelling portrait. He lacked the artistic skill, he told Schlesinger, to bring Matthews to life. He turned the piece into a general discussion for *Look* of Matthews's recent charge that "red propaganda has influenced 7,000 Protestant clergy"— a claim that had led to Matthews's dismissal from Senator McCarthy's committee staff when Eisenhower joined the chorus of outrage and termed the accusation "alien to America." Niebuhr called Matthews "almost as dangerous to democracy in the anti-Communist phase of his career as he was in its Communist phase"—a striking formulation since it had not occurred to Niebuhr until 1953 to regard Matthews's Communist games in the thirties as a danger to anyone. But in closing his article Niebuhr asserted

•

that "Matthews, who is fairly unscrupulous in handling total figures, is reasonably accurate when he actually names names. He has identified with considerable accuracy the slightly more than a dozen fellow travelers in the churches."

One of the dozen names named by Matthews and printed by *Look* was Guy Emery Shipler, editor of the *Churchman,* an independent progressive magazine with Episcopalian roots. Shipler was furious with Niebuhr, and with good reason, since the *Churchman* had as early as the thirties been critical of both communism and the Soviets—while also running articles by Harry Ward and other pro-Soviet figures. Shipler demanded evidence for Niebuhr's indirect but clear accusation that he was a fellow traveler and by implication disloyal to America. Niebuhr replied that he lacked the time to dig out "specific evidence" but had "honestly report[ed] my impressions after reading your journal for over a decade." Now Shipler was more indignant. No time to find evidence, but "time to write an article going to millions of Americans charging that I, among others, am a 'fellow traveler,' . . . a defender of or apologist for Russia." Impressions "fall far short of giving any man of integrity the moral right to make such a public statement."

> Frankly, it is a shocking experience to see you helping to whip up the witch hunt by aligning yourself with the Hearst Press, . . . Vernon Kaub, et al, by employing the very technique which has been used against you. . . . You will pardon me, I hope, for smiling a bit when I recalled that Kaub, to mention only one of the baiters, lists you in his "How Red is the Federal Council?" as being "affiliated with"—or whatever trick term he uses—fourteen "red front" organizations. You are two up on me, since he lists me with only twelve! Perhaps I ought to be envious! What would you think of me if I wrote an article calling you a fellow traveler on that kind of "evidence"?

Gradually Niebuhr came to see that his performance in print on both the Rosenbergs and Shipler had been shabby. A year after the *Look* article he finally apologized to Shipler and mailed a retraction to the magazine. "I am terribly sorry about that simple generalization about you as a 'fellow traveler.' . . . I am more and more apologetic for the injury I did you." It was too late to apologize to the Rosenbergs, who had been executed in June, 1953. In the *Look* article in November he already admitted his mistake on the clemency issue: "The President would have been well advised to commute the sentences to life imprisonment" in view of "the hysteria in Europe" over their execution. The Rosenbergs were guilty and deserved death, he believed, but political expediency could have justified sparing them. A year later he apparently repented: their execution, he granted in a public "conversation," was a "moral" as well as a "political" mistake.[4]

But in the tense political atmosphere of 1953 even a man steeped in the tradition of Biblical prophecy—and alive to the ironies of American history—was incapable of perceiving those wrongs. It was not just that Niebuhr the individual was once again—as a hyphenated German-American and as a sometime target of security investigations—trying to affirm his own loyalty to American institutions. That impulse was without doubt one reason for his stance on Lehmann, Shipler, and the Rosenbergs. Indeed,

•

Ursula's own application to become a naturalized American citizen was held up from 1951 to 1954 because of the same old accusations in his FBI file. Niebuhr had a strong personal interest in clearing his name.

Yet even more important was the conviction he shared with other liberal anti-Communists: that McCarthy should not be allowed to monopolize the anti-Communist issue. He and his friends detested McCarthy, and McCarthy vilified the ADA along with the Communists. As long as Tailgunner Joe was riding high they made sure everyone knew they were not soft on communism. Niebuhr went out of his way to praise the Senate Internal Security Committee of Senators McCarran and Jenner as "superb," as a responsible alternative to McCarthy's Sub-Committee on Permanent Investigations and Velde's HUAC. "No wild charges are made, the witnesses are not bulldozed, and the Communists are really ferreted out," he explained to a correspondent who objected to all such Congressional investigations. McCarthy's and HUAC's "indiscriminate charges against 'liberals,' even those who had a certain softness toward the Communist movement at one time," interfered with the genuine campaign against Communists. Only after McCarthy brought down his own crusade by taking on the US Army in televised hearings in mid-1954 did Niebuhr and other liberal anti-Communists relax their vigilance. The domestic Communist threat rapidly evaporated and Niebuhr finally issued his apology to Shipler and his apparent reversal on the Rosenbergs.

The chief literary product of Niebuhr's early confinement—and of his seething anti-communism of 1953—was the collection *Christian Realism and Political Problems,* which he delivered to Scribners in the summer. It was a potpourri of political and theological articles; only four of the eleven pieces were newly published and only one of those—"Augustine's Political Realism"—broke new ground. That essay was a finely nuanced exploration of Augustine's insight that the Neoplatonist quest for self-realization had to be confronted with Paul's Biblical view: self-love was the source of sin. But with one or two other exceptions the volume was scarcely memorable. His poor health prevented him from crafting a book out of disparate occasional writings. The embarrassingly inept proofreading, for which Niebuhr apologized to William Savage after the errors were published, was matched by the egregiously shallow analysis of chapters like "Why Is Communism So Evil?"—a militantly retitled copy of "The Evil of the Communist Idea" that had appeared in the *New Leader* ten days before the Rosenbergs' execution. That magazine, by far the most simplistically anti-Communist journal on the liberal side of the political spectrum, was so pleased with Niebuhr's contribution that it offered him a monthly column that began in 1954. It was a coup for the *New Leader* to acquire a writer of his prestige, and a sharp slap in the face for the *Nation,* Niebuhr's former home and the archenemy of the *New Leader.*

Bertram Wolfe of the State Department's Ideological Advisory Staff also liked Niebuhr's piece on the evil of communism, which in radio broadcast form became "Ideological Special No. 256" on June 30, 1953, ten days after the Rosenbergs were killed. The broadcast, Wolfe wrote, "was widely used by our language desks and greatly appreciated by them." They relished such Niebuhrian flourishes as his initial definition of communism: "an or-

•

ganized evil which spreads terror and cruelty throughout the world and confronts us everywhere with faceless men who are immune to every form of moral and political suasion." Rhetoric like that helped the government justify the Rosenbergs' fate to listeners around the world. Meanwhile Niebuhr had just complained to a correspondent on June 12 about the State Department's giving in to McCarthy by withholding passports from ideologically impure applicants. He was caught in a web of contradictions, unaware of his own part in creating the atmosphere of suspicion that he bemoaned. Ironies proliferated: while one organ of the federal government ran his alarmist message on the Communist threat, another held up his wife's citizenship because of the heightened fear of subversion.[5]

III

Far superior to *Christian Realism and Political Problems* was the volume he completed after the ideological fires began to cool in mid-1954. *The Self and the Dramas of History* was a phenomenal achievement for a man suffering serious physical and emotional ills. Like *Faith and History*, it was a reworking of certain themes in *The Nature and Destiny of Man*. But unlike *Faith and History*, it was well organized and made a novel contribution by elaborating on his critique of Freud. The book had a tranquil tone that marked it as a product of calmer times; but it was also a direct challenge to the more complacent culture of the midfifties. America, Niebuhr pointed out, was as enamored of Freud—and of the popular therapeutic goal of overcoming anxiety and erasing guilt—as the Communist nations were of Marx. Freud was in his view on the right track in positing a fundamental conflict within the self and between the self and the larger community. But he erred in not grasping the full range of these conflicts or their ultimate moral meaning. Freud illuminated the mechanism by which society imposed its will on the individual—the internalization of cultural norms by the "superego"—but neglected the self's "power to defy the community for the sake of its interests and for the sake of interests more inclusive than those of a given community." Men were not simply acted upon by society; they could react, and oppose the values of one community with those of another.

Freud furthermore tended to reduce the problem of guilt to the problem of neurotic guilt, which in Niebuhr's view had "little to do with the sense of guilt arising from the self's violations of norms accepted by it as valid and validated by the experience of other men." Some forms of guilt were destructive and ought to be overcome; others were not only normal but necessary signs of the serious moral life. In fact Niebuhr's complaint was less against Freud himself than against neo-Freudians like Erich Fromm, who imagined that human life might attain a state relatively free of anxiety. Niebuhr was much closer in spirit to Freud's *Civilization and Its Discontents* than he was to Fromm's *Man for Himself*. Freud and Niebuhr both insisted on an inevitable tension between psyche and society and within the psyche itself. Fromm offered an easier vision appropriate to a consumer culture: love was a "phenomenon of abundance" built on a necessary and legitimate "self-love." The "authoritarian" commands of religion could be jettisoned:

•

they made people needlessly guilty when they should be cultivating their personal resources.

The target of Niebuhr's attack was not just Freud and the neo-Freudians. It was also his own colleague Paul Tillich, who by the early 1950s was a close intellectual associate of the neo-Freudians. Tillich was the unacknowledged *éminence grise* of *The Self and the Dramas of History*. He was the "ontologist," the rationalist who reduced the dramatic, historical sensibility of Biblical religion to philosophical structures of "being." The church father Origen was the first, and Tillich the most recent, of those who tried to overcome "the absurdity of the self which is in time and yet beyond time . . . by reducing self to mind and identifying mind with form." When Niebuhr noted approvingly that "Augustine arrested for a time [Origen's] baneful absorption of a Biblical dramatic faith into an ontology," he was proclaiming his own intention as the modern Augustine to arrest Tillich's influence. "If Karl Barth is the Tertullian of our day," Niebuhr had written in a collection on Tillich in 1952, "abjuring ontological speculations for fear that they may obscure or blunt the kerygma of the Gospel, Tillich is the Origen of our period." He hesitated to place himself in print among the Big Three, but he divulged his preferred historic place to Scarlett several years later: "About Barth and Tillich and myself. I wouldn't want to be Tertullian. He was too obscurantist. I would rather emulate Augustine."[6]

Niebuhr and Tillich had been the best of friends in the 1930s, and continued to work closely together during the war in German relief and political affairs. But their relations were cooling even during the war and in the postwar years became increasingly strained. Their intellectual debate at midcentury was a serious one—his dialogue with Tillich, he told Scarlett, reflected age-old differences within the church—but it rested in part on a personal conflict that Niebuhr could not mention in print. Tillich had for years been engaged in a succession of sexual escapades. He was not just unfaithful to his wife, Hannah; he was exuberantly, compulsively promiscuous. Niebuhr once sent one of his female students to see Tillich during his office hours. He welcomed her warmly, closed the door, and—according to the student—began fondling her. She reported the episode to Niebuhr, who never forgave Tillich.

But even without that incident Niebuhr would not have been able to stomach either Tillich's behavior or the intellectual perspective to which it was related. Tillich's personal religion was deeply infused by aesthetics and psychology, and at times resembled a kind of nature worship; his ethics stressed not sin and responsibility, but establishing wholeness, experiencing the fullness of being. He was much more open than Niebuhr to novel experience, and to the worlds of art and music. He lived not just by his mind but by his senses. In earlier years he tried good-naturedly to interest Niebuhr in the flowers blossoming in the seminary courtyard ("They were there last year too," said Niebuhr as he rushed past), and in the afternoon clouds streaking over Manhattan. Niebuhr was oblivious to the beauty of the Berkshires in summer or the Hudson in winter. He could not open his senses, could not rest long enough to feel, smell, touch. Tillich thought Ernest Jones's description of Freud applied just as well to Niebuhr: "Someone whose instincts were far more powerful than those of the average man,

•

but whose repressions were even more potent." He did not mean it as a compliment.

Tillich, on the other hand, was so absorbed in his senses that he down-played the role of conscience that to Niebuhr lay at the heart of the moral life. He turned further and further away from the social and political interests that they had earlier shared. "Responsibility" for Tillich was coming to mean responsibility to one's own self: adjust, develop, reach for fulfillment. For Niebuhr, as he had preached forty years before in his first sermon, "he who seeks his own life shall lose it." Human fulfillment, such as it was, came as a by-product of participating in the historical struggles of one's time. It could not be sought directly, procured through therapy or the diligent pursuit of the good life. Tillich easily won their published debate over ontology versus Biblical drama, by showing that even Niebuhr could not dispense with such categories of being as "finite freedom." But the published debate was not the vital issue; it camouflaged a more visceral conflict over the meaning of moral commitment.

Of the two, Niebuhr was the more defensive by the midfifties. Tillich's star was rising relative to his own in the seminary, in the church, and in the wider society. Niebuhr's cultural influence had peaked in the crisis years of economic breakdown, war, and Cold War; he embodied steely resolve for a time of sacrifice and reconsecration. Tillich was the theologian for an era of abundance, ease, and self-satisfaction—and for the anxieties that inevitably pushed through the thick growth of contentment. Even atheists clutched copies of *The Courage to Be* and *The Shaking of the Foundations*. Of course Tillich was much more than a popular moralist. He was an original thinker of enormous distinction. As a professional philosopher and systematic theologian, he was out of Niebuhr's league, as Niebuhr well knew. Tillich's erudition and imagination awed him. After the war he did not even try to grapple with Tillich's ideas, just as he refused to study Barth. In his intellectual defensiveness he tended to shift the debate with each of them to the areas of his own strength: ethics and politics. If Barth was politically naive, his theology must have little to recommend it; if Tillich disregarded historical and ethical responsibility, his philosophy must be a maze of fruitless abstractions. The irony is that the cultural currents of the 1950s lifted Tillich to great renown even as an ethical thinker: an authority on coping with the dissatisfactions of modern existence.

Niebuhr's frustration finally erupted in print in 1956, but he made matters worse for himself by tackling Tillich on his home turf: modern art. In a television interview Tillich had called Picasso's *Guernica* a "Protestant" masterpiece. Niebuhr took umbrage at the label and at the artist himself, whom he designated with anachronistic alarm as "a well-known fellow traveler." The painting was not Protestant because Picasso "views the world at sixes and sevens or, in short, as disjointed and tragic"; there was no redemption, no path beyond tragedy. Niebuhr admitted awkwardly that "this is merely the reaction of an ignoramus" in matters of aesthetics, but cautioned his former friend that anyone like Tillich with "no more to say about Christianity and the arts . . . had better keep silent." Tillich, in reply, was composed and confident: let us welcome modern art, not fear it. From his position of strength he had no need to answer a petulant eruption that

•

rebutted itself. It was a fitting symbol of his new strength that he had just moved to Harvard in 1955 (after retiring from Union) to occupy the same university professorship that Conant had offered Niebuhr in 1942.[7]

For Niebuhr the *reductio ad absurdam* of Tillich's fixation on sensual fulfillment and Fromm's validation of self-love were the two Kinsey reports on human sexuality, which had appeared in 1948 and 1953 and become major cultural monuments despite their technical, scientific presentation. Kinsey the zoologist made the achievement of orgasm "a kind of *summum bonum.*" But "an apprenticeship in investigating gall wasps" did not prepare him to grasp that "sexual relations are necessarily relations between persons." Physical intimacy "becomes intolerable if undertaken without mutual respect and ultimately without mutual fidelity." Kinsey, in blissful ignorance of any deeper dimensions to human existence, made the sexual performance he could measure—frequency of orgasm—the essence of sexuality itself. He implicitly banished caring and long-term covenants from the realm of sex, and equated the quality of intimacy with the quantity of intercourse. As Niebuhr's neighbor Lionel Trilling pointed out, there was only one chapter "which hints that sex may be touched with tenderness": the one on "human-animal contacts." And Kinsey had created a new folk hero: "the 'scholarly and skilled lawyer' who for thirty years has had an orgasmic frequency of thirty times a week." Like Trilling, Niebuhr was appalled that Kinsey's "abysmal ignorance of the heights and depths of the human spirit should be cloaked and dignified by the prestige of 'science.' " The authority of science was being invoked to promote a culture of spiritless self-absorption. Not that the conventional religious legalism was much better. But he believed, as he wrote to a conscience-striken young correspondent, that sexual relations without "continuing mutual responsibility" are "bound to hurt one or the other partner. . . . I would not regard any sexual relations outside of marriage as a mortal sin, but I think the prohibition of them corresponds to the true facts of human nature and is not arbitrary."[8]

IV

For all his public berating of white-coated experts in human behavior, and his dismay at the spread of the therapeutic mentality, Niebuhr knew from painful family experience that professional therapy was in some cases a matter of necessity. By 1955 he realized that he too needed the psychiatric treatment that all his siblings had undergone. The strain of finishing *The Self and the Dramas of History* in August, 1954—only two hours a day on the typewriter, but many more mulling over the manuscript—brought on a prolonged weakness and depression that he tried in vain to escape. He had to cancel his trip to the World Council of Churches conference in Evanston, Illinois, where he was to deliver a major speech (it was read by his Heath neighbor Angus Dun). "Electrical treatment" for his lame left side at Saint Luke's in Manhattan brought no improvement. Counseling by his friend Dr. Lawrence Kubie helped a bit, but his spirits continued to sag. His own home remedy—more work—bore no fruit for either him or his readers. All he could manage were short articles, and the quality of his

•

monthly religious column—now published only by the *Lutheran, Episcopal Churchnews,* and his own denomination's *Messenger*—deteriorated seriously.

In the summer of 1955 he sought treatment at the Austin Riggs Center for the Study and Treatment of Neuroses in Stockbridge, Massachusetts. He received antidepressive medicine and psychotherapy from Dr. Edgerton Howard, and also consulted with Erik Erikson, a lay psychoanalyst in residence at Riggs since 1951. He confided in Erikson about the inferiority he felt in his scholarly profession, but Erikson did not attempt to analyze him. After his ten visits with Dr. Howard, Niebuhr felt mentally restored. Howard made him gradually aware, Niebuhr told his friend June Bingham, that he had been in a depression ever since his stroke over three years earlier, and that his emotional problem stemmed from "the violence of the shift from great activity to comparative impotence." Once again he was confident that he could work. "This human ego is even more complex than I had imagined. I learned a lot both about myself and about good psychiatry in the process this summer." He had new appreciation for the mystery of the self, he added to Scarlett: "We may know everything about ourselves rationally, and yet we need technically competent wisdom to get out of these kind of jams." He was grateful to Dr. Howard when he found he was able to do his seminary work with much more "zest and enjoyment" than the year before. In the summer of 1956 the Niebuhrs sold their cottage in Heath and bought a home in Stockbridge. The main reason for the move was to be closer to New York and within walking distance of a town center; a car was essential at Heath, and Niebuhr could no longer drive. An added benefit of the relocation was proximity to the Riggs Center.

Dr. Robert Coles, who knew Niebuhr before and after his stroke, believes that Niebuhr's friends and doctors may have led him to put too much faith in psychotherapy. His depression, Coles thinks, was in all likelihood organic in origin, a product of his stroke; it could have been permanently reversed only by antidepressant drugs that were not yet available in the 1950s. Psychotherapy with Dr. Howard, although temporarily helpful, may have generated false hopes which—when later disappointed—produced further depression. Niebuhr had been so miserable that his friends and doctors had naturally wanted to give him some kind of relief. Yet their very efforts to do good—in a classically Niebuhrian tangle—may have made matters worse in the end. Like William Carlos Williams, whom Coles also knew well, Niebuhr had suffered some brain damage as a result of a stroke. Coles suggests that a frank admission by the doctors that they were powerless to cure his depression might have been the best course. For Niebuhr possessed the capacity to put himself in perspective, and the ability to laugh despite his problems. Coles remembers that friends like W. H. Auden and Felix Frankfurter knew how to perk Niebuhr up as well as any psychiatrist. Indeed, it was Niebuhr's own natural suspicion of psychiatry's pretensions that led Coles—himself a psychiatrist—to value Niebuhr's work. He was far superior to Tillich, in Coles's view, because of his skepticism about psychological therapies. Building on that skepticism might have been the best therapeutic decision.[9]

Niebuhr always attributed his serious depression to feelings of uselessness that stemmed from decreased physical vitality; his own earlier productivity remained his norm, and he no longer measured up. He thought he was wallowing in inactivity in the mid- and late 1950s, when he was in fact doing a remarkable amount of work: in addition to teaching and writing he served as vice-president of the seminary. Still he bemoaned the change from his earlier whirlwind existence, and the loss of his unparalleled oratorical powers. Other disappointments may also have contributed to the severe stage of his depression in 1954 and 1955. One may well have been his losing battle against the cultural wave that Tillich was riding to the prominence of the Harvard chair. Another was ironically *The Self and the Dramas of History* itself. While he was working on it his depression eased. Once it was finished he began to dread an unfavorable critical response—the same syndrome that always afflicted Richard Niebuhr upon completing a manuscript. "The book depressed me very much upon rereading," he told June Bingham just as the reviews were beginning to appear in the spring of 1955. "I never had the same confidence [about my books] since my sickness. I have really gotten to be quite a different person."

A further irritant in late 1954 was a wrenching crisis in his relationship with Bingham herself. Wife of Jonathan Bingham, who had pushed him for the Yale presidency in 1949, she had first encountered Niebuhr at the ADA convention in Chicago earlier in that same year. His pep-rally address captivated her, and in her midthirties she became his ardent student and disciple. An experienced writer, she determined after his stroke to do a book about his life and work, an idea that embarrassed him since it might appear that he had promoted the venture. But he liked the Binghams, who were also close friends of the Schlesingers, and June's enthusiasm was contagious. He enjoyed bantering with her about the exploits of their respective poodles, and seeing the sudden illumination in her face when she grasped the meaning of a tough kernel of theology. He instructed his secretary Nola Meade to allow her to see his private files of correspondence and did not resist as she conducted scores of interviews with his intimates—including his mother, sister, and brother—and his far-flung acquaintances.

Unaccountably, in December, 1953, he changed his tune and asked her to put off the "biography." He claimed to be "engaged on a magnum opus"—*The Self and the Dramas of History*—and thought that the biography "might better come after I have more or less finished my 'system.' " She was crestfallen: only half in jest she called it her "banishment" for having tried "to eat the fruit of the tree of knowledge about Reinhold." But she accepted his condition that she publish her book only after a five-year wait and she persisted in collecting information. A year later, with Niebuhr already in his serious depression, she received a second shock. The biography, he informed her, would have to be scratched altogether. For Ursula had just confessed to him that her own abiding unhappiness about Bingham's project "was at least partially dictated by a long cherished desire to do a biography of me." He was duty-bound to give his wife priority despite the "serious injustice to you." Bingham could write an interpretation of his thought if she wished—as other authors had already done—but it could not be a biography.

Bingham was angry, and Niebuhr was left wondering why his wife had never mentioned her own desire to him before. "Ursula was not quite open with me about her plans," he told Schlesinger. He assumed she was reluctant to mention an idea for a project she might undertake only after his death. Bingham herself conjectured that Ursula "might feel threatened" by "my affection for R. Never tried to hide it. Am like Figaro [the Bingham poodle] with leash when R. mentioned"—ready to walk anywhere. "Loving R. makes me love . . . everyone else more rather than less. I have very little guilt about it—although not 100% pure: no love is. But it's unpossessive. U. rather than feeling threatened could feel glad for few pleasures R. has." If Niebuhr felt there had been any pleasures, however innocent, he was not prepared to acknowledge them. He apologized profusely to Bingham for his "indecisions, and ultimately a lack of complete honesty in regard to my embarrassment" about becoming the subject of a biography during his life. "I hope you will ultimately be able to make use of this facet of my character to give a really true picture of myself." Dwelling on his "embarrassment"—a term to which Niebuhr turned with extraordinary frequency when confronted with difficult feelings—concealed as much as it revealed. It allowed him to see himself as a humble innocent trying, with admitted awkwardness, to prevent a biography from advertising his significance. It absolved him of responsibility in the failure of communication with his wife or the grave injustice to Bingham. He suffered acute discomfort over the affair, which must have aggravated his depression, but could not probe the roots of it. Fascinated by the mysteries of the self, in this instance he kept his own safely at a distance.[10]

Embarrassed enough by biography, he was frozen by the thought of autobiography. Memoirs, he asserted again and again, were narcissistic, pretentious, only fitfully honest. When a collection devoted to his thought came out in 1956—four years after the same editors and publishers had brought one out on Tillich's—his opening twenty-page "intellectual autobiography" was long on the intellectual and short on the autobiography. In three pages he passed briskly over his personal formation. His memory for events was as fitfully accurate as he said it would be—as in his claim that he came to Union in 1928 "largely at the instigation of my friend Sherwood Eddy, who persuaded the seminary faculty to call me to a Chair of Christian Ethics." He was not given a chair until the Yale offer in 1930 forced Coffin's hand; it was Eddy who paid his entire salary for the first two years. Niebuhr's formulation was in this case not entirely a matter of forgetfulness. He had specifically asked June Bingham to keep Eddy's financial role out of her book. But since Eddy himself was proud of his role and soon described it truthfully in his own memoirs, Bingham got around the ban by referring to his published account. She deferred to her subject's wishes in part: she mentioned only that Eddy "contributed" to the salary.

Niebuhr's sketchy outline of autobiographical facts was much less revealing about himself than the moving story he recounted on the next page about "two old ladies" in Bethel Church. It was a classic New Testament parable. Each of the ladies was confronting death, but only one of them was facing it with faith. The faithless old lady was "too preoccupied with self, too aggrieved that Providence should not have taken account of her virtue in failing to protect her against a grievous illness." The faithful old lady, despite her cancer, "expressed gratitude for all the mercies of God

•

which she had received in life." She was one of "the true Christians who live by 'a broken spirit and a contrite heart,' " and a sign of "a mystery of grace which no one can fathom." Mired in his own depression as he wrote the essay, Niebuhr yearned for that kind of serenity, for deliverance from debilitating self-pity. He wondered if he belonged to the "invisible Church" of those who had died to self. He tended to doubt it. "One must come to the conclusion that none of us can be certain whether we have the faith or the courage to pass any final test."

His twenty-page "Reply" to his interpreters and critics was also more revealing about himself than his explicitly autobiographical remarks. He began by signaling his embarrassment that the critics had been "asked to consider a system of thought which does not deserve the attention which they were asked to give it." This was genuine humility, but with a subtle admixture of defensiveness: I'm not a theological scholar, therefore don't judge me as one, spare me your fine distinctions. Yet he did engage his critics in a far-ranging intellectual exchange of the sort that he had rarely had the time or patience to attempt before his stroke. He graciously conceded many of his critics' points: they were right to object to his use of the confusing term *myths* to describe the central truths of the Christian faith, right to find fault with his notion (in *The Nature and Destiny of Man*) of an "equality of sin and inequality of guilt." "Myth" conveyed a sense of falsity or fabrication; "equality of sin and inequality of guilt" reduced the mystery of human evil to falsely quantitative terms.

Niebuhr's readiness to retract earlier theological formulations was matched by his eagerness to dismiss his earlier political views. Reading Arthur Schlesinger's account of his political peregrinations made him "plead guilty" to the charge of clinging too long to "shreds of Marxist dogma." He found it "rather embarrassing to retrace one's pilgrimage . . . because it becomes so apparent that one was incredibly stupid in slowly arriving at a position which now seems valid but which required all the tragedies of history to clarify in one's own mind." The liberal pragmatism that he and Schlesinger embraced took on the character of trans-historical wisdom; despite his dialectical play of mind he could detect no hidden virtues in the vice of his earlier radical commitments. Like many intellectuals in the 1950s, he consigned those views to the period of youth, immaturity, recklessness. Branded with that label of irresponsibility they were not liable to re-emerge as prophetic levers against the certainties of the present.[11]

After the collection appeared, many readers found their appetites for his autobiographical reflections whetted. His friend William Lee Miller at *The Reporter* persuaded him to try his hand at a lengthier personal account, on the model of his earlier *Leaves*. His doctors and Ursula encouraged him: the effort might bear therapeutic as well as intellectual fruit. Niebuhr even hoped it might turn into his next book, now that he had finished his "system" with *The Self and the Dramas of History*. He produced four chapters: "Detroit," "England," "Germany," and "The Politics of the Thirties." All four were dull, meandering, and pocked with factual errors about himself: none of the spark of the original *Leaves,* none of the tension between pride and prophecy, belief and doubt. He tried revising, but grew "dubious" about "the whole mess," as he put it to Miller. To Bingham he vowed to "stick to my business of handling ideas and not try to dredge up memories. Autobiography requires more imagination than I have." Miller shared his view of the "later Leaves." The pieces lacked "the concreteness and vividness" of the first *Leaves,* and the *Reporter*'s editors rejected them. Over the years Niebuhr had suppressed the introspective impulses that produced *Leaves.* Ironically it was that volume itself which cast doubt on introspection—for the reason that it tended to morbidity. By the 1950s he was no longer capable of self-revelatory writing. He understood that. Paul Ramsey had written him shortly after his stroke about a planned *Festschrift* for Richard Niebuhr. Could Reinhold contribute a "biographical chapter" that traced "your own personal and intellectual relationship with your brother through the years"? The idea made him numb. Even if he were in good health, he replied, he would doubt "the propriety of a chapter by me."

> To write appreciatively of one's own family seems to violate some kind of canon, and to write biographically of a brother seems to me to be almost impossible. I wish I could see my way free to do this, but the more I try to think of how such a chapter should be written the more nonplussed I become.

His heart had not been in the "later Leaves" project; he had gone along with the idea since the doctors thought it might do some good. It was not just that "reminiscences are only precariously honest," as he wrote in the draft of "Detroit." It was also that too much self-examination threatened to undermine broader, communal commitments. It compromised historical responsibility. It was Richard's way, not his. For a quarter-century he had equated prolonged self-scrutiny with the passivity of a leisured consumer culture. Even in his enforced leisure of the 1950s he was not going to let down his guard against self-absorption.[12]

V

Niebuhr's cultural critique of passive self-regard fueled the political critique of the Eisenhower administration that he developed in the late 1950s: Ike was a do-nothing golfer, content to linger on the back nine while world problems worsened. In 1954 he had praised Eisenhower's refusal to save the French in Indochina; military intervention in Asian civil strife was foredoomed to failure. But with the Suez crisis in 1956 he and his liberal friends began clamoring for a new toughness in foreign policy. Niebuhr was not asking for a return to what he now termed the anti-Communist "psychosis" of 1953, but he wanted to rekindle a sense of crisis and struggle. Eisenhower was not standing up to the adversaries of freedom: like other self-satisfied Americans he was misled by de-Stalinization and by the Russians' warm embrace at the Geneva summit in 1955. He was in fact pursuing "a new pacifism and a new isolationism," ignoring the threat posed by Egypt's Nasser to the Suez Canal and to the survival of Israel. Naturally the British and French had in desperation colluded with the Israelis to protect their interests. In the end the only winner was the Soviet Union. It could pose as the defender of the United Nations and international law at the very

•

moment it was crushing the Hungarian revolt. The President and Secretary of State Dulles were abstract moralists out of touch with concrete configurations of power, wedded to a nuclear strategy of massive retaliation, and impotent in the face of subtle forms of subversion. "The one [Ike] is amiable and the other [Dulles] not," he intimated to Frankfurter, "but the stupidity is equal." The more imaginative Russians were content to play the waiting game of cultivating Third World leaders like Nasser.

Meanwhile, in the early stages of the Suez and Hungarian crises, Eisenhower crushed Stevenson again with a lopsided 58 percent of the vote. Niebuhr and Schlesinger commiserated over the "great holocaust," in Niebuhr's phrase. Ike's "mistakes and illusions" had managed to endear him to the voters all the more. That figured, said Niebuhr, since "the Eisenhower myth is partly dependent upon the desire of the American people to forget their anxieties and troubles." The leader and the led had their heads in the sand. "Eisenhower," Niebuhr informed Norman Thomas, "is becoming the Chamberlain of our day." He was risking the loss of "strategic fortresses" like Israel in the interest of " 'peace in our time,' " Niebuhr argued in print, "only to be forced to fight in the end without those fortresses." And a "prosperous and comfortable" people were glad to avoid responsibilities that might disturb their ease. "Totalitarian nations" could now "safely push forward everywhere, for we have announced beforehand that we will not assume any risks."

Yet the primary Soviet "push forward" was in Hungary, and Niebuhr knew the United States could do nothing to aid the freedom fighters. He, like Roosevelt, had conceded Eastern Europe to the Soviets at the end of the war. Americans, he thought, were "so enthralled" by the Hungarian resistance that they were in danger of forgetting about Israel, where United States power could make a difference. But if Americans were in a sense too preoccupied with Hungary, Karl Barth the "neutralist" was not. Niebuhr castigated Barth repeatedly for his "silence" on Hungary. He and *Christian Century* editors Harold Fey and Theodore Gill agreed the time was ripe to quash the "dangerous cult," in Gill's phrase, that was beginning to boom now that Barth's *Dogmatik* was coming out in English. It was a cult of eschatological irresponsibility that in Niebuhr's view paralleled Tillich's therapeutic irresponsibility. Barth had been an active adviser to the Hungarian Reformed Church and had urged it to cooperate with the Communist authorities; no human government was perfect, he told them, and none was diabolical. Granted, replied Niebuhr, but communism was demonic enough to stand up against. Even Jean-Paul Sartre had repented of his neutralism in the wake of the rumbling Russian tanks. Why could Barth not see that western capitalism—which he deprecated for its "dollar worship" and dismissed as a "fleshpot of Egypt"—was, unlike Communist "despotism," compatible with justice? From Niebuhr's standpoint Barthian neo-orthodoxy, like Tillich's ontological sensualism and Eisenhower's naive moralism, threatened to lull American churchpeople into a disregard of historical struggles for proximate justice.[13]

While Barthian influence was spreading in the American churches, so too, Niebuhr noted, was that of Billy Graham. His crusade was the driving force behind the American "religious revival" of the 1950s. On the surface

Barth and Graham had nothing in common: Barth's faith built upon critical Biblical scholarship, Graham's upon the old frontier certainties. But at a deeper level they shared an aversion to secularism and to the worldly quest for historical justice. Faced with what he considered European obscurantism and American fundamentalism, Niebuhr found himself pushed to a defense of the same liberal Social Gospel he had been repudiating for decades. It might have lacked "realism," but it was "infinitely more realistic than the pietistic individualism which it replaced," and which Graham was resurrecting. Niebuhr proposed to Graham that he make his appeal a shade tougher to accept, make his Christ a critic as well as a celebrator of culture. His evangelical message should "incorporate the demand of love transcending racial boundaries," become "a whole-souled effort to give the Negro neighbor his full due as a man and brother." Graham was certainly better, Niebuhr urged, than the popular religious therapists who dispensed with a God of judgment altogether, but his "evangelism has a blandness which befits the Eisenhower era."

When the New York City Protestant Council of Churches voted to sponsor Graham's New York crusade in June, 1957, Niebuhr was angry. "All the high pressure techniques of modern salesmanship" and "all the arts of the Madison Avenue crowd" were pressed into service. Local pastors were reduced to "ballyhoo helpers . . . to swell the Madison Square crowds." Henry Van Dusen liked the crusade, and criticized Niebuhr for insisting on a uniform "sophisticated" Gospel to "nourish the tough minds of 'intellectuals.'" What "the masses need first," he claimed, "is the pure milk of the Gospel in more readily digestible form." He was echoing Niebuhr's own defense of Billy Sunday's Detroit crusade forty years earlier. He reminded his colleague that "there are many, of whom I am one, who . . . would probably never have come within the sound of Dr. Niebuhr's voice . . . if they had not been first touched by the message of the earlier Billy." But Niebuhr was unpersuaded. The alliance between Graham's revivalism and Madison Avenue bespoke a new and dangerous cultural captivity for religion.

In fact Graham's crusade, and the larger religious revival, brought home to Niebuhr how secular he was. That perception was the unspoken theme of his motley collection of occasional papers *Pious and Secular America*, which Scribners released in late 1957. "Christians will have to agree with responsible and discriminating secularists," he wrote, that the preaching of

> [Graham's] simple version of the Christian faith as an alternative to the discredited utopian illusions [of the Social Gospel] is very ironic. It gives even simpler answers to insoluble problems than they. It cuts through all the hard antinomies of life and history by the simple promise that really good people will really be good. It does this at the precise moment when secularism, purged of its illusions, is modestly ready to work at tasks for which there are no immediate rewards and to undertake burdens for which there can be no promise of relief.

America, he observed, was more secular than any other nation, but also more religious. The best of its secularism drew on deep religious roots—

•

as in the civic virtue of secular Jews like Fred Butzel—while its popular religion aped the worst of secularism, the "frantic pursuit" of "success." The most thoughtful essay in the book—"The Relations of Christians and Jews in Western Civilization"—argued forcefully that Christians had no business trying to convert Jews, in part because of the secular fruits of Jewish piety.

The ironic essence of American culture was its curious compound of piety and secularism, parochialism and cosmopolitanism. Had he been inclined to autobiography he might have added that Reinhold Niebuhr was as paradoxical as America itself: he was the most religious of secular figures and the most secular of religious ones. He was so secular indeed that he had his doubts about going to church in the midst of a religious revival; easy piety perturbed him more than ever. His son, Christopher, he told Bingham, was very conventional about attending church every Sunday, though critical of every church he went to. His daughter, Elisabeth, now at Radcliffe, rarely attended the Harvard chapel—where Christopher had been a fixture—because she found it boring. Niebuhr sympathized with her view. He was "more and more skeptical" about "churchgoing per se." Three years later he was still seething at "the smugness of the current piety," as he put it to Frankfurter. Piety "has been reduced to triviality . . . in this seminary and indeed in the whole church. You can imagine my state of mind after having devoted all these decades to the religious enterprise."[14]

VI

Pious and Secular America was a clear demonstration that his literary interests were now primarily political and cultural, not theological. Once the nine essays—four previously published—were in Scribners' hands at the end of the spring term in 1957, he retired to Stockbridge for the summer to garden and read politics and history. Some months before he had accepted Robert Oppenheimer's invitation to spend the calendar year 1958 at Princeton's Institute for Advanced Study, and he was already feeling the pressure to prepare for it. His project, he told Frankfurter, would be a book on "The Morality of Nations," but "the prospect of doing this is both thrilling and frightening because I must elaborate an avocational interest into something which will not make the Institute look too silly." He sensed this might be his final chance to produce a serious political work, but he knew he was an amateur and wondered if he was overreaching himself. "I am spending so much of the summer on foreign policy," he told Scarlett, "that I feel an apostate from my calling." In late 1956 he had felt physically and emotionally strong enough to take on the challenge. By the summer of 1957 he was bothered by telltale symptoms of anxiety: recurrent and painful headaches.

A few days after moving to Princeton in early 1958 Niebuhr returned for an evening to New York so that the ADA could honor him at its New York City Roosevelt Day dinner. Ironically, official ADA honors had begun coming his way after he had virtually dropped out of the organization. The tenth anniversary convention in March, 1957, sent its "warmest greetings"

•

to him, regretted his absence, and proclaimed him "the spiritual father" of the ADA. Meanwhile he was telling June Bingham, "I must say, though this is rank heresy, that I am not as deeply committed to [the ADA] as I once was." The Roosevelt Day citation at the Waldorf-Astoria before seven hundred diners was Joseph Rauh's and his colleagues' way of celebrating former battles, but it may also have been an attempt to draw Niebuhr back into the fold. Niebuhr would of course not be able to come to meetings, but he could continue to sign statements and put his name on fund-raising appeals. Niebuhr did enjoy the dinner—a rare evening sortie—but he did not recommit himself to the ADA. His few hours of daily activity would go to his own work, and Ursula was standing firm guard over him to prevent any scattering of energies.[15]

At Princeton they occupied a new and architecturally striking apartment that made free use of glass construction. His wife was delighted to be circumscribed by innovative design, but Niebuhr called it a "modernistic horror." With her support he supposed he could stand it for a year. Ursula, understanding how emotionally frail he had become since his stroke, re-arranged her Barnard schedule so that she would commute to New York only three days a week. She devoted herself to keeping his spirits up and helping him make headway on his book. But the project went slowly in the spring and his confidence, shaky from the start, evaporated completely. He relapsed into the serious depression of 1954–1955. He tried to extricate himself by analyzing its causes. He told Scarlett in June that he had put in too many hours on the typewriter. Exhaustion came first, then depression, magnified by his shame at falling into the trap: "My basic difficulty derives from an almost neurotic compulsion to get things done. This enabled me to do a good deal of work in my lifetime but was unfortunate after my stroke." But he also knew that the cause of the problem was intellectual as well as physical and emotional. He wrote to Schlesinger for help on an historical point and confessed that "I don't feel I have enough historical knowledge for the chapter. . . . As a matter of fact, I don't have enough historical knowledge for any of the chapters that I have written." He was forced to ask himself "why I should have been foolhardy enough to write such a book . . . at the end of my days and with my physical powers, and perhaps my intellectual powers, on the wane."

By fall his condition was worse, despite treatment at the Riggs Center during the summer. His doctors considered shock treatments, but apparently ruled them out for fear of deleterious side effects. Scarlett suggested postponing the book, but "the trouble is," replied Niebuhr, "that I must work and would not know what to do with myself in idleness. I have no hobbies." The darkness was all-enveloping by mid-September: the "will to live," he announced starkly, "seems to have departed from me." He was committed to returning to Princeton for the fall term and dreaded it. On her own days in Princeton Ursula labored with him over the manuscript. George Kennan of the Institute's Historical School encouraged him with generally enthusiastic readings of his chapters, and by mid-December the manuscript was done. He wanted to call it no less than *Dominions in Nations and Empires: A Study of the Structures and Moral Dilemmas of the Political Order*

•

Relevant to the Perplexities of a Nuclear Age. T. S. Eliot at Faber and Faber, which had contracted to publish the book in Britain, was appalled, and urged the American editor, L. H. Brague, to hold out for something simple like *Nations and Empires*. "We didn't like the title either," Brague replied. "If you are able to persuade the author to agree to a less abstract and forbidding title, more power to you."[16]

Scribners had reason to be worried about more than the title. Niebuhr's friends George Kennan, Hans Morgenthau, and Kenneth Thompson did offer some reassurance with their prepublication plaudits. Yet even Kennan mixed some misgivings with glowing sentiments. He sensed, he wrote, a certain fatigue in Niebuhr's work. When *The Structure of Nations and Empires* appeared in August, 1959—with a twenty-two-word subtitle that Scribners buried in tiny print on the title page—it was apparent that Kennan's doubt was better placed than his praise. Niebuhr had shown great personal courage in completing the book at all, but the result was an intellectual disappointment. Even before the book's release he knew that it would not do well. "I have the suspicion," he confessed to Scarlett on the eve of publication, "that I have written my last book." The response to *Structure* was tepid when it was not silent or scornful. "The book has not been the success which I, in my egotism, expected. I thought it would make more of a contribution," he reported glumly. He had withdrawn from the theological and ethical studies where he had some claim to expertise, yet was "too much of an amateur to be regarded as competent for political studies."

The Structure of Nations and Empires announced itself as "a study of dominion and community in nations and empires in the whole of history." It was going to avoid the merely speculative tendencies of Toynbee and Spengler by following "rigorous empirical procedures in distinguishing the contingent and the novel from the permanent and the perennial in history." An impossible goal for even the most erudite of scholars. Niebuhr conducted the reader on a brisk survey of civilizations far and wide with the aid of a small number of secondary sources, and his writing lacked passion and precision. He had already expressed his key ideas on nations and empires in his articles, and done so more forcefully. America had more power than any of the ancient or modern empires, he claimed, but it lacked the prestige to exercise that power in a world of autonomous nations, which prided themselves on their recalcitrance. It could not even bring the western nations, much less the underdeveloped ones, together under its leadership. The Soviets, meanwhile, led a "real empire of traditional mold"—"with an ideological cement above the level of national loyalty"—but they too were confronted by the recalcitrance of autonomous nations: Poland and Hungary. Yet his book went so far afield from these central concerns that it became an amorphous heap of data and generalizations. It was no wonder that of the "many political scientists" who received advance copies, only his friend Arnold Wolfers bothered to acknowledge it. His literary future looked bleak. It was small consolation that the American Academy of Arts and Letters had admitted him in May to its elite fifty-member fellowship. Honors bestowed in recognition of past powers and achievements must have made his present quandary all the more painful to contemplate.[17]

•

VII

There were other reasons for sadness in 1959, besides the failure of his book and the apparent dead-end of his literary career. In April Hulda died suddenly at McCormick Seminary in Chicago, where she had taught Christian education since 1946. His doctors discouraged him from attending the funeral; Richard went out from New Haven for the service, and afterward took occasion to destroy all her correspondence, including his own and Reinhold's letters to her. He was determined to wipe out any evidence of his own or his siblings' private struggles. Lydia, now eighty-nine years old and again uprooted, came east to live with Richard, but frequently visited Reinhold in New York. When she did not visit, she wrote once or twice a week, as she had since moving to Chicago with Hulda in 1946. He was still her bow anchor. Soon she grew lonely for the midwest, and at the end of the year moved back to Lincoln, Illinois. "Yesterday I went to the station to bid my mother a sad farewell," he wrote to Scarlett. "She will be ninety on Christmas day and I doubt whether I will ever see her again. Such are the sadnesses of old age." A year later she died, he informed Bingham, "without suffering, in only two hours of illness." Again he was unable to travel to the funeral.

He also had to contend with the end of his teaching career at Union; his last full year began in the fall of 1959. Since 1928 the seminary had been the center that held all his fragmented activities together. It was his fellowship, indeed his church. The students were his favorite congregation, in chapel, in class, and in office hours. Whatever the press of his other activities, he had never compromised his commitment to them. He might have his packed suitcase beside the lectern at his last class of the week, he might be exhausted at his first class of the new week, but he did not cancel a class more than twice a term. No doubt he liked his students' adulation, but there was more to it than that. He was more at home with students than with anyone else. Like him, they were oblivious to social form and scornful of polite acquiescence. He admired their lack of cynicism, their willingness to believe that commitment mattered. Retirement for him was not just the end of a teaching career, but the disruption of a primary bond. At the final dinner in his honor in May, 1960, he wept openly. President Van Dusen announced the creation of the endowed Reinhold Niebuhr Professorship of Social Ethics, to which scores of his colleagues, friends, and admirers—W. H. Auden, Chester Bowles, T. S. Eliot, Hubert Humphrey, Walter Lippmann, Jacques Maritain, Adlai Stevenson, Norman Thomas, Paul Tillich, and Arnold Toynbee among them—contributed. It was entirely fitting that the very first contribution came from Niebuhr's early benefactor, eighty-nine-year-old Sherwood Eddy, who gave $5,000. It was also fitting that the chair's first occupant was John Bennett, his comrade and friend for three decades.[18]

Once the Niebuhrs had completed the move out of their seminary suite and into a new riverview apartment at 340 Riverside Drive he felt better. And soon he was immersed in politics, his favorite tonic. Robert Hutchins had invited him to spend the summer at the Fund for the Republic's Center for the Study of Democratic Institutions in Santa Barbara. He had been a well-paid consultant to the fund since 1957, and accepted the summer offer because, as he explained to Frankfurter, he needed the money. His seminary pension was only $300 a month, and up to half that sum, according to his wife, went to pay medical bills not covered by his insurance. Ursula had her Barnard salary, but she was angered by Union's paltry provision in view of President Van Dusen's success in raising a quarter of a million dollars from her husband's friends and admirers for the new Niebuhr chair. She made her resentment clear to Van Dusen in a stinging letter (she did not show it to Reinhold) that accused the seminary of cruelty in making money out of a man whose health and financial state were both fragile. The pressures of his last few weeks at the seminary, she claimed, had almost killed him; she did not hesitate to hold Van Dusen responsible. She was delighted with the California trip because it would take them far from the seminary. Once in Santa Barbara she wrote to Frankfurter and the Binghams that Reinhold had snapped out of the depression the seminary tension had caused and was flourishing. No doubt he felt better in part because she felt so much better herself.

Their stay in Santa Barbara coincided with the Democratic Convention in Los Angeles, and Hutchins made sure that political observers and participants trekked up from the LA Sports Arena to his intellectual oasis. Niebuhr had not been so close to the action in a decade. Adlai Stevenson, his own choice for the nomination once Hubert Humphrey's chances faded, powwowed with the fund consultants, along with Kennedy operative Abram Chayes, journalist William Shannon, and others. Niebuhr was very uneasy about Kennedy before and after the nomination. He had nothing against Catholic candidates, as he had long before shown in Mayor Smith's campaign in Detroit in 1925 and Governor Smith's Presidential race in 1928. Indeed, it was the "thinness" of Kennedy's religion, Niebuhr wrote to Scarlett, not the Catholic affiliation, that was troubling. His reasons for disliking Kennedy, he told Frankfurter, were that "I don't like Papa Kennedy at all and the two brothers, Jack and Bob, are . . . ruthless and unscrupulous. I know that that great magician of politics FDR was not always too scrupulous, but he had a heart, and he never bought primaries as Kennedy did in Wisconsin and West Virginia." To FDR biographer Arthur Schlesinger, who switched from Stevenson to Kennedy before the nomination, he was almost equally blunt. "The Kennedy machine is more ruthless than the bosses and I dread the prominence which young Bob will have in the campaign and administration." He felt like abstaining altogether, but after the nomination of Nixon he announced to Scarlett that "I shall probably hold my nose and vote for Kennedy."[19]

Schlesinger was not content to abandon Niebuhr to his sour acquiescence. He went right to work at converting him, and by Labor Day Niebuhr was coming around. He still bemoaned the influence of brother Bobby, but he recognized "the cool intelligence of the young Senator" and knew "he will be a good President, if not a great one, but even the latter is a possibility." During the campaign Niebuhr played a visible if circumscribed role. With John Bennett he held a well-reported news conference to reassure voters about Kennedy's Catholicism. And at Adolf Berle's suggestion he gave Kennedy his public benediction by introducing him for his acceptance speech at the Liberal Party nomination dinner. Trying to be lighthearted, Niebuhr began by remarking that Protestant fundamentalists were doing their best to make Kennedy responsible for everything the archbishop of Spain did. In fact, Niebuhr joked, Kennedy was not even responsible for what the archbishop of New York did. Kennedy sat rigid and unamused. He realized that New York Catholics (if they were listening to the live radio broadcast) might not appreciate the dig at Archbishop Spellman. Kennedy did not have to worry about press reports. The New York *Post* reporter, along with other pro-Kennedy journalists at the dinner, agreed not to mention Niebuhr's remark in their stories.

Despite his visible support for the Kennedy candidacy, Niebuhr still had his doubts. Not just, as he put it to Scarlett at the end of the campaign, because Kennedy lacked Stevenson's "depth." It was a problem of Kennedy's personal morality, which had bothered him since the senator's Presidential effort swung into gear in late 1958. As he had mentioned then to Bingham, he was "shocked" that some of their liberal friends did "not take serious sexual aberrations, such as compulsive adultery, seriously." Kennedy's aberrations could not be safely sequestered in a "private" sphere, far away from the "public" sphere of his political leadership. Deficiencies "in family fidelity and in ordinary honesty" were not to be lightly dismissed. For all Niebuhr's realism he was still the residual "Protestant purist," as he confessed to Frankfurter, who could not tolerate a purely amoral public arena. He of course could not endure pure Protestant moralism either. As usual he was in-between, insisting on the "moral ambiguity" of politics.

His choice of Kennedy over Nixon was a lesser-evil decision of the sort that had first led him to choose Roosevelt over Thomas and Landon in 1936. Nixon was anathema not just for his rabid, HUAC anti-communism of the early 1950s, but for his association with Eisenhower's "new pacifism," which Niebuhr had been condemning since the Suez crisis. Kennedy represented the new militance, the readiness to bear any burden and confront any foe. Niebuhr was worried about the "missile gap" and about overreliance on nuclear arms at the expense of conventional weapons. Kennedy, whatever his personal flaws, was eager to stand up to the Russians and to diversify the military: the United States had to prepare for small brushfires as well as atomic deadlock. Above all, he exuded resolution—the antidote, as Niebuhr wrote during the campaign, for the self-satisfaction of the Eisenhower era. The "decent but soft" Eisenhower "symbolize[d] both the essential decency and the love of ease of a great nation." America spoke "glibly of its 'moral leadership in the free world,' " but "consoled by its innumerable comforts," it lacked the "discipline and courage which would make that leadership effective." His tribute to the strenuous life and the vigilant spirit rivaled those of Kennedy's speech writers. His ideological and rhetorical accord with Kennedy was the foundation for Niebuhr's growing enthusiasm for the New Frontier after the election. "The young man has brains and shrewdness," he wrote to Bingham after a witty Kennedy news conference in early 1962. "I am sold."[20]

While Niebuhr was in Santa Barbara in 1960 he received a letter from his friend and editor at Scribners, Bill Savage, about June Bingham's book on his life and thought. Should Scribners publish it, Savage inquired. Nie-

buhr had known for some time that she had had no luck with other publishers. He had told Scarlett in April that he was not unhappy about her
bad luck: he was still uneasy about a biography in his lifetime. To Savage
too he claimed embarrassment; he would prefer the book to be published
in half a century, when, he said, there would probably be no reason to
publish it. But he was of two minds. Everyone who had read it, he told
Savage, had reported it was excellent. Go ahead with it if you like. It was
clearly within Niebuhr's power to veto the idea. Perhaps he felt the call of
friendship with Bingham. Perhaps he felt in his retirement that his "lifetime"
was in some sense complete, and ready for analysis. When the "biography"
appeared in 1961, he expressed his gratitude to her for a "work of art" that
imposed "form on the formless stuff," the key in his view to good biography. On one level he could not help liking it: it was a deeply felt appreciation and defense of his life's work. On another level he remained troubled.
"I feel unworthy of the extravagant praise dear June heaped on me," he
told Scarlett. "I should have been allowed to end my days without anyone
trying to make a 'prophet' out of me."

But it was not just Bingham who had made a prophet out of him. For
decades he had been fashioning his own prophetic identity, striving to build
up his authoritative voice while checking it against pretension. His many
admirers also built him up. He cherished his position on the pedestal but
also distrusted it as a threat to humility. His residual uneasiness about the
Bingham book stemmed in part from the prophet's abiding fear of success:
too many honors were a sign of softness, of submission to the dominant
culture. But it was difficult to preserve a critical edge when his energies
were dwindling and when depression sapped his self-confidence. Difficult
too when organs of mass diversion like the *Saturday Evening Post* were
willing to pay handsomely for the most fleeting of his reflections. The *Post*
paid him $2,500 for a single article on "The Religious Traditions of Our
Nation" in 1960; Bingham's report of the amount was one of the few
disclosures in the book that bothered him. He was for better or worse a
celebrity intellectual who could command a hefty fee for a few thoughts.
To his credit he rejected the temptations of the marketplace much more
consistently than many of his peers. He never reconciled himself to the role
of honored cultural sage. In the final decade of his life he was destined to
be much invoked and lauded as a venerable wise man while his own fragile
health and ebbing strength barred him from a fully productive life. "Are
[you and I] supposed to be status symbols?" he wrote to Trilling in 1961.
"What a curious destiny." It was a destiny that even in his declining years
he did a good deal to resist.[21]

TWELVE

GATHERED
TO
THE FATHERS

(1961–1971)

I

During the Kennedy administration Niebuhr managed, with his wife's constant support, to keep up a semblance of the active life. An appointment to Columbia University's Institute of War and Peace Studies and a Rockefeller Fellowship in 1960–1961 allowed him to start another book. He proposed a study of communism in relation to democracy—the theme that was trying to escape from the clutter of world history in *Structure*. One brief section of the work appeared at the end of the academic year; it revealed how closely attuned he was to the dominant foreign-policy ideas of the Kennedy forces. The chief conflict in the world, he wrote, was between democracy and communism—the same point he had been making since the 1940s.

But there was a new twist. His focus was no longer upon the democratic nations of Western Europe, which apart from a few trouble spots like Berlin were by this time relatively safe from Communist attack and immune to Communist propaganda. His stress was now upon "the new nations and the poor nations." For historical reasons western-style democracy was no simple possibility for them. Americans should not "despair if, on the fringes of the non-Communist world, we should see some serious defects in the attainment of democratic justice." Communist dictatorships were always baleful; non-Communist dictatorships could not be "regarded with complacency," but they had to be tolerated whenever they were the best that a particular people—with its historically ordained "political and moral capacities"—could do. "Realism" in foreign policy meant not expecting true democracy to flower where it had no roots.

Niebuhr knew that the Communist world was no longer a monolith.

•

But the splits within the Communist camp—which permitted American strategists to play more diplomatic cards—did not make Communist rule acceptable in any individual case. Communism was not merely a form of dictatorship or despotism. It was "a pretentious scheme of world salvation, a secularized religious apocalypse." In its "fantastic ambition to master all the variegated processes of history and press all its themes into one mold," it made a much more drastic attack on "freedom" than right-wing despotism. Dictatorships of the right were "uncreative," but "not as irrevocable as a Communist dictatorship." They abolished "democratic self-government," but "our cause is the cause of freedom in a wider sense than that of democratic political institutions." They could be tolerated because they were both less stable and less fanatical than Communist regimes.

Niebuhr did not explain what sort of freedom could persist in the absence of democracy. His own earlier works like *The Children of Light* insisted that the checks and balances of democratic rule were a precondition of freedom. Now he was contending that the mere absence of Communist rule was a significant form of freedom. He was making a lesser-evil argument: right-wing despotism did not destroy all the roots of the open society, while communism did. But his argument operated at such a level of abstraction that it did not meet the most obvious objection: in concrete cases right-wing despots might well equal their Communist peers in undermining freedom "in a wider sense." In some cases, no doubt, right-wing regimes were preferable to Communist ones. The danger of his own doctrine—which adumbrated a later generation's distinction between "authoritarian" and "totalitarian" states—was the ease with which it could be invoked to justify America's support for dictators of its choice. Such leaders could be tolerated, however vicious or corrupt in the present, because their societies had potential for freedom in some abstract future. Niebuhr might genuinely inveigh against "complacent" acceptance of dictatorship, but in other mouths the same warning could itself become complacent, rhetorical.

Niebuhr took his updated realism to Washington in January, 1961. For a month he was in residence at his old friend Arnold Wolfers's Center for Foreign Policy Research, which the Kennedy team was raiding for recruits like Paul Nitze. He enjoyed the heady rush of the administration-in-the-making. The Kennedy team, he told Scarlett in February, had "almost unbelievable morale and vigor. The young President has managed to put life into every department of government." Had Niebuhr been fifteen years younger he might have been tempted to remain longer among the dynamic young liberals who were streaming in from northeastern centers of law and academia. His own daughter Elisabeth, Radcliffe '60, joined the mass migration after spending a postgraduate year in Paris on a Fulbright. Elisabeth had credentials of her own and needed no special intercession to obtain her job at the State Department. Yet unbeknownst to her, highly placed parties were making inquiries on her behalf. "You will be interested to know," wrote Special Assistant to the President Arthur Schlesinger, "that a distinguished figure—indeed *the* most distinguished political leader in the land—called me the other night to inquire what was being done to get a job for Elisabeth. With support from this quarter we certainly should be able to do something for her." "Thank you for your word about Elisabeth," Nie-

•

buhr replied. "I am intrigued about the mystery of anyone telling the President about her existence."

It must have crossed his mind that the mystery had a certain practical import. Schlesinger and Kennedy both were eager for Niebuhr's support, and Schlesinger for one knew that Niebuhr's feelings about Kennedy were mixed, even if now mostly positive. Kennedy was scarcely a well-read Niebuhrian, but his special assistant recalls that he was "well aware of Niebuhr and well acquainted with his general approach." So were the rest of the New Frontiersmen. McGeorge Bundy called Niebuhr "probably the most influential single mind in the development of American attitudes which combine moral purpose with a sense of political reality." Niebuhr had indeed been a significant teacher for the generation of liberals in their thirties and forties, and they genuinely wished to honor his name. On another level they wanted to enlist the reputation of America's premier theologian. At sixty-nine Niebuhr was too old and frail to be mobilized in person. But his stature was separable from his day-to-day activity. He was a powerful political presence because his name itself summoned up an image of hard-earned wisdom and deep-seated commitment. Yet the Kennedy forces did not so much "use" Niebuhr's name as feel indebted to his perspective. He helped them maintain faith in themselves as political actors in a troubled—what he termed a sinful—world. Stakes were high, enemies were wily, responsibility meant taking risks: Niebuhr taught that moral men had to play hardball.[1]

Niebuhr the person was hardly an uncritical booster of the New Frontier. He did praise "the youthful President" for his forthright warning about "the burdens and responsibilities" of power that had to be borne "not for decades but perhaps for centuries." Kennedy realism pleased him, but some Kennedy policies did not. Niebuhr was upset about the hard line on Cuba—not just the Bay of Pigs fiasco initially planned by Eisenhower, but the embargo on Cuban products. "Our policy," he wrote in his monthly *New Leader* "has enabled Castro to blame all his economic problems on [us]. It has aroused the latent anti-Yankee resentment and fear of our power throughout the Hemisphere." It had also, he added, "robbed our cigar smokers of the pleasure of a good Havana." To his friend the special assistant to the President he was uncharacteristically blunt: "Our embargo on Castro is as mistaken as the original invasion."

The embargo disturbed him; the 1962 Senate campaign of younger brother Teddy in Massachusetts disgusted him. Niebuhr saw the campaign firsthand since he was teaching part-time at Harvard in 1961–1962—an appointment arranged in part through Schlesinger's good offices. The campaign heated up in June just as Niebuhr was passing his seventieth birthday. Schlesinger arranged a seven-line Presidential telegram for the occasion, but it did not dissuade Niebuhr from complaining to Schlesinger three days later about the effort "to foist young Ted on Massachusetts." To Scarlett he minced fewer words. "I hope the impudent young man will be soundly trounced by a Republican, not only for the sake of Massachusetts, but to teach the Kennedys a lesson where they need it desperately." To June Bingham he added that "if the Republicans were not so hopeless I would desert Kennedy on just this one issue, because it reveals a bland cynicism which is frightening." He did not desert Kennedy, but he did preside over

•

a well-publicized garden party for Teddy's Democratic primary opponent, State Attorney General Edward McCormick.

The Ted Kennedy flap, like the discussion of the President's sexual capers, revealed that there were firm—if ill defined—limits to Niebuhr's realism. The responsible statesman did have to dirty his hands in the pursuit of justice. But without personal probity a politician lost sight of justice, which was the social correlate of individual fair-dealing. Kennedy cynicism was Machiavellian, not Niebuhrian. Niebuhr frequently had to insist that his secular admirers were turning his realism into a world-weary manipulativeness that verged on moral nihilism. Political scientist Hans Morgenthau, for example, sometimes divorced the realm of politics so completely from the realm of morality that he doubted—as he told a conference of devoted Niebuhrian followers—whether one could be both "a successful politician and a good Christian." In his published response to Morgenthau, Niebuhr gently corrected him: "I do not think we will sacrifice any value in the 'realist' approach to the political order . . . if we define [it] in terms which do not rob it of moral content." There ought to be a place in "the Kingdom of God" for politicians like Abraham Lincoln. The Christian politician was the one who engaged in the statesmanlike compromises that a sinful world demanded, but who relentlessly subjected his actions to the test of the standard of justice. The Christian leader made use of the world's methods but did not resign himself to the world's ways. He cultivated an uneasy conscience—not merely a matter of breast-beating but of real self-criticism. His career was a perennial struggle, personal and political, to bring justice to bear in human relations. Politics was therefore not Morgenthau's realm of "amorality," as Niebuhr explained to Bingham, but a sphere of "moral ambiguity."[2]

II

Niebuhr's Christian realism was in one sense a more negative than positive perspective. It did not ordain specific positions on political issues. It demanded only that its adherents follow a middle path betwen the twin pitfalls of utopianism and resignation, sentimentality and cynicism. Niebuhrians disagreed vigorously among themselves on particular questions—even as they proclaimed their common devotion to the principle of justice. A good example was their debate in the early 1960s over nuclear weapons, in the course of which Niebuhr himself altered the specific content of his realism. Through the 1950s he had been a confident proponent of nuclear deterrence. Korea had demonstrated, he believed, that "small" wars need not turn into atomic holocausts. Deterrence was problematic, since it involved its adherents in the prospective guilt of destroying civilization in order to save it. But the only alternative to nuclear stalemate was "capitulation to the Russian tyranny." Disarmament was impossible "because the Russian price for such an agreement is that we quit Europe and expose it to the tender mercies of the Russian power."

The Berlin crisis in the summer of 1961 brought the issue home with frightening immediacy, and provoked a decided shift in his stance. The Russians had walled off East Berlin; there was talk of American tanks de-

•

stroying the wall, and fear that a nuclear exchange might follow. All the Christian realists accepted the necessity of retaliation if the Soviets initiated a nuclear war, though Niebuhr and Bennett did so with less equanimity than some. But there was sharp division on the use of "tactical" nuclear weapons in response to a conventional Russian advance in central Europe. In 1950 both Niebuhr and Bennett had favored preserving the option of "first use" to resist Russian tanks. Now they expressed their alarm at the term *tactical,* which described bombs of greater destructive force than those dropped on Japan. They insisted that, in Niebuhr's words, "the first use of the nuclear weapon is morally abhorrent and must be resisted." Niebuhr lamented "the disturbing fact that momentous decisions [about first use] have already been taken by military experts in behalf of 'free' nations without recourse to the democratic process." "Realists" like Kenneth Thompson were in turn disturbed by what they considered a weakening resolve on the part of both Bennett and Niebuhr. "If we declare we shall not use thermonuclear weapons except in the ultimate defense, we have assisted the Soviet Union in plotting a campaign of expansion and imperialism." Carl Mayer seconded Thompson and announced that Niebuhr had regrettably contributed to the apparent end "of what came to be known as Christian realism."

In reply Niebuhr pleaded guilty to the charge of inconsistency: he did believe both that the current balance of terror provided a real peace and that continued acquiescence in that balance of terror might be unjustified. The "general fear of a climax of escalation in nuclear weapons" did not incline him toward nuclear pacifism, but it did make him support a more flexible US position on disarmament. America might drop its "present insistence on foolproof inspection," which "is defined as unrealistic by most of the experts." It might be time to "take some risks for peace comparable to our ever more dangerous risks in the game of deterrence." He was subjecting his own Christian realism to a forceful ethical challenge. The proponents of first use—and even those like Thompson who advocated silence about the possibility of first use—were deficient in weighing "the moral consequences of initiating the dread conflict. Could a civilization loaded with this monstrous guilt have enough moral health to survive" even if it "won" the battle? He admitted privately to Bingham that "the President cannot tie our hands, but a private citizen ought to be able to say that it is morally inadmissible to start the nuclear catastrophe for the sake of Berlin even before we have seriously negotiated. There must be some limits to moral ambiguity. I don't know where they are but this may be the limit.[3]

While he was lecturing at Harvard in the fall of 1961—a course on democracy and communism attended by 450 students and auditors—Robert Hutchins signed him up to do a short book on the American character for his Fund for the Republic. Niebuhr put aside his other project on foreign policy and sat down to write *A Nation So Conceived.* He trotted out some of his old ideas about the transformation of America's original sense of innocence and mission, but Hutchins was dissatisfied with the result. Harvard professor Alan Heimert—former student of Niebuhr's friend and admirer Perry Miller—was brought in to contribute historical background. Niebuhr wrote just over half of the 150-page book, and his part was resoundingly mediocre. There were no new ideas, and the old ones were tired

•

husks left over from *The Irony of American History. A Nation So Conceived* contributed nothing to the vibrant debate over the national character sparked since the mid-1950s by writers like Louis Hartz and David Potter, because it failed to address itself to that debate. It was a pale reflection of Niebuhr's earlier work, as David Potter noted gently in his *Times* review.

Niebuhr was a consultant in 1961–1962 not only to the Fund for the Republic but to the Ford Foundation as well. The foundation asked him to attend six meetings "to talk about the state of the world and the most strategic area for their investment," as he put it to Frankfurter. "I have never before moved in the same circle as the Ford Foundation; but as they asked me not to give them advice on particular disbursements but to chew the rag on the general state of the world and the U.S.A., I was tempted." He was deeply impressed, and took the foundation as a sure sign of democratic vitality. It was one of many centers of decentralized power in America, he thought, and its programs tried to diversify power even further. In *Christianity and Crisis* he described it as a key manifestation of "the political virtue of a free society," which "disperses power into as many centers as possible . . . and refuses immunity from criticism and review to any center of power and prestige." His own earlier socialism had been the honest mistake of one who failed to grasp the "openness" of capitalist culture— who, "like many of my contemporaries, did not foresee that the auto union and the Ford Foundation, the latter the fruit of Federal tax laws, would change the distribution of power and of privilege."[4]

On the face of it, a curious juxtaposition: how could he put the Ford Foundation on a level with the UAW as an historical agent of justice? Perhaps because Henry Ford, the pious but nefarious engineer, had since the 1920s been his symbol of undisciplined capitalism. The Ford Foundation may not have changed the country, but it did help reform the model of Christian stewardship. It displaced Henry Ford's pretentious, self-serving prayerfulness with an apparently disinterested, professionalized efficiency. In Niebuhr's view it put community interest above individual gain. But he did not ask the tougher question: whether the foundation, like Ford himself, served ideological as well as philanthropic purposes. Perhaps its laudable programs had the effect of redistributing some power—but also the effect of making power in America appear to be more evenly shared than it really was. Henry Ford had constructed a benevolent image—the five-dollar day, the five-day week, the Ford hospital—that camouflaged assembly-line speed-ups, declining annual wages, and early, forced retirements. The foundation may have marked an improvement on Ford, but its image of streamlined, secular beneficence may also have distorted reality by encouraging the complacent belief that capitalism was now public spirited, responsible, producing an ever fairer society through incremental adjustment.

III

With the end of his teaching stint at Harvard in June, Niebuhr prepared nervously for his daughter's July wedding. "Elisabeth fell rather madly in

•

love," he confided to Scarlett, "which surprised me somewhat, showing that I don't know too much about the human heart, especially the feminine heart." He was anxious about his health holding up even for a small, family ceremony in a Stockbridge church; emotional intensity aggravated his pains. His chronic colon problem made it uncomfortable to sit down, and if that was not enough he was suffering from a severe case of bladder frequency. He had to have access to a toilet every forty-five minutes. With his nephew Richard Niebuhr (H. Richard's son) he was to officiate, but as the date approached his anxiety mounted. He told June Bingham that he did not care "share my apprehensions with the family, even with Ursula," because he feared another "periodic depression."

But two days before the wedding his own complaints evaporated: news arrived that his brother had died of a heart attack at his summer home in nearby Rowe, Massachusetts. Richard had been feeling fine as he approached his sixty-eighth birthday, despite the mild heart attack he had suffered earlier in the year. He was looking forward to further work on his ethical treatise *The Responsible Self*. Reinhold was deeply shaken, and consternated when the funeral was scheduled for the Yale Divinity School chapel on the same afternoon as the wedding. Elisabeth offered to postpone the ceremony for a week, but he did not want to upset her plans. On July 7 Richard's family attended the funeral and Reinhold's the wedding. Many friends—not understanding the frailty of Reinhold's state—were dismayed that he did not make the trip to New Haven. For his part he was thankful that he managed to get through a prayer for the bride and groom "without breaking down," as he wrote to Scarlett after the service. "My heart was in turmoil during the past days. It was not only the loss of a dearly beloved brother, who was my guide and counselor, particularly since the days of my illness. It was the fact that I could not express my gratitude for his life publicly by attending his funeral." He tried to express it in the many letters he typed in the following week. Richard, he told Van Dusen, was a confidant on whom he depended more and more as years passed. He was always, Niebuhr added, the better scholar and suffered from the greater renown he had himself achieved. As with Walter's death sixteen years before, feelings of guilt merged inevitably with the gratitude and the grief.[5]

Niebuhr had lost one of his own bow anchors, and his energies ebbed. He did have a part-time appointment in the Princeton humanities program in the fall, and a visiting position in his wife's religion department at Barnard in the spring. But there would be no more teaching posts after that; only an occasional informal seminar series at Union when he felt up to it. By the summer of 1963 he had abandoned his projected book on democracy and communism—the subject on which he lectured to 450 students at Princeton just as he had at Harvard. In May, 1963, working in their new smaller apartment at 404 Riverside Drive, he had tried to summon up enthusiasm for the project. "I am slowly finishing a book," he wrote to Schlesinger at the White House, "emphasizing that an 'open society' rather than self-government in the pure European sense must be regarded as the opposing value to Communism, because so many non-European cultures do not have the prerequisites for pure self-government, certainly not for a two-party or multi-party system." By August he had given it up. He quit writing, he told Scarlett sadly, when he realized it would be an inferior book. He and Ursula had decided "to devote the rest of our lives to collaborating on a book of conversations." But three days later he confessed to his friend that "I hope the Lord will take me before too long, much as I shall grieve to be separated from my family and friends."

His depression deepened as the academic year began—his first fall in thirty-five years without an academic appointment. His income suddenly shrank, and as he watched Ursula career through a heavy teaching schedule at Barnard and nurse's duties at home, he grew resentful—as she had been three years before—about his measly seminary pension. He complained to his friend and seminary board member Ed Miller, and the board quickly made amends by raising his annuity from $3,500 to $6,000. But he felt only a little better. He was still utterly dependent upon his wife and hated his own helplessness as well as the unavoidable imposition on her. As he remarked to Scarlett in early 1963, "I feel like sin and death and must be a great burden to my dear wife. . . . All I can do is to be grateful that Divine grace is mediated again and again through the love of a wife who loves me through thick and thin." But his gratitude did not dispel the "cloud which has enveloped me." A prostate operation in the fall made him even gloomier, and recovery was slow. It took the shock of President Kennedy's assassination in November to rouse him from self-pity.[6]

To Arthur Schlesinger, who was naturally in a state of shock, he offered sympathy in the form of a panegyric. No one in American history had combined intelligence and shrewdness, courage and prudence, as much as Kennedy. All of his policies—on civil rights, the economy, disarmament—challenged encrusted prejudices and conventional wisdom. He had touched the hearts of his countrymen more deeply than anyone had known. "The loss is simply incalculable. . . . We will be haunted for a long time about the tragedy of unfulfilled potentialities." To Scarlett he was more distanced and less celebratory. The American Presidency resembled an elected monarchy, he suggested, and thus the death of a president was traumatic for the nation. The youth and talent of this president made the emotional outpouring all the more intense. Niebuhr speculated that Kennedy's stand on civil rights would be recognized as a historic turning point, and that Lyndon Johnson would carry on the fight with the aid of "the aura of Kennedy's sacrificial death." Despite the detached analysis, Niebuhr did share in Schlesinger's sorrow. He dismissed W. H. Auden's claim that the exhibition of public grief was phony. To Scarlett he reported that Auden, "on whom we take pity in his bachelor loneliness on Christmas, despite his increasing habit to monopolize the conversation with his latest poetic idea," had dominated their Christmas dinner with his talk of the nation's crocodile tears. He insisted that "one could only mourn to the point of tears for an intimate friend or member of the family; and that all tears shed at Kennedy's death were therefore 'theatrical.' We were bored with . . . this absurd idea." To Niebuhr the grief was genuine; great leaders embodied the public spirit and the citizen's loss was personal.[7]

He was right that sacrificial death would bolster the movement for racial equality. President Johnson pressed for the Civil Rights Act, and in the course of that campaign Niebuhr's own ideas on racism underwent a

•

marked evolution. Civil rights had never been one of his preoccupations, though he had always scorned racial prejudice, battled southern racism through the Delta Farm, and allowed the NAACP Legal Defense Fund to add his name to its Committee of One Hundred in 1943. He had had serious doubts about the Supreme Court's 1956 decision to ban segregated schools—a toughening of the 1954 decision that Niebuhr had praised for its gradualism. The outright ban in 1956 was "morally right" but "pedagogically unfortunate, for it polarized the sentiments of the south and wiped out the moderate opinion which was making real progress before the decision." Southern white opposition did turn violent in the deep south in 1957. Yet when Martin Luther King, Jr., had approached Niebuhr to sign a petition for Presidential intervention, he refused. He explained to Frankfurter that pressure of that sort would do more harm than good. He believed the private visit of a group of southern preachers to the White House would exert more influence on Eisenhower. The reward for his moderation was another FBI examination of his file. The Bureau was studying "Communist infiltration" of the NAACP, and Niebuhr's name was added to the case: after all, he was on the Committee of One Hundred and had associated with over "forty Communist fronts."

Niebuhr continued to plead for an end to southern racism in the early 1960s. It was the very strength of his commitment to the notion of an "open society" that fueled his attack on the closed society of the deep south. "The question," he wrote in protesting the "Montgomery savagery" in 1961, "is simply whether we are prepared to treat our fellow man with the respect that his innate dignity as a human being requires and deserves." His dismay over the south was joined to a certain equanimity about the north, where he believed that "Negroes with high talent are breaking out of the enclave in increasing numbers, thus revealing the virtue of an open society, enlarging its openness, and refuting the libel about the 'innate inferiority' of their race." But in 1964 northern blacks became more vociferous in their demands for equality, and Niebuhr had to confront a challenge to his view of the open society—a challenge in his own backyard of Harlem. He granted to Scarlett that the school boycott there was a natural response to "wretched" schools. But he believed the black protesters were "overplaying their hands." The "massive desegregation" they sought would require cross-district busing, he thought, and that would probably provoke rioting. "Human nature is not that good and north and south are more similar than different. I imagine we will live for a long time in the throes of the Negro revolution."

He had lived on the border of the black ghetto for thirty-five years and was just beginning to understand the character of racism in New York. Even a comprehensive civil-rights bill of the type Johnson was pushing through Congress would not be enough. In mid-1963 he had still been able to write that "there is no 'increasing misery' among Negroes in this country," and therefore "no increasing revolutionary ardor." In the summer of 1964 he jettisoned that judgment. "We are in for . . . decades of social revolution," he intoned, because of the "despair and hopelessness" of young northern blacks. "The reason for this despair is obvious, but I for one was slow to gauge its import." It was persistent unemployment, not exclusion from voting booths or public accommodations. At the age of seventy-two he was forced to ponder his faith in the pluralist checks and balances of the free society. The structural racism of the economic marketplace had disrupted his vision of "an open society [which] prevents revolutions by allowing all economic, racial, and cultural groups to state their claims and adjust their interests."

In the early 1930s, before he had discovered the virtues of the open society, he had asserted that "the white race in America will not admit the Negro to equal rights if it is not forced to do so." He cautioned against any attempt by blacks to achieve freedom through "violent rebellion," but insisted that some form of nonviolent resistance was necessary. Now he returned to the doctrine of *Moral Man,* and vigorously supported Martin Luther King's strategy of civil disobedience. King, for his part, was profoundly influenced by Niebuhr's early perspective. Andrew Young, one of his aides, later told *Christianity and Crisis* editor Wayne Cowan that King always claimed to have been "much more influenced" by Niebuhr than by Gandhi; he considered his nonviolent technique to be "a Niebuhrian stratagem of power." By the mid-1960s Niebuhr was boosting King in his confrontation with "black power" enthusiasts like Stokely Carmichael and H. Rap Brown. King was too sentimental, he told one of his former students in 1966, but was still "the most creative Protestant, white or black." Black-power advocates who shouted about "the right of self-defense" were "terrible political leaders for a racial minority of only 10 percent." What he did not explain was how King's strategy could improve the lot of northern blacks. Nonviolent resistance might speed the end of Jim Crow in the south by spurring federal action and northern moral support. In the north it might be impotent in the face of discrimination in jobs, housing, and schools.[8]

IV

In mid-1964 he was worried about protecting the national commitment to southern blacks against the "primitivism" of the Republican right. He could scarcely believe the rise of Goldwater: it undermined his conviction that Americans shared a consensus about the mixed economy, international responsibility, and equal rights. European commentators who detected a hint of fascism in the far right, he asserted, ought not to be casually dismissed. The "parallels are rather frightening." For the first time ever, *Christianity and Crisis* endorsed a Presidential candidate. Johnson endorsed Niebuhr too: in September he awarded him the Medal of Freedom, the highest civilian honor in the land. Niebuhr kept up the attacks on Goldwater during the campaign. Even the grandson of Henry Ford, he pointed out in October, had endorsed Johnson. Intelligent capitalists understood that there was "a common national interest above and beyond particular interests."[9]

Johnson's promise to "seek no wider war" in Southeast Asia was one of the many reasons he was endorsed by Niebuhr and *Christianity and Crisis.* Niebuhr was actually of two minds on Vietnam, as he had been since the mid-1950s. On the one hand, since the Chinese revolution in 1949, he had been dead set against American military involvement in civil wars on the Asian mainland. On the other hand, since Korea, he was determined to

•

resist Russian- or Chinese-sponsored military aggression in Asia. Was Vietnam a civil war or another Korea? It was both, thought Niebuhr. In early 1962 he noted that the Diem regime had little political support and he expressed his ambivalent position. "The loss of South Vietnam to the Communists would mean a considerable strategic loss in Southeast Asia. But . . . the loss of moral prestige through the support of an unpopular and unviable regime is also a great hazard." Like other liberal anti-Communists, Niebuhr was on the horns of a painful dilemma. His anti-Communist stance convinced him, as he put it in 1963, that "if we withdraw the Communists will overrun the whole of Southeast Asia, including Thailand." But his liberal convictions had taught him that "if no moral content is put into the struggle the peasants will have to choose between two police states, the one not much better than the other." He did not expect Diem to be a democrat: Vietnam lacked the social basis for Western-style democracy. He did expect even an authoritarian government to be more enlightened than the tyrannical family of Diem and his sister-in-law, Madame Nhu.

When President Johnson, despite campaign promises, stepped up the bombing and began a major troop buildup in 1965, Niebuhr's doubts increased. A telltale sign of increased anxiety was his appeal to British wisdom: "Even our European allies, notably Britain, have been embarrassed by our policy in Vietnam." He knew the war was unwinnable. "The policy of restraining Asian Communism by sheer military might is fantastic," he wrote to Scarlett. But before moving into full-scale public opposition to American policy he had to persuade himself that the "loss" of Vietnam was tolerable. In September, 1965, he came up with a formula that demonstrated egregious ignorance of Southeast Asian realities, but at least permitted him to countenance American withdrawal: "It might be wise to persuade Thailand, for instance, to offer asylum to all anti-Communist warriors, and then defend this asylum with massive military power. This would be proof of our strength as well as our sense of honor to Asia."

Once again Christian realists split angrily on a concrete political issue. Niebuhr and Bennett began their steady movement into the ranks of the "doves"; Paul Ramsey was typical of the "hawks," who lamented that "even Reinhold Niebuhr signs petitions and editorials as if Reinhold Niebuhr never existed." The most painful moment for Niebuhr came when his old friend Vice-President Humphrey, a dutiful supporter of Johnson's escalation, arrived in New York on February 26, 1966, to deliver the major speech at the twenty-fifth anniversary dinner of *Christianity and Crisis*. Niebuhr could not attend since he found it too uncomfortable to sit down for more than a few minutes. Humphrey therefore came to his apartment for a half-hour before the talk and they discussed Vietnam. Niebuhr was appalled to discover that the Vice-President had not a sliver of doubt about American policy. "Hubert is too honest to have a private and public opinion as do [Robert] McNamara and [George] Ball," he explained to Scarlett. "He has to convince himself of the rightness of his official assignments. All very sad."

In his "Tribute to Reinhold Niebuhr" before the four hundred dinner guests at Riverside Church, Humphrey gave a rousing endorsement of Niebuhr's Lincolnian realism about human nature and community. "All to the end," Niebuhr told Scarlett, "of claiming my anti-Nazi stance of the thirties for the present war." The Vice-President was "in a tragic position of outdoing the Machiavelli in the White House, meanwhile losing all his friends." Niebuhr was aghast at Humphrey's ebullient leap into the Vietnam quagmire, but also worried about his own state of mind. He was not accustomed to preaching against American military ventures. "I am scared by my own lack of patriotism," he confessed in the spring of 1966. "For I take satisfaction in the embarrassment [of the United States] in a fantastic war." His capacity for antiwar work was limited because of his colon problem. His doctors could find nothing physical to account for it, and they resorted to hypnosis—unsuccessfully—to try to alleviate it. But he did what little he could from the sidelines. He actively supported the Clergymen Concerned About Vietnam by preparing a tape recording for their meetings. And he continuously blasted Lyndon Johnson's "error of regarding the issue [in Vietnam] as the containment of Communism, when we are in fact dealing with the nationalism of a small nation of Asia." Still he fretted about his love for his country. "For the first time I fear I am ashamed of our beloved nation," he admitted sadly to Scarlett.[10]

Niebuhr's modest writing output after 1964 was dominated by short editorials about Vietnam. His projected volume of conversations with his wife never materialized. But he did offer Scribners three short essays on historic conceptions of community that became *Man's Nature and His Communities* in 1965. Of much more interest than the essays themselves, which broke no new ground, was the fifteen-page introduction about his "Changing Perspectives." Here he made clear that his Protestant faith had been modified over the years by his increasing admiration not only for the Jewish but also for the Catholic tradition. In earlier years he had frequently lauded Catholics for their "organic," "social" sensibility, which "individualistic" Protestants lacked. But the Church had nevertheless struck him as fundamentally idolatrous: worshiping Mary as well as God, placing the Pope on a superhuman pedestal, regarding the Church itself as an unerring institution. Its "natural law" moral theory derived from the Stoics and Aristotle took insufficient account of the historically shifting character of human nature. Catholic opposition to "artificial" birth control was one unfortunate fruit of an absolutist conception of natural law. But the principled Catholic stance on civil rights in the south in the 1950s, and his friendship with liberal Catholics like John Courtney Murray and John Cogley at the Fund for the Republic, made him much more sympathetic. He still, as he put it to Scarlett in 1957, "alternate[d], as I think you do, between a violent anti-Catholicism and a measure of respect for what they are doing" on the race question. But the respect was growing. The hierarchal structure of authority in the Catholic Church permitted the bishops to discipline priests and laity alike; in the Protestant churches there was no authority "which can support a poor parson against the manias of his congregation. In this sad world we must pick up virtue wherever we can find it and also recognize weaknesses in our own position." The best compromise lay in Scarlett's own Episcopalian structure, which Bishop Williams in Detroit had first taught Niebuhr to appreciate. "I would settle for a Bishop who had as much authority as you have but not as much as a Catholic Bishop has."

·

By the mid-1960s, after Pope John XXIII's encyclicals, *Mater and Magister* and *Pacem in Terris,* and the Second Vatican Council, Niebuhr was consistently affirmative about the Catholic contribution. "It has always been one of the virtues of Catholicism," he wrote in 1961, "that it . . . skipped the whole period of classical economy and never doubted that political authority should exercise dominance over the economic sphere in the interest of justice." Protestants and Catholics could nurture one another, he wrote in 1969 in one of his last major articles, since they shared a common inheritance and each rightly stressed important virtues: the Catholics unity, order, and the social dimension of existence; the Protestants pluralism, liberty, and the individual transcendence of community.

Niebuhr's revaluation of Catholicism did not mean that he was coming to prefer a sacerdotal, or sacramental, view of the church. It is true that with his own preaching career at an end, he found it hard to abide Protestant pulpit-centered worship. There were not enough good preachers. The Catholic mass, he wrote privately in 1967, was "in many respects more religiously adequate than our Protestant worship," though there was still "superstitious belief in magic in the hearts of many worshipers." Many "intelligent Catholics" found the mass to be "a symbol of the mystery which makes sense out of life." He wished Protestants had an equally potent symbol. His own ecclesiology, such as it was, remained fundamentally Protestant in its stress on symbolism. There was no "real presence" of God in the sacrament, but a symbolic representation of God's presence. The church was a community of grace, but grace was mediated more through the Word that was preached than though the Eucharist that was received. Niebuhr's grace was verbal, active—a grace that confronted the believer and challenged even the church itself. A sacramental church was too liable to passivity, self-satisfaction, too prone to believe itself sanctified. Beginning at Bethel Church Niebuhr therefore emphasized the Jewish, prophetic roots of Christianity, and the role of the prophet as troubler of the worshiper's premature tranquility. The church was not the embodiment of God's grace or even the place where that grace was experienced; it was the place where people acknowledged their unworthiness and prayed for the fulfillment that came through self-giving instead of self-seeking. Niebuhr had a genuinely liturgical sensibility, but he restricted the expression of it to his prayers. He was afraid of offering too much reassurance, becoming too much the priest. His thirty-second prayers delivered after his sermons contained a concentrated dose of mystery, emotion, and celebration. They were verbal sacraments that often reached true poetic beauty. With this prayer Niebuhr closed his sermon at Saint George's Episcopal Church in New York in January, 1960:

> Eternal God, Father Almighty, maker of heaven and earth, we worship you. Your wisdom is beyond our understanding, your power is greater than we can measure, your thoughts are above our thoughts; as high as the heaven is above the earth, your majesty judges all human majesties. Your judgment brings princes to naught, and makes the judges of the earth as vanity; for before the mountains were brought forth or ever the earth and the world were made, even from everlasting to everlasting you are God.

•

Give us grace to apprehend by faith the power and wisdom which lie beyond our understanding; and in worship to feel that which we do not know, and to praise even what we do not understand; so that in the presence of your glory we may be humble, and in the knowledge of your judgment we may repent; and so in the assurance of your mercy we may rejoice and be glad.[11]

V

In Niebuhr's eyes religion was more a matter of "trust" than "belief." From his father, he wrote in 1965, he had inherited "an understanding of religious faith as trust in the meaning of human existence." True faith was "childlike in its single-heartedness" while avoiding the "childish belief that God is on the side of the believer." Yet it was just this basic trust that he had found it hard to maintain since his stroke. His "basic neurotic defect"—and the "work compulsion" with which he tried to overcome it—he had inherited, he told Scarlett, from his "good mother who was in persistent neurotic anxiety." It was in his relationship to Scarlett that he struggled as an old man to recapture the sense of trust. The bishop was his confessor, a stable source of encouragement. With him Niebuhr was able to reveal emotions, vent feelings of vulnerability and dependency. Scarlett in turn offered buoyant humor, strong advice, endless assurance. In moments of depression Niebuhr reached out for his letters and visits as a lifeline. If he did not hear from him on a regular schedule he grew restive. "Don't forget me!" he pleaded in 1954 after Scarlett had put off writing. In the late 1960s, as their other close friends like Felix Frankfurter died one by one, they confronted their own feelings about death. "We agreed that neither of us feared death," Niebuhr wrote in 1968.

> I can only hope that if I go first you will say a prayer at my funeral, even though I cannot promise, because of increasing weakness to return the mutual service of friendship. You have been a source of grace to all of us. . . . The Lord be with you and with us my good friend, in this year and in the years to come.

Scarlett helped him find the courage to accept his mortality and take comfort in viewing himself as a link between the generation of his father and that of his children. In one of his last published interviews, conducted by John Cogley for *McCall's,* the final question brought out his ultimate trust in the meaning of life despite the knowledge that he was soon to perish. Cogley asked if he was glad to have become a minister. Niebuhr concluded his answer with this reflection.

> I'm on the whole glad. I'm glad insofar as I have adequately exploited the vision of my father. You can't ever be fully glad when you survey a long life in your old age and know how many inadequacies there were in it. I might have been an historian, because I'm interested in history; but my critical daughter says, "Daddy, you're not enough of an empiricist to be a good historian."

From the wisdom of his father to the insight of his daughter; his own life was in balance.[12]

•

Beginning in 1967 Niebuhr spent more of each year, including the entire fall, in Stockbridge. He could write only an occasional article to break the monotony of his visits to hospitals, doctors, and dentists. He feared the dentists most of all—especially the repeated visits during which all of his lower teeth were extracted. Now he had to lie rather than sit most of the time, and announced to his friend that for the first time in his life he had stopped working. He was "reminded daily" that "in the midst of life we are in death." He could comment only fitfully on the events of the day. "Now that the Israelis have given Nasser and the Arab tribes their third resounding defeat," he observed in June, 1967, he wished to "thank God for the little nation, which mixes historic faith with superiority in the arts of war." The student antiwar movement in late 1967 drew his admiration. "Many of our young theology students have turned in their draft cards," he noted. "Heroic boys. I wonder if their sacrifices will change our fantastic course." But in the wake of the 1968 student strike at Columbia, which spread across Broadway to Union Seminary, he soured on youthful rebellion. The seminarians tried (unsuccessfully) to force the board to pay $100,000 in "reparations" to black families in New York. "These youngsters have all been going crazy," he complained. "I have an old man's peeve against the new generation."

During the 1968 election campaign, Humphrey and McCarthy organizations both approached him for endorsements. To the Humphrey managers he wrote that "despite our long friendship I *could not* endorse a candidate who is bound to the present futile policy in Vietnam." He liked McCarthy but did not know enough about his civil-rights stand to support him. There were two candidates he knew he did not like: Nixon and Bobby Kennedy, the two who he assumed would face each other in the fall. Had Rockefeller been nominated, he would have voted Republican for the first time in his life. With Nixon's nomination and Kennedy's assassination, he reluctantly backed Humphrey as the lesser evil.[13]

Nixon's victory brought Niebuhr into one final public controversy. In 1969 the President inaugurated Sunday worship services in the White House itself and invited a series of ministers from different faiths to preside. Leading off was Billy Graham. The combination of Graham and Nixon was potent enough to stir Niebuhr from his sickbed. In "The King's Chapel and the King's Court," he composed a biting put-down of religious complacency and ministerial collusion. There was an urgency to his prophetic satire; he was summoning up vestiges of the anti-establishment militance he had only rarely expressed since the mid-1930s. Billy Graham, "a domesticated and tailored leftover" from the wild frontier evangelists, was the modern equivalent of Amaziah, the king's chaplain who scorned the "critical radicalism" of Amos. Even the Jewish rabbi Louis Finkelstein (whom Niebuhr left unnamed) forgot "the warnings of Amos" and spoke during his service of "the finger of God" that "pointed to Richard Milhous Nixon." Niebuhr observed icily that "it is wonderful what a simple White House invitation will do to dull the critical faculties." He noted that Amos was Martin Luther King's favorite prophet. "It is unfortunate that he was murdered before he could be invited to that famous ecumenical congregation in the White House. But on second thought, . . . perhaps the FBI, which spied on him, had the

•

same opinion of him as Amaziah had of Amos." Nixon appears to have had the same opinion of Niebuhr. In October his lieutenant John Ehrlichman asked the FBI for a report on him. Niebuhr also received a pile of hate mail from Graham's legions, which according to his wife rather pleased him. So did the controversy that raged for two weeks in the New York *Times* letter columns after the initial report of his article. He felt again the rush of vitality that accompanied sharp rhetoric and firm commitment, but it was a brief moment, a reliving of memories.

There was no comparable lift from the publication in 1969 of his last "book," *The Democratic Experience,* since it provoked little interest in readers or reviewers. The book was co-authored by political scientist Paul Sigmund. Eighty-five pages were by Niebuhr, fragments of the project on democracy and communism that he had abandoned in 1963; ninety more—on the prospects for democracy in the developing world—were by Sigmund, who had taught with Niebuhr at Harvard in 1961. Niebuhr rewrote his 1961 "Reflections on Democracy as an Alternative to Communism," but in honor of the new President prefaced them with a decidedly anti–Republican Party statement. Democracy was not the product of "liberty"; it was the historic fruit of a particular convergence of cultural developments in Europe. On the one hand, as he had argued in 1961, democratic self-government could therefore not be imposed on societies that lacked the cultural preparation for it. On the other hand, Americans themselves were liable to forget that their own democracy was historically dependent on both a "united community" and a solution to the "industrial problems of collective justice." It was naive to "constantly extol liberty as if it were an absolute value without reference to either community or justice." By elevating the individual over the communal and valuing self-seeking over group responsibility for justice, Americans were undermining democracy, not shoring it up. The argument was only briefly sketched, and the book was as casual and incomplete as *A Nation So Conceived.* More remarkable than the book itself was its publisher: Frederick Praeger. For the first time since *An Interpretation of Christian Ethics* in 1935 he was not appearing under Scribners' imprint. Family loyalties were stronger. Elisabeth had gone to work at Praeger and he took the book there as a favor to her.[14]

In 1969 Niebuhr informed his old Bethel parishioner Otto Pokorny that he had trouble even writing letters. As he continued to decline, the letters he did manage to write took on a new equanimity. He was resigned but not frustrated; his weariness was tranquil. When an old Elmhurst and Eden classmate, Theophil Twente, reported to him on recent deaths among their childhood friends, he responded with a serene matter-of-factness. "Thus we are gathered to the fathers one by one. . . . I am ready to depart this life but my time may not be quite yet." To Scarlett, who himself spoke of "impending death," Niebuhr replied that "I am no longer surprised" by such reflections; "I have intimated to Ursula that this year may be my last."

> Remember the past when we used to speculate as to who would preside at the other's funeral. Vain thoughts. Now we will see each other at the throne of God. I will confess my sins and thank him for a lifelong friendship with a wonderful guy, who started at Phoenix, became Bishop of Missouri, and retired

in Maine. All the years he was a source of grace to this poor sinner whom he blessed with his friendship.

There were two major disturbances to his serenity in 1970. Nixon's "madness in extending an unpopular war he was elected to bring to an end," as he wrote to Bennett, was the first. It justified "all our opposition to this bloody, costly, and futile war"—including civil disobedience. One evening as he lay motionless on his bed, the television news flickered on a few feet away. When the image of Richard Nixon appeared, Niebuhr engaged in the only disobedience he could manage. He pushed himself up off the mattress and spat out the words, "That bastard!" Not a Christian sentiment, one might suppose. But Niebuhr thought that even the Christian needed a few good enemies. "God told us to love our enemies, not to like them," he would say. Having no enemies meant that one lacked strong convictions. It was one more of the human paradoxes in which he always delighted.[15]

The second disturbance arrived in a letter from Elson Ruff, editor of the *Lutheran,* who wondered whether Niebuhr's famous "Serenity Prayer" had perhaps really been authored by an eighteenth-century German theologian, Friedrich Oetinger. Others had written him over the years to ask whether it had come perhaps from Marcus Aurelius, Francis of Assisi, or another sage. Niebuhr was troubled by the suggestion that the prayer he had begun using at least by World War II was not his own. In the form in which he published it in a column in 1951, it read:

God, give us the serenity to accept what cannot be changed;
Give us the courage to change what should be changed;
Give us the wisdom to distinguish one from the other.

His friend Howard Chandler Robbins had asked during the war to use it in a collection of prayers he was editing for the Federal Council of Churches, and the USO distributed it to hundreds of thousands of servicemen. After the war Alcoholics Anonymous adopted it as an official prayer, and Hallmark Cards eventually paid Niebuhr for the commercial rights. He always claimed authorship of it, but never bothered to copyright it until Hallmark decided to use it in its 1962 Graduation Line.

Niebuhr never found out that a word-for-word German translation of his prayer had become just as universally known in post–World War II Germany as it was in America; in both countries it hung over family hearths stitched into mass-produced weavings. But in Germany it was always attributed to Oetinger. In fact the German version was not the work of Oetinger but the work of one Theodor Wilhelm, a writer who took the pseudonym Oetinger and (according to his own later recollection) put a German translation into circulation after receiving a copy from a Canadian friend in the 1940s. By the 1950s it was cropping up in statesmen's addresses as well as in common households. It even became the official motto of the West German Army academy—a fine irony, since it was from the service of the German military that Gustav Niebuhr had fled nearly a hundred years before. It was also ironic that the Anglophile Niebuhr, whose works were

·

(and are) rarely read in Germany, should nevertheless have insinuated one of his works so deeply into German culture.

But in 1970 a failing Niebuhr knew nothing of this. And his and Ursula's response to Ruff's question suggested that he was beginning to second-guess his own authorship. "Subconscious or even unconscious traces, of course, always play their part in all forms of art—in music as well as literature—and J. S. Bach, T. S. Eliot, Shakespeare (and Jesus, for that matter) often echoed material from the past." He must have wondered if he had subconsciously recorded a prayer used by his father or one that he had read somewhere years before. He was pained by the doubts of others—just as he must have been pained to receive a copy of an ad for the prayer that appeared in the Philadelphia *Inquirer* in 1970.

AMAZING EMBROIDERY OFFER
Beautiful "Silent Majority" Serenity Prayer Now Yours in Fabulous Crewel Stitchery. Spend Pleasant Moments Creating This Exquisite Full-Color Traditional Silent Prayer for Your Home. Complete Kit Only $2.95. Sure to Delight or Full Refund Guaranteed.

The commercialization was distressing enough. But having his prayer claimed for Nixon's "silent majority" was the final insult and the crowning irony.[16]

VI

Niebuhr's life, like all lives brought to self-consciousness or subjected to scrutiny, was a pattern of paradoxes and a sequence of ironies. The uniqueness of Reinhold Niebuhr lay in the energy and zeal with which he pursued paradox and irony in both life and thought. The prophet-priest seeking influence and humility. The German-American Anglophile. The religious-secular preacher chastising the pious and chiding the worldly. The teacher-academic who distrusted the scholars and hoped for their respect. The liberal crusader against liberalism. The Jamesian relativist who embraced the God of Abraham and the revelation of Jesus. The booming polemicist beset with hidden anxieties. Truth could be expressed only in paradox, he believed, and life lived as a succession of pregnant contradictions.

In *The Irony of American History* he had argued that the concept of irony was especially useful for illuminating the American experience. He hoped it would galvanize his readers into continuing the quest for personal and collective responsibility. The same concept of irony aids us in understanding Niebuhr. His career was "ironic," not "tragic" or "pathetic," just as he claimed the American experience to be. He did not choose his fate like a tragic hero; it was always partly chosen for him, beginning with the early "call" he accepted from his father. Nor was his fate imposed upon him by family, environment, or circumstance like that of a pathetic victim. His dynamic selfhood transcended psychic and social determinants even as it was indelibly marked by them. Perceiving his career as ironic provokes in us neither the tears of tragedy nor the pity of pathos. It promotes instead the sympathetic smile of critical understanding. He who sits in the heavens

·

shall laugh at the spectacle of human life, its greatness built on frailty. Those who contemplate the life of Niebuhr will marvel at the meaning his life disclosed and the mysteries it concealed. Now we know in part; only then, perhaps, shall we know face to face.

When Niebuhr's close friend Felix Frankfurter died in 1965, he tried to express the secret of his friend's life. "A part of the secret of Felix G. Frankfurter's life must be found in his unique gifts. Another part must be assigned to the open society of America, which, with all its faults, has the capacity to release the hidden potentialities of its children and of its immigrants' children." Had he tried autobiography he might have said the same of himself: uniquely gifted and well placed to seize the portion of opportunity offered a provincial German-American parson's son in early-twentieth-century America. He could not aspire to the heights of leadership and statesmanship inhabited by his heroes from Lincoln to MacDonald, Churchill, and Cripps. But America's own historic expansiveness was matched by the personal transformation he wrought. The midwestern preacher cultivated his hidden potentialities and at the same time helped transform American culture and the Protestant faith. Twentieth-century Protestant audiences quivered with instant recognition; he recalled deeply rooted ancestral memories. His language, rhythm, and intonation echoed the nineteenth-century Biblical culture that his older listeners remembered from childhood. The twentieth-century Christian church was shaken to its foundations by his piercing voice. So were the secular organizations of often agnostic liberals who flocked to him for inspiration. No one else could speak with such authority to Christian, Jew, and nonbeliever. He was assuredly an American phenomenon. With his modest educational preparation he could perhaps have risen to such stature only in America, where practical mastery could compensate for lack of credentials and absence of breeding.

In early January, 1971, Niebuhr leaned over to Erik Erikson, seated by his bed, and said, "Erik, I don't want to live." His bladder was tied to catheter tubes and he could not easily raise himself. "I know," said Erikson. In the late winter a bout of pneumonia weakened him, and as the weather turned warmer he suffered a pulmonary embolism and entered the hospital. He and Ursula agreed that his body would go to Harvard for medical research. They also agreed that their good friend Rabbi Abraham Heschel would participate in the memorial service along with several Protestant ministers. After going home in April, he rallied, but in May failed again. The end came quietly and peacefully at home on Tuesday evening, June 1, three weeks short of his seventy-ninth birthday and a half-year short of his fortieth anniversary.

Friends and family flocked to the First Congregational Church in Stockbridge—of which Jonathan Edwards had been an early pastor—for the memorial service on June 4. They recited the same psalm (the sixty-seventh) and sang the same hymns that the Niebuhrs had chosen for their wedding in 1931. A local reporter noted that Arthur Schlesinger, Joseph Rauh, William Shirer, Lionel and Diana Trilling, and Jonathan and June Bingham were present in the congregation of two hundred. So were two Appalachian Trail backpackers who had come down out of the Berkshires, bedrolls in hand, upon hearing of Niebuhr's death. The reporter did not recognize

·

eighty-seven-year-old Will Scarlett, who had managed to drive down alone from his home in Maine. He did not say a public prayer, but he added his silent reflections to Rabbi Heschel's words.

"The Lord has given, the Lord has taken,
Praised be the name of the Lord.
My flesh and my heart may fail,
But God is the strength of my heart.
He is my portion for ever."

Niebuhr had used the same passage from Job in informing Evangelical Synod readers of his father's death in 1913. Heschel continued: "He appeared among us like a sublime figure out of the Hebrew Bible. . . . Niebuhr's life was a song in the form of deeds, a song that will go on for ever. Revered, beloved Reinhold: In the words of the Psalmist:

"You are the fairest of the sons of men,
Grace is poured upon your lips
Therefore God has blessed you for ever."[17]

FULL
OF
GRACE AND GRIEF

Reinhold Niebuhr died only a decade and a half ago, but it is already difficult to hold him in focus. In retrospect his centrifugal career tends to fragment into its component parts. Latter-day disciples seize upon the particular Niebuhr they prefer. Neoconservatives flock to the Niebuhr of the late 1940s and 1950s: the vehement opponent of Soviet communism, the persistent adversary of left utopianism. Liberals and left-liberals take heart from the Niebuhr of the 1920s and 1930s: the zealous antagonist of business hegemony, the angry critic of the consumer culture. Theological scholars meanwhile debate his religious works, cut off from the historians and social scientists who analyze his political thought. In life Niebuhr always confounded those who stressed one side of his career or one segment of his standpoint at the expense of another. He confused his comrades as often as his detractors. At his most radical, before World War II, he chastised other radicals for their complacency; at his most conservative, after World War II, he did the same to conservatives. He was his own best critic because he was so aware of the risk of self-satisfaction. He undermined efforts to sum him up, plant him on a pedestal, appropriate his name. When he retired from Union Theological Seminary in 1960 he protested his friend Will Scarlett's letter of accolades: "I had a few thoughts and a tremendous urge to express myself. I spoke and wrote all over the place and now when the stuff is reviewed honestly most of it turns out to be slightly cockeyed or partly askew."

To offset the thick vein of pride that he knew lay behind even the humblest smile, he understated his own achievement. But he also displayed a sharp insight into his career. "I spoke and wrote all over the place." The unsettled, eruptive intelligence in perpetual motion. "A tremendous urge to express myself." The passionate hunger to preach his Word, a seed planted by his father and nourished by his own encounter with the beauties and tragedies of life. "Slightly cockeyed or partly askew." From a later vantage point he passed judgment on earlier inadequacies. He could never be content with his own viewpoint. He recognized its partiality. There was no virtue in consistency, he thought, since life overflowed with incongruities. In 1967 he told Scarlett that traditional terms of reassurance like "salvation" or "redemption" offered little comfort in the late twentieth century. Most modern people were "allergic" to them "because we all are conscious of the endless relativities of the human state." Christians occupied no privileged sanctuary beyond the insecurities of merely secular life. What distinguished them from most nonbelievers was the depth of their discontent. Like Job they felt themselves judged from beyond themselves, confronted in the darkness by a hidden God who, as Niebuhr liked to put it, "always confronts man first as an enemy, not as a friend." In the deep chill of that encounter the Christian "hoped against hope," affirmed an ultimate trust in a divine goodness that lay beyond the good and evil of human experience.[1]

Niebuhr lived and thought in intimate relation to the events of his time. While a Tillich, a Barth, or a Richard Niebuhr tried to lift himself out of the passing flux of history to mount sustained theological inquiries, he immersed himself in it. They were scholars of great erudition who wrote for the ages. He spoke and wrote with at least one eye firmly fixed on social and political forces. One wonders if he could have achieved such high distinction at any other historic juncture. So much of his influence stemmed from his knowledge of Germany and England at a time of unprecedented crisis for both nations. So much of it flowed from his eminence as a preacher in an era still marked by great preaching. One can easily picture Richard Niebuhr sitting today in his Yale Divinity School office writing his lectures on ethics, or Paul Tillich in his summer isolation at Easthampton composing his systematic theology. One cannot imagine Reinhold Niebuhr crisscrossing the east and midwest forty weekends a year on the college preaching circuit; that circuit no longer exists. The golden age of the intellectual preacher is past. Our intellectual gurus today are secular writers, academic popularizers, therapeutic counselors, psychological sages. We no longer generate theological celebrities. Niebuhr would have made a poor television personality.

He was not a man for all seasons. His social and political views cannot be ripped out of their context and pressed into service today. It is futile to wonder what he would have said today about Central American revolutions, about "free enterprise," about the women's movement. He would have evolved so much, so unpredictably, over the last quarter-century. And yet his mature vision of the "Christian realist" life is still a compelling model of the moral vocation. The moral life, he suggested, was not a restful state. It was the choice of aggravation over tranquility. The Christian was called to a continuous renegotiation of the balance between taking the world as it is and transforming it in the cause of justice. There could be only momentary deep breaths between assaults on complacent beliefs or outmoded structures. No political position was sacrosanct, above criticism. Likewise

•

none was to be dismissed without seeking the good that might be contained in it.

Niebuhr was always finding troubling questions where even his friends found easy answers. Take school prayer. By the early 1960s, when the Supreme Court banned organized, voluntary school prayer, liberals had reached a consensus: only benighted fundamentalists could support the right of a school system to enact a voluntary prayer. Niebuhr was not sure the fundamentalists were wrong on this issue. Justice Hugo Black's majority opinion in the New York Regents case amounted, he thought, to "the suppression of religion." The result would be "a consistently secular education, which the founding fathers certainly did not intend. They wanted a religiously neutral state, not one hostile to religion."

On one level he saw the court's decision as a "suppression" of religion, on another as an endorsement of one religion: secularism. As he had put it to Justice Felix Frankfurter years before, "the prevailing philosophy which is pumped into our public schools day after day is itself a religion . . . [which] preaches the redemption of man by historical development and . . . 'scientific objectivity.' It does not have to worry about the separation of church and state." The Regents' prayer itself verged on the innocuous, he granted, since it was written to offend the fewest people. And organized prayers in public places always tended toward banality. Still he feared the Court's decision. He felt that it assaulted the First Amendment itself, which barred the Congress from establishing any religion and also from prohibiting the free exercise of religion. Secularism was established and the free exercise of other religious beliefs was impeded.[2]

The fundamentalists must have reveled in Niebuhr's "dissenting opinion" on school prayer, but they could take no solace in most of his views, including those on religion. For all his disgust with the religion of secularism, he was scarcely more enamored of the religion of most Christians. He was put off by easy belief, angered by cost-free piety. He preferred to associate with secular liberals who slogged for justice without cosmic assurances than with religious ones who draped their actions in the rhetoric of salvation. He winced when religious people spoke of their religious "experiences," their "conversions," or (in Tillich's widely popular phrase) their "ultimate concern." Hearing that phrase made him feel like defecting to Sidney Hook's naturalistic secularism. To his friend June Bingham Niebuhr noted that there was no end to the things people could be ultimately concerned about. The question was, which ultimate concern merited our commitment, and what were we willing to sacrifice for that commitment?

Likewise he thought of faith not so much as an "experience," but as a foundation for experience. "Experiences are fleeting," he told Bingham. "Sometimes one has a strong awareness of the ultimate mystery of the divine, and sometimes one is troubled by what the mystics call periods of dryness. For me the point is that the experience of faith is a total attitude toward the mystery of God and life, which includes commitment, love, and hope." Believing in God was not like feeling warm inside. It was perceiving an outline of meaning in the midst of a broken existence. It was detecting "a mystery of grace . . . beyond the conscious designs and contrivances of men." Sidney Hook wondered why his friend had to go hunting

•

for mysteries. He figured Niebuhr had a permanent metaphysical itch. What Niebuhr had was a conviction that the self was in conflict with itself, deluding itself, subverting its own capacity for good with subtle intrusions of pride. To his Jewish friend Waldo Frank he wrote in 1938 of the "deeper sense of the tragic in Christianity, a greater certainty that life on every level may involve itself in self-destruction. Here it is both more profound and more imperiled than Judaism, more imperiled because it can so easily degenerate into other-worldliness."[3]

Niebuhr's was assuredly a faith for this world. His prime intellectual contribution was to weld together the tragic sense of life and the quest for justice. His work is a constant challenge to those who would accentuate one and neglect the other. The tragic character of human existence placed firm limits on the quest for justice: human community could never be perfected, never attain the level of harmonious fellowship. But the quest for justice undermined any premature appeal to tragic limits, any self-serving celebration of the social status quo. The "responsible" self made a measured response to the world, eschewing utopian enthusiasms yet rejecting counsels of acquiescence. Responsibility meant holding oneself in balance, poised in what Niebuhr's friend Lionel Trilling called "the middle of the journey": devoted to the principle of justice, skeptical and discriminating in concrete commitment.

Niebuhr was bounded by his times, but much of his work speaks directly to a later era in which many men and women have discerned the inadequacy of their political beliefs and moral viewpoints. Or discovered the shallowness of the political and moral wisdom dispensed by advice-giving agencies from schools and churches to popular books and mass advertising. The culture of the 1980s is permeated with appeals to unalloyed self-interest in politics and to fulfillment through personal "growth" in morals. Niebuhr knew that self-interest was a fact of political life, though he stressed that communal solidarity was the foundation for a just society. He was dismayed when Goldwater and the Republican right abstracted individual freedom from the web of social obligation, aghast when they attacked federal authority as an enemy of popular rights. "The resistance to 'big government' is frightening," he wrote in 1965, "particularly since all our problems are on a national scale."

Self-interest had its place in a realistic political theory, but as a moral ideal it repelled him. He was suspicious of all calls for self-fulfillment. He that findeth his life shall lose it. Personal contentment was a long-range by-product of communal engagement, not of a course in "growth." He was even uncomfortable with the traditional, Aristotelian notion of self-realization—the gradual development of talents and virtues, the acorn becoming the oak—because it was too complacent about the power of mind to discipline and control the self. "For the good that I would, I do not," Paul wrote to the Romans, "but the evil which I would not, that I do." Niebuhr knew, like Paul, that a law in his members warred against the law in his mind. Happiness could be found only on the other side of unhappiness, and it came as a gift, not an acquisition. The moral existence demanded a provisional unfulfillment. Yet the brokenness and brutality of the earthly vale of tears provoked not resignation but expectancy. For all his doubts

•

about the power of mind, he was sure that men and women were called to
enact justice, make their own history, in full awareness of the pride and
foolishness that would plague their efforts. All the while they could shake
their heads in wonder at the spectacle of a life that was forever, as he said
to Scarlett, "full of grace and grief."[4]

NOTES

The following abbreviations are used in the notes.

RN   Reinhold Niebuhr
HRN   Helmut Richard Niebuhr
UMN   Ursula M. Niebuhr

CC	*Christianity and Crisis*	N	*Nation*
CCY	*Christian Century*	NL	*New Leader*
CS	*Christianity and Society*	NR	*New Republic*
DN	Detroit *News*	NYT	New York *Times*
DT	Detroit *Times*	RR	*Radical Religion*
EH	*Evangelical Herald*	WT	*World Tomorrow*

Unless otherwise indicated in the notes, letters exchanged between RN and these correspondents are located in the following collections of the correspondents' papers.

John Baltzer, Eden Archives, Eden Seminary, Webster Groves, Missouri
John Bennett, John Bennett's possession
June Bingham, Box 26 of the RN Papers, Library of Congress
Sherwood Eddy, Kirby Page Papers, Southern California School of Theology, Claremont, California
Waldo Frank, Frank Papers, University of Pennsylvania
Felix Frankfurter, Frankfurter Papers, Library of Congress
James Loeb, Americans for Democratic Action Papers, State Historical Society of Wisconsin, Madison, Wisconsin
Lewis Mumford, Mumford Papers, University of Pennsylvania
Kirby Page, Page Papers, Southern California School of Theology
William Savage, Scribners Office Files, New York City
William Scarlett, Boxes 27 and 33 of the RN Papers, Library of Congress
Arthur Schlesinger, Jr., Schlesinger Papers, Kennedy Library, Waltham, Massachusetts

INTRODUCTION: DAY OF THE LORD

1. RN sermon, "Our Lord's Conception of the Providence of God," Feb. 3, 1952, tape recording available from Union Theological Seminary of Virginia, edited transcript published in RN, *Justice and Mercy*, ed. Ursula M. Niebuhr (New York, 1974), pp. 14–22; Amos 5:18–24, 6:1, 4, 7:14 (Revised Standard Version); Harlan B. Phillips, ed., *Felix Frankfurter Reminisces* (New York, 1960), p. 291.
2. RN to Savage, July 14, 1947, Aug. 8, 1960 [1947 letter in RN Papers]; RN remarks on topic "Has Twentieth Century Civilization Improved Mankind?" *Town Meeting of the Air*, Feb. 20, 1939, p. 5 [broadcast Feb. 16, 1939].

•

ONE: NEVER FAR FROM THE TREE (1892–1913)

1. Lincoln *Daily Courier*, Aug. 2, 1902, p. 3, Aug. 5, 1902, p. 2, Aug. 6, 1903, p. 2; V. Deacon Lile, "History of the Lincoln Chautauqua Association of Lincoln, Illinois" (MA thesis, State University of Iowa, 1938), pp. 22–31; Hugh A. Orchard, *Fifty Years of Chautauqua* (Cedar Rapids, Iowa, 1923), p. 311; Lawrence B. Stringer, *History of Lincoln County, Illinois,* vol. 1 (Chicago, 1911), pp. 466–468; author's interviews with Florence Niebuhr and George Opperman, Sr.

2. On Gustav Niebuhr's early life, William G. Chrystal, *A Father's Mantle* (New York, 1982), pp. 3–13; Karl Drüge to Chrystal, Mar. 28, 1979, Edgar Prasse to D. B. Robertson, Mar. 12, 1959, Mrs. Nelson Baumgartner to Chrystal, n.d. [1979], letters in Chrystal's possession; Lincoln *Daily News-Herald,* Apr. 21, 1913, p. 5; RN to June Bingham, n.d. [c. 1954]; Bingham notes on interview with Hulda Niebuhr, Jan. 20, 1954, RN Papers.

3. On the Evangelical Synod, Carl E. Schneider, *The German Church on the American Frontier* (St. Louis, 1939); David Dunn, et al., *A History of the Evangelical and Reformed Church* (Philadelphia, 1961); Ewald Kockritz, *Memorial Diamond Jubilee: German Evangelical Synod of North America* (St. Louis, 1915); Bureau of the Census, *Religious Bodies, 1906* (Washington, D.C., 1910); author's interview with Paul Lehmann.

4. On Edward Hosto and on Gustav Niebuhr's career between 1885 and 1902, Chrystal, *A Father's Mantle,* pp. 26–76; *News-Herald,* Apr. 21, 1913, p. 5; *Saint John's Church, 1860–1960* (Lincoln, Ill., 1960), p. 32.

5. Stringer, *History of Logan County,* pp. 15, 529–530; Bureau of the Census, *Twelfth Census of the United States, 1900,* Population and Agriculture volumes; interview with George Opperman; *Souvenir zum Goldenen Jubiläum der Evangelischen St. Johannes-Gemeinde zu Lincoln, Illinois, 23 Oktober, 1910* (Lincoln, Ill., 1910), p. 22; *News-Herald,* Apr. 21, 1913, p. 5.

6. Gustav Niebuhr, "Harnacks 'Das Wesen des Christentums,'" *Magazin für Evangelische Theologie und Kirche,* n.s., 4 (Mar., 1902), pp. 87, 92–93; Gustav Niebuhr, "In What Way and to What Extent Should the Church Exercise Influence on Social and Political Conditions?" *Messenger of Peace,* May 15, 1913, p. 2, June 1, 1913, pp. 1–2; Gustav Niebuhr, "Frauenberuf und Wissenschaft," *Evangelische Diakonissen-Herold* 3 (Nov., 1908), pp. 6–8; RN, *The Reminiscences of Reinhold Niebuhr* (New York [Columbia Oral History Research Office], 1953), pp. 7–16; interviews with Florence Niebuhr and George Opperman.

7. Stringer, *History of Logan County,* pp. 424–425, 429, 485; interview with George Opperman; *Courier,* May 16, 1903, p. 4, Oct. 28, 1904, p. 5, Apr. 22, 1907, p. 3; Sept. 13, 1909, p. 5; *News-Herald,* Sept. 5, 1912, p. 4, Dec. 21, 1912, pp. 4–5, July 10, 1914, p. 4, Sept. 3, 1914, p. 4.

8. Florence Denger to D. B. Robertson, Jan. 28, 1959, letter in Robertson's possession; Bingham interview with Hulda Niebuhr; RN to Floyd Brown, Apr. 17, 1957, RN Papers; RN, *Reminiscences,* pp. 1, 3; RN to Bingham, n.d. [c. 1954]; author's interviews with George Opperman and Raymond Gimbel.

9. RN quoted in Bingham, *Courage to Change* (New York, 1960), p. 55 (italics in original); L. W. Goebel to D. B. Robertson, Mar. 6, 1959, letter in Robertson's possession; RN, "Mein Lebenslauf" ["life story"], June 17, 1907, in his Elmhurst application, copy in possession of William Chrystal; *Courier,* Apr. 9, 1906, p. 5.

10. *Courier,* Oct. 24, 1906, p. 3; Eva Paine Carnes to RN, Jan. 31, 1933, letter in possession of UMN; RN to Bjarne Ullsvik, Nov. 6, 1953, RN Papers; *Festschrift zum Goldenen Jubiläum, June 5, 1921* (Elmhurst, Ill., 1921), p. 10; "Reminiscences of Reinhold Niebuhr by Theophil Twente," typescript, 1976, pp. 1–2, copy in Chrystal's possession; Chrystal, "Introduction," in Chrystal, ed., *Young Reinhold*

•

Niebuhr (St. Louis, 1977), p. 27; declassified FBI documents in author's possession [Elmhurst grade average]; RN, *Reminiscences*, pp. 2–4; Florence Denger to
RN, Jan., 1971, letter in possession of UMN; *Courier*, Aug. 10, 1909,
p. 5.

11. *Eden Seminary Catalogue*, 1911–1912, p. 32; Twente, "Reminiscences," p. 2; RN,
"Dr. Press and Evangelical Theology," typescript, 1941, p. 1, Eden Archives;
Carl E. Schneider, *History of the Theological Seminary of the Evangelical Church*
(St. Louis, 1925), p. 46; RN, "Religion: Revival and Education," in Chrystal,
Young Reinhold Niebuhr, pp. 46–52; RN, "Before and After," typescript, n.d.
[1912?], pp. 1–4, RN Papers; Bingham interview with Hulda Niebuhr [on Lin-
coln bull story]; "The Preliminary Debate," *Keryx*, Feb., 1912, pp. 18–19;
"Eden-Concordia Debate" and "First Intercollegiate Debate," *Keryx*, Apr., 1912,
pp. 9–11, 15; Theodore Seybold to Samuel Press, May 16, 1954, Paul Zwilling
to Press, Mar. 3, 1954, RN Papers; E. J. Friedrich to Chrystal, Sept. 27, 1979,
Franz Paul Puhlmann, "Reinhold Niebuhr," typescript, n.d., p. 1, both in
Chrystal's possession; "Bachelor and Anti-Bachelor Clubs," *Keryx*, Feb., 1912,
pp. 16–18.

12. Author's interview with Florence Niebuhr; RN, *Reminiscences*, pp. 6, 11; *Original
Records of Saint John's Church, 1865–1902* (Lincoln, Ill., n.d.), n.p.

13. *News-Herald*, Apr. 21, 1913, p. 5, Apr. 23, 1913, pp. 5, 8, Apr. 26, 1913, p. 4,
Apr. 28, 1913, p. 5, June 30, 1913, p. 5; Lincoln *Evening Star*, Apr. 23, 1913,
p. 5; *Saint John's Church, 1860–1960*, pp. 35–36; Florence Denger to D. B.
Robertson, Jan. 28, 1959; RN, "St. Johannes-Gemeinde," *Evangelisches Ge-
meindeblatt*, May 15, 1913, p. 2; Chrystal, "Introduction," p. 31.

14. John Cogley, "An Interview with Reinhold Niebuhr," *McCall's*, Feb., 1966,
p. 171; RN, "A Religion Worth Fighting For," *Survey*, Aug. 1, 1927, p. 444.

TWO: A MONGREL AMONG THOROUGHBREDS (1913–1915)

1. Lincoln *Daily News-Herald* reports on Lincoln churches and Union Services; RN,
"Sermon at Union Service," typescript, pp. 1–3, 5–6, RN Papers; *News-Herald*,
Aug. 20, 1913, p. 4, Aug. 30, 1913, p. 4; RN, *Reminiscences*, p. 11.

2. RN, *Reminiscences*, pp. 12–13; Roland Bainton, *Yale and the Ministry* (New York,
1957), pp. 198–211; Charles Reynolds Brown, *Faith and Health* (New York, 1910),
pp. 63, 144–145, 150, *The Social Message of the Christian Pulpit* (New York, 1906),
p. 239; *Bulletin of Yale University School of Religion, 1913–1914* (New Haven,
1913); *Yale Divinity Quarterly* 10 (Nov., 1913), p. 66, and 11 (Nov. 1914), p. 48.

3. RN to Samuel Press, Mar. 2, Apr. 6, 1914, RN Papers; RN, "Yale-Eden," in
Chrystal, *Young Reinhold Niebuhr*, p. 58; Information Flyer in Yale School of
Religion Scrapbook, Yale University Archives.

4. RN to Press, Apr. 6, 1914; HRN, "Value-Theory and Theology," in J. S. Bixler,
et al., eds., *The Nature of Religious Experience: Essays in Honor of Douglas Clyde
Macintosh* (New York, 1937), p. 96; RN, *Reminiscences*, pp. 16–17; RN, "The
Validity and Certainty of Religious Knowledge" (BD thesis, Yale Divinity School),
pp. 5, 11, 14, 19, 21, 26, 32–33, 35–36, RN Papers; Walter Rauschenbusch,
Christianizing the Social Order (New York, 1912), pp. 448–449, 455, 460; RN to
Bingham, June 14, 1954.

5. *News-Herald*, Sept. 21, 1914, p. 4; RN, *Reminiscences*, pp. 7–8; Ross E. Paulson,
*Radicalism and Reform: The Vrooman Family and American Social Thought, 1837–
1937* (Lexington, Ky., 1968), pp. 211–213.

6. Author's interview with Ferdinand Poffenberger; Cornelius Kruse reminiscences,
transcript in possession of William Chrystal, n.d., n.p.; Archibald MacLeish to
author, May 31, 1981; RN, "Yale-Eden," pp. 54–55; RN, *Reminiscences*, pp. 16–

•

17; *Yale Divinity Quarterly* 11 (May, 1915), p. 28 [announcement of Peace Prize essay].

7. William James, "The Moral Equivalent of War," in John J. McDermott, ed., *The Writings of William James* (Chicago, 1977), p. 669; RN, "Patriotism and Altruism," typescript, pp. 2–3, 5, 7, 9–11, 14, RN Papers.

8. RN to H. M. Bradley, Mar. 11, June 15, 1915, Church Record Book No. 5, pp. 223, 233, First Congregational Church of Derby; RN, "The Contribution of Christianity to the Doctrine of Immortality" (Master's thesis, Yale University), pp. 1, 32–33, 38, Yale University Library.

9. RN to Press, July 1, July 11, 1915, RN Papers [the second letter is dated June 11, but internal evidence establishes beyond any doubt that it was written after the July 1 letter]; Carl Vrooman Diary, entry for July 29, 1915, Vrooman Papers, Library of Congress; *Courier-Herald*, n.p., n.d. [mid-May, 1915], clipping in possession of Carol Niebuhr Buchanan; RN to George Moog, July 13, 1915, Bethel Church Papers, Emmanuel-Bethel United Church of Christ, Royal Oak, Michigan.

THREE: IF I WERE NOT OF GERMAN BLOOD (1915–1919)

1. Evangelical Bethel Congregation, *Secretary's Record Book, 1912–1923*, pp. 64–66, 70, Bethel Church Papers; RN to Press, Nov. 3, 1915; RN, *Leaves from the Notebook of a Tamed Cynic* (Chicago, 1929 [reissued, New York, 1957]), p. 26. On the origins of Bethel, Paul Jans, "A Brief History of Bethel Church," in *Anniversary Record Commemorating the Twenty-Fifth Anniversary of Bethel Evangelical Church* (Detroit, 1937), pp. 12–16. On his arrival at Bethel, RN, *Reminiscences*, p. 21.

2. RN, "The Failure of German-Americanism," *Atlantic*, July, 1916, pp. 16–18; RN to Münsterberg, Aug. 14, Sept. 4, 1916, Münsterberg Papers, Boston Public Library. On his budget and the *Atlantic* payment, June Bingham, undated interview with RN [c. 1954], notes in RN Papers. On Münsterberg—and on Hagedorn and Viereck—see Phyllis Keller, *States of Belonging: German-American Intellectuals and the First World War* (Cambridge, Mass., 1979), pp. 94–98, 226–230.

3. RN, "The Nation's Crime Against the Individual," *Atlantic*, Nov., 1916, p. 614; RN, "The War and Religion," typescript, pp. 6, 8, 11–12, RN Papers.

4. RN, "Billy Sunday—His Preachments and His Methods," *Detroit Saturday Night*, Oct. 14, 1916, p. 3; RN, *Leaves*, pp. 12, 19, 22, 26.

5. RN, "Report of the Secretary of the War Welfare Commission," Jan. 17, 1918, typescript, Eden Archives [all correspondence and memoranda cited in this chapter are, unless otherwise noted, located in the War Welfare Commission records, Eden Seminary, Webster Groves, Mo.]; RN, "Our Evangelical Boys in Military Camps," *Evangelical Tidings*, Mar. 3, 1918, p. 5; Eugene Baltzer to William Dresel, Jan. 9, 1918. On the commission, "Army and Navy Work of the Evangelical League," *Evangelical Tidings*, Aug. 26, 1917, p. 6; "The War Welfare Commission," *EH*, Nov. 15, 1917, p. 1; Margaret Renton, ed., *War-Time Agencies of the Churches* (New York, 1919), p. 44. I am indebted to William Chrystal for making available to me his copies of the files of the War Welfare Commission.

6. Wilson quoted in Frederick Luebke, *Bonds of Loyalty* (Dekalb, Ill., 1974), p. 234, which also surveys the campaign of repression; George Creel, *How We Advertised America* (New York, 1920), p. 85 ["Four Minute Men"]. Stephen Vaughn's study of CPI, *Holding Fast the Inner Lines* (Chapel Hill, N.C., 1980), p. 204, mentions Walter's role.

7. "Memorial to the Officers of the German Evangelical Synod of North America,"

•

Jan. 18, 1918; RN, "Love of Country," *EH*, Apr. 18, 1918, p. 2; RN, "The Present Task of the Sunday School" [*Evangelical Teacher*, July, 1918], in Chrystal, *Young Reinhold Niebuhr*, p. 91.

8. RN to Horstmann, Apr. 27, 1918; "Resolutions" of War Welfare Commission meeting, Apr., 1918, typescript; RN to Baltzer, May 3, 1918; Horstmann, "Have German-Americans Failed?" *EH*, Oct. 16, 1916, p. 1; RN to Horstmann, Jan. 2, 1917; Horstmann to RN, May 7, 1918; Baltzer to RN, May 15, 1918.

9. Baltzer to RN, May 15, 1918 [two letters of same date, one enclosing "Declaration of loyalty and patriotism"]; RN, *Leaves*, p. 32; RN to Baltzer, July 8, 1918.

10. RN to Baltzer, July 8, July 29, Sept. 9, Sept. 29, 1918; RN, *Leaves*, pp. 33–34; RN to Horstmann, Sept. 27, 1918; Baltzer to RN, Sept. 20, 1918.

11. Baltzer to RN, Feb. 14, 1919; RN to Baltzer, Feb. 9, 1919. On the merger question, RN to Baltzer, Nov. 26, 1918, Horstmann to RN, Dec. 6, 1918, and RN, "Where Shall We Go?" [*Magazin für Evangelische Theologie und Kirche*, Mar., 1919], in Chrystal, *Young Reinhold Niebuhr*, pp. 101–108.

12. RN to Baltzer, Feb. 9, May 13, 1919; Horstmann to RN, Oct. 18, Dec. 6, 1918; RN to Horstmann, Oct. 4, Oct. 22, 1918; RN, *Leaves*, pp. 40–41; RN, "The Twilight of Liberalism," *NR*, June 14, 1919, p. 218.

13. RN to Albert Katterjohn, Oct. 21, 1919; Bethel Congregation, *Secretary's Record Book*, pp. 97, 103–104.

FOUR: A NEW KIND OF MONASTICISM (1920–1925)

1. RN to Eddy, Feb. 12, 1924; RN, *Leaves*, pp. 57, 64–65, 87. On Detroit's growth, *DN*, Sept. 27, 1925, p. 1, Oct. 12, 1925, p. 18. On Bethel's, *Anniversary Record . . . of Bethel Evangelical Church*, pp. 17–18.

2. Bethel Congregation, *Secretary's Record Book*, pp. 67, 80, 94, 103; RN, *Reminiscences*, p. 31; RN to Baltzer, Mar. 10, 1921; Louis W. Goebel, "Detroit," *EH*, Mar. 9, 1922, p. 5; author's interview with Adelaide Buettner Poulin. On Bethel dedication, *DN*, Feb. 11, 1922, p. 11.

3. [RN,] "Repentance and Hope," *CCY*, Oct. 5, 1922, pp. 1214–1215; RN sermon notes for "Inward Sources of Happiness," Nov. 13, 1921, "Shall We Wait for Another?" Dec. 10, 1922, "The Strength of the Weak," Oct. 21, 1923, "The Greater Conquest," Nov. 23, 1923, RN Papers; RN, *Leaves*, pp. 106–107; RN to Eddy, Apr. 10, 1926.

4. RN, "What Are the Churches Advertising?" *CCY*, Nov. 27, 1924, pp. 1532–1533; RN, "A Far Journey," and Paul Jans's comment, *Bethel Brother*, Feb., 1924, pp. 2–4; "Another Travelogue," *Bethel Brother*, May, 1924, pp. 1, 4. See, e.g., the two-column ad in *DN*, Jan. 10, 1925, p. 11.

5. Author's interviews with Adelaide Buettner Poulin and Mrs. Lloyd Sherwood; RN to Otto and Grace Pokorny, Dec. 16, 1969, letter in possession of UMN; RN, *Leaves*, p. 70.

6. RN to Baltzer, Mar. 15, Mar. 19, Mar. 24, 1920, Baltzer to RN, Mar. 17, Mar. 25, 1920; RN, "The Evangelical Movement from the Viewpoint of a Liberal," *EH*, June 24, 1920, pp. 5, 8; RN, "The Church and the Industrial Crisis," *Biblical World* 54 (Nov., 1920), pp. 590–592.

7. RN to Speer, Mar. 4, 1921, RN Papers; RN, "Christian America," *EH*, Jan. 19, 1922, p. 6, Dec. 7, 1922, p. 6, Feb. 15, 1923, p. 105, Mar. 1, 1923, pp. 136–137.

8. RN, letter to the editor, *NR*, Feb. 22, 1922, p. 372; Morrison to RN, July 31, Sept. 27, Nov. 23, 1922, Feb. 23, Mar. 22, 1923, RN Papers; [RN,] "When Religion Is Good Copy," Jan. 10, 1924, p. 36; [RN,] "Protestantism in Ger-

•

many," Oct. 4, 1923, pp. 1258–1260, and "Roman Catholic Gains from the World War," Feb. 14, 1924, p. 196; [RN,] "On the Importance of Amendments" and "Deliver Us from Our Friends," May 8, 1924, pp. 588–589; [RN,] "The Church Speaks—And Is Silent," Mar. 22, 1923, pp. 357–358; RN to Baltzer, Apr. 22, 1925; Baltzer to RN, Apr. 27, 1925; RN to Page, May 18, 1925. I have attributed unsigned *CCY* editorials to RN only when internal and/or external evidence documents his authorship beyond reasonable doubt.

9. On the FCSO, Williams to Page, July 31, 1922, Page to Eddy, Nov. 10, 1922, Page Papers; Harold E. Fey, ed., *Kirby Page, Social Evangelist: The Autobiography of a Twentieth-Century Prophet for Peace* (Nyack, N.Y., 1975), p. 99; Charles Chatfield, *For Peace and Justice* (Knoxville, 1971), pp. 179–180.

10. RN, *Leaves*, pp. 93–94; RN to Mrs. Charles Williams, Feb. 15, 1923, Williams Papers, Bentley Historical Library, University of Michigan; RN, "A Voice Crying in the Wilderness," *Michigan Churchman*, Apr., 1923, p. 7; Williams, "Bishop Calls Industry War," *DN*, May 21, 1921, p. 9; RN, "The Church and the Middle Class," *CCY*, Dec. 7, 1922, pp. 1514–1515; RN, "Wanted: A Christian Morality," *CCY*, Feb. 15, 1923, p. 202.

11. Page Newsletter, July 27, 1923, Page Papers; Scarlett, "The Road Taken," typescript, 1965, pp. 182, 185, copy in possession of William G. Chrystal; RN, *Leaves*, pp. 67–69; RN, "A Trip Through the Ruhr," *EH*, Aug. 9, 1923, "Germany in Despair," *EH*, Sept. 13, 1923, "The Despair of Europe," *EH*, Sept. 20, 1923, in Chrystal, *Young Reinhold Niebuhr*, pp. 127, 129–130, 133, 135–136; RN, "Wanted: A Christian Morality," p. 202. On the English visit, "Astors Entertain Social Students," *NYT*, July 6, 1923, p. 13.

12. RN, "The Despair of Europe," p. 135; RN to Baltzer, Aug. 16, 1923; RN, "Germany," typescript, n.d. [1956], pp. 2–4, RN Papers (published posthumously in *Worldview*, June, 1973, pp. 13–18).

13. RN to Baltzer, Nov. 20, 1923; "Rev. R. Niebuhr Paints Vivid World Picture," *Vortexian*, Sept., 1923, n.p., RN Papers; Page to Harold Willoughby, Oct. 4, 1923; Page to RN, Jan. 10, Feb. 15, 1924; Page to Eddy, Feb. 15, Feb. 21, 1924; Eddy to Page, Feb. 18, Feb. 19, 1924; RN to Eddy, Feb. 12, 1924; RN to Page, Feb. 12, 1924, all in Page Papers. On the evangelistic team, Francis P. Miller to Van Dusen, Mar. 19, 1924, and Eddy to Van Dusen, Mar. 28, 1924, Van Dusen Papers, Union Theological Seminary.

14. Eddy to Page, Feb. 18, 1924; RN, "The Dawn in Europe," *EH*, Aug. 7, 1924, "Berlin Notes," *EH*, Sept. 18, 1924, "The Youth Movement in Germany," *EH*, Oct. 11, 1923, in Chrystal, *Young Reinhold Niebuhr*, pp. 151–152, 155–156, 138; RN, "Christianity and Contemporary Politics," *CCY*, Apr. 17, 1924, p. 498; [RN,] "Disproving Marxianism by Using the Truth in It," *CCY*, Dec. 18, 1924, pp. 1624–1625; RN, "Wanted: A Christian Morality," pp. 202–203; [RN,] "Liberal Faith, Not Ruthless Intellectualism," *CCY*, Mar. 15, 1923, p. 325.

15. Page to RN, Nov. 28, Dec. 15, 1924, RN to Page, May 18, 1925; Page to Alma Page, Apr. 20, 1925, Guthrie to Page, n.d. [mid-May, 1925] and n.d. [June, 1925], Guthrie to Alma Page, May 24, 1925, all in Page Papers; RN, *Leaves*, p. 185.

FIVE: HENRY FORD IS AMERICA (1925–1928)

1. "Calls America Hardest Preaching Field," *CCY*, June 4, 1925, p. 739; [RN,] "Booming Religion as a Business Proposition," *CCY*, May 21, 1925, pp. 658–659; [RN,] "Jesus as Efficiency Expert," *CCY*, July 2, 1925, p. 851; [RN,] "Seek Ye First the Kingdom," *CCY*, July 2, 1925, p. 848; RN, *Leaves*, pp. 103–105; RN, "Can Christianity Survive?" *Atlantic*, Jan., 1925, pp. 87–88; [RN,] "Birth Control," *CCY*, Aug. 27, 1925, p. 1066.

2. *DN*, Sept. 28, 1926, p. 20; "Our Negro Population," *Detroit Saturday Night*, Apr. 21, 1917, p. 13; Richard W. Thomas, "From Peasant to Proletarian: The Formation and Organization of the Black Industrial Working Class in Detroit, 1915–1945" (PhD thesis, University of Michigan, 1976), chs. 1–2; Kenneth T. Jackson, *The Ku Klux Klan in the City, 1915–1930* (New York, 1967), p. 129; RN to Page, Nov. 14, 1924. RN made passing reference to the racial situation in a number of articles, such as "The German Klan," *CCY*, Oct. 16, 1924, pp. 1330–1331, and "Is Protestantism Self-Deceived?" *CCY*, Dec. 25, 1924, p. 1661.

3. David Allen Levine, *Internal Combustion: The Races in Detroit, 1915–1926* (Westport, Conn., 1976), pp. 172ff; Sidney Fine, *Frank Murphy: The Detroit Years* (Ann Arbor, Mich., 1975), p. 98; *DN*, Sept. 12, 1925, pp. 1–2, Sept. 16, 1925, p. 27, Sept. 24, 1925, p. 24; *DT*, Nov. 2, 1925, p. 1; Detroit *Free Press*, Nov. 2, 1925, p. 1; *NYT*, Nov. 3, 1925, p. 8; RN to Eddy, Apr. 10, 1926.

4. RN to Page, Mar. 24, 1926; RN, "Detroit," typescript, n.d. [1956], pp. 4–6, copy in author's possession; RN, *Leaves*, pp. 214–215, 168–169; [RN,] "Race Prejudice in the North," *CCY*, May 12, 1927, pp. 583–584. There is no contemporary evidence to support Niebuhr's 1962 oral recollection that he was "Detroit chairman of the LaFollette campaign" (Paul Merkley, "Transcript of Conversation with Reinhold Niebuhr, Jan. 23, 1962," p. 1, copy in author's possession). That claim seems exaggerated in view of his more modest memory in the 1950s (Bingham, *Courage to Change*, p. 113) that he chaired "a meeting" for LaFollette in 1924. Had he been truly active in the campaign he would have written something about it in the summer or fall of 1924. Yet all he wrote about LaFollette was a moving, unsigned obituary a year later, "The Death of Senator LaFollette," *CCY*, July 2, 1925, pp. 847–848. On Butzel's active role on the race committee, see RN to Mayor John Lodge, Jan. 24, 1928, Detroit Mayor's Papers, Burton Historical Collection, Detroit Public Library.

5. RN, *Reminiscences*, p. 26; [RN,] "The Church Speaks—And Is Silent," *CCY*, Mar. 22, 1923, p. 358; Robert Littell, "Henry Ford," *NR*, Nov. 14, 1923, pp. 301–304; William Hard, "Mr. Ford Is So Good," *N*, Mar. 26, 1924, pp. 340–341. The *CCY* editorials appeared in the numbers of Aug. 13, Oct. 22, 1925, Jan. 14, Mar. 4, 1926. On Marquis and Ford's short-lived welfare paternalism, Allan Nevins and Frank Ernest Hill, *Ford: Expansion and Challenge, 1915–1933* (New York, 1957), pp. 332–354.

6. [RN,] "Henry Ford and Industrial Autocracy," *CCY*, Nov. 4, 1926, p. 1354; RN, "How Philanthropic Is Henry Ford?" *CCY*, Dec. 9, 1926, pp. 1516–1517; RN, *Leaves*, p. 181; RN, *Reminiscences*, p. 33; RN, "Detroit," pp. 3–4; Thomas, "From Peasant to Proletarian," pp. 10–32; Detroit Mayor's Interracial Committee, *The Negro in Detroit* (Detroit, 1926), employment tables reprinted in Melvin G. Holli, ed., *Detroit* (New York, 1976), p. 147; Nevins and Hill, *Ford*, p. 354. Cf. RN, "Ford's Five-Day Week Shrinks," *CCY*, June 9, 1927, pp. 713–714.

7. *NYT*, Oct. 6, 1926, p. 5; *DT*, Oct. 11, 1926, p. 1 [Wise quote]; *DN*, Oct. 11, 1926, p. 46; James M. Cain, "Courage in Detroit," *New York World*, Oct. 12, 1926, p. 14; RN, *Leaves*, p. 132; "What Happened in Detroit," *Federal Council Bulletin* 9 (Nov.–Dec., 1926), pp. 14–15; Donald B. Meyer, *The Protestant Search for Political Realism* (Berkeley, Calif., 1960), pp. 83–84. In *Reminiscences*, p. 29, Niebuhr unaccountably recollects that Communist Party member Jay Lovestone was the "labor speaker" at Bethel. According to the Detroit papers, it was Albert F. Coyle, editor of the Brotherhood of Locomotive Engineers' *Journal*.

8. RN, *Leaves*, pp. 132–133; [Morrison,] "Continuing Misrepresentation of Mr. Eddy," *CCY*, Dec. 2, 1926, pp. 1476–1477; [RN,] "Henry Ford and Industrial Autocracy," p. 1355; RN, "The Effects of Modern Industrialism on Personality," *Student World* 21 (Oct., 1927), p. 303–305. For Ford's own clear under-

•

standing of the link between assembly line speedup, more leisure, and the consumption of cars, "Ford Workers Win by Speed," *DN*, Nov. 14, 1926, p. 8.

9. [Morrison or Hutchinson,] "The Battle of Detroit," *CCY*, Oct. 21, 1926, pp. 1287–1289; RN, *Reminiscences*, p. 90; [RN,] "The Peril of the Stewardship Ideal," *CCY*, Nov. 18, 1926, p. 1414; RN, "Our World's Denial of God," *Intercollegian* 44 (Feb., 1927), pp. 128, 130 (reprinted as "The Practical Belief of Modern Civilization," in Francis P. Miller, ed., *Religion on the Campus* [New York, 1927], pp. 11–21). No contemporary account mentioned the debate with Studdert-Kennedy, including his own unsigned "The Religion of the Campus," *CCY*, Jan. 13, 1927, pp. 37–39.

10. RN, "A Critique of Pacifism," *Atlantic*, May, 1927, pp. 640–641; [RN,] "Graham Wallas and the Bishops," *CCY*, May 1, 1924, p. 556.

11. Francis J. McConnell, "A Challenge to Complacency," *CCY*, Feb. 16, 1928, p. 208; RN, *Does Civilization Need Religion?* (New York, 1927), pp. 200, 206–207. To Niebuhr, McConnell was "our most outstanding social prophet," "the most glorious figure in American church life." [RN,] "Religion: True or Useful?" *CCY*, Sept. 23, 1926, p. 1161; RN, *Leaves*, p. 220.

12. RN, "A New Defender of the Faith," *CCY*, Sept. 30, 1926, p. 1192; RN, "Science and the Modern World," *CCY*, Apr. 8, 1926, p. 449; RN, "Can Schweitzer Save Us from Russell?" *CCY*, Sept. 3, 1925, pp. 1094–1095; RN, *Does Civilization Need Religion?* chs. 1–3, 7 [on "personality"], pp. 192–198 [on Schweitzer], pp. 212–213 [on Whitehead]; Schweitzer to RN, July 27, 1926, RN Papers.

13. RN, "Capitalism—A Protestant Offspring," *CCY*, May 7, 1925, pp. 600–601; [RN,] "Can a Radical Be a Christian?" *CCY*, Aug. 6, 1925, pp. 993–994; [RN,] "Impotent Liberalism," *CCY*, Feb. 11, 1926, p. 167; RN, "How Civilization Defeated Christianity," *CCY*, July 15, 1926, pp. 895–896; RN, "Puritanism and Prosperity," *Atlantic*, June, 1926, pp. 722–725; RN, *Does Civilization Need Religion?* chs. 4–5 [on Weber and Tawney], ch. 9 [on the "new asceticism"]. Niebuhr told William Allen White in 1927 that he had been "plagiarizing" Weber's *Aufsätze in Religionsoziologie* for some time. RN to White, May 11, 1927, White Papers, Library of Congress.

14. [RN,] "Can a Radical Be a Christian?" p. 994; RN, *Does Civilization Need Religion?* ch. 6 and p. 209; [RN,] "The Peril of the Stewardship Ideal," p. 1415; *DN*, Apr. 21, 1928, p. 10.

15. "West Called Unchristian," *DN*, Dec. 30, 1927, p. 11.

16. Bingham notes on interview with Coffin, n.d. [early 1950s], RN Papers; Morgan Phelps Noyes, *Henry Sloane Coffin: The Man and His Ministry* (New York, 1964), p. 192; William Sloane Coffin, Jr., *Once to Every Man* (New York, 1977), p. 121; Henry Coffin to RN, Apr. 16, 1928, letter in possession of UMN; author's interviews with John C. Bennett and William Sloane Coffin, Jr.

17. RN to Page, Feb. 15, 1928, Page to RN, Feb. 25, 1928; *DN*, Apr. 23, 1928, pp. 1–2, Apr. 24, 1928, p. 4, May 23, 1928, p. 12; H. S. Dunbar to RN, May 1, 1928, and John C. Dancy to RN, Apr. 30, 1928, letters in possession of UMN; N. H. Bowen [associate editor, *Detroit Saturday Night*] to RN, May 31, 1928, RN Papers. Cf. *DT*, Apr. 24, 1928, p. 30.

18. RN, *Leaves*, pp. 12–13, 17–18, 113, 157–158, 220–221; "Publisher's Note" in Chicago edition, 1929, pp. v–vi; Baltzer to RN, Jan. 13, 1926.

19. RN, "Specialists and Social Life," *DT*, May 5, 1928, p. 18; [RN,] "The Minister's Salary," *CCY*, Dec. 10, 1925, p. 1534; [RN,] "Pooling Salaries," *CCY*, Aug. 26, 1926, p. 1055; RN, "The Philosopher's Chair," *Intercollegian* 46 (Nov., 1928), p. 48; RN, *Leaves*, p. 74. Cf. RN, "Religious Imagination and the Scientific Method," *Proceedings of the National Conference of Social Work, May 2–9,*

•

1928 (Chicago, 1928), p. 52; and RN, "The Minister as Expert," in G. Bromley
Oxham, ed., *Effective Preaching* (New York, 1929), p. 91.

SIX: A STATE OF JOY AND PAIN (1928–1932)

1. [RN,] "Puritan Versus Democrat," *CCY*, Apr. 16, 1923, p. 518; *DN*, Dec. 15,
   1925, p. 31; [RN,] "Puritan and Democrat," *CCY*, Oct. 20, 1927, p. 1224;
   "Independents and the Election," *CCY*, Sept. 13, 1928, p. 1098; RN, "Governor
   Smith's Liberalism," *CCY*, Sept. 13, 1928, pp. 1107–1108.
2. [RN,] "Anglo-Saxon Protestant Domination,"*WT*, Nov., 1928, pp. 438–439;
   RN, "Protestantism and Prohibition," *NR*, Oct. 24, 1928, pp. 266–267; RN,
   "Why We Need a New Economic Order," *WT*, Oct., 1928, pp. 397–398; RN,
   "Pacifism and the Use of Force," *WT*, May, 1928, pp. 218–220. In the mid-
   1950's Niebuhr mistakenly remembered himself as a Smith supporter. Although
   he in fact did not vote in 1928, having failed to establish residence in New York,
   he was clearly on the record for Thomas. RN, "The Politics of the Thirties,"
   typescript, n.d. [1956], p. 1, RN Papers.
3. "British Labor in Sweeping Victory" [headline], New York *Leader*, June 1,
   1929, p. 1. The New York Marxists around Hillquit were themselves gradualists
   who abhorred violence, but unlike Thomas they were committed to the "correct" formulation of doctrine. See Richard W. Fox, "The Paradox of Progressive
   Socialism: The Case of Morris Hillquit, 1901–1914," *American Quarterly* 26
   (May, 1974), pp. 127–140. Among the many biographies of Thomas, W. A.
   Swanberg, *Norman Thomas: The Last Idealist* (New York, 1976), gives a good
   account of the New York Socialist-pacifist-Protestant milieu in which Niebuhr
   circulated.
4. RN, "Barth—Apostle of the Absolute," *CCY*, Dec. 13, 1928, pp. 1523–1524;
   RN, "A Prophet Come to Judgment," *WT*, July, 1929, p. 313, and "Morals
   and Freedom," *DT*, June 1, 1929, p. 18 [reviews of Lippmann]; RN, "A Consistent Pessimist," *CCY*, May 1, 1929, pp. 586–587, and "The Unhappy Intellectuals," *Atlantic*, June, 1929, pp. 793–794 [on Krutch]. Niebuhr sent Lippmann
   a copy of his *WT* review. The New York *World* editor and columnist was
   "immensely gratified at what you say about my book," and thanked Niebuhr
   for his own illuminating writings. "I have learned to look immediately for
   anything that you write." Lippmann to RN, n.d. [1929], Lippmann Papers,
   Yale University.
5. *Yale Daily News*, Nov. 25, 1929, p. 1, Oct. 1, 1930, p. 1; Weigle to RN, Dec.
   27, 1929, Jan. 15, Mar. 29, 1930, Coffin to RN, Dec. 2, 1929, Angell to RN,
   Jan. 5, 1931, RN Papers. On his subsidy to Walter, RN to Page, Nov. 4, 1930.
6. *DN*, Oct. 21, 1929, p. 10, Dec. 7, 1929, p. 10; Edgar DeWitt Jones, "Detroit,"
   CCY, Jan. 15, 1930, p. 89; [RN,] "How to Resign a Pulpit," *CCY*, Dec. 18,
   1929, pp. 1568–1569; RN to Kenmitz, Jan. 2, 1930, Eden Archives; RN to
   Bethel Church council, Jan. 22, 1930, RN Papers.
7. RN to A. J. Helm, Jan. 17, 1930, RN Papers; RN, "The Race Issue in the
   Church," *DT*, Feb. 1, 1930, p. 18; Bethel Congregation, *Secretary's Record Book*,
   minutes of Apr. 13 and July 14, 1930 council meetings and July 29, 1930 congregational meeting, n.p., Bethel Church Papers; RN to Jerome Davis, Feb.
   12, 1930, Davis Papers, University of Oregon Library; RN, *Leaves*, pp. 219,
   222; RN, "It Was a Sermon on Love," *CCY*, Dec. 11, 1929, p. 1541; RN to
   Bingham, Oct. 25, 1956, Nov. 15, 1958; RN, "The Preaching of Repentance,"
   CCY, June 18, 1930, p. 781; RN, "The Speculation Mania," *WT*, Jan., 1930,
   p. 26.
8. HRN to RN, Feb. 14, 1930, letter in possession of UMN. For RN on "morbid

•

introspection," see, *inter alia*, *Leaves*, pp. 27, 158, "The Unhappy Intellectuals," p. 792, and the *NYT* report of one of his sermons, June 10, 1929, p. 34.

9. "Solomon and Niebuhr on Strong Senate Slate," *NL*, Aug. 16, 1930, pp. 1, 3. Niebuhr's first major piece in the *New Leader* was "Political Action and Social Change," Jan. 4, 1930, p. 4, reprinted from *WT*, Dec., 1929, pp. 491–493. On the initial push to nominate him for governor, RN to John Bennett, July 20, 1930.

10. RN to Bennett, June 10, July 20, 1930; HRN to RN, Feb. 14, 1930; HRN to Horstmann, June 26, July 29, Sept. 5, 1930, and Horstmann to HRN, July 10, 1930, Eden Archives; RN, "Political Currents in Germany" [July 9, 1930], *NL*, July 26, 1930, p. 5, "German Election Prospects" [July 25, 1930], *NL*, Aug. 16, 1930, p. 5, "Church Currents in Germany" [July 11, 1930], *CCY*, Aug. 6, 1930, pp. 959–960, "Europe's Religious Pessimism" [Aug. 3, 1930], *CCY*, Aug. 27, 1930, pp. 1032–1033.

11. RN, "The Church in Russia" [Aug. 21, 1930], *CCY*, Sept. 24, 1930, p. 1146, "The Land of Extremes" [Aug. 24, 1930], *CCY*, Oct. 15, 1930, p. 1241, "Glimpses from Soviet Russia" [Aug. 25, 1930], *NL*, Sept. 13, 1930, p. 5; HRN to Horstmann, July 29, Sept. 5, 1930, Eden Archives; Eddy to Joseph Stalin, July 29, 1932, Eddy Papers, Yale Divinity School [on his previous visits to Russia and the dismal tourist facilities]; author's interview with Florence Niebuhr. RN's other articles, all written between Aug. 17 and Aug. 24, appeared in *CCY* on Sept. 10, Sept. 17, and Oct. 1. Helmut's pieces appeared in *EH* on Oct. 2 and Oct. 9.

12. HRN to RN, n.d. [Oct. 1930], letter in possession of UMN; *NYT*, Nov. 5, 1930, p. 10; RN to Bennett, Nov. 5, 1930. For a tantalizing glimpse of intrigue in the Wall Street board room of the seminary's finance committee—complete with allusions to a "warning letter" against Niebuhr circulated by one "Colonel Denney"—see Coffin to RN, n.d. [1930], RN Papers.

13. Dietrich Bonhoeffer, *No Rusty Swords*, vol. 1, ed. Edwin H. Robertson (New York, 1965), pp. 87–91; Eberhard Bethge, *Dietrich Bonhoeffer* (New York, 1977), pp. 117–122. On Bonhoeffer's turn toward politics, RN, "The Death of a Martyr," *CC*, June, 1945, p. 6, and "Dietrich Bonhoeffer," *Union Seminary Quarterly Review* 1 (Mar., 1946), p. 3.

14. Author's interviews with UMN, Edwin Espy, King Gordon, Carl Hermann Voss, Albert Mollegen, Dorothy Fosdick, Langdon Gilkey, John Bennett, and D. B. Robertson; Myles Horton recollections, n.d. [1960s], Highlander Research and Education Center Records, State Historical Society of Wisconsin; Bingham, *Courage to Change*, p. 184 [the "courtship" adage]; RN to Bennett, May 12, June 16, 1931; HRN to RN, n.d. [May, 1931], letter in possession of UMN; UMN to Dombrowski, June 11, Aug. 20, 1931, Dombrowski Papers, State Historical Society of Wisconsin; RN, "The Common Root of Joy and Pain," in Elmore McNeill McKee, ed., *What Can Students Believe?* (New York, 1931), p. 130. Keppel-Compton was not, as asserted in Bingham, p. 183, "niece of an Anglican bishop."

15. RN to UMN, June 2, July 12, July 20, Aug. 1, Aug. 6, 1931, letters in possession of UMN; RN to Bennett, June 16, 1931; Hulda Niebuhr to Van Dusen, July 8, 1931, Van Dusen Papers, Union Theological Seminary; Page to Eddy, July 25, 1931, Page Papers; RN, "Fixed Salaries," *DT*, Nov. 29, 1930, p. 18; "Fellowship of Socialist Christians," *WT*, Feb., 1932, p. 39; author's interviews with John Bennett, King Gordon, and Albert Mollegen.

16. RN, "Property and the Ethical Life," *WT*, Jan., 1931, p. 20; RN to UMN, Aug. 6, 1931; RN, "Unemployment as a World Crisis," *The Unemployed*, Feb., 1931, pp. 13, 31; John Herling to author, Sept. 4, 1983; RN, *The Contribution of Religion to Social Work* [lectures delivered at the New York School of Social

Work] (New York, 1932), p. 83; RN, "The Religion of Communism," *Atlantic*, Apr., 1931, p. 468; "Christian Socialism," *Time*, May 11, 1931, p. 25. *Time*'s exuberant writer could have discovered from any of Niebuhr's associates that he was not "athletic." His "doctor's" degree was an in-house honor bestowed by Eden Seminary in 1930.

17. RN to UMN, Aug. 6, Sept. 26, Oct. 1, Oct. 6, Oct. 7, Oct. 16, Oct. 18, Oct. 20, 1931, letters in possession of UMN; RN, "What Chance Has Gandhi?" *CCY*, Oct. 14, 1931, pp. 1274–1276. I am indebted to Charles Chatfield for details on RN's role in the Fellowship of Reconciliation.

18. RN to UMN, Nov. 5, Nov. 14, Nov. 19, Nov. 24, Dec. 3, 1931, letters in possession of UMN; Fey, *Kirby Page*, p. 116; RN, *The Contribution of Religion to Social Work*, p. 73 (Cf. RN, *The Irony of American History* [New York, 1952]: "Nothing that is worth doing can be achieved in our lifetime. . . ." [p. 63]); Charles M. Styron to author, Jan. 16, 1981 ["damned pink vest"]; RN to Page, Jan. 28, 1932; Bingham, *Courage to Change*, pp. 187, 191; author's interview with UMN.

19. RN, "Peace Lessons from the Orient," *Christian Advocate*, May 19, 1932, pp. 523–524; [RN,] "The League and Japan," *WT*, Mar., 1932, p. 4; [RN,] "What Could Be Done in Manchuria?" *WT*, Dec., 1931, pp. 387–388; [RN,] "China Will Yet Win," *WT*, Jan., 1932, p. 5; Chatfield, *For Peace and Justice*, pp. 223–230.

20. HRN, "The Grace of Doing Nothing," *CCY*, Mar. 23, 1932, p. 379; RN, "Must We Do Nothing?" *CCY*, Mar. 30, 1932, pp. 416–417; HRN, "The Only Way into the Kingdom of God," *CCY*, Apr. 6, 1932, p. 447; author's interview with Florence Niebuhr.

21. Charles G. Profitt to RN, July 9, Aug. 1, 1932; RN to Profitt, July 12, 1932, Columbia University Press Papers, Columbia University; RN, *The Contribution of Religion to Social Work*, pp. 59, 68, 93.

22. RN to Page, July 21, July 26, July 30, Aug. 7, Aug. 10, 1932; *NL*, July 9, 1932, pp. 6–7; Louis Waldman, *Labor Lawyer* (New York, 1944), pp. 194, 202–203; author's interviews with UMN and John Bennett ["skunks"]. Maurice Goldbloom's recollection in the 1950s (quoted in Bingham, *Courage to Change*, p. 164) that Niebuhr ran for Congress "quite against his will" is contradicted by much evidence from the 1930s. John Herling also disputes it: "I would say that he was reluctant to run but did not run 'quite against his will.' " Herling to author, Sept. 4, 1983. Niebuhr was plainly worried about the demands on his time, but ran very eagerly once he had made up his mind. In the McCarthyite 1950s he, like Goldbloom, had reason to suggest that the commitment had been involuntary. (Goldbloom and Bingham mistakenly put the Congressional run in 1930 instead of 1932.)

23. RN, "The Stakes in the Election," *CCY*, Nov. 9, 1932, pp. 1379–1381; Edward Levinson to RN, Sept. 23, 1932, RN to Levinson, Sept. 24, 1932, Socialist Party Papers, Duke University (microfilm edition); *NL*, Sept. 17, 1932, pp. 3, 12, Oct. 8, 1932, pp. 12–13; RN, "Thomas for President!" *NR*, Aug. 17, 1932, p. 22; *Yale Daily News*, Oct. 22, 1932, p. 1; Herling to author ["Greens and Beans"]; *NYT*, Nov. 4, 1932, p. 1, Nov. 10, 1932, p. 7; author's interview with Roger Shinn [on Coffin]; Coffin, *A Half Century of Union Seminary* (New York, 1954), p. 149 [on reassuring the board]; FSC announcement in *CCY*, Dec. 7, 1932, p. 1520; [RN], "Ex Cathedra," *WT*, Dec. 21, 1932, p. 578. *NL*, Nov. 12, 1932, p. 6, rightly noted that Niebuhr's vote was more than 1,000 higher than the 1930 Socialist count in the district; it failed to add that his total amounted to a percentage decline of 0.4 percent.

24. "Doctrine of Christ and Marx Linked," *NYT*, Dec. 10, 1932, p. 13; RN, *Moral Man and Immoral Society* (New York, 1932), pp. xiii–xv, 171–172, 179, 190–191,

•

220, 223; RN, "Catastrophe or Social Control?" *Harper's*, June, 1932, p. 118. RN, "Pacifism and the Use of Force," *WT*, May, 1928, pp. 218–220, "Confessions of a Tired Radical," *CCY*, Aug. 30, 1928, pp. 1046–1047, and "What the War Did to My Mind," *CCY*, Sept. 27, 1928, pp. 1161–1163, are three crucial statements in his switch from "ideals" to "force."
25. RN, *Moral Man*, pp. 44–45, 82, 95, 21, 221, 277; Dewey, "Intelligence and Power," *NR*, Apr. 25, 1934, p. 306.
26. RN, *Moral Man*, pp. 112, 144, 19, 21; [RN,] "The Death of Liberalism," *WT*, May, 1931, pp. 136–137; RN, "Catastrophe or Social Control?" p. 118. Cf. RN, "Germany—A Prophecy of Western Civilization," *CCY*, Mar. 2, 1932, pp. 287–289.

SEVEN: LIKE A LONELY SOUL (1933–1935)

1. Hume review, *CCY*, Jan. 4, 1933, p. 18, and RN reply, *CCY*, Jan. 18, 1933, pp. 91–92; Thomas review, *WT*, Dec. 14, 1932, pp. 565, 567; Holmes review, *Books*, Jan. 8, 1933, p. 13; Miller to RN, Jan. 27, 1933, p. 4, Nevin Sayre Papers, Swarthmore Peace Collection [also in Van Dusen Papers]; Calhoun review, *Intercollegian*, Jan., 1933, p. 111; Van Dusen to Miller, Feb. 3, 1933, Van Dusen Papers; RN, "Optimism and Utopianism," *WT*, Feb. 22, 1933, pp. 179–180; Coe and RN letters to the editor, *CCY*, Mar. 15, 1933, pp. 362–363; RN to Miller, Mar. 1, 1933, RN Papers.
2. HRN to RN, n.d. [mid-Jan., 1933], RN Papers; HRN to RN, n.d. [fall, 1932], letter in possession of UMN; RN to Bennett, Aug. 1, 1929; HRN to Page, Oct. 25, 1932, Page Papers. Wilhelm Pauck, a close friend of both Niebuhrs and himself a student of Troeltsch, offered a fine discussion of their relationship to Harnack and Troeltsch (on whom Richard did his doctoral dissertation at Yale) in *Harnack and Troeltsch* (New York, 1968).
3. *NYT*, Apr. 18, 1933, p. 17, Apr. 20, 1933, p. 15; announcement of Taylor lectures, *CCY*, Apr. 12, 1933, p. 505. The lectures were not published, and apparently Niebuhr threw away his manuscript draft. Richard did read the lectures in manuscript six weeks before they were delivered. The lectures were a basis for *Reflections on the End of an Era*, but the book was a reformulation, not just a revision. HRN to RN, Mar. 9, 1933, letter in possession of UMN.
4. RN, "A Christian Philosophy of Compromise," *CCY*, June 7, 1933, pp. 746–748; Morrison, "Is Christianity Practicable?" *CCY*, June 21, 1933, pp. 805–807; Niebuhr and Morrison each issued two rebuttals: *CCY*, July 26, pp. 950–953, Aug. 9, pp. 1006–1008. Neither man granted his opponent a fair hearing; the rift Niebuhr had opened with his former pacifist associates was too deep.
5. RN, "Why German Socialism Crashed," *CCY*, Apr. 5, 1933, pp. 451–453; RN, "Democracy in Crisis," *WT*, May, 1933, p. 404; RN, "The Opposition in Germany," *NR*, June 28, 1933, p. 170; RN, "Religion and the New Germany," *CCY*, June 28, 1933, p. 844; [RN,] "Ex Cathedra," *WT*, Feb. 8, 1933, p. 122, and Apr. 19, 1933, p. 362; RN, "After Capitalism—What?" *WT*, Mar. 1, 1933, p. 204.
6. RN, "Germany and Modern Civilization," *Atlantic*, June, 1925, p. 843; [RN,] "The British Election," *WT*, Nov., 1931, p. 341, and "The Tory Victory," *WT*, Dec., 1931, pp. 389–390; RN, "Notes from a London Diary," *CCY*, July 12, 1933, p. 904; RN, "The Germans: Unhappy Philosophers in Politics," *American Scholar*, Oct., 1933, p. 418; RN, "A New Strategy for Socialists," *WT*, Aug. 31, 1933, p. 491. On Cripps, see H. N. Brailsford, "An English Heretic," *WT*, Feb. 15, 1934, pp. 80–81.
7. RN to Page, Aug. 17, 1933, and n.d. [late Aug., 1933]; RN, *Reflections on the*

End of an Era (New York, 1934), pp. ix–x, 115, 146–147, 168, 171, 284–285, 287, 293, 295.

8. Morrison, "Good Wholesome Pessimism," *CCY*, Mar. 7, 1934, p. 324; Van Dusen to RN, n.d. [1934], RN Papers; Holmes, "Reinhold Niebuhr's Philosophy of Despair," *Books*, Mar. 18, 1934, p. 7; Holmes to RN, Apr. 3, Apr. 13, 1934, RN Papers; Barnes review, *American Journal of Sociology* 40 (Nov., 1934), p. 403; Barnes, *Twilight of Christianity* (New York, 1929), pp. 382, 384; RN, "Conscience," *DT*, Apr. 20, 1929, p. 18, "Jesus and Christianity," *DT*, Nov. 16, 1929, p. 18, and *The Nature and Destiny of Man*, vol. 1 (New York, 1941), p. 94; author's interview with D. B. Robertson.

9. HRN to RN, n.d. [early 1934] and June 21, 1934, letters in possession of UMN. Richard's "dilemma" was explained in his prior letter of Jan. 2, 1934, RN Papers: he was exploring Catholicism as an alternative to his Evangelical faith.

10. RN to Page, Dec. 25, 1933; RN, "Why I Leave the FOR," *CCY*, Jan. 3, 1934, pp. 17–19; RN, "Shall We Seek World Peace or the Peace of America?" *WT*, Mar. 15, 1934, p. 132; RN, letter to editor, *CCY*, Jan. 31, 1934, p. 155; RN, quoted in Morrison editorial, *CCY*, Jan. 31, 1934, p. 156 [on RN's remaining in FOR]; Chatfield, *For Peace and Justice*, pp. 191–197. For RN's postmortem on the FOR split, "Ex Cathedra," *WT*, Jan. 18, 1934, p. 26.

11. HRN, "Inconsistency of the Majority," *WT*, Jan. 18, 1934, pp. 43–44; HRN to RN, Jan. 2, 1934.

12. FSC announcement, Feb. 26, 1934, Socialist Party Papers; FSC organizational data, FSC Papers, Union Theological Seminary; RN, "The Fellowship of Socialist Christians," *WT*, June 14, 1934, p. 297; Elizabeth Gilman to RN, Feb. 15, 1934, Howard Kester Papers, Southern Historical Collection, University of North Carolina, and RN to Norman Thomas, Sept. 20, 1934, RN Papers [on fund-raising for Kester]; author's interviews with John Bennett and Albert Mollegen.

13. [Devere Allen,] "The Socialist Party Comes Alive," *WT*, June 14, 1934, p. 295; [RN,] "Ex Cathedra," *WT*, July 26, 1934, p. 362; RN, "Comment," *WT*, Apr. 12, 1934, pp. 185–186 [on the Revolutionary Policy Committee]; [RN,] "Ex Cathedra," *WT*, June 28, 1934, p. 314.

14. Eddy to Page, May 15, 1934, Page Papers; Page, "Revolution: What Kind?" *WT*, June 14, 1934, pp. 300–303; RN to Page, July 28, 1934.

15. Coffin quoted in "Union Seminary to Curb Radicals," *NYT*, May 23, 1934, p. 21; Coffin remarks reported by Eddy, Eddy to Page, June 22, 1933, Page Papers; author's interview with Carl Hermann Voss; Hubert Herring, "Union Seminary Routs Its Reds," *CCY*, June 13, 1934, pp. 799–801. The Coffin Papers contain several letters from alumni infuriated about Ward's and Niebuhr's leading the students astray in the spring of 1934.

16. RN, "Eternity and Our Time," *WT*, Dec. 21, 1932, p. 596; June Bingham notes on interview with Tillich [early 1950s], RN Papers; Wilhelm and Marion Pauck, *Paul Tillich: His Life and Thought* (New York, 1976), p. 178; Tillich, "Autobiographical Reflections," in Charles W. Kegley and Robert W. Bretall, eds., *The Theology of Paul Tillich* (New York, 1952), p. 16; Tillich to Mann, May 23, 1943, reprinted in James R. Lyons, *The Intellectual Legacy of Paul Tillich* (Detroit, 1969), pp. 104–105; RN, "The Contribution of Paul Tillich," *Religion in Life*, Autumn, 1937, p. 575.

17. RN, *An Interpretation of Christian Ethics* (New York, 1935 [reissued, 1979]), pp. 3–4, 6–8, 13, 16–17, 51, 82, 116. On the urgent tone of the Rauschenbusch lectures, see "Rochester Holds Lecture Week," *CCY*, Apr. 18, 1934, p. 535.

18. RN, "Marx, Barth, and Israel's Prophets," *CCY*, Jan. 30, 1935, pp. 139–140; RN, "The Contribution of Paul Tillich," p. 575; RN, "A Footnote on Religion," *N*, Sept. 26, 1934, p. 358; RN to Page, Sept. 11, 1934; RN, *Leaves*, p. 70.

EIGHT: THIS SIDE OF CATASTROPHE (1935–1940)

1. [RN,] "Radical Religion," *RR* 1 (Fall, 1935), pp. 4–5; RN, "Is Religion Counter-Revolutionary?" *RR* 1 (Fall, 1935), p. 20; RN to Walter Warner, n.d. [Feb., 1936], FSC Papers, Union Theological Seminary [on Eddy's subsidy]; [RN,] "Bishop Paddock," *RR* 4 (Fall, 1939), p. 6; [RN,] "The United Front," *RR* 1 (Winter, 1936), p. 4; [RN,] "Fascism, Communism, and Christianity," *RR* 1 (Winter, 1936), p. 8; author's interviews with Albert Mollegen and John Bennett.
2. V. F. Calverton, "Marxism and Religion," *Modern Monthly* 8 (Feb., 1935), p. 715 [response to RN "Religion and Marxism," pp. 712–714]; Sidney Hook, "Marxism and Religion," *Modern Monthly* 9 (Mar., 1935), pp. 29–35; RN, "The Pathos of Liberalism," *N*, Sept. 11, 1935, p. 304 [on Dewey]; RN, "Is Social Conflict Inevitable?" *Scribner's*, Sept., 1935, p. 168; RN, "The Revival of Feudalism," *Harper's*, Mar., 1935, pp. 483–484, 488; RN, "The Revolutionary Moment," *American Socialist Quarterly* 4 (June, 1935), p. 13. Cf. RN's extended discussion of "Christian Politics and Communist Religion" in John Lewis, ed., *Christianity and the Social Revolution* (London, 1935), pp. 442–472.
3. RN, "Waldo Frank in Russia," *WT*, Sept. 14, 1932, p. 261; RN to Frank, Nov. 4, Dec. 31, 1934, Mar. 4, 1935; RN to Edmund B. Chaffee, Nov. 9, 1934, Chaffee Papers, Syracuse University; RN, "English and German Mentality—A Study of National Traits," *Christendom* 1 (Spring, 1936), p. 476; Frank, "Values of a Revolutionary Writer," in Henry Hart, ed., *American Writers' Congress* (New York, 1935), p. 73.
4. RN, "Sunday Morning Debate," *CCY*, Apr. 22, 1936, pp. 595–597; Elizabeth Kemlo to Coffin, Mar. 15, 1936, RN to Kemlo, Mar. 16, 1936, RN Papers.
5. RN to Page, June 3, 1936; RN, "Britain Bewildered," *CCY*, Aug. 12, 1936, p. 1081; [RN,] "Radicalism in British Christianity," *RR* 1 (Fall, 1936), pp. 7–8; RN, "Our Romantic Radicals," *CCY*, Apr. 10, 1935, p. 476. On Cripps, Colin Cooke, *The Life of Richard Stafford Cripps* (London, 1957), and Erik Estorick, *Stafford Cripps: A Biography* (London, 1949).
6. RN, "Meditations from Mississippi," *CCY*, Feb. 10, 1937, p. 184; [RN,] "Our Labor Church Fund," *RR* 2 (Winter, 1936), p. 9; Sherwood Eddy, "The Delta Cooperative's First Year," *CCY*, Feb. 3, 1937, pp. 139–140; [RN,] "The United Christian Council for Democracy," *RR* 2 (Winter, 1936), pp. 9–10; Robert F. Martin, "Critique of Southern Society and Vision of a New Order: The Fellowship of Southern Churchmen, 1934–1957," *Church History* 52 (Mar., 1983), p. 69; Robert Moats Miller, *American Protestantism and Social Issues, 1919–1939* (Chapel Hill, N.C., 1958), p. 95; Dwight Bradley to RN, Oct. 2, 1936, RN Papers; HRN to RN, Sept. 16, 1936, letter in possession of UMN; *Yale Daily News*, Nov. 2, 1936, p. 1; [RN,] "The National Election," *RR* 2 (Winter, 1936), pp. 3–4.
7. RN to Scarlett, Apr. 4, 1937; RN to Frank, n.d. [spring, 1937] and June 24, 1937; "Gifford Lectures—Recollections of Distinguished Men," Edinburgh *Evening News*, Apr. 29, 1939, p. 8; author's interview with John Macquarrie. The Burge lecture, "Do the State and Nation Belong to God or the Devil?" is reprinted in RN, *Faith and Politics*, ed. Ronald Stone (New York, 1968), pp. 83–101.
8. J. H. Oldham, *The Oxford Conference* (Chicago, 1937) (British edition entitled *The Church Faces Its Task*) pp. 25–27 [Oldham's summary of RN's speech]; Nicholas Berdyaev, *Freedom and the Spirit* (New York, 1935), p. 167; RN, "The Christian Faith and the Common Life," in *The Christian Faith and the Common*

Life, vol. 4 of Oxford preparatory papers (London, 1938), pp. 76–77, 97. A text of RN's speech—not an exact transcript of his spoken remarks—was published as "The Christian Church in a Secular Age," *Student World* 30 (Fall, 1937), pp. 291–305, and included in RN, *Christianity and Power Politics* (New York, 1940), pp. 203–226. For a summary of the conference proceedings, John A. Hutchison, *We Are Not Divided* (New York, 1941), pp. 246–264.

9. [Morrison,] "Vacancies at Edinburgh," *CCY*, Oct. 6, 1937, p. 1221; Van Dusen letter to editor, *CCY*, Oct. 27, 1937, pp. 1331–1332; author's interviews with Lord Redcliffe-Maud, Eric Fenn, Kathleen Bliss, David Paton, Oliver Tomkins, John Ross, and Ronald Preston; Roger Lloyd, *The Church of England, 1900–1965* (London, 1966), p. 309 [RN "influenced Christian thought in England as deeply or even more deeply than in America"]. On Eliot's participation at Oxford, see Roger Kojecky, *T. S. Eliot's Social Criticism* (New York, 1972), pp. 156–158.

10. RN, *Beyond Tragedy* (New York, 1937), pp. x–xi, 28–29, 61–62, 113, 148–149, 155, 164, 166, 168–169. RN made reference to both Nietzsche's *Birth of Tragedy* and *The Genealogy of Morals*, but showed no sign of having given either volume a careful reading.

11. Bennett review, *Journal of Religion* 18 (July, 1938), pp. 335–337; Richardson review, *Review of Religion* 11 (Mar., 1938), pp. 334–338; Haroutunian to RN, Nov. 15, 1938 [replying to and quoting RN to Haroutunian, Nov. 7, 1938], RN Papers; Winfred Garrison [literary editor of *CCY*] to RN, Mar. 4, 1938 [replying to and quoting RN to Morrison, Feb. 28, 1938], RN Papers; HRN to RN, n.d. [Nov. or Dec., 1937], RN Papers; RN, *Beyond Tragedy*, pp. 108, 128, 219.

12. RN to Frank, July 9, Nov. 15, 1937; RN, *Reflections on the End of an Era*, p. 118; [RN,] "The International Situation," *RR* 4 (Fall, 1938), p. 2; RN, "Russia and Karl Marx," *N*, May 7, 1938, p. 531; RN, "America and the War in China," *CCY*, Sept. 29, 1937, p. 1196; RN, "Japan and the Christian Conscience," *CCY*, Nov. 10, 1937, pp. 1390–1391; [RN,] "Brief Comments," *RR* 4 (Winter, 1938–1939), p. 7; RN to Gilbert S. Cox, Feb. 27, 1935, RN Papers; Robert Morss Lovett, *All Our Years* (New York, 1948), p. 264. On Lincoln as prophet-statesman par excellence, see *Beyond Tragedy*, pp. 66–68.

13. RN to Frank, Nov. 15, 1937, Jan. 7, Apr. 26, June 1, June 30, 1938; HRN to RN, Dec. 14, 1936, letter in possession of UMN; RN to Scarlett, Sept. 16, 1938, and n.d. [Dec., 1938]; RN to Page, July 11, 1934 [on Walter]; HRN to RN, n.d. [Nov. or Dec., 1937], RN Papers; RN to Bennett, n.d. [June, 1938], RN to Howard Kester, Aug. 28, 1938, Kester Papers, University of North Carolina; RN to Herman Reissig, Sept. 29, 1938, Reissig Papers, Columbia University.

14. RN to Frank, n.d. [Jan., 1939], Feb. 25, 1939; RN to Amberson, Jan. 25, Jan. 31, 1939, Amberson to RN, Feb. 22, 1939, RN Papers; Kester to RN, Aug. 14, 1939, RN to Kester, n.d. [July, 1939], Aug. 22, 1939, Apr. 1, 1940, Kester Papers. Cf. Eddy's letter of self-defense, *CCY*, June 14, 1939, pp. 774–775.

15. RN to Frank, Apr. 9, Apr. 21, 1939; RN to Wolf-Dieter Zimmermann, Dec. 28, 1955, reprinted in Zimmermann and Ronald Smith, eds., *I Knew Dietrich Bonhoeffer* (New York, 1966), p. 165; RN to Henry Leiper, May 1, 1939, and RN to Paul Lehmann, May 11, 1939, both reprinted in Bonhoeffer, *The Way to Freedom* (New York, 1966), pp. 211, 218; RN, "Dietrich Bonhoeffer," *Union Seminary Quarterly Review* 1 (Mar., 1946), p. 3; Bethge, *Dietrich Bonhoeffer*, pp. 543–544, 555–565.

16. "Gifford Lectures," Edinburgh *Evening News*, Apr. 29, 1939, p. 8; Baillie, "Niebuhr's Gifford Lectures," *Union Review* 2 (Mar., 1941), pp. 7–8; RN to Lehmann, May 11, 1939; RN to Frank, May 18, 1939; author's interview with Vernon Sproxton.

•

17. RN to Scarlett, n.d. [mid-June, 1939]; RN to Frank, n.d. [June or July, 1939];
Alan Richardson, "Swanwick, 1939," *The Student Movement* 42 (Oct., 1939),
p. 6; author's interviews with Ronald Preston, Eric Fenn, Kathleen Bliss, and
Daniel Jenkins.

18. W. A. Visser 't Hooft, *Memoirs* (London, 1973), pp. 100–101; author's interview
with Edwin Espy. RN's prepared text, "The Christian in a World of Conflict,"
was published in Denzil Patrick, ed., *Christus Victor* (Geneva, 1939), pp. 177–
184.

19. RN to Scarlett, n.d. [late Sept., 1939]; RN, "Leaves from the Notebook of a
War-Bound American," [note pun in "war-bound"], *CCY*, Oct. 25, 1939 [Aug.
23 and Sept. 1 entries], p. 1298, Nov. 15, 1939 [Sept. 19 and 21 entries],
p. 1406, Dec. 6, 1939 [Oct. 1 entry], p. 1503, Dec. 27, 1939 [Oct. 17 entry],
p. 1607; Baillie, "Niebuhr's Gifford Lectures," p. 7; RN to Frank, Aug. 7, 1939;
author's interview with Vernon Sproxton; RN's typescript "Britain," n.d. [1956],
p. 3, RN Papers, retells the Cripps story (published posthumously in *Worldview*,
July, 1974, pp. 30–33).

20. HRN to RN, Jan. 25, 1940, letter in possession of UMN; RN to Frank, n.d.
[late Feb. or early Mar., 1940], July 6, 1940; Nola Meade [RN's secretary] to
Oliver Hotz, Mar. 11, 1940, RN Papers; RN to Bennett, Apr. 19, May 31,
1940; RN to Mumford, July 17, 1940; Henry Coffin to George Stewart, Apr.
10, 1941, Coffin Papers.

NINE: WISER IN THEIR GENERATION (1941–1945)

1. Irving Barshop to RN, May 22, 1940, RN to Barshop, May 24, 1940, RN
Papers; RN, "An End to Illusions," *N*, June 29, 1940, p. 778; RN, *Christianity
and Power Politics* (New York, 1940), pp. 42, 47, 66–67, 69, 168, 172; RN, "If
America Is Drawn into War," *CCY*, Dec. 18, 1940, p. 1579.

2. RN to Frank, Nov. 26, 1940; W. H. Auden, "Tract for the Times," *N*, Jan. 4,
1941, pp. 24–25; UMN, "Memories of the 1940s," in Stephen Spender, ed.,
W. H. Auden: A Tribute (New York, 1975), p. 104; Humphrey Carpenter,
W. H. Auden: A Biography (Boston, 1981), p. 306; Morrison to RN, July 16, 1941,
RN to Morrison, July 19, 1941, RN Papers.

3. Francis Pickens Miller, *Man from the Valley: Memoirs of a Twentieth-Century
Virginian* (Chapel Hill, N.C., 1971), p. 70; [RN,] "A New Name," *RR* 5
(Winter, 1940), pp. 5–6; RN to Scarlett, Apr. 5, 1941 [on *CC* subscriptions].

4. RN to Charles Schweiso, Jr., May 20, 1940, RN Papers; RN, "The Politics of
the Thirties," typescript, n.d. [1956], pp. 11–12, RN Papers; [RN,] "Communists and the United Front," *RR* 4 (Summer, 1939), pp. 8–9; RN, "Communists and Unions," *N*, Mar. 15, 1941, p. 307; Adam Clymer, "The Union
for Democratic Action: Key to the Non-Communist Left" (senior honors thesis,
Harvard College, 1958), pp. 4–11; Bingham, *Courage to Change*, pp. 215–216
[on Gerson]; author's interviews with Benjamin Davidson, Robert Bendiner,
and James Loeb.

5. [RN,] "The Socialist Campaign," *CS* 5 (Summer, 1940), p. 4; [RN,] "Willkie
and Roosevelt," *CS* 5 (Fall, 1940), p. 5; [RN,] "Roosevelt's Election," *CS* 6
(Winter, 1941), p. 4; [RN,] "Social Justice in a Defense Economy," *CS* 6 (Spring,
1941), pp. 6–7. In 1952 the FBI obtained RN's voter registration record from
the New York Bureau of Elections. Declassified FBI documents in author's
possession.

6. *NYT*, Jan. 31, 1941, p. 1, Apr. 29, 1941, p. 9, May 11, 1941, p. 19; "Should
Our Ships Convoy Materials to Britain?" *Town Meeting of the Air* 6 (May 12,
1941), pp. 7–9, 19; Paul Merkley, *Reinhold Niebuhr: A Political Account* (Montreal,

•

1975), p. 149 [on the Senate]; author's interviews with Davidson, Bendiner, and Loeb.

7. RN to Samuel Cavert, Aug. 10, 1943 [enclosing "Open Letter"], Federal Council of Churches Papers, Presbyterian Historical Society, Philadelphia; Bruce Bliven, *Five Million Words Later* (New York, 1970), p. 311; RN to William Cochran, Nov. 27, 1942, RN Papers, and James Wechsler, *The Age of Suspicion* (New York, 1953), p. 212 [on the UDA budget]; James I. Loeb, "In Appreciation of Reinie," *ADA World*, Sept., 1971, pp. 7M–8M; David S. Wyman, *The Abandonment of the Jews* (New York, 1984), p. 320; author's interview with Loeb.

8. Herling to RN, May 12, 1941, RN Papers; RN to Melvyn Douglas, Feb. 20, 1940, RN Papers [on raising funds for Hagen in the 1930s]; RN to Cochran, Sept. 9, 1941, RN Papers; Hagen to Quincy Wright, Oct. 3, 1941, and "Statement of Policy, American Friends of German Freedom," Jan. 14, 1942, typescript, 3 pp., both in Wright Papers, University of Chicago; Bingham notes on interview with Karl Frank, 1954, RN Papers; author's interviews with Anna Loeb (formerly Mrs. Karl Frank) and Joseph Kaskell.

9. [Chambers,] "Sin Rediscovered," *Time*, Mar. 24, 1941, p. 38; [RN,] "White Man's Burden," *CS* 6 (Summer, 1941), pp. 3–5; [RN,] "Editorial Notes," *CS* 6 (Spring, 1941), p. 8; RN, "Imperialism and Responsibility," *CC*, Feb. 24, 1941, p. 6.

10. RN, *The Nature and Destiny of Man*, vol. 1, *Human Nature* (New York, 1941), pp. 124, 131, 260, 170–171, 182, 254; Calhoun, "A Symposium on *The Nature and Destiny of Man*," *Christendom* 6 (Autumn, 1941), p. 575; Calhoun review, *Journal of Religion* 21 (Oct., 1941), pp. 477–478; Calhoun to RN, Nov. 1, 1941, RN Papers; HRN to RN, n.d. [June, 1941], RN Papers; author's interview with Calhoun.

11. RN to Scarlett, Mar. 31, Apr. 5, 1941; RN to Mumford, n.d. [Mar., 1941], n.d. [Apr., 1941], and Dec. 29, 1942 [on UMN "rest cure"]; RN to Frank, Oct. 20, 1941; RN to Friess, Feb. 28, 1940, Friess Papers, Columbia University; author's interviews with Carol Niebuhr Buchanan, UMN [on RN as housekeeper], William Wolf, and June Bingham.

12. RN to Scarlett, Oct. 7, 1941; RN to Frankfurter, Nov. 17, 1941, Robbins to Frankfurter, Nov. 28, 1941, Burlingham to Frankfurter, Nov. 23, 1941, Welles to Frankfurter, Dec. 3, 1941, RN to MacLeish, Mar. 8, 1942, all in Frankfurter Papers, Library of Congress; Frankfurter to Burlingham, Dec. 4, 1941, Burlingham Papers, Harvard Law School.

13. MacLeish to RN, Feb. 10, Mar. 16, 1942, Frankfurter to RN, Mar. 10, 1942, RN Papers; RN to Frankfurter, n.d., enclosing copy of RN to MacLeish, Mar. 8, 1942, Frankfurter Papers; declassified FBI documents in author's possession; [Kirchwey,] untitled editorial paragraph, *N*, June 20, 1942, pp. 699–700; RN, *Leaves*, p. 32; RN, "The Limits of Liberty," *N*, Jan. 24, 1942, pp. 87–88; Baldwin, "Liberty in Wartime," *N*, Feb. 7, 1942, p. 275.

14. RN, "Jews After the War," *N*, Feb. 21, Feb. 28, 1942, pp. 214–216, 253–255; RN, "It Might Have Been," *EH*, Mar. 29, 1923, p. 202; [RN,] "The Rapprochement Between Jews and Christians," *CCY*, Jan. 7, 1926, pp. 9–11; RN, "Judah Magnes and the Zionists," *DT*, Dec. 28, 1929, p. 16; RN, "Germany Must Be Told!" *CCY*, Aug. 9, 1933, pp. 1014–1015; RN, letter to the editor, *CCY*, May 27, 1936, p. 771.

15. RN to Frank, Apr. 9, 1942; Frankfurter to RN, Dec. 24, 1941, RN Papers; RN, "Jews After the War," p. 255; author's interview with Isaiah Berlin. Cf. Carl Hermann Voss, "The American Christian Palestine Committee," in *Essays in American Zionism, 1917–1948: The Herzl Year Book*, vol. 8 (New York, 1978), pp. 246–248, and Hertzel Fishman, *American Protestantism and a Jewish State* (Detroit, 1973), pp. 68–77.

•

16. RN, "Jews After the War," p. 255; RN, "Plans for World Reorganization," CC, Oct. 19, 1942, pp. 3–6; RN, "Power and Justice," CS 8 (Winter, 1942), pp. 9–10; RN, "Russia and the West," N, Jan. 16, Jan. 23, 1943, pp. 82–84, 124–125; RN, "National Power and the Organization of the Peace," American Teacher 27 (Apr., 1943), pp. 23–26; RN, "American Power and World Responsibility," CC, Apr. 5, 1943, pp. 2–4.

17. RN to Frank, Apr. 9, 1942; RN to Kirchwey, June 19, 1942, Kirchwey Papers, Radcliffe College; Robert Sproul to RN, Jan. 10, 1942, RN Papers; RN to Scarlett, June 17, June 30, Oct. 2, 1942; HRN to RN, n.d. [late May, 1942], RN Papers; Coffin to RN, May 26, 1942, RN Papers; RN to Conant, Oct. 17, Nov. 7, Nov. 9, 1942, Feb. 15, 1943, RN Papers; RN to Bennett, Feb. 1, 1943.

18. RN, The Nature and Destiny of Man, Volume II: Human Destiny (New York, 1943), pp. 204, 244, 247–249; Calhoun review, Journal of Religion 24 (Jan., 1944), pp. 59–64; Bennett review, Union Review 4 (Mar., 1943), pp. 24, 26; RN to Bennett, Mar. 13, 1943; Haroutunian review, CS 8 (Spring, 1943), pp. 36–37; RN to Norman Kemp-Smith, Feb. 9, 1940, Kemp-Smith Papers, University of Edinburgh [I am indebted to William Clebsch for this reference]; RN to Frank, Apr. 26, 1938; Frank notebook entry, Mar. 17, 1943, Notebook 10, Box 47, Frank Papers [I am indebted to Casey Blake for this reference]. Georgia Harkness had complained about the paucity of Synoptic Gospel citations in volume one in her review in Christendom 6 (Autumn, 1941), p. 570.

19. Mumford, The Condition of Man (New York, 1944), pp. 132, 377; Randall review, Union Review 4 (Mar., 1943), pp. 22–24; Randall to RN, Dec. 2, Dec. 7, Dec. 9, 1942, RN to Randall, Dec. 5, Dec. 8, 1942, Mar. 21, 1943, Randall Papers, Columbia University; Hook, "The New Failure of Nerve," Partisan Review 10 (Jan.–Feb., 1943), pp. 2–23, "Metaphysics, War, and the Intellectuals," Menorah Journal 28 (Oct., 1940), pp. 326–337, and "Social Change and Original Sin: Answer to Niebuhr," NL, Nov. 8, 1941, pp. 5, 7; Farrell to Dewey, Mar. 31, 1941, Dewey Papers, Southern Illinois University [I am indebted to Robert Westbrook for this reference]; Dewey, "Anti-Naturalism in Extremis," Partisan Review 10 (Jan.–Feb., 1943), pp. 24–39; Dewey to Robert V. Daniels, Nov. 17, 1947, reprinted in Journal of the History of Ideas 20 (Oct.–Dec., 1959), p. 571.

20. RN reports from Britain, CC, June 28, 1943, pp. 4–6, July 12, 1943, p. 2; RN, "Great Britain's Post-War Role," N, July 10, 1943, pp. 39–40; RN, "Understanding England," N, Aug. 14, 1943, pp. 175–177; RN, "England Teaches Its Soldiers," N, Aug. 21, 1943, pp. 208–210; RN, "Archbishop Temple," CC, Nov. 13, 1944, p. 1; RN to Cavert, July 27, 1943, Federal Council of Churches Papers; Anson Phelps Stokes to RN, Sept. 21, 1943, RN to Stokes, Sept. 29, 1943, Stokes Papers, Yale University.

21. NYT, July 19, 1943, p. 11, Aug. 19, 1943, p. 11, Oct. 28, 1943, p. 22, Mar. 30, 1944, p. 1, July 28, 1944, p. 10; RN, "A Fourth Term for Roosevelt," New Statesman and Nation, May 15, 1943, pp. 315–316; RN to John Childs, July 14, 1944, RN Papers.

22. "The Churches and the War," Town Meeting 8 (Aug. 27, 1942), p. 15; "Can We Take Freedom to the Rest of the World?" Town Meeting 9 (Sept. 23, 1943), p. 19.

23. RN, The Children of Light and the Children of Darkness (New York, 1944), pp. xiii, 1, 10, 41, 79, 115, 117–118, 189–190; RN, "What Is at Stake?" CC, May 19, 1941, p. 1; RN, "Ideologies," NL, Aug. 16, 1941, p. 4; RN, "Study in Cynicism," N, May 1, 1943, p. 638; RN quoted in Clymer, "The Union for Democratic Action," p. 136.

24. RN to Hutchins, Dec. 5, 1946, Hutchins Papers, University of Chicago; "Dangers to Press Freedom" [editorial], Fortune, Apr., 1947, pp. 2–5; Hutchins, e

•

al., "A Free and Responsible Press," *Fortune*, Apr., 1947, supplement, 22 pp. [also published by University of Chicago Press]. Details on the commission's work are drawn from the collection of its papers, the Hutchins Papers, and the Charles Merriam Papers, all at the University of Chicago.

25. *What's Doing in the UDA?*, monthly newletter, fall issues, 1944, New York Public Library; RN to Ruth Shulsky [UDA secretary], Nov. 10, 1944, Americans for Democratic Action (ADA) Papers, State Historical Society of Wisconsin; Norman Thomas to RN, July 25, 1944, and RN to Thomas, Sept. 8, 1944, reprinted in Murray B. Seidler, *Norman Thomas, Respectable Rebel*, 2nd ed. (Syracuse, 1967), pp. 217–224 [cf. RN to Thomas, Jan. 5, 1944, Thomas Papers, New York Public Library]; "Dr. Niebuhr in Chicago," *CCY*, Dec. 27, 1944, pp. 1494–1495.

26. Robert Calhoun to RN, Nov. 27, 1944, copy in possession of James Gustafson; HRN, "War as the Judgment of God," *CCY*, May 13, 1942, p. 631, "Is God in the War?" *CCY*, Aug. 5, 1942, p. 954, "War as Crucifixion," *CCY*, Apr. 28, 1943, p. 515; RN to Mumford, Oct. 31, 1944; author's interviews with Robert Calhoun, Raymond Morris, James Gustafson, and Robert Michaelson.

TEN: THE HEAVENS SHALL LAUGH (1946–1952)

1. Federal Council of Churches, "Atomic Warfare and the Christian Faith," excerpted in "Theology and the Bomb," *CCY*, Apr. 10, 1946, p. 456; [RN,] "The Atomic Bomb," *CS* 10 (Fall, 1945), p. 4; Conant to RN, Mar. 6, 1946, RN to Conant, Mar. 12, 1946, RN Papers; RN, "Humor and Faith" and "Anger and Forgiveness," in *Discerning the Signs of the Times* (New York, 1946), pp. 21, 111; Schlesinger, "Niebuhr's Vision of Our Time," *N*, June 22, 1946, pp. 753–754; RN, "Spiritual Crisis in Our Culture," *NYT Book Review*, Feb. 3, 1946, p. 4.

2. [RN,] "The Victory of British Labor," *CS* 10 (Fall, 1945), pp. 7–9; [RN,] "The Atomic Issue," *CC*, Oct. 15, 1945, p. 6; RN, "American Liberals and British Labor," *N*, June 8, 1946, pp. 682–684; RN, "Statement" to Anglo-American Committee of Inquiry," typescript, RN Papers, excerpts in *Jewish Frontier* 13 (Feb., 1946), pp. 38–44; Richard Crossman, *Palestine Mission* (New York, 1947), p. 37; Wise to RN, Jan. 15, 1946, in Carl Hermann Voss, ed., *Stephen S. Wise: Selected Letters* (Philadelphia, 1970), p. 269; [RN,] "Editorial Notes," *CC*, May 27, 1946, p. 2; RN, "A New View of Palestine," *Spectator*, Aug. 16, 1946, p. 162; RN, "The Palestine Problem," *Messenger* [successor to *EH*], Aug. 20, 1946, p. 6; RN, "Palestine: British-American Dilemma," *N*, Aug. 31, 1946, pp. 238–239.

3. RN, "Europe, Russia, and America," *N*, Sept. 14, 1946, p. 288; [RN,] "Editorial Notes," *CC*, Sept. 16, 1946, p. 3; *NYT* report of Cambridge conference, Aug. 8, 1946, p. 8; RN, "The Conflict Between Nations and Nations and Between Nations and God," *CC*, Aug. 5, 1946, p. 4; Beatrice Braude to author, Mar. 11, 1981; RN, "Germany," p. 13; Donald Rohr to author, Jan. 23, 1981; RN to Beulah Niebuhr, Sept. 26, 1946, letter in possession of Carol Niebuhr Buchanan; Paul Limbert to author, Mar. 24, 1981 [reminiscences of the German trip].

4. RN, "The Fight for Germany," *Life*, Oct. 21, 1946, pp. 65–66, 72; RN to Ruml, Sept. 26, 1946, and RN, "Report on the Political and Religious Situation in Germany," typescript, n.d. [Sept., 1946], Merriam Papers, University of Chicago; *Time*, Oct. 21, 1946, p. 31; *Reader's Digest*, Jan., 1947, pp. 69–72; RN, "A Report on Germany," *CC*, Oct. 14, 1946, p. 7; RN, "Henry Wallace's Errors," *CC*, Oct. 28, 1946, pp. 1–2; [RN,] "Toward a Christian Approach to

•

International Issues," *CC*, Dec. 9, 1946, pp. 1–3; RN, "Our Chances for Peace," *CC*, Feb. 17, 1947, pp. 1–2.

5. RN and Loeb, "British Loan Held Vital" [letter to the editor], *NYT*, Apr. 18, 1946, p. 26; James Wechsler, *The Age of Suspicion* (New York, 1953), pp. 212–216; RN to Loeb, Nov. 14, 1946 and Loeb to RN, Nov. 26, 1946 [on the CIO speech]; RN to James Rowe, Jr., Nov. 29, 1946, ADA Papers; *NYT*, Jan. 5, 1947, p. 5, Jan. 6, 1947, p. 12; RN to Loeb, May 27, 1947; author's interviews with Loeb and Joseph Rauh.

6. Karl Barth quoted in Eberhard Busch, *Karl Barth* (Philadelphia, 1976), p. 342; RN, "European Impressions," *CC*, May 12, 1947, pp. 2, 4; RN, "American Power and European Health," *CC*, June 9, 1947, p. 1; RN, "Positive Defense," *CC*, Apr. 29, 1946, pp. 1–2; RN, "Editorial Notes" [on Hungary], *CC*, July 7, 1947, p. 2; RN, "Editorial Notes" and "Democracy as a Religion," *CC*, Aug. 4, 1947, pp. 1–2; "Faith to Combat Communism Urged," *NYT*, Oct. 22, 1947, p. 24; RN, "Can We Avoid Catastrophe?" *CCY*, May 26, 1948, pp. 504–506. On the liberal response to the Truman Doctrine and Marshall Plan, see Alonzo L. Hamby, *Beyond the New Deal: Harry S. Truman and American Liberalism* (New York, 1973), pp. 173–178, 185–186.

7. Loeb to RN, Jan. 27, 1948; typescript of RN address, Feb. 21, 1948, R. A. Landor to Loeb, Mar. 7, Mar. 23, 1948, Loeb to Landor, Mar. 20, 1948, all in ADA Papers; [Chambers,] "Faith for a Lenten Age," *Time*, Mar. 8, 1948, pp. 76, 79; RN quoted in Chambers, *Witness* (New York, 1952), p. 507; Savage to RN, Apr. 19, 1948; RN to Savage, Apr. 20, 1948; Richard Rovere, *The American Establishment and Other Essays* (New York, 1962), p. 13; RN, "For Peace, We Must Risk War," *Life*, Sept. 20, 1948, p. 38; Lionel Trilling, *The Middle of the Journey* (New York, 1947 [reissued 1975]), p. 300.

8. Karl Barth's Amsterdam address, excerpts reprinted as "No Christian Marshall Plan," *CCY*, Dec. 8, 1948, pp. 1330, 1332; RN's Amsterdam address, "The Christian Witness in the Social and National Order," in RN, *Christian Realism and Political Problems* (New York, 1953), p. 112; RN, "Protestantism in a Disordered World," *N*, Sept. 18, 1948, p. 312; RN, "We Are Men and Not God," *CCY*, Oct. 27, 1948, p. 1139. Barth and Niebuhr continued the battle in Barth, "Continental vs. Anglo-Saxon Theology," *CCY*, Feb. 16, 1949, pp. 201–204, and RN, "An Answer to Karl Barth," *CCY*, Feb. 23, 1949, pp. 234–236; J. H. Oldham article on the preparatory commissions, *Christian News-Letter*, Sept. 4, 1946, pp. 1–8; Edward Duff, *The Social Thought of the World Council of Churches* (New York, 1956), pp. 159–163, 170–180 [on Amsterdam itself].

9. RN, "God's Design and the Present Disorder of Civilization," introductory essay in *The Church and the Disorder of Society* (London, 1948), p. 22; RN, "The Situation in the U.S.A.," ibid, pp. 80–82; Jacques Ellul, "The Situation in Europe," ibid, pp. 56–58; Duff, *Social Thought of the World Council of Churches*, pp. 174–175; RN, "For Peace, We Must Risk War," *Life*, Sept. 20, 1948, p. 38; RN, "Protestantism in a Disordered World," p. 313; Loeb to RN, Sept. 17, 1948, RN to Loeb, Sept. 19, Oct. 25, 1948; RN to Scarlett, July 27, Nov. 8, 1948; RN, "The Presidential Campaign," *CC*, Nov. 1, 1948, p. 138; RN, "Editorial Notes," *CC*, Nov. 15, 1948, p. 146.

10. Loeb to RN, Sept. 30, 1948, RN to Loeb, Oct. 5, 1948; RN, *Faith and History* (New York, 1949), pp. 84, 101; Miller review, *N*, Aug. 6, 1949, p. 138; Kristol review, *Commentary*, July, 1949, pp. 99, 101; Frye, "The Rhythm of Growth and Decay" [1949], in Robert D. Denham, ed., *Northrop Frye on Culture and Literature* (Chicago, 1978), p. 145; Brunner, "Some Remarks on Reinhold Niebuhr's Work as a Christian Thinker," and RN, "Reply to Criticism and Interpretation," in Charles W. Kegley and Robert W. Bretall, *Reinhold Niebuhr: His*

•

Religious, Social, and Political Thought (New York, 1956), pp. 32–33, 431; author's interviews with Hans Frei and Florence Niebuhr.

11. RN to Loeb, May 25, 1949; Fosdick to Coffin, June 23, 1949, Coffin Papers; RN to Schlesinger, n.d. [June, 1949] and Nov. 13, 1949; author's interview with George Kennan; RN, "Editorial Notes," *CC*, Oct. 29, 1951, p. 139, and RN, *The Irony of American History* (New York, 1952), p. 148 [his critique of Kennan]; RN, "The Theory and Practice of UNESCO," *International Organization* 4 (1950), pp. 6, 10; "Problems Facing UNESCO," *University of Chicago Round Table*, Oct. 9, 1949, p. 12; Dean Acheson to June Bingham, May 19, 1959, RN Papers. On the Policy Planning Staff, Graham H. Stuart, *The Department of State* (New York, 1949), pp. 444–445. June Bingham quotes Kennan as saying (with respect to RN's foreign-policy perspective) "Niebuhr is the father of us all" (*Courage to Change*, p. 368). But her book has no footnotes and I have been unable to trace the citation to a prior source or to find any reference to it in her book file in the RN Papers.

12. RN to Schlesinger, Nov. 29, Dec. 14, and n.d. [early Dec.], 1949; RN, "The North Atlantic Pact," *CC*, May 30, 1949, pp. 65–66; RN, "Streaks of Dawn in the Night," *CC*, Dec. 12, 1949, pp. 162–164; RN, "At Our Wit's End," *Messenger*, Dec. 6, 1949, p. 9 [on Russian A-bomb].

13. RN, "Editorial Notes," *CC*, Feb. 6, 1950, p. 2; RN to Schlesinger, Feb. 23, 1950; RN to Scarlett, n.d. [fall, 1950], n.d. [summer, 1950]; RN, "Ten Fateful Years," *CC*, Feb. 5, 1951, p. 1; RN, "The Christian Conscience and Atomic War," and Federal Council of Churches, "Christian Conscience and Weapons of Mass Destruction," *CC*, Dec. 11, 1950, pp. 161–168; Bennett to author, Nov. 9, 1984; RN, "MacArthur Statements Contrasted" [letter to the editor], *NYT*, Dec. 6, 1950, p. 32; RN, "Our Position in Asia" [letter to the editor], *NYT*, Dec. 23, 1950, p. 14; RN, "Editorial Notes," *CC*, Dec. 25, 1950, p. 170 [on bargaining with China to prevent a Russian "advance" in Europe]; RN, "New Light on the Old Struggle," *CS* 15 (Fall, 1950), p. 4 [on Korean war as proof that atomic warfare was not imminent].

14. Declassified FBI documents in author's possession; *NYT*, May 7, 1951, p. 27 [on the finances of Resettlement Campaign]; American Council of Christian Laymen, *How Red Is the Federal Council of Churches?* (Madison, Wis.), 1949, p. 8, RN Papers; Verne Kaub to Edward Johnson, June 4, 1951, RN to Kaub, June 7, 1951, both in RN Papers; *NYT*, Jan. 14, 1951, pp. 1, 31; RN to Freda Kirchwey, Apr. 26, 1951, RN Papers; RN to Schlesinger, Mar. 27, 1951 [on timing his resignation with Bendiner's]; RN to Robert Hutchins, Mar. 16, Oct. 25, 1950, Hutchins Papers; RN to Charles Merriam, Sept. 7, 1950, Merriam Papers; RN to Dorothy Thompson, May 18, 1951, Thompson Papers, Syracuse University. Cf. RN, "Memorandum on Forgotten Intellectuals and Professionals," typescript, 3 pp., enclosed in RN to Kirchwey, Mar. 16, 1950, Kirchwey Papers, Radcliffe College.

15. RN, "Transatlantic Tension," *The Reporter*, Sept. 18, 1951, p. 16; Barth quoted in Busch, *Karl Barth*, pp. 395–396; author's interview with Robert Calhoun; RN, "The Problems of a World Church," *Messenger*, Aug. 21, 1951, p. 6; RN, "The 'Super-Theologians' Meet," *Union Seminary Quarterly Review* 7 (Jan., 1952), p. 26; RN to Francis Miller, Nov. 24, 1952, Miller Papers, University of Virginia.

16. RN, *Irony of American History*, pp. 133, 170; RN to Savage, Sept. 11, 1951, RN Papers; RN to Savage, Dec. 5, 1951; Daniel Boorstin, *The Genius of American Politics* (New York, 1953), and RN's review of it, *NL*, June 22, 1953, p. 15; author's interviews with Robert McAfee Brown and Samuel and Sara Terrien.

17. Peter Viereck, "Freedom Is a Matter of Spirit," *NYT Book Review*, Apr. 6,

•

1952, pp. 1, 24; Anthony West, "Night and Fog," *New Yorker*, May 3, 1952, p. 130; Morton White, "Of Moral Predicaments," *NR*, May 5, 1952, pp. 18–19; William Leuchtenburg, "Niebuhr: The Theologian and the Liberal," *NL*, Nov. 24, 1952, p. 24; author's interviews with Kennan, Schlesinger, C. Vann Woodward, and David Brion Davis; Henry May, *Ideas, Faiths and Feelings* (New York, 1983), pp. 215–216, 220–225. Cf. Richard Reinitz, *Irony and Consciousness: American Historiography and Reinhold Niebuhr's Vision* (Lewisburg, Pa., 1980).

18. RN photograph printed in RN, "Honesty in America," *Messenger*, July 31, 1951, p. 7; "Christian Action Statement of Purpose," *CC*, Oct. 1, 1951, pp. 126–127; RN to John Cartmell, Nov. 14, 1951, RN Papers [on transfer of assets of *CS*]; Bennett to author, Sept. 12, 1984 [quoting Liston Pope].

19. RN to Scarlett, n.d. [Jan., 1952], n.d. [late winter, 1952]; RN sermon, "Our Lord's Conception of the Providence of God," Feb. 3, 1952; RN to Pike, Feb. 11, 1952, Pike Papers, Syracuse University; RN to Vardis Fisher, Jan. 29, 1952, Fisher Papers, Beinecke Library, Yale University [on his end-of-semester workload]; Van Dusen press release, Feb. 19, 1952, and UMN to William Savage, Mar. 10, 1952, Scribners Office Files; Van Dusen to Coffin, Mar. 6, Mar. 11, 1952, Coffin Papers; RN to Fred Fox, Mar. 19, 1952, Fox Papers, Eisenhower Library, Abilene, Kansas; RN to Mumford, Apr. 1, 1952; RN, *Leaves*, p. 158.

ELEVEN: QUITE A DIFFERENT PERSON (1952–1960)

1. Louise Robbins's comments reported in Coffin to Van Dusen, Aug. 8, Aug. 23, 1952, Van Dusen Papers; UMN to Scarlett, Aug. 20, 1952, RN Papers; RN to Van Dusen, Oct. 14, 1952, RN Papers; RN to Schlesinger, May 29, July 3, July 14, July 27 ["enviable position"], Nov. 24, 1952; RN to Bennett, June 24, July 8, 1952; [RN,] "Television's Peril to Culture," *American Scholar* 19 (Spring, 1950), pp. 137–140; RN, *Irony of American History*, p. 59; RN, "Nixon Case Discussed" [letter to editor], *NYT*, Oct. 2, 1952, p. 55; Stevenson to RN, Aug. 13, 1952, in Walter Johnson, ed., *The Papers of Adlai Stevenson*, vol. 4 (New York, 1974), p. 42. On Schlesinger's career in these years, Michael Wreszin, "Arthur Schlesinger, Jr., Scholar-Activist in Cold War America, 1946–1956," *Salmagundi*, Spring-Summer, 1984, pp. 255–285.

2. RN to Lydia and Hulda Niebuhr, n.d. [summer, 1946], RN Papers; Wayne Cowan, "In 25 Years You Pick Up a Lot of Memories," *CC*, Sept. 17–Oct. 1, 1979, p. 211 ["aesthetic philistine"]; Lydia's and Hulda's recollections of Christopher, June Bingham interview, Jan. 20, 1954, notes in RN Papers; RN to Norman Kemp-Smith, Feb. 9, 1940, Kemp-Smith Papers, University of Edinburgh Library; RN to Scarlett, n.d. [late winter, 1952], n.d. [early spring, 1952], Oct. 10, 1952; UMN to Scarlett, Aug. 20, 1952; author's interviews with UMN, Christopher and Elisabeth Niebuhr, John Smith, Wayne Cowan, Robert McAfee Brown, Sydney Brown, June Bingham, and William Wolf.

3. RN, "Editorial Notes," *CC*, Mar. 16, 1953, p. 26; RN, "The French Do Not Like Us," *CS* 19 (Winter, 1953–1954), p. 12; Kristol to RN, Jan. 20, 1953, RN Papers; RN to Kristol, Jan. 20, 1953, Dwight Macdonald Papers, Yale University; author's interview with Lehmann. On the debate over McCarthyism and the ECLC, see William L. O'Neill, *A Better World* (New York, 1982), pp. 298–306.

4. RN to Schlesinger, Aug. 11, 1953; RN, "Communism and the Protestant Clergy," *Look*, Nov. 17, 1953, p. 37; Guy Shipler to RN, Nov. 18, Dec. 16, 1953, RN to Shipler, Nov. 20, Dec. 21, 1953, Oct. 1, Oct. 5, 1954, RN Papers; RN, quoted in Arnold W. Hearn, "Report on a Conversation: Niebuhr and DePury,"

•

CS 20 (Winter, 1954–1955), p. 22. On McMichael and his HUAC appearance, and on Shipler and the *Churchman*, see Ralph Lord Roy, *Communism and the Churches* (New York, 1960), pp. 298–316, 336–340.

5. RN to H. H. Lippincott, Jan. 29, 1954, RN Papers; UMN to C. C. Burlingham, Jan. 1, 1951, Burlingham Papers, Harvard Law School, and RN to Senator Herbert Lehman, Nov. 29, 1954, RN Papers [on Ursula's citizenship]; RN to Savage, Nov. 3, 1953, RN Papers; Bertram Wolfe to RN, July 6, 1953, RN Papers; RN, *Christian Realism and Political Problems*, New York, 1953, p. 34; RN to Stuart Schram, June 12, 1953, RN Papers.

6. RN, *The Self and the Dramas of History* (New York, 1955), pp. 10–11, 138–141, 99, 24, 100; RN, "Biblical Thought and Ontological Speculation in Tillich's Theology," in Charles W. Kegley and Robert W. Bretall, *The Theology of Paul Tillich* (New York, 1952), p. 217; RN to Scarlett, n.d. [Feb., 1958]; Cf. RN's review of Fromm's *Man for Himself*, in *CS* 13 (Spring, 1948), pp. 26–28.

7. RN to Scarlett, Jan. 31, 1958; Tillich quoted in Bingham, *Courage to Change*, p. 29; Tillich, "Reply to Interpretation and Criticism," in Kegley and Bretall, *Theology of Paul Tillich*, pp. 338–339; RN, "Editorial Notes," *CC*, Feb. 6, 1956, pp. 2–3; Tillich letter to the editor, *CC*, Mar. 5, 1956, p. 24; author's interviews with June Bingham, Langdon Gilkey, Wilhelm and Marion Pauck, and Hans Frei. On Tillich's personal life in New York, see Hannah Tillich, *From Time to Time* (New York, 1973), pp. 169–192.

8. RN, "Sex and Religion in the Kinsey Report," *Union Seminary Quarterly Review* 9 (Jan., 1954), pp. 4, 9 [reprinted from *CC*, Nov. 2, 1953, pp. 138–141]; RN, "More on Kinsey," *CC*, Jan. 11, 1954, p. 182; Lionel Trilling, "The Kinsey Report," in Donald Geddes, ed., *An Analysis of the Kinsey Reports* (New York, 1954), pp. 216, 218; RN to Carol Cade, Nov. 22, 1955, RN Papers.

9. RN to Bingham, Aug. 25, 1954, July 12, Sept. 8, 1955; RN to Scarlett, n.d. [Sept., 1954], Sept. 13, 1954, Mar. 7, July 12, 1955, Feb. 21, Aug. 5, Sept. 12, 1956; RN to Howard, Nov. 16, 1955, RN Papers; author's interviews with UMN, Erik Erikson, and Robert Coles.

10. RN to Bingham, Apr. 6, Apr. 11, 1955, Dec. 1, 1953, Nov. 9, Nov. 15, Nov. 16, 1954; RN to Schlesinger, Nov. 10, 1954; Bingham to RN, n.d. [handwritten draft of her reply to RN's of Nov. 15], and Bingham's handwritten personal notes, n.d. [Nov., 1954], RN Papers; author's interviews with Bingham and Schlesinger; UMN to author, Aug. 14, 1979. Schlesinger played a mediating role throughout the conflict over the biography.

11. RN, "Intellectual Autobiography," and "Reply to Interpretation and Criticism," in Kegley and Bretall, eds., *Reinhold Niebuhr*, pp. 6–8, 431, 436–437, 439; Sherwood Eddy, *Eighty Adventurous Years* (New York, 1955), p. 127; Bingham, *Courage to Change*, p. 138; Bingham's notes on interview with RN, Jan. 27, 1954, RN Papers.

12. RN to Bingham, May 31, June 28, 1956; RN to Miller, June 28, 1956, RN Papers; Miller to author, Oct. 1, 1979; RN, *Leaves*, p. 27; Ramsey to RN, Mar. 10, 1952, RN to Ramsey, Mar. 18, 1952, letters in Ramsey's possession; RN, "Detroit," p. 10.

13. RN, "The Cause and Cure of the American Psychosis," *American Scholar* 25 (Winter, 1955–1956), pp. 11–20; RN, "Seven Great Errors of U.S. Foreign Policy," *NL*, Dec. 24–31, 1956, p. 4; RN to Frankfurter, Feb. 19, 1957; RN to Schlesinger, Nov. 16, 1956; RN to Norman Thomas, Dec. 5, 1956, Thomas Papers, New York Public Library; RN, "Our Stake in the State of Israel," *NR*, Feb. 4, 1957, pp. 9, 12; RN, "Democracy and Foreign Policy," *NL*, Apr. 8, 1957, p. 10; RN, "Why Is Barth Silent on Hungary?" *CCY*, Jan. 23, 1957, pp. 108–110; RN, "Barth on Hungary," *CCY*, Apr. 10, 1957, pp. 454–445; Theo-

•

dore Gill to RN, Mar. 7, 1957, RN Papers; RN, "The Gospel in Future America," *CCY*, June 18, 1958, p. 715 ["dollar worship"]; RN, "The Quality of Our Lives," *CCY*, May 11, 1960, p. 571 ["fleshpot of Egypt"].

14. RN, "Literalism, Individualism, and Billy Graham," *CCY*, May 23, 1956, p. 641; RN, "Proposal to Billy Graham," *CCY*, Aug. 8, 1956, p. 921; RN, "The Billy Graham Campaign," *Messenger*, June 4, 1957, p. 5; "Graham Sermon in Garden on TV," *NYT*, June 2, 1957, p. 38; Van Dusen, "Billy Graham," *CC*, Apr. 2, 1956, p. 40, and author's interview with Hugh Van Dusen; RN, *Pious and Secular America* (New York, 1957), pp. 5, 11, 21–22, 91; RN to Bingham, Mar. 29, 1957; RN to Frankfurter, May 26, 1960. Graham later recollected of Niebuhr's criticism on the race question that "I thought about it a great deal. He influenced me and I began to take a stronger stand" (John Pollock, *Billy Graham* [New York, 1979], p. 157).

15. RN to Frankfurter, Dec. 31, 1956; RN to Scarlett, July 25, 1957; RN to John Bennett, Aug. 26, 1957; "Resolution of the Tenth Convention of the ADA, Mar. 29–31, 1957," enclosed in Joseph Rauh to RN, Apr. 5, 1957, RN Papers; RN to Bingham, Mar. 11, 1957; *NYT*, Feb. 1, 1958, p. 2; Bingham, *Courage to Change*, pp. 378–379.

16. RN to Bingham, Oct. 6, 1958 ["modernistic horror"]; RN to Scarlett, Jan. 31, Feb. 7, June 21, Sept. 10, Sept. 15, 1958, n.d. [fall, 1958]; RN to Schlesinger, July 30, Aug. 24, 1958, Jan. 6, 1959; Eliot to L. H. Brague, May 27, 1959, Brague to Eliot, June 3, 1959, Scribners Office Files. UMN believes that RN's letters to his intimate friend Will Scarlett do not provide an accurate view of his condition in the 1950s and 1960s. She considers them to have been a useful safety valve in discouraging times, but not a good gauge of his health or state of mind. Perhaps she is right that he did not always describe his condition with precision. Perhaps he did exaggerate his plight in order to prompt Scarlett to offer reassurance. If so, that exaggeration would itself provide a valuable clue to his state of mind. But there are reasons to assume the Scarlett letters to be generally reliable. The feelings and views RN expressed in them may sometimes have differed from those he voiced to his family not because they were inaccurate, but because he wished to spare his loved ones a litany of fears and complaints. He experienced profound guilt about being a constant imposition on his wife after his stroke in 1952; there is some evidence to suggest that he strived to ease her burden by keeping some of his anxieties to himself and to his letters. Finally, while his letters to Scarlett in the 1950s and 1960s are far more numerous than those to any other correspondent, they are not unique; he voiced the same feelings in his letters to Bingham and even at times to less intimate friends. UMN's main point still stands: one cannot be sure that any individual letter is a completely accurate report. None can be taken at face value. Yet it must also be said that the recollections of others many years later may themselves not always be precise. Oral history has its own pitfalls. UMN to author, Feb. 11, 1985.

17. Kennan to RN, Sept. 29, 1958, Scribners Office Files; author's interview with William Savage; RN to Scarlett, July 15, Aug. 29, 1959, n.d. [fall, 1959]; RN, *The Structure of Nations and Empires* (New York, 1959), pp. 3, 9; RN, "Power and Prestige in Empires and Alliances," *NL*, May 20, 1957, pp. 16–18.

18. RN to Scarlett, Nov. 12, Dec. 14, 1959; RN to Bingham, Feb. 7, 1961; author's interviews with Robert Michaelson, Florence Niebuhr, and James Gustafson; Van Dusen to Eddy, Jan. 5, 1960, Eddy Papers, Yale Divinity School.

19. RN to Scarlett, June 17, Aug. 22, 1960; RN and UMN to Frankfurter, July 23, 1960, Frankfurter Papers; UMN to Bingham, n.d. [summer, 1960], RN Papers; RN to Schlesinger, n.d. [c. July 23, 1960]. Schlesinger (*A Thousand Days* [Boston, 1968], p. 58) claims that Niebuhr supported Lyndon Johnson before the

nomination, but Niebuhr's correspondence shows that his choice was Stevenson (after the West Virginia primary, when Humphrey's chances faded).

20. RN to Schlesinger, Sept. 3, 1960; Bingham to Scarlett, Sept. 15, 1960, RN Papers [Liberal Party dinner]; RN to Scarlett, Nov. 5, 1960; RN to Bingham, Nov. 22, 1958, Jan. 25, 1962; RN to Frankfurter, July 23, 1960; RN, "The Eisenhower Era," *NL*, Oct. 3, 1960, p. 4; RN, "Balance of Terror: Credit and Debit," *NL*, Aug. 3–10, 1959, pp. 4–5 [on the "missile gap"].

21. RN to Savage, Aug. 8, 1960; RN to Bingham, Nov. 8, 1961; RN to Scarlett, Apr. 30, 1960, Aug. 20, 1962; RN, "The Religious Traditions of Our Nation," *Saturday Evening Post*, July 23, 1960, pp. 26–27, 45, 48; RN to Trilling, n.d. [Dec., 1961], Trilling Papers, Columbia University.

TWELVE: GATHERED TO THE FATHERS (1961–1971)

1. RN, "Reflections on Democracy as an Alternative to Communism," *Columbia University Forum*, Summer, 1961, pp. 16–17; RN to Scarlett, Feb. 5, 1961; Schlesinger to RN, Sept. 16, 1961, RN to Schlesinger, Sept. 25, 1961; Schlesinger to author, Apr. 9, 1984; McGeorge Bundy, "Foreign Policy: From Innocence to Engagement," in Arthur Schlesinger and Morton White, eds., *Paths of American Thought* (Boston, 1963), p. 306.

2. RN, "One Year of the New Frontier," *CC*, Feb. 5, 1962, p. 2; RN, "Drama on the Cuban Stage," *NL*, Mar. 5, 1962, p. 11; RN to Schlesinger, Mar. 30, June 23, 1962; Kennedy telegram to RN, June 20, 1962, copy in Schlesinger Papers; RN to Scarlett, n.d. (June, 1962), RN to Bingham, n.d. (Sept., 1962), Oct. 29, 1961; Hans Morgenthau, "The Influence of Reinhold Niebuhr in American Political Life and Thought," and RN, "Response," in Harold R. Landon, ed., *Reinhold Niebuhr: A Prophetic Voice in Our Time* (Greenwich, Conn., 1962), pp. 102, 121–122.

3. RN, "Our Moral Dilemma," *Messenger*, Nov. 5, 1957, p. 5; RN, "The Nuclear Dilemma: A Discussion," *CC*, Nov. 13, 1961, p. 202; Kenneth W. Thompson, ibid., p. 203; Carl Mayer, "Moral Issues in the Nuclear Dilemma," *CC*, Mar. 19, 1962, p. 38; RN, "Logical Consistency and the Nuclear Dilemma," *CC*, Apr. 2, 1962, p. 48; RN to Bingham, Oct. 29, 1961; John Bennett, "Christian Realism," *CC*, Apr. 16, 1962, pp. 51–52; RN, "Nuclear Dilemma," *Union Seminary Quarterly Review* 17 (Mar., 1962), pp. 239–242.

4. RN to William Savage, May 12, May 22, 1962; Potter review of RN and Alan Heimert, *A Nation So Conceived*, *NYT Book Review*, May 19, 1963, p. 22; RN to Frankfurter, Mar. 29, 1962; RN, "The Unintended Virtues of an Open Society," *CC*, July 24, 1961, p. 132; RN, "The Problem of the Modern Church: Triviality," *CC*, Dec. 10, 1962, p. 226.

5. RN to Scarlett, n.d. [1962], July 8, 1962; RN to Bingham, July 1, 1962; RN to Van Dusen, July 16, 1962, Van Dusen Papers; RN to Savage, July 11, 1962.

6. RN to Schlesinger, May 6, 1963; RN to Scarlett, Aug. 18, Aug. 21, Jan. 21, 1963.

7. RN to Schlesinger, Nov. 29, 1963, Jan 4, 1964; RN to Scarlett, Nov. 17, Nov. 25, Dec. 26, 1963.

8. RN, "The States' Rights Crisis," *NL*, Sept. 29, 1958, p. 7; RN to Frankfurter, Feb. 8, 1957; RN, "The Effect of the Supreme Court Decision," *CC*, Feb. 4, 1957, p. 3; FBI documents in author's possession; RN, "The Montgomery Savagery," *CC*, June 12, 1961, p. 103; RN, "Revolution in an Open Society," *NL*, May 27, 1963, pp. 7–8; RN to Scarlett, Feb. 3, 1964; RN, "The Struggle for Justice," *NL*, July 6, 1964, p. 10; RN, *Moral Man*, pp. 252–253; RN to D. B. Robertson, Aug. 26, 1966, letter in Robertson's possession; Wayne Cowan to RN, Apr. 13, 1970, RN Papers. On King's indebtedness to Niebuhr, see

•

Stephen B. Oates, *Let the Trumpet Sound* (New York, 1982), pp. 34–35, 40, and John J. Ansbro, *Martin Luther King, Jr.* (Maryknoll, N.Y., 1982), pp. 151–160, 188.

9. RN, "Triumph of Primitivism," *NL*, Aug. 17, 1964, p. 5; RN, "The Discontents of an Affluent Society," *CC*, Sept. 21, 1964, p. 169; RN, "Goldwater vs. History," *NL*, Oct. 26, 1964, p. 17.

10. RN "Can Democracy Work?" *NL*, May 28, 1962, p. 9; RN, "The Problem of South Vietnam," *CC*, Aug. 5, 1963, p. 143; RN, "Roosevelt and Johnson: A Contrast in Foreign Policy," *NL*, July 19, 1965, p. 8; RN to Scarlett, Sept. 18, 1965, Feb. 26, Mar. 9, Apr. 1, Apr. 4, 1966, Feb. 13, 1967; RN, "Consensus at the Price of Flexibility," *NL*, Sept. 27, 1965, p. 20; Paul Ramsey quoted in John Bennett, "From Supporter of War in 1941 to Critic in 1966," *CC*, Feb. 21, 1966, p. 13; Hubert H. Humphrey, "A Tribute to Reinhold Niebuhr," *CC*, May 30, 1966, pp. 120–123; RN, "Without Advice and Consent," *NL*, Aug. 28, 1967, p. 6.

11. RN to Scarlett, Mar. 26, 1957; RN, "Mater et Magister," *CC*, Aug. 7, 1961, p. 142; RN, "Toward New Intra-Christian Endeavors," *CCY*, Dec. 31, 1969, pp. 1663–1667; RN, "From the Sidelines" [1967], edited version published in *CCY*, Dec. 19–26, 1984, p. 1197; RN, *Justice and Mercy*, p. 37. On RN's sense of the church, see the exchange between John Bennett and Wilhelm Pauck in Landon, ed., *Reinhold Niebuhr*, p. 81.

12. RN, "Some Things I Have Learned," *Saturday Review*, Nov. 6, 1965, p. 63; RN to Scarlett, Mar. 6, 1965, Aug. 22, 1963, Sept. 24, 1954, Jan 4, 1968; John Cogley, "An Interview with Reinhold Niebuhr," *McCall's*, Feb., 1966, p. 171.

13. RN to Scarlett, June 16, Oct. 26, Nov. 2, 1967, Apr. 23, July 5, Oct. 5, 1968, May 14, 1969; RN to Otto and Grace Pokorny, Nov. 6, 1967, RN Papers.

14. RN, "The King's Chapel and the King's Court," *CC*, Aug. 4, 1969, pp. 211–212; FBI documents in author's possession; RN to Mumford, Sept. 2, 1969; Edward B. Fiske, "Niebuhr Is Critical of President's Sunday Services," *NYT*, Aug. 7, 1969, p. 24, and letter columns on Aug. 10, Aug. 13, Aug. 15, Aug. 19, 1969; RN and Paul Sigmund, *The Democratic Experience*, New York, 1969, p. 7; RN to Savage, May 27, 1963; Savage to RN, June 4, 1963.

15. RN to Otto Pokorny, Dec. 16, 1969, letter in possession of UMN; RN to Theophil Twente, July 11, 1969, letter in possession of William Chrystal; RN to Scarlett, Sept. 23, 1969; RN to Bennett, Apr. 6, 1970; author's interview with William Wolf.

16. Elson Ruff to Martin Marty, Apr. 30, 1970, copy to RN, RN Papers; RN, "To Be Abased and to Abound," *Messenger*, Feb. 13, 1951, p. 7; Theodor Wilhelm reminiscences, in Ludwig J. Pongratz, ed., *Pädagogik in Selbstdarstellungen II* (Hamburg, 1976), pp. 329–333 (I am deeply indebted to the Rev. Reinhard Neubauer for this reference); Loretta Evans (the Niebuhrs' secretary) to Ruff, May 11, 1970, RN Papers; advertisement in Philadelphia *Inquirer*, Feb. 22, 1970, copy in RN Papers.

17. RN, "Felix Frankfurter," *CC*, Apr. 5, 1965, p. 69; Erikson quoted in UMN to Mumford, Jan. 13, 1971, Mumford Papers; UMN to Bennett, Apr. 5, 1971; UMN to Wilhelm and Marion Pauck, May 11, June 29, 1971, single letter in Marion Pauck's possession; Abraham Joshua Heschel, "A Last Farewell," *Conservative Judaism* 25 (Summer, 1971), p. 63; "Four Friends Officiate at Services for Niebuhr," *Berkshire Eagle*, June 5, 1971, copy in RN Papers; author's interviews with UMN, Erikson, and Seymour Siegel.

•

EPILOGUE: FULL OF GRACE AND GRIEF

1. RN to Scarlett, June 23, 1960, June 20, 1967; RN talk on "Christian Faith and Humanism," Union Theological Seminary, Jan. 14, 1952, tape recording available from Union Theological Seminary of Virginia.
2. RN, "A Dissenting Opinion," *NL*, July 9, 1962, pp. 3–4, and "The Regents Prayer Decision," *CC*, July 23, 1962, pp. 125–126; RN to Frankfurter, Mar. 31, 1948; RN to Scarlett, June 19, June 26, July 12, 1962, and n.d. [summer, 1962].
3. RN to Bingham, Feb. 9, Mar. 6, 1956, May 20, 1959; RN to Frank, n.d. [1938].
4. RN to Scarlett, Feb. 10, July 5, 1965.

ACKNOWLEDGMENTS

AND

BIBLIOGRAPHY

This is not an official biography. The members of the Niebuhr family were nevertheless very helpful in offering recollections, suggesting leads, and recommending friends in America and Britain to interview. Conversations and correspondence with Ursula Niebuhr, Christopher Niebuhr, and Elisabeth Niebuhr Sifton were indispensable. I am especially grateful to Ursula Niebuhr for allowing me to see some of the important letters in her personal possession, including those from HRN to RN, and for reading and commenting on a portion of the manuscript. She was able to save me from a number of errors, and I regret it was not possible for her to read the entire manuscript. Florence Niebuhr, HRN's widow, and her son, Richard Reinhold Niebuhr, were very generous in granting multiple interviews and in making available their collection of family photographs. Carol Niebuhr Buchanan, Walter's daughter, provided photos, letters, and other documents and never tired of questions about her family. Niebuhr family members—even members of the same immediate family—did not always agree in their recollections and estimates of RN, or in their judgment of what material was relevant to his biography. The personal portrait I have drawn accords with their overall testimony, and that of many other people who knew him well. Oral recollections have been checked whenever possible against documentary evidence.

Among RN's friends and associates I have relied most on the assistance of John C. Bennett, Robert McAfee Brown, and William J. Wolf. All three gave me in-depth reminiscences, read the entire manuscript, and made detailed responses based on their close association with RN. In addition, John Bennett graciously sent me copies of the letters RN had written him in their forty-year correspondence. The devotion of all three to this task revealed both their affection for RN and their desire to support a fully critical (in the sense of impartial, not negative) account of his life. I am very deeply in their debt; without them this book would not have been possible.

Other friends, students, and colleagues of RN were also extremely helpful in providing reminiscences and documentary material. D. B. Robertson shared his bibliographical expertise as well as his memories, and kindly made copies of letters from and about RN. John Porter joined me in a lengthy quest for unknown RN works; in the Detroit Public Library microfilm room we exchanged disbelieving glances as we made the serendipitous discovery of RN's Detroit *Times* columns. King Gordon, Wilhelm and Marion Pauck, and Arthur Schlesinger, Jr., all spoke to me at length about RN and made available their correspondence with him. June Bingham granted me permission to use her collection of RN materials at

•

the Library of Congress, offered her memories and advice as an earlier RN biographer, and copied the photo of her friends RN and Will Scarlett. Latter-day students of RN's life and work are profoundly obligated to her for her diligence in interviewing RN, his family, and his friends in the 1950s. Had she done no more than to meet Samuel Press, and to obtain the letters RN wrote to him in the 1910s, she would have performed a major service. But she did much more. Her notes and correspondence are enormously rich for understanding RN's character and thought.

Among the dozens of friends, acquaintances, and associates of RN who offered oral reminiscences in person or by telephone, I wish especially to thank the following, whose contributions were the most important for the book. In the United States: Roland Bainton, Robert Bendiner, Sydney Brown, Robert Calhoun, William Sloane Coffin, Jr., Robert Coles (telephone), Wayne Cowan, John Crocker, Benjamin Davidson, John Dillenberger, Edwin Espy, Erik Erikson, Dorothy Fosdick, Langdon Gilkey, William Hamilton, Robert Handy, Alan Heimert, Joseph Kaskell, George Kennan (telephone), Edwin Kennedy, Paul Lehmann, Robert Lekachman, James Loeb, Albert Mollegen, George Opperman, Joseph Rauh, William Savage, Roger Shinn, Seymour Siegel, John Smith, William Spurrier, Samuel and Sara Terrien, and Carl Hermann Voss. In Great Britain: John Barnes, Isaiah Berlin, Kathleen Bliss (telephone), Eric Fenn, Daniel Jenkins, John Macquarrie, David Paton, Ronald Preston, John Redcliffe-Maud, Vernon Sproxton, Margaret Stansgate, Oliver Tomkins, and Geoffrey Wilson.

Among the many individuals who sent me useful written reminiscences of RN, I want particularly to thank Tony Benn, Beatrice Braude, Sidney Hook, David Jones, Paul Limbert, Archibald MacLeish, William Lee Miller, Lewis Mumford, Donald Rohr, Charles Styron, and Diana Trilling.

Several students and friends of HRN shed considerable light on RN and his relationship with his younger brother. James Gustafson, who also read and commented on the whole manuscript, kindly showed me correspondence and photographs. Hans Frei, Robert Michaelson, and Raymond Morris shared their close knowledge of HRN in interviews. A younger HRN researcher, Jon Diefenthaler, also added to my understanding of HRN.

In the younger generation of RN researchers, William G. Chrystal and J. Dell Johnson were very generous in making available the fruits of their labors. I owe a special debt to Chrystal. He gave me free run of his substantial personal archives of RN material, copied photographs, and took pleasure in tracking down further information about the young RN and about the Evangelical Synod. No one knows the denominational background of RN as Chrystal does. It was a joy to compare notes with him and to plumb his reservoir of knowledge.

It would be impractical to name all the librarians, archivists, and private individuals who helped me locate and obtain RN material. As a group they permitted me to assemble the substratum of this book, the documentary evidence, and I salute them all. But I do need to single out Charles Scribner, Jr., who opened the Scribners office files to me, and James Charles Janes, pastor of the Emmanuel-Bethel United Church of Christ in Royal Oak, Michigan, who allowed me to use the Bethel Archives. Two Yale University librarians deserve special mention for assistance that went far beyond the ordinary: Marilyn True in Inter-library Loan and Martha Smalley at the Yale Divinity School. And the staff of the Library of Congress Manuscript Room always made it a pleasure to do research—even before the days of air-conditioned comfort in the Madison Building.

For reading the final manuscript and giving me suggestions for improving it, my warm thanks go to Casey Blake, Charles Cannon, Diane Fox, David Hollinger, Ray Kierstead, Jackson Lears, Michael Novak, Paul Overby, Roger Shinn, Ronald Steel, and Christopher Wilson. Hollinger, Lears, Steel, and Wilson made especially valuable substantive criticisms that provoked painful but profitable revision. Lears and Wilson also rebelled at stylistic clichés; my gratitude to them for their editorial severity. Diane Fox not only read the manuscript but, with Rachel and Christopher Fox, made the far greater sacrifice of living with it. I give them my love as well as my thanks. At Pantheon Books, my publisher, André Schiffrin, and my editors, first Philip Pochoda and then James Peck, have earned my fond appreciation. Accomplished chemists, they know how to mix criticism and support in the right proportion. To Pochoda go my congratulations for years ago predicting exactly how long this would take. To Schiffrin my admiration for shrewd readings of early drafts. And to Peck my praise for his patient navigating at the end of the journey.

The starting point for research on RN is the collection of his papers at the Library of Congress. It contains his very important letters to June Bingham (204 letters in Box 26) and Will Scarlett (574 letters in Boxes 27 and 33), donated to the library by those correspondents. The nearly 800 letters he wrote to them, mostly in the 1950s and 1960s, are an unrivaled source for understanding the last twenty years of his life. In those letters he expressed his deepest feelings about his vocation and about the physical and emotional weakness that interfered with it. There are fifteen other boxes of correspondence at the Library of Congress, but they tend to be letters received, not sent, by RN. He rarely made copies of his outgoing correspondence; only those business letters typed by his Union Seminary secretary Nola Meade were typically done in duplicate. The vast majority of RN letters in those fifteen boxes are therefore organizational rather than personal in character. Nevertheless they are essential for grasping the multitude of activities in which he engaged. There are also another nineteen boxes of sermons, speeches, published and unpublished articles, lecture notes, book manuscripts, and clippings about RN. The five additional boxes of material donated by June Bingham contain not only her own notes for *Courage to Change*, but a variety of interesting manuscripts and reprints that RN gave her during her research. All forty-two boxes of the RN Papers, including the Bingham and Scarlett materials to which access was restricted until 1985, are now open to the public.

The most significant RN letters, apart from those to Press, Bingham, and Scarlett, are not in his Papers at the Library of Congress. His letters to Arthur Schlesinger, Jr., are in the Schlesinger Papers at the Kennedy Library, Waltham, Massachusetts (at least 109 letters); to John Baltzer, in the Eden Archives, Webster Groves, Missouri (at least 80); to John Bennett, in Ben-

•

nett's possession (at least 45); to Waldo Frank, in the Frank Papers, University of Pennsylvania (at least 38); to Kirby Page, in the Page Papers, Southern California School of Theology, Claremont, California (at least 36); to Lewis Mumford, in the Mumford Papers, University of Pennsylvania (at least 19); to Felix Frankfurter, in the Frankfurter Papers, Library of Congress (at least 36); to Sherwood Eddy, in the Kirby Page Papers (at least 6). His letters to the staff members of the UDA and ADA—mostly to James Loeb—are in the ADA Papers, State Historical Society of Wisconsin (over 30 letters). A small but useful collection of his letters to his Scribners editor William Savage is located at the Scribners headquarters in Manhattan (at least 11 letters). There are scattered RN letters—sometimes very important ones—in dozens of other places, both in archives and in private hands. The notes give the locations for those I have used.

Another very revealing primary source is the series of oral history interviews conducted in 1953 and 1954 by the Columbia University Oral History Research Office. They contain very useful memories of his childhood, his father, and his years at Yale and in Detroit (the interviewers put most stress on Detroit—probably because Columbia historian Allan Nevins, who ran the Oral History program, was at the time writing his multivolume biography of Henry Ford). Not that RN's memories were always accurate: a quarter-century and more after the events, he sometimes got the details wrong. But that makes the reminiscences all the more valuable, for they disclose what he remembered and how he remembered it in the relative inactivity of 1953 and 1954. He used some of the interview material in his own written recollections prepared in 1956 for possible publication by the *Reporter* magazine. The *Reporter* did not publish them, but drafts of three of the four pieces are available in the RN Papers: "The Politics of the Thirties" in Box 29, "Britain" and "Germany" (both published posthumously in *Worldview*) in Box 39. "Detroit," which draws most heavily on the Columbia Oral History, is not in the collection, but a number of RN friends and students, including D. B. Robertson, have copies. Of the many published interviews, the most interesting are Henry Beckett, "Niebuhr—The Grim Crusader," New York *Post*, April 20, 1943, p. 39, and John Cogley, "An Interview with Reinhold Niebuhr," *McCall's*, February 1966.

Perhaps the single most critical primary source for elucidating RN's family relationships and intellectual development is the set of letters he received from HRN. Five of them are in the RN Papers (Boxes 9 and 13), but the most important (at least 13 letters) are in UMN's possession. It is tragic that HRN felt compelled to destroy both the letters he received from RN and those that their sister Hulda received from them. It is also unfortunate that their mother Lydia's collection of family papers—including letters from RN in his youth and early adulthood, her husband Gustav's sermons, photos, and other family documents—was (as she told June Bingham in a 1954 letter) "lost in moving."

Since RN was always first a preacher, students of his career must consult the audio tape collection of his sermons, talks, and classroom lectures, available from the Union Theological Seminary of Virginia. Sadly, none of the fifty-three tapes predates the 1950s, and only two of them were recorded before his stroke in 1952. But those two—"Christian Faith and

•

Humanism," a lecture given a month before his stroke, and "Our Lord's Conception of the Providence of God," a sermon delivered two weeks before—supply a tantalizing sample of the power that infused his speech in the first four decades of his adult career.

At least two government agencies have files on RN: the FBI and the CIA. The documents that the CIA released to me were insignificant for my purposes, though interesting for the student of the CIA: they included a dispatch on domestic " 'Peace' Demonstrations" endorsed by RN in 1967. The FBI, by contrast, provided very useful material. The Bureau reviewed 635 pages of documents on RN and released 614 of them to me—although many of those were partially blacked out. In addition to the material gathered in the two major investigations of RN in 1942 and 1951–1952, there are valuable letters, memoranda, and clippings that were added to his file at other times. The Bureau was extremely diligent in tracking down out-of-the-way documents. The fact that it could not distinguish what was relevant and irrelevant to the issue of RN's "loyalty" makes the file all the more helpful to the historian. For sheer energy of accumulation of facts, opinions, and gossip, the Bureau may have had no match. A fine example of its zeal was its 1972 cross-checking exercise. Having discovered that "Reinhold Niebuhr" was misspelled more than thirty different ways in the Niebuhr file itself, FBI experts tested "all logical buildups, breakdowns, and variations" of his name to be sure that the Bureau had not inadvertently created more than one file on him.

The indispensable guide to RN's published works is D. B. Robertson's *Reinhold Niebuhr's Works: A Bibliography*. The revised edition published by University Press of America in 1983 contains a large number of new listings, including most of the previously unlisted RN writings that I found in the course of the research for this book. The most crucial of the new items are his Detroit *Times* columns (at least one hundred of them between 1928 and 1931) and his many unsigned *CCY* and *WT* editorials, which can be positively identified by either internal or external evidence. Between 1923 and 1928 RN wrote so many of the *CCY* editorials that it was not practical to list them all. After 1928 he also wrote countless unsigned pieces for *WT*, especially on England and Germany, in addition to his semi-anonymous column "Ex Cathedra," which began in 1932. My contribution to the preface of Robertson's revised edition gives more information about these materials.

No one will ever track down every last article that RN produced. He published too much, as he freely acknowledged, and did so in dozens of journals and newspapers at home and abroad. More items turn up regularly: for instance, his brief memorial to Perry Miller published in the *Harvard Review*, an undergraduate magazine, in 1964. Some of what he wrote, moreover, can never be identified. Between 1910 and 1915, when he was a high school student, seminarian, and graduate student, he wrote editorials and news stories for Walter's Lincoln *Courier*. Most appeared during the summer, but since there were no bylines, his articles cannot be differentiated from what Walter wrote. The two brothers shared the same interests in politics and foreign affairs, and RN had not yet developed his distinctive English prose style. RN later told Alan Heimert that he had written

•

about Eugene Debs for his brother's paper; it is a pity not to know what he said.

D. B. Robertson's bibliography contains a full listing of book-length treatments of RN, as well as an extensive sample of articles and dissertations about him. Three previous books that deal with both RN's life and thought are June Bingham, *Courage to Change* (New York, 1961), Ronald Stone, *Reinhold Niebuhr: Prophet to Politicians* (Nashville, 1972), and Paul Merkley, *Reinhold Niebuhr: A Political Account* (Montreal, 1975). Bingham's volume, written in the late 1950s, is the only one of the three to make extensive use of unpublished sources, but the absence of footnotes reduces the book's value. Given the constraints under which she worked—RN's own domi-nating presence and UMN's disapproval of her venture—it was a remarkable achievement, and all future researchers will remain firmly in her debt. Stone and Merkley focus mainly on RN's political interests, though they do ad-dress the connections between those interests and his theology. Merkley's book is the more provocatively argued and thoroughly researched of the two, but it tends to exaggerate the consistency of RN's role as a Cold Warrior. There was a tension in RN's stance even in the early 1950s that Merkley underestimates. Stone, who knew RN in the latter's final years at Union Seminary, found it difficult in his book (as Bingham did in hers) to maintain a critical distance from a subject he looked up to. He errs in a manner symmetrical to Merkley: he exaggerates the consistency of RN's prophetic detachment from Cold War ideology.

The truth lies not so much halfway between Merkley and Stone as on another plane altogether: in a more nuanced account of the development of RN's ideas and activities, an account that can do justice to the complexity of his own motives and perceptions. His desire for acceptance and influence warred with his quest for transcendence; he wanted to be a respected figure in his culture and an independent judge of it. To use HRN's terms, RN's Lord was a Christ in paradox with culture. Even at his most accommo-dationist, as in his virulent anti-communism of the early 1950s, there was a critical impulse that made him uncomfortable with his own complacency. Unfortunately Merkley and Stone did not have access to much of RN's correspondence, which is indispensable for documenting the tensions in his perspective. It is especially regrettable that Merkley, who came to his project with the requisite critical distance, was led to believe that there were no significant RN letters outside of the Library of Congress collection.

On RN's religious ideas, Gordon Harland, *The Thought of Reinhold Niebuhr* (New York, 1960), and Hans Hofmann, *The Theology of Reinhold Niebuhr* (New York, 1956), are still very useful, but each suffers from a lack of historical perspective and a failure to put the religious ideas in the broader context of RN's life. His theology cannot be fully understood if it is abstracted from his experience, treated as a systematic body of thought. A good start on a more profound analysis of the link between thought and practice in RN's work is Dennis McCann, *Christian Realism and Liberation Theology* (Maryknoll, N.Y. 1981). We are still waiting for a theologically and historically informed discussion of the transition from the liberal Prot-estantism of Harnack, Troeltsch, and Rauschenbusch to the updated liberal Protestantism of RN and the unique liberal-evangelical Protestantism of

HRN—although William R. Hutchison's *The Modernist Impulse in American Protestantism* (Cambridge, Mass., 1976) is an excellent foundation.

Two very insightful shorter discussions of RN's career are Arthur Schlesinger, Jr., "Reinhold Niebuhr's Role in American Political Thought and Life," in Charles W. Kegley, ed., *Reinhold Niebuhr: His Religious, Social, and Political Thought* (New York, 1984 [first published 1956]), and Donald B. Meyer, *The Protestant Search for Political Realism, 1919–1941* (Berkeley, Calif., 1960), chapters 13 and 14. Schlesinger rightly insists on RN's ambivalence toward Marxism even in his Marxian phase, and correctly underlines RN's constant distaste (from *Moral Man* on) for the notion of "intelligent planning" that he associated with Dewey. Even as he attacked FDR's "whirligig reforms" in the early 1930s, RN's "pragmatic" stance was in ironic accord with FDR's antitheoretical, makeshift politics. Schlesinger is on target in asserting that RN's embrace of FDR's gradualism was only a matter of time. But as a New Deal advocate he tends to interpret that shift as a movement from illusion to truth. This Dark Ages to Enlightenment model underestimates the potential even of "vital center" liberalism for "illusion." Donald Meyer's book, originally a doctoral dissertation advised by Schlesinger, offers often brilliant insight into the meaning of RN's career: the political meaning of his theological work and the theological meaning of his political work. It is a shame that Meyer did not have access to RN's letters. He would have known what to make of them. An earlier article of my own, also based on published sources, is "Reinhold Niebuhr and the Emergence of Liberal Realism, 1930–1945," *Review of Politics* 38 (April, 1976), pp. 244–265. It makes the same mistake that Merkley makes: exaggerating RN's role as a Cold Warrior. But it still provides a worthwhile discussion of the place of "myth" in RN's politics and theology, a discussion I have drawn on in this book. Likewise I have drawn on, but also modified, my analyses in three other earlier pieces: "Reinhold Niebuhr: Self-Made Intellectual," *Library of Congress Quarterly* 40 (Winter, 1983), pp. 48–55; "Who Can But Prophesy? The Life of Reinhold Niebuhr," in Kegley, ed., *Reinhold Niebuhr*, pp. 27–42; and "Reinhold Niebuhr's 'Revolution,' " *Wilson Quarterly* 8 (Autumn, 1984), pp. 82–93.

Many of the other twenty-one essays (besides Schlesinger's) in the Kegley collection (some of them—like John Bennett's—updated for the 1984 edition) are indispensable. So are the contributions by Bennett, Tillich, and Hans Morgenthau, and the concluding discussion among RN's assembled disciples, in Harold R. Landon, ed., *Reinhold Niebuhr: A Prophetic Voice in Our Time* (Greenwich, Conn., 1962). A memorial volume, Nathan A. Scott, ed., *The Legacy of Reinhold Niebuhr* (Chicago, 1975), contains valuable retrospective essays, most by leading scholars who knew RN.

Having consulted the aforementioned authoritative sources, the RN researcher would do well to examine the several letters (in the RN Papers) that one Floyd Brown of Toledo, Ohio, wrote to RN in the 1950s. Mr. Brown was not a theologian or a scholar. He wrote in longhand and pencil. But he knew that Reinhold Niebuhr was the genuine article and decided to start a conversation about the nature and destiny of man. Niebuhr is to be praised for many things—not least for finding the time to answer Floyd Brown.

AFTERWORD

One of the great pleasures of finishing this book has been to hear from scores of those who have read it. Most have sent me personal responses to the book. Some — ranging from Ursula and Christopher Niebuhr to my own mother — have improved the manuscript by noting minor factual or typographical errors, which have been corrected in this edition. Others have offered personal recollections of Reinhold Niebuhr. A few of their voices:

A nurse who cared for Niebuhr at St. Luke's in 1952 suspects that "there was too much medical attention. Sometimes less is better." She also stresses that his suffering was compounded after the stroke by the simple fact that he could no longer type with both hands. "He was so used to typing and thinking together." She adds that despite his pains he answered "all the letters I wrote to him."

A Yale choir member relates what it was like to watch from behind as Niebuhr preached in Battell Chapel. His body and voice were electric, he hurled down a string of lightning-bolt paradoxes, the students gaped and wondered in their quest to comprehend. When he had to sit down after the sermon and listen to the rest of the service, the chair could barely contain him. He shifted from one side to the other, rubbed his head and ears, and kept looking around at the choir with piercing blue eyes.

Several of Niebuhr's former students have also sent me reminiscences. "We did not know him well," writes one who attended Union in the 1950s. "Anyone who tells you we did is romanticizing. Sometimes we didn't understand him. But he was so incredibly *good* at teaching." He began one class by announcing that "the subject for our consideration today is what Augustine called perfidiousness. The Psalmist once wrote, 'In my haste, I said all men are liars.' The point

333

of view being taken here today? That he might well have said it at his leisure."

A seminarian from the early 1940s notes that while many professors were distant, aloof, Niebuhr was the "least difficult to know" of them all. "Nobody at Union entertained students in his apartment the way RN did." He also went far out of his way to do a favor: When a former student returned from a Navy chaplaincy, Niebuhr, who needed no car during the school year, offered him the use of his old Ford for the entire nine months.

The students' memories reinforce my conclusion that the seminary was Niebuhr's center, his home, after 1928. His teaching was not one activity among many. It was the foundation for all the others. He could put up with the maze of hotels and trains, with the numbing fatigue, because he could return to Union. Another seminarian from the 1930s still marvels at the "vast time" Niebuhr spent "with students and their problems, especially job placement." If he was hard to know, if he shielded some inner core from the admiring gallery and even from himself, he still had an exceptional gift for personal interchange, a warmth and glow in the eyes, a readiness to laugh *with* as well as speak *to*. A contagious spirit subverting assumed boundaries, enlivening those clustered around him with undisguised excitement about ideas, about politics, about people.

Economist Robert Lekachman, not one to be easily impressed, recalls Niebuhr's "impact on this unbeliever" in an issue of *Christianity and Crisis* (3 February 1980). "He had a marvelous tolerance for all manner of people who differed with him, an appreciation that extended even to obedient Catholics and secular types unappreciative of spiritual revelation of any variety." His tolerance, his delight in differences, is one key to his spirit. His humor is another. He could denounce, admonish, and pontificate because he relished disagreement and could deprecate himself.

Niebuhr marked countless individual lives. Even some who never knew him, as dozens of recent correspondents have reminded me. They, like me, have developed a relationship — perhaps a kind of friendship — with a man they have known only at a distance. But distance is a part of all friendship. Richard Niebuhr, in *The Meaning of Revelation*, meditated on the paradox that even our most intimate friends, even those we love, remain strangers to us. The better we know them the more we realize they are mysterious, unknown. The more we try to grasp their fullness the more it seeps through our fingers.

Writing the life of Niebuhr has been a curious process of trying to bring him to life. Not in the trivial sense of making him breathe on the page, but in the deep sense of giving him his life, letting him take his own fleshy independence. The biographer's natural tendency is to label, confine the subject, convert him to object; but the subject, if brought to life, resists the shaping, breaks the mold. If the biography is to succeed, it must be built on a tension between two critical spirits.

Shortly after finishing the book, I dreamt that I ran into Niebuhr in a hallway at Reed College. He chatted amiably about his cousins, and I confessed I didn't know much about them. He advised me that none of the members of the Union for Democratic Action were fellow-travellers, and I admitted I had no knowledge of the matter. He looked at his watch, smiled, muttered the words "Bless my soul," and hurried off down the corridor. As I watched him leave I wondered if those were going to be his last words before he died.

Finishing a biography is like saying goodbye to a close companion who is moving to another place. There may be further contact in years to come, but it will probably lose the vibrant intimacy forged during years of constant interchange. One releases one's friend even as one hopes for a lasting bond. The biographer must also release his subject. Niebuhr's life is still in the course of development. Others will meet him in different ways than mine, and new information may emerge from his family and friends. My portrait is the record of one encounter with Niebuhr a decade after his death. I believe it is objective — in taking account of and interpreting the evidence that is available to us about Niebuhr and his times — but it is not the only possible objective interpretation of Niebuhr's work and life. And it cannot be a final reading. No life is ever finished.

In the wake of the biography, a number of colleges, churches, and synagogues asked me to talk about Niebuhr. Suddenly I found myself in pulpits speaking — and tempted to preach — about the work of a preacher. Having wrestled with Niebuhr for so long, and listened to his sermons on tape, it was hard to avoid imitating him. In the question periods I found my own voice. What, I was always asked, would Niebuhr say about this or that contemporary issue: Soviet expansionism, abortion, genetic engineering, religious cults? I tried to speculate, but also tried to go beyond the question. I remain convinced that the best way to relate Niebuhr to the present is to remember what he thought about the relation between religion and politics.

His position is especially important at a time when liberalism is in near total disarray and — if one is a liberal — in drastic need of reconstruction. No longer can liberals get by with promises of higher living standards and government-guaranteed safety nets. Those left of center have joined those on the right in seeing the state as cold bureaucracy, potential or actual oppressor. More and more reformers share the conservative view that "private" action is superior to "public" action. "Public" means inefficient, unheroic, the dull gray corridor of an old post office. Liberals have got to reconceive the whole idea of public activity: dissociate the idea of the public from the idea of bureaucracy, validate the public as an arena worthy of active citizen participation.

It is hard to believe that as recently as the 1960s, when Niebuhr's work came to an end, the twentieth-century liberal commitment to the benevolent paternal state, to leadership by professionally trained experts, still seemed secure. Niebuhr shared the standard progressive faith in the power of enlightened government to discipline business and help establish justice. That faith was so potent precisely because beginning in the late nineteenth century it captured not only secular advocates, but theological spokesmen such as Niebuhr. Liberal Protestantism was a crucial institutional and ideological foundation for the Progressive and New Deal reform movements.

Yet Niebuhr also stressed that the state was "under God," under judgment since it was prone to self-aggrandizement. He sensed that public authority, like private authority, possessed imperial potential. Now that liberals too are broadcasting their doubts about the state, it is worth attending to the voice of a sceptic about government who still believed that public authority should discipline private authority. He rightly insisted that justice — the Christian's goal in society — was not an achievement of far-sighted corporations or of the free play of market forces. Even though he shared his generation's overconfidence in the state as guarantor, he also knew that justice always depended on organized action

·

by a mobilized citizenry.

Some liberals today are also joining conservatives in calling for the return of religion to the public sphere. Once again Niebuhr's stance is a valuable corrective. He insisted on the interpenetration of religion and politics, but the linkage was full of tension. In his view there could be no "Christian" politics. He hated "moral" parties, whether of left or right. He feared the fanaticism of true believers in politics. The secular realm had its own integrity, its own natural capacity for good. The place of religion was not to override the secular but to challenge it to live up to its potential, resist the impulse to degenerate into mere balance of power or conflict of interest. The secular was to be shielded from the imperial thrust of religion, yet religion was to provoke, galvanize the secular.

Chastising the secular also meant, paradoxically, chastising the churches. Niebuhr remains one of our most potent critics of tepid, therapeutic, feel-good religion. Today many evangelical and liberal ministers are equally content to preach it, along with armies of other pop psychologists, success strategists, and exercise faddists. For Niebuhr redeeming the secular—empowering it to achieve justice—meant pulling down the temples of self-enchantment. Responsibility, long-term commitment, fidelity to family, devotion to the interests of future generations, willingness to admit one's faults, readiness to accept one's limits: in themselves these are neither conservative, liberal, nor radical notions. But they are an indispensable foundation for any lasting cultural or political vision.

Portland, Oregon
September, 1986

INDEX